Fodor's

MONTANA & WYOMING

3rd Edition

Where to Stay and Eat
for All Budgets

Must-See Sights
and Local Secrets

Ratings You Can Trust

Fodor's Travel Publications   New York, Toronto, London, Sydney, Auckland
www.fodors.com

FODOR'S MONTANA & WYOMING
Editor: Eric B. Wechter

Editorial Production: Linda K. Schmidt
Editorial Contributors: Jean Arthur, Gil Brady, Linda Cabasin, Joyce Dalton, Jo Deurb-rouck, Dustin D. Floyd, T.D. Griffith, Amy Grisak, Andrew Mckean, Candy Moulton, Debbie Olson, Steve Pastorino, Ray Sikorski, Shauna Stephenson
Maps & Illustrations: David Lindroth, Ed Jacobus, Mark Stroud, and Henry Colomb, *cartographers;* Bob Blake, Rebecca Baer, and William Wu, *map editors*
Design: Fabrizio LaRocca, *creative director;* Guido Caroti, Siobhan O'Hare, *art directors;* Tina Malaney, Chie Ushio, Ann McBride, *designers;* Melanie Marin, *senior picture editor;* Moon Sun Kim, *cover designer*
Cover Photo: (Glacier National Park): Tom Bol
Production/Manufacturing: Matthew Struble

COPYRIGHT

3rd Edition

ISBN 978-1-4000-0726-4

ISSN 1549-3784

SPECIAL SALES

This book is available at special discounts for bulk purchases for sales promotions or premiums. Special editions, including personalized covers, excerpts of existing books, and corporate imprints, can be created in large quantities for special needs. For more information, write to Special Markets/Premium Sales, 1745 Broadway, MD 6-2, New York, New York 10019, or e-mail specialmarkets@randomhouse.com.

AN IMPORTANT TIP & AN INVITATION

Although all prices, opening times, and other details in this book are based on information supplied to us at press time, changes occur all the time in the travel world, and Fodor's cannot accept responsibility for facts that become outdated or for inadvertent errors or omissions. So **always confirm information when it matters,** especially if you're making a detour to visit a specific place. Your experiences—positive and negative— matter to us. If we have missed or misstated something, **please write to us.** We follow up on all suggestions. Contact the Montana & Wyoming editor at editors@fodors.com or c/o Fodor's at 1745 Broadway, New York, NY 10019.

PRINTED IN THE UNITED STATES OF AMERICA
10 9 8 7 6 5 4 3 2 1

Be a Fodor's Correspondent

Your opinion matters. It matters to us. It matters to your fellow Fodor's travelers, too. And we'd like to hear it. In fact, we need to hear it.

When you share your experiences and opinions, you become an active member of the Fodor's community. That means we'll not only use your feedback to make our books better, but we'll publish your names and comments whenever possible. Throughout our guides, look for "Word of Mouth," excerpts of your unvarnished feedback.

Here's how you can help improve Fodor's for all of us.

Tell us when we're right. We rely on local writers to give you an insider's perspective. But our writers and staff editors—who are the best in the business—depend on you. Your positive feedback is a vote to renew our recommendations for the next edition.

Tell us when we're wrong. We're proud that we update most of our guides every year. But we're not perfect. Things change. Hotels cut services. Museums change hours. Charming cafés lose charm. If our writer didn't quite capture the essence of a place, tell us how you'd do it differently. If any of our descriptions are inaccurate or inadequate, we'll incorporate your changes in the next edition and will correct factual errors at fodors.com immediately.

Tell us what to include. You probably have had fantastic travel experiences that aren't yet in Fodor's. Why not share them with a community of like-minded travelers? Maybe you chanced upon a beach or bistro or B&B that you don't want to keep to yourself. Tell us why we should include it. And share your discoveries and experiences with everyone directly at fodors.com. Your input may lead us to add a new listing or highlight a place we cover with a "Highly Recommended" star or with our highest rating, "Fodor's Choice."

Give us your opinion instantly at our feedback center at www.fodors.com/feedback. You may also e-mail editors@fodors.com with the subject line "Montana & Wyoming Editor." Or send your nominations, comments, and complaints by mail to Montana & Wyoming Editor, Fodor's, 1745 Broadway, New York, NY 10019.

You and travelers like you are the heart of the Fodor's community. Make our community richer by sharing your experiences. Be a Fodor's correspondent.

Happy Trails!

Tim Jarrell, Publisher

CONTENTS

About This Book. 5

What's Where. 6

When to Go 13

Quintessential Montana &
   Wyoming. 14

If You Like. 16

Glacier to Grand Teton
   Driving Tour. 22

Dakotas' Black Hills Driving Tour. . 24

1 YELLOWSTONE
   NATIONAL PARK 27

2 GRAND TETON
   NATIONAL PARK 65

3 NORTHWEST WYOMING. 91

4 SOUTHWEST MONTANA. . . . 130

5 GLACIER NATIONAL PARK . 189

6 NORTHWEST MONTANA. . . . 212

7 THE MONTANA PLAINS 262

8 CODY, SHERIDAN & NORTHERN
   WYOMING 309

9 CHEYENNE, LARAMIE &
   SOUTHERN WYOMING 347

10 THE SOUTH DAKOTA
   BLACK HILLS. 383

   MONTANA AND WYOMING
   ESSENTIALS 435

   INDEX. 452

   ABOUT OUR WRITERS 464

MAPS

Montana & Wyoming. 8

Glacier to Grand Teton
   Driving Tour. 23

Dakota Black Hills Driving Tour. . . 25

Yellowstone National Park . . . 28-29

Western Yellowstone. 33

Eastern Yellowstone. 34

Grand Teton National Park 67

Jenny Lake Trail 76

Northwest Wyoming 94

Jackson 96

Southwest Montana. 136

Bozeman 158

Helena 164

Glacier National Park. 191

Central Glacier NP. 202

Northwest Montana. 215

Missoula. 245

The Montana Plains. 265

Great Falls 268

Billings 282

Northern Wyoming 312

Southern Wyoming 350

Cheyenne. 353

Laramie. 359

The South Dakota Black Hills . . . 386

Wind Cave National Park . . 406–407

Subterranean Trail Network,
   Wind Cave NP. 414

Badlands National Park. . . . 418–419

ABOUT
THIS BOOK

Sometimes you find terrific travel experiences and sometimes they just find you. But usually the burden is on you to select the right combination of experiences. That's where our ratings come in.

As travelers we've all discovered a place so wonderful that its worthiness is obvious. And sometimes that place is so unique that superlatives don't do it justice: you just have to be there to know. These sights, properties, and experiences get our highest rating, **Fodor's Choice,** indicated by orange stars throughout this book.

Black stars highlight sights and properties we deem **Highly Recommended,** places that our writers, editors, and readers praise again and again for consistency and excellence.

By default, there's another category: any place we include in this book is by definition worth your time, unless we say otherwise. And we will.

Disagree with any of our choices? Care to nominate a place or suggest that we rate one more highly? Visit our feedback center at www.fodors.com/feedback.

Hotel and restaurant price categories from ¢ to $$$$ are defined within each chapter. For attractions, we always give standard adult admission fees; reductions are usually available for children, students, and senior citizens. Want to pay with plastic? **AE, D, DC, MC, V** following restaurant and hotel listings indicate whether American Express, Discover, Diner's Club, MasterCard, and Visa are accepted.

Unless we state otherwise, restaurants are open for lunch and dinner daily. We mention dress only when there's a specific requirement and reservations only when they're essential or not accepted—it's always best to book ahead.

Hotels have private bath, phone, TV, and air-conditioning and operate on the European Plan (aka EP, meaning without meals), unless we specify that they use the Continental Plan (CP, with a continental breakfast), Breakfast Plan (BP, with a full breakfast), or Modified American Plan (MAP, with breakfast and dinner) or are all-inclusive (AI, including all meals and most activities). We always list facilities but not whether you'll be charged an extra fee to

use them, so when pricing accommodations, find out what's included.

Many Listings
★	Fodor's Choice
★	Highly recommended
⊠	Physical address
⊕	Directions
⌖	Mailing address
☎	Telephone
🖷	Fax
⊕	On the Web
✍	E-mail
🎫	Admission fee
⊘	Open/closed times
Ⓜ	Metro stations
▭	Credit cards

Hotels & Restaurants
🏨	Hotel
⤹	Number of rooms
⟁	Facilities
⍾	Meal plans
✕	Restaurant
⌂	Reservations
⟍	Smoking
⌕	BYOB
✕🏨	Hotel with restaurant that warrants a visit

Outdoors
⚐	Golf
⛺	Camping

Other
☾	Family-friendly
⇨	See also
⊠	Branch address
☞	Take note

WHAT'S WHERE

YELLOWSTONE NATIONAL PARK	When mountain men like John Colter and Jim Bridger first saw the geyser basins of Yellowstone, in what's now Wyoming's northwest corner, they knew at once that this wondrous place was unique. Nearly 200 years later, the land that became Yellowstone National Park in 1872 remains just as alluring. Millions of people visit the park annually, but in Yellowstone you can still find solitude and listen to the sounds of nature: bubbling mud pots, steaming geysers, and the wind in the pine trees.

No matter where you enter Yellowstone, you'll find yourself driving in circles: the park's road system is laid out in a figure eight known as the Grand Loop. Along the road there are eight primary developed areas: Grant Village, Old Faithful, Madison, Norris, Canyon Village, Mammoth Hot Springs, Roosevelt–Tower Fall, and Lake Village/Fishing Bridge. They all have places to gas up your car at the very least, and some have hotels, restaurants, museums, and information centers.

The park's famous geysers are found throughout the area but are most prevalent in the western sections of the park near Old Faithful, Norris, and Mammoth. Yellowstone Lake attracts boaters and anglers, and the steep Yellowstone Canyon is a rich geological display spanning millions of years. Wildlife abounds everywhere, but particularly in open meadows and along the river valleys. You will see bison, elk, and coyotes in virtually all areas; bears are most visible in the Pelican Valley–Fishing Bridge area, near Dunraven Pass, and near Mammoth; wolves can often be spotted in the Lamar Valley and areas south of Mammoth. Watch for trumpeter swans and other waterfowl along the Yellowstone River and for sandhill cranes near the Firehole River and Madison Valley.

GRAND TETON NATIONAL PARK 	You might think Grand Teton National Park would suffer in comparison to its larger, more historic neighbor just to the north—Yellowstone—but when you see the Tetons rising out of Jackson Hole, you realize that the park is its own spectacular destination. Short trails lead through willow flats near Jackson Lake, connecting with longer trails that lead into the canyons of the Teton Range. Boats skim the waters of Jackson and Jenny lakes, depositing people on the wild western shore of Jenny, and guided float trips meander down a calm stretch of the tortuous Snake River. A trip to the backcountry—which has more than 200 mi of trails, from the

novice-accessible Cascade Canyon to the expert-level Teton Crest—reveals the majesty of what the Shoshone tribes called *Teewinot* (Many Pinnacles). Most people explore the park either from the south—usually out of Jackson—or from the north at Yellowstone National Park. There are two main routes through the park. U.S. 26/89/191/287 runs north–south along the eastern edge of the park; it remains open year-round. Teton Park Road diverges from this highway at Moose, running north through the center of the park and hooking up with the highway again near Jackson Lake. This second route—which is open seasonally, generally from May until October—more closely hugs the Teton Range.

NORTHWESTERN WYOMING

In this part of Wyoming you need to keep one thing straight: there is Jackson, and then there is Jackson Hole. The first is the small town, which serves as the area's cultural center; the second is the larger geographic area surrounding the town, home to world-class skiing (and called a hole because it is encircled by mountains). In addition to Jackson, Jackson Hole includes Grand Teton National Park and the small towns of Kelly, Moose, Moran, and Wilson. Also here is Teton Village, the center for the Jackson Hole Mountain Resort, best known for skiing in winter but popular for summer activities as well.

South of Jackson Hole is the Wind River mountain range. Learn about Native American traditions on the Wind River Reservation and find exceptional shops filled with arts and crafts locally made by Northern Arapaho and Eastern Shoshone tribal members. Towns here that make good bases for exploring the area include Pinedale on the west side of the range; Atlantic City, within the range itself; and Lander, Fort Washakie, and Dubois on the east side of the range.

SOUTHWEST MONTANA

Montana's southwest corner was built on the promise of gold-rush riches. More than 30,000 miners and merchants arrived in the five years after the first news of gold strikes on Grasshopper Creek started circulating in 1862. The gold and silver did not last long, but the unexpected discovery of a massive vein of copper beneath Butte ushered in the greatest era of Montana's colorful mining history. Today the region's real treasures are its untamed national forests, blue-ribbon trout streams, and state parks. The Gold West Country also has an ample supply of museums and art galleries, as well as

Montana & Wyoming

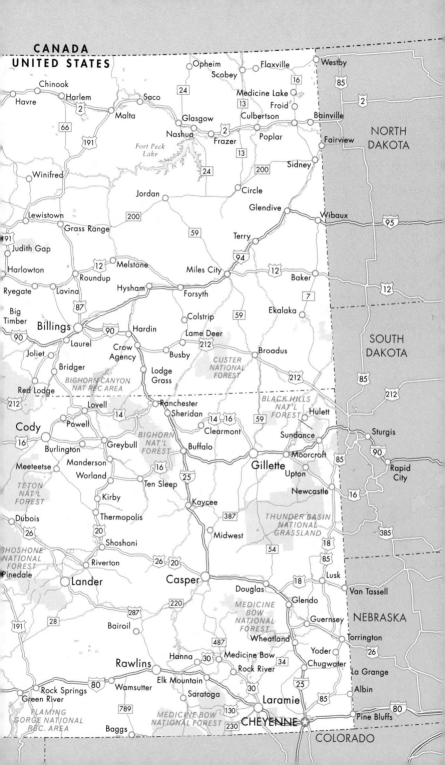

CANADA
UNITED STATES

NORTH DAKOTA

SOUTH DAKOTA

NEBRASKA

COLORADO

Chinook
Havre
Harlem
Saco
Malta
2
66
191
Winifred
Fort Peck Lake
Nashua
Glasgow
Frazer
2
Opheim
Scobey
24
Flaxville
Medicine Lake
13
Froid
Culbertson
Poplar
16
Westby
85
2
Bainville
Fairview
Sidney
200
13
24
200
Jordan
Circle
Lewistown
Grass Range
200
Judith Gap
191
Harlowton
Ryegate
Lavina
12
Melstone
Roundup
Hysham
87
59
Terry
94
Miles City
12
Glendive
Wibaux
95
Baker
7
12
Big Timber
Billings
90
Laurel
Hardin
90
Joliet
Bridger
Crow Agency
Busby
212
Lame Deer
Colstrip
59
Ekalaka
Red Lodge
212
Lovell
14
Lodge Grass
BIGHORN CANYON NAT REC AREA
CUSTER NATIONAL FOREST
Broadus
212
85
212
Cody
16
Powell
Burlington
Greybull
Manderson
Worland
Meeteetse
TETON NAT'L FOREST
Kirby
Thermopolis
20
Dubois
26
Ten Sleep
16
BIGHORN NAT'L FOREST
Ranchester
Sheridan
Clearmont
14
16
Buffalo
25
Kaycee
59
Sundance
Hulett
BLACK HILLS NAT'L FOREST
Moorcroft
Gillette
Upton
Newcastle
85
16
Sturgis
90
Rapid City
385
SHOSHONE NATIONAL FOREST
Pinedale
Shoshoni
Riverton
26
20
Lander
Casper
387
Midwest
THUNDER BASIN NATIONAL GRASSLAND
54
18
85
Lusk
Van Tassell
191
28
220
Bairoil
287
Rawlins
Hanna
30
Medicine Bow
487
MEDICINE BOW NATIONAL FOREST
Douglas
Glendo
18
Guernsey
Wheatland
34
Rock River
Yoder
Chugwater
NEBRASKA
Torrington
26
La Grange
80
Rock Springs
Green River
Wamsutter
789
Elk Mountain
Saratoga
FLAMING GORGE NATIONAL REC. AREA
Baggs
MEDICINE BOW NATIONAL FOREST
130
230
30
Laramie
25
85
Albin
CHEYENNE
Pine Bluffs
80

numerous historic sites—the Big Hole National Battlefield, the Grant-Kohrs Ranch, and the stately restored gold camps of Bannack, Virginia City, and Helena's Last Chance Gulch. Wildlife, water, and wilderness are the hallmarks of the region bordering Yellowstone National Park to the south. Three of Yellowstone's five entrances are here, as are the incredible Beartooth Highway, the Absaroka-Beartooth Wilderness, and the nation's longest free-flowing river. The region's cities and towns, including Bozeman, Livingston, Red Lodge, and West Yellowstone, sponsor year-round special events and are well equipped to welcome visitors.

GLACIER NATIONAL PARK

Glacier National Park occupies more than 1,500 square mi of Northwest Montana's most beautiful real estate. The rugged mountains that weave their way through the Continental Divide seem to have glaciers in every hollow, melting into tiny streams, raging rivers, and ice-cold mountain lakes. Each year 2 million visitors are both astonished and becalmed by the eye-popping blues and emerald greens of Glacier's waters. Hikers come from around the world for the backcountry trails and wilderness areas. More than 730 mi of hiking trails offer plenty of short, scenic routes and long treks in splendid isolation. Motorized access to the park is limited, but the few roads can take you from densely forested lowlands to craggy heights. Going-to-the-Sun Road snakes through the precipitous center of the park, revealing all the glory of this "Crown of the Continent," as it has come to be known.

NORTHWEST MONTANA

Crowned by Glacier National Park, flanked by the Bob Marshall Wilderness Area, and watered by the lakes of the Seeley Valley, northwest Montana is a wild realm encompassing nearly 3 million acres—roughly the size of Connecticut. Exquisite, land- and waterscapes such as the National Bison Range, the Jewel Basin Hiking Area, the Flathead River, and Flathead Lake—the largest body of fresh water in the West—provide some of Montana's most rewarding scenery. Tucked between the peaks and forests are numerous farms that yield such traditional crops as barley, wheat, seed potatoes, oats, and hay. But the peculiar soil and climate of the Flathead Valley also produce outstanding cherries, peppermint, Christmas trees, and champagne grapes. The largest city in the region, Missoula, is home to the University of Montana and the state's most thriving arts community.

THE MONTANA PLAINS	Nestled up against the eastern edge of the Rocky Mountains are the high plains of Montana, vast expanses of grassy prairie where cattle often outnumber people. Though much of the land has a lonesome, empty look to it, it's rich with the history of America's last frontier in places such as the Little Bighorn Battlefield National Monument, where Lakota and Cheyenne warriors scored a major victory over government troops, and in Ekalaka, where an entire town sprang up around a log saloon in the middle of nowhere. The region is also home to two metropolitan areas that serve as bastions of education, culture, and commerce: Billings, along the banks of the Yellowstone River just north of Wyoming, is the state's largest community and one of the largest industrial centers between Minneapolis and Seattle; and Great Falls, nestled at the base of the Rocky Mountains in the north, prides itself on its Western art tradition and beautiful parks.
CODY, SHERIDAN & NORTHERN WYOMING	Northern Wyoming is divided almost exactly in half by the Big Horn Mountains, an easterly Rocky Mountain range with peaks towering more than 13,000 feet above sea level. The wide-open plains of the Powder River Basin lie to the east of these mountains, extending for 150 mi to the Black Hills that straddle the Wyoming–South Dakota border. Although the centrally located and coal-rich town of Gillette is northern Wyoming's most populous city (19,646 residents), the city of Sheridan, with its proud ranching heritage and convenient location near the ski slopes and snowmobile trails of the Big Horns, is more visited by travelers. West of these lofty peaks is the Big Horn Basin, a giant earthen bowl almost as arid as most deserts. The storied settlement of Cody, founded by the great showman Buffalo Bill Cody, sits on its western edge near the border with Yellowstone National Park. Rodeos, museums, guest ranches, hiking trails, and winter sports are among the area's biggest draws.
CHEYENNE, LARAMIE & SOUTHERN WYOMING	Southern Wyoming spans the wheat fields of the southeast, the lush meadows of the Platte River and Bridger valleys, and the wide-open sagebrush lands of the southwest; the region is populated by the world's largest free-ranging pronghorn antelope herds, wild horses, deer, elk, and other wildlife. Cheyenne, Wyoming's state capital, anchors the southeast, and there are major services in Laramie, Rawlins, Rock Springs, Green River, and Evanston, towns that got their start because of the Union Pacific Railroad. Any trip across southern Wyo-

ming involves some miles on I–80, where you'll share the road with lots of 18-wheelers, but the best way to appreciate the region is to take side trips whenever possible. Between Cheyenne and Laramie, use Wyoming Route 210 (Happy Jack Road); follow the old Lincoln Highway—U.S. 30—between Laramie and Walcott Junction; cross the Snowy Range Scenic Byway (open from late May through early October) between Laramie/Centennial and Saratoga to see the rugged beauty of the Snowy Range mountains; and take Wyoming Route 70 (the Battle Highway) between Encampment and Baggs to explore the Medicine Bow National Forest and see the copper mines of the early 1900s. The Red Desert between Rawlins and Green River may seem stark, but in the early morning and late evening, shadows lengthen, adding depth and color to the landscape.

THE SOUTH DAKOTA BLACK HILLS

A few hundred miles east of the Rocky Mountains sit the Black Hills, an ancient mountain range that straddles the Wyoming–South Dakota border. A sacred land that was once the Great Sioux Indian Reservation, it saw America's last great gold rush. Western legends such as Deadwood Dick and the Sundance Kid roamed its creek-carved canyons and windswept prairies. Some, such as Calamity Jane and Wild Bill Hickok, never left. Today you can see their legacy in places such as Deadwood, the site of one of the country's largest ongoing historic preservation projects. You are unlikely to forget a visit to the weathered buttes and otherworldly canyons of Badlands National Park, or to the labyrinthine passages of Jewel Cave National Monument and Wind Cave National Park, two of the longest caves in the world. But the big draw for most visitors (2.5 million in 2007) is Mount Rushmore National Memorial, a mountain sculpted into the unblinking granite faces of George Washington, Thomas Jefferson, Theodore Roosevelt, and Abraham Lincoln.

WHEN TO GO

Hotels in tourist destinations book up early, especially in July and August, and hikers spread into the backcountry from June through Labor Day. Ski resorts buzz from December to early April, especially during Christmas and Presidents' Day holiday weeks.

If you don't mind capricious weather, spring and fall are opportune seasons to visit—prices drop and crowds are nonexistent. Spring's pleasures are somewhat limited, since snow usually blocks the high country well into June. But spring is a good time for fishing, rafting on rivers swollen with snowmelt, birding, and wildlife viewing. In fall, aspens splash the mountainsides with gold, and wildlife comes down to lower elevations. The fish are spawning, and the angling is excellent.

Climate

Summer in the area begins in late June or early July. Days are warm, with highs often in the 80s, and nighttime temperatures fall to the 40s and 50s. Afternoon thunderstorms are common over the higher peaks. Fall begins in September, often with a week of unsettled weather around mid-month, followed by four to six gorgeous weeks of Indian summer—frosty nights and warm days. Winter creeps in during November, and deep snows arrive by December. Temperatures usually hover near freezing by day, thanks to the warm mountain sun, dropping considerably overnight, occasionally as low as -20°F. Winter tapers off in March, though snow lingers into April on valley bottoms and into July on mountain passes. The Rockies have a reputation for extreme weather, but no condition ever lasts for long.

Forecasts Accu-Weather Provided by American Express (☎900/932–8437 75¢ per minute from a Touch-Tone phone. Also, visit ⊕www.weather.com for the most up-to-date weather forecasts for your area.)

Charts of average daily maximum and minimum temperatures for each month within the region.

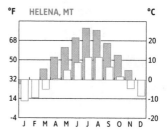

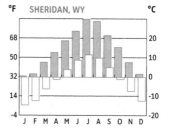

QUINTESSENTIAL MONTANA & WYOMING

Living with Animals

Whether they're wrangling a herd of cattle, waiting for a trout to bite, or sharing a trail with a mountain goat, people in these parts interact with other members of the animal kingdom to a degree you just don't find in many other places in the United States. Sharing the environment isn't some lofty concept—it's a part of everyday life.

What results is an unromanticized respect for animals and the places they live. It's an attitude worthy of emulation. Spotting the abundant, beautiful wildlife that populates Montana and Wyoming is a thrill, whether you're driving the Grand Loop in Yellowstone or hiking through the backcountry. The locals get a kick out of it, too—but they know to tread softly and keep a safe distance, for the animals' benefit as well as their own.

Rodeos, Rendezvous & Powwows

The Western tradition of working hard and then cutting loose is alive and well—look no further than Cheyenne Frontier Days, the rodeo extravaganza that's known simply as "The Daddy of 'Em All." It's the biggest event on the calendar, but it's hardly alone. In July and August a weekend doesn't go by without some sort of a celebration: there are rodeos, Native American powwows, and rendezvous (events commemorating 19th-century trappers and traders—the Green River Rendezvous in Pinedale, Wyoming, is one of the best).

Winter begins with torchlight ski parades and traditional Christmas celebrations, but as the season wears on, things turn wacky: In Whitefish, Montana, contestants race down the slopes in their favorite furniture, and it's golf on ice at the Wild West Winter Carnival in Riverton, Wyoming.

Montana and Wyoming are states where the buffalo still roam and a cowboy sensibility endures—people tend to look you in the eye, and they consider you a friend until proven otherwise. Below are a few classic elements of the regional culture worth keeping in mind.

Meat & Potatoes

You're in the land of the unrepentant carnivore here: fine dining first and foremost means steaks grilled to perfection. It's also prime hunting and fishing territory. Antelope, elk, venison, and grouse make regular appearances on menus, and you often have a choice of rainbow trout, salmon, and bass pulled from someone's favorite fishing spot. You can find adventurous chefs doing creative things in the kitchen, but nothing that smacks of "highfalutin'." No matter where you go, your server is likely to greet you with a smile, and blue jeans are always okay.

Microbreweries are another noteworthy phenomenon—a leader in the regional market is the Bozeman Brewing Co., but you'll find smaller local operations all over. And the fruits are exceptional: huckleberries are used in everything from muffins to ice cream, and apples, peaches, and pears from roadside stands are full of tree-ripened goodness.

The Big Sky

"The Big Sky State" is Montana's motto, but you can have the Big Sky experience in Wyoming, too. It happens when the vastness of the land (and the sky above it) becomes so great it nearly overwhelms you. The horizon heads off toward infinity in every direction, a few high clouds drift by overhead, and the only sign of civilization is the road beneath your feet.

Some people find the Big Sky exhilarating—a place where you can stretch your legs, take a deep breath, and consider your day-to-day life from a new, broader perspective. On the flip side, if you have a hint of agoraphobia in your blood, you'll feel it here. One way or the other, the Big Sky tends to provoke strong reactions.

IF YOU LIKE

Horseback Riding

Horseback riding in Montana and Wyoming can mean anything from a quick trot around a ring to a weeklong stay at a working dude ranch where guests rise at dawn and herd cattle.

Horse-pack trips are a great way to visit the backcountry, since horses can travel distances and carry supplies that would be impossible for hikers. Northwest Montana's Bob Marshall Wilderness Area is the perfect example: in the state's largest stretch of roadless wilderness, a horse-pack trip is just about the only way to travel the huge expanses. Although horsemanship isn't required for most trips, it's helpful, and even an experienced rider can expect to be a little sore for the first few days. June through August is the peak period for horse-pack trips; before signing up with an outfitter, ask what skills are expected.

Dude ranches fall roughly into two categories: working ranches and guest ranches. Working ranches, where guests participate in such activities as round-ups and cattle movements, sometimes require experienced horsemanship. Guest ranches offer a wide range of activities in addition to horseback riding, including fishing, four-wheeling, spa services, and cooking classes. At a typical dude ranch, guests stay in log cabins and are served meals family-style in a lodge or ranch house; some ranches now have upscale restaurants on-site, too. For winter, many ranches have added such snow-oriented amenities as sleigh rides, snowshoeing, and cross-country skiing.

The ranches are equipped to handle guests arriving with no gear, although all offer lists of what to bring for travelers who want to use their own gear. Jeans and cowboy boots are still the preferred attire for horseback, although hiking boots and Gore-Tex have long since become fashionable, especially in colder months and at higher altitudes. Long pants are a must either way. Layering is key; plan to have some kind of fleece or heavier outer layer no matter the time of year, since the mountains will be cooler the higher you go.

When choosing a ranch, consider whether the place is family-oriented or adults-only, and check on the length-of-stay requirements. Working ranches plan around the needs of the business, and thus often require full-week stays for a fixed price, whereas guest ranches operate more like hotels.

Gunsel Horse Adventures, Yellowstone. To get a taste of Yellowstone far from the traffic jams, pack up and head into the backcountry on trips ranging from 4 to 10 days.

Paradise Guest Ranch, Buffalo, Northern Wyoming. For a hundred years this ranch has been putting guests on horseback. You can take rodeo training, hit the trail for a multiday pack trip, and get out of the saddle for barbecues and square dances.

Seven Lazy P Guest Ranch, Bob Marshall Wilderness Area, Northwest Montana. From this comfortable all-inclusive ranch you can take rides into "the Bob," where the terrain has changed little since the days of Lewis and Clark.

Skiing & Snowboarding

The champagne powder of the Rocky Mountains can be a revelation for skiers and snowboarders familiar only with the slopes of other regions.

Forget treacherous sheets of rock-hard ice, single-note hills where the bottom can be seen from the top, and mountains that offer only one kind of terrain from every angle. In the Rockies, the snow builds up quickly, leaving a solid base that hangs tough all ski season, only to be layered upon by thick, fluffy powder that holds an edge, ready to be groomed into rippling corduroy or left in giddy stashes along the sides and through the trees. Volkswagen-size moguls and half-pipe–studded terrain parks are the norm, not the special attractions.

Skiing the Rockies means preparing for all kinds of weather, sometimes in the same day, because the high altitudes can start a day off sunny and bright but kick in a blizzard by afternoon. Layers help, as well as plenty of polypropylene to wick away sweat in the sun, and a water-resistant outer layer to keep off the powdery wetness that's sure to accumulate—especially if you're a beginner snowboarder certain to spend time on the ground. Must-haves: plenty of sunscreen, because the sun is closer than you think, and a helmet, because the trees are, too.

The added bonus of Rocky Mountain terrain is that so many of the areas have a wide variety of easier (green circle), intermediate (blue square), advanced (black diamond), and expert (double black diamond) slopes—often in the same ski resort. Turn yourself over to the rental shops, which are specialized enough at each resort to offer experts in helping you plan your day and the types of equipment you'll need. Renting is also a great chance for experienced skiers and snowboarders to try out the latest technology before investing in a purchase.

Shop around for lift tickets before you leave home. Look for package deals, multiple-day passes, and online discounts. Call the resort and ask if there are any off-site locations (such as local supermarkets) where discount tickets can be purchased. The traditional ski season usually runs from mid-December until early April, with Christmas, New Year's, and the month of March being the busiest times at the resorts.

Big Mountain, Whitefish, Northwest Montana. The highlight here is the long high-speed quad, the Glacier Chaser. The scene isn't as glamorous as Jackson Hole or Aspen, and skiers here think that's just fine.

Big Sky, Southwest Montana. An easygoing atmosphere combined with the second-greatest vertical drop in the United States makes for a first-rate ski destination.

Jackson Hole, Wyoming. The steep descents draw America's best skiers, but with thousands of ways to get down the mountain, this is a world-class experience no matter what your skill level.

Lone Mountain Ranch, Southwest Montana. If cross-country skiing is your thing, this is the place to go. The 50 mi of groomed trails are beautiful and wonderfully varied.

Hiking

Hiking is easily the least expensive and most accessible recreational pursuit. Sure, you could spend a few hundred dollars on high-tech hiking boots, a so-called "personal hydration system," and a collapsible walking staff made of space-age materials, but there's no need for such expenditure. All that's really essential are sturdy athletic shoes, water, and the desire to see the landscape under your own power.

Hiking in the Rockies is a three-season sport that basically lasts as long as you're willing to tromp through snow. (You could look at snowshoeing as winter hiking—the trails are often the same.) One of the greatest aspects of this region is the wide range of hiking terrain, from high-alpine scrambles that require stamina, to flowered meadows that invite a relaxed pace, to confining slot canyons where flash floods are a real danger and can be fatal to the unwary adventurer.

There are few real hazards to hiking, but a little preparedness goes a long way. Know your limits, and make sure the terrain you are about to embark on does not exceed your abilities. It's a good idea to check the elevation change on a trail before you set out—a 1-mi trail might sound easy, until you realize how steep it is—and be careful not to get caught on exposed trails at elevation during afternoon thunderstorms in summer. Dress appropriately by bringing layers to address changing weather conditions, and always carry enough drinking water. Also make sure someone knows where you're going and when to expect your return.

There are literally thousands of miles of hiking trails in Montana and Wyoming. The national parks have particularly well-marked and well-maintained trails, and admission to all trails is free. In fact, hiking is sometimes the only way to get close to certain highlights on protected land. Primarily for safety reasons, overnight hikers are usually expected to register with park or forest rangers. Also keep in mind that run-ins with bears and mountain lions are increasingly common.

Clear Creek Trail, Buffalo, Northern Wyoming. An easy 11-mi path goes through the historic town of Buffalo and out into nature, with good spots to stop for fishing and photography.

The Highline Trail, Glacier National Park. This gorgeous 7-mi hike leads from Logan Pass to Granite Chalet, a rustic National Landmark lodge where you can bed down for the night.

Jewel Basil Hiking Area, Flathead Lake, Northwest Montana. Thirty-five miles of well-maintained trails run past 27 trout-filled alpine lakes.

Yellowstone Association Institute, Yellowstone National Park. This is the group to contact for guided hikes through the park, from day trips to overnight backpacking in the backcountry.

Bicycling

The Rockies are a favorite destination for bikers. Wide-open roads with great gains and losses in elevation test and form road cyclists' stamina, although riders who prefer pedaling fat tires have plenty of mountain and desert trails to test their skills. Unmatched views often make it difficult to keep your eyes on the road.

Thanks to the popularity of the sport here, it's usually easy to find a place that rents bicycles if you'd prefer to leave yours at home. Shops often rent a variety of bikes from entry level to high end, though the latter come at a premium, and if you're in the market for a used bike, good deals can often be found when shops unload one season's rentals to make room for next year's models. Bike shops are also a good bet for information on local rides and group tours.

Mountain biking has a huge following—it's more popular in the region than touring on paved roads. The Montana-based Adventure Cycling Association ⊕ *www.adventurecycling.org* has mapped interconnecting back roads, logging and forest-service roads, and trails stretching from Canada to Mexico. Few people ride the whole route, which covers close to 2,500 mi, but it's easy to pick a segment to suit any rider's stamina. Although the route does follow, very approximately, the Continental Divide, the riding is not all big-mountain climbing and descending. Portions of the trip are negotiable by children as young as 10. The Adventure Cycling Association leads tours and can provide maps (complete with lodging and camping options), information, and advice for self-guided trips.

The rules of the road are the same here as elsewhere, though some areas are less biker-friendly than others. On the road, watch for trucks and stay as close as possible to the side of the road, in single file. On the trail, ride within your limits and keep your eyes peeled for hikers and horses (both have the right of way), as well as dogs. Always wear a helmet and carry plenty of water.

Adventure Cycling, Missoula, Southwest Montana. This organization is the first stop for mountain bikers looking for routes, maps, advice, and guided tours.

Mickelson Trail, Deadwood, South Dakota. More than 100 mi of former railroad line run the length of the Black Hills.

Railroad-Daly Loop, Darby, Northwest Montana. Sixteen miles of mountainous terrain provide lots of opportunities for spotting moose, deer, and elk.

Rimrocks, Billings, Montana Plains. Trails to suit every level of mountain biker are within easy reach in the terrain surrounding Billings.

Rafting

Rafting brings on emotions varying from the calm induced by flat waters surrounded with stunning scenery, back-country, and wildlife, to the thrill and excitement of charging a raging torrent of foam.

For the inexperienced, the young, and the aged, dozens of tour companies offer relatively tame floats ranging from one hour to one day starting at $20, which are ideal for anyone from 4 years old to 90. Others fulfill the needs of adventure tourists content only with chills, potential spills, and the occasional wall of water striking them smack-dab in the chest. Beginners and novices should use guides, but experienced rafters may rent watercraft.

Seasoned outfitters know their routes and their waters as well as you know the road between home and work. Many guides offer multiday trips in which they do everything, including searing your steak in a beach barbecue, setting up your tent, and rolling out your sleeping bag. Select an outfitter based on recommendations from the local chamber, experience, and word of mouth.

The International Scale of River Difficulty is a widely accepted rating system that ranks waters from Class I (the easiest) to Class VI (the most difficult—think Niagara Falls). Ask your guide about the rating on your route before you book. Remember, ratings can vary greatly throughout the season because of runoff and weather events.

Wear a swimsuit or shorts and sandals and bring along sunscreen and sunglasses. Outfitters are required to supply a life jacket for each passenger, although most states don't require that it be worn.

Midsummer is the ideal time to raft in the West, but many outfitters will stretch the season, particularly on calmer routes.

Numerous outfitters and guide services offer rafting trips in Wyoming and Montana, and the journey can vary from relaxing family outings to white-knuckled runs through raging waters. In all cases you'll discover scenery, wildlife, and an off-the-road experience that you'll never get looking through a windshield.

Alberton Gorge near Missoula, Northwest Montana. This canyon section of the Clark Fork River is perfect for a hot summer day.

North Platte River, near Casper, Northern Wyoming. Outfitters offer trips ranging from one hour to a full day on this tranquil stretch of water, ideal for the whole family.

Snake River Canyon, south of Jackson, Wyoming. Some of the wildest white water in the Rockies, a winding stretch lined with trees, steep granite walls, alpine meadows, and abundant wildlife.

Upper middle fork of the Flathead River, Northwest Montana. A white-water rafting adventure into the 286,700-acre Great Bear Wilderness.

Yellowstone River near Gardiner, Southwest Montana. Raft through Yankee Jim Canyon and experience Boxcar, Big Rock, and Revenge rapids.

Fishing

Trout do not live in ugly places.

And so it is in Montana and Wyoming, where you'll discover unbridled beauty, towering pines, rippling mountain streams, and bottomless pools. It's here that blue-ribbon trout streams remain much as they were when Native American tribes, French fur trappers, and a few thousand faceless miners, muleskinners, and sodbusters first placed a muddy footprint along their banks.

Those early-day settlers had one advantage that you won't—time. To make the best use of that limited resource, consider the following advice.

Hire a guide. You could spend days locating a great fishing spot, learning the water currents and fish behavior, and determining what flies, lures, or bait the fish are following. A good guide will cut through the options, get you into fish, and turn your excursion into an adventure complete with a full creel.

If you're comfortable with your fishing gear, bring it along, though most guides lend or rent equipment. Bring a rod and reel, waders, vest, hat, sunglasses, net, tackle, hemostats, and sunscreen. Always buy a fishing license.

If you're not inclined to fork over the $250-plus that most high-quality guides charge per day for two anglers and a boat, your best bet is a stop at a reputable fly shop. They'll shorten your learning curve, tell you where the fish are, what they're biting on, and whether you should be "skittering" your dry-fly on top of the water or "dead-drifting" a nymph.

Famed fisherman Lee Wolff wrote that "catching fish is a sport. Eating fish is not a sport." Most anglers practice "catch and release" in an effort to maintain productive fisheries and to protect native species.

Season is always a consideration. Spring runoffs can cloud the waters, summer droughts may reduce stream flows, and fall weather can be unpredictable. But, as many fishing guides will attest, the best time to come and wet a line is whenever you can make it.

Black Feet Reservation, near Browning, Northwest Montana. Twenty-some stocked reservoirs regularly yield lunker lake trout from 2 to 8 pounds.

Flaming Gorge Reservoir, Southern Wyoming. Home to state records for smallmouth bass, Kokanee salmon, brown trout, channel catfish, Utah chub, and lake trout.

Gallatin Canyon, south of Bozeman, Southwest Montana. The clarity and variety of water is outstanding; the scenery incredible.

North Fork of Shoshone River, west of Cody, Northern Wyoming. The river drops roughly 3,000 feet in 70 mi from the Silvertip Basin to Buffalo Bill Reservoir.

Platte River, near Casper, Northern Wyoming. With depths ranging from 1 to 15 feet, this blue-ribbon water attracts fishermen from all over the world.

Yellowstone National Park. Simply a tremendous fishing destination.

Yellowstone River through Paradise Valley, Southwest Montana. Fish surrounded by snowcapped peaks, free-roaming wildlife, and soaring hawks and eagles.

GLACIER TO GRAND TETON DRIVING TOUR

GLACIER NATIONAL PARK & MONTANA SCENIC BYWAYS

Day 1

After visiting ❶ **Glacier National Park,** with its 1,500 square mi of exquisite ice-carved terrain, plan to spend half a day (or more, depending on stops) driving on a scenic, 160-mi route through western Montana. Start off going southwest on U.S. 2 to ❷ **Kalispell,** then south on Highway 206 and Highway 83, through the Seeley–Swan Valley, where you'll have a view of the Mission Range to the west and the Swan Range to the east. South of ❸ **Seeley Lake** turn east on Route 200, and then take Route 141 to the small town of ❹ **Avon,** about 36 mi west of Helena. From here, turn west on U.S. 12 to connect with I–90. Continue southeast 10 mi to ❺ **Deer Lodge,** and 41 mi to the century-old mining town of ❻ **Butte,** where the lavish Copper King Mansion reveals what you could buy with an unlimited household budget back in the 1880s, when it was built. From Butte, follow I–90 to ❼ **Bozeman** or ❽ **Livingston.** Either town is a good place to spend the night and get a good night's sleep before exploring Yellowstone.

YELLOWSTONE NATIONAL PARK

Days 2 & 3

Dedicate the next two days to ❾ **Yellowstone National Park.** From Bozeman, you can reach ❿ **West Yellowstone** by following I–90 west 8 mi to U.S. 287, then driving south 106 mi. (From Livingston, enter the park from the north by driving south 57 mi on U.S. 89 through the Paradise Valley.) Spend the rest of your first day on the park's 142-mi Grand Loop Road.

THE PLAN

Distance: 850–1,000 mi

Time: 7 days

Breaks: Overnight in Glacier National Park, and Bozeman or Livingston, MT; and Yellowstone National Park, Grand Teton National Park, and Jackson, WY.

It passes nearly every major Yellowstone attraction, and you'll discover interpretive displays, overlooks, and short trails along the way. On your second day in the park, hike the park's trails, visit the geyser basins, or watch the wildlife. For your accommodations, you really can't go wrong with a stay at Old Faithful Inn, with its lodgepole-pine walls and ceiling beams, an immense volcanic rock fireplace, and green-tinted, etched windows.

GRAND TETON NATIONAL PARK

Days 4 & 5

On the final two days of your tour, experience Wyoming's other national treasure, ⓫ **Grand Teton National Park.** Its northern boundary is 7 mi from Yellowstone's south entrance. The sheer ruggedness of the Tetons makes them seem imposing and unapproachable, but a drive on Teton Park Road, with frequent stops at scenic turnouts, will get you up close and personal with the peaks. Overnight in one of the park lodges and spend your final day in the park hiking, horseback riding, or taking a river float trip, before continuing south to ⓬ **Jackson,** with its landmark elk antler arches in the town square, fine dining, art galleries, museums, and eclectic shopping.
—*Candy Moulton*

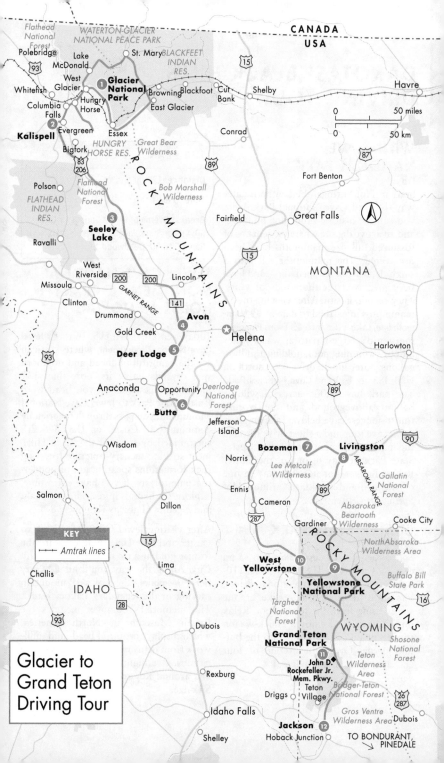

Glacier to
Grand Teton
Driving Tour

DAKOTAS' BLACK HILLS DRIVING TOUR

WIND CAVE NATIONAL PARK
Day 1

Start in Hot Springs, the southern gateway to Wind Cave National Park. Here you can see historic sandstone buildings and an active dig site where the remains of fossilized full-size mammoths have been discovered. The mammoths fell into a sinkhole, became trapped, died, and have been preserved for thousands of years. They remain in situ. After viewing the 55 mammoths unearthed to date at ❶ **Mammoth Site,** take a dip into ❷ **Evans Plunge**—the world's largest natural warm-water indoor swimming pool, holding 1 million gallons. After lunch, drive 6 mi north on U.S. 385 to ❸ **Wind Cave National Park.** The park has 28,000 acres of wildlife habitat aboveground and the world's fourth-longest cave below. Take an afternoon cave tour and a short drive through the park. Overnight at nearby Custer State Park or stay in one of the Custer Resort Lodges—or possibly stay in one of the bed-and-breakfasts around Hot Springs or Custer.

CUSTER STATE PARK
Day 2

Spend today at ❹ **Custer State Park,** 5 mi east of Custer on U.S. 16A. The 110-square-mi park has exceptional drives, lots of wildlife, and fingerlike granite spires rising from the forest floor. Relax on a hayride and enjoy a chuck-wagon supper, or take a Jeep tour into the buffalo herds. Overnight in one of four enchanting mountain lodges.

THE PLAN

Distance: 120 mi

Time: 5 days

Breaks: Overnight in Hot Springs or Custer, SD; Custer State Park, SD; Keystone, SD; Rapid City, SD; Deadwood, SD.

JEWEL CAVE NATIONAL MONUMENT & CRAZY HORSE MEMORIAL
Day 3

Today, venture down U.S. 16 to ❺ **Jewel Cave National Monument,** where you can see the beautiful nailhead and dogtooth spar crystals lining its more than 135 mi of passageways. As you head from Custer State Park to Jewel Cave National Monument, you pass through the friendly community of Custer on U.S. 385. It's surrounded by some of the Black Hills' most striking scenery—picture towering rock formations spearing out of ponderosa pine forests. If you have extra time, explore Cathedral Spires, Harney Peak, and Needles Highway (Highway 87).

After visiting Jewel Cave, head back to Custer and take U.S. 16/385 toward the former gold and tin mining town of Hill City. Along the way you'll hit ❻ **Crazy Horse Memorial,** the colossal mountain carving of the legendary Lakota leader. The memorial's complex includes the Indian Museum of North America, which displays beautiful bead- and quillwork from many of the continent's native nations. Overnight at one of the hotels in and around Keystone, such as the K Bar S Lodge.

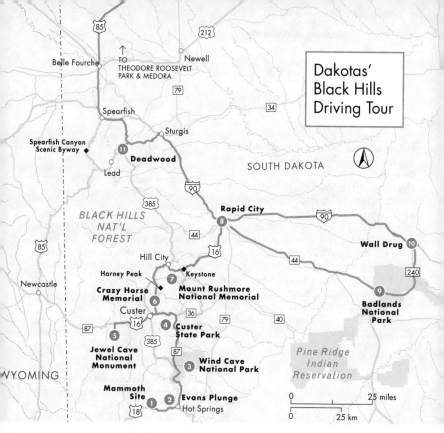

Dakotas' Black Hills Driving Tour

Belle Fourche

TO
THEODORE ROOSEVELT
PARK & MEDORA

Newell

Spearfish

Sturgis

Spearfish Canyon
Scenic Byway

Deadwood

Lead

SOUTH DAKOTA

Rapid City

BLACK HILLS
NAT'L
FOREST

Newcastle

Hill City

Harney Peak

Keystone

Crazy Horse
Memorial

Mount Rushmore
National Memorial

Custer

Custer
State Park

Jewel Cave
National
Monument

Wall Drug

Badlands
National
Park

WYOMING

Wind Cave
National Park

Pine Ridge
Indian
Reservation

Mammoth
Site

Evans Plunge

Hot Springs

0   25 miles

0   25 km

MOUNT RUSHMORE NATIONAL MEMORIAL
Day 4

This morning, travel 3 mi from Keystone (10 from Hill City) on Route 244 (the Gutzon Borglum Memorial Highway) to ⓐ Mount Rushmore National Memorial, where you can view the huge, carved renderings of Washington, Jefferson, Roosevelt, and Lincoln and have breakfast with the presidents. Afterward, head northwest on U.S. 16 to ⓑ Rapid City, western South Dakota's largest city and the eastern gateway to the Black Hills. Overnight here.

BADLANDS NATIONAL PARK
Day 5

Begin your day early and drive 55 mi on Route 44 to the North Unit of ⓒ Badlands National Park. Badlands Loop Road wiggles through this moonlike landscape for 32 mi. When you've had enough of this 380-square-mi geologic wonderland, head back to the hills. Exit onto Route 240 at the northeast entrance to catch I–90. For a fun excursion, take a little detour east to Wall for its world-famous ⓓ Wall Drug. Founded on the premise that free ice water would attract road-weary travelers, the emporium carries all manner of Westernalia.

Spend this afternoon and tonight in ⓔ Deadwood, reached via U.S. 14 and 14A. This Old West mining town has 80 gaming halls, including Old Style Saloon No. 10, which bills itself as "the only museum in the world with a bar." Upstairs, at the Deadwood Social Club, you can discover outstanding food at reasonable prices and the best wine selection in the state. To view rare artifacts from the town's colorful past, such as items that once belonged to Wild Bill Hickok, visit Adams Memorial Museum. Overnight in Deadwood's Franklin Hotel, where past guests have included Theodore Roosevelt, Babe Ruth, John Wayne, and country duo Big & Rich. —*T. D. Griffith and Dustin D. Floyd*

TIPS

■ Avoid the tour at the height of winter, when heavy snowfall can make roads impassable.

■ If you plan to be in the Black Hills in early August, when more than half a million motorcycle riders converge on Sturgis, make reservations several months in advance.

■ You cannot collect fossils. It is against federal law.

■ You *can* collect rocks in small amounts in the Black Hills National Forest, but no digging is allowed.

■ In certain areas you can pan for gold; contact forest personnel for locations and rules.

■ It's a good idea to pick up a Forest Service map if you plan to venture off the beaten path when in the Black Hills. The Black Hills National Forest intermixes with private property, so you'll want to know where you are at all times.

Yellowstone National Park

WORD OF MOUTH

"Oh, you will love Yellowstone! How much fun your young children will have seeing all the wildlife. (Please be safe and keep a big distance away.) The Beartooth Highway is a lovely drive. There are quite a number of places to pull over and enjoy the scenery, like the many glacial lakes with their turquoise blue waters."

—swisshiker

WELCOME TO YELLOWSTONE

TOP REASONS TO GO

★ **Going-off geysers:**
With more than 10,000 thermal features, Yellowstone is a natural war zone of steaming hot geysers, the most famous of all being Old Faithful.

★ **Fisherman's dream:**
Thousands of miles of streams and lakes, home to several types of trout, grayling, and mountain whitefish, make Yellowstone a fisherman's dream.

★ **Winter wonderland:**
Yellowstone can be a truly amazing place during the winter months, and navigating the park by snowmobile allows visitors to see all the park's main attractions.

★ **Volcanic ventures:** A combination of thinner-than-normal crust depth and a huge magma chamber beneath the park is the reason Yellowstone's surface is active with geysers, steaming pools, hissing fumaroles, bubbling mud pots, and warm seeps.

★ **Nature-calling:**
Yellowstone's mix of wildlife, mountains, geysers, and water showcases nature at her best.

1 **Grant Village/West Thumb.** Named for President Ulysses S. Grant, Grant Village is on the western edge of Yellowstone Lake. Early explorers thought the lake was shaped like a human hand; thus Grant Village is also called West Thumb.

2 **Old Faithful area.** This area is home to one of the most recognizable images in U.S. pop culture, Old Faithful. Famous for its regularity and awesome power, Old Faithful erupts every 94 minutes or so.

3 **Madison.** Here, the Madison River is formed by the joining of the Gibbon and Firehole rivers. Fly fishermen will find healthy stocks of brown and rainbow trout and mountain whitefish.

4 **Norris.** The Norris area is the hottest and most changeable part of Yellowstone National Park. Geysers can suddenly stop flowing and new ones can appear.

5 **Mammoth Hot Springs.** The Mammoth Hot Springs are a result of several key ingredients: rock fractures in the limestone allow heat and water to escape the earth's surface.

6 **Tower-Roosevelt.** This least-visited area of the park is the place to go for solitude, or at least a less crowded atmosphere.

7 **Canyon area.** Scientists believe that the Yellowstone area is home to one of the largest volcanic eruptions in history, which resulted in the formation of a large caldera and several canyons. The area continued to change over the centuries, and receding glaciers left the area in its current state.

8 **Yellowstone Lake area.** The largest body of water within the park, Yellowstone Lake is believed to have once been 200 feet higher than the present-day lake. In the winter months, the lake freezes over with ice depths ranging from a few inches to several feet.

WYOMING

GETTING ORIENTED

At more than 2.2 million acres, Yellowstone National Park is considered one of America's most scenic and diverse national parks. Established in 1872 in what is now the northwest corner of Wyoming, Yellowstone was the first national park in the world and was named for its location at the head of the Yellowstone River. At the time, people began to believe in preserving our natural wonders to ensure their longevity well into the future. As a result, Yellowstone is every bit as wondrous today as it was more than 130 years ago.

MONTANA

Cooke City
Silver Gate
Northeast Entrance

TO RED LODGE

Slough Creek
Pebble Creek

line lls

Blacktail Deer Plateau
6 Tower-Roosevelt
Roosevelt Lodge
Tower Fall

212

Lamar Valley
Specimen Ridge
Lamar Canyon Creek

Mount Washburn

Visitor Center

7 Inspiration Point
Artist Point
Yellowstone Falls

inia ade

ral Plateau

Hayden Valley
Grand Loop Road

Mud Volcano

Lake Yellowstone Hotel
Lake Village
Bridge Bay

Visitor Center

Avalanche Peak
East Entrance

TO CODY

Lake Butte

8 Yellowstone Lake
Sylvan Lake

14 16 20

1 West Thumb
Grant Village

Visitor Center

ewis ake
vis e

Continental

Heart Lake

Lewis Falls Mount Sheridan

Divide

RANGE

ABSAROKA

River

uth Entrance

gg Ranch

TO JACKSON

0   20 miles

0   35 km

KEY	
	Ranger Station
	Campground
	Picnic Area
	Restaurant
	Lodge
	Trailhead
	Restrooms
	Scenic Viewpoint
-----	Walking/Hiking Trails
......	Bicycle Path

YELLOWSTONE PLANNER

When to Go

There are two major seasons in Yellowstone: summer (May–September), when warm days give way to brisk evenings, and when by far the majority of visitors come; and winter (mid-December–February), when fewer people visit. Except for services at park headquarters at Mammoth Hot Springs, the park closes from October to mid-December and from March to late April or early May.

You'll find big crowds from mid-July to mid-August. There are fewer people in the park the month or two before and after this peak season, but there are also fewer facilities open. There's also more rain, especially at lower elevations. Except for holiday weekends, there are few visitors in winter. You must plan ahead if you want to visit during this time, as snowy conditions mean most roads are closed from early November to early May. Snow is possible year-round at high elevations.

If you've visited Yellowstone in summer, you might not recognize it after the first snowfall. Rocky outcroppings are smoothed over. Waterfalls are transformed into jagged sheets of ice. The most satisfying—and often the only—way to explore is by snowshoe, ski, or snowmobile.

Flora & Fauna

Yellowstone's scenery is astonishing any time of day, though the play of light and shadow makes the park most appealing in early morning and late afternoon. That is exactly when you should be out looking for wildlife, as most are active around dawn and dusk, when animals move out of the forest in search of food and water. May and June are the best months for seeing baby bison, moose, and other young arrivals. Spring and early summer find the park covered with wildflowers, and autumn is a great time to visit because of the vivid reds and golds of the changing foliage. Winter visitors are the ones who see the park at its most magical, with steam billowing from geyser basins to wreath trees in ice, and elk foraging close to roads transformed into ski trails.

Bison, elk, and coyotes populate virtually all areas; elk and bison particularly like river valleys and the geyser basins. Moose like marshy areas along Yellowstone Lake and in the northeast corner of the park. Wolves roam throughout the region but are most common in the Lamar Valley and areas south of Mammoth, and bears are most visible in the Pelican Valley–Fishing Bridge area, near Dunraven Pass, and near Mammoth. Watch for trumpeter swans and other waterfowl along the Yellowstone River and for sandhill cranes near the Firehole River and in Madison Valley.

Controversy swirls around the park's wolves, which were reintroduced in 1995, as well as its bison, which sometimes roam outside the park in winter. Both draw headlines because neighboring cattle ranchers see the creatures as a threat to their herds.

Getting There & Around

Yellowstone National Park is served by airports in nearby communities, including Cody, Wyoming, one hour east; Jackson, Wyoming, one hour south; Bozeman, Montana, 90 minutes north; and West Yellowstone, Montana, just outside the park's west gate, which has only summer service. The best places to rent cars in the region are at airports in Cody, Jackson, Bozeman, and West Yellowstone. There is no commercial bus service to Yellowstone.

Yellowstone is well away from the interstates, so drivers make their way here on two-lane highways that are long on miles and scenery. From Interstate 80, take U.S. 191 north from Rock Springs; it's about 177 mi to Jackson, then another 60 mi north to Yellowstone. From Interstate 90, head south at Livingston, Montana, 80 mi to Gardiner and the park's North Entrance. From Bozeman travel south 90 mi to West Yellowstone.

Yellowstone has five primary entrances. The majority of visitors arrive through the South Entrance, north of Grand Teton National Park and Jackson, Wyoming. Other entrances are the East Entrance, with a main point of origin in Cody, Wyoming; the West Entrance at West Yellowstone, Montana (most used during winter); the North Entrance at Gardiner, Montana; and the Northeast Entrance at Cooke City, Montana, which can be reached from either Cody, Wyoming, via the Chief Joseph Scenic Highway, or from Red Lodge, Montana, over the Beartooth Pass.

■TIP→ **The best way to keep your bearings in Yellowstone is to remember that the major roads form a figure eight, known as the Grand Loop, which all entrance roads feed into.** It doesn't matter at which point you begin, as you can hit most of the major sights if you follow the entire route.

The 370 mi of public roads in the park used to be riddled with potholes and had narrow shoulders—a bit tight when a motor home was pulled over to the side to capture wildlife or scenery on film. But because of the park's efforts to upgrade its roads, most of them are now wide and smooth. Road work is ongoing in a few areas, including a segment of the East Entrance Road over Sylvan Pass, with half-hour delays most days and complete nighttime closures through 2007. On holiday weekends, road construction halts so there are no construction delays for travelers. Check with park rangers to determine where you'll encounter delays or closures. Snow is possible any time of year in almost all areas of the park.

Winter Driving

All roads except those between Mammoth Hot Springs and the North Entrance, and Cooke City and the Northeast Entrance are closed to wheeled vehicles from mid-October to mid-April; they are open only to over-snow vehicles from mid-December to mid-March. Come spring, the roads don't open at the same time. The West Entrance and the road from Mammoth Hot Springs to Norris open mid-April. The East and South entrances open in early May. The road from Tower Fall to Canyon Village opens at the end of May.

Contact the Wyoming Department of Transportation (☎807/772–0824 or 800/996–7623) for travel reports October–April. For emergency situations dial 911 or contact the Wyoming Highway Patrol.

At present you can ride a snowmobile in winter if you have a guide and a four-stroke machine. But the controversy over snowmobile use in the park has continued for years, and further restrictions could be implemented. Snow coaches are the only certain means of motorized winter transportation. They range from bright-yellow Bombardier coaches to modern vans with their wheels converted to tracks. Snow coaches have guides, carry 6 to 12 passengers, make frequent stops, and serve as tour vehicles and shuttles.

Updated by
Steve Pastorino

FEW PLACES IN THE WORLD can match Yellowstone National Park's collection of accessible wonders—a "window on the earth's interior" is how one geophysicist described it. As you visit the park's hydro-thermal areas, you'll be walking on top of the Yellowstone Caldera—a 28-by-47-mi collapsed volcanic cone. The geyser basins, hot mud pots, fumaroles (steam vents), and hot springs are kept bubbling by an underground pressure cooker filled with magma. Above ground, the terrain yields rugged mountains, lush meadows, pine forests, free-flowing rivers, and the largest natural high-elevation lake in the United States.

The park has five entrances, each with its own attractions: the south has the Lewis River canyon; the east, Sylvan Pass; the west, the Madison River valley; the north, the beautiful Paradise Valley; and the northeast, the spectacular Beartooth Pass. Along the park's main drive—the Grand Loop—are eight primary "communities" or developed areas. Grant Village, near West Thumb, is the farthest south; Old Faithful and Madison are on the western side of the Lower Loop; Norris and Canyon Village are in the central part of the park, where the two loops intersect; Mammoth Hot Springs and Tower Roosevelt Fall lie at the northern corners of the Upper Loop; and the Yellowstone Lake area is along the eastern segment of the Lower Loop.

From south to north, these are the five main areas of the western part of the Grand Loop, as shown on the Western Yellowstone map.

Grant Village, along the western edge of Lake Yellowstone, is the first community you'll encounter from the South Entrance. It has basic lodging and dining facilities and gives you easy access to the West Thumb Geyser Basin. It takes about two hours to hike to Lake Overlook and explore West Thumb Geyser Basin.

★ **Old Faithful,** the world's most famous geyser, is the centerpiece of this area, which has extensive boardwalks through the Upper Geyser Basin and equally extensive visitor services, including several choices in lodging and dining. It is the one area of Yellowstone that almost all visitors include in their itinerary. In winter you can dine and stay in this area and cross-country ski or snowshoe through the Geyser Basin.

Madison, the area around the junction of the West Entrance Road and the Lower Loop, is a good place to take a break as you travel through the park, because you will almost always see bison grazing along the Madison River, and often elk are in the area as well. You'll find limited visitor services here, though there is an amphitheater for programs as well as a Yellowstone Association bookstore and a picnic area. There are no dining facilities, and the only lodging is a campground.

Norris, at the western junction of the Upper and Lower Loops, has the most active geyser basin in the park. The underground plumbing occasionally reaches such high temperatures—the ground itself has heated up in areas to nearly 200°F—that a portion of the basin is periodically closed for safety reasons. There are limited visitor services: you'll find two museums, a bookstore, and a picnic area. Allow at least half a day

Western Yellowstone

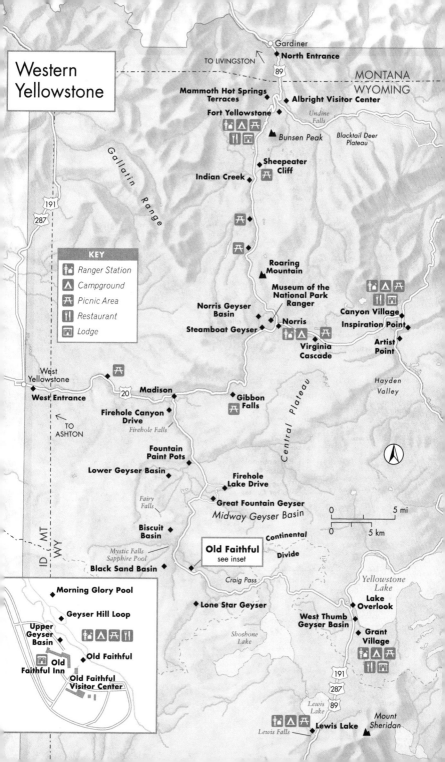

Gardiner
TO LIVINGSTON
North Entrance
89

MONTANA
WYOMING

Mammoth Hot Springs Terraces
Albright Visitor Center
Fort Yellowstone
Undine Falls

Bunsen Peak
Blacktail Deer Plateau

Sheepeater Cliff
Indian Creek

Roaring Mountain

191
287

Museum of the National Park Ranger

Norris Geyser Basin
Norris
Canyon Village
Inspiration Point

Steamboat Geyser

Virginia Cascade
Artist Point

Hayden Valley

KEY

Ranger Station
Campground
Picnic Area
Restaurant
Lodge

West Yellowstone

Madison
20
Gibbon Falls

Central Plateau

West Entrance

TO ASHTON

Firehole Canyon Drive
Firehole Falls

Fountain Paint Pots

Lower Geyser Basin

Firehole Lake Drive

Fairy Falls

Great Fountain Geyser
Midway Geyser Basin

Biscuit Basin

Mystic Falls
Sapphire Pool

Black Sand Basin

Old Faithful
see inset

Continental Divide

Craig Pass

0   5 mi
0   5 km

Yellowstone Lake

Lone Star Geyser

Lake Overlook

West Thumb Geyser Basin

Grant Village

Shoshone Lake

ID MT
WY

Morning Glory Pool

Geyser Hill Loop

Upper Geyser Basin

Old Faithful Inn

Old Faithful

Old Faithful Visitor Center

191
287
89

Lewis Lake

Lewis Falls
Lewis Lake

Mount Sheridan

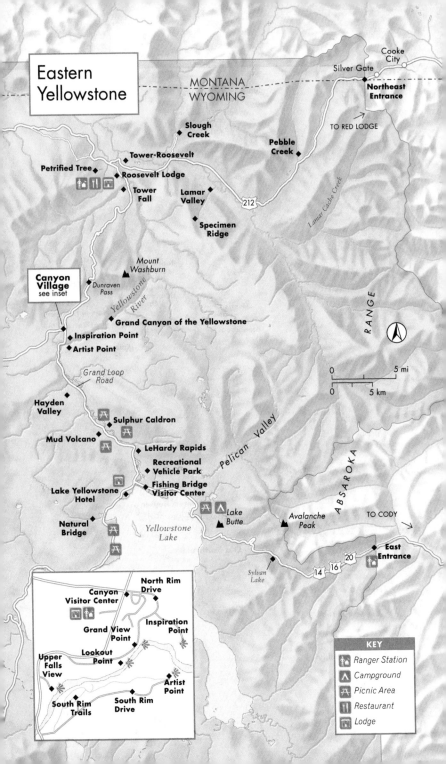

Eastern Yellowstone

Cooke City

Silver Gate

Northeast Entrance

TO RED LODGE

MONTANA
WYOMING

Slough Creek

Pebble Creek

Tower-Roosevelt

Petrified Tree

Roosevelt Lodge

Tower Fall

Lamar Valley

212

Lamar Cache Creek

Specimen Ridge

Mount Washburn

Canyon Village
see inset

Dunraven Pass

Yellowstone River

RANGE

Grand Canyon of the Yellowstone

Inspiration Point

Artist Point

Grand Loop Road

Hayden Valley

Sulphur Caldron

Mud Volcano

LeHardy Rapids

Pelican Valley

Recreational Vehicle Park

Fishing Bridge Visitor Center

Lake Yellowstone Hotel

Lake Butte

Avalanche Peak

TO CODY

ABSAROKA

Natural Bridge

Yellowstone Lake

20

14 16

East Entrance

Sylvan Lake

0   5 mi

0   5 km

Inset: Canyon Village

North Rim Drive

Canyon Visitor Center

Inspiration Point

Grand View Point

Lookout Point

Upper Falls View

Artist Point

South Rim Trails

South Rim Drive

KEY

🏚	*Ranger Station*
⛰	*Campground*
🍴	*Picnic Area*
🍽	*Restaurant*
🏠	*Lodge*

to explore Norris Geyser Basin. It's a good idea to consult with rangers at the Norris Geyser Basin Museum about when different geysers are expected to erupt and to plan your walk accordingly. Rangers also will know whether any areas of the geyser basin are closed.

Mammoth Hot Springs is known for its massive natural terraces, where mineral water flows continuously, building an ever-changing display. You will almost always see elk grazing here. In the early days of the park, it was the site of Fort Yellowstone, and the brick buildings constructed during that era are still used for various park activities. The Albright Visitor Center has information and displays about the park's history, including some of the original paintings Thomas Moran created on an 1871 government expedition to the area. There is a complete range of visitor services here as well. Schedule about half a day for exploration. There are lots of steps on the lower terrace boardwalks, so plan to take your time there.

From north to south, these are the three main areas of eastern Grand Loop, as shown on the Eastern Yellowstone map.

Tower-Roosevelt, the northeast region of Yellowstone, is the least-visited part of the park, making it a great place to explore without running into lots of other people. You can hike or ride horseback to sights in the area, such as a petrified tree and a ridge filled with fossil specimens. This is where wolves were first reintroduced to the park; packs are often seen in the Lamar Valley.

Canyon has waterfalls and steep canyon walls surrounding the Yellowstone River. This central part of the park is one of Yellowstone's most spectacular places. You will find all types of visitors' services and lots of hiking opportunities—as well as lots of other visitors.

Yellowstone Lake area, in the park's southeastern segment, is permeated by the tranquility of massive Yellowstone Lake. Near Fishing Bridge you might see grizzly bears. They like to hunt for fish spawning or swimming near the lake's outlet to the Yellowstone River. Visitor centers include Lake Yellowstone Hotel, Fishing Bridge RV Park (for hardsided vehicles only), and Bridge Bay Campground, the park's largest, with 432 sites.

SCENIC DRIVES

East Entrance Road. Crossing the Absaroka Range, this 16-mi drive descends from the 8,530-foot Sylvan Pass to idyllic views of Yellowstone Lake. The road hugs the lake shoreline between Lake Butte and Fishing Bridge, where some vistas may remind you of the northern California coast. ⊠ *Begin drive at East Entrance gate.*

Firehole Canyon Drive. Pick up this one-way, 2-mi detour off Grand Loop Road just south of Madison Junction. The narrow asphalt road twists through a deep canyon and passes the 40-foot Firehole Falls. In summer look for a sign marking a pullout and swimming hole. This is one of only two places in the park (Boiling River on the North Entrance

Road is the other) where you can safely and legally swim in the park's thermally heated waters. Also, look carefully for osprey and other raptors, plus animal bones in a small cave on the opposite bank of the river. ⊠ *1 mi south of Madison on Grand Loop Rd., Madison.*

Firehole Lake Drive. Eight miles north of Old Faithful, this one-way, 3-mi-long road takes you past **Great Fountain Geyser,** which shoots out jets of water reaching as high as 200 feet about twice a day. Rangers' predictions have a two-hour window of opportunity. Should you witness it, however, you'll be rewarded with a view of waves of water cascading down the terraces that form the edges of the geyser. Watch for bison, particularly in the winter. ⊠ *Firehole Lake Dr., 8 mi north of Old Faithful Old Faithful.*

Northeastern Grand Loop. A 19-mi segment of Grand Loop Road running between Canyon Village and Roosevelt Falls, this byway passes some of the park's finest scenery, twisting beneath a series of leaning basalt towers 40 to 50 feet high. That behemoth to the east is 10,243-foot Mt. Washburn. ⊠ *Between Canyon Village and Roosevelt Falls, Canyon Area.*

South Entrance Road. The sheer black lava walls of the Lewis River canyon make this a memorable drive. Turn into the parking area at the highway bridge for a close-up view of the spectacular Lewis River Falls, one of the park's most-photographed sights. ⊠ *Begin drive at South Entrance gate.*

Upper Terrace Drive. Limber pines as old as 500 years line this 1½-mi loop near Mammoth Hot Springs. You'll also spot a variety of mosses growing through white travertine, composed of lime deposited here by the area's hot springs. ⊠ *Approx. 2 mi by car from Mammoth Hot Springs Hotel on Grand Loop Rd. Reachable by foot from Lower Terrace Dr., Mammoth Hot Springs.*

West Entrance Road. One of the park's four grand drives through wildlife-filled valleys, this road follows the Madison River for 14 mi. From late summer through winter, you'll see bison and elk. Look up, too! Eagles, osprey, and even trumpeter swans may be seen here. ⚠ **At sunset, the drive west can be blinding.** ⊠ *Drive begins at West Entrance, West Yellowstone, MT.*

WHAT TO SEE

SCENIC STOPS

★ **Artist Point.** The most spectacular view of the Lower Falls of the Yellowstone River is seen from this point, which has two different viewing levels, one of which is accessible to wheelchairs. The South Rim Trail goes right past this point, and there is a nearby parking area open in both summer and winter. ⊠ *East end of South Rim Rd., Canyon.*

Back Basin. The trail through Back Basin is a 1½-mi loop guiding you past dozens of features highlighted by Steamboat Geyser. When it erupts fully (most recently in 1985), it's the world's largest, climbing 400 feet above the basin. More often, Steamboat growls and spits constantly, sending clouds of steam high above the basin. Kids will love the Puff 'n' Stuff Geyser and the mysterious cavelike Green Dragon Spring. Ask the Norris ranger for an anticipated schedule of geyser eruptions—you might catch the Echinus Geyser, which erupts almost hourly. ⊠*Grand Loop Rd. at Norris, Norris.*

Black Sand Basin. There are a dozen hot springs and geysers near the cloverleaf entrance from Grand Loop Road to Old Faithful. Emerald Pool is one of the prettiest. ⊠*North of Old Faithful on Grand Loop Rd., Old Faithful.*

Geyser Hill Loop. Along the 1⅓-mi Geyser Hill Loop boardwalk you will see active thermal features such as violent Giantess Geyser. Normally erupting only a few times each year, Giantess spouts 100 to 250 feet in the air for five to eight minutes once or twice hourly for 12 to 43 hours. Nearby Doublet Pool's two adjacent springs have complex ledges and deep blue waters, which are highly photogenic. Starting as a gentle pool, Anemone Geyser overflows, bubbles, and finally erupts 10 feet or more, every three to eight minutes. The loop boardwalk brings you close to the action, making it especially appealing to children intrigued with the sights and sounds of the basin. Also keep a lookout for elk and buffalo in this area. To reach Geyser Hill, head counterclockwise around the Old Faithful boardwalk ⅓ mi from the visitor center, crossing the Firehole River and entering Upper Geyser Basin. ⊠*Old Faithful, ⅓ mi from Old Faithful Visitor Center, Old Faithful.*

Gibbon Falls. Water rushes over the caldera rim in this 84-foot waterfall on the Gibbon River. ⊠*4 mi east of Madison on Grand Loop Rd., Madison.*

Fodor'sChoice
★ **Grand Canyon of the Yellowstone.** This stunning canyon is 23 mi long, but there is only one trail from rim to base. As a result, a majority of Park visitors clog the north and south rims to see Upper and Lower Falls. To compound problems, the North Rim Road has been closed for the 2008 season for construction, leaving many popular viewpoints reachable only by foot, if at all.

Unless you're up for the six-hour strenuous hike called Seven Mile Hole, you have no choice but to join the crowds on the rims to see this natural wonder. The red-and-ochre canyon walls are topped with emerald-green forest. It's a feast of color. Also look for ospreys, which nest in the canyon's spires and precarious trees. ⊠*Canyon.*

Grand Prismatic Spring. This is Yellowstone's largest hot spring, 370 feet in diameter. It's in the Midway Geyser Basin, and you can reach it by following the boardwalk. The spring is deep blue in color, with yellow and orange rings formed by bacteria that give it the effect of a prism. ⊠*Midway Geyser Basin off Grand Loop Rd., Old Faithful.*

Great Fountain Geyser. This geyser erupts twice a day; rangers predict when it will shoot some 200 feet into the air, but their prediction has a window of opportunity a couple of hours long. Should you see Great Fountain spew, however, you'll be rewarded with a view of waves of

A World of Geological Wonders

Spouting geysers, bubbling mud pots, and hissing steam vents have earned fame for Yellowstone, which has the greatest concentration of thermal features in the country—nearly 10,000 of them all told.

The past eruptions of cataclysmic volcanoes helped to create the steaming, vaporous landscape of Yellowstone today. The heat from the magma (molten rock) under the Yellowstone Caldera continues to fuel the park's most famous geyser basins—West Thumb, Upper, Lower, Midway, and Norris—which contain most of Yellowstone's 200 to 250 active geysers.

Other traces of the geological past include the basaltic columns near Tower and the steam that hisses from Roaring Mountain. The molten lava beneath the Yellowstone Caldera, one of the world's most active volcanoes,

has created two resurgent domes: Sour Creek, forming the eastern edge of Hayden Valley, and Mallard Lake, which overlooks Old Faithful from the Upper Geyser Basin, at Observation Point. In Firehole Canyon, the Firehole River runs between two lava flows; at West Thumb, a minor eruption created the Lake Yellowstone bay lined with hydrothermal features; in the park's forests, volcanic soils nurture lodgepole pine.

The superheated underground means Yellowstone is a constantly changing landscape. A geyser that is active one month may go dormant while a nearby thermal feature suddenly becomes quite intense. This potential for constant change makes Yellowstone a place where you can see something new and different each time you visit.

water cascading down the terraces that form the edges of the geyser. ⊠*Firehole Lake Dr., north of Old Faithful.*

Lake Butte. Reached by a spur road off the East Entrance Road, this wooded promontory rising 615 feet above Yellowstone Lake is a prime spot for watching the sun set over the lake. ⊠*Approx. 8½ mi east of Fishing Bridge on East Entrance Rd., Fishing Bridge.*

Lake Overlook. From this hilltop northwest of West Thumb and Grant Village you get an expansive view of the southwest portion of Yellowstone. You reach the promontory by taking a 1½-mi hiking trail through forest still recovering from the massive fires of 1988; the clearing caused by the fire makes this a prime area for sighting elk. ⊠*1½ mi northwest of Grant Village.*

LeHardy Rapids. Witness one of nature's epic battles as cutthroat trout migrate upstream to spawn in spring by catapulting themselves out of the water to get by, over, and around rocks and rapids here on the Yellowstone River. The quarter-mile forested loop takes you to the river's edge. Also keep an eye out for waterfowl and bears, which feed on the trout. ⊠*3 mi north of Fishing Bridge, Fishing Bridge.*

Lower Geyser Basin. Shooting more than 150 feet in the air, the Great Fountain Geyser is the most spectacular sight in this basin. Less impressive but more regular is White Dome Geyser, which shoots from a

20-foot-tall cone. You'll also find pink mud pots and blue pools at the basin's Fountain Paint Pots. ⊠*Midway between Old Faithful and Madison on Grand Loop Rd.*

Fodor's Choice
★ **Mammoth Hot Springs Terraces.** Multicolor travertine terraces formed by slowly escaping hot mineral water mark this unusual geological formation. It constantly changes as a result of shifts in water flow. You can explore the terraces via an elaborate network of boardwalks. The best is the Lower Terrace Interpretive Trail. If you start at Liberty Cap, at the area's north end, and head uphill on the boardwalks, you'll pass bright and ornately terraced Minerva Spring. It's about an hour walk. Along the way you may spy elk, as they graze nearby. Alternatively, you can drive up to the Lower Terrace Overlook on Upper Terrace Drive and take the boardwalks down past New Blue Springs to the Lower Terrace. This route, which also take an hour, works especially well if you can park a second vehicle at the foot of Lower Terrace. ⊠*Northwest corner of Grand Loop Rd., Mammoth Hot Springs.*

Midway Geyser Basin. Called "Hell's Half Acre" by writer Rudyard Kipling, Midway Geyser Basin is a more interesting stop than Lower Geyser Basin. A series of boardwalks wind their way to the Excelsior Geyser, which deposits 4,000 gallons of vivid blue water per minute into the Firehole River. Just above Excelsior is Yellowstone's largest hot spring, Grand Prismatic Spring. Measuring 370 feet in diameter, it's deep blue in color with yellow and orange rings formed by bacteria that give it the effect of a prism. ⊠*Between Old Faithful and Madison on Grand Loop Rd.*

☺ **Mud Volcano.** The ¾-mi round-trip Mud Volcano Interpretive Trail loops gently around seething, sulfuric mud pots with names such as Black Dragon's Cauldron and Sizzling Basin before making its way around Mud Volcano itself, a boiling pot of brown goo. ⊠*10 mi south of Canyon; 4 mi north of Fishing Bridge on Grand Loop Rd., Fishing Bridge.*

Natural Bridge. You can take an easy 1-mi hike or bicycle ride from Bridge Bay Campground to Natural Bridge, which was formed by erosion of a rhyolite outcrop by Bridge Creek. The top of the bridge is about 50 feet above the creek, and there is a trail to its top, though travel over the bridge itself is prohibited. ⊠*1 mi west of Bridge Bay Campground, Bridge Bay.*

☺ **Norris Geyser Basin.** From the Norris Ranger Station, choose either Porcelain Basin or Back Basin, or both. These volatile thermal features are constantly changing, although you can expect to find a variety of geysers and springs here at any time. The area is accessible via an extensive system of boardwalks, some of them suitable for people with disabilities. ⊠*Grand Loop Rd. at Norris, Norris.*

Fodor's Choice
★ **Northeast Entrance Road and Lamar Valley.** The 29-mi road features the richest diversity of landscape of the five entrance roads. Just after you enter the park from the northeast, you'll cut between 10,928-foot Abiathar Peak and the 10,404-foot Barronette Peak. You'll pass the extinct

geothermal cone called Soda Butte as well as the two nicest camp-grounds in the park, Pebble Creek and Slough Creek. Lamar Valley is the home to hundreds of bison, and the rugged peaks and ridges adjacent to it are home to some of the park's most famous wolf packs (reintroduced in 1995). The main wolf-watching activities in the park occur here during early-morning and late-evening hours year-round. As you exit Lamar Valley, the road crosses the Yellowstone River before leading you to the rustic Roosevelt Lodge. ⊠ *From Northeast Entrance near Cooke City to junction with Grand Loop Rd. at Roosevelt Lodge, Tower-Roosevelt.*

Ⓒ

Fodor'sChoice

★

Old Faithful. Almost every visitor includes the world's most famous geyser on his or her itinerary. Yellowstone's most predictable big gey-ser—although not its largest or most regular—sometimes reaches 180 feet, but it averages 130 feet. Sometimes it doesn't shoot as high, but in those cases the eruptions usually last longer. The mysterious plumbing of Yellowstone has lengthened Old Faithful's cycle somewhat in recent years, to every 94 minutes or so. To find out when Old Faithful is likely to erupt, check at the visitor center or at any of the lodging properties in the area. You can view the eruption from a bench just yards away, from the dining room at the lodge cafeteria, or from a guest room at the spectacular Old Faithful Inn (assuming you are lucky enough to spend the night there). The 1-mi hike to Observation Point yields yet another view—from above—of the geyser and its surrounding basin. ⊠ *Southwest segment, Grand Loop Rd., Old Faithful.*

Sulphur Caldron. You can smell the sulfur before you even leave your vehicle to walk to the overlook of Sulphur Caldron, where hissing steam escapes from a moonscapelike surface as superheated bubbling mud. ⊠ *9½ mi south of Canyon; 4½ mi north of Fishing Bridge on Grand Loop Rd., Fishing Bridge.*

Tower Fall. This is one of the easiest waterfalls to see from the roadside (follow signs to the lookout point); you can also view volcanic pin-nacles here. Tower Creek plunges 132 feet at this waterfall to join the Yellowstone River. A trail runs to the base of the falls, but it is closed at this writing (and for the foreseeable future) because of some erosion problems several hundred yards before you reach the bottom of the canyon; thus, there is no view of Tower Fall from this trail at present. ⊠ *2 mi south of Roosevelt on Grand Loop Rd.*

Upper Geyser Basin. With Old Faithful as its central attraction, this mile-square basin contains about 140 different geysers—one-fifth of the known geysers in the world. It's an excellent place to spend a day or more exploring. You will find a complex system of boardwalks and trails—some of them used as bicycle trails—that take you to the basin's various attractions. ⊠ *Old Faithful.*

Ⓒ **West Thumb Geyser Basin.** The primary Yellowstone caldera was cre-ated by a volcanic eruption 640,000 years ago, but West Thumb came about much more recently—"only" 150,000 years ago—as the result of another volcanic eruption. This unique geyser basin is the only place to see active geothermal features in Lake Yellowstone. Two boardwalk loops are offered; take the longer one to see features like "Fishing Cone," where fishermen used to catch fish, pivot, and drop their fish straight into boiling water for cooking without ever taking it off the hook. This area is particularly popular for winter visitors, who take advantage of the nearby warming hut and a stroll around the geyser basin before continuing their trip via snow coach or snowmobile. ⊠ *Grand Loop Rd., 22 mi north of South Entrance, West Thumb.*

Ⓒ **Yellowstone Lake.** One of the world's largest alpine lakes, encompassing
Fodor's Choice 132 square mi, Yellowstone Lake was formed when glaciers that once
★ covered the region melted into a caldera—a crater formed by a volcano. The lake has 141 mi of shoreline, less than one-third of it followed by the East Entrance Road and Grand Loop Road, along which you will often see moose, elk, waterfowl, and other wildlife. In winter you can sometimes see otters and coyotes stepping gingerly on the ice at the lake's edge. Many visitors head here for the excellent fishing—streams flowing into the lake give it an abundant supply of trout. ⊠ *Intersection of East Entrance Rd. and Grand Loop Rd., between Fishing Bridge and Grant Village.*

VISITOR CENTERS

Ⓒ **Albright Visitor Center.** Serving as bachelor quarters for cavalry officers from 1886 to 1918, this red-roof building now holds a museum with exhibits on the early inhabitants of the region and a theater showing films about the history of the park. There are original Thomas Moran paintings of the park on display here as well. Kids and taxidermists will love extensive displays of park wildlife, including bears and wolves. ⊠ *Mammoth Hot Springs* ☎ *307/344-2263* ⊗ *Late May–Aug., daily 8–7; Sept., daily 8–5; Oct.–May, daily 9–5.*

Ⓒ **Canyon Visitor Center.** This gleaming new visitor center is the pride of
★ the park service with elaborate, interactive exhibits for adults and kids. The focus here is volcanoes and earthquakes, but there are also exhibits on Native Americans and park wildlife, including bison and wolves. The video titled "Water, Heat & Rock" is a riveting look at the geo- and hydrothermal basis for the park. As at all visitor centers, you can obtain park information, backcountry camping permits, etc. The adjacent bookstore, operated by the Yellowstone Association, is the best in the park with guidebooks, trail maps, gifts, and hundreds of books on the park, its history, and the science surrounding it. ⊠ *Canyon Village, Canyon Area* ☎ *307/242-2552* ⊗ *Late May–Aug., daily 8–7; Sept., daily 8–6; Oct. 1–14, daily 9–5.*

Ⓒ **Fishing Bridge Visitor Center.** This distinctive stone-and-log building, which was built in 1931, has been designated a National Historic Landmark. If you can't distinguish between a Clark's nut hatch and an ermine (note: one's a bird, the other a rodent), check out the extensive exhibits on park wildlife. Step out the back door to find yourself on one of the beautiful black obsidian beaches of Yellowstone Lake. The Yellowstone Association bookstore here features books, guides, and other educational materials, but you can't buy coffee. ⊠ *East Entrance Rd.,*

PARK RANGER MARY WILSON'S TIPS FOR VISITING YELLOWSTONE

1. Before your trip, go online to get information from the park's official Web site, www.nps.gov/yell.

2. Upon arrival at the park, stop at the nearest visitor center for information and updates.

3. Pack for all types of weather no matter what time of year.

4. Avoid the crowds by getting an early start to your day in the park.

5. Stay at least 75 feet away from wildlife (300 feet for bears).

6. Stay on geyser basin boardwalks to prevent serious thermal burns.

7. Drive defensively, and allow more time than you think you need.

8. Try to be to your destination before dark to avoid hitting wildlife on park roads.

9. Take a friend when you go hiking; it's safer and a lot more fun!

10. Don't try to see and do everything. You need two to three days just to visit the park highlights.

1 mi from Grand Loop Rd. ☎307/242–2450 ⊙Memorial Day–Labor Day, daily 8–7; Sept. (after Labor Day), daily 9–6.

Grant Village Visitor Center. Each visitor center in the park tells a small piece of the park's history. This one tells the story of fire in the park. A seminal moment in Yellowstone's historical record, the 1988 fire burned 36% of the total acreage of the park and forced multiple federal agencies to reevaluate their fire control policies. Watch an informative video, purchase maps or books, and learn more about the 25,000 firefighters from across America who fought the 1988 fire. ✉*Grant Village ☎307/242–2650 ⊙Late May–Labor Day, daily 8–7; Labor Day–Sept. 30, daily 9–6.*

Madison Information Center. In this National Historic Landmark, the ranger shares the space with a Yellowstone Association bookstore, which features high-quality books, guides, music, and learning aids. You may find spotting scopes set up for wildlife viewing out the rear window; if this is the case, look for eagles, swans, bison, elk, and more. Rangers will answer questions about the park, provide basic hiking information and maps, and issue permits for backcountry camping and fishing. Picnic tables, toilets, and an amphitheater for summer-evening ranger programs are shared with the nearby Madison campground. ✉*Grand Loop Rd. at West Entrance Rd., Madison ☎307/344–2821 ⊙June–Sept., daily 9–5.*

Old Faithful Visitor Center. Unfortunately, the most visited place in the park does not have an adequate visitor center at this writing. A temporary trailer has housed an information center and Yellowstone Association bookstore since 2006. Park officials hope to open a new visitor center in 2010, but construction had not yet begun as of January 2008. Even with its limitations, this is the best place to inquire about geyser eruption predictions. Backcountry and fishing permits are handled out of the ranger station adjacent to the Old Faithful Snow Lodge. ✉*Old*

Faithful Bypass Rd., Old Faithful ☎*307/545–2750* ☉*Daily, late Apr.–May, 9–5; June–Aug., 8–7; Sept., 8–6; Oct.–mid-Nov., 9–5; late Dec.–early Mar., 9–5.*

West Thumb Information Station. This historic log cabin houses a Yellowstone Association bookstore and doubles as a warming hut in the winter. There are restrooms in the parking area. Check for informal ranger-led discussions "beneath the old sequoia tree" in the summer. ✉ *West Thumb* ☉ *Late May–Sept., daily 9–5.*

SPORTS & THE OUTDOORS

BICYCLING

Park management does not encourage bicycling in the park. It considers the vast majority of the park's roads "unimproved" and unsafe for bicyclists. A brochure titled "Bicycling in Yellowstone National Park" is available at some visitor centers and at the park Web site (⊕*www. nps.gov/yell*), but is not widely promoted or disseminated. Still, many long-distance cyclists do ride in Yellowstone, despite heavy traffic and narrow roads. If you choose to ride the Grand Loop Road or entrance roads, be safe, ride single file, and wear a helmet and reflective gear. Be cautious in May and June, as high snowbanks can make riding the park's narrow roads particularly dangerous. Remember that some routes, such as those over Craig Pass, Sylvan Pass, and Dunraven Pass, are especially challenging because of their steep climbs.

Outfitter & Expeditions Free Heel and Wheel (✉*40 Yellowstone Ave., West Yellowstone, MT* ☎*406/646–7744* ⊕*www.freeheelandwheel. com*), just outside the West Entrance, rents bikes, dispenses advice, and sells hiking and cross-country skiing gear. The staff here can also recommend road cycling routes outside the park. Rates are $8 per hour, or $25 per day, including helmet and water bottle.

BOATING

Motorized boats are allowed only on Lewis Lake and Yellowstone Lake. Kayaking or canoeing is allowed on all park lakes except Sylvan Lake, Eleanor Lake, Twin Lakes, and Beach Springs Lagoon; however, most lakes are inaccessible by car, so accessing the park's lakes requires long portages. Boating is not allowed on any park river, except for the Lewis River between Lewis Lake and Shoshone Lake, where nonmotorized boats are permitted.

You must purchase a seven-day, $5 permit for boats and floatables, or a $10 permit for motorized boats at Bridge Bay Ranger Station, South Entrance Ranger Station, Grant Village Backcountry Office, or, occasionally, Lewis Lake Ranger Station (at the campground). Nonmotorized permits are available at the Northeast and West entrances; backcountry offices at Mammoth, Old Faithful, and Canyon; Bechler Ranger Station; West Yellowstone Chamber of Commerce; and locations where motorized permits are sold. Annual permits are also available.

Outfitter & Expeditions Watercraft from rowboats to powerboats are available at **Bridge Bay Marina** by the hour or by the day for trips on Yellowstone Lake. You can even rent 22- and 34-foot cabin cruisers. ⊠*Grand Loop Rd., 2 mi south of Lake Village, Bridge Bay* ☎*307/344–7311* ⌨*$70–$90 per hour for guided sightseeing or fishing boats; $9.50 per hr for rowboat; $45 per hr for small boat with outboard motor* ◷*June–mid-Aug., daily 8–8; mid-Aug.–mid-Sept., daily 8–5:30.*

⟳ **Yellowstone Lake Scenic Cruises,** run by Xanterra Parks & Resorts, oper-
★ ates the *Lake Queen II* from out of Bridge Bay Marina on Yellowstone Lake. The one-hour cruises make their way to Stevenson Island and then return to Bridge Bay. Boats depart throughout the day. ⊠*Bridge Bay Marina, Bridge Bay* ☎*307/344–7311* ⌨*$11.25* ◷*June–mid-Sept., daily.*

FISHING

Anglers flock to Yellowstone beginning the Saturday of Memorial Day weekend, when fishing season begins. By the time the season ends in November, thousands have found a favorite spot along the park's rivers and streams. Native cutthroat trout are one of the prize catches, but four other varieties—brown, brook, lake, and rainbow—along with grayling and mountain whitefish inhabit Yellowstone's waters. Popular sportfishing opportunities include the Gardner and Yellowstone rivers as well as Soda Butte Creek, but the top fishing area in the region is Madison River, known to fly-fishermen throughout the country.

Yellowstone fishing permits are required for people over age 16. Montana and Wyoming fishing permits are not valid in the park. Yellowstone fishing permits cost $15 for a three-day permit, $20 for a seven-day permit, or $35 for a season permit. Anglers ages 12 to 15 must have a nonfee permit or fish under direct supervision of an adult with a permit. Anglers younger than 12 don't need a permit but must be with an adult who knows the regulations. Permits are available at all ranger stations, visitor centers, and Yellowstone general stores.

Outfitter & Expeditions The park concessionaire **Xanterra Parks & Resorts** offers guided Yellowstone Lake fishing charters on boats large enough for as many as six guests. The cost of a charter includes your guide plus fishing gear. Charters are on 22- and 34-foot cabin cruisers that accommodate as many as three people fishing at one time. ⊠*Grand Loop Rd., 2 mi south of Lake Village, Bridge Bay* ☎*307/344–7311* ⌨*$70–$90 per hr* ◷*Mid-June–early Sept.*

HIKING

Your most memorable Yellowstone moments will likely take place along a park hiking trail. Encountering a gang of elk in the woods is unquestionably more exciting that watching them graze on the grasses of Mammoth Hot Springs Hotel. Hearing the creak of lodgepole pines on a breezy afternoon feels more authentic than listening to idle tourist chatter as you jostle for the best view of Old Faithful on a recycled-plastic boardwalk for 94 minutes or so.

Even a one-day visitor to Yellowstone can—and should—get off the roads and into the "wilderness." Since the park is a wild place, however, even a half-mile walk on a trail puts you at the mercy of nature, so be sure to prepare yourself accordingly. As a guide on an Old Yellow Bus Tour said, "You don't have to fear the animals—just respect them."

Fodor'sChoice
★ **Outfitter & Expeditions** If you are interested in having a park expert, whether a naturalist, geologist, or wildlife specialist, accompany you, the **Yellowstone Association Institute** offers daylong hiking excursions; multiday "Lodging and Learning" trips geared around hikes, some of them designed for families (there are age restrictions on some trips); and full-blown backcountry backpacking trips. The Lodging and Learning trips include nightly accommodations at park facilities, but for the hikes you bring your own personal gear; they provide group gear and instruction plus permits as needed and some meals. The association also offers courses on topics ranging from nature writing to wolf biology. Taught by college professors or other experts, most courses are for people age 18 and older. ⌂ *Box 117, Yellowstone National Park, WY 82190* ☎ *307/344–2293* ☐ *307/344–2486* ⊕ *www.yellowstoneassociation. org* ⌨ *From $80 for 1-day trips to $1,000+ for 5-night trips, including lodging.*

EASY **Back Basin Trail.** A 1.5-mi loop passes Emerald Spring, Steamboat Geyser, Cistern Spring (which drains when Steamboat erupts), and Echinus Geyser. The latter erupts 50 to 100 feet every 35 to 75 minutes, making it Norris's most dependable big geyser. ⊠ *Grand Loop Rd., Norris* ⌔ *Easy.*

Fountain Paint Pots Nature Trail. Take the easy ½-mi loop boardwalk of Fountain Paint Pot Nature Trail to see fumaroles (steam vents), blue pools, pink mud pots, and mini-geysers in this thermal area. It's popular in both summer and winter because it's right next to Grand Loop Road. ⊠ *Lower Geyster Basin, between Old Faithful and Madison* ⌔ *Easy.*

Mud Volcano Interpretive Trail. This ¾-mi round-trip trail loops gently around seething, sulfuric mud pots with such names as Sizzling Basin and Black Dragon's Cauldron and around Mud Volcano itself. ⊠ *10 mi south of Canyon Village on Grand Loop Rd., Canyon* ⌔ *Easy.*

Old Faithful Geyser Loop. Old Faithful and its environs in the Upper Geyser Basin are rich in short-walk options, starting with three connected loops that depart from Old Faithful visitor center. The 0.75-mi loop

What to Take on a Hike

CLOSE UP

No matter how short the hike, the following items are essential, not discretionary:

Bear spray. At $40 a can and available for sale in the park, it's not cheap, but it's a critical deterrent if you run into one. Know how to use it, too. Be aware that sometimes supplies are sold out.

Food and water. Your "meal" can be as simple as a protein bar and a bottle of water, but the properly prepared hiker has an energy-boosting snack, and it's just foolish to head out without some drinking water.

Appropriate clothing. Watch the forecast closely (available at every lodging office and visitor center). Bring a layer of clothing for the opposite extreme if you're hiking at least half the day. Yellowstone is known for fierce afternoon storms, so be ready with gloves, hat, and waterproof clothing.

Altitude awareness. Yes, this is rather intangible, but much of Yellowstone lies more than 7,500 feet above sea level, significantly higher than Denver. The most frequent incidents requiring medical attention are respiratory problems, not animal attacks. Be aware of your physical limitations—as well as those of your young children or elderly companions if they are with you.

simply circles the benches around Old Faithful, filled nearly all day long in summer with tourists. Currently erupting approximately every 94 minutes, Yellowstone's most frequently erupting big geyser—although not its largest or most regular—reaches heights of 100 to 180 feet, averaging 130 feet. ⊠ *Old Faithful Village, Old Faithful* ☞ *Easy.*

Porcelain Basin Trail. At Norris Geyser Basin, this ¾-mi, partial-boardwalk loop leads from the north end of Norris Museum through whitish geyserite stone and past extremely active Whirligig and other small geysers. ⊠ *Grand Loop Rd., Norris* ☞ *Easy.*

☼ **Storm Point Trail.** Well marked and mostly flat, this 1½-mi loop leaves the
★ south side of the road for a perfect beginner's hike out to Yellowstone Lake. The trail rounds the western edge of Indian Pond, then passes moose habitat on its way to Yellowstone Lake's Storm Point, named for its frequent afternoon windstorms and crashing waves. Heading west along the shore, you're likely to hear the shrill chirping of yellow-bellied marmots, rodents that grow as long as 2 feet. Also look for ducks, pelicans, and trumpeter swans. You will pass several small beaches where kids can explore on warm summer mornings. ⊠ *3 mi east of Lake Junction on East Entrance Rd., Fishing Bridge* ☞ *Easy.*

MODERATE **Beaver Ponds Loop Trail.** The hike to Beaver Ponds is a 2½-hour, 5-mi round-trip starting at Liberty Cap in the busy Lower Terrace of Mammoth Hot Springs. You enter Yellowstone backcountry within minutes as you climb 400 feet through spruce and fir, passing several ponds and dams, as well as a glacier-carved moraine, before emerging on a windswept plain overlooking the 45th parallel (Montana/Wyoming border), Boiling River, and the North Entrance. Look up to see Everts

Peak to the east, Bunsen Peak to the south, and Sepulcher Mountain to the west. Bear, elk, bighorn sheep, coyote, and fox may frequent the area. Your final descent into Mammoth Springs offers great views of Mammoth Springs. ⊠ *Grand Loop Rd. at Old Gardiner Rd., Mammoth Hot Springs* ☞ *Moderate.*

Bunsen Peak Trail. Past the entrance to Bunsen Peak Road, the moderately difficult trail is a 4-mi, three-hour round-trip that climbs 1,300 feet to Bunsen Peak for a panoramic view of Blacktail Plateau, Swan Lake Flats, the Gallatin Mountains, and the Yellowstone River valley. (Use a topographical map to find these landmarks.) ⊠ *Grand Loop Rd., 1½ mi south of Mammoth Hot Springs* ☞ *Moderate.*

Mystic Falls Trail. From the Biscuit Basin boardwalk's west end, this trail gently climbs 1 mi (3½ mi round-trip from Biscuit Basin parking area) through heavily burned forest to the lava-rock base of 70-foot Mystic Falls. It then switchbacks up Madison Plateau to a lookout with the park's least-crowded view of Old Faithful and the Upper Geyser Basin. ⊠ *3 mi north of Old Faithful Village off Grand Loop Rd., Old Faithful* ☞ *Moderate.*

★ **North Rim Trail.** Offering great views of the Grand Canyon of the Yellowstone, the 1¾-mi North Rim Trail runs from Inspiration Point to Chittenden Bridge. You can wander along small sections of the trail or combine it with the South Rim Trail. Especially scenic is the 0.5-mi section of the North Rim Trail from the Brink of the Upper Falls parking area to Chittenden Bridge that hugs the rushing Yellowstone River as it approaches the canyon. ⚠ **Portions of this trail may be affected, or closed, by the closure of the North Rim Road for all of 2008, so check with park rangers.** ⊠ *1 mi south of Canyon Village, Canyon* ☞ *Moderate.*

Observation Point Loop. A 2-mi round-trip from the temporary Old Faithful Visitor Center leaves Geyser Hill Loop boardwalk and becomes a trail shortly after the boardwalk crosses the Firehole River; it circles a picturesque overview of Geyser Hill with Old Faithful Inn as a backdrop. You may also see Castle Geyser erupting as well. Even when 1,000-plus people are crowded on the boardwalk to watch Old Faithful, expect to find fewer than a dozen here. ⊠ *Old Faithful Village, Old Faithful* ☞ *Moderate.*

Purple Mountain Trail. Climbing a steady 1,500 feet from start to finish, this 6-mi round-trip trail takes you through lodgepole-pine forest. At the end of the trail catch views of Firehole and Gibbon valleys. ⊠ *¼ mi north of Madison Junction, on Madison-Norris Rd.*

Shoshone Lake–Shoshone Geyser Basin Trail. A 22-mi, 11-hour, moderately difficult overnight trip combines several shorter trails. The trail starts at the DeLacy Creek Trail, gently descending 3 mi to the north shore of Shoshone Lake. On the way, look for sandhill cranes and browsing moose. At the lake turn right and follow the North Shore Trail 8 mi, first along the beach and then through lodgepole-pine forest. Make sure you've reserved one of the several good backcountry campsites (reservations can be made at any ranger station in the park). Take time to explore the Shoshone Geyser Basin, reached by turning left at the fork at the end of the trail and walking about ¼ mi before bedding down for the night. On your second morning, turn right at the fork, follow Shoshone Creek for 2 mi, and make the gradual climb over Grant's Pass. At the 17-mi mark the trail crosses the Firehole River and divides; take a right onto Lone Star Geyser Trail and continue past this geyser through Upper Geyser Basin backcountry to Lone Star Geyser Trailhead. ⊠ *8 mi east of Old Faithful Village on north side of Grand Loop Rd., Old Faithful* ⚐ *Moderate.*

Fodor'sChoice   **Slough Creek Trail.** Starting at Slough Creek Campground, this trail
★   climbs steeply along a historic wagon trail for the first 1½ mi before reaching expansive meadows and prime fishing spots, where moose are common and grizzlies occasionally wander. From this point the trail, now mostly level, meanders another 9½ mi to the park's northern boundary. Anglers absolutely rave about this trail. ⊠ *7 mi east of Tower-Roosevelt off Northeast Entrance Rd.* ⚐ *Moderate.*

South Rim Trail. Partly paved and fairly flat, this 4½-mi loop along the south rim of the Grand Canyon of the Yellowstone affords impressive views and photo opportunities of the canyon and falls of the Yellowstone River. It starts at Chittenden Bridge. Along the way you can take a break for a snack or a picnic, but you'll need to sit on the ground, as there are no picnic tables. Beyond Artist Point, the trail crosses a high plateau and meanders through high mountain meadows, where you're likely to see bison grazing. ⊠ *Chittenden Bridge, off South Rim Dr., Canyon* ⚐ *Moderate.*

DIFFICULT   **Avalanche Peak.** On a busy day in summer, maybe six parties will fill out
Fodor'sChoice   the trail register at the Avalanche Peak trailhead, so you won't have
★   a lot of company on this hike. Yet many say it's one of the best-kept secrets in the park. Starting across from a parking area on the East Entrance Road, the difficult 4-mi, 4-hour round-trip climbs 2,150 feet to the peak's 10,566-foot summit, from which you'll see the rugged Absaroka Mountains running north and south. Some of these peaks have patches of snow year-round. Look around the talus and tundra near the top of Avalanche Peak for alpine wildflowers and butterflies. Don't try this trail before late June or after early September—it may be covered in deep snow. Also, rangers discourage hikers from attempting this hike in September or October because of bear activity. Whenever you decide to go, carry a jacket: the winds at the top are strong. ⊠ *2 mi east of Sylvan Lake on north side of East Entrance Rd., Fishing Bridge* ⚐ *Difficult.*

Heart Lake–Mt. Sheridan Trail. This very difficult 24-mi, 13-hour round-trip provides one of the park's top overnight backcountry experiences. After traversing 5½ mi of partly burned lodgepole-pine forest, the trail descends into Heart Lake Geyser Basin, reaching Heart Lake at the 8-mi mark. This is one of Yellowstone's most active thermal areas; the biggest geyser here is Rustic Geyser, which erupts to a height of 25 to 30 feet about every 15 minutes. Circle around the northern tip of Heart Lake and camp at one of five designated backcountry sites on the western shore (remember to get your permit beforehand). Leave all but the essentials here as you take on the 3-mi, 2,700-foot climb to the top of 10,308-foot Mt. Sheridan. To the south, if you look carefully, you can see the Tetons. ⊠ *1 mi north of Lewis Lake on east side of South Entrance Rd., Grant Village* ⚲ *Difficult.*

SKIING, SNOWSHOEING & SNOWMOBILING

Yellowstone can be the coldest place in the continental United States in winter, with temperatures of -30 degrees not uncommon. Still, winter-sports enthusiasts flock here when the park opens for its winter season the last week of December. Until early March, the park's roads teem with over-snow vehicles like snowmobiles and snow coaches. Its trails bristle with cross-country skiers and snowshoers.

Snowmobiling is an exhilarating way to experience Yellowstone. It's also controversial: there's heated debate about the pollution and disruption to animal habitats. The number of riders per day is limited, and you must have a reservation, a guide, and a four-stroke engine (which is less polluting than the more common two-stroke variety). About a dozen companies have been authorized to lead snowmobile excursions into the park from the North, West, South, and East entrances. Prices vary, as do itineraries and inclusions—be sure to ask about insurance, guides, taxes, park entrance fees, clothing, helmets, and meals. Regulations are subject to change.

Lone Star Geyser Trail is an easy 2.3-mi ski to the Lone Star Geyser, starting south of Keppler Cascades. You can ski back to the Old Faithful area. ⊠ *Shuttle at Old Faithful Snow Lodge; trailhead 3½ mi west of Old Faithful Village, Old Faithful.*

Five ski trails begin at the **Madison River Bridge** trailhead. The shortest is 4 mi and the longest is 14 mi. ⊠ *West Entrance Rd., 6 mi west of Madison, Madison.*

Outfitter & Expeditions **Free Heel and Wheel** (⊠ *40 Yellowstone Ave., West Yellowstone, MT* ☎ *406/646–7744* ⊕ *www.freeheelandwheel. com*), outside the West Yellowstone entrance gate, is a source for cross-country ski gear and advice. Expect to pay $20 to $30 per day for ski rentals.

Jackson-based **National Park Adventures** (⊠ *650 W. Broadway, Jackson, WY* ☎ *307/733–1572 or 800/255–1572* ⊕ *www.anpatours. com*)specializes in one-, two-, and multiday guided snowmobile trips into Yellowstone, centering on Canyon and Old Faithful. Lodging is sometimes within the park, sometimes just outside. No riders under six years old are permitted. Day trips, including meals, cost $235 per driver, $110 per passenger to Old Faithful; $250 per driver, $110 per passenger to Canyon. It's approximately $425 per person for multiday trips, including meals and lodging. Park admission fees are not included.

The **Yellowstone Association Institute** (⊡ *Box 117, Yellowstone National Park, WY 82190* ☎ *307/344–2293* ⊕ *www.yellowstoneassociation. org*) offers everything from daylong cross-country skiing excursions to multiday "Lodging and Learning" trips geared around hiking, skiing, and snowshoeing treks. Ski instruction is available. Expect to pay $120 to $500 for excursions; $545 to $1,000 or more for Lodging and Learning trips.

Yellowstone Tour & Travel (⊠ *211 Yellowstone Ave., West Yellowstone, MT* ☎*406/646–9310 or 800/221–1151* ⊕*www.yellowstone-travel. com*) rents snowmobiles and leads trips into the park from West Yellowstone. Longer packages may include lodging in West Yellowstone. Rentals cost $164 to $239 per day with guide. At Mammoth Hot Springs Hotel and Old Faithful Snow Lodge, **Xanterra Parks & Resorts** (☎*307/344–7901* ⊕*www. travelyellowstone.com*) rents skis and snowshoes. Ski rentals (includ-

> **GET ON THE BUS!**
>
> Xanterra's, **Historic Yellow Bus Tours** on White Motors' 14-passenger buses are the most elegant way to see and learn about the park. The soft-top convertibles allow you to bask in the sun if it's warm enough—and keep you plenty warm when it's not. Well-trained guides amuse and educate you through more than a dozen itineraries ranging from one hour to the entire day. Reservations are essential during peak summer season but can usually be made a few days in advance. ☎*307/344–7901* ⊕*www.travel yellowstone.com* ⌫*$12.50–$87* ⊙*Late May–late Sept.*

ing skis, poles, gloves, and gaiters) are $11 per half day, $16 per full day. Snowshoes rentals are $9 per half day, $12 per full day. Shuttle service is $13.50 from Snow Lodge, $14.50 from Mammoth. Group and private lessons are available. Skier shuttles run from Mammoth Hotel to Indian Creek and from Old Faithful Snow Lodge to Fairy Falls.

WHAT'S NEARBY

Cody sits near the park's East Entrance. It is a good base for hiking trips, horseback-riding excursions, and white-water rafting on the North Fork of the Shoshone or the Clarks Fork of the Yellowstone. Because of its proximity to both Grand Teton and Yellowstone, **Jackson** is the region's busiest community in summer and has the widest selection of dining and lodging options. Meanwhile, the least well-known gateway, the little town of **Dubois,** is a great base if you want to stay far from the madding crowds. Jackson and Dubois are near the park's South Entrance.

The most popular gateway from Montana, particularly in winter, is **West Yellowstone,** near the park's West Entrance. Affectionately known among winter recreationists as the "snowmobile capital of the world," this town of 1,000 is also a good place to go for fishing, horseback riding, and downhill skiing. There's also plenty of culture, as this is where you'll find the Museum of the Yellowstone. As the only entrance to Yellowstone that's open the entire year, **Gardiner** is always bustling. The Yellowstone River slices through town, beckoning fishermen and rafters. There are quaint shops and good restaurants. To the north of

Gardiner is **Livingston,** a town of 7,500 known for its charming historic district.

With both Yellowstone and the Absaroka-Beartooth Wilderness at its back door, the village of **Cooke City** is a good place for hiking, horseback riding, mountain climbing, and other outdoor activities. Some 50 mi to the east, **Red Lodge** provides a lot more options for dining and lodging. Cooke City and Red Lodge guard the Northeast Entrance—though it's the least used of all entry points to the park, it's by far the most spectacular. Driving along the Beartooth Scenic Byway between Red Lodge and Cooke City, you'll cross the southern tip of the Beartooth range, literally in the ramparts of the Rockies.

For more information on nearby towns see Chapters 2, 3, and 4.

WHERE TO STAY & EAT

ABOUT THE RESTAURANTS
When traveling in Yellowstone it's always a good idea to bring along a cooler—that way you can carry some snacks and lunch items for a picnic or break and not have to worry about making it to one of the more developed areas of the park, where there are restaurants and cafeterias. Generally you'll find burgers and sandwiches at cafeterias and full meals at restaurants. There is a good selection of entrées such as free-range beef and chicken; game meats such as elk, venison, and trout; and organic vegetables. At the several delis and general stores in the park you can purchase picnic items, snacks, and sandwiches.
■ TIP➔ Reservations at all the sit-down, full-service restaurants are a must for dinner during the height of the summer season.

ABOUT THE HOTELS
Park lodgings range from two of the national park system's magnificent old hotels to simple cabins to bland modern motels. Make reservations at least two months in advance for July and August for all park lodgings. Old Faithful Snow Lodge and Mammoth Hot Springs Hotel are the only accommodations open in winter; rates are the same as in summer. Ask about the size of beds, bathrooms, thickness of walls, and room location when you book, especially in the older hotels, where accommodations vary and upgrades are ongoing. Telephones have been put in some rooms, but there are no TVs. All park lodging is no smoking. There are no roll-away beds available.

ABOUT THE CAMPGROUNDS
Yellowstone has a dozen campgrounds scattered around the park. Most have flush toilets; some have coin-operated showers and laundry facilities. Most are operated by the National Park Service and are available on a first-come, first-served basis. Those campgrounds run by Xanterra Parks & Resorts—Bridge Bay, Canyon, Fishing Bridge, Grant Village, and Madison—accept bookings in advance. To reserve, call ☎307/344–7311. Larger groups can reserve space in Bridge Bay, Grant, and Madison from late May through September.

There are about 300 backcountry sites available in the park; camping outside designated areas is prohibited, with exceptions during the winter season (October 15–May 15). All overnight backcountry camping requires a free backcountry-use permit, which must be obtained in person from the Backcountry Office no more than 48 hours before the planned trip. In summer you can usually obtain the permits seven days a week, from 8 AM to 4:30 PM, at most visitor centers and ranger stations. Sites can be reserved for $20, regardless of the duration of the stay or the number in the group. Reserve a site by visiting any ranger station or by mailing the Backcountry Office, Box 168, Yellowstone National Park, WY 82190. All backcountry campsites have restrictions on group size and length of stay. Pit fires are prohibited at certain campsites.

WHAT IT COSTS					
	¢	$	$$	$$$	$$$$
RESTAURANTS	under $8	$8–$12	$13–$20	$21–$30	over $30
HOTELS	under $50	$50–$100	$101–$150	$151–$200	over $200

Restaurant prices are for a main course at dinner. Hotel prices are for two people in a standard double room in high season, excluding taxes and service charges.

WHERE TO EAT

$$$–$$$$

Fodor's Choice

★

✕ **Lake Yellowstone Hotel Dining Room.** Opened in 1893 and renovated by Robert Reamer beginning in 1903, this double-colonnaded dining room off the hotel lobby is the most elegant dining experience in the park. It is an upgrade from Old Faithful Inn in every way—service, china, view, menu sophistication, and even the quality of the crisp salads. Arrive early and enjoy a beverage in the airy sunroom. The menu includes elk medallions, buffalo prime rib, and fettuccine with wild smoked salmon. The wine list focuses on wines from California, Oregon, and Washington—with prices as high as $120 for a bottle of Mondavi Reserve Cabernet. ⊠ *Lake Village Rd., Lake Village* ☎ *307/344–7311* ⚑ *Reservations essential* ▤ *AE, D, DC, MC, V* ⊗ *Closed early Oct.–mid-May.*

$$–$$$$

★

✕ **Obsidian Dining Room.** From the wood-and-leather chairs etched with figures of park animals to the intricate lighting fixtures that resemble snowcapped trees, there's lots of atmosphere at Old Faithful Snow Lodge. The huge windows give you a view of the Old Faithful area, and you can sometimes see the famous geyser as it erupts. Aside from Mammoth Hot Springs Dining Room, this is the only place in the park where you can enjoy a full lunch or dinner in winter. The French onion soup will warm you up on a chilly afternoon; among the main courses, look for elk, beef, or salmon. ⊠ *Old Faithful Village, far end of Old Faithful Bypass Rd., Old Faithful* ☎ *307/344–7311* ▤ *AE, D, DC, MC, V* ⊗ *Closed mid-Oct.–mid-Dec. and mid-Mar.–mid-May.*

$$–$$$$

✕ **Old Faithful Inn Dining Room.** Just behind the lobby, the original dining room designed by Robert Reamer in 1903—and expanded by him in 1927—has lodgepole-pine walls and ceiling beams and a giant volcanic rock fireplace graced with a contemporary painting of Old Faithful by the late Paco Young. Note the etched-glass panels featuring partying cartoon animals that separates the dining room from the Bear Pit Lounge. These are reproductions of oak panels commissioned by Reamer in 1933 to celebrate the end of Prohibition. A buffet offers quantity over quality: bison, chicken, shrimp, two salads, two soups, and a dessert. You're better off choosing from nearly a dozen entrees on the à la carte menu, including grilled salmon, baked chicken, prime rib, and bison rib eye. Expect at least one vegetarian entrée (pasta and/or tofu) in addition to a choice of salads and soups (roasted red pepper and Gouda, for example). Save room for a signature dessert such as the Caldera, a chocolate truffle torte with a molten middle. The most extensive wine list in the park offers more than 50 (all American) choices, including sparkling and nonalcoholic varieties (from $20 to $70 per bottle). ⊠ *Old Faithful Village, Old Faithful* ☎ *307/344–7311* ◬ *Reservations essential* ▭ *AE, D, DC, MC, V* ⊘ *Closed late Oct.–early May.*

$–$$$ ✕ **Grant Village Dining Room.** The floor-to-ceiling windows of this lakeshore restaurant provide views of Yellowstone Lake through the thick stand of pines. The most contemporary of the park's restaurants, it makes you feel at home with pine-beam ceilings and cedar-shake walls. You'll find dishes ranging from pork and duck to prime rib; in late season you'll find a sandwich buffet on Sundays. ⊠ *Grant Village* ☎ *307/344–7311* ◬ *Reservations essential* ▭ *AE, D, DC, MC, V* ⊘ *Closed late Sept.–late May.*

$–$$$ ✕ **Mammoth Hot Springs Dining Room.** A wall of windows overlooks an expanse of green that was once a military parade and drill field at Mammoth Hot Springs. The art deco–style restaurant, decorated in shades of gray, green, and burgundy, has an airy feel with its bentwood chairs. Beef, pork, and chicken are on the menu as well as a selection of pasta and vegetarian dishes. ⊠ *Mammoth Hot Springs* ☎ *307/344–7311* ◬ *Reservations essential* ▭ *AE, D, DC, MC, V* ⊘ *Closed mid-Oct.–mid-Dec. and mid-Mar.–mid-May.*

$–$$$ ✕ **Roosevelt Lodge Dining Room.** At this rustic log cabin in a pine forest, the menu ranges from barbecued ribs and Roosevelt beans to hamburgers and french fries. For a real Western adventure, call ahead to join the popular chuck-wagon cookout that includes an hour-long trail ride or a stagecoach ride. ⊠ *Tower-Roosevelt* ☎ *307/344–7311* ◬ *Reservations essential for cookout* ▭ *AE, D, DC, MC, V* ⊘ *Closed early Sept.–early June.*

¢–$$ ✕ **Canyon Lodge Cafeteria.** This busy lunch spot serves such traditional and simple American fare as country-fried steak and hot turkey sandwiches. It stays open for light dinners as well, and for early risers, it also has a full breakfast menu. ⊠ *Canyon Village* ☎ *307/344–7311* ▭ *AE, D, DC, MC, V* ⊘ *Closed mid-Sept.–early June*

¢–$$ ✕ **Lake Lodge Cafeteria.** This casual eatery, popular with families, serves hearty lunches and dinners such as spaghetti, pot roast, and fried chicken. It also has a full breakfast menu. ⊠ *Lake Village Rd., Lake Village* ☎ *307/344–7311* ▭ *AE, D, DC, MC, V* ⊘ *Closed mid-Sept.–early June.*

¢–$$ ✕**Old Faithful Lodge Cafeteria.** Serving kid-friendly fare such as pizza,
☺ this noisy, family-oriented eatery also has some of the best views of Old
Faithful. ⊠*South end of Old Faithful Bypass Rd.* ☎*307/344–7311*
🞸*AE, D, DC, MC, V* ☾*Closed mid-Sept.–mid-May.*

¢–$ ✕**Bear Paw Deli.** You can grab a quick bite and not miss a geyser erup-
tion at this snack shop off the lobby in the Old Faithful Inn. Burgers,
chicken sandwiches, and chili typify your choices for hot meals. ⊠*Old
Faithful Village, Old Faithful* ☎*307/344–7311* 🞸*AE, D, DC, MC, V*
☾*Closed early Oct.–late May.*

¢–$ ✕**Mammoth Terrace Grill.** Although the exterior looks rather elegant,
this restaurant in Mammoth Hot Springs serves only fast food, ranging
from biscuits and gravy for breakfast to hamburgers and veggie burg-
ers for lunch and dinner. ⊠*Mammoth Hot Springs* ☎*307/344–7311*
🞸*AE, D, DC, MC, V* ☾*Closed late Sept.–mid-May.*

PICNIC AREAS

There are 49 picnic areas in the park, ranging from secluded spots
with a couple of tables to more popular stops with a dozen or more
tables and more amenities. Only nine areas—Snake River, Grant Vil-
lage, Spring Creek, Nez Perce, Old Faithful East, Bridge Bay, Cascade
Lake Trail, Norris Meadows, and Yellowstone River—have fire grates.
Only gas stoves may be used in the other areas. None have running
water; all but a few have pit toilets.

Keep an eye out for wildlife; you never know when a herd of bison
might decide to march through. In that case, it's best to leave your food
and move a safe distance away.

Firehole River. The Firehole River rolls past and you might see elk graz-
ing along its banks. This picnic area has 12 tables and one pit toilet.
⊠*Grand Loop Rd., 3 mi south of Madison.*
Fishing Bridge. This picnic area has 11 tables within the busy Fishing
Bridge area. It's walking distance to the amphitheater, store, and visi-
tor center. ⊠*East Entrance Road, 1 mi from Grand Loop Rd., Fish-
ing Bridge.*
Gibbon Meadows. You are likely to see elk or buffalo along the Gibbon
River from one of nine tables at this area, which has a wheelchair-
accessible pit toilet. ⊠*Grand Loop Rd., 3 mi south of Norris.*

WHERE TO STAY

See Grand Teton National Park for more area lodging and camping.

$$–$$$$ 🏨**Lake Yellowstone Hotel.** More Kennebunkport than Western, this dis-
★ tinguished hotel is the park's oldest. Dating from 1891, the white-and-
pastel-color hotel has maintained an air of refinement that Old Faithful
Inn can't because of its constant tour buses full of visitors. Just off
the lobby, a spacious sunroom offers priceless views of Lake Yellowstone at sunrise or sunset. It's also a great place to play cards, catch up
on a newspaper from the gift shop, or just soak in the grandeur of a
117-year-old National Historic Landmark. Note the tile-mantel fireplace, the etched windows of the gift shop, and the beautiful bay win-

dows. Rooms have white wicker furnishings, giving them a light, airy feeling; some have lake views. There is one two-room suite with lake views that has been used as accommodations for more than one U.S. president. The least expensive rooms are in an annex, not the original building. **Pros:** An oasis of elegance in the park, with the best views of any park lodging. **Cons:** The most expensive property in the park (even Old Faithful Inn has some rooms under $100), restaurant expensive and not particularly kid-friendly. ⊠ *Lake Village Rd., Lake Village* ☎ *307/344–7901* ⊕ *www.travelyellowstone.com* ⌘ *194 rooms* ⚲ *In-room: no a/c, no TV. In-hotel: restaurant, bar, no-smoking rooms* ⊚| *EP* ⊟ *AE, D, DC, MC, V* ⊘ *Closed early Oct.–mid-May.*

$$$ 🏨 **Cascade Lodge.** Pine wainscoting and brown carpets set the tone in this lodge built in 1992 in the trees above the Grand Canyon of the Yellowstone. The location is at the farthest edge of the Canyon Village, which means it's quite a hike to the nearest dining facilities—and you have to pass through rows upon rows of cabins, parking lots, and roads to get anywhere; the payoff is a much quieter environment because it's away from the major traffic. **Pros:** Canyon location is central to the entire park. Cons: Far from dining and other service, with children you'll need to drive to restaurants. ⊠ *North Rim Dr. at Grand Loop Rd., Canyon Village* ☎ *307/344–7901* ⊕ *www. travelyellowstone.com* ⌘ *40 rooms* ⚲ *In-room: no a/c, no TV. In-hotel: bar, no elevator, no-smoking rooms* ⊚| *EP* ⊟ *AE, D, DC, MC, V* ⊘ *Closed mid-Sept.–late May.*

$$$ 🏨 **Old Faithful Inn.** It's no accident that this Robert Reamer signature
☯ building has been declared a National Historic Landmark—and has
Fodor'sChoice been a favorite of five generations of park visitors. The so-called Old
★ House was originally built in 1904 and is worth a visit regardless of whether you are staying the night. The lobby has a 76-foot-high, eight-sided fireplace; bright red iron-clad doors, and two balconies (both open to the public) as well as a fantasylike "tree house" of platforms, ladders, and dormer windows high above the foyer. Believe it or not, you can stay in 1904-era rooms with thick wood timber walls and ceilings for less than $100 if you are willing to forsake a private bathroom. Rooms with bathrooms in either the Old House or the "modern" wings (built in 1913 and 1927) can rent for as high as $200-plus, especially if they have geyser views. Renovations in the hotel will continue throughout 2008 but shouldn't compromise one of America's most distinctive buildings. **Pros:** A truly historic property, Old House rooms are truly atmospheric with lodgepole-pine walls and ceilings. **Cons:** Waves of tourists in the lobby, some rooms lack private bathrooms. ⊠ *Old Faithful Village, Old Faithful* ☎ *307/344–7901* ⊕ *www.travelyellowstone.com* ⌘ *324 rooms, 246 with bath; 6 suites* ⚲ *In-room: no a/c, no phone (some), no TV. In-hotel: restaurant, bar, no-smoking rooms* ⊚| *EP* ⊟ *AE, D, DC, MC, V* ⊘ *Closed late Oct.–early May.*

$$$ 🏨 **Old Faithful Snow Lodge.** Built in 1998, this massive structure brings back the grand tradition of park lodges by making good use of heavy timber beams and wrought-iron accents in a distinctive facade. Inside you'll find soaring ceilings, natural lighting, and a spacious lobby with a stone fireplace. Nearby is a long sitting room, where writing desks

and overstuffed chairs invite you to linger. Guest rooms combine traditional style with modern amenities. This is one of only two lodging facilities in the park that are open in winter, when the only way to get here is on over-snow vehicles. **Pros:** The most modern hotel in the park, lobby, and adjacent hallway are great for relaxing, the only property on the interior of the park open in winter. **Cons:** Pricey, but you're paying for location. ⊠*Far end of Old Faithful Bypass Rd., Old Faithful* ☎*307/344–7901* ⊕*www.travelyellowstone.com* ✎*100 rooms* ♿*In-room: no a/c, no TV. In-hotel: restaurant, bicycles, no-smoking rooms* ⊙*EP* ⊟*AE, D, DC, MC, V* ⊘*Closed mid-Oct.–mid-Dec. and mid-Mar.–early May.*

$$ 🏨 **Grant Village Lodge.** The six humble lodge buildings that make up this facility have rough pine exteriors painted gray and rust. Grant Village is a great location to visit the southern half of the park, but the lodge itself is reminiscent of a big-city motel, the complex offering basic rooms with few features beyond a bed and nightstand. **Pros:** Excellent location to explore southern half of park, many nearby facilities. **Cons:** Merely the basics, with absolutely no extras. ⊠*Grant Village* ☎*307/344–7901* ⊕*www.travelyellowstone.com* ✎*300 rooms* ♿*In-room: no a/c, no TV. In-hotel: 2 restaurants, bar, no-smoking rooms* ⊟*AE, D, DC, MC, V* ⊘*Closed mid-Sept.–late May* ⊙*EP.*

$$ 🏨 **Lake Yellowstone Hotel Cabins.** Located behind the Yellowstone Lake Hotel, these cabins were renovated and brightened up with yellow paint in 2003–04. The simple duplexes provide basic, no-frills accommodations, but unlike some cabins in the park, all of these have private bathrooms. **Pros:** Active area for bison and other wildlife. **Cons:** The cabins feel like they were plunked adjacent to the unattractive rear parking lot without much thought, nearby Lake Lodge cabins are a better deal in a nicer setting. ⊠*Lake Village Rd., Lake Village* ☎*307/344–7901* ⊕*www.travelyellowstone.com* ✎*110 cabins* ♿*In-room: no a/c, no TV. In-hotel: restaurant, no-smoking rooms* ⊟*AE, D, DC, MC, V* ⊘*Closed mid-Oct.–mid-May.*

$–$$ 🏨 **Lake Lodge Cabins.** Just beyond the Lake Yellowstone Hotel lies one
♻ of the park's hidden treasures: Lake Lodge, built in 1920. The 140-foot lobby and porch offer one of the best views of sunrise in the park. The lodge itself no longer offers rooms. Rather, check in at the lobby (make a note to return to enjoy the two fireplaces, a visiting speaker, or a meal), and then head for your cabin, which is just north of the lodge. The accommodations are basic Yellowstone no-frills style—clean, with one to three beds, and a sink (some also have a shower/tub). There are views of the lake from the lodge but not from the rooms. **Pros:** The best front porch at a Yellowstone lodge and a great lobby, affordability, good for families. **Cons:** Absolutely no frills of any kind. ⊠*Lake Village Rd., Lake Village* ☎*307/344–7901* ⊕*www.travelyellowstone. com* ✎*186 rooms, 100 with bath* ♿*In-room: no a/c, no phones, no TV. In-hotel: restaurant, bar, no-smoking rooms* ⊙*EP* ⊟*AE, D, DC, MC, V* ⊘*Closed mid-Sept.–mid-June.*

$–$$ 🏨 **Mammoth Hot Springs Hotel and Cabins.** Built in 1937, this hotel has a spacious art deco lobby, where you'll find an espresso cart after 4 PM. The rooms are smaller and less elegant than those at the park's other two historic hotels, but the Mammoth Hot Springs Hotel is less expensive and usually less crowded. In summer the rooms can get hot, but you can open the windows, and there are fans. More than half the rooms do not have their own bathrooms; shared baths are down the hall. The cabins, set amid lush lawns, are the nicest inside the park, but most do not have private bathrooms, and only two very expensive suites have TVs. This is one of only two lodging facilities open in winter. Some cabins have hot tubs, a nice amenity after a day of cross-country skiing or snowshoeing. **Pros:** Great rates for a historic property, beautiful setting near picturesque Fort Yellowstone, no better place to watch elk in the fall. **Cons:** Those elk grazing on the lawn can create traffic jams, many hotel rooms and cabins without private bathrooms, rooms can get hot during the day. ⊠*Mammoth Hot Springs* ☎*307/344–7901* ⊕*www.travelyellowstone.com* ⤶*97 rooms, 67 with bath; 2 suites; 115 cabins, 76 with bath* ♿*In-room: no a/c, no phones (some), no TV. In-hotel: restaurant, bar, no-smoking rooms* |○|*EP* ⊟*AE, D, DC, MC, V* ⊘*Closed early Oct.–late-Dec. and mid-Mar.–early May.*

$ ⌂**Old Faithful Lodge Cabins.** There are no rooms inside the Old Faithful Lodge, though there are 97 cabins sitting at the northeast end of the village. Typical of cabins throughout the park, these are very basic—lacking most amenities (including bathrooms in about one-third of the cabins), views, or character. However, the location can't be beat—cabins are almost as close to the geyser as Old Faithful Inn. If you plan to spend a day or three exploring the geyser basins or the central area of the park, this is a great budget-conscious option to lay down your head since you'll be out and about most of the time anyway. **Pros:** A stone's throw from Old Faithful Geyser, all area services are within walking distance. **Cons:** Some cabins lack private bathrooms, they're pretty basic. ⊠*South end of Old Faithful Bypass Rd.* ☎*307/344–7901* ⊕*www.travelyellowstone.com* ⤶*96 cabins, 60 with bath* ♿*In-room: no a/c, no phone, no TV. In-hotel: restaurant, no-smoking rooms* |○|*EP* ⊟*AE, D, DC, MC, V* ⊘*Closed mid-Sept.–mid-May.*

$ ⌂**Roosevelt Lodge Cabins.** Near the beautiful Lamar Valley in the park's northeast corner, this simple lodge dating from the 1920s surpasses some of the more expensive options. All lodging is in rustic cabins set around a pine forest. Some cabins have bathrooms, but most do not, though there is a bathhouse nearby. Roughrider cabins may have woodstoves as the only heating system. You can make arrangements here for horseback and stagecoach rides. **Pros:** Closest cabins to Lamar Valley and its world-famous wildlife, authentic Western ranch feel, Roughrider cabins are the most inexpensive in the park. **Cons:** Cabins are very close together and many lack private bathrooms, you may have to draw straws to stoke the fire at 3 AM if your Roughrider cabin has only a woodstove. ⊠*Tower-Roosevelt Junction on Grand Loop Rd., Tower-Roosevelt* ☎*307/344–7901* ⊕*www.travelyellowstone. com* ⤶*80 cabins, 14 with bath* ♿*In-room: no a/c, no TV. In-hotel: restaurant, no-smoking rooms* |○|*EP* ⊟*AE, D, DC, MC, V* ⊘*Closed early Sept.–early June.*

CAMPGROUNDS & RV PARKS

If the kids enjoy camping and spending time in the great outdoors, any of the properties listed below will be good. Fishing Bridge RV Park is the only campground offering water, sewer, and electrical hookups, and it is for hard-sided vehicles only (no tents or tent-trailers are allowed).

⚠️**Bridge Bay.** The park's largest campground, Bridge Bay rests in a wooded grove above Lake Yellowstone and adjacent to the park's major marina. Ask for one of the few sites with a lake view. Xanterra tries to keep tent and RV campers separate—make sure you ask if you have a preference. If you end up on one of the inner loops, you may find yourself surrounded. You can rent boats at the nearby marina, take guided walks, or listen to rangers lecture about the history of the park. Don't expect solitude, as there are more than 400 campsites. Generators are allowed from 8 AM to 8 PM. Hot showers and laundry are 4 mi north at Fishing Bridge. ♿ *Flush toilets, dump station, drinking water, showers, bear boxes, fire pits, picnic tables, public telephone, ranger station* 🛏432 sites ✉3 mi southwest of Lake Village on Grand Loop Rd., Bridge Bay ☎307/344–7311 ⊕www.travelyellowstone.com ▭AE, D, DC, MC, V ⊙Late May–mid-Sept.

🔆 ⚠️**Canyon.** A massive campground with 400-plus sites, the Canyon campground accommodates everyone from hiker/biker tent campers to large RVs. The campground is accessible to Canyon's many short trails. Nearby Canyon Village offers every service—stores, laundry, ranger station, ice, etc.—which makes this campground a hit with families. The location is near laundry facilities and the visitor center. Generators are allowed from 8 AM to 8 PM. ♿ *Flush toilets, drinking water, guest laundry, showers, bear boxes, fire pits, picnic tables, public telephone, ranger station* 🛏272 sites ✉North Rim Dr., ¼ mi east of Grand Loop Rd., Canyon Village ☎307/344–7311 ⊕www.travelyellowstone.com ▭AE, D, DC, MC, V ⊙Mid-June–early Sept.

⚠️**Fishing Bridge RV Park.** Xanterra emphasizes "Park" not "Campground" in this area. There are no picnic tables or fire pits at individual RV sites here. However, full hookups are available for RVers to empty septic tanks, refill their potable water tank, and plug in to electricity, but plan on parking your RV and spending the majority of your time away from the park. Boat access is via nearby Bridge Bay Marina. This is the only facility in the park that caters exclusively to recreational vehicles. Because of bear activity in the area, only hard-sided campers are allowed. Liquid propane, as well as basic RV supplies, are available upon check-in. Generators are allowed from 8 AM to 8 PM. ♿ *Flush toilets, full hookups, dump station, drinking water, guest laundry, showers, bear boxes, public telephone, ranger station* 🛏344 sites ✉East Entrance Rd. at Grand Loop Rd., Fishing Bridge ☎307/344–7311 ⊕www.travelyellowstone.com ▭AE, D, DC, MC, V ⊙Mid-May–late Sept.

⚠️**Grant Village.** The park's second-largest campground, Grant Village has some sites with great views of Yellowstone Lake. Some of the sites are wheelchair accessible. The campground has a boat launch but no dock. Generators are allowed from 8 AM to 8 PM. ♿ *Flush toilets, dump* *station, drinking water, guest laundry, showers, bear boxes, picnic tables, public telephone, ranger station* ⇥*425 sites* ⊠*South Entrance Rd., 2 mi south of West Thumb* ☎*307/344–7311* 🖷*307/344–7456* ⊕*www.travelyellowstone.com* ▤*AE, D, DC, MC, V* ⊗*Late June–late Sept.*

🏕 **Indian Creek.** In a picturesque setting next to a creek, this campground is in the middle of a prime wildlife-viewing area. There are some combination sites that can accommodate trailers up to 45 feet. ♿*Pit toilets, bear boxes, fire pits, picnic tables* ⇥*75 sites* ⊠*8 mi south of Mammoth Hot Springs on Grand Loop Rd.* ☎*307/344–2017* ▤*No credit cards* ⊗*Early June–mid-Sept.*

🏕 **Lewis Lake.** Set among lodgepole-pine trees that didn't burn in 1988, this hilly campground above Lewis Lake has comfort and character. Used primarily by visitors from Grand Teton, fishermen, and backcountry hikers, it's fairly quiet. Launch your boat into Lewis Lake, hike several popular trails, and otherwise avoid the crowds of the Grand Loop campgrounds—if you can get a spot here. It's a bit off the beaten track, which means this campground south of Grant Village is quieter than most. This is the only campground besides Bridge Bay and Grant Village that has a boat launch. ♿*Pit toilets, drinking water, bear boxes, fire pits, picnic tables* ⇥*85 sites* ⊠*6 mi south of Grant Village on South Entrance Rd.* ☎*307/344–2017* ▤*No credit cards* ⊗*Mid-June–early Nov.*

🏕 **Madison.** The largest National Park Service–operated campground (meaning no advance reservations are accepted), Madison has eight loops and nearly 300 sites. The outermost loop backs up to the Madison River, but other sites feel a bit claustrophobic. You can't beat the location, though; you're minutes from Old Faithful, five different geyser basins, and three picturesque rivers (the Firehole, Madison, and Gibbon). Visit the adjacent ranger station (a National Historic Landmark) and view National Park Mountain. This campground can accommodate trailers up to 45 feet. Generators are allowed from 8 AM to 8 PM. ♿*Flush toilets, dump station, drinking water, bear boxes, fire pits, picnic tables, public telephone, ranger station* ⇥*277 sites* ⊠*Grand Loop Rd., Madison* ☎*307/344–7311* ⊕*www.travelyellowstone.com* ▤*AE, D, DC, MC, V* ⊗*Early May–Oct.*

🏕 **Mammoth Hot Springs.** At the base of a sagebrush-covered hillside, this campground can be crowded and noisy in the summer. It's surrounded on three sides by the North Entrance Road, so expect to hear a lot of auto traffic encircling you and to see vehicles climbing the hill to Mammoth Hot Springs. The campground lacks shade, so it's one of the few places in the park that can get pretty hot in the summer. Just 4 mi from the North Entrance and adjacent to the busy Mammoth village, it fills up early in busy season. Be extremely aware of bison, mule deer, and, in particular, elk, which are especially active in autumn because of their annual mating patterns. There are wheelchair-accessible sites at this campground. Generators are allowed from 8 AM to 8 PM. ♿*Flush toilets, drinking water, bear boxes, fire pits, picnic tables, public telephone, ranger station* ⇥*85 sites* ⊠*North Entrance Rd., Mammoth Hot Springs* ☎*307/344–2017* ▤*No credit cards* ⊗*Year-round.*

⚠ **Norris.** Straddling the Gibbon River, this is a quiet, popular campground. A few of its "walk-in" sites are among the best in the park (if you don't mind carrying your tent, food, and other belongings a few yards). Anglers love catching brook trout and grayling here. The campground can accommodate trailers up to 45 feet. Generators are allowed from 8 AM to 8 PM. ♿ *Flush toilets, drinking water, bear boxes, fire pits, picnic tables, ranger station* ⤤ *116 sites* ⊠ *Grand Loop Rd., Norris* ☎ *307/344–2177* ⊟ *No credit cards* ☉ *Mid-May–late Sept.*

★ ⚠ **Pebble Creek.** For 9 of the past 10 years, Darlene and Ray Rathmell have served as campground hosts here. It's no wonder. Beneath multiple 10,000-foot peaks (Thunderer, Barronnette Peak, and Mt. Norris) this easternmost campground in the park is set creek-side in a forested canopy. Pebble Creek is a babbling stream here, but hike a few yards north of the canyon to see the small canyon the river has carved. Great fishing, hikes, and wildlife abound in the vicinity. Along with nearby Slough Creek, this is the best campground in the park. Because of its small size, it fills up by 10 AM on busy days. It's also smaller than most, which means it tends to be a little quieter. Sites can accommodate trailers up to 45 feet. ♿ *Pit toilets, bear boxes, fire pits, picnic tables* ⤤ *32 sites* ⊠ *Northeast Entrance Rd., 22 mi east of Tower-Roosevelt Junction* ☎ *307/344–2017* ⊟ *No credit cards* ☉ *June–late Sept.*

★ ⚠ **Slough Creek.** Down the most rewarding 2 mi of dirt road in the park, Slough Creek is a gem. Nearly every site is adjacent to the creek, which is prized by anglers. The campground sits at the edge of the wildlife-rich Lamar Valley, and one of the famous wolf packs introduced in 1995 has taken residence several miles up the river and bears the name Slough Creek Pack. Listen carefully for grunting bison, howling wolves, and bugling elk. If you want to stay here in the summer, make this your first stop in the morning—on many days it fills up by 10 AM. ♿ *Pit toilets, bear boxes, fire pits, picnic tables* ⤤ *29 sites* ⊠ *Northeast Entrance Rd., 10 mi east of Tower-Roosevelt Junction* ☎ *307/344–2017* ⊟ *No credit cards* ☉ *Late May–Oct.*

YELLOWSTONE ESSENTIALS

To research prices, get advice from other travelers, and book travel arrangements, visit www.fodors.com.

ACCESSIBILITY

Yellowstone has long been a Park Service leader in providing for people with disabilities. Restrooms with sinks and flush toilets designed for those using wheelchairs are in all developed areas except Norris and West Thumb, where more rustic facilities are available. Accessible campsites and restrooms are at Bridge Bay, Canyon Village, Madison, Mammoth Hot Springs, and Grant Village campgrounds, and accessible campsites are found at both Lewis Lake and Slough Creek campgrounds. Ice Lake has an accessible backcountry campsite. An accessible fishing platform is about 3½ mi west of Madison at Mount Haynes Overlook. For details, contact the accessibility coordinator for the park or pick up a free copy of *Visitor Guide to Accessible Features in Yellowstone National Park.* It's available at all park visitor centers. You can also order it by mail.

Information **Park Accessibility Coordinator** (⬚ *Box 168, Yellowstone National Park, WY 82190-0168* ☎ *307/344–2017 or 307/344–2386 TDD*).

ADMISSION FEES

Entrance fees are $25 per car, $20 per motorcycle, and $12 per visitor arriving on foot, ski, bicycle, or in a noncommercial bus. Entrance fees entitle visitors to seven days in both Yellowstone and Grand Teton. Guests 15 and younger are exempt from paying an entrance fee. An annual pass to the two parks costs $50. A Senior Pass is $10 for U.S. citizens or permanent residents of the United States who are 62 or older. Access Pass allows free admission to citizens or permanent residents of the United States who have been determined to be blind or permanently disabled and present such documentation.

AUTOMOBILE SERVICE STATIONS

In 2008 all service stations in the park will accept credit cards (AE, Conoco, D, MC, V) at the pump, 24 hours a day. The adjacent convenience stores are open roughly from dawn to dusk during the summer season (7 AM–10 PM during July and August). They carry a limited selection of snacks, beverages, and ice, but no magazines, alcohol, or tobacco.

Repair services are available at Canyon, Fishing Bridge, Grant Village, and Old Faithful from late May through early September. Towing service is available from mid-May through mid-October. Repair stations can fix all common problems (including electronics, fuel pumps, alternators, brakes, bearings)—and carry a selection of replacement parts. They also receive daily, overnight parts deliveries in the summer.

No services are available for automobiles in the winter, but fuel for over-snow vehicles is available at Mammoth Hot Springs. The nearest gasoline stations in the winter are in Gardiner and West Yellowstone.

Contacts **Canyon Village Service Station** ✉ *Canyon* ☎ *406/848–7333* ☉ *Closed mid-Oct.–mid-May.* **Fishing Bridge Service Station** ✉ *Fishing Bridge* ☎ *406/848–7333* ☉ *Closed mid-Sept.–mid-May.* **Grant Village Service Station** ✉ *Grant Village* ☎ *406/848–7333* ☉ *Closed late Sept.–mid-May.* **Mammoth Hot Springs Service Station** ✉ *Mammoth Hot Springs* ☎ *406/848–7333* ☉ *Closed mid-Oct.–early May.* **Old Faithful Lower Station** ✉ *Old Faithful Village, Old Faithful* ☎ *406/848–7333* ☉ *Closed mid-Oct.–early May.* **Old Faithful Upper Station** ✉ *Old Faithful Village, Old Faithful* ☎ *406/848–7333* ☉ *Closed early Sept.–late May.* **Tower Junction Service Station** ✉ *Tower Junction, Tower-Roosevelt* ☎ *406/848–7333* ☉ *Closed early Sept.–early June.*

EMERGENCIES

In case of emergency, dial 911 or visit one of the park's clinics or ranger stations. In addition to public phones throughout the park, there are phones outside each clinic for after hours use.

Mammoth Clinic ☎ *307/344–7965* is next to the post office in Mammoth Hot Springs. It is the only medical facility in the park open year-round. An MD is on duty all day Monday through Thursday and Friday mornings. Call for an appointment unless you have an emergency condition or new work injury. **Lake Clinic** is behind the Lake Hotel in Lake village. It is staffed with a physician's assistant or nurse practitioner and two nurses. No appointments are taken. **Old Faithful Clinic** ☎ *307/545-7325.* is in the parking lot behind Old Faithful Inn. It is staffed with one physician's assistant or nurse practitioner and two nurses. No appointments are taken. There are hospitals with 24-hour emergency rooms in Jackson, Cody, and Bozeman.

Contacts **General Emergencies** (☎ *911 or 307/344-7381).*

Bozeman Deaconess Hospital (✉ *915 Highland Blvd., Bozeman MT* ☎ *406/585-5000).* **Lake Clinic** (✉ *Lake Village* ☎ *307/242-7241* ☉ *Late-May-late-Sept., daily 8:30-8:30).* **Mammoth Clinic** (✉ *Mammoth Hot Springs* ☎ *307/344-7965* ☉ *May-Sept., daily 8:30-5; Sept.-May, Mon.-Thurs., 8:30-5 and Fri. 8:30-1).* **Old Faithful Clinic** (✉ *Old Faithful* ☎ *307/545-7325* ☉ *Mid-May-mid-Sept., daily 7-7; mid-Sept.-early Oct., Thurs.-Mon., 8:30-5).* **St. John's Medical Center** (✉ *625 E. Broadway Ave., Jackson, WY* ☎ *307/733-3636).* **West Park Hospital** (✉ *707 Sheridan Ave., Cody, WY* ☎ *307/527-7501).*Yellowstone Family Medical Clinic (✉ *11 S. Electric Ave., West Yellowstone, MT* ☎ *406/646-0200* ☉ *May-Sept., weekdays 8-5; Oct.-Apr., weekdays 9-4).*

PERMITS
Fishing permits are required if you want to take advantage of Yellowstone's abundant lakes and streams. Live bait is not allowed, and for all native species of fish, a catch-and-release policy stands. Anglers 16 and older must purchase a $15 three-day permit, a $20 seven-day permit, or a $35 season permit. Those 12 to 15 need a free permit or must fish under direct supervision of an adult with a permit. Children 11 and under do not need a permit but must be supervised by an adult. Fishing permits are available at ranger stations, visitor centers, and Yellowstone General Stores.

All camping outside of designated campgrounds requires a free backcountry permit. Horseback riding also requires a free permit.

All boats, motorized or nonmotorized, including float tubes, require a permit. Boat permits for motorized vessels are available for $20 (annual) or $10 (seven days). Permits for nonmotorized vessels are $10 (annual) or $5 (seven days). Permits from Grand Teton National Park are valid in Yellowstone, but owners must register their vessel in Yellowstone.

ROAD INFORMATION & EMERGENCY SERVICES
Contact the Wyoming Department of Transportation for road and travel reports October–April. For emergency situations dial 911 or contact the Wyoming Highway Patrol. Most cell phones work in the developed areas of the park, and there are emergency phones along some park roads.

Information **Montana Highway Patrol** (☎ *406/388-3190 or 800/525-5555* ⊕ *www.mdt.mt.gov).* **Wyoming Department of Transportation** (☎ *307/777-4484, 307/772-0824 from outside Wyoming for road conditions, 888/996-7623 from within Wyoming for road conditions* ⊕ *www.wyoroad.info).* **Wyoming Highway**

1

Patrol (☎ *307/777–4301, 800/442–9090 for emergencies, #4357 [#HELP] from a cell phone for emergencies).*

VISITOR INFORMATION

Check *Yellowstone Today,* the newspaper available at all entrances and visitor centers, for details, dates, and times. The Park Service and its concessionaires make a concerted effort to ensure that all information is up-to-date and accurate. If you need them, be sure to ask for publications titled "Beyond Road's End," "Backcountry Trip Planner," "Ranger Programs," "Boating Regulations," "Bicycling in Yellowstone National Park," and "Fishing Regulations," as well as one-sheet fliers on day hikes (by region) and historical attractions in the park.

The park Web site makes all these publications available online, in addition to the *Yellowstone Resources and Issues Handbook,* a 200-page book used by park naturalists to answer many basic questions.

Information **Yellowstone National Park** ✉ *Box 168, Mammoth, WY 82190-0168* ☎ *307/344–7381, 307/344–2386 TDD* ⊕ *www.nps.gov/yell.*

West Yellowtone Visitor Information Center ✉ *30 Yellowstone Ave. West Yellowstone, MT* ☎ *406/646–4403* ⊕ *www.nps.gov/yell.*

Grand Teton National Park

WORD OF MOUTH

"We're thinking of going to Yellowstone/Grand Teton around some holidays this summer. When's the best time to go—good weather, decent sighting of wildlife, hopefully, less crowds?"

–JC98

"We were in YNP & GTNP this past September and had a wonderful trip. Tons of wildlife, little or no crowds, and the weather was nice, leaves golden and red, even got a little snow."

–BayouGal

WELCOME TO GRAND TETON

TOP REASONS TO GO

★ **Heavenward hikes:** Trek where grizzled frontiersmen roamed. Jackson Hole got its name from mountain man David Jackson; now there are dozens of trails for you to explore.

★ **Wildlife big and small:** Keep an eye out for little fellows like short-tailed weasels and beaver, as well as bison, elk, wolves, and both black and grizzly bears.

★ **Waves to make:** Float the Snake River or take a canoe onto Jackson Lake or Jenny Lake.

★ **Homesteader history:** Visit the 1890s barns and ranch buildings of Mormon Row or Menor's Ferry.

★ **Rare bird-watching:** Raise the binoculars—or just your head—to see more than 300 species of birds, including trumpeter swans, bald eagles, and osprey.

★ **Trout trophies:** Grab your rod and slither over to the Snake River, where cutthroat trout are an angler's delight.

1 Antelope Flats. Buffalo and antelope frequently roam across this sagebrush-covered area of the park northeast of Moose, and it is also where homesteader barns along Mormon Row still dot the landscape. It's a popular place for wildflower viewing and leisurely bicycle rides.

2 Jenny Lake. Nestled at the base of the Tetons, Jenny Lake is a microcosm of the park. In this developed area, you can visit the visitor center, purchase supplies, or talk to a ranger—plus ride a boat across the lake, hike around it, have a picnic, or camp nearby.

3 Moose. Just north of Craig Thomas Discovery & Visitor Center, this historical area is home to the Chapel of the Transfiguration, and was once the stomping grounds of early settlers at Menor's Ferry. The ferry has been re-created so you can see how it provided transportation across the Snake River before there were bridges.

4 Oxbow Bend. At this famously scenic spot the Snake River, its inhabitants and the Tetons all converge, especially in early morning or near dusk. You're likely to see moose feeding in willows, elk grazing in aspen stands, and birds such as bald eagles, osprey, sandhill cranes, ducks, and American white pelicans.

GETTING ORIENTED

Grand Teton's immense peaks jut dramatically up from the Jackson Hole valley floor. Without any foothills to soften the blow, the sight of these glacier-scoured crags is truly striking. Several alpine lakes reflect the mountains, and the winding Snake River cuts south along the eastern side of the park. The northern portion of the park is outstanding wildlife-watching territory—you can see everything from rare birds to lumbering moose to the big predators (mountain lions, and black and grizzly bears). Two main roads run through the 310,000-acre park; Highway 26/89/191 curves along the eastern or outer side; and Teton Park Road (also called the inner park road, which is closed during winter) runs closer to the mountain range.

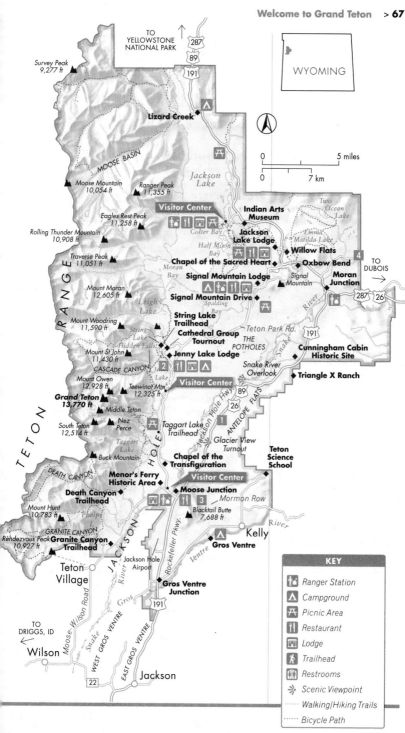

WYOMING

2

TO
YELLOWSTONE
NATIONAL PARK

Survey Peak
9,277 ft

Lizard Creek

MOOSE BASIN

Moose Mountain
10,054 ft

Ranger Peak
11,355 ft

Eagles Rest Peak
11,258 ft

Rolling Thunder Mountain
10,908 ft

Traverse Peak
11,051 ft

RANGE

Mount Moran
12,605 ft

Mount Woodring
11,590 ft

Mount St John
11,430 ft

CASCADE CANYON

Mount Owen
12,928 ft

Teewinot Mtn
12,325 ft

**Grand Teton
13,770 ft**

Middle Teton

South Teton
12,514 ft

Nez Perce

TETON

Buck Mountain

DEATH CANYON

Mount Hunt
10,783 ft

GRANITE CANYON

Rendezvous Peak
10,927 ft

**Granite Canyon
Trailhead**

Teton
Village

TO
DRIGGS, ID

Wilson

Jackson Lake

Jackson Lake

Half Moon
Bay

Moran
Bay

Leigh
Lake

String
Lake

Hidden Falls

String Lake

Jenny
Lake

Taggart
Lake

Phelps
L.

JACKSON

Snake River

Moose-Wilson Road

Jackson Hole
Airport

Gros

191

West Gros Ventre

East Gros Ventre

22

Jackson

Two
Ocean
Lake

Emma
Matilda Lake

Visitor Center

Colter Bay

**Indian Arts
Museum**

**Jackson
Lake Lodge**

Willow Flats

Chapel of the Sacred Heart

Oxbow Bend

Signal Mountain Lodge

Signal
Mountain

**Moran
Junction**

TO
DUBOIS

287 26

Signal Mountain Drive

Spalding

Teton Park Rd.

191

Cathedral Group
Tournout

THE
POTHOLES

Snake
River

**Cunningham Cabin
Historic Site**

Jenny Lake Lodge

2

Snake River
Overlook

Triangle X Ranch

Jenny
Lake

Visitor Center

89

26

ANTELOPE FLATS

Jackson Hole Hwy.

1

**Taggart Lake
Trailhead**

Glacier View
Turnout

**Teton
Science
School**

**Chapel of the
Transfiguration**

Visitor Center

Moose Junction

3 Mormon Row

Blacktail Butte
7,688 ft

River

Kelly

Gros Ventre

Rockefeller Pkwy.

Ventre

**Death Canyon
Trailhead**

**Menor's Ferry
Historic Area**

**Gros Ventre
Junction**

0 ——— 5 miles
0 ——— 7 km

KEY	
🏚	*Ranger Station*
⛺	*Campground*
🏕	*Picnic Area*
🍴	*Restaurant*
🏠	*Lodge*
🥾	*Trailhead*
🚻	*Restrooms*
✳	*Scenic Viewpoint*
-----	*Walking/Hiking Trails*
·····	*Bicycle Path*

GRAND TETON NATIONAL PARK PLANNER

When to Go

In July and August all the roads, trails, and visitor centers are open, and the Snake River's float season is in full swing. **To have full access to services without competing with peak use by summer visitors, plan a trip between May and June or September and October.**

The lowest rates and smallest crowds can be found in spring and fall, but services and roads are more limited. Grand Teton Lodge Company, the park's major outfitter, winds down its activities in September, and most of Teton Park Road closes from late October through early May.

Towns just outside the park rev up in winter. Teton Village and Jackson both buzz with the energy of Snow King Resort and Jackson Hole Mountain Resort, the former being the older of the two, also conveniently in town, and the latter an international skiing hot spot deep in the valley. (Prices, accordingly, rise along with the hotel occupancy rates.) Because of this onslaught of skiers, U.S. Highway 26/191/89 stays open all winter.

Flora & Fauna

Grand Teton's short growing season and arid climate create a complex ecosystem and hardy plant species. The dominant elements are big sagebrush, which gives a gray-green cast to the valley, lodgepole-pine trees, quaking aspen, and ground-covering wildflowers such as bluish-purple lupine, arrow leaf, arnica, scarlet gilia, balsamroot, and Indian paintbrush, Wyoming's state flower. In spring and early summer you will see the vibrant yellow arrow leaf, balsamroot, and the delicate blue camas, a plant prized by Native Americans for its nutritional value. The growing season in Jackson Hole is short, but gives rise to spectacular, though short-lived displays of wildflowers. The best time to see these natural displays are mid-June to early July, although the changing of the aspen and cottonwood leaves in early fall can be equally spectacular.

Your best chance to see wildlife is at dawn or dusk, along forest edges. The best place to view elk in summer is on Teton Park Road because some of the animals summer in the area. During winter they migrate out of the surrounding mountains, and about 7,500 spend the winter south of the park on the National Elk Refuge. Oxbow Bend and Willow Flats are good places to look for moose, beaver, and otter any time of year. Pronghorn antelope and bison appear in summer along Highway 26/191/89 and Antelope Flats Road. Occasionally, the animals are on or crossing the road; remember in all cases they have the right-of-way. On almost any trip to Grand Teton, you will see bison, antelope, moose, and coyotes. Rarely will you see a black or grizzly bear or a mountain lion or wolf. Because bears and lions live in the park, campers should always follow safe-camping practices by storing food in bear-proof containers and never in their tents. The park's smaller animals, yellow-bellied marmots and golden-mantled ground squirrel, as well as a variety of birds and waterfowl, are commonly seen along park trails and waterways. Watch for elk along the forest edge. Black and grizzly bears inhabit the forests, but are rarely spotted. Seek out the water sources—the Snake River, the alpine lakes, and marshy areas—to see birds such as bald eagles, ospreys, ducks, and trumpeter swans.

Getting There & Around

The best way to see Grand Teton National Park is by car. Unlike Yellowstone's Grand Loop, Grand Teton's road system doesn't allow for easy tour-bus access to all the major sights. Only a car will get you close to Jenny Lake, into the remote east Jackson Hole hills, and to the top of Signal Mountain. You can stop at many points along the roads within the park for a hike or a view. Be extremely cautious in winter, when whiteouts and ice are not uncommon. There are adequate road signs throughout the park, but a good road map is handy to have in the vehicle.

Jackson Hole Highway (U.S. Highway 26/191/89) runs the entire length of the park, from Jackson to Yellowstone National Park's south entrance. (This highway is also called Route 26/191 south of Moran Junction and U.S. 287/26 north of Moran Junction.) This road is open all year from Jackson to Moran Junction and north to Flagg Ranch, 2 mi south of Yellowstone. Depending on traffic, the southern (Moose) entrance to Grand Teton is about 20 minutes from downtown Jackson via Highway 89/189 (Broadway Avenue), then right onto Wyoming 22 west and right at Wyoming 390 north (aka Moose–Wilson Road). Coming from the opposite direction on the same road, the northern boundary of the park is about 15 minutes south of Yellowstone National Park. Also open year-round, U.S. 26/287 runs east from Dubois over Togwotee Pass to the Moran entrance station, a drive of roughly an hour.

Grand Teton Lodge Company has shuttle service to its lodging properties, but if you drive, which is recommended, there is plenty of free parking at all developed areas and adequate parking at waysides and historic sites. Although break-ins aren't common, use good sense when leaving your vehicle for an extended period of time by locking valuables out of sight or taking them with you.

Two back-road entrances to Grand Teton require high-clearance or good-performing vehicles. Both are closed by snow from November through May and are heavily rutted through June. The Moose–Wilson Road (or Route 390) starts at its intersection with Route 22 in Wilson (4 mi west of Broadway Avenue in Jackson) and travels 7 mi north past Teton Village, then turns into an unpaved road for almost 1 mi until the Moose entrance. It's closed to large trucks, trailers, and RVs. Even rougher is 60-mi Grassy Lake Road, which heads east from Route 32 in Ashton, Idaho, through Targhee National Forest. It connects with U.S. 89/287 in the John D. Rockefeller Jr. Memorial Parkway sandwiched between Grand Teton and Yellowstone.

Festivals & Events

Throughout the year Grand Teton Music Festival presents monthly concerts featuring solo performers as well as duos and groups at Walk Festival Hall in Teton Village. Tickets are about $25 for adults, $5 for students. ☎ *307/733–3050* ⊕ *www.gtmf.org.*

March The **Pole-Pedal-Paddle** is a minimarathon ski-cycle-canoe relay race held every March, starting at Jackson Hole Ski Resort and finishing down the Snake River. ☎ *307/733–6433* ⊕ *www.polepedalpaddle.com.*

May Jackson's **Old West Days** includes a rodeo, Native American dancers, a Western swing-dance contest, Mountain Man Rendezvous, and cowboy poetry readings. ☎ *307/733–3316.*

May–Sept. Between Memorial Day and Labor Day, gunslingers stage **The Shootout** daily at 6:15 PM, except Sunday, on the southeast corner of the Jackson Town Square. Don't worry, the bullets aren't real. ☎ *307/733–3316.*

Updated by
Gil Brady

YOUR JAW WILL PROBABLY DROP the first time you see the Teton Range jabbing up from the Jackson Hole valley floor. With no foothills to get in the way, you'll have a close-up, unimpeded view of magnificent, jagged, snowcapped peaks. This massif is long on natural beauty. Before your eyes, mountain glaciers creep imperceptibly down 12,605-foot Mt. Moran. Large and small lakes gleam along the range's base. Many of the West's iconic animals (elk, bears, bald eagles) call this park home.

SCENIC DRIVES

Antelope Flats Road. Off U.S. 191/89/26, about 2 mi north of Moose Junction, this narrow road wanders eastward over rolling plains, rising buttes, and sagebrush flats. The road intersects Mormon Row, where you can turn off to see abandoned homesteaders' barns and houses from the turn of the 20th century. Less than 2 mi past Mormon Row is a four-way intersection where you can turn right to loop around past the town of Kelly and Gros Ventre campground and rejoin U.S. 191/26/89 at Gros Ventre Junction. Keep an eye out for pronghorn, bison, moose, and mountain bikers.

Jackson Hole Highway (U.S. 191/26/89). Slicing through the middle of Jackson Hole, this busy highway passes views of the Teton Range along most of its distance, with a turnout at the Snake River Overlook and another picturesque Snake River view at Oxbow Bend.

Fodor's Choice
★

Jenny Lake Scenic Drive. This 4-mi, one-way loop provides the park's best roadside close-ups of the Tetons as it winds south through groves of lodgepole-pine and open meadows. Roughly 1.5 mi off Teton Park Road, the Cathedral Group Turnout faces 13,770-foot Grand Teton (the range's highest peak), flanked by 12,928-foot Mt. Owen and 12,325-foot Mt. Teewinot. ⊠ *Jenny Lake.*

Fodor's Choice
★

Signal Mountain Road. This exciting drive climbs Signal Mountain's 1,040-foot prominence along a 5-mi stretch of switchbacks. As you travel through forest you can catch glimpses of Jackson Lake and Mt. Moran. The trip ends with a sweeping view—from 7,720 feet above sea level—of Jackson Hole and the entire 40-mi Teton Range. Sunset is the best time to make the climb up Signal Mountain. The road is not appropriate for long trailers and is closed in winter. ⊠ *Oxbow Bend.*

Teton Park Road. Linking Moose Junction with Jackson Lake Junction, this 20-mi drive is the closest to the Teton Range and it ties in with the Jenny Lake Scenic Drive. The main road skirts Jackson Lake, with Signal Mountain looming to the east. Farther south, turnouts give you excellent views of Mt. Moran and the Cathedral Group (the three highest peaks in the Teton Range).

GRAND TETON IN ONE DAY

Begin the day by packing a picnic lunch or picking one up at a Jackson eatery. Arrive at **Moose Visitor Center** in time for a 9 AM, two-hour, guided Snake River float trip (make reservations in advance with one of the dozen or so outfitters that offer the trip). When you're back on dry ground, drive north on Teton Park Road, stopping at scenic turnouts—don't miss Teton Glacier—until you reach Jenny Lake Road, which is one-way headed south. After a brief stop at **Cathedral Group Turnout**, park at the Jenny Lake ranger station and take the 20-minute boat ride to **Cascade Canyon** trailhead for a short hike. Return to your car by midafternoon, drive back to Teton Park Road, and head north to Signal Mountain Road to catch a top-of-the-park view of the Tetons. In late afternoon descend the mountain and continue north on Teton Park Road. At Jackson Lake Junction, you can go east to **Oxbow Bend** or north to **Willow Flats**, both excellent spots for wildlife viewing before you head to **Jackson Lake Lodge** for dinner and an evening watching the sun set over the Tetons. Or if you'd like to get back on the water, drive to **Colter Bay Marina,** where you can board a 1½-hour sunset cruise across Jackson Lake to Waterfalls Canyon. You can reverse this route if you're heading south from Yellowstone: start the day with a 7:30 AM breakfast cruise from Colter Bay and end it with a sunset float down the Snake River.

WHAT TO SEE

HISTORIC & CULTURAL SITES

Fodor'sChoice
★ **Chapel of the Transfiguration.** This tiny chapel built in 1925 on land donated by Maud Noble is still a functioning Episcopal church. Couples come here to exchange vows with the Tetons as a backdrop, and tourists come to take photos of the small church with its awe-inspiring view. ⊠ *Turn off Teton Park Rd. onto Chapel of the Transfiguration Rd., 1.1 mi north of Moose Junction, Moose* ☉ *Late May–late Sept., Sun.: Eucharist 8 AM, service 10 AM.*

☾ **Indian Arts Museum.** This collection's standout exhibits include Plains Indian weapons and clothing. You will see Crow blanket strips with elegant beadwork, sashes from the Shawnee and Hopi tribes, and various weapons, games and toys, flutes and drums, and a large collection of moccasins from many tribes. From June through early September, you can see crafts demonstrations by tribal members, take ranger-led tours of the museum, and listen to a daily 45-minute ranger program on Native American culture. ⊠ *2 mi off U.S. 89/191/287, 5 mi north of Jackson Lake Junction inside Colter Bay Visitor Center, Oxbow Bend* ☏ *307/739–3594* ☏ *Free* ☉ *Mid-May–mid-June and Sept., daily 8–5; mid-June–Labor Day, daily 8–7.*

Fodor'sChoice
★ **Menor's Ferry Historic Area.** Down a path from the Chapel of the Transfiguration, the ferry on display is not the original, but it's an accurate re-creation of the double-pontoon craft built by Bill Menor in 1894. It demonstrates how people crossed the Snake River before bridges

were built. In the cluster of turn-of-the-20th-century buildings there are historical displays, including a photo collection of historic shots taken in the area; one building has been turned into a small general store. You can pick up a pamphlet for a self-guided tour. Check out the nearby general supplies store where candy and pop are sold in the summer. The ferry typically runs after spring runoff, between June and August, and only when a park ranger is available to operate it. ⊠ ½ *mi off Teton Park Rd., 1 mi north of Moose Junction, Moose* ⊙ *Year-round, dawn–dusk.*

SCENIC STOPS

FodorsChoice
★

Jackson Lake. The biggest of Grand Teton's glacier-carved lakes, this body of water in the northern reaches of the park was enlarged by construction of the Jackson Lake Dam in 1906. You can fish, sail, and windsurf on the lake, or hike trails near the shoreline. Three marinas (Colter Bay, Leeks, and Signal Mountain) provide access for boaters, and several picnic areas, campgrounds, and lodges overlook the lake. ⊠ *U.S. 89/191/287 from Lizard Creek to Jackson Lake Junction, and Teton Park Rd. from Jackson Lake Junction to Signal Mountain Lodge, Oxbow Bend.*

★ **Jenny Lake.** Named for the Native American wife of mountain man Beaver Dick Leigh, this alpine lake south of Jackson Lake draws paddlesports enthusiasts to its pristine waters and hikers to its tree-shaded trails. ⊠ *Off Teton Park Rd. midway between Moose and Jackson Lake, Jenny Lake.*

Laurance S. Rockefeller Preserve & Center. This new preserve includes 8 mi of trails. You can access the preserve via the Valley Trail, 1.75 mi north of the Granite Canyon trailhead and ½ mi south of the Death Canyon turnoff. For the first time, hikers can admire the new public viewpoint from the south–southwestern shore of Phelps Lake. ⊠ *On east side of Moose–Wilson Rd., about 4 mi south of park headquarters and 3 mi north of Granite Canyon Entrance Station, Moose.*

FodorsChoice
★

Oxbow Bend. This peaceful and much-admired spot overlooks a quiet backwater left by the Snake River when it cut a new southern channel. White pelicans stop here on their spring migration (many stay on through summer), sandhill cranes and trumpeter swans visit frequently, and great blue herons nest amid the cottonwoods along the river. Use binoculars to search for bald eagles, ospreys, moose, beaver, and otter. The Oxbow is known for the reflection of Mt. Moran that marks its calm waters in early morning. ⊠ *U.S. 89/191/287, 2.5 mi east of Jackson Lake Junction, Oxbow Bend.*

★ **Willow Flats.** You will almost always see moose grazing in the marshy area of Willow Flats, in part because it has a good growth of willow trees, which moose both eat and hide in. This is also a good place to see birds and waterfowl. ⊠ *U.S. 89/191/287, 1 mi north of Jackson Lake Junction. Oxbow Bend.*

2

VISITOR CENTERS

If you plan to do any hiking or exploring on your own, it is important to stop at a visitor center to get up-to-date information about weather conditions. Rangers also will know if any trails are temporarily closed because of wildlife activity. Before beginning any backcountry explorations, you must obtain permits, which you can get at visitor centers.

★ **Colter Bay Visitor Center.** The auditorium here hosts several free daily programs about Native American culture and natural history. Also, at 11 and 3 daily, a 30-minute "Teton Highlights" ranger lecture provides tips on park activities. ⊠*Colter Bay, ½ mi west of Colter Bay Junction on Hwy. 89/191/287, Oxbow Bend* ☎*307/739–3594* ⊙*Mid-May–early June, daily 8–5; early June–early Sept., daily 8–7, Sept.–early Oct., daily 8–5.*

Craig Thomas Discovery & Visitor Center. This brand-new center has interactive and interpretive exhibits dedicated to themes of preservation, mountaineering, and local wildlife. There's also a 3-D map of the park and streaming video along a footpath showing the area's intricate natural features. ⊠*½ mi west of Moose Junction, Moose* ⊙*Early June–early Sept., 8–7; early Sept.–early June, 8–5.*

Jenny Lake Visitor Center. Geology exhibits, including a relief model of the Teton Range, are on display here. ⊠*S. Jenny Lake Junction, 8 mi north of Moose Junction on Teton Park Rd., Jenny Lake* ☎*307/739–3392* ⊙*Early June–late Sept., daily 8–4:30.*

SPORTS & THE OUTDOORS

BICYCLING

Grand Teton has few designated bike paths, so cyclists should be very careful when sharing the road with vehicles, especially RVs and trailers. A bike lane allows for northbound bike traffic along the one-way Jenny Lake Loop Road, a one-hour ride. The River Road, 4 mi north of Moose, is an easy four-hour mountain-bike ride along a ridge above the Snake River on a dirt road. Bicycles are not allowed on trails or in the backcountry.

⇨*Outfitters & Expeditions box for bike rentals and expeditions.*

BIRD-WATCHING

With more than 300 species of birds in the park, the Tetons make for excellent bird-watching country. Here you might spot both the calliope hummingbird (the smallest North American hummingbird) and the trumpeter swan (the world's largest waterfowl). The two riparian habitats described below draw lots of attention, but there are many other bird-busy areas as well. Birds of prey circle around Antelope Flats Road; for instance, the surrounding fields are good hunting turf for red-tailed hawks and prairie falcons. At Taggart Lake you'll see woodpeckers, bluebirds, and hummingbirds. Look for songbirds, such as pine and evening grosbeaks and Cassin's finches, in surrounding open pine and aspen forests.

Oxbow Bend. Some seriously impressive birds tend to congregate at this quiet spot (⇨ *Scenic Stops*). In spring white pelicans stop by during their northerly migration; in summer, bald eagles, great blue herons, and osprey nest nearby. Year-round you'll have a good chance of seeing trumpeter swans. Nearby Willow Flats has similar birdlife, plus sandhill cranes. ⊠ *U.S. 89/191/287, 2 mi east of Jackson Lake Junction.*

Phelps Lake. The moderate 2-mi round-trip Phelps Lake Overlook Trail takes you up conifer- and aspen-lined glacial moraine to a view that's accessible only by trail. Expect abundant birdlife: Western tanagers, northern flickers, and ruby-crowned kinglets thrive in the bordering woods, and hummingbirds feed on scarlet gilia beneath the overlook. Don't neglect the newly opened Phelps Lake Trail (*see* ⇨ *Hiking, below*). ⊠ *Moose–Wilson Rd., about 3 mi off Teton Park Rd., 1 mi north of Moose Junction.*

BOATING & WATER SPORTS

Water sports in Grand Teton are diverse. You can float the Snake River, which runs high and fast early in the season (May and June) and more slowly during the latter part of the summer. Canoes and kayaks dominate the smaller lakes and share the water with motorboats on the impressively large Jackson Lake. Motorboats are allowed on Jenny, Jackson, and Phelps lakes. On Jenny Lake, there's an engine limit of 10 horsepower. You can launch your boat at Colter Bay, Leek's Marina, Signal Mountain, and Spalding Bay.

If you're floating the Snake River on your own, you are required to purchase a permit that costs $10 per raft and is valid for the entire season, or one for $5 per raft for seven days. Permits are available year-round at Moose Visitor Center and at Colter Bay, Signal Mountain, and Buffalo (near Moran entrance) ranger stations in summer. Before you set out, check with park rangers for current conditions.

You may prefer to take one of the many guided float trips through calm-water sections of the Snake; outfitters pick you up at the float-trip parking area near Moose Visitor Center for a 10- to 20-minute drive to upriver launch sites. Ponchos and life preservers are provided. Early-morning and evening floats are your best bets for wildlife viewing, but be sure to carry a jacket or sweater. Float season runs mid-April to December.

Colter Bay Marina. All types of services are available to boaters, including free parking for boat trailers and vehicles, free mooring, boat rentals, guided fishing trips, and fuel. ⊠ *On Jackson Lake.*

Leek's Marina. Both day and short-term parking for boat trailers and vehicles are available for up to three nights maximum. There are no boat rentals, but you can get fuel, and there's free short-term docking plus a pizza restaurant. This marina is operated by park concessionaire Signal Mountain Lodge. ⊠ *U.S. 89/191/287, 6 mi north of Jackson Lake Junction* ☎ *307/543–2831* ☉ *Mid-May–mid-Sept.*

Signal Mountain Lodge Marina. The marina rents pontoon boats, deck cruisers, motorboats, kayaks, and canoes by the hour or for full-day cruising; rates range from $12 an hour for a kayak to $62 an hour for a pontoon boat. ⊠ *Teton Park Rd., 3 mi south of Jackson Lake Junction* ☎ *307/543–2831* ⊗ *Mid-May–mid-Sept.*

⇨ *Outfitters & Expeditions box for boating outfitters.*

CLIMBING

The Teton Range offers the nation's most diverse general mountaineering. Excellent rock, snow, and ice routes abound for climbers of all experience levels. Unless you're already a pro, it's recommended that you take a course from one of the area's climbing schools before tackling the tough terrain.

⇨ *Outfitters & Expeditions box for outfitters.*

FISHING

Rainbow, brook, lake, and native cutthroat trout inhabit the park's waters. The Snake's 75 mi of river and tributary are world renowned for their fishing. To fish in Grand Teton National Park, you need a Wyoming fishing license. A day permit for nonresidents is $10, and an annual permit is $65 plus a $10 conservation stamp; for state residents a license costs $15 per season plus $10 for a conservation stamp. Children under age 14 can fish free with an adult who has a license. You can buy a fishing license at Colter Bay Marina, Moose Village Store, Signal Mountain Lodge, and at area sporting-goods stores, where you will also be able to get solid information on good fishing spots and the best flies or lures to use. Or you can get one direct from **Wyoming Game and Fish Department** (⊠ *420 N. Cache St., Box 67, Jackson 83001* ☎ *307/733–2321*).

⇨ *Outfitters & Expeditions box for guided fishing expeditions.*

HIKING

Of the more than 250 mi of maintained trails, the most popular are around some of the lakes, including Jenny Lake, the Leigh and String lakes area, and Taggart and Bradley lakes (particularly the Taggart Lake Trail with its views of Avalanche Canyon and the Grand Teton). Must-do trails that will whip your legs into mountain shape without too much strain include Taggart Lake via Beaver Creek and Phelps Lake. Front country or backcountry, you may see moose, bears, or mountain lions; keep your distance and don't run from mountain lions. Instead, make lots of noise. Pets are not permitted on trails or in the backcountry, but you can take them on paved front-country trails so long as they're on a short leash. Always sign in at trailheads, let someone know where you are going and when you expect to return, and carry plenty of water, snacks, and a cell phone.

EASY **Cascade Canyon Trail.** Take the 20-minute boat ride from the Jenny Lake ⓒ dock to the start of a gentle, ½-mi climb to 200-foot Hidden Falls, the park's most popular and crowded trail destination. With the boat ride, plan on a couple of hours to experience this trail. Listen here for the distinctive bleating of the rabbitlike pikas among the glacial boulders and pines. The trail continues ½ mi to Inspiration Point over a rocky path that is moderately steep. There are two points on the climb that

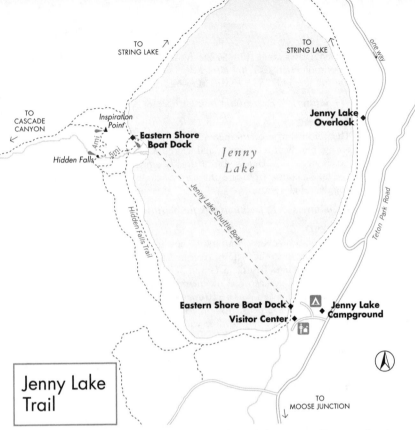

afford good views of Jenny Lake and the surrounding area, but keep climbing; after passing a rock wall you'll finally reach the true Inspiration Point, with the best views. To avoid crowds, try to make your way to Inspiration Point in early morning or late afternoon. To reach the Cascade Canyon trailhead, go to the Jenny Lake Visitor Center to catch a ride across Jenny Lake with **Jenny Lake Boating**. ⊠ *Jenny Lake Rd., 2 mi off Teton Park Rd., 12 mi south of Jackson Lake Junction* ☎ *307/734–9227* 🖻 *$5–$7* ⊘ *June–early Sept.*

Colter Bay Nature Trail Loop. This easy, 1¾-mi round-trip excursion treats you to views of Jackson Lake and the Tetons. As you follow the level trail from Colter Bay Visitor Center and along the forest's edge, you may see moose and bald eagles. Allow yourself two hours to complete the walk. ⊠ *2 mi off U.S. 89/191/287, 5 mi north of Jackson Lake Junction.*

Lunchtree Hill Trail. One of the park's easiest trails begins at Jackson Lake Lodge and leads ½ mi to the top of a hill above Willow Flats. The area's willow thickets, beaver ponds, and wet, grassy meadows make it a birder's paradise. Look for sandhill cranes, hummingbirds, and the many types of songbirds described in the free bird guide available at the visitor centers. You might also see moose. The round-trip walk takes no more than half an hour. ⊠*U.S. 89/191/287, ½ mi north of Jackson Lake Junction.*

Phelps Lake Trail. This easy-to-moderate hike starts at the Death Canyon Trailhead, which is 5.6 mi from the Moose–Wilson entrance to the park (the turnoff to the trailhead is 4 mi from Moose Junction). At less than 2 mi, it's ideal for beginners, those scouting for an ideal place to campout in the boondocks, and couples seeking a romantic outing. You'll summit at the spectacular 700-foot, forested overlook of Phelps Lake and the lower Jackson Hole valley. The turnoff for Whitegrass Road, which leads to the Death Canyon Trailhead parking lot, is about 3 mi southwest of the Moose Visitor Center; the last mile or so is dirt and can get rough, so be sure your vehicle is adequate for the task. The trail to the Phelps Lake Overlook is relatively short (less than a mile), but you'll travel a total of 4 mi if you go down to the lake itself. ⊠*Turn off Moose–Wilson Rd. at Whitegrass Rd., 4 mi southwest of Moose Junction.*

MODERATE **Jenny Lake Trail.** You can walk to Hidden Falls from Jenny Lake ranger ☺ station by following the mostly level trail around the south shore of the ★ lake to Cascade Canyon Trail. Jenny Lake Trail continues around the lake for 6½ mi. It's an easy trail—classed here as moderate because of its length—that will take you two to three hours. You'll walk through a lodgepole-pine forest, have expansive views of the lake and the land to the east, and hug the shoulder of the massive Teton range itself. Along the way you are likely to see elk, pikas, golden mantle ground squirrels, and a variety of ducks and waterbirds, plus you may hear elk bugling, birdsong, and the chatter of squirrels. ⊠*S. Jenny Lake Junction, ½ mi off Teton Park Rd., 8 mi north of Moose Junction.*

Leigh Lake Trail. The flat trail follows String Lake's northeastern shore to Leigh Lake's south shore, covering 2 mi in a round-trip of about an hour. You can extend your hike into a moderate 7½-mi, four-hour round-trip by following the forested east shore of Leigh Lake to Bearpaw Lake. Along the way you'll have views of Mt. Moran across the lake, and you may be lucky enough to spot a moose. ⊠*String Lake trailhead, ½ mi west of Jenny Lake Rd., 14 mi north of Moose Junction.*

String Lake Trail. This moderate 3½-mi, three-hour loop around String Lake lies in the shadows of 11,144-foot Rockchuck Peak and 11,430-foot Mt. Saint John. This is also a good place to see moose, hear songbirds, and view wildflowers. This trail is a bit more difficult than other midlength trails in the park, which means it is also less crowded. ⊠*½ mi west of Jenny Lake Rd., 14 mi north of Moose.*

Taggart Lake–Beaver Creek Trail. Hike 1½ mi from the trailhead to the lake and then continue on a 4-mi route around the lake where the terrain becomes steeper near Beaver Creek. There are views of Avalanche Canyon and areas where you might spot a moose. Plan on two to three hours to enjoy this trail. ⊠*½ mi south of Jenny Lake on Teton Park Rd.*

OUTFITTERS & EXPEDITIONS

BICYCLING

Teton Cycle Works. The oldest cycle shop in town offers mountain- and road-bike rentals, sales, accessories, and repairs. ⊠ *175 N. Glenwood St., Jackson* ☎ *307/733–4386* ⊙ *Mar.–Oct.*

Teton Mountain Bike Tours. Mountain bikers of all skill levels can take guided half-, full-, or multiday tours with this company into both Grand Teton and Yellowstone national parks, as well as to the Bridger-Teton and Caribou–Targhee national forests. ⊕ *Box 7027, Jackson 83002* ☎ *307/733–0712 or 800/733–0788* ⊕ *www.wybike.com* ✉ *$55–$125 for half- to full-day trips; multiday trips $379–$400 per day* ⊙ *May–Sept.*

BOATING & WATER SPORTS

Barker-Ewing Scenic Float Trips. Travel the peaceful parts of the Snake River looking for wildlife as knowledgeable guides talk about area history, plants, and animals. ⊕ *Box 100–J, Moose 83012* ☎ *307/733–1800 or 800/365–1800* ⊕ *www.barkerewingscenic.com* ✉ *$50* ⊙ *May–Sept.*

Grand Teton Lodge Company. You can rent motorboats, row boats, and canoes at Colter Bay Marina. ⊠ *2 mi off U.S. 89/191/287, 5 mi north of Jackson Lake Junction* ☎ *307/543–3100, 307/543–2811, or 800/628–9988* ⊕ *www.gtlc.com* ✉ *Motorboats $25 per hr, rowboats and canoes $11 per hr* ⊙ *Early June–late Sept.*

Grand Teton Lodge Company Snake River Float Trips. Choose from a scenic float trip with lunch, or an evening trip with a steak-fry dinner. Make reservations at the activities desk at Colter Bay Village

or Jackson Lake Lodge. ☎ *307/543–3100 or 800/628–9988* ⊕ *www.gtlc.com* ✉ *Scenic float $45, lunch float $53, steak-fry float $60* ⊙ *June–Aug.*

Lewis and Clark River Expeditions. Get in touch with these folks for an exhilarating wet-and-wild ride or a more leisurely scenic float. ⊠ *335 N. Cache St., Box 720, Jackson 83001* ☎ *307/733–4022 or 800/824–5375* ⊕ *www.lewisandclarkexpeds.com* ✉ *$43–$79* ⊙ *Mid-May–mid-Sept.*

Mad River Boat Trips. This company leads a variety of white-water and scenic float trips, some combined with breakfast, lunch, or dinner. ⊠ *1255 S. U.S. 89, Jackson* ☎ *307/733–6203 or 800/458–7238* ⊕ *www.mad-river.com* ✉ *$44–$83* ⊙ *Mid-May–Sept.*

Snake River Kayak and Canoe. Get some instruction in the fine art of paddling here, then test yourself on the river. ⊕ *Box 4311, Jackson 83001* ☎ *307/733–9999 or 800/529–2501* ⊕ *www.snakeriverkayak.com* ✉ *Raft trips $63–$95, 1-day clinics $175–$280, multiday instruction $275–$900* ⊙ *Apr.–Oct.*

Triangle X Float Trips. This company offers subdued river trips in Grand Teton National Park, including a sunset supper float. ⊠ *2 Triangle X Ranch Rd., Moose* ☎ *307/733–5500 or 888/860–0005* ⊕ *www.trianglex.com* ✉ *$48–$58* ⊙ *Mid-May–late Sept.*

CLIMBING

Exum Mountain Guides. You'll find a variety of climbing experiences here, ranging from one-day mountain climbs to ice climbing to backcountry adventures on skis and snowboards. ⬚ *Box 56, Moose 83012* ☎*307/733-2297* ⊕*www.exumguides.com* ✉*1-day climbs $200–$340, climbing schools $105–$170* ⏱*Year-round.*

Jackson Hole Mountain Guides. Mountain climbers get a leg up in the Tetons from this outfit, which offers instruction for beginning to advanced climbers in both rock and ice climbing. ✉*165 N. Glenwood St., Jackson* ☎*307/733-4979 or 800/239-7642* ⊕*www.jhmg.com* ✉*1-day guided climbs $195–$225, climbing classes $125–$275* ⏱*Year-round.*

FISHING

Grand Teton Lodge Company. The park's major concessionaire operates guided Jackson Lake fishing trips that include boat and tackle, and guided fly-fishing trips on the Snake River. Make reservations at the activities desks at Colter Bay Village or Jackson Lake Lodge, where trips originate. ✉*Colter Bay Marina or Jackson Lake Lodge* ☎*307/543-3100 or 800/628-9988* ⊕*www.gtlc.com* ✉*$130–$375 and up* ⏱*June–Sept.*

Signal Mountain Lodge. A variety of guided Lake Jackson fishing trips leave from the marina here. ✉*Teton Park Rd., 3 mi south of Jackson Lake Junction* ☎*307/543-2831* ⊕*www.signalmountainlodge.com* ✉*$65 per hr* ⏱*Mid-May–mid-Sept.*

HORSEBACK RIDING

Colter Bay Village Corral. One- and two-hour rides leave Colter Bay Village for a variety of destinations, and half-day trips—for advanced riders only—go to Hermitage Point; some rides include a trailside breakfast or dinner. ✉*2 mi off U.S.*

89/191/287, 5 mi north of Jackson Lake Junction ☎*307/543-3100 or 800/628-9988* ⊕*www.gtlc.com* ✉*Short rides $30–$42, breakfast rides $50, dinner rides $56; wagon rides $30 for breakfast and $40 for dinner* ⏱*June–Aug.*

Jackson Lake Lodge Corral. One-hour trail rides give an overview of the Jackson Lake Lodge area; two-hour rides go to Emma Matilda Lake, Oxbow Bend, and Christian Pond. Experienced riders can take a half-day ride to Two Ocean Lake. Some rides include breakfast or dinner eaten along the trail. ✉*U.S. 89/191/287, ½ mi north of Jackson Lake Junction* ☎*307/543-3100 or 800/628-9988* 🖶*307/543-3143* ⊕*www.gtlc.com* ✉*Short rides $30–$42, breakfast rides $50 ($30 by wagon), dinner rides $56 ($40 by wagon)* ⏱*June–Aug.*

WINTER SPORTS

Jack Dennis Outdoor Shop. This place stocks skis and snowboards for sale and rent, and outdoor gear for any season. ✉*50 E. Broadway Ave., Jackson* ☎*307/733-3270 Jackson, 307/733-6838 Teton Village* ⊕*www.jackdennis.com* ✉*Ski rental $25–$44, snowboard and boot rental $25–$35* ⏱*Year-round.*

Pepi Stiegler Sports Shop. You can buy or rent skis or snowboards at this Teton Village shop, at the base of the Jackson Hole ski mountain. ✉*3395 McCollister Dr., Teton Village 83025* ☎*307/733-4505* ⊕*www.pepistieglersports.com* ✉*Ski rental $25–$44, snowboard and boot rental $25–$35* ⏱*Nov.–Apr.*

DIFFICULT   **Death Canyon Trail.** This 7½-mi trail is a strenuous hike with lots of hills to traverse, ending with a climb up into Death Canyon. Plan to spend most of the day on this steep trail. ✉ *Off Moose–Wilson Rd., 4 mi south of Moose Junction.*

HORSEBACK RIDING

You can arrange a guided horseback tour at Colter Bay Village and Jackson Lake Lodge corrals or with a number of private outfitters. Most offer rides of an hour or two up to all-day excursions. ⇨ *Outfitters & Expeditions box for rentals and riding expeditions.*

WINTER SPORTS

Grand Teton has some of North America's finest and most varied cross-country skiing. (And don't forget the nearby Jackson Hole Mountain Resort; ⇨ *Chapter 3.*) Ski the gentle 3-mi Swan Lake–Heron Pond Loop near Colter Bay Visitor Center, the mostly level 10-mi Jenny Lake Trail, or the moderate 4-mi Taggart Lake–Beaver Creek Loop and 5-mi Phelps Lake Overlook trail. Advanced skiers should head for the Teton Crest Trail. In winter, overnight backcountry travelers must register or make a reservation at park headquarters in Moose for a permit costing $25 for each reservation. Those wanting to access the backside of the Tetons toward Idaho should check with Jackson Hole Mountain Resort to see if their new tram will access that backcountry.

You can snowmobile on the Continental Divide snowmobile trail as well as on Jackson Lake. You must first purchase a permit—$15 permit for one day, $20 for seven days—at a park entrance station. Snowmobilers wishing to proceed north from Flagg Ranch into Yellowstone National Park must be with a commercial tour guide. The Flagg Ranch Information Station closed for the 2007–08 winter season, and consequently ski and snowshoe trails went unmarked. Any references to marked or flagged trails on brochures should be disregarded until further notice. For a ranger-guided snowshoe walk, call the Craig Thomas visitor center (⇨ *Visitor Centers, above*).

⇨ *Outfitters & Expeditions box for winter-sports outfitters.*

EDUCATIONAL OFFERINGS

PROGRAMS & TOURS

Grand Teton Lodge Company Bus Tours. Half-day tours depart from Colter Bay Village or Jackson Lake Lodge and include visits to scenic viewpoints, visitor centers, and other park sites. Interpretive guides provide information about the park geology, history, wildlife, and ecosystems.

ACCESSIBLE TOURS

Many Grand Teton bus tours, float trips, fishing trips, lake cruises, and wagon rides are fully or partially accessible; ask the independent operators for details. One company, **Access Tours,** caters specifically to people with physical disabilities. The company can also give you general information about places that are easily accessible in Teton, Glacier, and Yellowstone. 🖂 *Box 499, Victor, ID 83455* ☎ *208/787–2338 or 800/929–4811* ⊕ *www.access-tours.org.*

Buy tickets in advance at Colter Bay Marina or Jackson Lake Lodge activities desks. Tours include Grand Teton, Yellowstone, or a combination of the two parks. ⊠ *Colter Bay Village or Jackson Lake Lodge* 🕾*307/543–2811 or 800/628–9988* 🖃*$40–$80* ☉ *Mid-May–early Oct., daily.*

Gray Line Bus Tours. Full-day bus tours provide an overview of Grand Teton National Park. They depart from Jackson, and you will learn about the park's geology, history, birds, plants, and wildlife. ⊠ *16 W. Martin La., Jackson* 🕾*307/733–4325 or 800/443–6133* 🖃*$80 plus $12 park entrance fee* ☉ *Memorial Day–Sept.*

Jackson Lake Cruises. Grand Teton Lodge Company runs 1½-hour Jackson Lake scenic cruises from Colter Bay Marina throughout the day as well as breakfast cruises, and sunset steak-fry cruises. One cruise, known as Fire and Ice, shows how forest fires and glaciers have shaped the Grand Teton landscape. ⊠ *2 mi off U.S. 89/191/287, 5 mi north of Jackson Lake Junction* 🕾*307/543–3100, 307/543–2811, or 800/628–9988* ⊕*www.gtlc.com* 🖃*Scenic cruise $21; breakfast cruise $33; steak-fry cruise $55* ☉ *Late May–mid-Sept.*

Teton Wagon Train and Horse Adventures. Multiday covered-wagon rides and horseback trips follow Grassy Lake Road on the "back side" of the Tetons. You can combine the trip with a river trip and a tour of Yellowstone and Grand Teton. ⬚ *Box 10307, Jackson 83001* 🕾*307/734–6101 or 888/734–6101* ⊕*www.tetonwagontrain.com* 🖃*Wagon trip $895; combination trip $1,859* ☉ *June–Aug.*

RANGER PROGRAMS

Jackson Lake Lodge Ranger Talks. Visit the Wapiti Room to hear a slide-illustrated ranger presentation on topics such as area plants and animals, geology, and natural history. Also, you can chat with the ranger on the back deck of the lodge 6:30–8 PM daily, early June through early September. ⊠ *U.S. 89/191/287, ½ mi north of Jackson Lake Junction* 🕾*307/739–3300* ☉ *Late June–mid-Aug., nightly at 8:30.*

ৎ **Ranger Walks.** Rangers lead free walks throughout the park in summer, from a one-hour lakeside stroll at Colter Bay to a three-hour hike from Jenny Lake. The talks focus on a variety of subjects from wildlife to birds and flower species to geology. Call for itineraries, times, and reservations. 🕾*307/739–3300, 307/739–3400 TTY* ☉ *Early June–early Sept.*

ৎ **Young Naturalist Program.** Children ages 8–12 learn about the natural world of the park as they take an easy 2-mi hike with a ranger. Kids should wear old clothes and bring water, rain gear, and insect repellent. The hike, which takes place at Jenny Lake or Colter Bay, is 1½ hours long and is limited to 12 children. ⊠ *Jenny Lake: meet at flagpole at visitor center; Colter Bay: meet at visitor center* 🕾*307/739–3399 or 307/739–3594* ☉ *Mid-June–mid-Aug., daily 1:30.*

WHAT'S NEARBY

The major gateway to Grand Teton National Park is **Jackson**—but don't confuse this with Jackson Hole. Jackson Hole is the mountain-ringed valley that houses Jackson and much of Grand Teton National Park. The town of Jackson, south of the park, is a small community (around 9,000 residents) that gets flooded with more than 3 million visitors annually.

If it's skiing you're after, **Snow King Resort** is the oldest resort in the valley, and its 7,808-foot mountain overlooks the town of Jackson and the National Elk Refuge. It's at the end of Snow King Avenue. **Teton Village,** on the southwestern side of Grand Teton National Park, is a cluster of businesses and restaurants around the facilities of the Jackson Hole Mountain Resort—a ski and snowboard area with gondola and various other lifts. There are plenty of places to eat, stay, and shop here.

Dubois, about 85 mi east of Jackson is the least known of the gateway communities to Grand Teton and Yellowstone, but this town of 1,000 has most of the services of the bigger towns. You can still get a room for the night here during the peak summer travel period without making a reservation weeks or months in advance (though it's a good idea to call a week or so before you intend to arrive). About two hours south of Jackson is **Pinedale,** another small Wyoming town with lodging, restaurants, and attractions. Energy development has made the area a hopping place these days, so be sure to plan ahead if you want to stay in town, as many hotels are filled with mineral-field workers.

For more information on nearby towns and attractions, *see* Chapter 3.

WHERE TO STAY & EAT

ABOUT THE RESTAURANTS

Though the park itself has some excellent restaurants, don't miss dining in Jackson (⇨ Chapter 3), where restaurants combine game, fowl, and fish with the enticing spices and sauces of European cuisine and the lean ingredients, vegetarian entrées, and meat cuts that reflect the desires of health-consciousness diners. Steaks are usually cut from grass-fed Wyoming beef, but you'll also find bison and elk on the menu; poultry and pasta are offered by most restaurants, and you'll find fresh salads and fish (trout, tilapia, and salmon are most common). Just about everywhere, you can order a burger or a bowl of homemade soup. Casual is the word for most dining both within and outside the park. An exception is Jenny Lake Lodge, where jackets are suggested for men at dinner. Breakfast is big: steak and eggs, pancakes, biscuits and gravy; lunches are lighter, often taken in a sack to enjoy on the trail.

ABOUT THE HOTELS

The choice of lodging properties within the park is as diverse as the landscape itself. Here you'll find simple campgrounds, cabins, and basic motel rooms. You can also settle into a homey bed-and-breakfast, or a luxurious suite in a full-service resort. Between June and August, room rates go up and are harder to get without advanced reservations. Nonetheless, if you're looking to stay in a national park that's tailored to individual pursuits, this is it. Although this park is becoming more popular and crowded each year, it's still closer to the original vision of a haven for man to interact with nature (while contemplating it), as its idealistic founders first imagined back in 1929 and again in 1950.

For information on lodging and dining (as well as tours) in the park, contact the park's largest concessionaire, **Grand Teton Lodge Company.** *Box 250, Moran, WY 83013* ☎*307/543–3100 or 800/628–9988* ⊕*www.gtlc.com.*

You can reserve rooms near the park through two agencies. **Jackson Hole Central Reservations** (☎*888/838–6606* ⊕*www.jacksonholewy.com*) handles hotels as well as B&Bs. **Resort Reservations** (☎*307/733–6331 or 800/329–9205* ⊕*www.jacksonhole.net*) is the place to call for reservations for most motels in Jackson.

ABOUT THE CAMPGROUNDS

You can camp in the park's backcountry year-round, provided you have the requisite permit and are able to gain access to your site. Between June 1 and September 15, backcountry campers in the park are limited to one stay of up to 10 days. Campfires are prohibited in the backcountry except at designated lakeshore campsites. You can reserve a backcountry campsite between January 1 and May 15 for a $25 nonrefundable fee (social security numbers must be included on all checks) by faxing a request or writing to **GTNP-Backcountry Permits** (*Box 170, Moose, WY 83012* ☎*307/739–3443*). You can also take a chance that the site you want will be open when you show up, in which case you pay no fee at all, but park officials seem less inclined recently to accommodate walk-ins.

At this writing the Jackson Hole Mountain Resort tram will not be running during the entire summer season of 2008. Consequently, there is no access to the park's backcountry except on foot, so backcountry campers should plan accordingly. Updates are posted on the park's Web site.

WHAT IT COSTS					
	¢	$	$$	$$$	$$$$
RESTAURANTS	under $8	$8–$12	$13–$20	$21–$30	over $30
HOTELS	under $50	$50–$100	$101–$150	$151–$200	over $200

Restaurant prices are for a main course at dinner. Hotel prices are for two people in a standard double room in high season, excluding taxes and service charges

WHERE TO EAT

$$$$
★
✕ **Jenny Lake Lodge Dining Room.** Elegant yet rustic, this is one of Grand Teton National Park's finest dining establishments, with jackets suggested for men. The menu is ever changing and offers fish, pasta, chicken, and beef; the wine list is extensive. Gourmet five-course dinners are prix-fixe; lunch is à la carte. Unless children are particularly well behaved, families with youngsters should probably find a babysitter or go elsewhere. ⊠ *Jenny Lake Rd., 2 mi off Teton Park Rd., 12 mi north of Moose Junction, Jenny Lake* ☎ *307/733–4647 or 800/628–9988* ⚘ *Reservations essential* ▭ *AE, MC, V* ⊘ *Closed early Oct.–late May. No lunch.*

$$$-$$$$
Fodor'sChoice
★
✕ **Jackson Lake Lodge Mural Room.** If you're looking for upscale, this fine-dining restaurant might be the ultimate in Wyoming's national parks' culinary experiences. This large room houses a 700-square-foot mural painted by late-20th-century Western artist Carl Roters that details an 1837 Wyoming mountain man rendezvous. Select from a menu that includes trout, elk, lamb, beef, and pasta. The cedar-plank salmon is a great choice, or try a buffalo steak. One cannot exaggerate the scene beyond the windows of this establishment. The riparian area below and Willow Flats, where moose love to feast, compete with Jackson Lake and the Teton's Cathedral Group. If you can, book a window table at sunset and drink in the luscious panorama. Other delicious sights include Roters's mural, which covers two walls of the dining room. This elegant restaurant might not work as a first choice for casual or budget-conscious diners. ⊠ *U.S. 89, 5 mi north of Moran Junction* ☎ *307/543–2811 Ext. 3463 or 800/628–9988* ▭ *AE, MC, V* ⊘ *Closed mid-Oct.–late May.*

$$$-$$$$
✕ **The Peaks.** Part of Signal Mountain Lodge, this casual room has exposed ceiling beams and big square windows creating a rustic atmosphere overlooking southern Jackson Lake and the Tetons. The emphasis here is on fish: Rocky Mountain trout is marinated, lightly floured, and grilled, or simply grilled and topped with lemon-parsley butter. But there's also filet mignon and elk stew, not to mention free-range chicken and vegetable lasagna for the health-conscious or vegetarian diner. Families should call about menu selections in advance. ⊠ *Teton Park Rd., 4 mi south of Jackson Lake Junction, Oxbow Bend* ☎ *307/543–2831* ▭ *AE, D, MC, V* ⊘ *Closed mid-Oct.–mid-May.*

$$-$$$
☺
★
✕ **Dornan's Chuck Wagon.** This legendary chuck wagon operates only in summer and has been feeding hungry wranglers, cowboys, travelers, and dudes since 1948. It is owned and operated by the same family as Dornan's restaurant and operates on the same grounds. Locals know that here they can catch a hearty meal of beef stew, short ribs, steak, prime rib, trout, chicken, cowboy beans, mashed potatoes, with lemonade or hot coffee, and cobbler for dessert in the spring and summer. At breakfast, count on old-fashioned staples such as sourdough pancakes, eggs, bacon, sausage, or biscuits and gravy. You can eat your chuck-wagon meal inside one of Dornan's tepees if it happens to be raining or windy (which kids are sure to enjoy). Otherwise, sit at outdoor picnic tables with pristine views of the Snake River and the Tetons. In recent years the food at Dornan's chuck wagon has not been as consistently

good as that of the Bar J in Wilson; however, the quick service and inexpensive prices make this a good choice for families or travelers on a budget. ⊠*200 Moose St., at Moose Entrance to Grand Teton National Park, off Teton Park Rd. at Moose Junction, Moose* ☎*307/733–2415* ☐*AE, MC, V* ⊗*Closed Oct.–May.*

¢–$$ ✕**Jackson Lake Lodge Pioneer Grill.** With its old-fashioned soda fountain, frontier antiques, friendly service, and seats along a winding counter, this eatery recalls a 1950s-era luncheonette. It serves breakfast, lunch, and dinner and is a good spot for hikers starting out to grab a bagel, eggs, or flapjacks before hitting the trails. The grill also offers buffalo burgers, turkey dinners, and fried trout. Diners looking for something more substantial or sophisticated should look elsewhere. ⊠*U.S. 89, 5 mi north of Moran Junction, Oxbow Bend* ☎*307/543–2811 Ext. 1911* ☐*AE, MC, V* ⊗*Closed early Oct.–late May.*

¢–$ ✕**John Colter Café Court.** This Colter Bay Village resting spot serves Mexican-America fare such as tacos, burritos, and quesadillas as well as ice cream. You can also buy a boxed lunch and take it to the beach. It's just right for what it is, but don't expect the moon. ⊠*Just under 5 mi north of Jackson Lake Lodge, Colter Bay* ☎*307/543–2811* ☐*AE, MC, V* ⊗*Closed Oct.–mid-May.*

PICNIC AREAS

The park has 11 designated picnic areas, each with tables and grills, and most with pit toilets and water pumps or faucets. In addition to those listed here you can find picnic areas at Colter Bay Village Campground, Cottonwood Creek, Moose Visitor Center, the east shore of Jackson Lake, South Jenny Lake, and String Lake trailhead.

Chapel of the Sacred Heart. From this intimate lakeside picnic area you can look across southern Jackson Lake to Mt. Moran. For wedding information contact Our Lady of the Mountains Catholic Church in Jackson. ⊠*¼ mi east of Signal Mountain Lodge, off Teton Park Rd., 4 mi south of Jackson Lake Junction, Oxbow Bend.*

Chapel of the Transfiguration & Maud Noble Cabin. Near Menor's Ferry the tiny chapel built in 1925 is still an active Episcopal church. The nearby homesteader's cabin of Maud Noble is the original 1917 meeting site where the plan to set aside a portion of Jackson Hole as a national recreation area for the people of the United States was hatched. In summer you can have ice cream and soda, or eat a packed lunch, at the old General Store by Menor's Ferry. Just walk northeast down the footpath along the Snake River. ⊠*½ mi off Grand Teton Park Rd., 2 mi north of Moose Junction in Grand Teton National Park* ⊗*Late Sept.–late May.*

☾ **Hidden Falls.** Adjacent to the Jenny Lake shuttle-boat dock is a shaded,
Fodor'sChoice pine-scented scenic trail. An easy ½-mi hike takes you to the falls.
★ Because of problems with bears, park rangers advise that hikers to the falls refrain from eating there. You might also want to pack "bear spray" to repel any sudden unwanted visitors. At the least, hikers should take extra precautions to carefully wrap food in bear-proof containers and not leave behind scraps or crumbs. Take the shuttle

boat across Jenny Lake to reach the Cascade Canyon trailhead. ⊠ *At Cascade Canyon trailhead, Jenny Lake.*

Signal Mountain Lodge. Slightly less crowded than the picnic area at Colter Bay Visitor Center, this lakeside picnic area has staggeringly beautiful views of the surrounding landscape, meadows, and mountains but contains only a few tables. Flush toilets and stores are nearby. ⊠ *Teton Park Rd., 4 mi south of Jackson Lake Junction, Oxbow Bend.*

Two Ocean Lake. One of the park's most isolated and uncrowded picnic sites is about 6 mi northwest of the Moran entrance station at the east end of Two Ocean Lake. About 1 mi north of the entrance station, turn east onto Pacific Creek Road, and about 2 mi in from U.S. 191/287 take a left (turning north) on the first dirt road. Two Ocean Lake is about 2½ mi down Two Ocean Lake Rd. ⊠ *Off Pacific Creek Rd., 2 mi east of U.S. 26/89/191, Oxbow Bend.*

WHERE TO STAY

$$$$ ⊞ **Jenny Lake Lodge.** This lodge (the most expensive lodging in any U.S. national park) has been serving tourists, sportspeople, and travelers since the 1920s. Nestled off the scenic one-way Jenny Lake Loop Road, bordering a wildflower meadow, its guest cabins are well spaced in lodgepole-pine groves. Cabin interiors, with sturdy pine beds and handmade quilts and electric blankets, live up to the elegant rustic theme, and cabin suites have fireplaces. Breakfast, bicycle use, horseback riding, and dinner are always included the price. Room telephones are provided only on request. **Pros:** Maximum comfort in a pristine setting; perhaps the best hotel in the national park system. **Cons:** Very expensive; not suitable for families with kids under 17; pretty formal for a national park property. ⊠ *Jenny Lake Rd., 2 mi off Teton Park Rd., 12 mi north of Moose Junction, Jenny Lake* ☎ *307/733–4647 or 800/628–9988* ⊕ *www.gtlc.com* ⇆ *37 cabins* ♿ *In-room: no TV, no a/c. In-hotel: restaurant, bicycles, public Internet, no elevator* ▭ *AE, DC, MC, V* ☉ *Closed early Oct.–late May* †⊙† *MAP.*

$$$–$$$$ ⊞ **Dornan's Spur Ranch Cabins.** Near Moose Visitor Center in Dornan's all-in-one shopping-dining-recreation development, these one and two-bedroom cabins have queen-size beds as well as great views of the Tetons and the Snake River. Each cabin has a full kitchen, with electric stove, toaster, pots, pans, dishes, coffeemaker, and utensils as well as a generously sized living-dining room and a furnished porch with a Weber grill in summer. However, at this writing, there's only one microwave on-site, so you'll want to request it early. **Pros:** Cabins are simple but clean; full kitchens allow you to make your own meals to save money. **Cons:** Proximity of cabins means not much privacy; cabins have little atmosphere and no fireplaces. ⊠ *10 Moose Rd., off Teton Park Rd. at Moose Junction, Moose* ☎ *307/733–2522* ⊕ *www. dornans.com* ⇆ *8 1-bedroom cabins, 4 2-bedroom cabins* ♿ *In-room: kitchen, no a/c, no TV. In-hotel: 2 restaurants, bar, no elevator* ▭ *D, MC, V* †⊙† *EP.*

2

$$$–$$$$ 🏠**Jackson Lake Lodge.** This large, full-service resort stands on a bluff with spectacular views across Jackson Lake to the Tetons. (And we do mean full service: there's everything from live music in the bar to in-house religious services.) The upper lobby has 60-foot picture windows and a collection of Native American artifacts and Western art. Many of the guest rooms have lake and mountain views, but others have little or no view, so ask when you book. **Pros:** Central location for visiting both Grand Teton and Yellowstone; heated outdoor pool; on-site medical clinic. **Cons:** Rooms without views are pricey for what you get; the hotel hosts many large meetings. ✉ *U.S. 89/191/287, ½ mi north of Jackson Lake Junction, Oxbow Bend* ☎ *307/543–3100 or 800/628–9988* ⊕ *www.gtlc.com* 🛏 *385 rooms* △ *In-room: refrigerator (some), no a/c, no TV, dial-up. In-hotel: 2 restaurants, public Wi-Fi, bar, pool, airport shuttle, some pets allowed* ☰ *MC, V* ☉ *Closed early Oct.–mid-May.*

$–$$$
Fodor's Choice
★
🏠**Moulton Ranch Cabins.** Along Mormon Row, these stand a few dozen yards south of the famous Moulton Barn, which you see on brochures, jigsaw puzzles, and photographs of the park. The land was once part of the T. A. Moulton homestead, and the cabins are still owned by the Moulton family. The quiet property has views of the Teton and the Gros Ventre ranges, and the owners can regale you with stories about early homesteaders. There's a dance hall in the barn, making this an ideal place for family and small group reunions. No smoking is allowed on the premises. **Pros:** Quiet and secluded. **Cons:** Fairly basic accommodations, little nightlife nearby. ✉ *Off Antelope Flats Rd., U.S. 26/89/191, 2 mi north of Moose Junction, Antelope Flats* ☎ *307/733–3749 or 208/529–2354* ⊕ *www.moultonranchcabins.com* 🛏 *5 units* △ *In-room: kitchen (some), no TV, no a/c. In-hotel: no-smoking rooms, no elevator* ☰ *MC, V* ☉ *Closed Oct.–May. No Sun. check-in.*

$$ 🏠**Signal Mountain Lodge.** These relaxed, pine-shaded log cabins sit on Jackson Lake's southern shoreline. The main building has a cozy lounge and a grand pine deck overlooking the epic lake. Some cabins are equipped with sleek kitchens and pine tables. The smaller log cabins are in shaded areas, and eight of them have a fireplace. Rooms 151–178 have lake views. **Pros:** Restaurants and bar are popular hot spots; on-site gas station; general store sells ice. **Cons:** Rooms are pretty motel-basic; fireplaces are gas. ✉ *Teton Park Rd., 3 mi south of Jackson Lake Junction, Oxbow Bend* ☎ *307/543–2831* ⊕ *www.signalmountainlodge.com* 🛏 *79 rooms, 32 cabins* △ *In-room: kitchen (some), refrigerator (some), no a/c, no TV. In-hotel: 2 restaurants, bar, no elevator* ☰ *AE, D, MC, V* ☉ *Closed mid-Oct.–mid-May.*

¢–$$ 🏠**Colter Bay Village.** Near Jackson Lake, this complex of Western-style cabins—some with one room, others with two or more rooms—are within walking distance of the lake. The property has splendid views and an excellent marina and beach for the windsurfing crowd (you'll need a wet suit because of the cold). There are also tent cabins, which aren't fancy (*see Where to Camp, below*) and share communal baths, but they do keep the wind and rain off. There's also a 116-space RV park. **Pros:** Prices are good for what you get; many nearby facilities. **Cons:** Little sense of privacy; not all cabins have bathrooms. ✉ *2 mi*

off U.S. 89/191/287, 10 mi north of Jackson Lake Junction, Colter Bay
☎*307/733–3100 or 800/628–9988* ⊕*www.gtlc.com* ⤴*166 cabins,*
66 tent cabins ♿*In-room: no a/c, no phone, no TV. In-hotel: 2 res-*
taurants, bar, laundry facilities, some pets allowed, no elevator ☰*AE,*
MC, V ☾*Closed late Sept.–late May.*

WHERE TO CAMP

🏕 **Colter Bay Tent Village & RV Park.** Adjacent to the National Park Service, this concessionaire-operated campground is the only RV park in
Grand Teton Park. And you'll find showers here, too. ♿*Flush toilets,*
full hookups, drinking water, guest laundry, showers, bear boxes, fire
grates, picnic tables ⤴*66 tent cabins, 112 RV sites* ✉*2 mi off U.S.*
89/191/287, 10 mi north of Moran Junction, Colter Bay ☎*307/543–*
2811 or 800/628–9988 ⤴*Campground is first-come, first-served. RV*
park takes reservations ☰*AE, D, MC, V* ☾*June–Sept.*

★ 🏕 **Colter Bay Campground.** Busy, noisy, and filled by noon, this campground has both tent and trailer/RV sites. One of its great advantages:
it's centrally located. Try to get a site as far from the nearby cabin
road as possible. This campground also has hot showers at Colter Bay
Village. The maximum stay is 14 days. ♿*Flush toilets, dump station,*
drinking water, guest laundry, showers, bear boxes, fire grates, picnic
tables ⤴*350 tent or RV sites* ✉*2 mi off U.S. 89/191/287, 5 mi north*
of Jackson Lake Junction, Colter Bay ☎*307/543–2100 or 800/628–*
9988 ⤴*Reservations not accepted* ☰*AE, MC, V* ☾*Late May–late*
Sept.

🏕 **Gros Ventre.** The park's biggest campground is in an open, grassy
area on the bank of the Gros Ventre River, away from the mountains and 2 mi southwest of Kelly. Try to get a site close to the river.
The campground usually doesn't fill until nightfall, if at all. There's
a maximum stay of 14 days. ♿*Flush toilets, dump station, drinking*
water, bear boxes, fire grates, picnic tables ⤴*360 tent or RV sites, 5*
group sites ✉*4 mi off U.S. 26/89/191, 1½ mi west of Kelly on Gros*
Ventre River Rd., 6 mi south of Moose Junction, Moose ☎*307/739–*
3603 or 800/628–9988 ⤴*Reservations not accepted* ☰*AE, MC, V*
☾*May–mid-Oct.*

★ 🏕 **Jenny Lake.** Wooded sites and Teton views make this the most desir-
able campground in the park, and it fills early. The small, quiet facility
allows tents only, and limits stays to a maximum of seven days. There's
a maximum of one vehicle per campsite, no longer than 14 feet. ♿*Flush*
toilets, drinking water, bear boxes, fire grates, picnic tables ⤴*50 tent*
sites (10 walk-in) ✉*Jenny Lake Rd., ½ mi off Teton Park Rd., 8 mi*
north of Moose Junction, Jenny Lake ☎*800/628–9988* ⤴*Reserva-*
tions not accepted ☰*No credit cards* ☾*Mid-May–late Sept.*

🏕 **Lizard Creek.** Views of Jackson Lake, wooded sites, and the relative isolation of this campground make it a relaxing choice. You can
stay here no more than 14 days. No vehicles over 30 feet are allowed.
♿*Flush toilets, drinking water, bear boxes, fire grates, picnic tables*

🛏61 *tent/trailer sites* ☒ *U.S. 89/191/287, 13 mi north of Jackson Lake Junction* ☎307/543–2831 *or* 800/672–6012 ⚳ *Reservations not accepted* ⊟ *No credit cards* ☾ *Early June–early Sept.*

🔺 **Signal Mountain Campground.** This campground in a hilly setting on Jackson Lake has boat access to the lake. Campsites offer spectacular views of the Tetons across Jackson Lake. No vehicles or trailers over 30 feet are allowed. There's a maximum stay of 14 days. ⚲ *Flush toilets, dump station, drinking water, fire grates, picnic tables* 🛏81 *tent or RV sites* ☒ *Teton Park Rd., 3 mi south of Jackson Lake Junction, Oxbow Bend* ☎ *No phone* ⚳ *Reservations not accepted* ⊟ *AE, D, MC, V* ☾ *Early May–mid-Oct.*

GRAND TETON ESSENTIALS

ACCESSIBILITY

The frontcountry portions of Grand Teton are largely accessible to people using wheelchairs. There's designated parking at most sites, and some interpretive trails are easily accessible. There are accessible restrooms at visitor centers. TDD telephones are available at Colter Bay Visitor Center and Moose Visitor Center. For an "Easy Access" guide to the park, stop by any visitor center or call the park's general information number.

Contacts Colter Bay Visitor Center (☎307/739–3544). **Grand Teton National Park** (☎ *307/739–3600, 307/739–3400 TTY* ⊕ *www.nps.gov/grte*). **Moose Visitor Center** (☎307/739–3400).

ADMISSION FEES

Park entrance fees are $25 per car, truck, or RV, $20 per motorcycle or snowmobile, and $12 per person entering on foot or bicycle, good for seven days. Annual park passes are $40. You can also buy a $25 pass that's good for seven days in both Grand Teton and Yellowstone parks. A winter day-use fee is $5.

ADMISSION HOURS

The park is open 24/7 year-round. The Craig Thomas Discovery and Visitor Center is closed only on Christmas Day. All park visitor centers are open 8 to 7 from Memorial Day through Labor Day. The park is in the Mountain time zone.

AUTOMOBILE SERVICE STATIONS

Automobile service stations are in the park at Colter Bay Village, Dornan's, Jackson Lake Lodge, and Signal Mountain Lodge. Auto and RV repair is available at Colter Bay Village.

EMERGENCIES

In case of a fire, medical, or police emergency in the park, dial 911. Park law enforcement rangers are at ranger stations (at Colter Bay, Jenny Lake, and Moose). Dial 307/739–3301 for park dispatch. The Grand Teton Medical Clinic at Jackson Lake Lodge is open daily from

10 to 6 in summer. The closest hospital to the park is St. John's Hospital in Jackson.

Contacts **General Emergencies** (☎ *911*). **Medical Emergencies** (☎ *307/739–3300*).

Grand Teton Medical Clinic (✉ *Jackson Lake Lodge, ½ mi north of Jackson Lake Junction* ☎ *307/543–2514 or 307/733–8002*). **St. John's Hospital** (✉ *625 E. Broadway Ave., Jackson* ☎ *307/733–3636 or 800/877–7078*).

LOST & FOUND
The park's lost-and-found is at Moose.

Contact **Lost & Found** (☎ *307/739–3450*).

PERMITS
Backcountry permits, which must be obtained in person at Craig Thomas visitor center, Colter Bay visitor centers, or Jenny Lake ranger station, are $25 and required for all overnight stays outside designated campgrounds. Seven-day boat permits, available year-round at Moose Visitor Center and in summer at Colter Bay and Signal Mountain ranger stations, cost $20 for motorized craft and $10 for nonmotorized craft and are good for seven days. Annual permits are $40 for motorized craft and $20 for nonmotorized craft.

POST OFFICES
Contacts **Moose Post Office** (✉ *Visitor Center, Box 9998, Moose 83012* ☎ *307/733–3336*).**Moran Post Office** (✉ *Moran Junction, 1 Central Station, Moran 83013* ☎ *307/543–2527*).

RESTROOMS
Public restrooms may be found at all park visitor centers, campgrounds, and ranger stations. There are restrooms at the picnic area north of Moose on Teton Park Road, and at String Lake and Colter Bay picnic areas.

SHOPS & GROCERS
Both Signal Mountain Lodge and Dornan's have general stores with basic grocery items (Signal Mountain Lodge sells ice). Other, better-stocked and cheaper stores can be found in Jackson or Wilson.

Contacts **Dornan's Moose Trading Post & Deli** (✉ *10 Moose Rd., off Teton Park Rd. at Moose Junction* ☎ *307/733–2415*). **Hungry Jack's General Store** (✉ *Teton Park Rd., 3 mi south of Jackson Lake Junction, Oxbow Bend* ☎ *307/543–2831* ⊙ *Closed mid-Oct.–mid-May*)

VISITOR INFORMATION
Contact **Grand Teton National Park** ⓓ *Drawer 170, Moose, WY 83012* ☎ *307/739–3300, 307/739–3400 TTY* ⊕ *www.nps.gov/grte*.

Northwest Wyoming

WITH JACKSON & THE WIND RIVER RANGE

WORD OF MOUTH

"Jackson Hole is wonderful around late April/early May! Everything is green and fresh. It's still a bit chilly, but not too bad. A light jacket would be helpful. This time is the 'down time' for Jackson."

—DM5

"Jackson is great, but the town itself is not primarily a ski town. The ski area, Jackson Hole, called Teton Village, is about 15-min drive out of town at the base of the mountains. Snow King Ski area is small and more in town, but it's dead in summer. Jackson as a town is fun in itself but LOADED with tourists during summer. Lots to do with Teton Nat'l Park and Yellowstone nearby!"

—Dayle

Updated by
Gil Brady

NORTHWEST WYOMING IS MOUNTAIN COUNTRY, where high peaks— some of which remain snowcapped year-round—tower above deep, glacier-carved valleys. In addition to the tallest, most spectacular peaks in the state, there's a diverse wildlife population that includes wolves, grizzly bears, Rocky Mountain bighorn sheep, and antelope. Here you can hike through mountain meadows, challenge white water, explore Native American culture, and trace the history of westbound 19th-century emigrants.

Jackson Hole, the valley to the east of the Tetons, is a world-class ski destination, with literally thousands of ways to get down the slopes. In the valley the town of Jackson works to maintain its small-town charm while at the same time serving as the area's cultural center. In the Wind River Mountains the Oregon-California-Mormon trail sites near South Pass merit a visit, and you can learn about Native American traditions on the Wind River Reservation.

> ## TOP REASONS TO GO
>
> ■ The Grand Teton range and sweeping Snake River . . . breathtaking, awe-inspiring
>
> ■ Wildlife: Moose, bald eagles, elk, grizzlies, mountain lions . . . a living menagerie and natural treasure to behold without the artificiality of even the best zoo
>
> ■ Restaurants: Some of the best food in the region, not just western fare, is available here.
>
> ■ People: Jacksonites are friendly and knowledgeable, if slightly prideful, of their beautiful town.

Wildlife watching in northwest Wyoming ranks among the best in the state: look for Rocky Mountain bighorn sheep at Whiskey Mountain near Dubois; buffalo, elk, and even wolves in Jackson Hole; and moose near Pinedale or north of Dubois. One of the best ways to admire the landscape—mountain flowers, alpine lakes, and wildlife ranging from fat little pikas to grizzly bears—is to pursue an outdoor activity.

Adventure . . . From skiing; to hiking, kayaking and parasailing . . . the only limit on things to do here appears to be one's imagination. Name an outdoor activity and you can probably do it here. You can hike or ride a horse along one of the backcountry trails near Grand Teton National Park, Dubois, or Lander; scale mountain peaks in the Wind River or Grand Teton ranges; or fish or float the Snake River near Jackson. Come winter take a sleigh ride through the National Elk Refuge, snowmobile on hundreds of miles of trails, cross-country ski throughout the region, or hit the slopes at Snow King Mountain, Grand Targhee, or Jackson Hole Mountain Resort, one of the greatest skiing destinations in the country.

There's more to northwest Wyoming than the great outdoors. A handful of museums, well worth a few hours of your trip, offer a window on the history of the American West. The Jackson Hole Museum concentrates on the early settlement of Jackson Hole, and the Museum of the Mountain Man in Pinedale takes an informative look at the trapper heritage.

PLANNING YOUR TIME

Any tour of northwest Wyoming should include a day or two, at minimum, in Jackson Hole, where you can explore Grand Teton National Park (⇨ Chapter 2). Also in Jackson Hole is the small but bustling town of Jackson, with its one-of-a-kind town square entered through elk antler arches and a stagecoach that gives rides throughout the day in summer. In winter, action is concentrated at nearby Teton Village, where you'll find unparalleled winter sports offerings at the Jackson Hole Mountain Resort. You're likely to share the slopes with Olympic champion skiers and snowboarders.

If you can extend your stay, travel over Togwotee Mountain Pass to little Dubois, where you can stay at a guest ranch, ride horses in the Bridger-Teton National Forest, learn about local history at the Wind River Historical Center, and glimpse the region's wildlife at the National Bighorn Sheep Interpretive Center. After Dubois and environs, head south onto the Wind River Indian Reservation to find exceptional shops filled with arts and crafts locally made by Northern Arapaho and Eastern Shoshone tribal members.

Spend some time in Lander and explore the Wind River Mountains before heading south and then west to South Pass City State Historic Site, near Atlantic City. From here, follow the emigrant trail corridor west and then northwest to Pinedale and its excellent Museum of the Mountain Man.

EXPLORING NORTHWEST WYOMING

You will need a car to tour northwest Wyoming; to reach the really spectacular backcountry a four-wheel-drive vehicle is best. Major routes through the area include U.S. 191, which runs north–south through Jackson, on the western edge of the state, and U.S. 26/287, which runs east of Grand Teton National Park (also on the western edge of the state, within the Jackson Hole valley) toward Dubois. Much of the driving you do here will take you through the mountains—including the Absaroka and Wind River ranges that dominate the region.

ABOUT THE RESTAURANTS

Northwest Wyoming has many restaurants. Anyplace you go you'll find basic Western fare such as steaks, chicken, and burgers; in Jackson there's a wider selection, with menus listing everything from Chinese and Thai dishes to trout, buffalo, and elk. There are also a few fine-dining establishments in the region. Arguably the best steaks in all of Wyoming are prepared at Svilars, a steak house in the tiny community of Hudson, east of Lander.

ABOUT THE HOTELS

No other part of Wyoming has such a variety of lodging properties that appeal to all budgets. Lodging options in the area include elegant and expensive properties such as the Amangani resort in Jackson Hole, guest ranches in the Dubois and Jackson areas, historic inns, simple cabins, and dozens of chain motels.

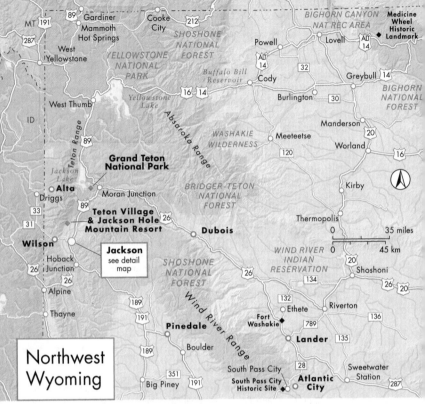

It's a good idea to reserve well ahead for lodging in the town of Jackson in July and August. You should also reserve lodgings at Teton Village well in advance for skiing at Jackson Hole Mountain Resort.

WHAT IT COSTS					
	¢	$	$$	$$$	$$$$
RESTAURANTS	under $7	$7–$11	$12–$16	$17–$22	over $22
HTOELS	under $10	70–$110	$111–$160	$161–$220	over $220

Restaurant prices are for a main course at dinner, excluding sales tax of 4%–7%. Hotel prices are for two people in a standard double room in high season, excluding service charges and 5%–10% tax.

TIMING

Most people visit northwest Wyoming in summer, although winter draws skiing enthusiasts (the ski season generally lasts December through March). The months between Memorial Day and Labor Day are the busiest, with all attractions operating at peak capacity. If you don't mind a few limitations on what you can do and where you can stay and eat, the best times to visit the region are in late spring (May) and early fall (September and October). Not only will you find fewer people on the roads and at the sights, but you also will have some of the best weather (although springtime can be wet, and it can and does snow here every month of the year). In general, spring is the best time to see wildlife, particularly young animals. Fall brings a rich blaze of colors, painting the aspen and cottonwood trees with a palette of red, gold, and orange. The days are warm, reaching into the 60s and 70s, and the nights are cool in fall. There are also fewer thunderstorms than in midsummer, plus fewer biting insects (such as mosquitoes) to bother you.

JACKSON

Most visitors to northwest Wyoming come to Jackson, which remains a small but booming Western town that's "howdy" in the daytime and hopping in the evening. For active types, it's a good place to stock up on supplies before heading for outdoor adventures in Grand Teton National Park, Yellowstone, and the surrounding Jackson Hole area. It's also a great place to kick back and rest your feet awhile while taking in the wealth of galleries, Western-wear shops, varied cuisines, a new $35 million arts center, and active nightlife centering on bars and music.

Unfortunately, Jackson's charm and popularity have put it at risk. On busy summer days, traffic often slows to a crawl on the highway that doglegs through downtown. Proposals for new motels and condominiums sprout like the purple asters in the spring as developers vie for a share of the upscale vacation market. Old-timers suggest that the town—in fact, the entire Jackson Hole—has already lost some of its dusty charm from when horses stood at hitching rails around Town Square. However, with national parks and forests and state lands occupying some of the most beautiful real estate in the country, there's only 3%–4% in unprotected ground on which to build. These limitations, along with the cautious approach of locals, may yet keep Jackson on a human scale.

EXPLORING JACKSON

Numbers correspond to the Jackson map.

The best way to explore Jackson's downtown, which is centered on vibrant Town Square, is on foot, since parking can be a challenge during the busy summer months. To go beyond downtown—the National Wildlife Art Museum or National Elk Refuge, for example—you'll need to hop into your car.

TIMING If you don't plan to shop on Town Square, you can easily do this tour in a few hours. But if you want to hit the stores, budget in a full day for this tour. Note, the Jackson Hole Museum is closed from October through May.

Jackson Hole
Historical
Society **3**

Jackson Hole
Museum **2**

National Elk
Refuge **5**

National Museum
of Wildlife Art ...**4**

Town Square **1**

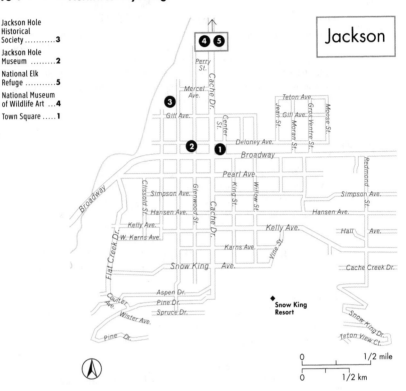

Jackson

WHAT TO SEE

🐾 **2** **Jackson Hole Museum.** For some local history, visit this museum, where you can get acquainted with the early settlers and find out how Dead Man's Bar got its name. You'll also learn how Jackson elected the first all-female town government, not to mention a lady sheriff who claimed to have killed three men before hanging up her spurs. Kids can try on vintage clothes and hats and see what they'd look like as homesteaders. Among the exhibits are Native American, ranching, and cowboy artifacts. ⊠ *Glenwood St. and Deloney Ave.* ☎ *307/733–2414* ⊕ *www. jacksonholehistory.org* ⊠ *$3* ⊙ *Memorial Day–Sept., Mon.–Sat. 9:30– 6, Sun. 10–5.*

🐾 **5** **National Elk Refuge.** Wildlife abounds on this 25,000-acre refuge year-
Fodor'sChoice round at the foot of "Sleeping Indian" mountain. But from around late
★ November through March, the real highlight is the more than 7,500 elk, many with enormous antler racks, that winter here. There are also buffalo, and limited hunts, depending on population size, to cull the herds. The Refuge Road entrance lies about 1 mi from the Town Square just past St. John's hospital on East Broadway. Elk can also be observed from various pullouts along U.S. 191 or up close by slowly driving your car on the refuge's winding unpaved roads. There's also a horse-drawn sleigh ride, giving visitors the chance to see the elk stand or eat calmly

A GOOD TOUR

Start your visit at the corner of Cache and Broadway at **Town Square** ❶, easily identifiable by its elk-antler arches and bustle of activity. Stroll around the square and visit the many shops and galleries here. Walk one block west to Glenwood Street and the **Jackson Hole Museum** ❷ for a lesson on local history, a collection of artifacts from Native American and early frontier life, and a compilation of Hollywood movie memorabilia from westerns shot on location here. For $4 you can also pick up a self-guided walking tour. Once you've done the town, hop into your car and drive 3 mi north on Cache Drive to the **National Wildlife Art Museum** ❹,

with its wonderful collection of timeless western talents like Charles Russell and Frederic Remington. The museum is devoted to the fine art of depicting wildlife in all its natural splendor. From a deck at the museum, between November and March, you can see the real thing: thousands of elk, plus waterfowl, mountain sheep, and coyotes wintering at the elk refuge below. The museum also hosts periodic lectures covering international wildlife issues and cultural events. For those who want to see the animals up close, you can drive down to the **National Elk Refuge** ❺ in the valley below. In winter you can take a sleigh ride to the refuge.

as sleighs loaded with families and supplied with alfalfa pellets move in their midst. Among the other animals that make their home here are buffalo, coyote, mountain sheep, trumpeter swan, and other waterfowl. Arrange for sleigh rides through the Jackson Hole & Greater Yellowstone Visitor Center at 532 N. Cache. (⊕ *www.fws.gov/nationalelkrefuge)* in Jackson; wear warm clothing, including hats, gloves, boots, long johns, and coats. ⊠ *532 N. Cache Dr.* ☏ *307/733–5771* ⊜ *Sleigh rides $16* ⊙ *Year-round; sleigh rides mid-Dec.–Mar.*

★ ❹ **National Museum of Wildlife Art.** Among the paintings and sculptures of bighorn sheep, elk, and other animals of the West you'll find fine-art representations and photographs of wildlife by such artists as John J. Audubon, Frederick Remington, George Catlin, Tucker Smith, and Charles M. Russell. The collection includes works in various media and styles, the earliest pieces dating to 2000 BC. A deck here affords views across the National Elk Refuge, where, particularly in winter, you can see wildlife in a natural habitat. ⊠ *2820 Rungius Rd., 3 mi north of Jackson* ☏ *307/733–5771* ⊕ *www.wildlifeart.org* ⊜ *$6* ⊙ *Daily 9–5.*

❶ **Town Square.** You can spend an entire day wandering around Jackson's always-bustling Town Square, a parklike area crisscrossed with walking paths and bedecked with arches woven from hundreds of elk antlers. Various shops and restaurants surround the square, and there's often entertainment going on in the square itself, including a rip-roaring "shoot-out" most summer evenings at approximately 6:30. At the southwest corner of the square you can board a stagecoach for a ride around the area; it costs about $6 per adult.

ALSO WORTH SEEING

③ **Jackson Hole Historical Society.** Displays at this log cabin illuminate local history. In addition to historic artifacts and photographs, the society houses manuscripts, maps, and an oral-history collection. ✉ *105 Mercill Ave.* ☎ *307/733–9605* 🌐 *www.jacksonholehistory.org.*

**OFF THE
BEATEN
PATH**

Granite Hot Springs. Soothing thermal baths in pristine outback country awaits in the heart of the Bridger-Teton National Forest, just a short drive south of Jackson. Concerted local and federal efforts have preserved the wild lands in this hunter's and fisherman's paradise where ranches dot the Teton Valley floor. The Snake River turns west and the contours sheer into steep vertical faces. By Hoback Junction there's white-water excitement. The drive south along U.S. 191 provides good views of the river's bends and turns and the life-jacketed rafters and kayakers who float through the Hoback canyon. At Hoback Junction, about 11 mi south of Jackson, head east (toward Pinedale) on U.S. Highway 189/191 and follow the Hoback River east through its beautiful canyon. A tributary canyon 10 mi east of the junction is followed by a well-maintained and marked gravel road to Granite Hot Springs, in the Bridger-Teton National Forest. Drive 9 mi off U.S. 189/191 (northeast) on Granite Creek Road to reach the hot springs. People also come for the shady, creek-side campground and moderate hikes up Granite Canyon to passes with panoramic views. You'll want to drive with some caution, as there are elevated turns, the possibility of a felled tree, and wandering livestock that can own the road ahead on blind curves. In winter there's a popular snowmobile and dogsled trail from the highway. The 93°F to 112°F thermal baths at the end of the road are pure physical therapy, but they're closed from November through mid-December. There's also an admission price of $6 per person.

SPORTS & THE OUTDOORS

For more listings of sports outfitters serving the Jackson area, see Outfitters & Expeditions box in Chapter 2.

BICYCLING

The trip up to **Lower Slide Lake,** north of town, is a favorite of cyclists. Turn east off U.S. 26/89/191 to Kelly, and then follow Slide Lake Road. Cyclists ride the **Spring Gulch Road,** part pavement, part dirt, off Route 22, along the base of Gros Ventre Butte, rejoining U.S. 26/89/191 near the Gros Ventre River.

Bike rentals for all skill levels and age groups are available at **Edge Sports** (✉ *490 W. Broadway* ☎ *307/734–3916*); the company also does on-site repairs. You can rent a mountain bike to explore on your own or take a tour at **Hoback Sports** (✉ *520 W. Broadway* ☎ *307/733–5335*). General tours are geared to intermediate and advanced riders, but Hoback can also custom-design a tour to suit your abilities and interests. The store also sells bike, ski, skate, and snowboard apparel and equipment.

CANOEING, KAYAKING & RAFTING

South of Jackson, where the Hoback joins the Snake River and the canyon walls become steep, there are lively white-water sections. But the Snake, whose rating is Class I and II, is a river for those who value scenery over white-water thrills. For the most part, floating rather than taking on rapids is the theme of running the Snake (with trips usually incorporating Jackson Lake, at the foot of the Tetons). As such, it's a good choice for families with children. What makes the trip special is the Teton Range, looming as high as 8,000 feet above the river. This float trip can also be combined with two or more days of kayaking on Jackson Lake. Raft trips take place between June and September. Experienced paddlers run the Hoback, too.

The Snake River's western Idaho portion has earned a strange footnote in history. It's the river that Evel Knievel tried (and failed miserably) to jump over on a rocket-powered motorcycle in the mid-1970s.

Rendezvous River Sports (✉ *945 W. Broadway* ☎ *307/733–2471 or 800/ 733–2471* ⊕ *www.jacksonholekayak.com*) is the premiere paddle-sports outfitter in the region, offering expert instruction so you can test yourself on western Wyoming's ancient rivers and lakes. The company also schedules more relaxed and scenic trips, including guided tours of Jackson, Slide, and String lakes, and rapid-shooting rides on the Hoback River down Granite Creek to the Snake River while you marvel at south Jackson's majestic canyons. Raft and canoe rentals are also available.

DOGSLEDDING

Dogsledding excursions are available through **Iditarod Sled Dog Tours** (✉ *11 Granite Creek Rd.* ☎ *307/733–7388 or 800/554–7388* ⊕ *www. jhsleddog.com*). Veteran Iditarod racer Frank Teasley leads half-day introductory trips and full-day trips to Granite Hot Springs. It's a great way to see wintering native wildlife such as moose, elk, bighorn sheep, deer, and bald eagles in the Bridger-Teton National Forest. Sled trips are offered only in season, which can begin as early as November and run as late as April.

HIKING

Bridger-Teton National Forest (✉ *340 N. Cache St., Box 1888, 83001* ☎ *307/739–5500* ⊕ *www.fs.fed.us/btnf*) covers hundreds of thousands of acres of western Wyoming and shelters abundant wildlife. Permits for backcountry use of the forest are necessary only for groups and commercial operators such as outfitters. Contact the forest office for more information.

The guides at **the Hole Hiking Experience** (✉ *Box 7779, 83002* ☎ *866/733–4453 or 307/690–4453* ⊕ *www.holehike.com*) will take you to mountain meadows or to the tops of the peaks on half- or full-day tours. Some outings are suitable for the very experienced, others for any well-conditioned adult, and still others for families.

SKIING

Ⓒ **Snow King Resort** (✉ *400 E. Snow King Ave.* ☎ *307/733–5200 or 800/ 522–5464* ⊕ *www.snowking.com*), at the western edge of Jackson, has 400 acres of ski runs for daytime use and 110 acres suitable for night skiing, plus an extensive snowmaking system on Snow King Mountain. You'll also find a snow-tubing park. In summer there's a 2,500-foot alpine slide and miles of biking and hiking paths, all the way to the mountaintop. For $10 and under a person, you can also ride the scenic chairlift to the top and back. Or you can stop off at the summit, which is 7,751 feet above sea level, for a picnic and feast on the stunning 50-mi view of Jackson. From up here, on a clear day, you can see over the neighboring buttes and count the clouds passing around the Tetons. **Spring Creek Ranch** (✉ *1800 Spirit Dance Rd.* ☎ *307/733–8833 or 800/443–6139*) offers lessons and use of its groomed cross-country trails for a fee.

SLEIGH RIDES

Ⓒ Sleigh rides into the National Elk Refuge last about 45 minutes and depart from in front of the **Jackson Hole & Greater Yellowstone Visitor Center** (✉ *532 N. Cache Dr.* ☎ *307/733–5771*) daily in winter, 10 to 4, about every 20 minutes. Dinner sleigh rides are available through **Spring Creek Ranch** (✉ *1800 Spirit Dance Rd.* ☎ *307/733–8833 or 800/443– 6139*), with dinner at its Granary restaurant.

SNOWMOBILING

Numerous companies in the Jackson area rent snowmobiles. **Rocky Mountain Snowmobile Tours** (✉ *1050 S. U.S. 89* ☎ *307/733–2237 or 800/ 647–2561* ⊕ *www.rockymountainsnow.com*) guides one- to five-day trips beginning at $200 per day, to such areas as Granite Hot Springs, Togwotee Pass, Gros Ventre Mountains, Grey's River near Alpine, and Yellowstone National Park.

WHERE TO EAT

$$$–$$$$ ✕ **The Blue Lion.** For 30 years, consistently excellent, distinctive fare has been the rule at this white-and-blue clapboard house two blocks from Town Square. The sophisticated offerings range from Dijon-mustard-rubbed rack of lamb to grilled elk with port wine sauce to fresh fish dishes, including rainbow trout. There's patio dining in summer and a wine list. Early-bird specials (6–6:30 PM) are a great value in an otherwise pricey restaurant. This is a no-smoking establishment. ✉ *160 N. Millward St.* ☎ *307/733–3912* ⊟ *AE, D, MC, V* ☉ *Closed Tues. and Oct. and Mar. No lunch.*

$$$–$$$$ ✕ **Burke's Chop House.** Offering fine dining in casual elegance, Burke's is
★ considered by many to be Jackson's best steak house. The menu ranges from a variety of game dishes—venison, elk, and buffalo—to haute cuisine such as beef tournedos with truffles and foie gras. The wine list is extensive. The food and service here are first-rate, but the restaurant is usually crowded and can be noisy. A kids' menu is available, and this is a completely no-smoking restaurant. Its semiprivate dining room seats up to 26. ✉ *72 S. Glenwood* ☎ *307/733–8575* ⊟ *AE, D, MC, V.*

$$$–$$$$ ✕**The Gun Barrel Steak & Game House.** At Jackson's legendary game and steak lodge, all dishes are slow-cooked over an open river-rock mesquite grill. The dining atmosphere is rustic and fun, with an Old West collection of mounted game, wildlife, and memorabilia. Service is always friendly. The menu offers a wide variety of unique dishes, but some, such as velvet elk, may be too rich for those unaccustomed to game. The bar has an ample list of bourbons, scotches, and wines to sample if you just want a drink. ⊠*862 W. Broadway, approximately 1 mi from Town Square in Grand Teton Plaza* ☎*307/733–3287* ▭*MC, V* ⊘*No lunch.*

$$$–$$$$ ✕**Snake River Grill.** Dine in Western, fireside elegance, with white table-cloths and an excellent wine list aimed at true oenophiles. Those looking for a brew may find the beer list lacking. Choose from fresh fish, free-range meats, and organic produce at this second-floor restaurant overlooking the Town Square and Snow King Mountain. Buffalo cowboy steaks, vegetarian pasta with mushrooms and artichokes, and grilled elk chops are among the standout entrées, but some may find the prices on the high side. A room for private parties right off the bar seats up to 16. Kids are welcome; however, there are no high chairs and there's no children's menu. Reservations are recommended, but walk-ins will be accommodated if there is room. ⊠*84 E. Broadway* ☎*307/733–0557* ▭*AE, MC, V* ⊘*Closed Apr. and Nov. No lunch.*

$$$–$$$$ ✕**Sweetwater Restaurant.** Imaginative takes on salmon, pork tenderloin, buffalo, and pot roast are on the dinner menu in this historic log building built in 1915 with antique oak furnishings. The atmosphere is rustic, homey, and comforting. There's a great dessert menu, too. Try lemon raspberry cake with extra homemade whipped cream if they have it. For lunch, you can have a wrap, salad, or sandwich in the outdoor dining area (weather permitting), though even there the views aren't great. Reservations are essential in busy seasons. ⊠*85 S. King St.* ☎*307/733–3553* ▭*AE, D, MC, V.*

$–$$$ ✕**The Bunnery.** Lunch is served year-round and dinner is served in summer at the Bunnery, but it's the breakfasts of omelets and home-baked pastries that are irresistible; the coffee is also very good. All of the breads are made on the premises, most from OSM flour (oats, sunflower, millet). It's elbow to elbow inside, so you may have to wait to be seated on busy mornings, but any inconvenience is well worth it. There's also a decent vegetarian selection here. Try a giant almond stick, sticky bun, or a piece of Very Berry Pie made from raspberries, strawberries, and blueberries. In summer there's outdoor seating. On-street parking can be hard to find here. ⊠*Hole-in-the-Wall Mall, 130 N. Cache Dr.* ☎*307/734–0075* ▭*D, MC, V* ⊘*No dinner Sept.–May.*

Fodor's Choice ★

$–$$$ ✕**Jedediah's House of Sourdough.** Friendly, noisy, and elbow knocking, this restaurant a block east of Town Square—which also has a branch at the airport—makes breakfast and lunch for those with big appetites. There are plenty of excellent "sourjacks" (sourdough flapjacks) and biscuits and gravy. Burgers are mountain-man size. The menu at the airport location tends to be more expensive than in the restaurant downtown, but it's open later. ⊠*135 E. Broadway* ☎*307/733–5671* ⊠*1250 Airport Rd.* ☎*307/733–6063* ▭*AE, D, DC, MC, V* ⊘*No dinner.*

$$ ✕ **Billy's Giant Hamburgers & Cadillac Grille.** True to its name, Billy's serves big—really big—burgers and waffle fries that are really, really good, albeit greasy. Not to be outdone, there are also hot dogs and several deli-style sandwiches that you can munch around a 1950s-style lunch counter with clear views of the Town Square. The portions in general are huge. Service is quick and unpretentious. Billy's shares space with the more refined but equally fun Cadillac Grille, where you can enjoy a casual atmosphere of a few booths and tables or grab a stool—if you can find one—around its usually jam-packed circular bar. ⊠55 N. Cache Dr. ☎307/733-3279 ▭AE, MC, V.

¢-$$ ✕ **Bubba's Barbecue Restaurant.** Succulent baby back ribs and mouthwatering spareribs are the specialties at this busy barbecue joint, which evokes the Old West with its large wooden porch, wooden booths, Western paintings, and antique signs. Sandwiches and a huge salad bar with plenty of nonmeat choices are also available. This is also one of the most affordable breakfast options in Jackson, but whenever you go there can be long waits. The desserts include homemade pies of the chocolate-buttermilk and fudge-pecan variety. ⊠515 W. Broadway ☎307/733-2288 ▭AE, D, MC, V.

¢-$$ ✕ **Teton Thai.** For the best Thai this side of San Francisco—and maybe
Fodor's Choice the entire inner-mountain west—this family-owned local favorite tops
★ the list of everyone in Jackson. Just one block off Town Square—across from the Teton Theatre and next to Gaslight Alley—it's always packed. In winter there's inside counter seating right in the kitchen or you can get takeout, but in summer you can sit on the patio outside, where the atmosphere can become boisterous. Service can sometimes be slow, but the *tom kha gai* (coconut milk, lemongrass, and chicken soup) or tofu curry dishes are always worth the wait. ⊠135 N. Cache Dr. ☎307/733-0022 ▭No credit cards ⊙Closed mid-Oct.–mid-Nov. No lunch weekdays.

WHERE TO STAY

There are three reservations services for Jackson Hole. You can make reservations for most lodgings in Jackson through **Central Reservations** (☎888/838-6606). Properties managed by **Jackson Hole Resort Lodging** (☎800/443-8613 ⊕www.jacksonholewy.com) include rooms, condominiums, and vacation homes at Teton Village, Teton Pines, and the Jackson Hole Racquet Club. **Mountain Property Management** (⊠250 Veronica La., Box 2228, 83001 ☎800/992-9948 ⊕www.mpmjh. com) offers condominium, cabin, and luxury-home rentals throughout Jackson Hole.

$$$$ ▥**Amangani.** This exclusive resort built of sandstone and redwood
★ melds into the landscape of Gros Ventre Butte, affording beautiful views of Spring Creek Valley from its cliff-top location. The warm hospitality is Western, but the setting is that of Eastern (as in Asian) simplicity, with tall ceilings, clean lines, and rooms with platform beds, large soaking tubs, and plenty of space. The amenities here are the best in Jackson Hole, and include horseback riding, tennis, and nearby cross-country

skiing and sleigh rides in winter. **Pros:** Extremely luxurious, impeccable service, excellent views of the Tetons. **Cons:** Very expensive; too detached from the mundane world below (even by Jackson standards); decor seems a bit too exotic for western Wyoming. ⊠*1535 N.E. Butte Rd., 83002* ☎*307/734–7333 or 877/734–7333* ⊕*www.amangani. com* ⟗*40 suites* ☐*In-room: safe, refrigerator, VCR, DVD. In-hotel: restaurant, room service, bar, tennis courts, pool, spa, laundry service, airport shuttle* ⊟*AE, D, DC, MC, V* ◉|*EP.*

$$$$ 🏨**Rusty Parrot.** An imposing river-rock fireplace in the cathedral lounge lends warmth to this timber inn near the center of Jackson. You can walk the four blocks to shops, galleries, and restaurants on Town Square. Handcrafted wooden furnishings fill the rooms, some of which have fireplaces and oversize whirlpool tubs. With body wraps, massages, and facials, the spa is a nice extra. Have dinner at the Wild Sage Restaurant ($$$$), which serves duck, pork, halibut, and Montana Legend Beef. Children under 12 are strongly discouraged. **Pros:** In town yet off the beaten path; fine dining in the charming restaurant; good off-season deals. **Cons:** Not family-friendly; limited views. ⊠*175 N. Jackson St., 83001* ☎*307/733–2000 or 800/458–2004* ⊕*www. rustyparrot.com* ⟗*31 rooms* ☐*In-room: Wi-Fi, VCR, DVD. In-hotel: restaurant, room service, spa, public Wi-Fi, no-smoking rooms, no elevator* ⊟*AE, D, DC, MC, V* ◉|*CP.*

$$$–$$$$ 🏨**Parkway Inn.** From the moment you enter its ground floor "salon,"
★ a vintage ambience soothes the soul in period furniture and black-and-white photographs, showing the rise of east Jackson. Each room has a distinctive look—with oak or wicker furniture—and each is filled with antiques from the 19th century onward. The overall effect is homey and delightful, especially if you plan to stay a few days or longer. Continental breakfast is served in an antiques-filled lounge. This quiet property is three blocks from Town Square. **Pros:** Convenient location; boutique atmosphere. **Cons:** Not a full-service hotel; no restaurant on premises. ⊠*125 N. Jackson St., 83001* ☎*307/733–3143 or 800/247–8390* ⊕*www.parkwayinn.com* ⟗*37 rooms, 14 suites* ☐*In-room: dial-up. In-hotel: pool, gym, public Wi-Fi, public Internet, no-smoking rooms* ⊟*AE, D, MC, V* ◉|*CP.*

$$$–$$$$ 🏨**Spring Creek Ranch.** Outside Jackson on Gros Ventre Butte, this luxury resort has beautiful views of the Tetons. Among the numerous amenities are horseback riding, tennis, and cross-country skiing and sleigh rides in winter. Aside from hotel rooms, there's a mix of studios and condos; many of the accommodations have wood-burning fireplaces and lodgepole-pine furniture. Wi-Fi in the lobby is free. Among the fine dishes served at the Granary ($$$–$$$$) are Alaskan halibut, fillet of beef, elk tenderloin, and New Zealand lamb. You can also eat in the Rising Sage Café. A naturalist is on the property, and astronomy lectures are offered twice weekly in summer. **Pros:** Scenic mountaintop location; expert staff, meals included in some packages. **Cons:** Not for budget-conscious; can be a tricky, winding drive in winter. ⊠*1800 Spirit Dance Rd., Box 4780, 83001* ☎*307/733–8833 or 800/443–6139* ⊕*www.springcreekranch.com* ⟗*36 rooms, 76 studios and condominiums* ☐*In-room: kitchen, Ethernet. In-hotel: restaurant,* *room service, bar, tennis courts, pool, spa, public Wi-Fi, no-smoking rooms, no elevator* ⊟AE, DC, MC, V ▯EP.

$$$-$$$$

FodorsChoice

★

The Wort Hotel. This brick Victorian hotel near Town Square, built in 1941, seems to have been around as long as the Tetons, but it feels fresh inside (there's even Wi-Fi in the lobby, though it's not free, yet). A fireplace warms the lobby, and a sitting area is just up the stairs. Locally made Western-style furnishings of lodgepole-pine beds, pine dressers, carpets, drapes, and bed coverings are in warm, muted blues and mauves. You can sip a drink in the Silver Dollar Bar & Grill ($–$$$$)—aptly named for the 2,032 silver dollars embedded on top of the bar—or amble through swinging doors into the restaurant for a fine meal. **Pros:** Charming old building with lots of history; convenient location in town; some good-value packages offered. **Cons:** Limited views; must drive to parks and mountains. ⊠*50 N. Glenwood St., 83001* ☎*307/733–2190 or 800/322–2727* ⊕*www.worthotel.com* ⇆*59 rooms, 5 suites* ♿*Inroom: Wi-Fi, dial-up. In-hotel: restaurant, room service, bar, gym, public Wi-Fi, public Internet, no-smoking rooms* ▯EP ⊟AE, D, MC, V.

$$-$$$$

Trapper Inn. This motel is within walking distance of Town Square and has some of the best-appointed rooms in Jackson for people with disabilities. It's also undergone a major renovation geared toward turning it into an executive-stay hotel. Downstairs you'll find an open reception desk with friendly and helpful staff, free coffee, plenty of tall windows, ample sitting space, free Wi-Fi, a stone fireplace, and vintage trapper gear big enough to snare a grizzly. **Pros:** Some package deals include breakfast; walking distance to town; small pool and Jacuzzi. **Cons:** Limited views; must drive to mountains. ⊠*235 N. Cache St., 83001* ☎*307/733–2648* ⊕*www.trapperinn.com* ⇆*80 rooms, 48 suites* ♿*In-room: kitchen (some), refrigerator. In-hotel: pool, laundry facilities, no-smoking rooms* ⊟AE, DC, MC, V ▯EP.

$-$$$

Cowboy Village Resort. Stay in your own small log cabin with covered decks and barbecue grills. There is a ski-waxing room, and both the START Bus and Targhee Express buses that serve the ski areas stop here. **Pros:** Near town; late-night dinner option next door; grills available for cooking outside. **Cons:** Crowded in summer; few amenities,;more like a motel with cabins than a true resort. ⊠*120 S. Flat Creek, 83001* ☎*307/733–3121 or 800/962–4988* ⊕*www.townsquareinns.com* ⇆*82 cabins* ♿*In-room: kitchen (some). In-hotel: laundry facilities, no-smoking rooms* ⊟AE, D, MC, V ▯EP.

¢-$$$

Antler Inn. Perhaps no motel in Jackson has a better location than the Antler, one block south of Town Square. Some rooms have fireplaces, two have Jacuzzis, but otherwise they're standard motel rooms. In winter there's a complimentary ski shuttle. **Pros:** Restaurants nearby; family-run operation with owner on premises; good prices in the off-season. **Cons:** Frequently booked in summer; can get rowdy during "Hill Climb;" a snowmobile festival in March at nearby Snow King. ⊠*43 W. Pearl St., 83001* ☎*307/733–2535 or 800/483–8667* ↪*110 rooms* ⚭*In-hotel: some pets allowed* ¶◎¦*EP* ⊟*AE, D, DC, MC, V.*

CAMPING

⚠ **Curtis Canyon.** Numerous trees surround this simple campground northeast of Jackson Hole. Part of Bridger-Teton National Forest, the campground is near a popular mountain-biking area and sits at an elevation of 6,600 feet. No trailers longer than 30 feet. Ten-day limit. ⚭*Pit toilets, drinking water, fire pits, picnic tables* ↪*11 sites* ⊠*From Elk Refuge Headquarters in Jackson, take Flat Creek Road northeast 7 mi* ☎*307/739–5400 or 307/543–2386* ⊕*www.fs.fed.us/btnf/* ⚭*Reservations not accepted* ⊟*No credit cards* ☉*June–Sept.*

⚠ **Granite Creek.** Part of Bridger-Teton National Forest, this wooded, 52-site campground is a big, noisy place convenient to hiking and mountain-biking trails. An added bonus is the small pools of Granite Hot Springs. The elevation is 7,100 feet and there are wheelchair-accessible sites. ⚭*Flush toilets, pit toilets, drinking water, fire pits, picnic tables* ↪*52 sites* ⊠*Granite Creek Rd. off U.S. 189/191, 35 mi southeast of Jackson* ☎*307/739–5400 or 307/543–2386* ⊕*www. fs.fed.us/btnf* ⚭*Reservations not accepted* ⊟*No credit cards* ☉*Late May–Sept.*

NIGHTLIFE & THE ARTS

NIGHTLIFE

There's never a shortage of live music in Jackson, where local performers play country, rock, and folk. Some of the most popular bars are on Town Square. At the **Million Dollar Cowboy Bar** (⊠*25 N. Cache St.* ☎*307/733–2207*) everyone dresses up in cowboy garb and tries to two-step into the Old West, or mosey over to the bar and slide into authentic horse-saddle seats. There are plenty of pool tables, and there's good pub grub and live country music most nights but Sunday, not to mention free country-western dance lessons on Thursday. Downstairs is a popular restaurant serving certified Black Angus steaks. **43 North** (⊠*645 S. Cache Dr.* ☎*307/733–0043*), at the base of Snow King Mountain, serves continental cuisine for both lunch and dinner, with outdoor seating (weather permitting) and a stellar view of the mountain in summer. You can also curl up inside by the stone fireplace at this locals' hangout and grab a drink at a table or the antique bar. There's lots of free parking and frequent live music; call for a schedule of events. Come to the **Virginian Saloon & Lodge** (⊠*750 W. Broadway* ☎*307/733–2792*) to shoot a game of pool, throw darts, grab a pitcher at a table, sip a drink by the fireplace, watch sports from one of four TVs, or listen to live music.

THE ARTS

Center for the Arts (⊠*240 S. Glenwood* ☎*307/734–8956* ⊕*www.jhcenterforthearts.org*) is Jackson's new $35 million center dedicated to supporting the fine and performing arts, including theater, film, and dance. It also hosts lectures on global issues, rotating exhibits, and showcases of star talent from Hollywood to Broadway. Classes for adults are included in the center's mission.

Artists who work in a variety of media show and sell their work at the **Jackson Hole Fall Arts Festival** (☎*307/733–3316*), with special events highlighting art, poetry, and dance. Festival events take place throughout town in September, and many art galleries in Jackson have special programs and exhibits.

For those seeking a more contemporary theater experience, **Off-Square Theatre** (⊠*Center for the Arts, 240 S. Glenwood, 83001* ☎*307/733–3021*) is a space for children and adults where theater professionals and nonprofessionals strut their stuff and sometimes go outside the box. The company is one of the leading theater companies in the region.

SHOPPING

Jackson's peaceful Town Square is surrounded by storefronts with a mixture of specialty and outlet shops—most of them small scale—with moderate to expensive prices. North of Jackson's center, on Cache Street, is a small cluster of fine shops on Gaslight Alley.

BOOKS

One of Gaslight Alley's best shops is **Valley Bookstore** (⊠*125 N. Cache St.* ☎*307/733–4533*). It ranks among the top bookstores in the region, with a big selection of regional history, guidebooks on flora and fauna, and fiction by Wyoming and regional authors.

CLOTHING

Fodor'sChoice **Hide Out Leather** (⊠*40 N. Center St.* ☎*307/733–2422*) carries many
★ local designs and has a diverse selection of men's and women's coats, vests, and accessories such as pillows and throws. Try **Corral West** (⊠*840 W. Broadway* ☎*307/733–0247*) for authentic women's, men's, and children's Western wear.

CRAFT & ART GALLERIES

★ Jackson's art galleries serve a range of tastes. **Di Tommaso Galleries** (⊠*172 Center St.* ☎*307/734–9677*) has a collection of 19th- and 20th-century art as well as contemporary pieces; the gallery specializes in painting and sculpture of Western life, wildlife, and Native America by artists Kate Starling, Harry Jackson, Melvin Johansen, and Conrard Schwring. Fine nature photography by Tom Mangelson from around the globe is displayed and sold at his **Images of Nature Gallery** (⊠*170 N. Cache St.* ☎*307/733–9752*). **Trailside Galleries** (⊠*105 N. Center St.* ☎*307/733–3186*) sells traditional Western art and jewelry. The photography of Abi Garaman is highlighted at **Under the Willow Photo Gallery** (⊠*50 S. Cache St.* ☎*307/733–6633*). He has been photographing Jackson Hole for decades and has produced a wide selection of images of wildlife, mountains, barns, and both summer and winter scenes. **Wilcox Gallery** (✉ *1975 N. U.S. 89* ☎ *307/733–6450*) showcases wildlife and landscape paintings, sculpture, pottery, and other works by contemporary artists. At **Wild By Nature Gallery** (✉ *95 W. Deloney Ave.* ☎ *307/733–8877*) 95% of the images are of local wildlife and landscape photography by Henry W. Holdsworth; there's also a selection of books and note cards. **Wild Exposures Gallery** (✉ *60 E. Broadway* ☎ *307/739–1777*) represents photographers Jeff Hogan, Scott McKinley, and Andrew Weller, all of whose work has appeared on National Geographic and BBC programs.

SPORTING GOODS

Jackson's premier sports shop, **Jack Dennis Sports** (✉ *50 E. Broadway* ☎ *307/733–3270*) is well stocked with the best in outdoor equipment for winter and summer activities. It also has a store at Teton Village. **Skinny Skis** (✉ *65 W. Deloney Ave.* ☎ *307/733–6094*) offers everything a cross-country skier might need. **Teton Mountaineering** (✉ *170 N. Cache St.* ☎ *307/733–3595*) specializes in Nordic-skiing, climbing, and hiking equipment and clothing. **Westbank Anglers** (✉ *3670 N. Moose-Wilson Rd.* ☎ *307/733–6483*) can provide all the equipment necessary for fly-fishing.

AROUND JACKSON HOLE

Although you might headquarter in Jackson, most of the outdoor activities in the region occur out in Jackson Hole and "The Valley." The valley has a world-class ski mountain and hiking and biking trails, and the Snake River, ideal for fishing or floating, runs right through the middle of it.

TETON VILLAGE & JACKSON HOLE MOUNTAIN RESORT

11 mi northwest of Jackson via Hwy. 22 and Teton Village Rd.

Teton Village resounds with the clomping of ski boots in winter and with the sounds of violins, horns, and other instruments at the Grand Teton Music Festival in summer. The village mostly consists of the restaurants, lodging properties, and shops built to serve the skiers who flock to Jackson Hole Mountain Resort. This is possibly the best ski resort area in the United States, and the expanse and variety of terrain are incredible. In summer folks come here to hike, ride the tram, and attend high-caliber concerts.

As it travels to the summit of Rendezvous Peak, the **Aerial Tramway** has always afforded spectacular panoramas of Jackson Hole. There are several hiking trails at the top of the mountain. The tram was closed and dismantled in September 2006, and at this writing, its replacement was not expected to be online until late in 2008 or early in 2009, though the opening date was still very much in flux. ✉ *Teton Village* ☎ *307/733–2292 or 800/333–7766.*

DOWNHILL SKIING & SNOWBOARDING

Fodor'sChoice A place to appreciate both as a skier and as a voyeur, **Jackson Hole**
★ **Mountain Resort** (⌂ *Box 290, Teton Village 83025* ☎*307/733–2292 or 800/333–7766* ⊕*www.jacksonhole.com*) is truly one of the great skiing experiences in America. There are literally thousands of ways of getting from top to bottom, and not all of them are hellishly steep, despite Jackson's reputation. First-rate racers such as Olympic champion skier Tommy Moe and snowboarders Julie Zell, A.J. Cargill, and Rob Kingwill regularly train here. As Kingwill has put it, "nothing really compares to Jackson Hole . . . This place has the most consistently steep terrain. You can spend years and years here and never cross your trail."

On the resort map, about 111 squiggly lines designate named trails, but this doesn't even begin to suggest the thousands of different skiable routes. The resort claims 2,500 skiable acres, a figure that seems unduly conservative. And although Jackson is best known for its advanced to extreme skiing, it is also a place where imaginative intermediates can go exploring and have the time of their lives. It is not, however, a good place for novices.

⚠ **High snowfall some winters can lead to extreme avalanche danger in spite of efforts by the Ski Patrol to make the area as safe as possible.** Before venturing from known trails and routes, check with the Ski Patrol for conditions. Ski with a friend, and always carry an emergency locator device. Ski passes range from $58 to $81 for adults, depending on the day of the week.

BACKCOUNTRY   Few areas in North America can compete with Jackson Hole when it
SKIING comes to the breadth, beauty, and variety of backcountry opportunities. For touring skiers, one of the easier areas (because of flatter routes) is along the base of the Tetons toward Jenny and Jackson lakes. Telemark skiers (or even skiers on alpine gear) can find numerous downhill routes by skiing in from Teton Pass, snow stability permitting. A guide isn't required for tours to the national park lakes but might be helpful for those unfamiliar with the lay of the land; trails and trail markers set in summer can become obscured by winter snows. When you are touring elsewhere, a guide familiar with the area and avalanche danger is a virtual necessity. The Tetons are big country, and the risks are commensurately large as well.

Alpine Guides (⊠ *Teton Village* ☎*307/739–2663*) leads half-day and full-day backcountry tours into the national parks and other areas near the resort, for more downhill-minded skiers. Arrangements can also be made through the Jackson Hole Ski School. **Jackson Hole Mountain Guides** (⊠*165 N. Glenwood St., Jackson* ☎*307/733–4979* ⊕*www. jhmg.com*) leads strenuous backcountry tours. The **Jackson Hole Nordic Center** (⊠*Teton Village* ☎*307/739–2629 or 800/450–0477*) has cross-country, telemark, and snowshoe rentals and track and telemark lessons. The center also leads naturalist tours into the backcountry. Rental packages begin at $28 and lessons start at $75, including rental equipment and a $13 trail pass. Forest Service rangers lead free snowshoe tours; the Nordic Center also runs snowshoe tours, starting from $80. Sled dog tours available (call to inquire about prices).

FACILITIES 4,139-foot vertical drop; 2,500 skiable acres; 10% beginner, 40% intermediate, 50% expert; 1 gondola, 6 quad chairs, 2 triple chairs, 2 double chair, 1 magic carpet.

HELI-SKIING In general, heli-skiing is best done when there has been relatively little recent snowfall. For two or three days after a storm, good powder skiing can usually be found within the ski area. Daily trips can be arranged through **High Mountain Helicopter Skiing** (⊠ *Jackson Hole Mountain Resort base area, Teton Village* ☎ *307/733–3274* ⊕ *www. heliskijackson.com*).

LESSONS & Half-day group lessons at the **Jackson Hole Ski & Snowboard School**
PROGRAMS (⊠ *Teton Village* ☎ *307/733–2292 or 800/450–0477*) start at $90. There are extensive children's programs, including lessons for kids 6 to 13 years old and day care for children from 6 months to 2 years old. Nordic-skiing lessons start at $45. For expert skiers, the **Jackson Hole Ski Camps** (⊠ *Teton Village* ☎ *307/739–2779 or 800/450–0477*), headed by such skiers as Tommy Moe, the 1994 Olympic gold medalist, and top snowboarders like Julie Zell, A. J. Cargill, and Jessica Baker, run for five days, teaching everything from big-mountain free-skiing to racing techniques. The cost is $890 per person.

LIFT TICKETS Lift tickets cost $58 to $81. You can save about 10% to 30% if you buy a five- to seven-day ticket.

RENTALS Equipment can be rented at ski shops in Jackson and Teton Village. **Jackson Hole Sports** (⊠ *Teton Village* ☎ *307/739–2649 or 800/443–6931*), at the Bridger Center at the ski area, offers ski and snowboard rental packages starting at $22 a day. You can buy or rent skis or snowboards at **Pepi Stegler Sports Shop** (⊠ *3395 W. McCollister Dr., Teton Village* ☎ *307/733–4505* ⊕ *www.pepistieglersports.com*), which is run by the famous Stiegler family. Daughter Resi, who calls Jackson Hole home, competed in the 2006 Olympics in Torino, Italy. Pepi, her father, is a native of Austria who won a bronze in the giant slalom at the 1964 Innsbrook games. Ski rentals cost between $25 and $44; snowboard rentals are $25. The store is at the base of Rendezvous Peak.

TRACK SKIING The **Jackson Hole Nordic Center** (⊠ *Teton Village* ☎ *307/739–2629 or 800/450–0477* ⊕ *www.jacksonhole.com*) is at the ski-resort base. The scenic 17 km (10½ mi) of groomed track is relatively flat. Because the Nordic Center and the downhill ski area are under the same management, downhill skiers with multiday passes can switch over to Nordic skiing in the afternoon for no extra charge. Otherwise the cost is $13 for a day pass. Rentals and lessons are available; alpine lift tickets are also good at the Nordic Center.

WHERE TO STAY & EAT

In the winter ski season, it can be cheaper to stay in Jackson, about 20 minutes away; in summer it's generally cheaper to stay at Teton Village.

$$$$ ✕**Solitude Cabin Dinner Sleigh Rides.** Climb aboard a horse-drawn sleigh and ride through the trees to a log cabin for a dinner of prime rib, broiled salmon, or a vegetarian entrée. Live entertainment is provided; a children's menu is available. ⊠*Jackson Hole Mountain Resort, Teton Village* ☎*307/739–2603* ⊟*AE, D, DC, MC, V* ⚓*Reservations essential* ⊘*Closed Apr.–early Dec.*

$$$–$$$$ ✕**Mangy Moose.** Folks pour in off the ski slopes for a lot of food and talk at this two-level restaurant with a bar and an outdoor deck. There's a high noise level but decent food consisting of Alaska king crab legs, buffalo meat loaf, and fish and pasta dishes. The place is adorned with antiques, including a full-size stuffed caribou and sleigh suspended from the ceiling. It's a popular nightspot, with live music and frequent concerts by top bands. ⊠*3295 Village Dr., Teton Village* ☎*307/733–4913* ⊟*AE, MC, V.*

$$$–$$$$ 🏠**R Lazy S Ranch.** Jackson Hole, with the spectacle of the Tetons in the background, is true dude-ranch country, and the R Lazy S is one of the largest dude ranches in the area. Horseback riding and instruction are the main attraction, with a secondary emphasis on fishing, either in private waters on the ranch or at other rivers and streams. One of the regular activities is a scenic float on the Snake River. You stay in log-cabin guest cottages and gather for meals in the large main lodge. **Pros:** Authentic dude ranch experience; very popular with older kids and preteens, an absolutely beautiful setting. **Cons:** Few modern trappings; not for the high-maintenance traveler. ⊠*1 mi north of Teton Village on outskirts of Grand Teton National Park 83025* ☎*307/733–2655* ⊕*www.rlazys.com* ⟿*14 cabins* ⚫*In-room: no a/c, no TV. In-hotel: no kids under 7, no elevator, no-smoking rooms* ⊟*No credit cards* ⊘*Closed Oct.–mid-June* ⦙◎⦙*FAP* ⌁*1-week minimum; rates based on double occupancy.*

$$–$$$$ 🏠**Alpenhof Lodge.** This small Austrian-style hotel is in the heart of Jackson Hole Mountain Resort, next to the tram. Hand-carved Bavarian furniture fills the rooms. All the deluxe rooms have balconies, and some have fireplaces and bathtub jets. Standard rooms are smaller and don't have balconies. Entrées such as wild-game loaf, Wiener schnitzel, and fondue are served in the dining room, and a relatively quiet nightclub also offers casual dining. **Pros:** Quaint; old-world feel; cozy surroundings. **Cons:** Some rooms are more small than cozy; especially for the price. ⊠ *Teton Village, 83025* ☎*307/733–3242 or 800/732–3244* ⊕*www.alpenhoflodge.com* ⟿*42 rooms* ⚫*In-room: Wi-Fi. In-hotel: bar, pool, spa, no-smoking rooms* ⊟*AE, D, DC, MC, V* ⊘*Closed mid-Oct.–Dec. 1 and early Apr.–May 1* ⦙◎⦙*BP.*

¢–$ 🏠**The Hostel X.** Although the classic hostel accommodations at this lodge-style inn are basic, you can't get any closer to Jackson Hole Mountain Resort for a better price. It's popular with young, budget-conscious people. Rooms, some of which have twins, bunks, and king beds, sleep from two to four people. Downstairs common areas include a lounge with a fireplace, game room, movie room, library, and ski-waxing room. There's no smoking in any of the hostel's public areas. **Pros:** Superb deal for the upscale locale; true convivial and communal atmosphere. **Cons:** Not family-friendly; little privacy; no matter how you slice it this is still a hostel. ✉ *3315 McCollister Dr., Teton Village 83025* ☎ *307/733–3415* ⊕ *www.hostelx.com* ⇆ *55 rooms* ᴥ *In-room: no a/c, no phone, no TV. In-hotel: laundry facilities, public Internet, public Wi-Fi, no elevator* ▤ *MC, V.*

WILSON

6 mi south of Teton Village on Teton Village Rd., 4 mi west of Jackson on Hwy. 22.

If you want to avoid the hustle and bustle of Jackson, Wilson makes a good alternative base for exploring Grand Teton National Park or skiing at Jackson Hole Mountain Resort. This small town takes its name from Nick Wilson, one of the first homesteaders in the area, a man who spent part of his childhood living with the Shoshone Indians.

WHERE TO EAT

$$$–$$$$
Fodor'sChoice
★
✗ **Bar J Chuckwagon.** At the best bargain in the Jackson Hole area, you'll get a true ranch-style meal in a long hall along with some of the liveliest Western entertainment you'll find in the region. The food, served on a tin plate, includes barbecued roast beef, chicken, or rib-eye steak, plus potatoes, beans, biscuits, applesauce, spice cake, and ranch coffee or lemonade. The multitalented Bar J Wranglers sing, play instruments, share cowboy stories and poetry, and even yodel. "Lap-size" children eat free. The doors open at 5:30, so you can explore the Bar J's Western village—including a saloon and several shops—before the dinner bell rings at 7:30. The dining area is covered, so no need to worry if the sun isn't shining. Reservations are strongly suggested. ✉ *4200 Bar J Chuckwagon Rd., Wilson, 83014* ☎ *307/733–3370* ▤ *D, MC, V.*

$$–$$$$
Fodor'sChoice
★
✗ **Nora's Fish Creek Inn.** Nora's is one of those inimitable Western places that have earned its keeping as a local treasure among its many loyal customers. Look for the giant trout on the roof outside. It's a great spot to catch a hearty weekend breakfast of pancakes or huevos rancheros that barely fit on your plate and dinner among the talkative locals. Among the imaginative dishes served at this casual log inn are honey-hickory baby back ribs, prime rib, elk tenderloin with blackberry-wine sauce, and nut-crusted trout, plus nightly specials. Soups such as pumpkin warm your bones, and there's wine by the glass and a kids' menu. You can dine in one of two large rooms or sit at the counter for quick service. Breakfast, but not lunch, is served on weekends. ✉ *Hwy. 22, 6 mi outside Jackson at base of pass* ▤ *AE, D, MC, V* ⊗ *No lunch weekends.*

$–$$$
★
✗ **Merry Piglets.** No pork is served here, hence the name! But otherwise, you'll get more than generous portions of Mexican fare, over a mesquite grill if you like, with a range of homemade sauces from mild to spicy for those who like the heat. Favorites include sizzling fajitas, carne asada, shrimp mango wraps, and even Tex-Mex–style seafood chimichanga. It's usually noisy and jam-packed, but there's a full-service bar whipping up frozen strawberry margaritas that you can sip in this festive atmosphere while waiting for your table. ✉ *160 N. Cache Dr., Jackson, near Teton Theatre* ☎ *307/733–2966* ᴥ *Reservations not accepted* ▤ *AE, D, MC, V.*

CLOSE UP

The Bear Essentials

The northern Rockies are bear country—grizzlies and black bears are a presence throughout the region. Seeing one across a valley, through a pair of binoculars, is fun, but meeting one at closer range isn't. There have been few fatal encounters, but almost every summer there are incidents involving bears.

Wherever you venture in Wyoming and Montana, keep in mind these tips for travel in bear country:

PRACTICAL PRECAUTIONS

Avoid sudden encounters. Whenever possible, travel in open country, during daylight hours, and in groups. Make noise—talking or singing is preferable to carrying "bear bells"—and leave your dog at home. Most attacks occur when a bear is surprised at close quarters or feels threatened.

Stay alert. Look for signs of bears, such as fresh tracks, scat, matted vegetation, or partially consumed salmon.

Choose your tent site carefully. Pitch the tent away from trails, streams with spawning salmon, and berry patches. Avoid areas that have a rotten smell or where scavengers have gathered; these may indicate the presence of a nearby bear cache, and bears aggressively defend their food supplies.

Keep food away from campsites. Cook meals at least 100 feet from tents, and store food and other items that give off odors (including personal products such as soap, shampoo, lotions, and even toothpaste) away from campsites. Hang food between trees where possible, or store your food in bear-resistant food containers. Avoid strong-smelling foods, and clean up after cooking and eating.

Store garbage in airtight containers or burn it and pack up the remains.

IF YOU ENCOUNTER A BEAR

Identify yourself. Talk to the bear, to identify yourself as a human. Don't yell. And don't run. Running will trigger a bear's predatory instincts, and a bear can easily outrun you. Back away slowly, and give the bear an escape route. Don't ever get between a mother and her cubs.

Bigger is better. Bears are less likely to attack a larger target. Therefore, increase your apparent size. Raise your arms above your head to appear larger and wave them slowly, to better identify yourself as a human. With two or more people, it helps to stand side by side. In a forested area it may be appropriate to climb a tree, but remember that black bears and young grizzlies are agile tree climbers.

As a last resort, play dead. If a bear charges and makes contact with you, fall to the ground, lie flat on your stomach or curl into a ball, hands behind your neck, and remain passive. If you are wearing a pack, leave it on. Once a bear no longer feels threatened, it will usually end its attack. Wait for the bear to leave before you move. The exception to this rule is when a bear displays predatory behavior. Instead of simply charging, a bear hunting for prey will show intense interest while approaching at a walk or run and it may circle, as if stalking you. But remember that such circumstances are exceedingly rare and most often involve black bears, which are much smaller and less aggressive than grizzlies (and can be driven off more easily).

WHERE TO STAY

$$$$ ⚐ **The Wildflower Inn.** This log country inn built in 1989 is cozy, clean, comfortable, and serves gourmet breakfasts. Just down the road from Jackson Hole Mountain Resort and Teton Village, the inn is surrounded by 3 acres of aspen and pine trees frequented by moose, deer, and other native wildlife. Each room has a private decks and bathroom, handcrafted log bed piled high with comforters, and its own alpine theme. There's also a plant-filled solarium, hot tub, and sunlit dining room. **Pros:** Excellent views; perfectly situated for outdoor activities and exploration parks. **Cons:** Books far in advance; 12 mi from Jackson itself. ⊠ *3725 Teton Village Rd., 83001* ☎ *307/733–4710* ⊕ *www. jacksonholewildflower.com* ⇖ *5 rooms* ⚐ *In room: refrigerator (some), Wi-Fi. In-hotel: no-smoking rooms* ⊟ *MC, V* ❚◎❚ *BP.*

$$$–$$$$ ⚐ **Teton Tree House.** On a steep hillside and surrounded by trees, this is a real retreat. Ninety-five steps lead to this cozy lodgepole-pine bed-and-breakfast tucked away in the forest. Decks abound, rooms are full of wood furniture and warm Southwestern colors, and an inviting common area has a two-story old-fashioned adobe fireplace. **Pros:** Scenic locale; good breakfast. **Cons:** Not open in winter; must drive to town; small climb up to the B&B. ⊠ *6175 Heck of a Hill Rd., 83014* ☎ *307/733–3233* ⇖ *6 rooms* ⚐ *In-room: no a/c, no TV. In-hotel: no kids under 6, no elevator, no-smoking rooms* ⊟ *D, MC, V* ⊘ *Closed Oct.–Apr.* ❚◎❚ *BP.*

NIGHTLIFE

The **Stagecoach Bar** (⊠ *5575 W. Hwy. 22* ☎ *307/733–4407*) fills to bursting when local bands play. Disco Night is on Thursday and attracts a packed house of swingers. "The Coach" is a good place to enjoy a drink and conversation at other times, and there's now a Mexican café and kitchen where you can grab a quick bite.

ALTA

27 mi northwest of Wilson via Hwy. 22 to Hwy. 33 (in Idaho) to Alta cutoff (back to Wyoming).

Alta is the site of the Grand Targhee Ski and Summer Resort, famed for its deep powder and family atmosphere. The slopes never feel crowded, but to experience complete solitude, try a day of Sno-Cat skiing in untracked powder.

SPORTS & THE OUTDOORS

⚙ An average of 500 inches of powdery "white gold" attracts skiers to **Grand Targhee Ski & Summer Resort** (⊠ *Ski Hill Rd.* ☎ *307/353–2300 or 800/TARGHEE* ⊕ *www.grandtarghee.com*), with 2,000 acres, 1,000 of which are dedicated to powder Sno-Cat skiing and 15 km (9 mi) to cross-country trails. 'Boarders have two trick terrain parks and lots of freestyle areas with rails and mailboxes to tear it up. There are four lifts and one rope tow, and the vertical drop is 2,419 feet. Lift tickets are about $60 per day; Nordic trail permits $10. Classes by expert instructors are also available. Lifts operate 8:30–4 daily.

WHERE TO STAY

$–$$$$ 🏨 **Grand Targhee Ski and Summer Resort.** This modern facility perched
☼ on the west side of the Tetons has a handsome, natural-wood look and
the atmosphere of an alpine village. Clustered around common areas
with fireplaces, the motel-style rooms are simply furnished with West-
ern furniture; the condominium rooms are brighter and more spacious.
Targhee Steakhouse ($–$$$$) is the resort's foremost restaurant. The
Trap Bar and Grille and Wild Bill's Grille serve quicker, less expensive
food, and Snorkel's has bakery items, espresso, and deli sandwiches.
⊠3300 E. Ski Hill Rd., 83414 ☎307/353–2300 or 800/827–4433
⊕www.grandtarghee.com ⤳96 rooms, 50 suites ⚲In-hotel: 5 res-
taurants, pool, spa, airport shuttle ☱AE, D, MC, V.

THE WIND RIVER RANGE

Rising to the east and southeast of Jackson Hole is the Wind River
Range, which remains snowcapped year-round and still holds small
glaciers. Much of this range is rugged wilderness, ideal for backcountry
hiking and horseback riding. Several towns here make good bases for
exploring the area, including Pinedale on the west side of the range;
Atlantic City, within the range itself; and Lander, Fort Washakie, and
Dubois on the east side of the range.

PINEDALE

77 mi southeast of Jackson on Hwy. 191.

A southern gateway to Jackson Hole, Pinedale has much to offer on
its own, for the spirit of the mountain man lives on here. Fur trappers
found the icy streams of the Green River watershed to be among the
best places to capture beaver. In the mid-1800s they gathered on the
river near what is now Pinedale for seven annual rendezvous. Now, the
Museum of the Mountain Man preserves their heritage, and modern-
day buckskinners continue to meet in the area each summer.

To the east are millions of acres of Bridger-Teton National Forest, much
of it off-limits to all but foot and horse traffic. The peaks reach higher
than 13,000 feet, and the area is liberally sprinkled with more than a
thousand high-mountain lakes where fishing is generally excellent.

Contact the **Bridger-Teton National Forest, Pinedale Ranger District** (⊠29 E.
Fremont Lake Rd., Box 220, 82941 ☎*307/367–4326* ⊕*www.fs.fed.
us/btnf)* for more information. Although outdoor activities still beckon
in the forest, an oil and gas boom in the area keeps motel rooms full
year-round and restaurants often busy.

☼ The **Museum of the Mountain Man** depicts the trapper heritage of the
★ area with displays of 19th-century guns, traps, clothing, and beaver
pelts. There's also an interpretive exhibit devoted to the pioneer and
ranch history of Sublette County as well as an overview of the Western
fur trade. In summer the museum hosts living-history demonstrations,
children's events, a reenactment of the early 19th-century Green River

3

Rendezvous, and lectures. ✉ *700 E. Hennick Rd.* ☎ *307/367–4101 or 877/686–6266* ⊕ *www.museumofthemountainman.com* ☜ *$5* ⊙ *May–Sept., daily 9–5; fall daily 9–4.*

WORD OF MOUTH

"If you are in Pinedale spend a few hours at the Museum of the Mountain Man."

–RedRock

SPORTS & THE OUTDOORS

Encompassing parts of the Wind River Range, the **Bridger-Teton National Forest, Pinedale Ranger District** (✉ *Forest office, 29 E. Fremont Lake Rd.* ☎ *307/367–4326* ⊕ *www.fs.fed.us/btnf*) holds hundreds of thousands of acres to explore. The fishing is generally excellent in the numerous mountain lakes, and you can also hike, horseback ride, snowmobile, camp, and picnic here.

At the **Half Moon Lake Resort** (☎ *307/367–6373* ⊕ *www.halfmoonlake.com*) you'll find modern lakefront cabins with electricity and phones. Pastimes here include boating, fishing, camping, and hiking around this jewel of the Wind River Range. Trout, whitefish, and mackinaw await anglers and ice fishers, too. There are also guided horseback rides, a boat launch, and a campground with picnic tables, trailer pull-throughs, vault toilets, fire grates, and refuse containers. The lake has a beach where children can build sand castles and bigger kids can enjoy canoeing, water skiing, and inner tubing. The resort area is open May–October. It's about 10 mi northeast of Pinedale. Take Fremont Lake Road north out of Pinedale; the turnoff for Half Moon Lake is about 8 mi from town along a narrow, winding gravel road.

WHERE TO EAT

$$$ ✕**Stockmen's Restaurant.** The salad bar is shaped like a tepee and there's
★ a 1903 map of the United States at this locals' hangout since 1933. On the menu are burgers, salads, prime rib, steaks, and seafood. It's a perfect stop for dessert and coffee (try the thick, crumbly cheesecake served warm). Early risers can grab breakfast here before 6 AM flanked by mineral-field workers. The restaurant serves lunch, too. Smoking is allowed, so it can get hazy at times. Or you can sit in the no-smoking section. After eating you can get a drink, shoot a game of pool, or relax in the roomy, low-lighted lounge. There's also a beer and package store for those on the run. ✉ *117 W. Pine St.* ☎ *307/367–4562 bar, or 307/367–4563 restaurant* ▤ *MC, V.*

$–$$$ ✕**Moose Creek Trading Company.** As the name suggests, this downtown restaurant employs a moose motif, reflected, for example, in the wrought-iron bar tables with carvings of the animal. But the local palate, as evidenced by a new Chinese restaurant in this classic Western town, is expanding beyond chuck-wagon fare. Moose Creek's menu includes tasty sandwiches, fresh bread, and steaks for dinner plus espresso and homemade pies for dessert. Try the chunky chicken salad for a light summer meal. ✉ *44 W. Pine St.* ☎ *307/367–4616* ☏ *307/367–4616* ▤ *AE, D, DC, MC, V* ⊙ *No dinner.*

$$ ✕**Bottoms Up Brewery & Grill.** Microbrewery and grill that serves award-winning grog and quality pub grub from steaks and sandwiches to daily specials. ✉ *402 W. Pine St.* ☎ *307/367–2337* ▤ *AE, D, MC, V.*

TOP REASONS TO GO

History: From ancient Native American settlements; to early pioneer trails, towns and red rock canyons and mountains . . . nearly anywhere you look out here, man and nature have left their indelible marks.

Space: The drive westward and from the southeast never fails to enchant newcomers with one of America's least populated frontiers.

Sights: As you approach Dubois from the flatlands of Riverton and enter the ascending Wind River

Range, keep an eye peeled for mule deer and robust wildlife.

Sounds: Park the car at any scenic overlook, or camp out at the right time of year, and you'll understand why "The Wind River" area resounds with timeless music.

Colors: Yellowed, tawny prairies in late summer and early fall; ochre-stained geology around Dubois; and lazy sunsets that paint the skys indigo and red cast a spell on unhurried visitors.

¢–$$ ✕**China Gourmet.** Serving full-fare, Cantonese-style "Western" Chinese food, this might be the only joint in America where you'll find a Budweiser sign over the door, Asian decor on the walls, large-screen TVs playing all the big games, and ketchup on a table aside a bowl of egg-drop soup. It's good for families with picky eaters, as the menu carries more than 100 items—spanning from lo mein and mu shu shrimp to hamburgers, pork chops, and fried chicken. Many dishes also come with mushrooms and barbecue sauce; some even have spaghetti. ⊠*44 W. Pine St.* ☎*307/367–4788*.

WHERE TO STAY

$–$$$ ⚏**Best Western Pinedale Inn.** On the north side of town, this hotel is within five blocks of downtown shopping and restaurants. The rooms aren't large, but they have contemporary furniture. **Pros:** Swimming pool; continental breakfast; good location. **Cons:** Check cancellation policy (reportedly locked by computer); prices not always best around. ⊠*864 W. Pine St., 82941* ☎*307/367–6869* 🖷*307/367–6897* ⊕*www. bestwestern.com* ⋽*84 rooms* ⌂*In-room: refrigerator (some). In-hotel: pool, no-smoking rooms, some pets allowed, no elevator* ⊟*AE, D, DC, MC, V* ❍|*CP*.

$–$$ ⚏**Chambers House B&B.** Huge pine trees surround this 1933 log home
★ filled with the owner's family antiques. Downstairs there's a sitting room where you can relax with a book or chat with other guests. The master bedroom, with a fireplace, private bathroom, and private entrance, is also on the ground floor. Three of the upstairs bedrooms share bathroom facilities; a fourth has a private bathroom and a fireplace. **Pros:** Charming old house; solid breakfast; recently renovated. **Cons:** Limited reading materials and games; some rooms share bathroom. ⊠*111 W. Magnolia St., 82941* ☎*307/367–2168 or 800/567–2168* ⊕*www. chambershouse.com* ⋽*5 rooms, 2 with bath* ⌂*In-room: no a/c, no phone (some), no TV (some). In-hotel: no-smoking rooms, no pets, no elevator* ⊟*AE, D, DC, MC, V* ❍|*BP*.

$-$$ ⚏**The Lodge at Pinedale.** This three-story motel is across a parking lot from the town's movie theater and bowling alley. Green carpeting and bed coverings decorate the rooms. **Pros:** Jacuzzi; pool; complimentary evening cookies. **Cons:** Complaints have been lodged about occasional maintenance problems; doesn't offer a classic, rustic experience. ⊠*1054 W. Pine St., 82941* ☎*307/367–8800 or 866/995–6343* 🖨*307/367–8812* ⊕*www.lodgeatpinedale.com* 🗪*41 rooms, 2 suites* ♿*In-room: refrigerator, Wi-Fi. In-hotel: pool, no-smoking rooms, some pets allowed* ⊟*AE, D, DC, MC, V* ⎮⦿⎮*CP.*

SHOPPING

The Cowboy Shop (⊠*129 W. Pine St.* ☎*877/567–6336* ⊕*www.cowboyshop.com*) stocks Western and cowpoke clothing for all ages, including hats and boots, and also sells leather goods and regional books.

EN ROUTE As you drive south of Pinedale along U.S. 191, the mountains of the Wind River Range seem to fade down to a low point. This is **South Pass,** the area through which some 500,000 emigrants traveled over the Oregon, Mormon, and California trails between 1843 and 1870.

ATLANTIC CITY

36 mi south of Pinedale via U.S. 191 to Farson, then 45 mi east on Hwy. 28. Look for green sign "Atlantic City" and take wide dirt road for about 4 mi. More than likely, you'll need four-wheel drive in snow season.

A near ghost town amid the real ghost towns of Miner's Delight and South Pass City, this bygone gold rush–era settlement still has a few residents, a couple of tourist-oriented businesses, dirt streets, late-19th-century buildings, and a whole lot of character. Formed in 1868 when gold rushers flocked to the area seeking their fortunes and known for its red-light district, Atlantic City was where Wyoming Territory's first brewery opened in the late 1860s. Once the gold boom went bust less than a decade later, however, residents deserted the town. Atlantic City had a few more smaller rushes over the years, but none ever matched its early days.

South Pass City, 2 mi west of Atlantic City, was established in 1867 after gold was discovered in a creek called Sweetwater in 1842. In its heyday, by various accounts, before the gold thinned out in the 1870s, there were between 1,500 and 4,000 residents. After Sioux and Cheyenne raids, over settlers hunting indigenous game herds and miners poisoning their drinking water, the town still boomed until going bust and dropping to double digits by 1872. Its well-preserved remains are now the **South Pass City State Historic Site.** You can tour many of the original surviving buildings that have been restored, and you can even try your hand at gold panning. With artifacts and photographs of the town at its peak, the small museum here gives an overview of the South Pass gold district.

Fodor's Choice
★

South Pass City has another claim to fame. Julia Bright and Esther Hobart Morris are two of the women from the community who firmly believed that women should have the right to vote. It is suspected that they encouraged Bright's husband, Representative William Bright, to introduce a bill for women's suffrage in the Wyoming Territorial Legislature. He did so, the bill was ratified, and South Pass went down in history as the birthplace of women's suffrage in Wyoming. In 1870 Morris became the first female justice of the peace in the nation, serving South Pass City. ⊠*South Pass City Rd., off Hwy. 28, South Pass* ☎*307/332–3684* ⊕*wyoparks.state.wy.us/index.asp* ⊠*$2* ☉*Mid-May–early Sept., daily 9–5:30.*

WHERE TO STAY & EAT

$–$$$ ✕**Atlantic City Mercantile.** The town's oldest saloon, known as the
★   "Merc," serves refreshments in a room that has seen its share of gold miners, perhaps an outlaw or two, and certainly some ruffians. When you step through the doors of this 1893 building with tin ceilings, a massive back bar, and an assortment of mismatched oak tables and chairs, you may feel as though you've walked directly into an episode of *Gunsmoke.* At times a honky-tonk piano player is on hand. The menu includes steak, chicken, and seafood, plus sandwiches and big burgers. ⊠*100 E. Main St.* ☎*307/332–5143* ▭*D, MC, V.*

¢–$ ✕**Miner's Grub Stake.** Drop in for pancakes, French toast, omelets, and coffee for breakfast; or a buffalo burger, tuna salad, or Reuben sandwich for lunch. You can also warm your bones with beef vegetable soup, chili, and hot cider before stocking up on paper goods, groceries, sunscreen, soft drinks, two-cycle motor oil, pet food, and other supplies. Daily specials include meat loaf on Friday and pork loin, chops, and ribs on Saturday. ⊠*150 W. Main St.* ☎*307/332–0915* ☉*Closed Nov.* ▭*MC, V.*

$ ▦**Miner's Delight Inn & B&B.** Live like the prospectors did in the olden days
★   and stay in one of the authentic, rustic cabins. Each has a small washstand with a bowl and a pitcher of water, and it's a short walk to the main house's bathroom and shower. Rooms in the lodge, built in 1904 as the town's hotel, are larger, have private bathrooms, cost a couple bucks more, and share a kitchen downstairs. There are patchwork curtains and ample bed coverings. The red velvet wallpaper was reportedly hung by Georgina Newman, who, along with her husband, Paul, no relation to the actor, ran the place in the 1960s. Legend has it this chic New York couple started a "Jazz Age" revival in a ghost town, replete with gourmet dinners and Paris gowns. Current innkeepers Barbara and Bob Townsend are gracious raconteurs whose breakfast salon doubles as a gallery featuring top local artists. The inn borrows its name from the real, nearby ghost town of Miner's Delight. Writers are encouraged to finish and hawk their works here. And there are plenty of smooth-sipping spirits at the well-stocked "two bit" Cowboy saloon by the downstairs fireplace. **Pros:** True west ghost town charm; gracious hosts; late night saloon and fireplace. **Cons:** Remote location; no Internet/TV; some rooms share bath. ⊠*290 Atlantic City Rd., 82520* ☎*307/332–*

0248 or 888/292–0248 ⊕www.minersdelightinn.com ⌐3 lodge rooms, 5 cabins without bath ≥In-room: no a/c, no phone, no TV. In-hotel: no-smoking rooms, no elevator ⊟AE, D, MC, V ⍭⏐BP.

SHOPPING

South Pass Mercantile (⊠50 South Pass Main ☎307/332–9935 or 307/332–8120 ⊕www.south-pass.com) sells Wyoming-made products ranging from clothing to the largest selection of books in the area by regional authors, plus gold mining and prospecting supplies.

LANDER

About 31 mi northeast of Atlantic City via Hwy. 28/U.S. 287.

At the southwestern edge of the Wind River Indian Reservation and in the heart of country held dear by Chief Washakie (circa 1804–1900), one of the greatest chiefs of the Shoshone tribe, and his people, Lander has always had a strong tie to the Native American community. East of the Wind River Range, Lander makes a good base for pursuing mountain sports and activities ranging from backcountry hiking to horse-packing trips.

At **Sinks Canyon State Park,** the Popo Agie (pronounced pa-*po*-sha, meaning "Tall Grass River" to the Crow Indians) flows into a limestone cavern. The crashing water "sinks" into fissures only to resurface ½ mi downstream in the "rise," where it reemerges and huge fish (mainly rainbow and brown trout) swim in the calm pool. Wildflowers, Rocky Mountain bighorn sheep, black bears, golden eagles, moose, mule deer, marmots, and other wildlife wander the grounds. The park is ideal for hiking, camping, and picnicking. No fishing is allowed, but visitors can toss fish food to the trout from the observation deck. ⊠3079 Sinks Canyon Rd., 6 mi south of Lander on Hwy. 131 ☎307/332–3077 ⊕wyoparks.state.wy.us/Parks/SinksCanyon/index.asp ⍰Park free, camping $4 ⍟Park daily 24 hrs; visitor center Memorial Day–Labor Day, daily 9–7.

SPORTS & THE OUTDOORS

For more than 35 years, adventurers and students have been exploring the remote Wind River range to learn all aspects of mountaineering—from low-impact camping and horse packing to rock climbing and fly-fishing—by taking a course from the **National Outdoor Leadership School** (⊠284 Lincoln St. ☎307/332–6973 ⊕www.nols.edu).

FISHING   There's great fishing on the Wind River Indian Reservation, but you must first obtain a tribal license; contact **Shoshone and Arapaho Tribes** (⊠Fish and Game Dept., Box 217, Fort Washakie 82514 ☎307/332–7207) for more information. **At Sweetwater Fishing Expeditions,** (☎307/332–3986 ⊕www.sweetwaterfishing.com) George Hunker, Orvis guide of the year, and his crew lead small guided horseback and backpacking camping trips into the Wind River Mountains as well as day trips along smaller streams.

HORSEBACK   **Allen's Diamond Four Ranch,** the highest-altitude dude ranch in Wyoming,
RIDING   arranges mountain horse-pack trips, big-game hunts, and guided fishing and other horseback excursions. Some trips originate at the ranch,
where you stay in cabins and take day rides; others are overnight backcountry adventures. Children must be seven or eight years old to go on
extended pack trips. Also available are drop-camp services. No pets are
allowed. Call or check the Web site for directions. ⊠ *Off U.S. 287, 35
mi northwest of Lander.* ☎*307/332–2995 or 307/330–8625* ⊕*www.
diamond4ranch.com).* Ride the Oregon Trail, take pack trips into the
high country, or participate in an "outlaw ride" with **Rocky Mountain
Horseback Adventures** (☎*307/332–4993 or 800/408–9149).*

WHERE TO EAT

$$$-$$$$ ✕**Cowfish.** At this funky restaurant you can dine on a cozy, outdoor
patio and select from sandwiches and haute cuisine from both land
and water. For starters try pot stickers and seared ahi tuna. Entrées
range from 16-ounce rib-eye steaks, fillets, prime rib (served Friday
only), slow-cooked baby back ribs, and hamburgers made from local
beef, to wild Alaskan salmon and beer-battered shrimp. Rounding
out the menu are pasta dishes like prosciutto and chicken with vodka
cream or fillet tips on penne pasta smothered in tequila cream sauce.
An on-site microbrewery and organic garden of fresh vegetables and
herbs adds a distinctive flair to each meal. ⊠*128 Main St., Lander*
☎*307/332–8227* ⊟.

$$$-$$$$ ✕**Svilars' Bar & Dining Room.** This small, dark, family-owned restaurant
Fodor$Choice   with vinyl booths has what many locals say are the best steaks in all
★   of Wyoming. It's rivaled only by the Club El Toro steak house across
the street. A meal here usually begins with *sarma* (cabbage rolls) and
other appetizers. Your server will then place before you one of the big-
gest, if not *the* biggest, and best steaks you've likely ever seen. There's
even baked lobster. ⊠*173 S. Main St., 10 mi east of Lander, Hudson
82515* ☎*307/332–4516* ⊟*MC, V* ⊗*Closed Sun. and alternate Mon.
No lunch.*

¢–$$$ ✕**Gannett Grill.** This crowded, noisy place serves large sandwiches, never-
frozen half-pound hamburgers, and hand-tossed New York–style pizzas.
In spring and summer you can sit on the garden deck while the kids play
in the yard. ⊠*126 Main St.* ☎*307/332–7009* ⊟*D, MC, V.*

WHERE TO STAY

$–$$$ ⊞**The Inn at Lander.** This two-story Best Western motel sits on a hill
overlooking Lander and is beautifully landscaped with grassy areas
and trees. It's within walking distance of restaurants and discount-
store shopping. The small outdoor area has picnic tables. Children
12 and under stay free with one paying adult. **Pros:** Good-size clean
rooms; close to downtown; bar/café. **Cons:** Close to highway; can get
crowded during conferences; no indoor pool. ⊠*260 Grandview Dr., at
U.S. 287/789, WY 82520* ☎*307/332–2847* ⊕*www.bestwestern.com*
⇆*109 rooms* ⌂*In-room: safe, refrigerator, Wi-Fi. In-hotel: pool, spa,
no-smoking rooms, no elevator* ⊟*AE, D, MC, V* ⏍*CP.*

3

$ ⌂**Blue Spruce Inn.** Highlights of this 1919 home built by a wealthy sheep rancher and named for five enormous spruce trees on the property include a front porch with a swing where you can sip tea or coffee. The interior design is from the Arts and Crafts period, and there are hardwood floors and beautiful gardens. The sunporch is a nice spot to curl up with a book and a cup of tea. Three rooms are on the second floor, accessible only by a staircase. The Floral Room is a garden-level basement. **Pros:** Lovely old home; hospitable innkeepers; close to downtown. **Cons:** No TV (some rooms); books fast in summers, reservations recommended. ⊠677 S. 3rd St., 82520 ☎307/332–8253 or 888/503–3311 ☐307/332–1386 ⊕www.bluespruceinn.com ⤴4 rooms ᗚIn-room: no a/c, no TV (some), Wi-Fi. In-hotel: no-smoking rooms, no elevator ⊟AE, D, MC, V ⏽BP.

CAMPING ⚠**Sleeping Bear Ranch.** There's a re-created Old West ghost town of Dallas, Wyoming, at this RV park and campground that sits beside the Little Popo Agie River. There are lots of amenities here, including a restaurant, shops, and horseshoes, and you can take a hayride or swim in the river. Horses and pets are welcome. ᗚFlush toilets, full hookups, drinking water, guest laundry, showers, picnic tables, general store, play area, swimming (river) ⤴58 full hookups, 8 partial hookups, 10 tent sites; 7 cabins ⊠U.S. 287, 9 mi southeast of Lander, 1 mi east of Rawlins turnoff ☎307/332–5159 or 888/757–2327 ⊟D, MC, V.

⚠**Sleeping Bear RV Park.** Next to a golf course, this campground and RV park has lots of grass and shade trees. You can enjoy various activities here, including basketball, horseshoes, volleyball, and video games. There's often evening entertainment in the form of campfires and storytelling. ᗚFlush toilets, full hookups, partial hookups (electric and water), drinking water, showers, picnic tables, public telephone, general store, play area ⤴22 full hookups, 23 partial hookups, 10 tent sites ⊠715 E. Main St., 82520 ☎307/332–5159 or 888/757–2327 ⊕www.sleepingbearrvpark.com ⊟D, MC, V.

NIGHTLIFE

On weekends the **Lander Bar & Grill** (⊠126 Main St. ☎307/332–7009) gets crowded with people who come to dance and listen to live country bands.Local bands often jam at **Folklore Coffeehouse** (⊠311 Main St. ☎No phone).

THE ARTS

☺ June through August the **Native American Cultural Program** (☎307/332–5546 or 800/433–0662) has dance exhibitions in nearby Riverton City Park most Thursday evenings. Native American traditional dancing is part of the **Yellow Calf Memorial Powwow** (☎307/332–6120 or 800/433–0662), usually held in early June in Ethete to honor Chief Yellow Calf, the last chief of the Arapaho tribe; 16 mi north of Lander on the Wind River Indian Reservation. For information on area cultural events, such as the Shoshone tribe's Chokecherry Festival in Lander's City Park (3rd and Fremont Street) in late August, call 307/332–4932. You can also find a calendar of Wind River Indian activities at (⊕www.wind-river.org) under "Things to Do."

SHOPPING

The shelves at **Main Street Books** (⊠*300 W. Main St.* ☎*307/332–7661*) are lined with classic, regional, and best-selling books that you can peruse at the coffee bar. Antiques and one-of-a-kind treasures are sold at **Charlotte's Web** (⊠*228 Main St.* ☎*307/332–5884*).

Distinctive, flamboyant clothing, unique jewelry, and local art are available at **Whippy Bird** (⊠*306 Main St.* ☎*307/332–3444*), in an old mercantile store.

DUBOIS

86 mi east of Jackson via U.S. 26, U.S. 287, and U.S. 89/191.

The mountains around Dubois attracted explorers as early as 1811, when members of the Wilson Price Hunt party crossed through the region en route to Fort Astoria in Oregon. These high peaks still attract folks who like to hike, climb, ride horses, camp, and experience wilderness. The largest concentration of free-ranging bighorn sheep in the country—more than 1,400—lives here, roaming the high country in summer and wintering just above town on Whiskey Mountain.

South and east of Grand Teton and Yellowstone, Dubois is the least well known of the gateway communities to the parks, but this town of 1,000 provides all the services a visitor in Jackson or Cody might need. You can still get a room during the peak summer season without making a reservation months in advance, although it's a good idea to call a week or so before you arrive.

Displays at the **Wind River Historical Center** focus on Wind River tie hacks (workers who cut ties for railroads), local geology, and the archaeology of the Mountain Shoshone. Outbuildings include the town's first schoolhouse, a saddle shop, a homestead house, and a bunkhouse. The center also offers Elderhostel programs for senior citizens. With advance notice you can examine the historical-photograph collection, oral-history tapes, and library. ⊠*909 W. Ramshorn Ave.* ☎*307/455–2284* ⊡*$1* ☉*June–mid-Sept., daily 9–6; mid-Sept.–May, daily 10–4.*

☺ Friday nights at 8 in the summer, the "Bad Boys of Bull Riding" kick up a ruckus in the downtown Clarence Allison Memorial Arena for one of the west's best rodeos. It's $5 for adults; children get in free.

☺ You can learn about bighorn sheep, including Rocky Mountain big-
★ horn, at the **National Bighorn Sheep Interpretive Center** on the north side of Dubois. Among the mounted specimens here are the "super slam," with one of each type of wild sheep in the world, and two bighorn rams fighting during the rut. Hands-on exhibits illustrate a bighorn's body language, characteristics, and habitat. Winter tours (reserve ahead) to Whiskey Mountain provide an opportunity to see the wild sheep in its natural habitat; reservations are required and cost $25 per person. ⊠*907 Ramshorn Ave.* ☎*307/455–3429 or 888/209–2795* ⊡*$2 adults; $5 family* ☉*Memorial Day–Labor Day, daily 9–8; Labor Day–Memorial Day, daily 9–5; wildlife-viewing tours mid-Nov.–Mar.*

OFF THE BEATEN PATH

Brooks Lake Recreation Area. About 20 mi west of Dubois, easy to moderate hiking trails lead around Brooks Lake, across alpine meadows, and through pine forest to high mountain points with expansive views of Brooks Lake Mountain and the Pinnacles. You can picnic here, and boat, fish, or swim on the lake. Brooks Lake Lodge, a private dude ranch, stands on the lakeshore. ☒ *20 mi west of Dubois on U.S. 26/287, then 7 mi northeast on gravel road to Brooks Lake Recreation Area* ☎ *307/578–1200* ∰ *www.fs.fed.us/r2/shoshone.*

SPORTS & THE OUTDOORS

CROSS-COUNTRY SKIING

Among the best places for cross-country skiing is **Togwotee Pass,** east of Jackson and north of Dubois on U.S. 26/287, in Bridger-Teton and Shoshone national forests.

MOUNTAIN CLIMBING

Much of the appeal of the Wind River Range, which you can access from the west near Pinedale, or the east near Lander and Dubois, is the (relatively difficult) access to major peaks, the most significant of which is Gannett Peak, at 13,804 feet the highest mountain in Wyoming. The trip to the base of Gannett Peak can take two days, with considerable ups and downs and stream crossings that can be dangerous in late spring and early summer. The reward for such effort, however, is seclusion: climbing Gannett Peak might not be as dramatic as climbing the Grand Teton to the west, but you won't have to face the national-park crowds at the beginning or end of the climb. Wind River is a world of granite and glaciers, the latter (though small) being among the last active glaciers in the U.S. Rockies. Other worthy climbs in the Wind River Range are Gannett's neighbors Mount Sacajawea and Fremont Peak. **Jackson Hole Mountain Guides** (☒ *165 N. Glenwood St., Jackson* ☎ *307/733–4979* ∰ *www.jhmg.com*) leads trips in the area.

WHERE TO EAT

$$$–$$$$
Fodor'sChoice
★

✕ **Rustic Pine Steakhouse.** The 1930s-era, 40-foot, hand-carved pinewood bar reveals a menagerie of trophy game. This is one of Wyoming's more memorable package stores and watering holes, where locals and visitors congregate to shoot pool and share news about hunting or hiking. The adjoining restaurant serves mouthwatering steaks, seafood, and pastas in a quaint, remodeled barn with a stone fireplace, white tablecloths, and candles. Get your greens at the salad bar. ☒ *119 E. Ramshorn Ave.* ☎ *307/455–2772 restaurant,307/455–2430 bar* ▤ *MC, V* ⊘ *No lunch.*

$–$$$
☺
★

✕ **Paya Deli Pizza & Catering.** Don't be fooled by the Podunk picnic tables where you can hang out and eat on the sheltered porch while people-watching on the main drag in this one-horse cow town. Inside, amid the pastel walls, whimsical photos, and pub-style table seating, chef Barb from Seattle tosses perhaps the tastiest gourmet pizzas baked in a wood oven in Wyoming. She's also stocking the soup and salad bar with hot broths and chowders. In the deli you'll find fresh antipasto and big-city sandwiches like a Reuben on real rye bread. ☒ *112 Ramshorn Ave., 82513* ☎ *307/450–3331* ▤ *MC, V* ⊘ *Closed Tues. and Wed.*

¢–$$$

✕ **Cowboy Café.** Among the homemade, blue-ribbon dishes served at this small restaurant in downtown Dubois are sandwiches, steaks, buffalo burgers, chicken, pork, baby back ribs, and fish. For dessert the peach caramel crisp and chocolate bourbon pecan pie are not soon forgotten. You can also grab a hearty breakfast and sip coffee alongside the cowboy clientele. ⊠*115 E. Ramshorn Ave.* ☎*307/455–2595* ⊟*AE, D, MC, V.*

WHERE TO STAY

$$$$

Fodor'sChoice

★

Brooks Lake Lodge. This mountain lodge on Brooks Lake combines great scenery with service and amenities. Built in 1922, the lodge has massive open-beam ceilings, spacious rooms, subtle lighting, and log, leather, and wicker furnishings. Each of the lodge bedrooms and cabins has handcrafted lodgepole-pine furniture. Some cabins have wood-burning stoves; the lodge suite has a full kitchen, living room, two-person Jacuzzi tub, and king-size beds. All cabins have panoramic views of the Wind River Range; some overlook Brooks Lake. Take a guided hike, go horseback riding, or fly-fish or canoe on the lake in summer. In winter you can take dogsled or snowmobile rides with outfitters. Dinner is served in the lodge dining room, or you can enjoy a drink in the small bar or tea in the adjoining den. Many evenings include music and other entertainment before or during dinner. **Pros:** Warm, hospitable staff; diverse menu; year-round activities; rustic location. **Cons:** No TV/phone; not accessible by car in winters. ⊠*458 Brooks Lake Rd., 23 mi west of Dubois, 82513* ☎*307/455–2121* ⊕*www.brookslake.com* ⇩*7 rooms, 6 cabins* △*In-room: no a/c, no TV. In-hotel: restaurant, bar, gym, spa, no-smoking rooms, no elevator* ⊟*AE, MC, V* ⊺⊙⊺*FAP.*

$$$

Absaroka Ranch. Surrounded by mountains, this ranch with four comfortable cabins offers traditional activities such as horseback riding, hiking, fishing, and relaxing. Five Mile Creek runs right through the property, which is 16 mi west of Dubois. There are special programs for children, and you can take an overnight pack trip deep into mountain country. The ranch takes weeklong bookings only in July and August, and there's a three-night minimum in June and September. **Pros:** Lots of activities in ideal wilderness location; professional staff; comfortable cabins. **Cons:** 16 mi to town; minimum stays; no TV or a/c. ⊠*306 Dunoir, off U.S. 26/287, 82513* ☎*307/455–2275* ⊕*www.absarokaranch.com* ⇩*4 cabins* △*In-room: no a/c, no TV. In-hotel: children's programs (ages 8–12), no-smoking rooms, no elevator* ⊟*No credit cards* ⊗*Closed mid-Sept.–mid-June* ⊺⊙⊺*FAP.*

$$$

T Cross Ranch. At this traditional guest ranch in an isolated valley 15 mi north of Dubois, the eight cozy cabins have porches with rocking chairs, fireplaces or woodstoves, and handmade log furniture. You can snuggle under a down quilt by night and spend your days riding horses. Hosts Ken and Garey Neal have been in the guest-ranch business for decades, and they know how to match people to horses. Weeklong and three-night stays are available. **Pros:** A genuine dude ranch, surrounded by the beautiful Shoshone National Forest with a focus on horses, hiking, backpacking and fishing. **Cons:** Tennis players and golfers should book elsewhere. Those wishing to vacation closer to Yellowstone and Grand Teton national parks might find themselves too far and on the wrong side of the mountains here. ⊠*15 mi north of Dubois off Horse Creek Rd., 82513* ☎*307/455–2206 or 877/827–6770* 🖷*307/455–2720* ⊕*www.tcross.com* ⇩*8 cabins* △*In-room: no* *a/c, no phone, no TV. In-hotel: children's programs (ages 6 and up), laundry facilities, no-smoking rooms, no elevator* ☰*No credit cards* ⊘*Closed mid-Sept.–mid-June* ⦶*FAP.*

¢–$$ ⊡**Longhorn RV & Motel.** Recently remodeled, this family-owned lodging has cabins and a small camping area/RV park in a cottonwood grove. It's 2 mi east of Dubois, with a view of the painted badlands. **Pros:** Good shade and trees; long pull throughs. **Cons:** Some sites still rough from remodel; Wi-fi signal varies. ⊠*5810 U.S. 26, 82513* ☎*307/455–2337 or 877/489–2337* ⊕*www.duboislonghornrvresort.com* ⇌*22 rooms, 51 RV sites, 10 tent sites* ♿*In-room: Wi-Fi. In-hotel: laundry facilities, no-smoking rooms, some pets allowed* ☰*D, MC, V.*

¢–$ ⊡**Stagecoach Motor Inn.** This locally owned downtown motel has a large backyard with a picnic area and playground equipment, and there's even a reproduction stagecoach for kids to climb on. But the play area is bordered by Pretty Horse Creek, so young children need some supervision. Some rooms have full kitchens; others have refrigerators only. **Pros:** Walking distance to town; pool; friendly staff; pets. **Cons:** Might not satisfy all the high-tech needs of a business traveler. ⊠*103 E. Ramshorn Ave., 82513* ☎*307/455–2303 or 800/455–5090* ⊟*307/455–3903* ⇌*50 rooms, 4 suites* ♿*In-room: kitchen (some), refrigerator (some). In-hotel: pool, laundry facilities, airport shuttle, some pets allowed, no-smoking rooms, no elevator* ☰*AE, D, MC, V.*

SHOPPING

Fodor'sChoice From leather couches to handmade lamps, painted hides, and lodge-
★ pole-pine and aspen furniture, you can furnish your home with the Western-style items sold at **Absaroka Western Designs & Tannery** (⊠*1414 Warm Springs Dr.* ☎*307/455–2440* ⊕*www.absarokawesterndesign. com*). The sounds of Native American music set the tone at **Stewart's Trapline Gallery & Indian Trading Post** (⊠*120 E. Ramshorn Ave.* ☎*307/455–2800*). You'll find original oil paintings, old-pawn silver Native American jewelry, Navajo rugs, katsina dolls, Zuni fetishes, and high-quality Plains Indian artwork.

NORTHWEST WYOMING ESSENTIALS

To research prices, get advice from other travelers, and book travel arrangements, visit www.fodors.com.

AIR TRAVEL

CARRIERS

American, Delta Connection, and United Airlines/United Express provide multiple flights to Jackson daily, with connections in Chicago, Denver, and Salt Lake City. Scheduled jet service increases during the ski season. United flies between Denver and Riverton.

Airlines & Contacts **American Airlines** (☎*800/433–7300* ⊕*www.aa.com*). **Great Lakes Aviation** (☎*307/587–7683 or 800/554–5111* ⊕*www.greatlakesav.com*). **Delta** (☎*800/221–1212* ⊕*www.delta-air.com*). **United Airlines/United Express** (☎*800/241–6522* ⊕*www.united.com*).

AIRPORTS

The major airports in the region are Jackson Hole Airport, about 10 mi north of Jackson in Grand Teton National Park and nearly 50 mi south of Yellowstone National Park. Riverton Airport in Riverton is 30 mi northeast of Lander and about 76 mi southeast of Dubois.

Many lodgings have free shuttle-bus service to and from Jackson Hole Airport. Superior Ride, Alltrans, and Jackson Hole Transportation are shuttle services that serve the Jackson Hole Airport. If you're coming into the area from the Salt Lake City or Idaho Falls airport, you can travel to Jackson and back on a Jackson Hole Express shuttle for about $140 round-trip.

Airport Information **Jackson Hole Airport** (⊠ *1250 E. Airport Rd., Jackson Hole* ☎ *307/733–7682*). **Riverton Regional Airport** (⊠ *4800 Airport Rd., Riverton* ☎ *307/856–1307* ⊕ *www.flyriverton.com*).

Transfer Information **Alltrans** (☎ *307/733–3135 or 800/443–6133*). **Jackson Hole Express** (☎ *307/733–1719 or 800/652–9510*). **Superior Ride** (☎ *307/690–8005*).

BUS TRAVEL

During the ski season, START buses shuttle people between Jackson and the Jackson Hole Mountain Resort as well as Star Valley to the south. The fare is free around town, $3 one-way to Teton Village, and $1 along the Teton Village Road. Buses operate from 6 AM to 11 PM. In summer START buses are free, operating from 5:45 AM to 10:30 PM. They stop at more than 45 locations in Jackson. People with disabilities must make reservations 48 hours in advance for START buses.

The Targhee Express runs between Jackson and the Grand Targhee Ski and Summer Resort, with pickups at various lodging properties in Jackson and Teton Village. The cost is $35 per day, or you can buy a combination shuttle/Grand Targhee lift ticket for $73. Advance reservations are required. All Star Transportation runs a nightly shuttle bus between Jackson and Teton Village; the cost is $25 round-trip per person.

Bus Information **All Star Transportation** (☎ *307/733–2888*). **START** (☎ *307/733–4521*). **Targhee Express** (☎ *307/733–1719 or 800/652–9510*).

CAR RENTAL

If you didn't drive to Wyoming, rent a car once you arrive. The airports have major car-rental agencies, which offer four-wheel-drive vehicles and ski racks. Aspen Rent-A-Car, a local agency in Jackson, rents cars, full-size vans, and sport utility vehicles; another local agency in Jackson, Eagle Rent-A-Car, provides cars and package deals with sport utility vehicles and snowmobiles. Rent-A-Wreck, in Lander, rents used cars.

Contacts **Aspen Rent-A-Car** (⊠ *345 W. Broadway, Jackson* ☎ *307/733–9224*). **Avis** (⊠ *Jackson Hole Airport* ☎ *307/733–3422*). **Budget** (⊠ *Yellowstone Regional Airport* ☎ *307/587–6066 or 800/527–0700*). **Eagle Rent-A-Car** (⊠ *375 N. Cache Dr., Jackson* ☎ *307/739–9999 or 800/582–2128*). **Hertz** (⊠ *Jackson Hole Airport* ☎ *800/654–3131* ⊠ *Riverton Regional Airport* ☎ *307/856–2344*). **Rent-A-Wreck**

(⊠ *715 E. Main St., Lander* ☎ *307/332–9965*). **Thrifty** (⊠ *Jackson Hole Airport* ☎ *307/734–8312*).

CAR TRAVEL

Northwest Wyoming is well away from the interstates, so drivers make their way here on two-lane highways that are long on miles and scenery. To get to Jackson from I–80, take U.S. 191/189 north from Rock Springs for about 177 mi. From I–90, drive west from Sheridan on U.S. 14 or Alternate U.S. 14 to Cody. U.S. 14 continues west to Yellowstone National Park, and you can also hook up with U.S. 191, which leads south to Jackson.

Be extremely cautious when driving in winter; game crossings, white-outs, and ice on the roads are not uncommon. Contact the Wyoming Department of Transportation for road and travel reports. For emergency situations dial 911 or contact the Wyoming Highway Patrol.

Contacts Grand Teton Park Road Conditions (☎ *307/739–3682*). **Wyoming Department of Transportation** (☎ *307/777–4375 from outside Wyoming for road conditions, 888/WYO–ROAD or log on to* ⊕ *www.wyoroad.info*). **Wyoming Highway Patrol** (☎ *307/777–4301, 800/442–9090 for emergencies, #4357 [#HELP] from a cell phone for emergencies*).

EMERGENCIES

There are hospitals in Jackson and Riverton and clinics in most other towns throughout the region.

Ambulance or Police Emergencies (☎ *911*).

Hospitals & Clinics Grand Teton Medical Clinic (⊠ *Next to Jackson Lake Lodge* ☎ *307/543–2514 or 307/733–8002 after hours*). **Riverton Memorial Hospital** (⊠ *2100 West Sunset Dr., Riverton* ☎ *307/856–4161* ⊕ *www.riverton-hospital. com*). **St. John's Medical Center** (⊠ *625 E. Broadway, Jackson* ☎ *307/733–3636* ⊕ *www.tetonhospital.org*).

LODGING

APARTMENT & CABIN RENTALS

There are three reservations services for Jackson Hole.

Contacts Jackson Hole Central Reservations (☎ *888/838–6606* ⊕ *www. jacksonholewy.com*). **Jackson Hole Resort Lodging** (✎ *Box 510, Teton Village 83025* ☎ *800/443–8613* ⊕ *www.jhrl.com*). **Mountain Property Management** (⊠ *250 Veronica La., Box 2228, Jackson 83001* ☎ *800/992–9948* 🖶 *307/739–1686* ⊕ *www.mpmjh.com*).

CAMPING

There are numerous campgrounds within Grand Teton National Park and Bridger-Teton, Shoshone, and Targhee national forests (Targhee National Forest borders Grand Teton National Park on the west; most of the forest lies within Idaho). Few of these campgrounds accept reservations. Campgrounds in the national forests tend to fill up more slowly than those in Grand Teton.

Reservations can be made for a small number of national-forest campgrounds near Jackson through U.S. Forest Reservations.

Contacts **Bridger-Teton National Forest** (☎ *307/739–5500*). **Grand Teton National Park** (☎ *307/739–3300*). **Targhee National Forest** (☎ *208/524–7500*). **U.S. Forest Service Recreation Reservations** (☎ *800/280–2267*).

SAFETY

You can encounter a grizzly bear, mountain lion, wolf, or other wild animal anywhere in the Yellowstone ecosystem, which encompasses the mountains and valleys around Pinedale, Dubois, Jackson, and both Grand Teton and Yellowstone national parks. If you plan on hiking on backcountry trails, be sure to carry bear repellent, make noise, and travel with a companion. Check with forest or park rangers for other tips to protect yourself. (There are different tactics, depending on the animal species.) Always let someone know where you are going and when you plan to return.

Take particular care with female animals, particularly moose and bear, with young by their side. These animal mothers are fiercely protective of their offspring. Buffalo can and do charge visitors every year. The best safety rule with all animals is to give them plenty of space.

SPORTS & THE OUTDOORS

FISHING

To fish in Wyoming you must obtain a fishing license, usually available at sporting-goods stores; you can also request a license through the Wyoming Game and Fish Department.

The Wind River Indian Reservation has some of the best fishing in the Rockies. A separate license is required here. Contact Shoshone and Arapaho Tribes.

Contacts **Shoshone and Arapaho Tribes** (✉ *Fish and Game Dept., 1 Washakie, Fort Washakie 82520* ☎ *307/332–7207*). **Wyoming Game and Fish Department** (✉ *360 N. Cache Dr., Box 67, Jackson 83001* ☎ *307/733–2321* ⊕ *http://gf.state. wy.us/*).

SKIING

For up-to-date information on ski conditions and snowfall at the Jackson Hole Mountain Resort, contact the number below or visit the Web site.

Information **Snow report** (☎ *888/DEEP–SNO* ⊕ *www.mountainweather.com*). Boarders and skiers can view updated snow and avalanche reports, including Web cams, for all area ski resorts, plus lots more.

TOURS

Information For leisurely appreciation of the area, try a multiday covered-wagon and horseback trip with Teton Wagon Train and Horse Adventure. Wild West Jeep Tours has naturalist guides who will show you the backcountry.

Teton Wagon Train and Horse Adventure (⌂ *Box 10307, Jackson 83002* ☎ *888/734–6101* ⊕ *www.tetonwagontrain.com*). **Wild West Jeep Tours** (⌂ *Box 7506, Jackson 83002* ☎ *307/733–9036* ⊕ *www.wildwestjeeptours.com/wyomingtours.htm*).

VISITOR INFORMATION

Dubois Chamber of Commerce (⌂ *Box 632, Dubois 82513* ☎ *307/455–2556* 🖷 *307/455–3168* ⊕ *www.duboiswyoming.org*). **Grand Teton National Park** (⌂ *Drawer 170, Moose 83012* ☎ *307/739–3300* ⊕ *www.nps.gov/grte*). **Jackson Hole Chamber of Commerce** (✉ *990 W. Broadway, Box 550, Jackson 83001* ☎ *307/733–3316* 🖷 *307/733–5585* ⊕ *www.jacksonholechamber.com*). **Jackson Hole Mountain Resort** (⌂ *Box 290, Teton Village 83025* ☎ *307/733–2292 or 800/443–6931* 🖷 *307/733–2660* ⊕ *www.jacksonhole.com*). **Lander Chamber of Commerce** (✉ *160 N. 1st St., Lander 82520* ☎ *307/332–3892 or 800/433–0662* 🖷 *307/332–3893* ⊕ *www.landerchamber.org*). **Pinedale Chamber of Commerce** (✉ *32 E. Pine St., Box 176, Pinedale 82941* ☎ *307/367–2242* 🖷 *307/367–6830* ⊕ *www.pinedaleonline.com*).**Snow King Resort** (⌂ *Box SKI, Jackson 83001* ☎ *307/733–5200 or 800/552–KING* 🖷 *307/733–4086* ⊕ *www.snowking.com*).

Southwest Montana

BOZEMAN, HELENA, NORTH OF YELLOWSTONE

4

WORD OF MOUTH

"Don't rule out Helena for an overnight stay. Although it isn't a college town it's about half way between Glacier and Yellowstone along a much shorter route than Missoula is. . . . Helena has a beautifully restored capitol building, the state historical society museum with its Charlie Russell collection, and a picturesque downtown (don't miss the Parrot candy shop)."

—ternstail

"Bozeman—can't say enough about this delightful town. We LOVED it—the Museum of the Rockies is a MUST for kids—the dinosaur egg clutches are worth the ticket alone. Be sure to catch the film as it shows how they find and extract the dino bones."

—explorefamily

Updated by
Joyce Dalton &
Ray Sikorski

GLISTENING, GLACIATED, AND GRAND, THE Absarokas, Crazies, Gallatins, and other mountains send cooling summer winds to roil among the grasslands and forests of southwest Montana. This is a wild place inhabited by hundreds of animal species. Abundant wildlife is a daily sight, from the pronghorn sprinting across grasslands to the 17,000-strong northern elk herd in and north of Yellowstone National Park. Bald eagles and ospreys perch in tall snags along the rivers, watching for fish. Mules and white-tailed deer spring over fences (and across roads, so watch out when driving). Golden eagles hunt above hay fields. Riparian areas come alive in spring with ducks, geese, pelicans, and great blue herons. The south-central area known as Yellowstone Country shares the topography, wildlife, rivers, and recreational opportunities of its namesake national park.

> **TOP REASONS TO GO**
>
> ■ Fly-fishing the gorgeous Gallatin River.
>
> ■ For a scenic and exhilarating drive, the Beartooth Highway can't be topped.
>
> ■ State Capitol Building, Helena: From Charlie Russell's Lewis and Clark painting to the Goddess of Liberty crowning the copper dome, the capitol is a masterpiece inside and out.
>
> ■ The Museum of the Rockies houses the world's largest collection of dinosaur fossils.
>
> ■ Wilderness skiing at the remote Big Sky Ski Resort.

4

Critters outnumber people in southwest Montana, which should come as no surprise when you consider that some counties have fewer than one person per square mile. The region's ranches are measured in the thousands of acres, though they are bordered by ranchettes of fewer than 20 acres around the towns of Bozeman, Big Timber, Red Lodge, and Dillon. But even the most densely populated area, Yellowstone County, has only about 34 people per square mile. That leaves thousands of square miles in the region wide open for exploration. Hiking, fishing, mountain biking, and rock climbing are popular outdoor activities in summer, and in winter the thick pillows of snow make skiing and snowmobiling conditions near perfect.

Southwest Montana's human history reaches back only about 12,000 years, and the non–Native American presence dates back only 200 years. Yet this place is full of exciting tales and trails, from the path followed by the Lewis and Clark Expedition to the Bozeman and Nez Perce trails. To the west, in Montana's southwesternmost corner, is Gold West Country, which includes the gold-rush towns of Helena, Virginia City, and Bannack. Roadside historic signs along various routes in the region indicate the sites of battles, travels, and travails.

EXPLORING SOUTHWEST MONTANA

A private vehicle is far and away the best means of exploring southwest Montana, as it allows you to appreciate the grandeur of the area. Wide-open terrain affords startling vistas of mountains and prairies, where you're likely to see abundant wildlife. I–90 is the major east–west artery through the region; I–15 is the major north–south route. Most of the other routes here are paved and in good shape, but be prepared for gravel and dirt roads the farther off the beaten path you go. Driving through the mountains in winter can be challenging; a four-wheel-drive vehicle, available from most car-rental agencies, is best.

ABOUT THE RESTAURANTS
This is ranch country, so expect numerous Angus-steer steak houses. Many restaurants also serve bison meat and various vegetarian meals but few ethnic dishes. Restaurants here are decidedly casual: blue jeans, crisp shirts, and cowboy boots are dressy for the region.

ABOUT THE HOTELS
Lodging varies from national chain hotels to mom-and-pop motor inns. More and more guest ranches are inviting lodgers, historic hotels are being restored, and new bed-and-breakfasts are opening their doors. If you plan to visit in summer or during the ski season (December–mid-March), it's best to reserve rooms far in advance.

WHAT IT COSTS					
	¢	$	$$	$$$	$$$$
RESTAURANTS	under $7	$7–$11	$12–$16	$17–$22	over $22
HOTELS	under $70	$70–$110	$111–$160	$161–$220	over $220

Restaurant prices are for a main course at dinner. Hotel prices are for two people in a standard double room in high season, excluding service charges and a 7% bed tax.

TIMING
December through March is the best time to visit for skiers, snowboarders, snowshoers, and people who love winter. Summer draws even more visitors. That's not to say that southwest Montana gets crowded, but you may find more peace and quiet in spring and fall, when warm days and cool nights offer pleasant vacationing under the Big Sky.

Temperatures will drop below freezing in winter (and in fall and spring in the mountains) and jump into the 80s and 90s in summer. The weather can change quickly, particularly in the mountains and in the front range area north of Helena, and temperatures have been known to vary by as much as 70°F within a few hours, bringing winds, thunderstorms, and the like.

NORTH OF YELLOWSTONE

This mountainous stretch of land from the town of Red Lodge west to the resort region at Big Sky is mostly roadless, glaciated, and filled with craggy heights. Winter often refuses to give up its grasp on this high alpine region until late spring. Snowpack assures that streams feeding the mighty Yellowstone River will flow throughout the hot summer, satiating the wildlife, native plants, and numerous farms downstream.

MAKING THE MOST OF YOUR TIME

Southwest Montana encompasses a multitude of landscapes, from rolling plains and creek-carved coulees to massive mountain ranges and raging rivers fed by snowfields atop towering peaks. The region's beauty is best experienced at a leisurely pace—one that allows you to do some wildlife viewing, to spend an afternoon on the banks of a stunning stream, and to watch the slow descent of the sun as it drops behind ragged mountains.

Growing numbers of city-dwellers are immigrating to southwest Montana in search of their own slice of paradise. Fortunately, state and federal management of massive land holdings and the enduring strength of the ranch economy and lifestyle have kept development in check. Millions of acres of the region remain much as they have been for time immemorial.

For the best tour of southwest Montana, drive the unforgettable roadways that seem to reach the top of the world, make frequent stops in historic towns and parks. Drive up the Beartooth Pass from Red Lodge and, between late May and early October, hike along myriad trails right from the highway. Stop in Big Timber to sample small-town Western life, ride a white-water raft on the Stillwater River, or fly-fish the Yellowstone River with a knowledgeable outfitter. From Livingston, home to several museums, drive south into ever more beautiful countryside, through the Paradise Valley toward Yellowstone National Park. A float trip on this section of the Yellowstone, combined with a stay at Chico Hot Springs, is the stuff of which great memories are made.

In summer in Virginia City, Ennis, or Three Forks, return to gold-rush days along the historic streets or live for today with a fly rod in hand and a creel waiting to be filled beside you. Trail rides, float trips, steam trains—not to mention long walks in the long-gone footsteps of Lewis and Clark, Sacajawea, and a few thousand forgotten trappers, traders, cavalry soldiers, and Native Americans—all await you around these towns.

Bozeman, Big Sky, and the Gallatin Canyon are premier destinations in any season, with more than enough museums, galleries, historical sites, and scenic stops to fill your itinerary. Southwest Montana offers ample opportunities for outdoor recreation even when the snow flies. In places like Big Sky, Bridger Bowl, the Gallatin National Forest, and Moonlight Basin you can experience some of the best skiing and snowmobiling in America, and after a day on the slopes or the trails plunge into the hot springs in Bozeman, Butte, or Boulder.

In making the most of your time, pause to breathe in the air filtered through a few million pines, to listen to the sounds of nature all around, to feel the chill of a mountain stream or the welcome warmth of a thermal spring. Small moments like these stick with you and become the kind of memories that will beckon you back to this high, wide, and handsome land.

RED LODGE

> **WORD OF MOUTH**
>
> "We spent two nights in Red Lodge. I think it is worth at least a night after driving the Beartooth Highway. We enjoyed walking through the town, visiting the Beartooth Nature center and going to dinner and pig races at the Bear Creek Saloon."
>
> –wtm003

60 mi southwest of Billings via U.S. 212.

Nestled against the foot of the pine-draped Absaroka-Beartooth Wilderness and edged by the Limestone Palisades, this little burg is listed on the National Register of Historic Places and has become a full-blown resort town, complete with a ski area, trout fishing, access to backcountry hiking, horseback riding, and a golf course. Red Lodge was named for the Crow Indians' custom of marking their tepee lodges with paintings of red earth. It became a town in the late 1880s, when the Northern Pacific Railroad laid tracks here to take coal back to Billings. One of Red Lodge's most colorful characters from this time was former sheriff "Liver Eatin'" Jeremiah Johnson, the subject of much Western lore and an eponymous movie starring Robert Redford. This Area is a favored stop-over for motorcyclists and others heading over the Beartooth Highway to Yellowstone National Park. Free brochures for self-guided historical walking tours of the town and driving tours of the county are available at the Chamber and the museum.

The folks in Red Lodge, all 2,300 of them, relish festivals. For a complete list and exact dates, contact the **Red Lodge Area Chamber of Commerce** ✉*601 N. Broadway, 59068* 📫 *Box 988* ☎*406/446–1718 or 888/281–0625* 🌐*www.redlodge.com.*

Each August the **Festival of Nations** (🌐*www.festivalofnations.us*) celebrates the varied heritages of early settlers, many of whom migrated to work in now-defunct coal mines. The weekend festival includes ethnic music, food, and dance.

From kindergartners to seniors, fiddlers of all ages head for Red Lodge each July to compete in the two-day **Montana State Old-Time Fiddlers Contest** 🌐*www.montanafiddlers.org.*

For 10 days in July, the fur trade/mountain man era lives again during **Rendezvous at Red Lodge** (🌐*www.redlodge.com/rendezvous*). Participants from around the country set up tents, don period dress, and trade tools, beads, and other items at this historical reenactment.

When the snow flies in late February, the annual **Winter Carnival** (🌐*www.redlodgemountain.com*) draws skiers, snowboarders, and other fans of the cold to three days of events such as the zany Classic Cardboard Downhill Race with construction materials limited to cardboard, glue, and tape. Other events include kids activities, and live music.

The **Beartooth Nature Center** provides a home for more than 70 injured or orphaned mammals and raptors, including bears, mountain lions, bobcats, wolves, and golden eagles. ✉*615 2nd Ave. E, 59068* ☎*406/446–*

1133 ⊕*www.beartoothnaturecenter.org* ⊠*$6* ⊙*June–Oct., daily 10–5; Nov.–May, daily 10–2.*

In addition to memorabilia that once belonged to rodeo greats, the Ridin' Greenoughs and Bill Linderman, the **Carbon County Historical Society Museum** houses a historic gun collection, simulated coal and hard rock mines, and Crow Indian and Liver Eatin' Johnson exhibits. ⊠*224 N. Broadway, 59068* ☎*406/446–3667* ⊕*www.carboncounty history.com* ⊠*$3* ⊙*Late May–early Sept., Mon.–Sat. 10–5; Sept.– May, Tues.–Sat. 11–3.*

OFF THE BEATEN PATH

A bar and a museum may seem an unlikely pairing, but Shirley Smith, owner of the **Little Cowboy Bar & Museum** (⊠*105 W. River St., Fromberg, 20-mi east on Hwy. 308, then 19-mi north on Hwy. 72, 59029* ☎*406/668–9502* ⊠*Free*), makes it work. A rodeo enthusiast and lover of local lore, Smith has packed the one-room museum with rodeo memorabilia and objects ranging from projectile points to bottled beetles.

SPORTS & THE OUTDOORS

DOWNHILL SKIING ⊙

There are 84 ski trails on 1,600 acres at **Red Lodge Mountain Resort** (⊠*305 Ski Run Rd., 59068* ☎*406/446–2610 or 800/444–8977* ⊕*www.red lodgemountain.com*). The family-friendly resort has a 2,400-foot vertical drop, a large beginner area, plenty of groomed intermediate terrain, and 30 acres of extreme chute skiing. Slopes are accessed by two high-speed quads, one triple, and four double chairs. Lift tickets are $46. The season runs late November–early April.

FISHING

Montana Trout Scout (⊠*213 W. 9th St., 59068* ☎*406/855–3058* ⊕*www. montanatroutscout.com*) conducts fly-fishing float trips and wade fishing on local streams and rivers such as the Yellowstone, Clark's Fork, Stillwater, and Rock Creek.

GOLF

The surrounding mountains form a backdrop for the 18-hole, par 72 **Red Lodge Mountain Golf Course** (⊠*828 Upper Continental Dr., 59068* ☎*406/446–3344 or 800/444–8977*).

HORSEBACK RIDING ⊙

With **Whispering Winds Horse Adventures** (⊠*55 Ladvala Rd., Roberts, 59070* ☎*406/671–6836*) enjoy riding lessons in the ranch's arena or daytime or sunset trail rides among rolling hills. Lunch or dinner are optional. A half-day Family Fun program customizes the riding experience. ⚠*Reservations required.*

NORDIC SKIING

At the **Red Lodge Nordic Ski Center,** escape to the solitude of forests along 14½ km (9 mi) of groomed trails at the base of the Beartooth Mountains. You also can experience on- and off-trail backcountry skiing and snowboarding. Trails are maintained by volunteers, and there is no lodge. ✛*1 mi from town on Hwy. 78, then 2 mi west on Fox Trail* ☎*406/446–1771* ⊕*www.beartoothtrails.org* ⊙*Dec.–Mar.*

WHITE-WATER RAFTING

The Stillwater River's foaming white water flows from the Absaroka-Beartooth Wilderness, providing exhilarating rafting with **Adventure Whitewater** (⊠*310 W. 15th St., 59068* ☎*406/446–3061 or 800/897– 3061* ⊕*www.adventurewhitewater.com*).

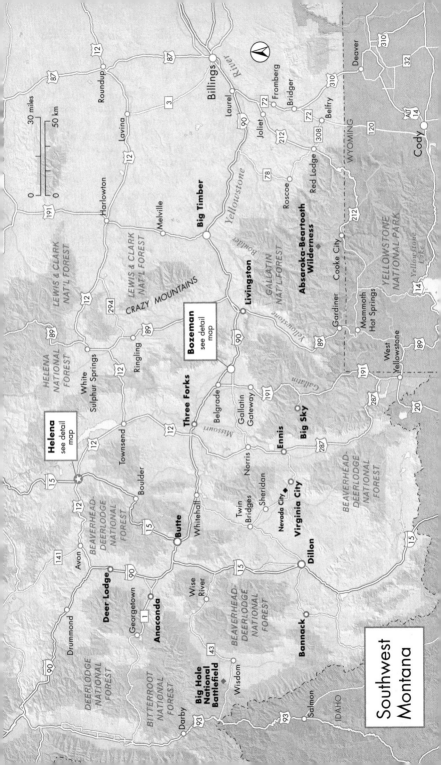

Southwest Montana

WHERE TO EAT

$$–$$$$ ✕**Bridge Creek Backcountry Kitchen & Wine Bar.** This restaurant's signature entrée is naturally raised Montana strip loin, dry-aged for 28 days to enhance flavor. Bridge Creek has an extensive wine list, occasional wine tastings, theme buffets in the off-season, and patio dining in summer. ✉*116 S. Broadway, 59068* ☎*406/446–9900* ⊕*www.eatfooddrinkwine. com* ▭*MC, V.*

$–$$$ ✕**Bogart's.** Not surprisingly, Bogie's photos and memorabilia cover the walls. But this casual eatery's most notable features are great Mexican food, margaritas, burgers, and specialty pizzas. ✉*11 S. Broadway, 59068* ☎*406/446–1784* ▭*MC, V.*

$–$$ ✕**Foster and Logan's Pub & Grill.** Multiple TVs, each tuned to a different sport, line the brick walls of this friendly place. The bar claims 20 beers on tap, the better to enjoy what locals call the town's best hamburgers. In winter opt for buffalo chili. ✉*17 S. Broadway, 59068* ☎*406/446–9080* ▭*AE, D, MC, V.*

WHERE TO STAY

$$–$$$ ▦**Gallagher's Irish Rose B&B.** A large stone fireplace serves as the focal point of the living room, while gas or electric stoves or fireplace lend a cozy feel to each guestroom as do quilts and artwork, both by the owners. Baked apple pecan French toast with homemade syrup is a popular breakfast choice. Pros: Food products organically grown; easy walk to shops, galleries, and restaurants. Cons: Stairs pose a problem for some; no parking lot but street parking plentiful. ✉*302 S. Broadway, 59068* ⌂ *Box 1237* ☎*406/446–0303 or 877/446–0303* ⊕*www. irishrosehost.com* ⇆*3 rooms* ♿*In-room: no phone, DVD (some), no TV (some), Wi-Fi. In-hotel: no elevator* ▭*AE, D, MC, V* ⊗*Closed 3rd week Mar.–3rd week May; Dec. 1–28* ◍*BP.*

$$–$$$ ★ ▦**Pollard Hotel.** This 1893 landmark in the heart of Red Lodge's historic district has been restored to the charms of an earlier era, when the likes of Calamity Jane and Liver Eatin' Johnson frequented the hotel. Reproduction Victorian furniture give a fin de siècle feel, and handsome oak paneling adds a rich touch to some public rooms. The Pollard's restaurant ($$–$$$$) specializes in steaks, chops, duck, and fresh fish. Pros: Near most shops and attractions; sauna and hot tub welcome after a day on the ski slopes. Cons: Front desk staff often in office rather than visible. ✉*2 N. Broadway, 59068* ⌂*Box 650* ☎*406/446– 0001 or 800/765–5273* 📠*406/446–0002* ⊕*www.pollardhotel.com* ⇆*39 rooms* ♿*In-hotel: restaurant, gym* ▭*AE, D, MC, V* ◍*BP.*

$$ ▦**Rock Creek Resort.** A wooden bear's raised paw welcomes you to this 35-acre getaway, where a Southwestern motif decorates the wood, log, and stone lodge, cabin, and condos perched beside a babbling, boulder-strewn creek. Some of the rooms have hot tubs and/or fireplaces. A historic old cabin holds the wonderful Old Piney Dell restaurant ($$–$$$$), where the steaks, Wiener schnitzel, and Sunday brunch are especially popular. In summer the Kiva restaurant serves breakfast and lunch. Pros: Creek and woods make for pleasant surroundings; restaurant offers superb food and views. Cons: Lack of public transport necessitates a car; reception personnel could be friendlier. ✉*6380 U.S. 212 S, 5 mi south of Red Lodge, 59068* ☎*406/446–1111 or 800/667–*

1119 🖶*406/237–9851* ⊕*www.rockcreekresort.com* 🛏*38 rooms, 48 condos, 1 cabin* ⚭*In-room: kitchen (some), dial-up. In-hotel: 2 restaurants, bar, tennis courts, pool, laundry facilities, elevator in lodge only* ▤*AE, D, DC, MC, V* ¶◎¶*CP.*

CAMPING   🔺**Greenough Campground and Lake.** Pine trees, a small trout-stocked lake, and gentle hiking trails provide summer respite in Greenough, one of a dozen U.S. Forest Service campgrounds in the Red Lodge vicinity. There's fishing for kids in small shallow lake ⚭*Vault toilets, drinking water, fire grates, picnic tables* 🛏*18 sites* ✉*10½ mi south of Red Lodge on U.S. 212, then 1 mi west on Hwy. 421, 59068* 🖶*406/446–2103* ⊕*www.fs.fed.us/r1/custer* 🖉*Reservations essential* ▤*AE, D, MC, V only if reservations made through National Reservation Service* 🖶*877/444–6777* ⊕*www.recreation.gov* ◎*May–Sept.*

🅲   🔺**Red Lodge KOA.** With its heated pool, playground, trout-filled brook, and access to Rock Creek for fishing, this tidy campground is ideal for families. Sites are along the banks of small creeks and among shady willows and pine trees. ⚭*Pool, laundry facilities, flush toilets, full hookups, partial hookups (water), drinking water, showers, fire grates, picnic tables, food service, electricity, public telephone, play area, public Wi-Fi* 🛏*13 full hookups, 35 partial hookups, 20 tent sites; 6 cabins* ✉*7464 U.S. 212, 4 mi north of Red Lodge, 59068* 🖶*406/446–2364 (disconnected in winter) or 800/562–7540* ⊕*www.koa.com* 🖉*Reservations essential during July* ▤*AE, D, MC, V* ◎*Mid-May–Sept.*

NIGHTLIFE & THE ARTS

NIGHTLIFE   You can sit back with a beer and watch the Bearcreek Downs' Pig Races at the **Bearcreek Saloon & Steakhouse** (✉*108 W. Main St., 7 mi east of Red Lodge on Hwy. 308, Bearcreek, 59007* 🖶*406/446–3481*). Oinkers in numbered jerseys streak around an outdoor oval while patrons bet on their favorites; proceeds fund local scholarships. The races take place summer evenings at 7, Thursday through Sunday.

THE ARTS   Located in a 1889 train depot the **Carbon County Arts Guild & Depot Gal-**
★   **lery** (✉*11 W. 8th St., 59068* 🖶*406/446–1370* ⊕*www.carboncounty*
★   *depotgallery.org*) showcases paintings and sculptures by some 200 Western artists. The **Coleman Gallery and Studio** (✉*223 S. Broadway, 59068* 🖶*406/446–1228 or 800/726–2228* ⊕*www.colemangallery.biz*) features works by photographer Merv Coleman. Natural scenery and wildlife are his specialties. Internationally recognized painter Kevin Red Star, whose works draw on his Crow Indian heritage, displays his oils, acrylics, lithographs, and etchings at **Kevin Red Star Gallery** (✉*1 N. Broadway, 59068* 🖶*406/446–4646* ⊕*www.kevinredstar.com*). Red Star's works are in the permanent collections of the Smithsonian Institution, the Institute of American Indian Art, and the Pierre Cardin Collection in Paris. The **Red Lodge Clay Center** (✉*123 S. Broadway, 59068* 🖶*406/446–3993* ⊕*www.redlodgeclaycenter.com*) promotes local, regional, and national ceramic artists. Exhibits change monthly.

SHOPPING

You'll find high-end Western-style decor pieces, woven blankets and rugs, art, and jewelry at **Common Ground** (⊠ *3 N. Broadway, 59068* ☎ *406/446–2800* ⊕ *www.comngrndartgallery.com*). Pick up a paper bag and fill it from the bushel baskets overflowing with what once was called "penny candy" at the **Montana Candy Emporium** (⊠ *7 S. Broadway, 59068* ☎ *406/446–1119*).

Distinctive clothing, handmade jewelry, china, and gifts are just some of the offerings at **Twin Elk** (⊠ *6382 U.S. 212, 59068* ☎ *406/446–3121 or 877/894–6355*), at the Rock Creek Resort.

EN ROUTE

Fodor's Choice
★

Driving south from Red Lodge along the 68-mi **Beartooth Highway** (U.S. 212) will take you over the precipitous 11,000-foot **Beartooth Pass** as the road winds its way through lush alpine country to the "back door" of Yellowstone National Park in Wyoming. With multiple steep climbs and switchbacks, this officially designated All American Road was a feat of 1930s engineering. The highway is usually open from mid-May to mid-October, but snow can close it at any time of the year. Several hiking trails lead off the highway; for hiking maps and more information, contact the **Beartooth Ranger District** (☎ *406/446–2103*) in Red Lodge.

4

ABSAROKA-BEARTOOTH WILDERNESS

The two main access routes are 12 mi south of Red Lodge via Beartooth Hwy. and 10 mi west of Red Lodge via Rock Creek Rd.

Although millions of summer visitors swarm into Yellowstone National Park to the south, the Absaroka-Beartooth Wilderness is blissfully unpeopled year-round, except for dedicated backcountry travelers who come precisely for its emptiness. Unlike in Yellowstone, no paved roads lead into the wilderness area, although a four-wheel-drive vehicle is not essential for access. The wilderness encompasses Montana's highest mountains, including 12,799-foot Granite Peak; because of that, the prime hiking season (August) is relatively short. Many of the 640 high-mountain lakes may remain partially frozen even into August, especially in the high plateau region. Hikes are moderate to strenuous. Perhaps the most popular trails are those in the East Fork–Rosebud Creek area (35 mi one-way), where numerous lakes rest in alpine basins above 9,000 feet. Keep in mind that this is grizzly-bear country. You can get information and permits from Custer National Forest in Billings, or Gallatin National Forest in Bozeman.

For information on the western half of the wilderness, contact **Gallatin National Forest** (⊠ *Federal Bldg., 3017 Fallon St., Suite C, Bozeman, 59718* ☎ *406/522–2520* ⊕ *www.fs.fed.us/r1/gallatin*).

For information on the eastern half of the wilderness, contact **Custer National Forest** (⊠ *1310 Main St., Billings* ☎ *406/657–6200* ⊕ *www. fs.fed.us/r1/custer*).

SPORTS & THE OUTDOORS

Because the Beartooths are rugged and remote, it's best to get outfitted in Billings, Red Lodge, or another city before heading here. Climbing guides and horse-pack trail guides—recommended unless you are familiar with the backcountry—can lead trips to remarkable and scenic places, safely. Most important, know backcountry rules regarding travel in grizzly-bear country.

> **WORD OF MOUTH**
>
> "I go to Yellowstone frequently, but had never driven the Beartooth. Last summer I finally made it. I went out the Silvergate entrance and drove to Red Lodge and stayed overnight. Really enjoyed Red Lodge! From there I cut over northwest to meet Interstate 90, past Billings and down through the gorgeous Paradise Valley to Gardiner."
>
> – Dayle

HORSEBACK RIDING Ride the high alpine wilderness trails on one- to five-day pack trips with **Beartooth Plateau Outfitters** (✉ *819 Clear Creek Rd., 13 mi north of Red Lodge on U.S. 212, Roberts, 59070* ☎ *406/445–2293 or 800/253–8545* ⊕ *www.beartoothoutfitters.com*).

MOUNTAIN CLIMBING Experienced climbers from **Beartooth Mountain Guides** (✉ *Box 1985, 59068* ☎ *406/446–9874* ⊕ *www.beartoothmountainguides.com*) lead climbs to the top of Montana's tallest mountain, the challenging 12,799-foot Granite Peak. They also offer one-day and multiday backpacking trips devoted to rock climbing, alpine and ski mountaineering, and ice climbing for beginners and experts.

BIG TIMBER & THE BOULDER RIVER

88 mi northwest of Red Lodge via Hwy. 78 north and I–90 west; 81 mi west of Billings via I–90.

People come to Big Timber for its small-town (population 1,600) Western ambience, to fly-fish the blue-ribbon trout streams, float the Yellowstone River, or unwind in front of the Crazy Mountains (so called because a homesteader supposedly went crazy from living in such a remote setting). South of town you can follow the Boulder River in its mad dash out of the Absaroka-Beartooth Wilderness. This journey along Highway 298 will take you into wild country, with craggy peaks rising on either side of a lush, ranch-filled valley.

The **Sweet Grass Chamber of Commerce** (✉ *I–90, Exit 367, 59011* ☎ *406/ 932–5131* ⊕ *www.bigtimber.com*) can provide information about sightseeing in the region; of particular interest in the area are a prairiedog park and a natural bridge. ۞ *June–early Sept.*

Drop by the **Yellowstone River Trout Hatchery,** a five-minute drive from the town center, to view and learn about cutthroat trout. The best time to visit the hatchery is in spring, when you can see the fingerlings. ✉ *Fairgrounds Rd., 59011* ☎ *406/932–4434* 🎫 *Free* ۞ *Daily 8–5.*

A striking lodge-style building constructed with native stone and logs houses the **Crazy Mountain Museum**, with exhibits on Big Timber's history and people, as well as the Crazy Mountains. Highlights include the famous Cremer Rodeo, sheep and wool exhibits, and a room dedicated to pioneers that includes artifacts dating from the late 1890s. ⊠*2 Cemetery Rd., Exit 367 off I–90, 59011* ☎*406/932–5126* ⊕*www.bigtimber.com* ⊠*Donations accepted* ☉*Late May–early Sept., Tues.–Sun. 1–4:30 or by appointment.*

[⟳] The comical critters at **Greycliff Prairie Dog Town State Park** pop out of their underground homes, stand upright, sound their chirping alarms, and dash to another hole. Explorers Meriwether Lewis and William Clark referred to these "barking squirrels" in their journals. At this 98-acre protected habitat, you can catch the action from your car or wander the trails. Watch out for rattlesnakes. ⊠*I–90, Exit 377, Greycliff, 59033* ☎*406/247–2940* ⊕*www.fwp.state.mt.us* ⊠*$2 per vehicle; no charge for Montana license plate* ☉*Daily dawn–dusk.*

> **PAMPLONA PRIMER**
>
> The annual one-day **Running of the Sheep** (⊠*I–90, Exit 392, 25 mi west of Big Timber, Reed Point, 59069* ☎*406/326–2325*), held the Sunday of Labor Day weekend, celebrates the sturdy Montana-bred sheep and the state's agriculture history with humor. In addition to the sheep run (the sheep are let loose down the main street, sort of like the bulls in Pamplona, Spain, only a lot tamer), you can see a parade of antique cars, covered wagons, and a stagecoach (robbed, of course, by bandits on horseback).

At **Natural Bridge State Monument**, the Boulder River disappears underground, creating a natural bridge, then reappears as roaring falls in the Boulder River canyon. Hiking trails and interpretive signs explain how this geologic wonder occurred. The Main Boulder Ranger Station, a few miles past the bridge, is one of the oldest in the United States and is now an interpretative center. ⊠*Hwy. 298, 27 mi south of Big Timber* ☎*406/247–2940* ⊕*www.fs.fed.us/r1/gallatin/* ⊠*Free* ☉*Daily.*

SPORTS & THE OUTDOORS

FISHING You're likely to see white pelicans, bald eagles, white-tailed deer, and cutthroat trout on single- or multiday float and fishing trips on the Yellowstone River with **Big Timber Guides and Rollin' Boulder Outfitters** (⊠*529 E. Boulder Rd., last 6 mi on gravel, McLeod, 59052* ☎*406/932–4080* ⊕*www.finditlocal.com/bigtimber/flyfish.html*).

You can fish in a private lake or streams at the vast working cattle ranch, **Burns Ranch** (⊠*333 Swamp Creek Rd., 59011* ☎*406/932–4518* ☉*Apr.–Oct.*). The 40-acre Burns Lake, with rainbow, cutthroat, brown, and brook trout, is limited to a few anglers a day. This is a registered lake, so no license is necessary. The cost is $100 per rod, and reservations are required. The ranch is 4 mi north of Big Timber on U.S. 191 and then another 4 mi west on Swamp Creek Road.

HORSEBACK RIDING **Montana Bunkhouses Working Ranch Vacations LLC** is an organization of more than a dozen (and counting) ranches working cooperatively on the European agro-tourism model to give visitors a non-gussied-up ranching experience. At least seven are in the Big Timber area. Join the rancher in his daily tasks, take part in cattle drives, trail rideshead for the nearest trout stream, or just relax. Accommodations range from ranch houses to remote cabins to bunkhouses. *Box 693, Livingston 59047* ☎*406/222–6101* ⊕*www.montanaworkingranches.com.*

WHERE TO STAY & EAT

¢–$ ✕**Cole Drug.** Behind the historic brick-front facade of this pharmacy is an old-fashioned 1930s soda fountain, where friendly folks whip up Italian sodas, milk shakes, and the giant Big Timber, with nine scoops of ice cream and 12 toppings. ⊠*136 McLeod St., 59011* ☎*406/932– 5316 or 888/836–4146* ⊟*AE, D, MC, V* ☉*Closed Sun. No dinner.*

$$–$$$ 🏠**The Homestead Bed & Breakfast.** There's nothing rustic about this homestead. Situated in a tree-lined historical residential district, this 1903 house claims period furnishings throughout, a 52-inch TV for guests, and fireplaces in the parlor, library, music room, and one guest room. The original oak staircase leads to three of the guest rooms, each with private bath and individually controlled thermostat. Popular breakfast dishes include puffed pancakes filled with fresh fruit. During the winter, the Homestead hosts concerts sponsored by the local Jazz Society. Pros: Quiet neighborhood; most bathrooms are quite large. Cons: Town offers few dining options; no parking lot but street parking no problem. ⊠*614 McLeod St., 59011* *Box 466* ☎*406/932–3033* *4 rooms* *In hotel: no elevator* ⊟*MC, V* ❍*BP.*

¢–$ 🏠**Grand Hotel.** Fine dining and an 1890s saloon are two of the attrac-
★ tions of this classic Western hotel in downtown Big Timber. The attractive 1890 Room ($$–$$$$) serves steaks, seafood, and lamb for dinner, plus decadent desserts. For lunch, the 1890 Saloon claims to have served "cattlemen, cowboys, sheepherders, miners, railroad men and travelers" for more than 100 years. Guest rooms are small, clean, and comfortable with period furnishings—the kind of accommodations you might find over the Longbranch Saloon in *Gunsmoke*. Pros: Virtually shrieks once-grand Old West; restaurant decor and food still qualify as grand. Cons: Claw-foot tubs in hallway baths notwithstanding, the dearth of en suite facilities won't please all; on a given day the "chef's choice" breakfast might not coincide with "guest's choice." ⊠*139 McLeod St., 59011* *Box 1242* ☎*406/932–4459* 📠*406/932–4248* ⊕*www.thegrand-hotel.com* *11 rooms, 4 with bath* *In-room: no TV (some). In-hotel: restaurant, bar, no elevator* ⊟*D, MC, V* ❍*BP.*

CAMPING ⚠**Halfmoon Campground.** At the end of a dusty road leading into the lovely Crazy Mountains, this respite with tent or camper sites is ideal for scenic picnicking, hiking, and fishing. *Vault toilets, drinking water, fire grates (some), picnic tables, swimming in melted-snow creek (cold!)* *12 sites* ⊠*11 mi north of Big Timber on U.S. 191, then 12 mi west on Big Timber Canyon Rd., 59011* ☎*406/932–5155* ⊕*www. fs.fed.us/r1/gallatin* *Reservations not accepted* ⊟*No credit cards.*

⚠**West Boulder Campground and Cabin.** Shady and cool, this remote setting is known for good fishing, access to the Absaroka-Beartooth Wilderness, and quiet camping. The cabin has electricity, a woodstove, a refrigerator, and water in summer. Reservations, available through National Reservation Service (☎877/444–6777 ⊕*www.recreation. gov*), are essential for the cabin. ⚬ *Vault toilets, drinking water, fire pits, picnic tables* ⊠ *West Boulder Rd.; head 16 mi south of Big Timber on U.S. 298 to McLeod, 6½ mi southwest on Rd. 30, and 8 mi southwest on West Boulder Rd., 59052* ☎406/932–5155 ⊕*www.fs.fed.us/ r1/gallatin* 🛏️*10 tent sites; 1 cabin* ⚬*Reservations not accepted for campsites* ▤*No credit cards for campsites; AE, D, MC, V for cabin.*

NIGHTLIFE & THE ARTS

NIGHTLIFE The name may evoke unsavory images, but that doesn't stop fly-fishing anglers, ranchers, and curious tourists from filling the **Road Kill Cafe and Bar** (⊠*1557 Boulder Rd., U.S. 298, 15 mi south of Big Timber, McLeod 59052* ☎406/932–6174). Beer, burgers, and Road Kill T-shirts are big sellers. Weekly movie nights are complete with popcorn.

THE ARTS **Raging Bull Antiques Mall** (⊠*38 McLeod St., 59011* ☎406/932–7777) is packed full of Western pieces, including many, such as a stuffed musk ox, that are quite unusual. If oxen aren't to your taste, consider chaps, spurs, saddles, or an antler chandelier.

LIVINGSTON & THE YELLOWSTONE RIVER

35 mi west of Big Timber via I–90, 116 mi west of Billings via I–90.

The stunning mountain backdrop to the town of Livingston was once Crow territory, and a chief called Arapooish said about it, "The Crow country is good country. The Great Spirit has put it in exactly the right place. When you are in it, you fare well; when you go out of it, you fare worse."

Livingston, along the banks of the beautiful Yellowstone River, was built to serve the railroad and white settlers brought. The railroad still runs through the town of just over 7,000, but now tourism and outdoor sports dominate the scene, and there are some 15 art galleries. Robert Redford chose the town, with its turn-of-the-20th-century flavor, to film parts of the movie *A River Runs Through It.*

Antique creels, fly rods, flies, and aquarium exhibits are among the displays at the Federation of Fly Fishers' **Fly Fishing Discovery Center,** housed in a former school. The museum–education center hosts year-round classes. ⊠*215 E. Lewis St., 59047* ☎406/222–9369 ⊕*www. fedflyfishers.org* 💲*$3* 🕐*June–Sept., Mon.–Sat. 10–6, Sun. noon–5; Oct.–May, weekdays 10–4.*

The 1902 **Livingston Depot Center in the Northern Pacific Depot** served as the gateway to Yellowstone for the park's first 25 years. It is now a museum with displays on Western and railroad history. ⊠*200 W. Park St., 59047* ☎406/222–2300 ⊕*www.livingstonmuseums.org* 💲*$3* 🕐*Late May–mid-Sept., Mon.–Sat. 9–5, Sun. 1–5.*

The **Yellowstone Gateway Museum,** on the north side of town in a turn-of-the-20th-century schoolhouse, holds an eclectic collection, including finds from a 10,000-year-old Native American dig site and a flag fragment associated with the Battle of the Little Bighorn. Outdoor displays include an old caboose, a sheep wagon, a stagecoach, and other pioneer memorabilia. ⊠ *118 W. Chinook St., 59047* ☎ *406/222–4184* 🖃 *$4* ⊙ *Late May–early Sept., daily 8–5; rest of Sept., Tues.–Sat. noon–4.*

Just south of Livingston and north of Yellowstone National Park, the **Yellowstone River** comes roaring down the Yellowstone Plateau and flows through Paradise Valley. Primitive public campsites (available on a first-come, first-served basis; for information contact Montana Fish, Wildlife and Parks Department at ☎ 406/247–2940) and fishing access sites can be found at various places along the river, which is especially popular for trout fishing, rafting, and canoeing. With snowcapped peaks, soaring eagles, and an abundance of wildlife, a float on this section of the Yellowstone is a lifetime experience. U.S. 89 follows the west bank of the river, and East River Road runs along the east side.

Since the 1920s cowboys and cowgirls have ridden and roped at the annual **Livingston Roundup Rodeo,** held at the Park County Fairgrounds. All members of the Professional Rodeo Cowboy Association (PRCA), participants descend on Livingston from around the United States. ⊠ *46 View Vista Dr., 59047* ☎ *406/222–0850 Livingston Chamber* ⊕ *www.livingston-chamber.com* 🖃 *$12* ⊙ *July 2–4, nightly at 8* PM.

Since the 1950s the **Wilsall Rodeo** (⊠ *U.S. 89 N, east on Clark St. past grain elevator to rodeo grounds, Wilsall 59086* ☎ *406/578–2371*) has been showcasing cowboy and cowgirl events in mid-June at this ranching community at the base of the Crazy Mountains 35 mi east of Livingston.

OFF THE
BEATEN
PATH

Paradise Valley Loop. A drive on this loop takes you along the spectacular Yellowstone River for a short way and then past historic churches, schoolhouses, hot springs, and expansive ranches, all behind the peaks of the Absaroka-Beartooth Wilderness. From Livingston head 3 mi south on U.S. 89, turn east onto East River Road, and follow it over the Yellowstone River and for 32 mi through the tiny towns of Pine Creek, Pray, Chico, and Emigrant. You'll eventually hit U.S. 89 again, where roadside historic markers detail early inhabitants' lives; follow it north to Livingston. ☎ *406/222–0850* ⊕ *www.livingston-chamber.com.*

SPORTS & THE OUTDOORS

The Yellowstone River and its tributary streams draw fly-fishers from around the globe to the blue-ribbon streams for Yellowstone cutthroat, brown, and rainbow trout. Hiking trails lead into remote accesses of surrounding peaks, often snowcapped through June.

BOATING With **River Source Outfitters** (⊠ *5237 Hwy. 89, 59047* ☎ *406/223–5134* ⊕ *www.riversourcerafting.com*) you can take multiday canoe trips on the Yellowstone or Marias rivers, half- or full-day whitewater (class II and III rapids) rafting trips, or kayak lessons and tours. Boaters eager to explore the Yellowstone River will find a one-stop shop at **Rubber Ducky River Rentals** (⊠ *15 Mt. Baldy Dr., 59047* ☎ *406/222–3746* ⊕ *www.riverservices.com*). Aside from guide and drop-off services, the store rents and sells boats and equipment, including its own line of rafts

Welcome to Fly-Fishing Heaven

Montana has the best rainbow, brown, and brook trout fishing in the country. This is the land of *"A River Runs Through It,"* the acclaimed Norman Maclean novel that most people know as a movie. Although the book was set in Missoula, the movie was filmed in the trout-fishing mecca of southwest Montana and the Gallatin River played the role of Maclean's beloved Big Blackfoot. Several rivers run through the region, notably the Madison, Gallatin, and Yellowstone (more or less parallel to one another flowing north of Yellowstone National Park), as well as the Big Hole River to the west. All are easily accessible from major roads, which means that in summer you might have to drive a ways to find a fishing hole to call your own.

If you're only a casual angler, all you'll really need is a basic rod and reel, some simple tackle (hooks, sinkers, floaters, and extra line) and a few worms, which can all be bought at most outfitting and sporting-goods stores for less than $40. Many non-fly-fishers use open-face reels with lightweight line and spinners, which makes for a nice fight when they connect with trout. If you would like to try your hand at the more elegant stylings of fly-fishing, hire a local guide. Not only will he show you the good fishing holes, but a knowledgeable outfitter can teach you how not to work waters into a froth. Many guide services will provide you with fly-fishing equipment for the day.

and kayaks. Guided rafting and kayaking trips down the Yellowstone, Gallatin, and Madison rivers are available from the **Yellowstone Raft Company** (⊠*406 Hwy. 89, Gardiner 59030* ☎*800/858–7781* ⊕*www.yellowstoneraft.com*). Be sure to make reservations for your trip in advance.

FISHING **George Anderson's Yellowstone Angler** (⊠*5256 U.S. 89 S, 59047* ☎*406/222–7130* ⊕*www.yellowstoneangler.com*) specializes in catch-and-release fly-fishing float trips on the Yellowstone River, wade trips on spring creeks, access to private lakes, and fly-casting instruction.

The fishing experts at **Dan Bailey's Fly Shop** (⊠*209 W. Park St., 59047* ☎*406/222–1673 or 800/356–4052* ⊕*www.dan-bailey.com*) can help you find the right fly, tackle, and outdoor clothing. Rental equipment, fly-fishing clinics, and float and wade trips are also available at this world-renowned shop.

HORSEBACK **Bear Paw Outfitters** (⊠*136 Deep Creek Rd., 59047* ☎*406/222–6642* RIDING *or 406/222–5800*) runs day rides and pack trips in Paradise Valley, the Absaroka-Beartooth Wilderness, and Yellowstone National Park.

WHERE TO EAT

$–$$$ ╳**Montana's Rib & Chop House.** Here, in the middle of cattle country, you can expect the juiciest, most tender steaks—such as the flavorful hand-cut rib eye—all made from certified Angus beef. Jambalaya, baby back ribs, and catfish are also on the menu. ⊠*305 E. Park St., 59047* ☎*406/222–9200* ▤*AE, D, MC, V.*

¢–$ ✕**Paradise Valley Pop Stand & Grill.** You can dine in or order takeout from this 1950s-style burger and ice-cream joint. The ice cream is made locally. ⌧*5060 U.S. 89, 2 mi south of Livingston, 59047* ☎*406/222–2006* ⊟*MC, V.*

WHERE TO STAY

$$$$ ⊡**63 Ranch.** Owned by the same family since 1929, this 2,000-acre working cattle ranch is one of Montana's oldest dude ranches. Only weeklong packages are available, and they include a full range of activities, from horseback riding to fishing to helping check or move cattle. The rustic cabins are commodious yet comfortable, with log furniture and private baths. Pros: Guests describe the number of riding trails as inexhaustible; even cautious riders report feeling secure accompanied by wranglers. Cons: The 5,600-foot altitude might take some getting used to; no credit card policy equals loss of air miles. ⌧*Off Bruffey La., 12 mi southeast of Livingston* ⌕*Box 979, 59047* ☎*406/222–0570* 🖷*406/222–6363* ⊕*www.sixtythree.com* ➷*12 cabins* &*In-room: no a/c, no phone, no TV. In-hotel: no elevator, laundry facilities* ⊟*No credit cards* ⊙*Closed mid-Sept.–mid-June* ⦿*FAP.*

$$$$ ⊡**B Bar Ranch.** In winter this 9,000-acre working cattle ranch invites
★   guests for spectacular winter adventures in cross-country skiing and wildlife tracking. The ranch shares a 6-mi boundary with Yellowstone National Park, in Tom Miner Basin, 36 mi south of Livingston. Sleigh rides and naturalist-led trips into Yellowstone are some of the activities. Rates include meals and activities, and there's a two-night minimum stay. Pros: A rare chance to enjoy winter ranch activities; owners' strong commitment to ecology is evident. Cons: Ranch access involves travel on gravel roads. Pro or con: absence of phone and TV is a blessing or a curse. ⌧*818 Tom Miner Creek Rd., Emigrant 59027* ☎*406/848–7729* 🖷*406/848–7793* ⊕*www.bbar.com* ➷*6 cabins, 3 lodge rooms* &*In-room: no a/c, no phone, no TV. In-hotel: no elevator* ⊟*MC, V* ⊙*Mid-Dec.–Feb.* ⦿*FAP.*

$$$$ ⊡**Mountain Sky Guest Ranch.** This full-service guest-ranch resort in the middle of scenic Paradise Valley and 30 mi north of Yellowstone National Park is a family favorite. The cabins feel luxurious after a day in the saddle. The children's programs offer age-appropriate activities such as hiking, swimming, crafts, hayrides, campfires, and a talent show. Dinners range from Western barbecue to gourmet treats such as grilled lamb loin topped with fig-and-port-wine glaze. There's a seven-night minimum stay in summer only. Pros: Variety, preparation, and abundance of food win raves; fresh fruit delivered to cabins daily. Cons: 100% occupancy means 90 guests. ⌧*Big Creek Rd.; U.S. 89 S, then west 4½ mi on Big Creek Rd., Emigrant 59027* ⌕*Box 1219, Bozeman 59715* ☎*406/333–4911 or 800/548–3392* 🖷*406/333–4537* ⊕*www. mtnsky.com* ➷*30 cabins* &*In-room: no a/c, no phone, refrigerator, no TV. In-hotel: bar, tennis court, pool, no elevator, children's programs (ages 1–18), laundry facilities, airport shuttle, public Internet* ⊟*MC, V* ⦿*FAP.*

¢–$$ ⊡**Chico Hot Springs Resort & Day Spa.** The Chico Warm Springs Hotel
★   opened in 1900, drawing famous folks such as painter Charlie Russell (1864–1926) to the 96°F–103°F hop-spring pools. The hotel is sur-

4

rounded by two large outdoor soak pools, a convention center, and upscale cottages that open to views of 10,920-foot Emigrant Peak and the Absaroka-Beartooth Wilderness beyond. The dining room ($$$–$$$$) is considered among the region's best for quality of food, presentation, and service. Pine nut–encrusted halibut with fruit salsa and Gorgonzola filet mignon are among the biggest draws. Pros: Chef can't be beat; setting encourages closeness to nature. Cons: All guest rooms are not equal; not situated for dining around. ✉ *1 Old Chico Rd., Pray 59065* ☏*406/333–4933 or 800/468–9232* ✉*406/333–4694* ⊕*www.chicohotsprings.com* ↝*82 rooms, 4 suites, 16 cottages* ♿*In-room: no a/c (some), kitchen (some), refrigerator (some), no TV, dial-up. In-hotel: restaurant, room service, bar, pool, spa, no elevator, some pets allowed* ▭*AE, D, MC, V.*

$ 🏨**The Murray Hotel.** Even cowboys love soft pillows, which is why they come to this 1904 town centerpiece, whose floors have seen silver-tipped cowboy boots, fly-fishing waders, and the polished heels of Hollywood celebrities. Antiques reflect a different theme in each guest room. Ask to see the third-floor suite that film director Sam Peckinpah once called home. Historic photos, a player piano, and stuffed game animals decorate the lobby and surround the antique elevator, which is still in use. Pros: Easy stroll to shops and galleries; metal beds, claw-foot tubs, and pedestal sinks maintain period ambience. Cons: elevator requires an operator; some areas show their age. ✉ *201 W. Park St., 59047* ☏*406/222–1350* ✉*406/222–2752* ⊕*www.murrayhotel.com* ↝*30 rooms* ♿*In-room: dial-up. In-hotel: bar* ▭*AE, D, MC, V.*

CAMPING ⛺**Paradise Valley/Livingston KOA.** Set among willows, cottonwoods, and small evergreens, this full-service campground is well situated along the banks of the Yellowstone River, 40 mi north of Yellowstone National Park. It's popular with families, who enjoy the heated pool. It's a good idea to reserve ahead. ♿*Laundry facilities, flush toilets, full hookups, dump station, drinking water, showers, fire grates, picnic tables, electricity, public telephone, general store, swimming (indoor pool)* ↝*82 RV sites, 27 tent sites; 22 cabins, 2 cottages* ✉*163 Pine Creek Rd.; 10 mi south of Livingston on U.S. 89, then ½ mi east on Pine Creek Rd., 59047* ☏*406/222–0992 or 800/562–2805* ⊕*www.livingstonkoa.com* ▭*D, MC, V* ☾*May–mid-Oct.*

⛺**Pine Creek Campground.** A thick growth of pine trees surrounds this Paradise Valley campground at the base of the mountains. It's near the trailhead for challenging hikes to Pine Creek Waterfalls and the Absaroka-Beartooth Wilderness. There's live music on weekends. ♿*Toilets, drinking water, fire pits, picnic tables, playground* ↝*26 sites* ✉*9 mi south of Livingston on U.S. 89, then 2.5 mi east on Pine Creek Rd., 59047* ☏*406/222–1892 or 877/444–6777 (latter is National Reservation Service)* ⊕*www.fs.fed.us/r1/gallatin* ▭*AE, MC, V (cards through National Reservation Service only)* ☾*Late May–early Sept.*

NIGHTLIFE & THE ARTS

NIGHTLIFE With dancing and country music, microbrews, video poker, and keno, the **Buffalo Jump Steakhouse & Saloon** (✉*5237 U.S. 89 S, 59047* ☏*406/222–2987*) has livened up many a Saturday night in Livingston.

Locals voted the jukebox at the **Murray Bar** (⊠*201 W. Park St., 59047* ☎*406/222–6433* ⊕*www.themurraybar.com*) the best in town and its staff the friendliest. There's live music most weekends. Friday and Saturday evenings June through August, the **Pine Creek Cafe** (⊠*2496 E. River Rd., 59047* ☎*406/222–3628*) serves up live bluegrass music, barbecue burgers, and beer under the stars. The fun starts at 7.

THE ARTS Livingston's beauty has inspired artists, as evidenced by the many fine-
★ art galleries in town. Subtle, moody images by renowned artist Russell Chatham line the walls of **Chatham Fine Art** (⊠*120 N. Main St., 59047* ☎*406/222–1566* ⊕*www.russellchatham.com*). Works on display include oils, lithographs, drawings, and posters. The **Danforth Gallery** (⊠*106 N. Main St., 59047* ☎*406/222–6510*) is a community art center that displays and sells paintings, sculptures, and jewelry. **Visions West Gallery** (⊠*108 S. Main St., 59047* ☎*406/222–0337* ⊕*www.visions westgallery.com*) specializes in contemporary Western and wildlife art, including numerous works on the fly-fishing theme, from paintings and bronzes to hand-carved flies.

The historic district's **Blue Slipper Theatre** (⊠*113 E. Callender St., 59047* ☎*406/222–7720*) presents various full-length productions, including one-act plays, popular melodramas, and an annual Christmas variety show. The **Firehouse 5 Playhouse** (⊠*Sleeping Giant Trade Center, 5237 U.S. 89 S, 59047* ☎*406/222–1420*) stages comedies, dramas, and musicals year-round.

SHOPPING

★ At **the Cowboy Connection** (⊠*110 S. Main St., 59047* ☎*406/222–0272*) you'll find two rooms filled with pre-1940 Western boots, art, photos, spurs, holsters, even the occasional bullet-riddled hat. For contemporary Western and Native American items, such as fringed jackets and skirts, and rattlesnake earrings, visit **Gil's Indian Trading Post** (⊠*207 W. Park St., 59047* ☎*406/222–0112*). The floorboards creak as you walk through **Sax and Fryer** (⊠*109 W. Callender St., 59047* ☎*406/222–1421*), an old-time bookstore specializing in Western literature, especially books by Montana authors. It's the oldest store in Livingston.

In addition to selling outdoor clothing, boots, and bicycles, **Timber Trails** (⊠*309 W. Park St., 59047* ☎*406/222–9550*) helps mountain bikers, hikers, and cross-country skiers with trail maps, directions, and friendly advice.

THREE FORKS

51 mi west of Livingston via I–90, 29 mi west of Bozeman via I–90.

Although the scenery in Three Forks is striking, it's the historical sites that make this place worth a visit. Sacajawea (circa 1786–1812) traveled in the area with her Shoshone family before she was kidnapped as a child by a rival tribe, the Hidatsas. Five years later she returned here as part of the Lewis and Clark expedition. In 1805 they arrived at the forks (of the Madison, Jefferson, and Gallatin rivers), now in Missouri Headwaters State Park, looking for the river that would lead them to the Continental Divide. A plaque in the city park commemorates her contribution to the expedition's success.

★ The Madison, Jefferson, and Gallatin rivers come together to form the mighty Missouri River within **Missouri Headwaters State Park,** a National Historic Landmark. At 2,540 mi, the Missouri is the country's longest river, after the Mississippi. Lewis and Clark named the three forks after Secretary of the Treasury Albert Gallatin, Secretary of State James Madison, and President Thomas Jefferson. The park has historical exhibits, interpretive signs, picnic sites, hiking trails, and camping. ⊠*Trident Rd., 3 mi northeast of Three Forks on I–90, exit at Three Forks off-ramp, then go east on 205 and 3 mi north on 286, 59752* ☎*406/994–4042* ⊕*www.fwp.state.mt.us* ≋*$5 per vehicle, includes admission to Madison Buffalo Jump; free with Montana license plate* ⊙*Daily dawn–dusk.*

Within the **Madison Buffalo Jump** historic site is a cliff where Plains Indians stampeded bison to their deaths for more than 2,000 years, until European guns arrived in the West. An interpretive center explains how the technique enabled Native Americans to gather food and hides. Picnic areas provide a restful break from touring. Be on the lookout for rattlesnakes here, and avoid wandering off the paths. ⊠*Buffalo Jump Rd., 5 mi east of Three Forks on I–90, exiting at Logan, then 7 mi south on Buffalo Jump Rd., 59752* ☎*406/994–4042* ⊕*www.fwp. state.mt.us* ≋*$5 per vehicle, includes admission to Missouri Headwaters State Park; free with Montana license plate* ⊙*Daily dawn–dusk.*

⟳ The **Lewis and Clark Caverns,** Montana's oldest state park, hold some of the most beautiful underground landscapes in the nation. Two-hour tours lead through narrow passages and vaulted chambers past colorful, intriguingly varied limestone formations. The temperature stays in the 50s year-round; jackets and rubber-sole shoes are recommended. Note that the hike to the cavern entrance is mild. Each cave area is lighted during the tour, but it's still a good idea to bring a flashlight. A campground sits at the lower end of the park. ⊠*Hwy. 2, 19 mi west of Three Forks, 59752* ☎*406/287–3541* ≋*$10* ⊙*Mid-June–mid-Aug., daily 9–6:30; May–mid-June and mid-Aug.–Sept., daily 9–4:30.*

Thousands of local historical artifacts are on display in the **Headwaters Heritage Museum,** including a small anvil and all that is left of a trading post, Fort Three Forks, established in 1810. ⊠*Main and Cedar Sts., 59752* ☎*406/285–4778* ≋*Donations accepted* ⊙*June–Sept., Mon.–Sat. 9–5, Sun. 1–5; Oct.–May by appointment.*

SPORTS & THE OUTDOORS

BOATING In addition to arranging guided fly-fishing float trips, **Canoeing House and Guide Service** (⊠*11227 U.S. 287, 59752* ☎*406/285–3488*) rents canoes and kayaks.

WHERE TO STAY & EAT

¢–$ ✕**Wheat Montana.** At any of the Wheat Montana restaurants/stores around the state, you can enjoy tasty sandwiches, freshly baked bread, and pastries like gigantic cinnamon rolls. You can even purchase grind-your-own flour from several kinds of wheat, including Prairie Gold Whole Wheat and Bronze Chief Hard Red Spring Wheat. ✉ *10778 Hwy. 287, I–90 at Exit 274, 59752* ☎ *406/285–3614 or 800/535– 2798* ▤ *AE, MC, V* ⊙ *Daily 6* AM*–7* PM; *summer, 6* AM*–8* PM.

$ ⛉**Sacajawea Hotel.** The original portion of this hotel, built in 1910 by the Old Milwaukee Railroad, was rolled on logs from a site about a mile away to its current location, where it became a railroad hotel for travelers heading to Yellowstone National Park. The lofty lobby and cozy rooms retain their period style, and the front porch has rockers where you can relax and watch the sunset. The restaurant offers such selections as steaks, chops, meat loaf, and walleye at reasonable prices, and the bar serves lighter fare. Pros: A tourist attraction in its own right; the view's not much but love those rockers on the veranda. Cons: Town offers little in the way of shops or eateries; rambling hotel can seem a bit empty at times. ✉ *5 N. Main St., 59752* ☎ *406/285–6515 or 888/722–2529* 🖷 *406/285–4210* ⊕ *www.sacajaweahotel.com* 🛏 *30 rooms, 1 suite* ⛉ *In-room: dial-up. In-hotel: restaurant, bar, no elevator, some pets allowed* ▤ *AE, D, DC, MC, V* ⊙|*CP.*

CAMPING ⛺ **Missouri Headwaters State Park.** Tent sites are strewn among the cottonwood trees of the campground at this park. Three pavilions detail the Lewis and Clark adventure through the area. Be prepared for mosquitoes and rattlesnakes along the 4 mi of hiking trails. Reservations are taken only for groups. ⛉ *Flush toilets, pit toilets, drinking water, fire grates, picnic tables* 🛏 *23 sites* ✉ *Hwy. 286; 4 mi northeast of Three Forks on Hwy. 205, then north on Hwy. 286, 59752* ☎ *406/994–6934* ⊕ *www.fwp.state.mt.us* ▤ *No credit cards* ⊙ *May–Sept.*

BIG SKY & GALLATIN CANYON

75 mi southeast of Three Forks via I–90 and then U.S. 191; 43 mi southwest of Bozeman via I–90, then U.S. 191.

The name of Lone Peak, the mountain that looms over the isolated community beneath Big Sky, is a good way to describe **Big Sky Ski and Summer Resort,** one of the most remote major ski resorts in the country. Here you can ski a true wilderness. Yellowstone National Park is visible from the upper mountain ski runs, as are 11 mountain ranges in three states. The park's western entrance at West Yellowstone is about 50 mi away, along a route frequented by elk, moose, and bison (use caution when driving U.S. 191).

Conceived in the 1970s by national TV newscaster Chet Huntley, the resort area is the solitary node of civilization in otherwise undeveloped country, between Bozeman and West Yellowstone. Getting here invariably means at least one plane change en route to Bozeman and about an hour's drive to the resort through Gallatin Canyon, a narrow gorge of rock walls, forest, and the frothing Gallatin River.

This is not to suggest that Big Sky is primitive. Indeed, being just a few decades old and growing rapidly, the resort is quite modern in its design and amenities. You won't find crowds among all this rugged nature, but you will discover that all the perks of a major summer and ski vacation spot are readily available in Big Sky's three villages. One is in the Gallatin Canyon area along the Gallatin River and U.S. 191. Another, Meadow Village, radiates from the 18-hole Big Sky Golf Course. The third enclave, 9 mi west of U.S. 191, is the full-service ski resort itself, overlooking rugged wilderness areas and Yellowstone National Park.

Major real-estate developments around Big Sky have started to impinge upon the resort-in-the-wild atmosphere with exclusive developments such as Spanish Peaks and the gated Yellowstone Club. The latter claims Bill Gates among its homeowners and has its own ski mountain. Still, outdoor pleasures abound. In addition to skiing, golfing, hiking, horseback riding, and other activities, Big Sky hosts many festivals, musical events, races, and tournaments. ⊠*1 Lone Mountain Tr., Big Sky 59716* ⊕*Box 160001* ☎*406/995–5000 or 800/548–4486* ⊕*www.bigskyresort.com.*

A restored early-20th-century homestead and cattle ranch, **Historic Crail Ranch** makes a pleasant picnic spot in the midst of Big Sky's Meadow Village area. To get here drive west on Big Sky Spur Road, make a right on Little Coyote, go past the chapel, and make a left onto Spotted Elk Road in Meadow Village. ⊠*Spotted Elk Rd. 59716* ☎*406/995–2160* ⊕*www.bigskychamber.com* ✍*Free* ☉*Memorial Day–Labor Day, daily dawn–dusk.*

SPORTS & THE OUTDOORS

FISHING
Fodor'sChoice
★
Rivers such as the **Gallatin**, which runs along U.S. 191, the Madison (one valley west), and the Yellowstone (one valley east) have made southwest Montana famous among fly-fishers, most of whom visit during the nonwinter months.

East Slope Outdoors (⊠*47855 Gallatin Rd., U.S. 191, 59716* ☎*406/995– 4369 or 888/359–3974* ⊕*www.eastslopeoutdoors.com*) arranges guides for winter and summer fly-fishing. You can also rent or buy flies, rods and reels, clothing, and gifts here. Flies, rods and reels, clothing, equipment rentals, and guides are available at **Gallatin Riverguides** (⊠*47430 Gallatin Rd., U.S. 191, 59716* ☎*406/995–2290 or 888/707–1505* ⊕*www.montanaflyfishing.com*). **Wild Trout Outfitters** (⊠*47520 Gallatin Rd. (U.S. 191), 59716* ☎*406/995–2975 or 800/423–4742* ⊕*www. wildtroutoutfitters.com*) offers fly-fishing instruction, full-day horseback fishing trips, float tube fishing, and drift boat trips with stops for wade fishing at prime runs.

GOLF
The 18-hole Arnold Palmer–designed **Big Sky Golf Course** (⊠*Black Otter Rd., Meadow Village 59716* ☎*406/995–5780 or 800/548–4486*) has challenging holes along the fork of the Gallatin River, breezes from snowy Lone Peak, and the occasional moose, elk, or deer on the green.

HORSEBACK RIDING
☖
Jake's Horses & Outfitting (⊠*U.S. 191 and Beaver Creek Rd., 59716* ☎*406/995–4630 or 800/352–5956* ⊕*www.jakeshorses.com*) will take you on one- to six-hour rides along mountainous trails on Forest Service lands year-round. Summer dinner rides and multiday pack trips

inside Yellowstone National Park are also available. **Canyon Adventures** (✉ *47200 Gallatin Rd., U.S. 191, 59716* ☎ *406/995–4450 or 800/520–7533*) leads one- and two-hour trail rides May through September in the Gallatin Canyon. There's also a ride-and-raft combo.

KIDS'
ACTIVITIES
☺

The kids-only Outdoor Youth Adventures program at **Lone Mountain Ranch** (✉ *4 mi west of U.S. 191 on Lone Mountain Tr., Hwy. 64 and ½ mi down gravel ranch Rd., 59716* ☎ *406/995–4644 or 800/514–4644*) includes building snow caves, tubing, snowshoeing, playing snow kickball, and cross-country skiing over snowy trails and through obstacle courses. From June through August, **Camp Big Sky** (✉ *Box 161433* ☎ *406/995–3194*) runs a day camp for visiting and local kids ages prekindergarten through middle school. Activities such as tennis, dance, golf, nature study, and soccer are held at Big Sky Community Park in Meadow Village and at other sites.

RAFTING

Geyser Whitewater Expeditions (✉ *46651 Gallatin Rd., U.S. 191, 59730* ☎ *406/995–4989 or 800/914–9031*) has guided raft trips on the Gallatin River. **Montana Whitewater** (✉ *63960 Gallatin Rd., U.S. 191, 59730* ☎ *406/763–4465 or 800/799–4465* ⊕ *www.montanawhitewater.com*) arranges half- or full-day rafting trips on the Gallatin, Madison, and Yellowstone rivers. The company also offers paddle and saddle combos and a five-day teen kayaking school.

SNOW-
MOBILING

Far and away the most popular nonskiing activity in the region is snowmobiling into and around Yellowstone National Park. West Yellowstone, about 50 mi south of Big Sky on U.S. 191, prides itself on being the "Snowmobile Capital of the World." The most popular excursion is the 60-mi round-trip between West Yellowstone and Old Faithful. Recent attempts to ban snowmobiling in the park have ended up in court, but to date, the sleds are still allowed. **Canyon Adventures** (✉ *47100 Gallatin Rd., U.S. 191, 59716* ☎ *406/994–4450 or 800/520–7533*) arranges snowmobiling excursions.

SNOWSHOEING

You can rent snowshoes through **Big Sky Rentals** (✉ *Snowcrest Lodge, Plaza Area 59716* ☎ *406/995–5841*) for use on the resort's 2-mi Moose Tracks trail, which wends through aspen groves. Quiet and picturesque snowshoe trails lead through the woods and meadows of **Lone Mountain Ranch** (✉ *4 mi on Lone Mountain Tr., Hwy. 64, and ½ mi down gravel ranch road, 59716* ☎ *406/995–4644 or 800/514–4644*), where you can get a trail map and rent snowshoes and poles.

DOWNHILL SKIING & SNOWBOARDING

For many years, the attitude of more advanced skiers toward Big Sky was "big deal." There wasn't nearly enough challenging skiing to keep expert skiers interested for long, and certainly not for an entire ski week. As a remedy, the Big Sky people strung up the Challenger chairlift, one of the steepest in the country, and then installed a tram to the summit of Lone Peak, providing access to an array of steep chutes, open bowls, and at least one scary-steep couloir. The tram also gave Big Sky the right to claim the second-greatest vertical drop—4,350 feet—of any resort in the country.

CLOSE UP | Hitting the Slopes

It's called "cold smoke"—the exceedingly light, dry snow that falls on the mountains of southwest Montana—and it doesn't go to waste. All told, the region has six downhill ski areas and more than 390 km (245 mi) of cross-country trails. The season generally begins in late November or early December and runs through early to mid-April.

Downhill ski areas like Bridger Bowl, Discovery, Moonlight Basin, Maverick, and Red Lodge Mountain are family friendly, inexpensive, and relatively uncrowded. For steep skiers, one of the country's largest resorts, Big Sky, has more than 500 turns on a single slope; it's also a fine mountain for beginner and intermediate skiers.

The cross-country tracks of Lone Mountain Ranch stand out among the 40 or 50 trails in southwest Montana. They're groomed daily or weekly and are track-set for both classic and skate skiing. Backcountry skiing has no limits, with hundreds of thousands of skiable acres on public land.

None of that, however, has diminished Big Sky's otherwise easy-skiing reputation. There is still a good deal of intermediate and lower-intermediate terrain, a combination of wide-open bowl skiing higher up and trail skiing lower down. Additionally, there are 75 km (47 mi) of groomed cross-country skiing trails nearby at Lone Mountain Ranch.

The other plus about skiing Big Sky is its wide variety of exposures. Many of the ski areas here are built on north-facing slopes, where snow usually stays fresher longer, protected from the sun. In addition to these, Big Sky also has plenty of runs facing south and east, and the differing snow textures that result make for more interesting skiing.

FACILITIES 4,350-foot vertical drop; 3,812 skiable acres; 150 runs on 3 mountains; 17% beginner, 25% intermediate, 37% advanced, 21% expert; 1 aerial tram, 1 4-passenger gondola, 4 high-speed quads, 1 quad chair, 4 triple chairs, 6 double chairs, 3 surface lifts.

LESSONS & PROGRAMS Half-day group-lesson rates at the **ski school** (☎406/995–5000 or 800/548–4486) are $64. Powder, mogul, and snowboarding clinics are also available. There's also a ski school just for kids—whether they're first-timers or speedsters—with enthusiastic instructors.

LIFT TICKETS Lift tickets cost $75. Multiday tickets (up to 10 days) offer savings of up to $12 per day. Kids 10 and under ski free. The Lone Peak Pass lift ticket ($89) allows access to both Big Sky Resort and Moonlight Basin, which comprise the largest connected skiable terrain in the United States (5,500 acres).

RENTALS The resort's **Big Sky Ski Rentals** (☎406/995–5841) at the base of the mountain offers rental packages for $32, and high-performance ski packages for $48. At **Gallatin Alpine Sports** (✉3091 Pine Dr., Meadow Village 59716 ☎406/995–2313) rentals run $24 with discounts for multidays; performance skis are $30 and demos, $35.

MOONLIGHT BASIN

The Big Sky resort still dominates downhill skiing in the area, but don't overlook the resort at **Moonlight Basin** (⊠ *1020 Hwy. 64, 59716* ☎ *Box 160040* ☎ *406/993–6000 or 877/822–0430* ⊕ *www.moonlight basin.com*), with north-facing slopes overlooking the Lee Metcalf Wilderness Area. The runs here may not be as lengthy as they are next door at Big Sky, but Moonlight's 1,900 acres offer some unique knolls, chutes, and glades. Vertical drop is 4,150 feet, and runs are rated 23%

beginner, 41% intermediate, and 36% advanced. Lift tickets cost $51. Purchase of a Lone Peak Pass ($89) gives access to 5,500 connected skiable acres at both Moonlight and Big Sky. Lifts from each resort meet at the top.

NORDIC SKIING

★ **Lone Mountain Ranch** (☎ *406/995–4644 or 800/514–4644* ⊕ *www. lmranch.com*) is a rare bird in cross-country and snowshoeing circles. Not only are there 75 km (47 mi) of groomed trails, but the network is superb, with everything from a flat, open, golf-course layout to tree-lined trails with as much as 1,600 feet of elevation gain (and loss). Much of the trail network provides a genuine sense of woodsy mountain seclusion. If there is a drawback, it's that moose sometimes wander onto the trails.

WHERE TO EAT

$$$$ ✕ **Moonlight Dinners.** For a unique dining experience, rendezvous at the Summit Hotel in Mountain Village to ride a Sno-Cat into the pristine land of Big Sky for a meal under the stars. While the chef prepares French onion soup, filet mignon, garlic mashed potatoes, and chocolate fondue with fresh fruit on a woodstove, you can sled on hills under the light of the moon and tiki lamps or relax around a bonfire. Yurt dining is accompanied by live music and candlelight. ☎ *Box 160815, 59716* ☎ *406/995–3880* ☎ *Reservations essential* ☐ *MC, V* ☉ *Late Nov.–mid-Apr.*

$$–$$$$ ✕ **By Word of Mouth.** By day this café is filled with sunlight, and by night, with noise, particularly Friday nights, when the after-ski crowd gathers for an all-you-can-eat fish fry. The menu includes coriander-dusted Alaskan sockeye salmon with apricot, pine nut, and sun-dried tomato, and sugar-and-spice-rubbed baby back ribs. The wine list is lengthy, and there are several local beers on tap. ⊠ *2815 Aspen Dr., in Westfork Meadows, 59716* ☎ *406/995–2992* ⊕ *www.bigskycatering. com* ☐ *AE, D, MC, V.*

$$$ ✕ **Bugaboo Cafe.** This spacious café, possibly the best value in the area, serves contemporary fare, from breakfasts that feature a blue-crab omelet to dinners centered around rib eye, fish, and pork. On weekends brunch is set out from 7 AM to 2 PM. ⊠ *47995 Gallatin Rd., U.S. 191, 59716* ☎ *406/995–3350* ☐ *AE, D, MC, V* ☉ *Closed Mon. No dinner Sun.*

Westfork Meadows has several tasty eat-in or take-out spots. At **Wrap Shack** (☎406/995–3099) wraps start out the size of a pizza, and stuffed, aren't a whole lot smaller. Choose as many fillings as you can handle. **Hungry Moose** (☎406/995–3045) serves up deli sandwiches as well as basic grocery items. **Blue Moon Bakery** (☎406/995–2305) sets out a tempting array of scones, muffins, cakes, and cookies.

WHERE TO STAY

$$$$

Fodor'sChoice

★

☐ **The Big EZ.** Atop a mountain at a 7,500-foot elevation, the Big EZ lodge overlooks other mountains and the Gallatin River drainage. All guest rooms are appointed with Western-style furnishings, an eclectic collection of fine art, and flat-screen TVs. Guests are housed in the main lodge and the Inn (a separate structure); the suite is in its own little stone building. The property includes a wine cellar, an 18-hole, par-72 championship putting course, and one of the state's largest outdoor hot tubs. Dinners are unusual, elegant, and savory: try pan-roasted caribou loin or African pheasant, and save room for Tasmanian-honey crème brûlée. Pros: River rock fireplaces in guest rooms; massage room. Cons: not the easiest property to reach; not best choice for singles or those with disabilities. ☒7000 Beaver Creek Rd. ☎Box 160070, 59716 ☎406/995–7000 or 877/244–3299 ☎406/995–7007 ⊕www.bigezlodge.com ☞12 rooms, 1 suite ☐In-room: no a/c (some), dial-up. In-hotel: restaurant, bar, no elevator (Inn only), laundry service, concierge, airport shuttle ☐AE, MC, V ┤◯┤FAP.

$$$$

☐ **Lone Mountain Ranch.** Four-night to one-week packages include seasonal activities such as naturalist-guided trips to Yellowstone, cross-country ski lessons, downhill skiing, fishing on the Gallatin, Madison and Yellowstone rivers, and kids' camps. The ranch, known for its Nordic Ski Center, maintains 80 km (48 mi) of groomed trails for classic and skate cross-country skiing. An additional four trails totaling 10 km (6 mi) are for snowshoers only. Some activities cost extra, such as horse packing trips to alpine lakes. Lodging ranges from historic cabins to an elegant log lodge. Partake of a night of backcountry sleigh rides, dinner, and entertainment. Pros: Guests praise the cozy lodgings; wide variety of adventure and nature-oriented activities. Cons: Not a working ranch; accommodations range from old cabins to modern lodge. ☒4 mi on Lone Mountain Tr., and ½ mi down gravel ranch road ☎Box 160069, 59716 ☎406/995–4644 or 800/514–4644 ☎406/995–4670 ⊕www.lmranch.com ☞23 cabins, 7 rooms ☐In-room: no a/c, no phone, no TV. In-hotel: restaurant, bar, children's programs (ages 4–18), airport shuttle, no elevator ☐D, MC, V ☺Closed Oct., Nov., Apr., and May ┤◯┤FAP.

$$$–$$$$

Fodor'sChoice

★

☐ **Rainbow Ranch Lodge.** Lovely log-accented cabins and a fully updated 1919 log lodge perch alongside the Gallatin River. Fish from the riverbank or in the rainbow trout–stocked pond (catch and release). An outdoor fireplace stands beside the infinity hot tub. Animal and fishing motifs decorate the spacious guest rooms, which have wood-burning fireplaces (most), TVs discreetly hidden behind pictures, filtered water, lodgepole-pine beds, and down comforters. The exceptional restaurant ($$$$), decorated with Western paintings, has the state's largest collection of wines, 6,500 bottles, displayed in the Bacchus Room, where

4

groups of up to 14 can dine. Fresh fish is flown in daily. Among the game dishes are mesquite-grilled elk tenderloin and Gorgonzola-crusted bone-in buffalo rib eye. Pros: Guest room decks overlook the river; great use of wood, even in baths. Cons: Situated along highway rather than in resort area; only coffee, tea, and some pastries put out in morning. ⊠*42950 Gallatin Rd., U.S. 191, 59716* ☝*Box 160336* ☎*406/995–4132 or 800/937–4132* 🖷*406/995–2861* ⊕*www.rainbowranch.com* ↪*21 rooms, 3 cabins* ⌂*In-room: Wi-Fi. In-hotel: restaurant, bar* ▤*AE, D, MC, V* ⧀*CP.*

$$$–$$$$ 🏨 **Summit at Big Sky.** The rooms of this slope-side, full-service hotel
★ take in the full view of Lone Mountain and several ski runs. A Euro-Western flavor decorates the spacious rooms and suites, which are ideal for discriminating business travelers and families looking to be at the center of the mountain action. The best things about the Summit just may be the underground, heated parking garage, unusual in Montana, and the outdoor, year-round soaking pool. Pros: All the facilities one could wish; located near slopes, shops, and restaurants. Cons: Some miss the intimacy of smaller properties; attracts conventions. ⊠*1 Lone Mountain Tr., Mountain Village 59716* ☝*Box 160001* ☎*406/995–5000 or 800/548–4486* 🖷*406/995–8095* ⊕*www.bigskyresort.com* ↪*213 rooms, 8 suites* ⌂*In-room: kitchen, Wi-Fi. In-hotel: 2 restaurants, room service, bar, pool, gym, spa, bicycles, concierge, children's programs (ages 2–12), airport shuttle* ▤*AE, D, DC MC, V* ⧀*Mid-Apr.–late May and early Oct.–late Nov.* ⧀*FAP.*

CAMPING ⛺ **Greek Creek.** This Forest Service campground with tent sites snuggles up to the Gallatin River under a canopy of tall evergreens. ⌂*Vault toilets, drinking water, fire grates, picnic tables, swimming (river)* ↪*15 sites* ⊠*U.S. 191, 13 mi south of Bozeman* ☎*406/522–2520 or 877/444–6777 (latter is National Reservation Service)* ⊕*www.fs.fed.us/r1/gallatin* ▤*AE, D, MC, V (cards through National Reservation Service only)* ⧀*Early May–late Sept.*

NIGHTLIFE & THE ARTS

NIGHTLIFE Some weekends the **Corral** (⊠*42895 Gallatin Rd., U.S. 191, 59730* ☎*406/995–4249)* rocks to the house band. Other entertainment comes from quirky bartenders, pool-table bets, and legions of skiers, snowmobilers, and locals in for the Montana brews. With live music year-round on weekends the dance floor at **Half Moon Saloon** (⊠*45130 Gallatin Rd., U.S. 191, 59716* ☎*406/995–2928)* rivals the saloon's long bar, mountain views, and pool tables as a draw. There's live rock music at **Whiskey Jack's** (⊠*Mountain Mall, 1 Lone Mountain Tr., 59716* ☎*406/995–3999)*, where the dancing often spills out onto the deck for a boogie in ski boots.

THE ARTS Every July and August, the **Music in the Mountains** (⊠*Meadow Village*
★ *Pavilion, 59716* ☎*406/995–2742 or 877/995–2742)* summer concert series showcases such headliners as Taj Mahal, Willie Nelson, and the Bozeman Symphony Orchestra in outdoor venues. **Gallatin River Gallery** (⊠*50 Meadow Village Dr., Brewski Bldg., upper level, Meadow Village* ☎*406/995–2909)*, the only contemporary gallery in Big Sky,

showcases one-of-a-kind jewelry, paintings, sculptures, and photography from international, national, and local artists.

SHOPPING

Top-of-the-line ski and snowboard equipment and outerwear are sold at **Big Sky Sports** (⊠*Mountain Mall, 1 Lone Mountain Tr., 59716* ☎*406/995–5840*). Jewelry and women's and children's clothing, including ski wear, are among the offerings at **Willow Boutique** (⊠*Meadow Village 59716* ☎*406/995–4557*). Be sure to check out the fancy belts.

BOZEMAN

4

This recreation capital offers everything from trout fishing to whitewater river rafting to backcountry mountain biking to skiing. The arts have also flowered in Bozeman, the home of Montana State University. The mix of cowboys, professors, students, skiers, and celebrities make it one of the more diverse communities in the northern Rockies as well as one of the fastest-growing towns in Montana.

Bozeman has a strong Western heritage, readily evident at local museums, downtown galleries, and even the airport. In 1864 a trader named John Bozeman led his wagon train through this valley en route to the booming goldfields of Virginia City and southwest Montana. For several years this was the site of Fort Ellis, established to protect settlers making their way west along the Bozeman Trail, which extended into Montana Territory.

EXPLORING BOZEMAN

You can easily maneuver downtown Bozeman's mix of Old West bars, saddle shops, upscale stores and restaurants, and espresso cafés on foot or by bicycle. To appreciate the town's diversity, stroll the residential area near the university where mansions, bungalows, and every style in-between coexist side by side. A vehicle is necessary—in winter, a four-wheel-drive vehicle is best—to explore the parks, trails, and recreation areas in the mountain ranges surrounding Bozeman.

Free maps for self-guided historical walking tours are available at the **Bozeman Area Chamber of Commerce** (⊠*2000 Commerce Way, 59715* ☎*406/586–5421*) and at the Gallatin Pioneer Museum listed below.

TIMING This tour should take about three hours, including time for visiting the museums. Note that some of the downtown businesses close on Sunday. It's a good idea to carry a jacket around, even on warm days, in case of sudden changes in the weather.

THE MAIN ATTRACTIONS

❷ **Emerson Cultural Center.** A school until 1990, this 1918 Gothic Revival brick building now houses 37 galleries, studios, and classrooms, plus a performing-arts hall. You can watch craftspeople at work, purchase artwork, take a class, or catch a performance here, plus enjoy a tasty

Emerson Cultural
Center 2

Museum of the
Rockies 3

Pioneer
Museum 1

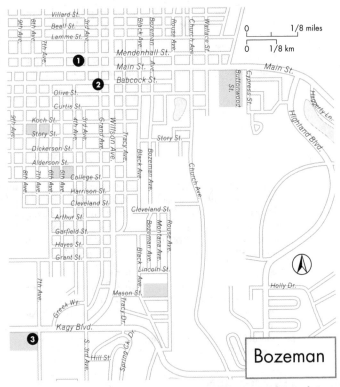

Bozeman

lunch or dinner at the on-site Emerson Grill. ⊠*111 S. Grand Ave.,
59715* ☎*406/587–9797, 406/586–5247 for Grill* ⊕*www.theemerson.
org* ⊠*Free* ⊘*Daily 10–5 and for scheduled evening performances.*

❸ Museum of the Rockies. Here you'll find a celebration of the history of the
Rockies region, with exhibits ranging from prehistory to pioneers, plus
Fodor'sChoice a planetarium with laser shows. Most renowned is the museum's Siebel
★ Dinosaur Complex housing one of the world's largest dinosaur fossil
collections along with the largest known T-rex skull, a Mesozoic Media
Center, and a Hall of Giants complete with sound effects. Children
love the hands-on science activities in the Martin Discovery Room and
the outdoors Tensley Homestead, with home-crafts demonstrations,
including butter churning, weaving, and blacksmithing. May through
mid-September, sheep, donkeys, and horses graze among the tall pasture grasses of the homestead. ⊠*600 W. Kagy Blvd., south end of university campus, 59718* ☎*406/994–3466* ⊕*www.museumoftherockies.
org* ⊠*$10 museum and planetarium combo, $5 planetarium laser
shows* ⊘*Mon.–Sat. 9–5, Sun. 12:30–5; daily 8–8 in summer.*

❶ Pioneer Museum. West of downtown, this redbrick former jail, built in
1911, serves as a reminder of the rough-and-tumble days of the past.
Inside, the Gallatin County Historical Society displays Native American artifacts, a model of Fort Ellis, a reconstruction of an 1870s log

cabin, a research library, photo archives, and a bookstore. ⊠ *317 W. Main St., 59715* ☎ *406/522-8122* ⊕ *www.pioneermuseum.org* ☑ *$3* ☉ *June–Sept., Mon.–Sat. 10–5; Oct.–May, Tues.–Fri. 11–4.*

ALSO WORTH SEEING

Bozeman Hot Springs. You can soak for an hour or a day at Bozeman Hot Springs, with nine indoor pools, one outdoor pool, a sauna, spa, gym, and juice bar. ⊠ *81123 Gallatin Rd., 5 mi west of Bozeman at Four Corners Junction of Huffine La. and U.S. 191, 59718* ☎ *406/586-6492* ☑ *$7.50* ☉ *Mon.–Thurs. 7 AM–10 PM, Fri. 7 AM–dusk, Sat. dusk–11 PM, Sun. 8 AM–10 PM.*

SPORTS & THE OUTDOORS

BICYCLING

Two Bozeman bike shops can supply all the equipment, repairs, and info that bike addicts might wish. **Bangtail Bicycle Shop** (⊠ *508 W. Main St., 59715* ☎ *406/587-4905*) is a full-service shop selling bikes and gear along with rentals and maps. The staff at **Summit Bike & Ski** (⊠ *26 S. Grand, 59715* ☎ *406/587-1064*) Sells bikes, supplies, maps, and biking guidebooks. They don't do rentals.

FISHING

The **Bozeman Angler** (⊠ *23 E. Main St., 59715* ☎ *406/587-9111*) sells fly rods and gear and arranges guided trips on several lakes, streams, and rivers, including the Gallatin, Madison, and Yellowstone rivers.

SKIING

Located 20 minutes from downtown Bozeman, **Bridger Bowl** (⊠ *15795 Bridger Canyon Rd., 59715* ☎ *406/587-2111 or 800/223-9609* ⊕ *www.bridgerbowl.com*) is known for skiing in "cold smoke," light, dry powder. The terrain, from steep, rocky chutes to gentle slopes and meadows, is the headline act at this city-owned mountain, where lift tickets ($43) are almost half the price of those at upscale resorts. One quad, four double, and two triple chair lifts access 71 named runs, which are ranked 25% beginner, 35% intermediate, and 40% advanced. The mountain is open early December–early April. Fresh powder on the mountain? Look for a flashing blue beacon atop the former Baxter Hotel on Main Street.

Bohart Ranch & Cross-Country Ski Center (⊠ *16621 Bridger Canyon Rd. 59715* ☎ *406/586-9070*) maintains 27 km (17 mi) of groomed trails on ranch and Forest Service permit land for classic and skate technique skiing. Lessons and rentals are available. The season runs December 1–April 1. In summer the trails are open for hiking, mountain biking, and horseback riding. There's also an 18-hole Frisbee golf course.

WHERE TO EAT

$$$–$$$$ ✗**Boodles.** With a wine list of 230 selections, including 20 by the glass, it's not surprising that this trendy spot has won the Wine Spectator Award of Excellence six years running. The kitchen attracts its own

share of attention with entrées such as grilled bison tenderloin medallions served with Montana huckleberry sauce. ⊠ *215 E. Main St., 59715* ☎ *406/587–2901* ⊟ *AE, D, MC, V.*

$–$$$$ ✕ **Montana Ale Works.** A cavernous brick building, the former Northern Pacific Railroad depot houses a brewery, a full bar, and a restaurant. In addition to the 37 beers on tap, the Ale Works serves bison

burgers, baked pasta dishes, Caribbean and Spanish dishes, and nightly specials such as fresh grilled yellowfin tuna and blue marlin. ⊠ *611 E. Main St., 59715* ☎ *406/587–7700* ⊟ *AE, D, MC, V* ☉ *No lunch.*

$–$$$ ✕ **Cafe International.** African batiks and masks decorate the walls of this popular eatery where a large selection of hot and cold salads and sandwiches greet the lunch crowd. For dinner the portobello-mushroom lobster soup and fillet Madagascar are big favorites. ⊠ *622 Mendenhall, 59715* ☎ *406/586–4242* ⊟ *AE, D, MC, V.*

$–$$$ ✕ **Cateye Café.** Some call it funky; all call it good food at a fair price.
★ Named for the shape of Grandma Annable's glasses, this small restaurant serves three meals a day, including a "Cat'serole" (the café's term) of the Day at lunch and honey-fried chicken and a seafood curry at dinner. ⊠ *23 N. Tracy St., 59715* ☎ *406/587–8844* ⊟ *MC, V.*

$–$$ ✕ **Western Café.** A deer head sporting sunglasses surveys the cowboys and families that pack the counter stools and tables at this down-home breakfast and lunch spot. Peruse the local paper as you work your way through biscuits and gravy, eggs with corned-beef hash, or pork chops. There's nothing fancy outside or in, but for local color, this is it. ⊠ *443 E. Main St., 59715* ☎ *406/587–0436* ⊟ *No credit cards* ☉ *No dinner.*

WHERE TO STAY

$$$$ ⊞ **Gallatin River Lodge.** On the property of a 350-acre ranch, this full-service, year-round fly-fishing lodge perches on the banks of the river for which it is named. Fly-fishing packages include a guide, 3 meals per day, airport transfers, and accommodations; a 3-day minimum applies for packages. The elegant country inn has six suites, with Mission-style furniture, Western art, Jacuzzi tubs, fireplaces, and views of the river. Pros: Owner is member of Trout Unlimited; lodge earns praise for matching guests with activities. Cons: Most opt for 3- to 7-night packages, so single night reservations scheduled only 2 weeks in advance. If fly-fishing isn't your thing, not the best choice. ⊠ *9105 Thorpe Rd., 59718* ☎ *406/388–0148 or 888/387–0148* ☐ *406/388–6766* ⊕ *www. grlodge.com* ⊅ *6 suites* ⚘ *In-room: no a/c, Wi-Fi. In-hotel: restaurant, bar, no elevator, airport shuttle* ⊟ *AE, MC, V* ⊚ *BP.*

$$–$$$ ⊞ **Gallatin Gateway Inn.** Back in 1927 the Milwaukee Railroad built this inn as a stopping-off point for visitors to Yellowstone National Park. Carved beams crisscross the 23-foot ceiling of the long, rectan-

gular lobby, and a modern, Western style decorates the guest rooms painted in soothing pastels. The bathrooms are fitted with original tile work and brass fixtures. Crisp white linens and candlelight set the formal tone in the restaurant ($$$–$$$$), which serves regional cuisine. Pros: Tile and brass uphold early-20th-century ambience; handicapped-accessible rooms. Cons: Staff could be a bit friendlier; long, somewhat sparse lobby doesn't invite relaxation. ⊠ *76405 Gallatin Rd., U.S. 191, Gallatin Gateway 59730* ☎ *406/763–4672 or 800/676–3522* ⊕ *www. gallatingatewayinn.com* ⬅ *33 rooms* ⬅ *In-hotel: restaurant, bar, tennis court, pool, public Wi-Fi* ⊟ *AE, MC, V* ⦿ *CP.*

$$–$$$ ⊞ **Hilton Garden Inn.** This comfortable property with a friendly staff is a 10-minute drive from downtown. Since the hotel attracts business travelers, guest rooms are equipped with additional phone lines, microwaves, and other extras. There is a sumptuous breakfast buffet (extra charge) with omelets made to order and room service from Old Chicago next door. Pros: Decor a step up from usual chain hotel look; staff helpful and pleasant. Cons: Located in busy mall area; no restaurant. ⊠ *2023 Commerce Way, 59715* ☎ *406/582–9900 or 877/782–9444* 🖷 *406/582–9903* ⊕ *www.bozeman.stayhgi.com* ⬅ *122 rooms* ⬅ *In-room: refrigerator, dial-up. In-hotel: room service, pool, gym, laundry facilities, public Wi-Fi* ⊟ *AE, D, DC, MC, V.*

$$–$$$ ⊞ **Lehrkind Mansion.** Built in 1897 for a wealthy master-brewer, this
Fodor'sChoice   B&B's gables, bays, and corner tower exemplify Queen Anne archi-
★   tecture. The current owners scoured antique stores in five states to find the perfect furniture, art, and decorative items, including a 7-foot tall Regina music box which plays 27" tin disks. Guest rooms have en suite bath. **Pros:** Grand oak staircase and carefully selected antique furnishings; proprietors happy to relate history of home. **Cons:** Opt for Garden House if stairs are a problem; breakfast at set time. ⊠ *719 N. Wallace Ave., 59715* ☎ *406/585–6932 or 800/992–6932* ⊕ *www. bozemanbedandbreakfast.com* ⬅ *9 rooms* ⬅ *In-room: no a/c, no TV. In-hotel: no elevator* ⊟ *AE, D, MC, V* ⦿ *BP.*

$–$$ ⊞ **Voss Inn.** This B&B occupies an elegant 1883 Victorian house and
★   is lavishly furnished with antiques and knickknacks. Four guest rooms have fireplaces. Guests enjoy afternoon tea in the parlor where they chat, watch TV, and share sightseeing info. Huge breakfasts are served in rooms or in the parlor. Pros: Fringed lamps and metal beds true to Victorian era; warming oven for morning coffee built into hallway radiator upstairs. Cons: Decor, such as dark flowered wallpaper, lends formal touch; only one guest room on first floor if stairs are a problem. ⊠ *319 S. Willson Ave., 59715* ☎ *406/587–0982* 🖷 *406/585–2964* ⊕ *www.bozeman-vossinn.com* ⬅ *6 rooms* ⬅ *In-room: no a/c (some), no TV. In-hotel: no elevator* ⊟ *AE, D, MC, V* ⦿ *BP.*

NIGHTLIFE & THE ARTS

NIGHTLIFE

A smoke-free downtown saloon, the **Rocking R Bar** (⊠ *211 E. Main St. 59715* ☎ *406/587–9355*) draws a young crowd with its classic-rock bands and original local acts, suds, and dancing. **The Filling Station,** affectionately dubbed the Filler by locals, (✉️*2005 N. Rouse, 59715* ☎️*406/587–0585*) features live music on weekends and often during the week, ranging from bluegrass to hip-hop. Ranchers and co-eds share the dance floor.

THE ARTS

The **Bozeman Symphony Society** (✉️*1822 W. Lincoln, Suite 3, 59715* ☎️*406/585–9774* ⊕*http://bozemansymphony.org*) runs a year-round concert series, often featuring talented university students and traveling artists. Performances take place at the Willson Auditorium, and there's one outdoor summer concert each year in Big Sky. During the summer months Shakespeare in the Parks performs several plays in repertoire. Most performances take place on the Montana State University campus. ✉️*354 Strand Union Bldg., MSU 59717* ☎️*406/994–1220* ⊕*www2.montana.edu/shakespeare/indexSIP.html* 🎫*Free.*

Chaparral Fine Art (✉️*24 W. Main St., 59715* ☎️*406/585–0029* ⊕*www.chaparralfineart.com*) specializes in contemporary impressionist works by local and national artists.

SHOPPING

The two levels of **Country Bookshelf** (✉️*28 W. Main St., 59715* ☎️*406/587–0166*) house a large Montana and Western section, including many autographed works, as well as more general offerings. Outdoor wear, cross-country skiing equipment, and boating gear are sold at **Northern Lights Trading Co.** (✉️*1716 W. Babcock St., 59715* ☎️*406/586–2225* ⊕*www.northernlightstrading.com*). Don't be surprised to see any of the helpful staff members out on the trails, tracks, or rivers beside you. **Schnee's Powderhorn Outfitters** (✉️*35 E. Main St., 59715* ☎️*406/587–7373* ⊕*www.schnees.com*), in business since 1946, sports two rooms filled with fishing gear and Western clothing.

HELENA

Montana's state capital is a city of 28,000, with 25 city parks, several museums, a thriving arts community, and its own minor-league baseball team. The southern part of the city, near the State Capitol Building and neighboring museums, mansions, and parks, is hilly and thick with lush greenery in summer. This quiet town started as a rowdy mining camp in 1864 and became a banking and commerce center in the Montana Territory. At the turn of the 20th century, Helena had more millionaires per capita than any other town in the country. Some of that wealth came from ground now occupied by Main Street: called Last Chance Gulch, it was the first of several gulches that yielded more than $15 million in gold during the late 1800s. With statehood came a fight between the towns of Anaconda and Helena over which would be the capital. In a notoriously corrupt campaign in which both sides bought votes, Helena won. The iron ball of urban renewal has since robbed the town of much of its history, but Helena still has ornate brick-and-granite historic buildings along Last Chance Gulch.

EXPLORING HELENA

The downtown historic area has a pedestrian-only mall on Last Chance Gulch with shops, coffeehouses, and restaurants. There are several historic sights here that you can see on foot, but other sights are spread out in the city and best accessed by automobile.

The **Helena Area Chamber of Commerce** (✉*225 Cruse Ave.* ☎*406/442–4120* 🌐*www.helenachamber.com*) near Helena's historic downtown can provide a brochure for a self-guided walking tour.

TIMING If you wish to hit all of the major sights in town, set aside an entire day for a walk. Plan on spending at least two hours strolling around the historic district and another two hours visiting the capitol, Montana Historical Society Museum, and the Governor's Mansion.

4

THE MAIN ATTRACTIONS

10 **Cathedral of St. Helena.** Modeled after the cathedral in Cologne, Germany, this Gothic Revival building has stained-glass windows from Bavaria and 230-foot-tall twin spires that are visible from most places in the city. Construction began in 1908 and was completed 16 years later. Note the white marble altars, statues of Carrara marble, and gold leaf decorating the sanctuary. Guided tours are available with one day's advance notice. ✉*530 N. Ewing St.* ☎*406/442–5825* *Donations accepted* *Daily 7–6.*

12 ★ **Exploration Works.** Rotating exhibits and interactive science displays—which can include a transparent anatomical woman or the dissection of sheep brains—are the main attractions at Helena's newest museum. ✉*995 Carousel Way* ☎*406/457–1800* 🌐*www.explorationworks.org* *$8 adults, $5.50 kids* *MC, V* *Tues. and Thurs.–Sat. 10–6, Wed. 10–8, Sun. noon–5.*

11 **Great Northern Carousel.** Hand-carved grizzly bears, mountain goats, bighorn sheep, and river otters gallop through the center of town on this carousel, open 363 days a year (closed Thanksgiving and Christmas). You can buy locally made premium ice cream and fudge here. ✉*989 Carousel Way* ☎*406/457–5353* 🌐*www.gncarousel.com* *$1.50* *Sun.–Thurs. 11:30–8, Fri. 11:30–9, and Sat. 10–9.*

3 **Last Chance Gulch.** Four down-and-out prospectors designated this spot their "last chance" after they'd followed played-out gold strikes across the West. Their perseverance paid off when they discovered the first of several gold deposits here, which propelled Helena to the ranks of Montana's leading gold producers. Many of the mansions and businesses that resulted from the discovery of gold still stand on this historic route, also known as Main Street.

7 **Montana Governor's Mansion.** Governors lived in this Victorian mansion between 1913 and 1959. You can take a scheduled guided tour, but call ahead, because some tours are unexpectedly canceled. ✉*304 N. Ewing St.* ☎*406/444–4789* 🌐*www.montanahistoricalsociety.org* *$4* *Tours May–Sept., Tues. and Sat. at noon, 1, 2, and 3. Oct.–Apr., Sat. noon–4.*

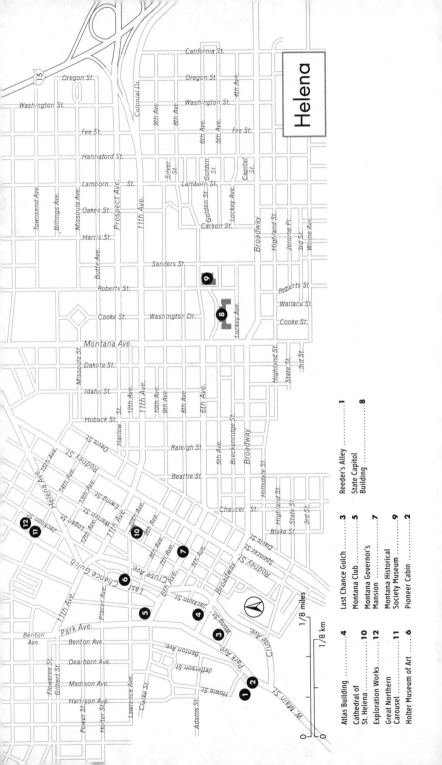

Helena

Atlas Building **4**	Last Chance Gulch **3**	Reeder's Alley **1**
Cathedral of	Montana Club **5**	State Capitol
St. Helena **10**	Montana Governor's	Building **8**
Exploration Works **12**	Mansion **7**	
Great Northern	Montana Historical	
Carousel **11**	Society Museum **9**	
Holter Museum of Art ... **6**	Pioneer Cabin **2**	

9 Montana Historical Society Museum. Highlights here include the MacKay Gallery, which displays one of the most important collections of Western artist Charlie Russell's work, and the Haynes Gallery, where early black-and-white photos of Yellowstone National Park taken by F. Jay Haynes are on display. The expansive Montana Homeland exhibit, which contains nearly 2,000 historical artifacts, documents, and photographs, takes a thorough look at Montana from the time of the first settlers to the present. The venue also hosts special events and family days in summer, including programs on folk music, Native American culture, and cowboys. Call ahead for information on upcoming events. Out in front of the Historical Society Museum, catch the **Last Chance Train Tour** (☎406/442–1023 or 888/423–1023) for an hour-long tour through historic neighborhoods of miners' mansions on the west side to the site where four miners made their first gold discovery on the gulch. Train tours cost $6 and take place Monday–Saturday at 11, 1, 3, and 5:30 in July and August, 11, 1, and 3 Memorial Day weekend–June 30, and 11 and 3 September 1–15. ✉225 N. Roberts St., across from state capitol ☎406/444–2694 or 800/243–9900 ⊕www. montanahistoricalsociety.org ☜$5 ⊙Memorial Day–Labor Day, Mon.–Sat. 9–5; Labor Day–Memorial Day, Tues.–Sat. 9–5.

2 Pioneer Cabin. This 1864 hand-hewn log structure now houses a museum of the gold-rush days of the 1860s. This is Helena's oldest extant home. ✉212 S. Park Ave. ☎406/449–6688 ⊕www.reeders alley.com ☜Donation ⊙Mid-May–mid-Sept., call for tour schedule; group tours available year-round by appointment.

1 Reeder's Alley. Miners' houses and distinctive shops built in the 1870s line this carefully restored area of old Helena along with restaurants and a visitor center. Note the stone pillars and wooden stringers of the Morelli Bridge, spanning a walking trail that leads to the Mount Helena Trail System. ✉Near south end of Last Chance Gulch.

8 State Capitol Building. The Greek Renaissance capitol is topped by a dome of Montana copper and holds Charlie Russell's largest painting, a 12-by-25-foot depiction of Lewis and Clark. Self-guided-tour booklets are available. This building was thought so beautiful, South Dakota modeled its capitol in Pierre on the same design. ✉6th Ave. and Montana Ave. ☎406/444–4789 or 800/243–9900 ☜Free ⊙May–Sept., Mon.–Sat. 9–3, Oct.–Apr., Sat. 10–2.

ALSO WORTH SEEING

4 Atlas Building. A statue of Atlas and two lizards and a salamander crown this recently restored 1887 neo-Romanesque building, home to the Upper Missouri Artists Gallery. ✉7 Last Chance Gulch ☎406/457–8240 or 800/457–8240 ☜Free ⊙Wed.–Sat. 10–5:30, Sun. 11–3.

6 Holter Museum of Art. Displays at this museum include folk art, crafts, photography, painting, and sculpture, with an emphasis on homegrown Montana artists. ✉12 E. Lawrence Ave. ☎406/442–6400 ⊕www. holtermuseum.org ☜Donations accepted ⊙Tues.–Fri. 10–5:30, Sat. 10–4:30, Sun. 11:30–4. Closed Mon.

⑤ The Montana Club. Built in 1905 by architect Cass Gilbert, who also designed the United States Supreme Court Building, the Montana Club was once the tallest building in the state. It's notable for its stone archways and contemporary I-beam construction underneath its classical facade. ⊠*24 W. 6th Ave., corner of Fuller* ☎*406/442–5980* ▨*Free.*

SPORTS & THE OUTDOORS

To stretch your legs, consider taking an hour-long hike to the top of Mt. Helena, which towers over the Last Chance Gulch pedestrian mall on the west edge of town. From the summit, you'll have panoramic views of the city, the Helena Valley, and the Rocky Mountains to the west.

BICYCLING

Old logging roads such as the MacDonald Pass area, 20 mi west of town on the Continental Divide, offer challenging mountain biking. Other trails closer to town, such as the Mount Helena Ridge Trail, the Birdseye Loop, and the Helena Valley Loop, lead to mining towns and thick forests.

To find out more about bike routes, check the Web site of the **Helena Bicycle Club** (⊕*www.helenabicycleclub.org*). The **Helena National Forest** (☎*406/449–5201*) can provide bike route information by phone.

BOATING

The more than 75 mi of shoreline of the **Canyon Ferry Recreation Area** (⊠*Hwy. 284, near Helena, Townsend* ☎*406/475–3310*) are a great place to fish, boat, sail, camp, and watch wildlife. The Missouri River once flowed freely here, though now a dam has created a lake. You can rent canoes, Jet Skis, and pontoon, fishing, and pedal boats from **Kim's Marina, RV Park and Store** (⊠*8015 Canyon Ferry Rd., 2 mi east of dam on Hwy. 284* ☎*406/475–3723*).

★ In their travels on the Missouri River, Lewis and Clark made note of towering limestone cliffs. **Gates of the Mountains** (⊠*Off I–15, 20 mi north of Helena* ☎*406/458–5241* ⊕*www.gatesofthemountains.com* ☉*Memorial Day–mid-Sept.*) boat tours take you past these same great stone walls, which rise 1,200 feet above the river.

FISHING

Western Rivers Outfitters (⊡*Box 772, East Helena 59635* ☎*406/227–5153*)offers day trips, overnight camping, and base-camp fishing excursions, and float trips on the Bitterroot, Blackfoot, Clark Fork, Missouri, Madison, Gallatin, and Jefferson rivers.

WHERE TO EAT

$$$$ ✕**The Caretaker's Cabin.** Located next to the Pioneer Cabin, the 1865-built Caretaker's Cabin is one of the oldest houses in Helena. The cabin was recently transformed into a cozy fine-dining restaurant, which offers a constantly changing menu of five-course, prix-fixe meals. These could include herbed rack of lamb, king crab legs, Greek shrimp, pork enchiladas, or New York strip teriyaki stir-fry, and they all feature local,

seasonal, and organic items as available. Price of the meals includes two appetizers, soup and salad du jour, dessert, and coffee or tea. Wine and beer is BYOB. ⊠*212 S. Park Ave.* ☎*406/449–6848* ⚎*Reservations essential* ⊟*No credit cards* ⊗*Closed Sun.–Tues. No lunch.*

$$$$ ✕**Last Chance Ranch.** An all-you-can-eat prime rib dinner follows a ★ wagon ride (included in the price). Dinner, served family-style at 7 PM in Montana's largest teepee, includes salads, potatoes, and huckleberry cheesecake, all accompanied by a singing cowboy. ⊠*Transportation from Helena to ranch, 8 mi southwest of town, is included in price* ☎*406/442–2884 or 800/505–2884* ⊕*www.lastchanceranch.biz* ⚎*Reservations essential* ⊟*MC, V* ⊗*Closed Oct.–May.*

$$–$$$$ ✕**On Broadway.** Wooden booths, discreet lighting, and brick walls contribute to the comfortable ambience at this Italian-fusion restaurant. Popular dishes include rib-eye steak and pasta puttanesca (sautéed Greek olives, artichoke hearts, red bell peppers, red onions, capers, and pine nuts tossed in linguine). When the state legislature is in session, representatives make this a boisterous place. ⊠*106 Broadway* ☎*406/443–1929* ⚎*Reservations not accepted* ⊟*AE, D, MC, V* ⊗*Closed Sun. N o lunch.*

$$$ ✕**Benny's Bistro.** An art deco–inspired interior fills out this small but spacious restaurant, which started out serving comfort food but branched into more exotic fare. It's known for its creamy tomato soup with fresh rosemary and its smoked-trout martini appetizer: local smoked trout with capers, cucumbers, baguette, and seasoned cream cheese, served in a martini glass. The bistro features live music, usually jazz, on Friday and Saturday at 7 PM. ⊠*108 E. 6th Ave.* ☎*406/443–0105* ⊟*AE, D, MC, V* ⊗*Closed Sun. No dinner Mon. and Tues.*

$$–$$$ ✕**Windbag Saloon & Grill.** This historic restaurant in the heart of down- ★ town was called Big Dorothy's until 1973, when a crusading county attorney forced Dorothy to shut down. Now it's a family restaurant, named for the political debates you're likely to hear while dining on burgers, quiche, salads, and sandwiches. It also has a large selection of imported beer, on tap and in bottles. A bounty of cherrywood give the place a warm, comfortable feel. ⊠*19 S. Last Chance Gulch* ☎*406/443–9669* ⊟*AE, D, MC, V* ⊗*Closed Sun.*

$ ✕**Toi's Thai.** Possibly the best Thai restaurant in Montana, the tiny Toi's ★ is always crowded. Every dish is hand-cooked by Thai native Toi Areya Tyler. Specialties include pad thai, panang—a beef curry dish—and green curries. ⊠*423 N. Last Chance Gulch* ☎*406/443–6636* ⚎*Reservations essential* ⊟*MC, V* ⊗*Closed Sun. and Mon.*

¢–$ ✕**The Staggering Ox.** The unique deli sandwiches here have even more unique, often political, names. Try the Capitol Complex (loaded with different deli meats and cheese), or the Nuke (ham, turkey, roast beef, and three cheeses). The "clubfoot" sandwiches are served on specialty breads shaped like a can of beans. Zany decor ranges from old records dangling from the ceiling to various artists' paintings. ⊠*Lundy Center, 400 Euclid St.* ☎*406/443–1729* ⊟*MC, V.*

WHERE TO STAY

$–$$$ 🏠 **Canyon Ferry Mansion.** Saved from inundation in 1954 when the Can-
★   yon Ferry Reservoir was created, this former cattle baron's home was
relocated to a premier perch above the lake. Antiques, many of which
are for sale, accent the frilly modern furnishings and lovingly restored
woodwork throughout the B&B. In addition to several private rooms,
there's a dorm-style bunkhouse that sleeps seven. Outdoorsy types
come here for summer water sports, winter ice boating, and year-round
fishing. Pros: Meticulously restored home; friendly host. Cons: Remote
location. ⊠*7408 U.S. 287, 30 mi southeast of Helena at mile marker
74, Townsend 59644* ☎*406/266–3599 or 877/933–7721* 🖷*406/266–
4003* ⊕*www.canyonferrymansion.com* 🛏*7 rooms, 3 with bath;
1 bunkhouse; 1 wheelchair-accessible cabin* ♿*In-room: Wi-Fi. In-
hotel: spa, beachfront, bicycles, concierge, no-smoking rooms, no ele-
vator* ☰*AE, D, MC, V* ⎟◯⎢*BP.*

$$ 🏠 **The Sanders Bed and Breakfast.** Colonel Wilbur Sanders, one of the first
Fodor'sChoice   senators of Montana, built this three-story Victorian mansion in 1875.
★   The colonel's rock collection is still in the front hall, and the B&B has
retained his furnishings. Most of the rooms overlook mountain-ringed
downtown Helena. Breakfasts are a work of art: Grand Marnier French
toast, orange soufflé, or gingerbread waffles. Pros: Incredibly accommodating hosts, first-class breakfasts, warm, relaxing atmosphere. Cons:
Dim reading light in room. ⊠*328 N. Ewing St., 59601* ☎*406/442–
3309* 🖷*406/443–2361* ⊕*www.sandersbb.com* 🛏*7 rooms* ♿*In-room:
Ethernet.* ☰*AE, MC, V* ⎟◯⎢*BP.*

CAMPING

⛺ **Cromwell-Dixon Campground.** High above Helena on MacDonald Pass
at 6,320 feet, this forested spot is frequented by migrating birds in
spring and fall. ♿*Pit toilets, drinking water, fire grates, picnic tables*
🛏*15 sites* ⊠*MacDonald Pass, U.S. 12* ☎*406/449–5490* ⊕*www.
fs.fed.us/r1/helena* ⊙*Early June–early Oct.*

NIGHTLIFE & THE ARTS

Late May through mid-September, live music plays in downtown parks
and plazas Wednesday evenings from 5 to 9 as part of the **Alive at Five**
(☎*406/447–1535* ⊕*www.downtownhelena.com*) series. The type of
music and the venues vary, but it's always free and good family fun.

In a remodeled historic stone jail, the **Myrna Loy Center for the Performing Arts** (⊠*15 N. Ewing St.* ☎*406/443–0287* ⊕*www.myrnaloycenter.
com*)—named after the Montana-born actress—hosts live performances by nationally and internationally recognized musicians and
dance troupes. Two theaters show foreign and independent films.

SHOPPING

★   Since 1951, many of the nation's best ceramic artists have come to
work in residency at the **Archie Bray Foundation** (⊠*2915 Country Club
Ave.* ☎*406/443–3502* ⊕*www.archiebray.org*). Wander near the five

antiquated, 8-foot-high, dome-shape brick kilns on a self-guided walking tour, and visit the gift shop, which sells work produced by foundation artists. It's open Monday–Saturday 10–5 and Sunday 1–5.

The **Made in Montana Store and Gallery** (⊠*21 N. Last Chance Gulch* ☎*406/442–3136 or 800/700–3136* ⊕*www.madeinmontanastore. com*) stocks a huge selection of Montana-made foods and gifts, including huckleberry and chokecherry treats, T-shirts, and books. There's also an Old West photo studio. A refreshing stop in the historic center of town, the independent **Montana Book and Toy Company** (⊠*331 N. Last Chance Gulch* ☎*406/443–0260* ⊕*www.mtbookco.com*) lines its shelves with regional and hard-to-find books, unique toys, games, and gifts.

4

⟳ For an old-fashioned sweet treat, pull up a stool at the **Parrot Confectionery** (⊠*42 N. Last Chance Gulch* ☎*406/442–1470*), a soda fountain and candy store built in the 1920s that sells everything from chocolate malts with homemade ice cream to hand-dipped chocolates and a regional favorite, a cherry phosphate.

THE SOUTHWEST CORNER

In Montana Territory days, the mineral wealth of this remote area drew hard-drinking miners, women of easy virtue, thieves, and the people who became rich on it all. Abundant winter snowfall coats the mountains and feeds the lush valleys, where ranching and forestry are the main industries and where remnants of the mining era abound.

DEER LODGE

60 mi southwest of Helena via U.S. 12 and I–90.

Deer Lodge, a quiet community of 3,400 residents, maintains a complex of history museums in and near its old penitentiary. Many locals make their living by ranching, which came to the 55-mi-long Deer Lodge Valley in 1862, when John Grant built the area's first cabin and began a cattle operation, selling beef to miners. Ranching remained the primary industry as the town of Deer Lodge developed. Its name derives from a 40-foot-high geothermal mound that used to emit steam from its top; Native Americans thought it resembled a large medicine lodge. The minerals and water attracted deer, and so the Native Americans named the place Deer Lodge. The mound is hidden behind trees and buildings at the Warm Springs State Hospital.

A single admission charge ($9) grants you access to the Old Montana Prison Museum, the Montana Auto Museum, the Frontier Montana Museum, and Yesterday's Playthings.

Built in 1871, the old Montana Territorial Prison did not shut down until 1979. It's now the **Old Montana Prison Museum,** where you can enter cells and learn about early Montana law. Also on display is the gallows tree taken from town to town in territorial days to hang convicted prisoners. ✉*1106 Main St.* ☎*406/846–3111* ⊕*www.pcmaf.org* 🖃*$9, includes admission to other 3 complex museums* ⊘*June–Aug., daily 8–8; Sept.–May, daily 9–5.*

The **Montana Auto Museum** is a car buff's delight. Displays include more than 150 vintage Mopars, Chevys, Fords, and Studebakers dating from 1903 to the 1970s, including such rarities as a 1928 REO Speedwagon. Admission here also grants you entrance to the Old Montana Prison Museum, the Frontier Montana Museum, and Yesterday's Playthings doll and toy museum. ✉*1106 Main St.* ☎*406/846–3111* ⊕*www. pcmaf.org* 🖃*$9, includes admission to other 3 complex museums* ⊘*Late May–early Sept., daily 8–8; early Sept.–Oct. and Apr.–late May, daily 9–5. Call for hrs rest of yr.*

The **Frontier Montana Museum** displays hats, saddles, spurs, chaps, and all things cowboy. Also here are Civil War items, Native American artifacts, and Desert John's Saloon, complete with whiskey memorabilia. Admission here also grants you entrance to the Old Montana Prison Museum, the Montana Automobile Museum, and Yesterday's Playthings doll and toy museum. ✉*1106 Main St.* ☎*406/846–0026* ⊕*www.pcmaf.org* 🖃*$9, includes admission to other 3 complex museums* ⊘*Mid-May–Sept., daily 10:30–5:30.*

Whimsical old toys inhabit **Yesterday's Playthings.** Admission here grants you access to the Montana Auto Museum, Frontier Montana Museum, and the Old Montana Prison Museum. ✉*1106 Main St.* ☎*406/846–1480* ⊕*www.pcmaf.org* 🖃*$9, includes admission to 3 other museums* ⊘*Mid-May–Sept., daily 10–6. Closed in winter.*

The **Powell County Museum** focuses on local history; it includes an antique gun collection, photographs, mining memorabilia, and a 1926 Model T Ford. ✉*1193 Main St.* ☎*406/846–1694* ⊕*www.pcmaf.org* 🖃*Free* ⊘*June–Sept., daily 11–6; closed in winter.*

⟳ Daily tours of the 1,600-acre **Grant-Kohrs Ranch National Historic Site,** a working cattle ranch run by the National Park Service, give insight into ranching life in the 1850s. You can learn about roping steers, watch blacksmith demonstrations, and bounce along on a hayride. The annual Grant-Kohrs Ranch Days, with demonstrations and kids' programs, takes place in mid-July. ✉*Grant Circle, ½ mi off I-90* ☎*406/846–2070* ⊕*www.nps.gov/grko* 🖃*Free* ⊘*June–Aug., daily 8–5:30; Sept.–May, daily 9–4:30.*

WHERE TO STAY & EAT

¢–$ ✕ **Yak Yak's.** Remember to save room for one of the 40 different milk shakes and malts at this Western-front eatery, which serves a bit of everything: breakfast items, burritos, cold and grilled sandwiches, salads, and baked potatoes. ✉*200 Main St.* ☎*406/846–1750* ⚠*Reservations not accepted* ⊘*Closed Sun.*

¢–$ 🏨 **Scharf's Motor Inn.** Directly across from the Old Montana Prison complex of museums, this nondescript, conveniently located motel offers a family-style restaurant (¢–$$) with no-nonsense fare such as ham and eggs, burgers, and chicken-fried steak. Pros: Near museums and town, playground for the kids, the price is right. Cons: Generic rooms. ⊠*819 N. Main St., 59722* ☎*406/846–2810* 🖷*406/846–3412* ⊕*www.scharfsmontana.com* ⇆*42 rooms, 1 9-person house* ⌂*In-room: Wi-Fi. In-hotel: no-smoking rooms, some pets allowed, no elevator* ⊟*AE, D, DC, MC, V.*

CAMPING ⚠ **Indian Creek Campground.** Set among brush and flats, this campground along tiny Indian Creek has large campsites, plus cable TV hookups and Wi-Fi. It's a good idea to make reservations. ⌂*Flush toilets, full hookups, drinking water, guest laundry, showers, picnic tables, electricity, public telephone, general store* ⇆*61 full hookups, 10 tent sites* ⊠*745 Maverick La.* ☎*406/846–3848 or 800/294–0726* ⊟*MC, V* ⊙*Mid-Apr.–Oct.*

ANACONDA

22 mi south of Deer Lodge via I–90.

Nicknamed the Smelter City, Anaconda is a window on the age of the copper barons, who ran this town in the 1880s through the 1950s. A number of sites preserve traces of Anaconda's rough-and-tumble history, including the dormant 585-foot smokestack, visible for miles, of the copper-smelting works around which the town was built. Copper is no longer the chief industry here, but even the Jack Nicklaus–designed golf course uses smelter-tailings slag for sand traps. Anaconda is also an ideal spot for fishing and hiking, and it sits at the base of the rugged Pintler Mountains, popular for cross-country skiing, downhill skiing, and backcountry adventures.

The **Anaconda Visitor Center,** in a replica railroad depot, displays memorabilia of the town's copper history. Here you can board a 1931 **Vintage Bus** for a tour of historic Anaconda. ⊠*306 E. Park Ave.* ☎*406/563–2400* ⊕*www.anacondamt.org* 🖼*Visitor center free, bus $7* ⊙*Visitor center weekdays 9–5, mid-May–mid-Sept., Sat. 9:30–4. Bus mid-May–mid-Sept., Mon.–Sat. at 10 and 2.*

The **Copper Village Museum and Arts Center** houses displays on the area's history along with local artwork. The center also hosts musical performances and special events. ⊠*401 E. Commercial St.* ☎*406/563–2422* 🖼*Free* ⊙*Tues.–Sat. 10–4.*

The classic art deco **Washoe Theatre** (⊠*305 Main St.* ☎*406/563–6161*), built in 1931, was ranked by the Smithsonian as the fifth-most-beautiful theater in the nation. Murals and ornamentation in silver, copper, and gold leaf are some of the highlights of this theater, which is open nightly for movies and other events.

At 585 feet tall, "the Stack" at **Anaconda Smoke Stack State Park** is a solid reminder of the important role the Anaconda Copper Company played in the area's development. Built in 1919, the stack, one of the tallest freestanding brick structures in the world, is listed on the National Register of Historic Places. Smelting operations ceased in 1980. There's a viewing and interpretive area with displays and historical information, but you cannot access the smokestack itself. ☒*Hwy. 1* ☎*406/542–5500* ⊕*http://fwp.mt.gov* ⊠*Free* ☉*Daily dawn–dusk.*

OFF THE BEATEN PATH

Anaconda-Pintler Wilderness. Overlapping three ranger districts of the Beaverhead-Deerlodge National Forest, the 159,000-acre Anaconda-Pintler wilderness area extends more than 30 mi along the Continental Divide to the southwest of Anaconda. Elevations range from 5,400 feet near the Bitterroot River to 10,793 feet at the summit of West Goat Peak. Glaciation formed many spectacular cirques, U-shape valleys, and glacial moraines in the foothills. The habitat supports mountain lions, deer, elk, moose, bears, and many smaller animals and birds. About 280 mi of Forest Service trails cross the area. If you hike or ride horseback along the Continental Divide, at times you can view the Mission Mountains to the northwest and the mountains marking the Idaho-Montana border to the southwest. If you want to explore the wilderness, you must obtain a detailed map and register your plans with a Forest Service office. Stock forage is scarce, so if you're riding a horse, bring concentrated feed pellets. Note that no motorized travel is permitted in the wilderness area. There are more than 20 access points to the area, including popular ones at Moose Lake, Georgetown Lake, and the East Fork of the Bitterroot River. ☒*Access to East Fork of Bitterroot River via U.S. 93* ☎*406/821–3201* ⊠*Free* ☉*Daily 24 hrs.*

Pintler Scenic Highway. The 63 mi of mountain road on this highway pass a ghost town, historic burgs, and Georgetown Lake. The road begins in Anaconda and ends on I–90 at Drummond, backdropped by the 159,000-acre Anaconda-Pintler Wilderness. ☎*406/563–2400 for information on highway.*

SPORTS & THE OUTDOORS

BICYCLING

Check with **Sven's Bicycles of Anaconda** (☒*220 Hickory St.* ☎*406/563–7988*) for local advice, including the best mountain-biking routes, from back roads to challenging mile-high trails. In winter Sven's rents ice skates and cross-country skiing equipment and can provide ski-trail maps and telemarking suggestions.

CROSS-COUNTRY SKIING

Beautifully groomed skate and classic-ski trails climb nearly to the Continental Divide at the **Mt. Haggin Cross-Country Ski Trails** area, the state's largest wildlife management area, with more than 54,000 acres. There's a warming hut but there are no services. Ski rentals and information are available at Sven's Bicycles on Hickory Street (☎*406/563–7988*). To get to the area from Anaconda, head southwest on Highway 1, cross the railroad tracks, and look for the sign to Wisdom; from here make a left onto Highway 274 and follow it for 11 mi to the parking area.

DOWNHILL SKIING

Powder skiing at **Discovery Ski Area** (☒*Hwy. 1, 23 mi northwest of Anaconda at Georgetown Lake* ☎*406/563–2184* ⊕*www.skidiscovery.com*), an inexpensive family resort, offers thrills on the extreme steeps and extensive beginner and intermediate runs.

GOLF

At the public 18-hole, Jack Nicklaus–designed **Old Works Golf Course** (☒*1205 Pizzini Way* ☎*406/563–5989*), on the site of Anaconda's historic Old Works copper smelter, hazards are filled with smelter-tailings slag instead of sand.

WHERE TO STAY & EAT

$$$ ✕ **Rocky Mountain Brewing Company.** Although the shape of the building
★ seems vaguely familiar, little else would hint that this tastefully remodeled brewery/grill was once a fast-food restaurant—least of all the gourmet menu. Accompany your Smelter Stack Stout or Pintler Wilderness Wheat with a grilled swordfish steak or macadamia-crusted chicken breast. ⊠ *315 E. Commercial St.* ☎ *406/563–3317* 🖃 *AE, MC, V.*

$$ ▥ **Fairmont Hot Springs Resort.** This resort between Anaconda and Butte
🌣 is a great option for families. Although not much to look at, the Fairmont has naturally heated indoor and outdoor swimming pools, a 350-foot waterslide, a playground, and a wildlife zoo in a beautiful setting. There's also an 18-hole golf course on the grounds. Pros: The huge, hot pools are great for kids of any age. Cons: Water slide not included with room charge; detractors point to outdated facilities and lackluster food. ⊠ *1500 Fairmont Rd., Fairmont 59711* ☎ *406/797–3241 or 800/332–3272* 🖷 *406/797–3337* ⊕ *www.fairmontmontana.com* ⇆ *153 rooms, 23 suites* ⚭ *In-room: Wi-Fi. In-hotel: restaurant, bar, golf course, tennis courts, pools, no-smoking rooms* 🖃 *AE, D, MC, V.*

¢–$ ▥ **Seven Gables Resort.** At Georgetown Lake, this simple, clean lodge has views of the Pintler Mountains and is 4 mi from skiing and across the road from fishing. The restaurant ($–$$$) serves simple fare such as pressure-fried chicken and burgers; there's also a salad bar. Pros: Convenient to fishing. Cons: Miles from most services. ⊠ *20 Southern Cross Rd., 59711* ☎ *406/563–5052* ⊕ *www.sevengablesmontana.com* ⇆ *9 rooms* ⚭ *In-room: Wi-Fi, refrigerator, no a/c. In-hotel: restaurant, bar, beachfront, no-smoking rooms* 🖃 *AE, D, MC, V.*

CAMPING ⛺ **Lost Creek State Park.** A short trail at this scenic recreation area leads to the Lost Creek Falls. Views of limestone cliffs rising 1,200 feet above the canyon floor, and frequent sightings of bighorn sheep and mountain goats are some of the attractions of this park. The campground has hiking trails and creek fishing. ⚭ *Pit toilets, drinking water, fire grates, picnic tables, swimming (creek)* ⇆ *25 sites, 1 wheelchair-accessible with toilet* ⊠ *1½ mi east of Anaconda on Hwy. 1, then 2 mi north on Hwy. 273, then 6 mi west* ☎ *406/542–5500* ⊕ *www.state.mt.us* ⌂ *Reservations not accepted* ⊙ *May 1–Nov. 30.*

BUTTE

30 mi east of Anaconda via Hwy. 1 and I–90, 79 mi northwest of Virginia City via Hwy. 287 and Hwy. 55.

Dubbed the "Richest Hill on Earth," Butte was once a wealthy and rollicking copper-, gold-, and silver-mining town. During its heyday, 100,000 people from around the world lived here; by 1880 Butte had generated about $22 billion in mineral wealth. The revived historic district, Uptown Butte, is now a National Historic Landmark area. Numerous ornate buildings recall the Old West, and several museums preserve the town's past. Today about 34,000 people live in the Butte–

Silver Bow County area. The city maintains a strong Irish flavor, and its St. Patrick's Day parade is one of the nation's most notorious.

Butte's uptown district, with several historic buildings and museums, is easily walkable, but you'll want a car to drive to some of the outlying attractions.

> ## WORD OF MOUTH
>
> "Butte is rich in mining history, the city itself is built half on a hill dotted with gallows frames and the "no longer operational" Berkely Pit. Butte was once known as the richest hill on earth. So if you have an interest in mining, etc., Butte's your place."
>
> –Lynn 5

You can catch narrated tours on a red trolley at the **Butte-Silver Bow Chamber of Commerce Visitor and Transportation Center** (✉ *1000 George St.* ☎ *800/735–6814 or 406/723–3177* ⊕ *www.buttechamber.org*), just off I–90 at Exit 126. You also can pick up free information about the area and take a stroll down the scenic Blacktail Creek Walking Path.

TIMING Like most places in Montana, many attractions in Butte are either closed or have limited hours in winter. Summer or autumn are the ideal seasons for visiting the city, as the warm weather allows for walks through the old mining town's historic uptown district. It takes at least half a day to visit the house-museums and explore the shops and eateries. Another half day can be spent visiting worthwhile locations outside the city, including Our Lady of the Rockies.

THE MAIN ATTRACTIONS

Keeping watch over Butte is **Our Lady of the Rockies,** on the Continental Divide. The 90-foot-tall, 80-ton statue of the Virgin Mary is lighted at night. For a 2½-hour bus tour, stop by the visitor center, run by a nonprofit, nondenominational organization. ✉ *3100 Harrison Ave., at Butte Plaza Mall* ☎ *406/782–1221 or 800/800–5239* ⊕ *www.ourlady oftherockies.com* ☎ *Call for rates* ☼ *June–Sept., Mon.–Sat. at 10 and 2, Sun. at 11 and 2, weather permitting.*

Thanks to old mining waste, Butte has the dubious distinction as the location of the largest toxic-waste site in the country. Some underground copper mines were dug up in the 1950s, creating the **Berkeley Open Pit Mine,** which stretches 1½ by 1 mi, reaches 1,800 feet deep, and is filled with toxic water some 800 feet deep. A viewing platform allows you to look into the now-abandoned mammoth pit where more than 20 billion pounds of copper, 704 million ounces of silver, and 3 million ounces of gold were extracted from the Butte mining district. ✉ *Continental Dr. at Park St.* ☎ *406/723–3177 or 800/735–6814* ☎ *$2* ☼ *May–Sept., daily 8–dusk, weather permitting.*

William Clark, one of Butte's richest copper barons, built the **Copper King Mansion** between 1884 and 1888. Tours of the house take in the hand-carved oak paneling, nine original fireplaces, antiques, a lavish ballroom, and frescoes. The house doubles as a bed-and-breakfast. ✉ *219 W. Granite St.* ☎ *406/782–7580* ⊕ *www.thecopperkingmansion.com* ☎ *$7* ☼ *May–Sept., daily 9–4; Oct.–Apr. by appointment.*

ALSO WORTH SEEING

Built in 1890 as a sporting house, the **Dumas Brothel Museum** was America's longest-running house of ill repute: it was shut down in 1982 and reopened as a museum. Tours are available of the building and of Butte's red-light district, Venus Alley. ☒*45 E. Mercury St.* ☎*406/494– 6908* ⊕*www.thedumasbrothel.com* ☒*Free; guided tours $10* ⊗*May– Aug., daily 10–5.*

More than 1,300 mineral specimens are displayed at Montana Tech University's **Mineral Museum,** including a 27½-troy-ounce gold nugget and a 400-pound smoky quartz crystal. ☒*1300 W. Park St.* ☎*406/496–4414* ⊕*www.mbmg.mtech.edu* ☒*Free* ⊗*Late May–early Sept., daily 9–6; early May–late May and mid-Sept.–Oct., weekdays 9–4, weekends 1–5.*

The **Mai Wah Museum** contains exhibits on the history of the Chinese and other Asian settlers of Butte. The two historic buildings it occupies were constructed to house Chinese-owned businesses: the Wah Chong Tai Company and the Mai Wah Noodle Parlor. ☒*17 W. Mercury St.* ☎*406/723–3231* ⊕*www.maiwah.org* ☒*Donations accepted* ⊗*June–Sept., Tues.–Sat. 11–5; open in winter by appointment.*

★ The **Clark Chateau Museum,** an elegant 1898 four-story Victorian mansion that was owned by Charles Clark, eldest son of Copper King W.A. Clark, now serves as a gallery. The collection includes 18th- and 19th-century furniture, textiles, and collectibles as well as artwork. ☒*321 W. Broadway* ☎*406/723–7600* ☒*$5* ⊗*May–Sept., Tues.–Sat. 10–4.*

OFF THE BEATEN PATH **Sheepshead Mountain Recreation Area.** At this designated Wildlife Viewing Area you might glimpse elk, deer, moose, waterfowl, and birds of prey. The area is wheelchair-accessible, and offers paved walking trails, a fishing dock, picnic tables, a rentable pavilion, horseshoe pits, and drinking water. ☒*13 mi north of Butte on I–15 to Exit 138, Elk Park, west on Forest Service Rd. 442, follow signs for 6 mi* ☎*406/494–2147* ⊕*www.fs.fed.us/r1/bdnf* ☒*Free* ⊗*Memorial Day–Labor Day, daily.*

SPORTS & THE OUTDOORS

FISHING **Tom's Fishing and Bird Hunting Guide Service** (☒*3460 St. Ann St.* ☎*406/ 723–4753 or 800/487–0296*) arranges float and wade trips for blue-ribbon trout fishing.

HORSEBACK RIDING **Cargill Outfitters** (☒*40 Cedar Hills Rd., Whitehall* ☎*406/494–2960* ⊕*www.ironwheel.com*), which is just over the Continental Divide, 20-minutes east of Butte, offers two-hour to full-day horseback riding into the Highland Mountain range.

You can speed-skate on ice at the **U.S. High Altitude Sports Center** (☒*5155 Continental Dr.* ☎*406/494–7570*) with international speed skaters or beginners. The ice track is open for general ice skating as well; call for times. Skate rentals are available.

WHERE TO EAT

$$$–$$$$ ✕**Spaghettini's.** This Italian trattoria brings a bit of the Mediterranean into Butte's former Great Northern Hotel. Tuck into seafood and pasta wonders such as shrimp spaghettini, with shrimp, asparagus, prosciutto. A piano player entertains on Friday and Saturday nights. ⊠*801 Front St.* ☎*406/782–8855* ▤*AE, D, MC, V* ☉*Closed Sun.*

$$–$$$$ ✕**Acoma.** Renovations haven't altered the authentic art deco decor of this restaurant on the National Register of Historic Places. Dine on pork osso buco, a pork shank roasted and served with duchess potatoes and a sauce Robert, or veal Acoma sautéed with artichoke hearts and mushrooms and finished with white-wine cream sauce. ⊠*60 E. Broadway* ☎*406/782–7001* ▤*AE, D, MC, V.*

$$$ ✕**Freds Mesquite Grill.** This spacious newcomer to the Butte scene has made its mark by offering contemporary spins on old favorites, all of which are cooked in the restaurant's mesquite grill. Menu items range from hamburgers and barbecue chicken sandwiches to halibut, filet mignon, and kebabs. The Caesar dressing is made fresh every day, and the bar offers a wide variety of Northwestern microbrews. ⊠*205 S. Arizona* ☎*406/723–4440/* ▤*MC, V.*

¢–$$$ ✕**Broadway Café.** This turn-of-the-20th-century building is the place for pizzas and salads. Try the ginger tahini salad or the "madhouse" pizza, with red onions, sun-dried tomatoes, olives, artichokes, feta, and mozzarella cheese. Friday nights there's live music, usually contemporary jazz. It's right near the Berkeley Open Pit Mine. ⊠*302 E. Broadway* ☎*406/723–8711* ▤*AE, D, MC, V* ☉*Closed Sun.*

¢   ✕**Town Talk Bakery.** No visit to Butte is complete without trying a pasty, the traditional miner's dinner of meat, potatoes, and onion baked inside a pastry shell. This bakery is one of the best of several eateries that serve these pocket-size meals; they also sell doughnuts, cookies, cakes, and breads. There are no tables; all items are takeout. ⊠*611 E. Front St.* ☎*406/782–4985* ▤*No credit cards* ☉*Closed Sun. and Mon.*

WHERE TO STAY

$–$$$
Fodor'sChoice
★   ▥**Toad Hall Manor Bed and Breakfast.** Built as a private home in the early 1990s, this mansion has a historic feel thanks to hardwood accents, marble tile, and a classic redbrick exterior. Each of the four guest rooms is named after a character from Kenneth Grahame's *The Wind in the Willows.* The ground-floor Papa Otter's Place, with its Victorian-style furnishings, marble-accented Jacuzzi, and French doors opening to a private garden, probably offers the best value. Sir Badger's Suite, which takes up the entire fifth floor with two bedrooms, a two-person Jacuzzi, walk-in closet, and loft-style windows, ranks as the most luxurious option. ⊠*1 Green La., 59701* ☎*406/494–2625 or 866/443–8623* ▤*406/494–8025* ⊕*www.toadhallmanor.com* ↪*4 rooms* ♿*In-hotel: no-smoking rooms, Internet* ▤*AE, D, MC, V* ▮○▮*BP.*

$–$$ ▥**Best Western Butte Plaza Inn.** Butte's largest lodging is convenient to shopping, sports events, and the interstates. The rooms are clean and comfortable, if somewhat bland. Pros: No surprises; decent breakfast bar; full-service restaurant attached. Cons: Generic; can be loud; not walking distance to the Uptown Butte sights. ⊠*2900 Harrison Ave., 59701* ☎*406/494–3500 or 800/543–5814* ▤*406/494–7611* ⊕*www.*

bestwestern.com ⇆134 rooms ☝In-room: Wi-Fi. In-hotel: restaurant, bar, pool, laundry facilities, airport shuttle, parking (no fee), no-smoking rooms, some pets allowed, no elevator ⊟AE, D, MC, V ⦿BP.

¢–$ ▦**Copper King Mansion Bed and Breakfast.** Completed in 1888 as the home of notorious Copper King William Andrews Clark, the mansion remains much in its original state, and is the only privately owned mansion in Montana accessible to the public through seasonal tours. Five of the mansion's 35 rooms are used as a bed-and-breakfast, and the owners have attempted to re-create the experience of living like a turn-of-the-century millionaire, with such furnishings as a hand-carved fireplace, burled walnut bed, and a circular shower that hits you from all sides. Pros: Where else can you live like a Copper King? The furniture, the stories, and the history are all genuine and first-rate. Cons: Even Copper Kings get hot without air-conditioning. ⊠*219 W. Granite St.* ☎*406/782–7580* ⊕*www.thecopperkingmansion.com* ⇆*4 rooms, 2 suites* ☝*No-smoking rooms, no elevator, no a/c.* ⦿*BP* ⊟*MC, V.*

¢–$ ▦**Hotel Finlen.** In continuous operation since it opened in 1924, Finlen, with its lobby of ornate chandeliers and pillars, stands in testament to Butte's heyday, when the hotel played host to the likes of Charles Lindbergh and Mrs. Herbert Hoover. Once boasting more than 200 rooms under the mansard roof of this nine-story, French Second Empire structure, most of those are now apartments, with only 20 hotel rooms remaining—plus another 32 in the adjacent Finlen Motor Inn. The rooms are unremarkable, but some provide excellent views of Uptown Butte. Pros: Elegant, historic lobby; excellent value; best location in Uptown Butte. Cons: Not all rooms have views; small parking lot; tiny bathrooms. ⊠*100 E. Broadway, 59701* ☎*406/723–5461* ⇆*20 hotel rooms, 3 suites, 32 motel rooms* ☝*In-hotel: Wi-Fi, laundry, no-smoking rooms* ⊟*AE, D, DC, MC, V.*

CAMPING   ⛺**Butte KOA.** This large and grassy campsite with cottonwood trees has a playground and allows fishing in the on-site Silver Bow Creek. It's next to a tourism office and is easily accessed from the interstate. It's a good idea to reserve ahead. ☝*Flush toilets, full hookups, partial hookups (water), dump station, drinking water, guest laundry, showers, picnic tables, food service, electricity, public telephone, general store, pool* ⇆*100 RV sites (full or partial hookups), 20 tent sites; 4 cabins* ⊠*1601 Kaw Ave., off I–90 at Exit 126* ☎*406/782–8080 or 800/562–8089* ⊕*www.koa.com* ⊟*D, MC, V* ⦿*Mid-Apr.–Oct.*

SHOPPING

Find everything from Butte collectibles to fine porcelain and antique furniture at **D&G Antiques** (⊠*16 N. Montana St.* ☎*406/723–4552*), one of eight antiques shops in the historic district. Montana's largest bookstore, **Second Edition Books** (⊠*112 S. Montana St.* ☎*406/723–5108 or 800/298–5108*), buys, sells, and trades books on many different subjects but specializes in hard-to-find regional tomes. While visiting the historic district, stop at the **Uptown Butte Farmers' Market** (⊠*Main St. between Park St. and Broadway* ☎*406/723–3177 or 800/735–6814*) for fresh garden produce, fruit, flowers, baked goods, and local crafts. It's open Saturday in summer from 9 to 1.

VIRGINIA CITY

72 mi southeast of Butte via Hwys. 2, 41, and 287.

Remnants of Montana's frontier days, Virginia City and its smaller neighbor, Nevada City, are two of the state's standout attractions. Boardwalks pass in front of partially restored historic buildings, and 19th-century goods stock the stores. Virginia City prospered when miners stampeded into Montana Territory after the 1863 discovery of gold. The diggings were rich in Alder Gulch, and Virginia City eventually became Montana's second territorial capital. Enticed by the city's wealth, criminals came to prey on the miners. In turn, vigilance committees held lightning-fast trials and strung up the bad guys. The outlaws were buried atop Boot Hill, overlooking town.

Begin a visit at the **Virginia City Depot Visitor Center,** where you can get information on theater, historic accommodations, and gold panning. ✉*430 W. Wallace St.* ☎*406/843–5239* ⊕*www.virginiacitymt.com* ⊠*Free* ☉*Memorial Day–Labor Day, daily 9–5.*

The eclectic assortment of items dating from 1860 to 1900 at the **Thompson-Hickman Memorial Museum** includes a petrified wedding cake, the eponymous limb of "Club Foot" George Lane, rifles, and numerous photographs. The collection is made up of the heirlooms of three local families. The local library is upstairs. ✉*Wallace St.* ☎*406/843–5238* ⊠*Donations accepted* ☉*May–Sept., daily 10–5.*

A 1910 narrow-gauge steam train, the **Baldwin Locomotive No. 12,** Montana's only operating steam locomotive run by volunteer crews, travels between Virginia City and Nevada City on weekends from July 4 through Labor Day, as well as Memorial Day weekend. On weekdays, a smaller locomotive, the **Alder Gulch Shortline Railroad,** makes the same journey. ☎*406/843–5247* ⊕*www.virginiacitymt.com* ⊠*$10.*

Full-moon evenings of June, July, and August feature **Moonlight and Steam Trains,** in which a moonlight train ride is topped off with drinks and munchies at Virginia City's Bale of Hay Saloon. ⊠*$15, includes drink* ☉*Memorial Day–Labor Day, 5 trips daily, on either Baldwin or Alder Gulch.*

★ The living-history **Nevada City Open Air Museum,** down the road from Virginia City, preserves the town as it was at the turn of the 20th century, with restored buildings, thousands of artifacts from the gold-rush era, and weekend demonstrations. New to the collection is the **Frontier House Museum,** from the PBS television series of the same name. ✉*U. S. 287, 1½ mi west of Virginia City* ☎*406/843–5247* ⊕*www.virginia citymt.com* ⊠*$8* ☉*Mid-May–mid-Sept., daily 9–6.*

After they were hanged by vigilantes, the outlaws who preyed on miners ended up in graves at **Boot Hill** cemetery. Have a look at the old markers and take in the hill's view. ✉*From Wallace St. turn north on Spencer St. and follow signs for* ROAD AGENTS' GRAVES ☎*406/843–5555 or 800/829–2969* ⊕*www.virginiacitychamber.com.*

SPORTS & THE OUTDOORS

Spend a day moving cattle from high in the saddle with **Upper Canyon Outfitters/Tate Ranch** (⊠*2149 Upper Ruby Rd., 35 mi southwest of Virginia City* ☎*800/735–3973* ⊕*www.ucomontana.com*). The ranch also offers fly-fishing and summer vacations in its lodge and four kitchen-equipped cabins.

WHERE TO STAY & EAT

¢ ✕**City Bakery.** Fresh pastries and gingerbread keep people coming back for more at this bakery. Wash your order down with a huckleberry iced tea. There's no seating in the bakery, but there are benches on the sidewalk outside. ⊠*325 W. Wallace St.* ☎*406/843–5227* ⚞*Reservations not accepted* ☰*MC, V* ⊗*Closed Oct., Nov., and Jan.–May.*

$$–$$$ 🏨**Upper Canyon Outfitters.** Along with cattle herding, hunting, and fly-fishing adventures, this secluded guest ranch offers rooms in its spacious Western-style lodge or kitchen-equipped log cabins. Hearty ranch meals are available in the lodge. Pros: An all-inclusive Western experience. Cons: It's a far cry from Disneyland. ⊠*2149 Upper Ruby Rd., 35 mi southwest of Virginia City* ☎*800/735—3973* ⊕*www.ucomontana.com* ⚞*Lodge: 5 rooms, 1 suite. Cabins: 3 2-bedroom cabins, 1 1-bedroom cabin.* ⚘*In-room: Lodge: Mini-fridge. Cabins: Stove, oven, refrigerator, utensils. In-hotel: Fly shop, gift shop, fly-tying area, no smoking rooms, no elevator (lodge is handicapped-accessible).*

$ 🏨**Stonehouse Inn Bed & Breakfast.** Period charm pervades this 1884 Gothic Revival home with antiques, brass beds, 12-foot ceilings, and a teddy-bear collection. The full breakfast might include strawberry French toast with cream cheese and fresh fruit. ⊠*306 E. Idaho St., 59755* ☎*406/843–5504* ⊕*www.stonehouseinnbb.com* ⚞*5 rooms* ⚘*In-room: Wi-Fi, no a/c, no phone. In-hotel: laundry facilities, no-smoking rooms, no elevator* ☰*MC, V* ⑧*BP.*

¢–$ 🏨**Fairweather Inn and the Nevada City Hotel and Cabins.** Virginia City's Fairweather Inn is a classic Western-Victorian hotel with balconies in the heart of the area's gold-mining country. The two-story 1863 Nevada City Hotel is 1½ mi away in Nevada City; there are Victorian-style hotel rooms, plus rustic miners' cabins. Pros: Historic hotel; convenient location, comfortable rooms. Cons: No air-conditioning; most rooms have shared bath; no frills. ⊠*305 W. Wallace St., 59755* ☎*406/843–5377 or 800/829–2969* 📠*406/843–5235* ⚞*Fairweather Inn: 14 rooms, 5 with bath. Nevada City Hotel: 11 rooms, 2 suites, 17 cabins* ⚘*In-room: no phone, no TV. In-hotel: no-smoking rooms, no elevator* ☰*D, MC, V* ⊗*Closed Oct.–mid-May.*

CAMPING 🏕**Virginia City RV Park.** It's a good idea to reserve ahead at this RV park, which also has seven grassy campsites. ⚘*Flush toilets, full hookups, partial hookups, dump station, drinking water, showers, picnic tables, electricity* ⚞*10 full hookups, 15 partial hookups, 7 tent sites* ⊠*Hwy. 287, ¼ mi east of Virginia City* ☎*406/843–5493 or 888/833–5493* ⊕*www.virginiacityrvpark.com* ☰*MC, V* ⊗*Mid-May–mid-Sept.*

NIGHTLIFE & THE ARTS

NIGHTLIFE   Weekend evenings in summer there's often live rock music at **Banditos** (⊠*320 Wallace St.* ☎*406/843–5556*), in the historic Wells Fargo building. The **Brewery Follies** (⊠*H. S. Gilbert Brewery building, Cover St.* ☎*406/843–5218 or 800/829–2969*) are contemporary comedies (ages 12 and up); shows take place Wednesday through Monday evenings from late May through August.

THE ARTS   The historic **Opera House** (⊠*338 W. Wallace St.* ☎*406/843–5314 or 800/829–2969* ⊕*virginiacityplayers.com*) is the oldest continuously ★   operating summer theater in the West, in operation since 1949. Early June through early September, the theater hosts an amusing vaudeville show by the Virginia City Players on Tuesdays through Sundays at 7 PM, with Wednesday and Saturday matinees at 2 PM. The cost is $15.

SHOPPING

Opened in 1864 **Rank's Mercantile** (⊠*411 Wallace St.* ☎*406/843–5454 or 800/494–5442*) is Montana's oldest continuously operating store. Period clothing, books, toys, gifts, and groceries are for sale here.

ENNIS

14 mi east of Virginia City via Hwy. 287.

In addition to being a hub of ranching in the area, this tiny town sits among some of the best trout streams in the West. People come from around the world for the area's blue-ribbon fishing, particularly in the area of Beartrap Canyon. Welcoming you to town is a sign that reads 600 PEOPLE, 11,000,000 TROUT.

Consistently rated among the most exciting and challenging rodeos in Montana, the July 3 and 4 **Ennis Rodeo** (☎*406/682–4700*) attracts top cowpokes each year.

Each year at the **Ennis National Fish Hatchery** six strains of rainbow trout produce 23 million eggs used to stock streams throughout the United States. Note that the 10-mi access road leading here is bumpy. ⊠*180 Fish Hatchery Rd.* ☎*406/682–4847 or 800/344–9453* ⊕*www.fws. gov/ennis/* ☜*Free* ☉*Daily 7:30–5.*

For a bit of relaxation, nothing beats soaking in the natural hot water of the **Norris Hot Springs** pool. Live musical acts perform on the poolside stage Thursday through Sunday nights, starting at 7 PM. ⊠*Hwy. 84, 16 mi north of Ennis on U.S. 287, then ¼ mi east through town, or 33 mi west of Bozeman on Hwy. 84 Norris* ☎*406/685–3303* ⊕*www. norrishotsprings.com* ☜*$5* ☉*Wed.–Fri. 4–10, weekends 2–10.*

OFF THE   **Beartrap Canyon.** In this part of the Lee Metcalf Wilderness, you can
BEATEN   hike, fish, and go white-water rafting on the Madison River. A picnic
PATH   area and access to Trail Creek are at the head of the canyon below Ennis Lake. To get here, drive north out of Ennis on U.S. 287 to the town of McAllister and turn right down a bumpy dirt road (no number), which takes you around to the north side of the lake across the dam. Turn left

after the dam onto an unmarked road and drive across the river to the Trail Creek access point. ☎*406/683–2337* 🖂*Free* ⊙*Daily.*

SPORTS & THE OUTDOORS

FISHING The fly-fishing specialists of **Eaton Outfitters** (🖂*307 Jeffers Rd.* ☎*406/682–4514 or 800/755–3474*) lead trips on the Madison, Beaverhead, Big Hole, and Ruby rivers. The **Tackle Shop** (🖂*127 E. Main St.* ☎*406/682–4263 or 800/808–2832*) offers guided float and wade fishing on the Madison, Big Hole, and other rivers. The full-service Orvis fly shop also sells luggage, clothing, and fishing accessories.

HORSEBACK RIDING Ride the dusty trails with **Bar 88 Horses** (🖂*Box 1109, 59729* ☎*406/682–4827*) on half- and full-day adventures in the Beaverhead National Forest.

4

WHERE TO STAY & EAT

$$$–$$$$ ✕**Continental Divide.** This bistro-style restaurant is a pleasant surprise in an area with numerous steak houses. Among the specials are local free-range duck slow roasted with apricot glaze, and lobster cannelloni. 🖂*47 Geyser St., 1½ mi north of Ennis on Hwy. 287* ☎*406/682–7600* ⊟*AE, D, MC, V* ⊙*Closed Dec.–Apr.*

¢–$ 🏨**Fan Mountain Inn.** This simple but clean family motel has wonderful views of the Madison Range and is within walking distance of downtown shops and galleries. There's a cozy fireplace in the lobby. 🖂*204 N. Main St., 59729* ☎*406/682–5200 or 877/682–5200* 🖷*406/682– 5266* ⊕*www.fanmountaininn.com* ⇆*27 rooms* ⌂*In-room: Wi-Fi, refrigerator (some). In-hotel: no-smoking rooms, some pets allowed, no elevator* ⊟*AE, D, MC, V.*

CAMPING 🏕**Ennis RV Village.** An 8-acre wetlands park with hiking trails is adjacent to this RV park, with views of the Madison, Gravelly, and Tobacco Root ranges. Reservations are recommended. ⌂*Flush toilets, full hookups, partial hookups, dump station, drinking water, guest laundry, showers, fire pits, picnic tables, electricity, public telephone, general store* ⇆*76 full hookups, 10 partial hookups, 4 tent sites* 🖂*15 Geyser St., just off Hwy. 287 1 mi north of Ennis* ☎*406/682–5272 or 866/682–5272* 🖷*406/682–5245* ⊕*www.ennisrv.com* ⊟*AE, MC, V* ⊙*Apr.–Oct.*

NIGHTLIFE & THE ARTS

NIGHTLIFE Live music Friday nights at the **Claim Jumper Saloon** (🖂*305 E. Main St.* ☎*406/682–5558*) ranges from blues to classic rock. The saloon's **Roadmaster Grille** features booths crafted from 1950s-era American automobiles.

THE ARTS The **River Stone Gallery** (🖂*219 E. Main St.* ☎*406/682–5243*) displays original paintings, sculptures, pottery, and contemporary jewelry by Western artists. Local stones are often used in the jewelry. One-of-a-kind abstract sculptures are made of copper and brass at the **Trudi Gilliam Metal Sculpture Studio and Gallery** (🖂*100 W. Main St.* ☎*406/682–7772*).

DILLON

65 mi south of Butte via I–90 west and I–15 south.

From Dillon you can hike and mountain-bike into the nearby Ruby and Tendoy mountains. Blue-ribbon trout fishing on the Beaverhead River attracts thousands of fly fishermen and anglers year-round. A capital of southwest Montana's ranch country, Dillon began as a cattle- and wool-shipping point between Utah and the goldfields of Montana. From the mid-1860s until the early 1900s cattle and sheep remained the primary cargo shipped out of here on the Union Pacific Railroad.

The **Beaverhead County Museum** exhibits Native American artifacts, ranching and mining memorabilia, a homesteader's cabin, agricultural artifacts, a one-room schoolhouse, research center, and a boardwalk imprinted with the area's ranch brands. ⌧*15 S. Montana St.* ☎*406/683–5027* ⌸*$2* ⊙*Memorial Day–Labor Day, Mon.–Sat. 9–5, Sun. noon–5; Labor Day–Memorial Day, weekdays 9–5.*

Everyone is a cowboy for the annual **Dillon Jaycee Labor Day Rodeo and Parade** (⌧*Fairgrounds, Railroad St.* ☎*406/683–5511*), which has been staged here since 1914. Among the activities that take place at this four-day festival running late August through early September are a fair, rodeo, and concert.

Clark's Lookout State Park. Captain William Clark of the Lewis and Clark Expedition climbed to the top of this limestone bluff and took three compass readings; the maps he made from these readings became an important resource for future travelers. A ¼-mi gravel loop trails take visitors to the top of the bluff, where interpretive signs include a replica of Clark's sketched map of the area. ⌧*1 mi north of Dillon on Hwy. 91* ⊕*www.fwp.state.mt.us* ⌸*Free* ⊙*Daily 8–dusk.*

OFF THE
BEATEN
PATH

Red Rock Lakes National Wildlife Refuge. In the undeveloped and remote Centennial Valley, this 45,000-acre refuge shelters moose, deer, and antelope but is primarily a sanctuary for 230 species of birds, including trumpeter swans. Once threatened with extinction, these elegant birds have survived thanks to refuge protection; today, they build their nests and winter here among the 14,000 acres of lakes and marshes. ⌧*27820 Southside Centennial Rd., 60 mi south of Dillon on I–15 to Monida; follow signs east 28 mi on gravel and dirt road, Lima* ☎*406/276–3536* ⊕*www.fws.gov/redrocks* ⌸*Free* ⊙*Daily 7:30–4.*

SPORTS & THE OUTDOORS

FISHING   Whether they're discussing nymphs, caddis flies, or crane flies, the guides of **Backcountry Angler** (⌧*426 S. Atlantic St.* ☎*406/683–3462* ⊕*www.backcountryangler.com*) know the art of fly-fishing. They lead overnight fishing-lodging trips, plus wade- and float-fishing day adventures. **Uncle Bob's Outdoors, Inc.** (⌧*11 Pierce Dr.* ☎*406/683–2692 or 888/683–7637*) arranges float- and wade-fishing trips on private creeks and ponds and the Beaverhead, Big Hole, Jefferson, and Ruby rivers.

HORSEBACK   Horse and mule day rides and pack trips traverse the Continental
RIDING   Divide and the Lima Peaks with **Centennial Outfitters** (⌧*Box 92, 45 mi*

south of Dillon via I–15, Lima ☎406/276–3463). **Diamond Hitch Out-fitters** (✉*3405 10 Mile Rd., 4 mi west of Dillon* ☎406/683–5494 or 800/368–5494) takes you by horse or mule to high rocky summits, past endless flowery meadows, and along trout fisheries on hourly rides, cookout rides, and overnight pack trips.

SKIING A fun family attraction, **Maverick Mountain Ski Area** (✉*Hwy. 278 [Maverick Mountain Rd.], 40 mi west of Dillon* ☎406/834–3454 ⊕*www.skimaverick.com*) has a top elevation of 8,620 feet, a vertical drop of 1,927 feet, and 24 runs. Lessons and ski and snowboard rentals and sales are available for kids and adults.

WHERE TO EAT

$$–$$$$ ✕**Cross Ranch Cookhouse.** Dine in a cookhouse with working ranch
★ hands. In addition to salads, bread, and dessert, there's "pitchfork fondue"—Angus beef sirloin, skewered and then deep-fried in a cauldron via pitchfork. A local fiddle, banjo, and guitar band plays country music. ✉*12775 Bannack Rd.; south on I–15, Exit 44, on Hwy. 324 12 mi to Bannack turnoff, right 2 mi ahead on right* ☎406/681–3133 ✍*Reservations essential* ▭*No credit cards* ⊘*Closed Sun. and Jan.*

¢–$ ✕**Sweetwater Coffee.** This warm and friendly coffee shop offers salads, sandwiches, and pasta along with its espresso drinks. Try the Blue Dorris Salad. ✉*26 E. Bannack* ☎406/683–4141 ▭*No credit cards* ⊘*Closed Sat. and Sun.*

WHERE TO STAY

$$ ⌂**Goose Down Ranch.** Darling cabins, one log and one clapboard, have mountain views all around and are near the famed Poindexter Slough blue-ribbon fly-fishing spot on the Beaverhead River. The cabins both have two bedrooms, fireplaces, and cozy couches. Pros: Great fishing, full-service cabins. Cons: Only two cabins means advance reservations are essential. ✉*2409 Carrigan La., 59725* ☎406/683–6704 or 406/925–1619 ⎙406/683–8390 ⊕*www.goosedownranch.com* ⟳*2 cabins* ⌂*In-room: no phone, kitchen, VCR, laundry facilities. In-hotel: no-smoking rooms, no elevator* ▭*MC, V.*

$$ ⌂**The River's Edge Lodge Bed and Breakfast.** Located 10 mi south of Dillon on a stretch of the Upper Beaverhead River, this year-round bed-and-breakfast caters to fishermen. Although the amenities of town may be a good ways down the road, this secluded barnlike lodge—constructed from wood of a wide variety of species—was designed to put its guests as close to this first-class fly-fishing river as possible. ✉*765 Henneberry Rd., 59725* ☎406/683–6214 or 406/925–1494 ⟳*5 rooms* ⌂*In-hotel: no-smoking rooms, no a/c, no elevator, some pets allowed* ▭*No credit cards* †⊙*BP.*

$ ⌂**Guest House Inn & Suites.** This hotel is affordable, clean, and quiet and has an outdoor sundeck off the indoor pool. The staff can direct you to interesting local sights, scenic viewpoints, and perhaps even a good local fishing hole. Pros: Full breakfast; indoor pool; not overpriced—it's one of the nicer places to stay in Dillon. Cons: Detractors speak of inattentive management; and a buffet that didn't last until the advertised time. ✉*580 Sinclair St., 59725* ☎406/683–3636 or 800/214–8378 ⎙406/683–3637 ⊕*www.guesthouseintl.com* ⟳*58*

4

rooms & *In-room: kitchen (some), refrigerator, VCR, Wi-Fi. In-hotel: pool, exercise room, no-smoking rooms, some pets allowed, no elevator* ⊟*AE, D, MC, V* ⏚*BP.*

¢–$ ⛰**The Grasshopper Inn.** In the spectacular Pioneer Mountains, this mountain lodge is ideally situated for snowmobiling, hiking, and fishing. The tidy, colorful rooms have log beds and views of the mountains. The restaurant's back bar dates from the 1800s. The simple yet filling meals ($$) include burgers, steak, and fish. You can rent snowmobiles nearby in winter. Pros: Cozy, secluded getaway; reasonably priced. Cons: Miles from services. ⊠*3900 Pioneer Scenic Byway, 45 mi west of Dillon, Polaris 59746* ☎*406/834–3456* 📠*406/834–3507* 📲*10 rooms* & *In-room: no phone, no a/c. In-hotel: restaurant, bar, no-smoking rooms, no elevator* ⊟*D, MC, V.*

CAMPING ⛰**Dillon KOA.** Pine, aspen, and birch trees shade this campground on the banks of the Beaverhead River. The campground, which is on the edge of Dillon, has views of the Pioneer Mountains and other peaks. &*Flush toilets, full hookups, dump station, drinking water, guest laundry, showers, picnic tables, electricity, public telephone, general store, play area, swimming (pool)* 📲*68 full hookups, 30 tent sites; 4 cabins* ⊠*735 W. Park St.* ☎*406/683–2749 or 800/562–2751* ⊕*www.koa. com* ⊟*D, MC, V.*

SHOPPING

Original paintings of flowers, dragonflies, sticks, stones, skulls, bones, and other scenes from nature are for sale at the **Cathy Weber–Artmaker** (⊠*26 N. Idaho St.* ☎*406/683–5493*) studio. Antiques and collectibles are for sale in **Gracie's Antiques** (⊠*140 W. Bannack St.* ☎*406/683–9552*).

BANNACK

24 mi west of Dillon via I–15 and U.S. 278.

Bannack was Montana's first territorial capital and the site of the state's first major gold strike, on July 28, 1862, at Grasshopper Creek. Now **Bannack State Historic Park,** this frontier boomtown has historic structures lining the main street, and picnic and camping spots. It was here that the notorious renegade Sheriff Henry Plummer and several of his gang members were caught and executed by vigilantes for murder and robbery. A re-creation of the gallows on which Plummer was hanged still stands. Rumors persist that Plummer's stash of stolen gold was hidden somewhere in the mountains near here and never found. To get to Bannack from Dillon, follow Highway 278 west for 17 mi and watch for a sign just after Badger Pass; take the paved road for 4 mi. ☎*406/834–3413* ⊕*www.bannack.org* 🎫*$5 per vehicle* ⊗*Park Memorial Day–Labor Day, daily 8–9; Labor Day–Memorial Day, daily 8–5. Visitor center late May–early Sept., daily 10–6; Sept. daily 11–5; Oct. weekends 11–5; limited hrs in May.*

For two days in mid-July **Bannack Pioneer Days** (☎*406/834–3413* ⊕*www.bannack*.org) celebrates life in Montana's first territorial capital with wagon rides, a main-street gunfight, old-time music and dancing, and pioneer-crafts demonstrations.

OFF THE
BEATEN
PATH

Pioneer Mountain Scenic Byway. Mountains, meadows, lodgepole-pine forests, and willow-edged streams line this road, which runs north–south between U.S. 278 (west of Bannack) and Highway 43. Headed north, the byway skirts the Maverick Mountain Ski Area and Elkhorn Hot Springs and ends at the town of Wise River on the Big Hole River. ☎406/683–5511.

CAMPING

⚠ **Bannack Campgrounds.** Grasshopper Creek, where gold was discovered in 1862, flows not far from this rustic campground, which has few amenities but is close to Bannack. Grocery stores and restaurants are in nearby Dillon. It's a good idea to reserve ahead for the single tepee. △ *Vault toilets, drinking water, fire pits, picnic tables* ⇆*28 tent sites; 1 tepee* ⊠*4200 Bannack Rd.* ☎*406/834–3413* ⊕*www.bannack.org* ▭*MC, V.*

4

BIG HOLE NATIONAL BATTLEFIELD

60 mi northwest of Bannock via Hwy. 278 northwest and Hwy. 43 west; 87 mi southwest of Butte via I–90 west, I–15 south, and Hwy. 43 west.

At Big Hole, a visitor center overlooks meadows where one of the West's greatest and most tragic stories played out. In 1877 Nez Perce warriors in central Idaho killed some white settlers as retribution for earlier killings by whites. Knowing the U.S. Army would make no distinction between the guilty and the innocent, several hundred Nez Perce fled, beginning a 1,500-mi, five-month odyssey that has come to be known as the Nez Perce Trail. The fugitives engaged 10 separate U.S. commands in 13 battles and skirmishes. One of the fiercest of these was at Big Hole, where both sides suffered losses. From here the Nez Perce headed toward Yellowstone. The Big Hole battlefield remains as it was when the battle unfolded; tepee poles erected by the park service mark the site of a Nez Perce village and serve as haunting reminders of what transpired here. Ranger-led programs take place daily in summer; group tours can be arranged with advance request. The park stays open for winter snowshoeing and cross-country skiing on a groomed trail through the battlefield's sites. Big Hole National Battlefield is one of 38 sites in four states that make up the **Nez Perce National Historic Park** (☎*208/843–3155* ⊕*www.nps.gov/nepe*), which follows the historic Nez Perce Trail. ⊠*Hwy. 43, 10 mi west of Wisdom* ☎*406/689–3155* ⊕*www.nps.gov/biho* ⊠*Free* ⊙*May–Labor Day, daily 9–6; Labor Day–Apr., daily 10–5.*

The annual **Commemoration of the Battle of Big Hole** (☎*406/689–3155* ⊕*www.nps.gov/nepe*), in early August, includes traditional Nez Perce music, ceremonies, and demonstrations, along with cavalry exhibitions.

SPORTS & THE OUTDOORS

You can cross-country ski (with your own equipment) or snowshoe through the historic trails of **Big Hole Battlefield** (⊠ *Hwy. 43, 10 mi west of Wisdom* ☎ *406/689–3155* ⊕ *www.nps.gov/biho*). A few pairs of snowshoes are available for use for free at the visitor center.

WHERE TO STAY

¢–$ 🏨 **Jackson Hot Springs Lodge.** Lewis and Clark cooked their dinner in the hot springs near the site of this spacious log lodge decorated with elk antlers, a stuffed mountain lion, and other critters. Accommodations are in cabins, many with fireplaces, and there's also tent and RV camping. The Olympic-size outdoor pool is filled with artesian hot water that averages 103°F year-round. The dining room ($$–$$$$) specializes in wild game dishes such as pheasant, bison, and elk steaks. Pros: First-class dining; relaxing pool; classic Western lodge. Cons: Detractors complain of stubborn room temperatures; facilities in need of upkeep; overpriced. ⊠ *Main St., Box 808; 30 mi northwest of Big Hole, Jackson 59736* ☎ *406/834–3151 or 888/438–6938* 📠 *406/834–3157* ⊕ *www.jacksonhotsprings.com* 🛏 *20 cabins* ♿ *In-room: no a/c, no phone, no TV. In-hotel: restaurant, bar, pool, no-smoking rooms, some pets allowed, no elevator* ▭ *AE, MC, V.*

CAMPING ⛺ **Miner Lake Campground.** Campsites have a view of the Beaverhead Mountains at this quiet, out-of-the-way lakeside spot. You can fish in 30-acre Miner Lake, which is also popular for nonmotorized boats. ⛺ *Pit toilets, drinking water, fire grates, picnic tables, swimming (lake)* 🛏 *18 tent sites* ⊠ *Forest Rd. 182, 11.5 mi west of Hwy. 278, 12 mi southwest of Jackson Jackson* ☎ *406/689–3243* 📠 *406/689–3245* ⊕ *www.fs.fed.us/r1/* ▭ *No credit cards* ☼ *June–mid-Sept.*

SOUTHWEST MONTANA ESSENTIALS

AIR TRAVEL

CARRIERS Several daily flights link Bozeman's Gallatin Field Airport to Butte, Denver, Minneapolis, Salt Lake City, and Seattle. Butte Airport has service from Bozeman, Salt Lake City, and Seattle. Helena Airport has service from Billings, Great Falls, Minneapolis, and Salt Lake City. Note that major air carriers tend to use smaller planes to serve the area.

AIRLINES & CONTACTS

Delta (☎ *800/221–1212* ⊕ *www.delta.com*). **Alaska Airlines/Horizon Air** (☎ *800/547–9308* ⊕ *www.alaskaair.com*). **Northwest** (☎ *800/225–2525* ⊕ *www. nwa.com*). **Skywest** (☎ *800/453–9417* ⊕ *www.skywest.com*). **United/United Express** (☎ *800/241–6522* ⊕ *www.united.com*).

AIRPORTS

Butte Airport is 7 mi south of downtown. Gallatin Field Airport is 16 mi west of Bozeman. Helena Airport is 3 mi from downtown.

Information Butte Airport (⊠ *101 Airport Rd., Butte* ☎ *406/494–0090*). **Gallatin Field Airport** (⊠ *850 Gallatin Field Rd., Belgrade* ☎ *406/388–8321* ⊕ *www. gallatinfield.com*). **Helena Airport** (⊠ *2850 Skyway Dr., Helena* ☎ *406/442–2821* ⊕ *www.helenaairport.com*).

BUS TRAVEL

Greyhound Lines serves several communities along I–90, including Billings, Livingston, Bozeman, and Butte. Karst Stage/4x4 Stage has regional service in the Bozeman area, plus service from Bozeman to Big Sky. Rimrock Trailways, which is based in Billings, serves major communities in the state.

Information **Greyhound Lines** (☎ *800/231–2222* ⊕ *www.greyhound.com*). **Karst Stage/4x4 Stage** (☎ *800/845–2778* ⊕ *www.karststage.com*). **Rimrock Trailways** (☎ *800/255–7655* ⊕ *www.rimrocktrailways.com*).

CAR RENTAL

You can rent anything from an economy car on up at the Bozeman and Butte airports; a four-wheel-drive vehicle may be necessary for some winter travel.

Contacts **Avis** (☎ *406/388–6414 or 800/331–1212* ⊕ *www.avis.com*). **Budget** (☎ *406/388–4091 or 800/527–0700* ⊕ *www.budget.com*). **Hertz** (☎ *406/388–6939 or 800/654–3131* ⊕ *www.hertz.com*). **National** (☎ *406/388–6694 or 800/227–3768* ⊕ *www.nationalcar.com*). **Thrifty** (☎ *406/388–3484 or 877/283–0898* ⊕ *www.thrifty.com*).

CAR TRAVEL

Major routes are paved and well maintained, but there are many gravel and dirt roads off the beaten track. When heading into remote regions, be sure to fill up the gas tank, and check road reports for construction delays or passes that may close in severe winter weather. Always carry a flashlight, drinking water and some food, a first-aid kit, and emergency overnight gear (a sleeping bag and extra, warm clothing). Most important, make sure someone is aware of your travel plans. While driving, be prepared for animals crossing roads, livestock on open ranges along the highway, and other hazards such as high winds and dust- or snowstorms.

When driving in the mountains in winter, make sure you have tire chains, studs, or snow tires.

Information **Montana Highway Patrol** (☎ *406/388–3190 or 800/525–5555* ⊕ *www.doj.mt.gov/enforcement/highwaypatrol/*). **Statewide Road Report** (☎ *800/226–7623* ⊕ *www.mdt.mt.gov/travinfo/*).

LODGING

Contacts **Montana Bed & Breakfast Association** (☎ *406/582–8440* ⊕ *www.mtbba.com*). **Montana Dude Ranchers' Association** (☎ *888/284–4133* ⊕ *www.montanadra.com*). **Mountain Home–Montana Vacation Rentals** (☎ *406/586–4589 or 800/550–4589* ⊕ *www.mountain-home.com*). **Montana Innkeepers Association** (☎ *406/449–8408* ⊕ *www.montanainnkeepers.com*).

CAMPING There are numerous campsites throughout the region, and they vary from rustic (with pit toilets) to relatively plush (with cabins and heated swimming pools). When camping, ask about bears in the area and whether or not food must be stored inside a hard-side vehicle (not a tent). Avoid bringing pets to campgrounds—it can lead to confrontations with the wildlife, and it's against the rules at most campgrounds.

Contact Montana Fish, Wildlife & Parks for information on camping in state parks and the U.S. Forest Service for information on camping at national parks in the area.

Information **Montana Fish, Wildlife & Parks** (☎ *406/444–2535* ⊕ *www.fwp.state. mt.us/parks*). **U.S. Forest Service** (☎ *406/329–3511* ⊕ *www.fs.fed.us/r1*).

SPORTS & THE OUTDOORS

When you are heading into the backcountry, it's best to hire a guide or outfitter who knows the local trails, weather patterns, and unique features of the region.

BICYCLING   Adventure Cycling can create route maps and provide other resources for cycling in the region.

Information **Adventure Cycling** (✉ *150 E. Pine St., Missoula 59802* ☎ *406/721– 1776* ⊕ *www.adventurecycling.org*).

FISHING   Fishing Outfitters Association of Montana and Montana Outfitters and Guides Association can help you find outfitters who lead fishing excursions throughout the state.

Contacts **Fishing Outfitters Association of Montana** (⌂ *Box 67, Gallatin Gateway 59730* ☎ *406/763–5436* ⊕ *www.foam-montana.org*). **Montana Outfitters and Guides Association** (⌂ *2033 11th Ave. #8, Helena 59601* ☎ *406/449–3578* ⊕ *www.montanaoutfitters.org*).

SKIING   The best information for downhill and cross-country skiing is available through the state tourism bureau, Travel Montana. There's detailed information on the Web site, and you can order a free winter guide.

Contacts **Travel Montana** (✉ *301 S. Park Ave., Helena 59620* ☎ *406/841–2870 or 800/847–4868* ⊕ *www.visitmt.com*).

VISITOR INFORMATION

Travel Montana is the state's tourism bureau.

Tourist Information **Beaverhead Chamber of Commerce** (✉ *10 W. Reeder, Box 425, Dillon 59725* ☎ *406/683–5511* ⊕ *www.beaverheadchamber.org*). **Big Sky Chamber of Commerce** (⌂ *Box 160100, Big Sky 59716* ☎ *406/995–3000 or 800/943–4111* ⊕ *www.bigskychamber.com*). **Bozeman Chamber of Commerce** (✉ *2000 Commerce Way, Bozeman 59715* ☎ *406/586–5421 or 800/228–4224* ⊕ *www.bozemanchamber.com*). **Gold West Country** (✉ *1105 Main St., Deer Lodge 59722* ☎ *406/846–1943 or 800/879–1159* ⊕ *www.goldwest.visitmt.com*). **Helena Chamber of Commerce** (✉ *225 Cruse Ave., Helena 59601* ☎ *406/442–4120 or 800/743–5362* ⊕ *www.helenachamber.com*). **Red Lodge Chamber of Commerce** (✉ *601 N. Broadway, Red Lodge 59068* ☎ *406/446–1718 or 888/281–0625* ⊕ *www.redlodge.com*). **Travel Montana** (✉ *301 S. Park Ave., Helena 59620* ☎ *406/841–2870 or 800/847–4868* ⊕ *www.visitmt.com*). **Yellowstone Country** (✉ *1820 W. Lincoln, Bozeman 59715* ☎ *406/556–8680* ⊕ *www.yellowstonecountry. net*).

Glacier National Park

WORD OF MOUTH

"Be sure to drive into Many Glacier. One of the best places to see grizzly. They also have some great trails if not snowed in. [You] could also visit Two Medicine area, which is lower in elevation. Outside of Walton is the goat overlook, where mountain goats come down to eat mineral salts out of the ground."

–Photodog

WELCOME TO GLACIER

TOP REASONS TO GO

★ **Witness the Divide:** The rugged mountains that weave their way through Glacier and Waterton along the Continental Divide seem to have glaciers in every hollow melting into tiny streams, raging rivers, and icy-cold mountain lakes.

★ **Just Hike It:** There are more than 700 mi of trails that cater to hikers of all levels—from all-day hikes to short strolls. It's little wonder the readers of *Backpacker Magazine* rated Glacier the number-one backcountry hiking park in America.

★ **Go to the Sun:** Crossing the Continental Divide at the 6,646-foot-high Logan Pass, Glacier's Going-to-the-Sun Road is a spectacular drive.

★ **View the Wildlife:** This is one of the few places in North America where all native carnivores, including grizzlies and wolves, still survive. Bighorn sheep, mule deer, coyotes, grizzly bears, and black bears can often be seen from roadways.

1 West Glacier. Known to the Kootenai people as "sacred dancing lake," Lake McDonald is the largest glacial water basin lake in Glacier National Park.

2 Logan Pass. At 6,646 feet, this is the highest point on the Going-to-the-Sun Road. From mid-June to mid-October, a 1½-mi boardwalk leads to an overlook that crosses an area filled with lush meadows and wildflowers.

3 East Glacier. St. Mary Lake and Many Glacier are the major highlights of the eastern side of Glacier. Services and amenities are at both sites.

4 Backcountry. This is some of the most incredible terrain in North America and provides the right combination of beautiful scenery and isolation. Although Waterton is a much smaller park, its backcountry trails connect with hiking trails in both Glacier and British Columbia's Akamina-Kishinena Provincial Park.

MONTAN

Polebridge

GETTING ORIENTED

In the rocky northwest corner of Montana, Glacier National Park encompasses 1.2 million acres (1,563 square mi) of untrammeled wilds. Within the park, there are 37 named glaciers (which are ever-so-slowly diminishing), 200 lakes, and 1,000 mi of streams. Neighboring Waterton Lakes National Park, across the border in Alberta, Canada, covers another 130,000 acres. In 1932 the parks were unified to form the Waterton-Glacier International Peace Park—the first international peace park in the world—in recognition of the two nations' friendship and dedication to peace.

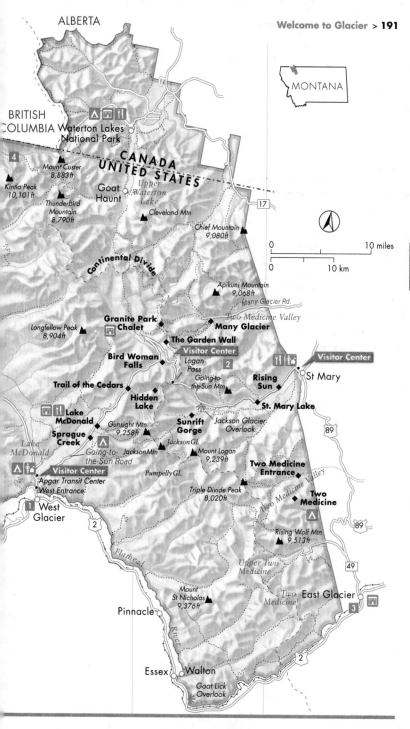

ALBERTA

MONTANA

BRITISH
COLUMBIA

Waterton Lakes
National Park

CANADA
UNITED STATES

4

Mount Custer
8,883 ft

Kintla Peak
10,101 ft

Thunderbird
Mountain
8,790 ft

Goat
Haunt

Upper
Waterton
Lake

Cleveland Mtn

Chief Mountain
9,080 ft

17

0   10 miles

0   10 km

5

Continental Divide

Apikuni Mountain
9,068 ft

Many Glacier Rd.

Two Medicine Valley

Longfellow Peak
8,904 ft

Granite Park
Chalet

Many Glacier

The Garden Wall

Visitor Center

Bird Woman
Falls

Logan
Pass

2

Going-to-
the-Sun Mtn

Rising
Sun

Visitor Center

St Mary

Trail of the Cedars

Hidden
Lake

St. Mary Lake

Lake
McDonald

Gunsight Mtn
9,258 ft

Sunrift
Gorge

Jackson Glacier
Overlook

89

Sprague
Creek

Jackson Gl.

Lake
McDonald

Going-to-
the-Sun Road

Jackson Mtn

Mount Logan
9,239 ft

Pumpelly Gl.

Two Medicine
Entrance

Two Medicine Valley

Two
Medicine

Visitor Center

Apgar Transit Center
West Entrance

Triple Divide Peak
8,020 ft

89

1 West
Glacier

2

Rising Wolf Mtn
9,513 ft

Flathead

Upper Two
Medicine

49

Mount
St Nicholas
9,376 ft

Two
Medicine

East Glacier

Pinnacle

River

3

2

Essex

Walton

Goat Lick
Overlook

GLACIER NATIONAL PARK PLANNER

When to Go

Getting There & Around

Of the 2 million annual visitors to Glacier, **the vast majority drive through the gates between July 1 and September 15,** when Going-to-the-Sun Road is plowed free of snow, providing visitors with spectacular vistas. Spring and fall are the quiet seasons, but they're becoming increasingly popular. By October, snow forces the closing of most park roads.

Snow removal on the alpine portion of Going-to-the-Sun Road is usually completed by mid-June, and the opening of Logan Pass at the road's summit marks the summer opening of Glacier.

On the east, U.S. 89 accesses Many Glacier and St. Mary; Route 49 reaches Two Medicine. On the west, U.S. 2 goes to West Glacier. The nearest airports are in Great Falls and Kalispell, Montana.

The roads are either paved or gravel and deteriorate from moisture freezing and thawing. Drive slowly and anticipate that rocks and wildlife may be around the corner. Road reconstruction is part of the park experience, as there are only a few warm months in which road crews can complete projects. Scenic pullouts are frequent; watch for other vehicles pulling in or out, and watch for children in parking areas. It's also courteous to pull over if you are traveling slowly and there are cars behind you. Most development and services center around St. Mary Lake on the east, and Lake McDonald on the west.

Glacier Park, Inc. operates a shuttle along the Going-to-the-Sun Road from July 1 to Labor Day. Buses make stops at major trailheads, campgrounds, and other developed areas between Lake McDonald Lodge and Rising Sun Motor Inn. For schedules and fares call ☎406/226–4041 or see ⊕ *www.glacierparkinc.com.* Reservations are suggested. To get between the parks, take Chief Mountain Highway from June to September.

Flora & Fauna

In summer a profusion of new flowers, grasses, and budding trees covers the landscape high and low. Spring attracts countless birds, from golden eagles riding thermals north to Canada and Alaska, to rare harlequin ducks dipping in creeks. Snow-white mountain goats, with their wispy white beards and curious stares, are seen in alpine areas, and sure-footed bighorn sheep graze the high meadows in the short summers. The largest population of grizzly bears in the lower 48 states lives in the wild in and around the park. Feeding any animal is illegal.

Visiting Glacier in winter makes for easy tracking of many large animals like moose, elk, deer, mountain lions, wolf, lynx, and their smaller neighbors the snowshoe hare, pine marten, beaver, and muskrat.

In park lakes, sportfishing species include burbot (ling), northern pike, whitefish, grayling, Westslope cutthroat, rainbow, lake (Mackinaw), kokanee salmon, and brook trout.

Tours

Glacier Park, Inc. schedules driver-narrated van tours that cover most of the park accessible by road. The tour of Going-to-the-Sun Road is a favorite, with plenty of photo opportunities at roadside pullouts. Some of the tours are conducted in "Jammers," vintage 1936 red buses with roll-back tops. Their white vans operate on the east side of the park, taking groups to East Glacier, Many Glacier, and Waterton. Short trips and full-day trips are available. Reservations are essential. ✉ Box 2025, Columbia Falls, MT 59912 ☎ 406/892-2525 ⊕ www.glacierparkinc.com ☞ $25–$75 ⊗ June–late Sept.

Safety Tips

Never approach a bear or any other park animal, no matter how cute, cuddly, and harmless it appears. If you encounter a bear, don't run. Back away slowly and assume a nonthreatening posture. If a grizzly bear charges, drop into the fetal position, protect your head and neck, and do not move. Don't plan on climbing a tree since many in the area don't have adequate branches, plus grizzlies have been known to "climb" up to 31 feet by sheer momentum. If a black bear or mountain lion approaches you, act aggressively, throw rocks or sticks, and try to look large by holding up a pack or branches. If attacked, fight back, aiming for the eyes and nose. Some people carry bear spray, a capsaicin repellent used as a last resort in an attack situation. Pick up information on how to prevent and handle aggressive encounters, or talk with a park ranger before venturing on the trails.

To minimize the risk of contact with bears and mountain lions, hike only during the day, hike in groups, and make lots of noise by singing, talking loudly, and clapping hands, especially near blind corners and streams. If you discover a carcass anywhere near the trail, leave the area immediately and report it to a park ranger.

Check for ticks after walking through shrubs and high grasses. They are a problem especially in spring.

Updated by
Amy Grisak

THE MASSIVE PEAKS OF THE Continental Divide in northwest Montana are the backbone of Glacier National Park and its sister park in Canada, Waterton Lakes, which together make up the International Peace Park. From their slopes, melting snow and alpine glaciers yield the headwaters of rivers that flow west to the Pacific Ocean, north to the Arctic Ocean, and southeast to the Atlantic Ocean via the Gulf of Mexico. Coniferous forests, thickly vegetated stream bottoms, and green-carpeted meadows provide homes and sustenance for all kinds of wildlife.

SCENIC DRIVES

Fodor'sChoice
★

Going-to-the-Sun Road. This magnificent, 50-mi highway—a National Historic Civil Engineering Landmark—crosses the crest of the Continental Divide at Logan Pass and traverses the towering Garden Wall. The Federal Highway Administration and the park have embarked on a multiyear road rehabilitation, which will see this narrow, curving highway undergo structural repair. A shuttle system is provided by the National Park Service to decrease the amount of traffic during the construction.

Many Glacier Road. This 12-mi drive enters Glacier on the northeast side of the park, west of Babb, and travels along Sherburne Lake for almost 5 mi, penetrating a glacially carved valley surrounded by mountains. It passes through meadows and a scrubby forest of lodgepole pines, aspen, and cottonwood. The farther you travel up the valley, the more clearly you'll be able to see Grinnell and Salamander glaciers. The road passes Many Glacier Hotel and ends at the Swift Current Campground. It's usually closed from October to May.

WHAT TO SEE

To decrease traffic during the rehabilitation of Going-to-the-Sun Road, the free **Glacier Park Shuttle Service** is available from July 1 to Labor Day. Starting points are the Apgar Transit Center and St. Mary Visitor Center with 16 stops, and riders can get on or off the shuttle at any point of the route. No reservations are required. Be sure to take everything you need with you. For more information on specific routes and recommendations, see the Glacier National Park Web site (⊕*www.nps.gov/glac*).

Apgar. On the southwest end of Lake McDonald, this tiny hamlet has a few stores, an ice-cream shop, motels, ranger buildings, a campground, and a historic schoolhouse. From November to mid-May, no services remain open, except the weekend-only visitor center. ⊠*2 mi north of the west entrance.*

☾ The **Apgar Discovery Cabin,** across the street from the Apgar Visitor Center, is filled with animal posters, kids' activities, and maps. ☎*406/888–7939* ☾*Mid-June–Labor Day.*

CLOSE UP

Going-to-the-Sun Road

Going-to-the-Sun Road, arguably the most beautiful drive in the country, connects Lake McDonald on the west side of Glacier with St. Mary Lake on the east. Turnoffs provide views of the high country and glacier-carved valleys. The sights below are listed in order from west to east.

The Garden Wall. An abrupt and jagged wall of rock juts above the road and is visible for about 10 mi as it follows Logan Creek from just past Avalanche Creek Campground to Logan Pass. ⊠ *24–34 mi from West Glacier.*

Logan Pass. At 6,660 feet this is the highest point in the park accessible by motor vehicle. It presents unparalleled views of both sides of the Continental Divide and is frequented by mountain goats, bighorn sheep, and grizzly bears. It is extremely crowded in July and August. ⊠ *34 mi from West Glacier, 18 mi from St. Mary.*

Hidden Lake Overlook. Take a walk from Logan Pass up to see the crystalline Hidden Lake, which often still has ice clinging to it in early July. It's a 1½-mi hike on an uphill grade, partially on a boardwalk that protects the abundant wildflowers. ⊠ *1½ mi from Logan Pass, Going-to-the-Sun Rd.*

Jackson Glacier Overlook. On the east side of the Continental Divide, you come into view of Jackson Glacier looming in a rocky pass across the upper St. Mary River valley. If it isn't covered with snow, you'll see sharp peaks of ice. The glacier is shrinking and may disappear in another 100 years. ⊠ *5 mi east of Logan Pass.*

St. Mary Lake. When the breezes calm, the lake mirrors the snow-capped granite peaks that line the St. Mary Valley. The Sun Point Nature

Trail follows the lake's shore 1 mi each way. You can buy an interpretive brochure for 50¢ at the trailhead on the north side of the lake, then drop it off at the box at the trail's end to be recycled. ⊠ *1 mi west of St. Mary.*

■TIP➜ **The drive is susceptible to frequent delays in summer. To avoid traffic jams and parking problems, take the road early in the morning or late in the evening** (when the lighting is ideal for photography and wildlife is most likely to appear). Vehicle size is restricted to under 21 feet long, 10 feet high, and 8 feet wide, including mirrors, between Avalanche Creek Campground and Sun Point. From late October to late May or June, deep snows close most of Going-to-the-Sun Road.

If you don't want to drive the Going-to-the-Sun Road, consider making the ride in a Jammer, an antique red bus operated by **Glacier Park, Inc.** (☎ *406/892–2525* ⊕ *www. glacierparkinc.com*). The drivers double as guides, and they can roll back the tops of the vehicles to give you improved views. Reservations are required.

5

SCENIC STOPS

⇨ *Going-to-the-Sun Road box for stops along that road.*

Goat Lick Overlook. Mountain goats frequent this natural salt lick on a cliff above the Middle Fork of the Flathead River. ⊠ *2½ mi east of Walton Ranger Station on U.S. 2.*

Grinnell and Salamander Glaciers. These glaciers formed about 4,000 years ago as one ice mass. In 1926 they broke apart and have been shrinking ever since. The best viewpoint is reached by the 5½-mi Grinnell Glacier Trail from Many Glacier. ⊠ *5½ mi from Swiftcurrent Campground on Grinnell Glacier Trail.*

Lake McDonald. This beautiful 10-mi-long lake is accessible year-round on Going-to-the-Sun Road. Take a boat ride to the middle for a view of the surrounding glacier-clad mountains. You can go fishing and horseback riding at either end, and in winter, snowshoe or cross-country ski. ⊠ *2 mi from west entrance at Apgar.*

Running Eagle Falls (Trick Falls). Cascading near Two Medicine, this is actually two different waterfalls from two different sources. In spring, when the water level is high, the upper falls join the lower falls for a 40-foot drop into Two Medicine River; in summer, the upper falls dry up, revealing the lower 20-foot falls that start midway down the precipice. ⊠ *2 mi east of Two Medicine entrance.*

Two Medicine Valley. Rugged, often windy, and always beautiful, the valley is a remote 9-mi drive from Route 49 and is surrounded by some of the park's most stark, rocky peaks. On and around the valley's lake you can rent a canoe, take a narrated boat tour, camp, and hike. Be aware that bears frequent the area. The road is closed from late October through late May. ⊠ *Two Medicine entrance, 9 mi east of Hwy. 49* ☎ *406/888–7800, 406/257–2426 boat tours.*

VISITOR CENTERS

☾ **Apgar Visitor Center.** This is a great first stop if you're entering the park from the west. Here you can get all kinds of information, including maps, permits, books, and the *Junior Ranger* newspaper. You can plan your route on a large relief map to get a glimpse of where you're going. In winter the rangers offer free snowshoe walks—they provide the snowshoes, too. ☎ *406/888–7800* ☼ *Mid-May–Oct., daily 8–8; Nov.–mid-May, weekends 9–4.*

Logan Pass Visitor Center. Built of stone, this center stands sturdy against the severe weather that forces it to close in winter. Books, maps, and more are stocked inside. Rangers staff the center and give 10-minute talks on the alpine environment. ⊠ *34 mi from West Glacier, 18 mi from St. Mary* ☎ *406/888–7800* ☼ *Mid-June–Labor Day, daily 9–7.*

St. Mary Visitor Center. The park's largest visitor complex is undergoing a major renovation, including the construction of a new parking lot. The lot and most of the center's interior are due to be finished by mid-June 2008. Some of the permanent exhibits won't be ready until 2010 but in the meantime, there's a 15-minute video that orients

GLACIER IN ONE DAY

It's hard to beat the **Going-to-the-Sun Road** for a one-day trip in Glacier National Park. This itinerary takes you from west to east—if you're starting from St. Mary, take the tour backward. First, however, call Glacier Park Boat Tours ☎406/257–2426 to make a reservation for the **St. Mary Lake or Lake McDonald boat tour**, depending on where you end up. Then, drive up Going-to-the-Sun Road to **Avalanche Creek Campground** and take a 30-minute stroll along the fragrant **Trail of the Cedars.** Afterward, continue driving up—you can see views of waterfalls and wildlife to the left and an awe-inspiring, precipitous drop to the right. At the summit, **Logan Pass**, your arduous climb is rewarded with a gorgeous view of immense peaks, sometimes complemented by a herd of mountain goats. Stop in at the **visitor center**, then take the 1½-mi **Hidden Lake Trail** up to prime wildlife-viewing spots. Picnic at the overlook above Hidden Lake. In the afternoon, continue driving east over the mountains. Stop at the **Jackson Glacier Overlook** to view one of the park's largest glaciers. Continue down; eventually the forest thins, the vistas grow broader, and a gradual transition to the high plains begins. When you reach **Rising Sun Campground,** take the one-hour St. Mary Lake boat tour to St. Mary Falls. If you'd rather hike, the 1-mi **Sun Point Nature Trail** also leads to the falls. (Take the boat tour if you're driving from east to west.) The Going-to-the-Sun Road is generally closed from early October to late May.

visitors. Rangers host evening presentations during the peak summer months. Traditional Blackfeet dancing and drumming performances are offered throughout the summer. Check with the center for exact dates and times. The center has books and maps for sale, backcountry camping permits, and large viewing windows facing the 10-mi-long St. Mary Lake. ⊠ *Going-to-the-Sun Rd. off U.S. 89* ☎*406/732–7750* ⊗*Mid-May–mid-June and Sept.–Oct., daily 8–5; late June–Labor Day, daily 7–9.*

SPORTS & THE OUTDOORS

OUTFITTER &
EXPEDITIONS
Glacier Heli Tours. This outfitter offers one-hour and half-hour tours of Glacier or up to six people, weather permitting. The half-hour tour covers the park's major glaciers and lakes, while the one-hour tour encompasses the entire park. Headsets allow you to hear the pilot's narration. ⊡*11950 Hwy 2 E, West Glacier, MT 59936* ☎*406/387–4141 or 800/879–9310* ⊕*www.glacierhelitours.com* ⊠*Tours $100–$780 per person* ⊗*May–Oct.*

BICYCLING

Cyclists in Glacier must stay on roads or bike routes and are not permitted on hiking trails or in the backcountry. Bicyclists practically have the park to themselves in April and May before the roads are open to vehicle traffic. This is an ideal time to enjoy it before the summer bustle. The one-lane, unpaved Inside North Fork Road from Apgar to

Polebridge is well suited to mountain bikers. Two Medicine Road is an intermediate paved route, with a mild grade at the beginning, becoming steeper as you approach Two Medicine Campground. Bicycles are not permitted past Apgar campground on Going-to-the-Sun Road from 11 to 4, although during the summer full moons, groups of bicyclists pedal to Logan Pass and cruise back down in the bright moonlight. Other restrictions apply during road construction.

BOATING & RAFTING

Glacier has many stunning lakes and rivers, making boating a popular park activity. Glacier Park Boat Company offers guided tours of Lake McDonald, St. Mary Lake, and Two Medicine Lake, as well as Swiftcurrent and Josephine lakes at Many Glacier from June to midSeptember. You can rent small boats at Lake McDonald, Apgar, Two Medicine, and Many Glacier (⇨ *Glacier Park Boat Company below*). Watercraft such as Sea-Doos or Jet Skis are not allowed in the park.

Many rafting companies provide adventures along the border of the park on the Middle and North forks of the Flathead River. The Middle Fork has some excellent white water, and the North Fork has both slow-moving and fast-moving sections. If you bring your own raft or kayak, stop at the Hungry Horse Ranger Station in the Flathead National Forest near West Glacier to obtain a permit.

OUTFITTERS & **Glacier Park Boat Company** gives tours on five lakes. A **Lake McDonald**
EXPEDITIONS **cruise** takes you from the dock at Lake McDonald Lodge to the middle
★ of the lake for an unparalleled view of the Continental Divide's Garden Wall. Cruises on **Swiftcurrent Lake** and **Lake Josephine** depart from Many Glacier Lodge and provide views of the Continental Divide. **Two Medicine Lake cruises** leave from the dock near the ranger station and lead to several trails. **St. Mary Lake cruises** leave from the launch near Rising Sun Campground and head to Red Eagle Mountain and other spots. The tours last 45–90 minutes. You can rent kayaks, canoes, rowboats, and small motorboats at Lake McDonald, Apgar, Two Medicine, and Many Glacier. ☎406/257–2426 ⊕*www.glacierparkboats. com* 🖃*Tours under $20; rentals $12–$22/hr* ☉*June–Oct.*

Glacier Guides and Montana Raft Company will take you on raft trips through the stomach-churning white water of the Middle Fork of the Flathead and combine it with a hike, horseback ride, or barbecue. The company also offers guided hikes and fly-fishing trips. ⊠*11970 U.S. 2 E, 1 mi west of West Glacier* ☎*406/387–5555 or 800/521–7238* ⊕*www.glacierguides.com* 🖃*$47–$102* ☉*May–Oct.*

Great Northern Whitewater offers half-day, full-day, and multiday whitewater, kayaking, and fishing trips, and rents Swiss-style chalets with views of Glacier's peaks. ⊠*12127 U.S. 2 E, 1 mi south of West Glacier* ☎*406/387–5340 or 800/735–7897* ⊕*www.gnwhitewater.com* 🖃*$44–$295* ☉*May–Oct.*

⇨*Multisport Outfitters box for more options.*

FISHING

Within Glacier there's an almost unlimited range of fishing possibilities, with a catch-and-release policy encouraged. You can fish in most waters of the park, but the best fishing is generally in the least accessible spots. A fishing license is not required inside the park boundary, but you must stop by a park office to pick up a copy of the regulations. The fishing season runs from the third Saturday in May to November 30.

> ### GLACIERS AWAY?
>
> Call it global warming or call it a natural progression, but the glaciers at Glacier National Park are feeling the heat. By 2050, or earlier, it is estimated that all of the glaciers in the park will have melted. Currently there are 37 named glaciers in the park (at one time there were 200).

■ TIP→ **Fishing on both the North Fork and the Middle Fork of the Flathead River requires a Montana conservation license ($10) plus a Montana fishing license ($15 for two consecutive days or $60 for a season).** They are available at most convenience stores, sports shops, and from the Montana Department of Fish, Wildlife, and Parks (☎406/752–5501).

GOLF

Glacier Park Lodge has a 9-hole, par-36 course, and a 9-hole pitch-and-putt course. Watch out for moose. ⊠ *Off U.S. 2, East Glacier* ☎*406/226–9311.*

HIKING

With 730 mi of marked trails, Glacier is a hiker's paradise. Trail maps are available at all visitor centers and entrance stations. Before hiking, ask about trail closures because of bear or mountain lion activity. Never hike alone. For backcountry hiking, pick up information on closures and a map from park headquarters (☎406/888–7800) or the Apgar backcountry office near Glacier's western entrance (☎406/888–7939).

EASY **Avalanche Lake Trail.** From Avalanche Creek Campground, take this 3-mi trail leading to mountain-ringed Avalanche Lake. The walk is relatively easy (it ascends 500 feet), making this one of the most accessible backcountry lakes in the park. Crowds fill the parking area and trail during July and August, and on sunny weekends in May and June. ⊠ *15 mi north of Apgar on Going-to-the-Sun Rd.*

Baring Falls. For a nice family hike, try the 1.3-mi path from the Sun Point parking area. It leads to a spruce and Douglas fir wood; cross a log bridge over Baring Creek and you arrive at the base of gushing Baring Falls. ⊠ *11 mi east of Logan Pass on Going-to-the-Sun Rd..*

★ **Hidden Lake Nature Trail.** This uphill, 1½-mi trail runs from Logan Pass southwest to Hidden Lake Overlook, from which you get a beautiful view of the lake and McDonald Valley. In spring, ribbons of water pour off the rocks surrounding the lake. ⊠ *Logan Pass Visitor Center.*

☺ **Trail of the Cedars.** This wheelchair-accessible, ½-mi boardwalk loop
★ through an ancient cedar and hemlock forest is a favorite of families with small children and people with disabilities. Interpretive signs describe the habitat and natural history of the rain forest. ⊠ *Avalanche Creek Campground, 15 mi north of Apgar on Going-to-the-Sun Rd.*

MODERATE **Highline Trail.** From the Logan Pass parking lot, hike north along the
Fodor'sChoice Garden Wall and just below the craggy Continental Divide. Wildflow-
★ ers dominate the 7½ mi to Granite Park Chalet, a National Historic Landmark, where hikers with reservations can overnight. Return to Logan Pass along the same trail or hike down 4½ mi (a 2,500-foot descent) on the Loop Trail. ⊠ *Logan Pass Visitor Center.*

Iceberg Lake Trail. This moderately strenuous 9-mi round-trip hike passes the gushing Ptarmigan Falls, then climbs to its namesake, where icebergs bob in the chilly mountain lake. Mountain goats hang out on sheer cliffs above, bighorn sheep graze in the high mountain meadows, and grizzly bears dig for glacier lily bulbs, grubs, and ground squirrels. Rangers lead hikes here almost daily in summer, leaving at 8:30 AM. ⊠ *Swiftcurrent Inn parking lot off Many Glacier Rd.*

DIFFICULT **Grinnell Glacier Trail.** The strenuous 5½-mi hike to Grinnell Glacier, the
★ park's largest and most accessible glacier, is marked by several spectacular viewpoints. You start at Swiftcurrent Lake's picnic area, climb a moraine to Lake Josephine, then climb to the Grinnell Glacier overlook. Halfway up, turn around to see the prairie land to the northeast. You can short-cut the trail by 2 mi each way by taking two scenic boat rides across Swiftcurrent and Josephine lakes. From July to mid-September, a ranger-led hike departs from the Many Glacier Hotel boat dock most mornings at 8:30. ⊠ *Josephine boat dock.*

Two Medicine Valley Trails. One of the least developed parts of Glacier, the lovely southeast corner of the park is a good place for a quiet day hike, although you should look out for signs of bears. The trailhead to Upper Two Medicine Lake and Cobalt Lake begins west of the boat dock and camp supply store, where you can make arrangements for a boat pickup or drop-off across the lake. ⊠ *Two Medicine Campground, 9 mi west of Rte. 49.*

HORSEBACK RIDING

Horses are permitted on many trails within the parks; check for seasonal exceptions. Horseback riding is prohibited on paved roads. You can pick up a brochure about suggested routes and outfitters from any visitor center or entrance station. The Sperry Chalet Trail to the view of Sperry Glacier above Lake McDonald is a tough 7-mi climb.

OUTFITTERS & **Glacier Gateway Outfitters** offers one-hour or full-day rides in the Two
EXPEDITIONS Medicine area with a Blackfeet cowboy as your guide. Rides begin across the road from Glacier Park Lodge and climb through aspen groves to high-country views of Dancing Lady and Bison mountains. You can enjoy a rodeo every Tuesday evening. All riders must be older than seven. Walk-ins are welcome, or reservations are handled through

MULTISPORT OUTFITTERS

Glacier Raft Company and Outdoor Center. In addition to running white-water, scenic, and fishing trips, this outfitter will set you up with camping, backpacking, and fishing gear. There's a full-service fly-fishing shop and outdoor store. You can stay in one of nine cabins that sleep from 6 to 14 people. ✉ *11957 U.S. 2 E, West Glacier* ☎ *406/888–5454 or 800/235–6781* ⊕ *www.glacierraftco. com* 🖅 *$46–$83* ⊗ *Year-round; rafting mid-May–Sept.*

Wild River Adventures. These guys will paddle you over the Middle Fork of the Flathead, and peddle tall tales all the while. They also provide trail rides, and scenic fishing trips on rivers around Glacier Park. ✉ *11900 U.S. 2 E, 1 mi west of West Glacier* ☎ *406/387–9453 or 800/700–7056* ⊕ *www.RiverWild.com* 🖅 *$47–$76* ⊗ *Mid-May–Sept.*

Glacier Park, Inc. (☎ 406/892–2525). ⌂ *Box 411, East Glacier 59434* ☎ *406/338—5560 for info in winter* 🖅 *$25–$175* ⊗ *June–Sept.*

Swan Mountain Outfitters have corrals at Apgar, Lake McDonald, and Many Glacier. Trips range from one hour to all day, and can accommodate most riding levels. Children must be at least seven years old to ride on the west side, and eight to ride from Many Glacier. No riders over 250 pounds are allowed. Reservations are essential. ⌂ *Box 5081, Swan Lake 59911* ☎ *877/888–5557, 800/919–4416 in winter* ⊕ *www.swanmountainoutfitters.com* 🖅 *$32/hr, $135/full day* ⊗ *Mid-May–mid-Sept.* ▤ *MC, V.*

SKIING & SNOWSHOEING

Cross-country skiing and snowshoeing are increasingly popular in the park. Glacier distributes a free pamphlet titled *Ski Trails of Glacier National Park,* with 16 noted trails. You can start at Lake McDonald Lodge and cross-country ski up Going-to-the-Sun Road. The 2½-mi Apgar Natural Trail is popular with snowshoers. No restaurants or stores are open in winter in Glacier.

OUTFITTERS & EXPEDITIONS **Glacier Park Ski Tours** leads one-day or multiday guided ski trips on the park's scenic winter trails. They have full-moon tours from 7 to 11 PM, or you can stay in a snow hut or tent on an overnight excursion. ⌂ *Box 4833, Whitefish 59937* ☎ *406/892–2173* ⊕ *www.glacierpark skitours.com* 🖅 *$35–$200* ⊗ *Mid-Nov.–May.*

EDUCATIONAL OFFERINGS

CLASSES & SEMINARS

☾ **Glacier Institute.** Based near West Glacier at the Field Camp and on the remote western boundary at the Big Creek Outdoor Education Center, this learning institute offers more than 75 field courses for kids and adults. Year-round, experts in wildlife biology, native plants, and river

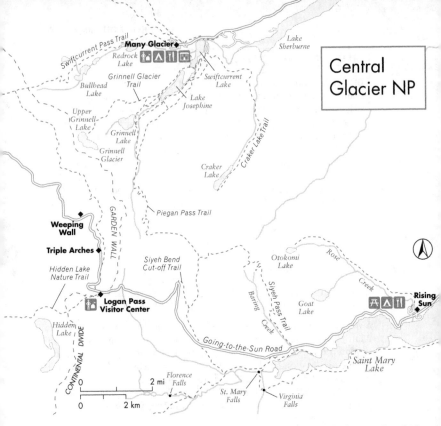

Central Glacier NP

ecology lead treks into Glacier's backcountry on daylong and multiday programs. ✉ *Box 1887, Kalispell 59903* 📞 *406/755–1211* 🌐 *www. glacierinstitute.org.*

KIDS' CAMPS

🕑 **Adventure Camps.** Youngsters ages 7–8 can partake of one-day naturalist courses, older children have hiking or fly-fishing and aquatic ecology courses, and kids 14–16 can take weeklong hiking and rafting trips. Some camps involve backcountry camping, and others are based out of the Big Creek or Glacier Park field camps. Subjects range from ecology and birding to wildflowers, predators and prey, and backcountry medicine. ✉ *137 Main St., Box 1887, Kalispell 59903* 📞 *406/755–1211* 🌐 *www.glacierinstitute.org* 💲 *$95–$350.*

RANGER PROGRAMS

These programs are free to visitors. Most run daily, July through Labor Day. For information on ranger programs, call 406/888–7800.

🕑 **Children's Programs.** Kids learn about bears, wolves, geology, and more via hands-on activities, such as role-playing skits and short hikes. Check the Apgar Education Cabin or Apgar Visitor Center for schedules and locations.

Evening Campfire Programs. Rangers lead discussions on the park's wildlife, geology, and history. The programs occur at park campgrounds, beginning at 8 or 9 PM. Topics and dates are posted at campgrounds, lodges, and the St. Mary Visitor Center.

☺ **Junior Ranger Program.** Year-round, children ages 6–12 can become a Junior Ranger by completing activities in the *Junior Ranger* newspaper. ⊕*www.nps.gov/learn/juniorranger.htm.*

Naturalist activities. Evening slide programs, guided hikes, and boat tours are among the ranger-led activities held at various sites in the park. A complete schedule of programs is listed in *Glacier Explorer.*

TOURS

★ **Sun Tours.** Members of the Blackfeet Nation lead bus tours along Going-to-the-Sun Road. Guides discuss historic and current aspects of Blackfeet culture, and there are plenty of photo ops at scenic spots like the Jackson Glacier Overlook. In summer tours depart every morning from East Glacier, Browning, and St. Mary in air-conditioned coaches. ⊠*29 Glacier Ave., East Glacier* ☎*406/226–9220 or 800/786–9220* ⊕*www. glacierinfo.com* ⌁*$40–$70* ☺*June–Sept., daily.*

NEARBY TOWNS

You can easily spend a week exploring Glacier, but you may wish to take in some nearby sights as well. Outside Glacier National Park are the gateway towns of **East Glacier**, **West Glacier**, and **Columbia Falls**, where you can find tour operators, accommodations, restaurants, and stores. Not far from the park are the towns of **Essex**, **Kalispell**, **Whitefish**, **Browning**, and **Bigfork.** Here you will find some excellent golf courses, terrific cross-country and downhill skiing, summer and winter festivals, and plenty of places to stay and eat.

On the banks of the North Fork of the Flathead River on Glacier National Park's western edge, the tiny community of **Polebridge** (pop. 25) has just one store, one restaurant and saloon, one camp store, and one hostel, yet it is a gem in the wilderness. The entrance station (staffed in summer only) is the gateway to Bowman and Kintla lakes, as well as Logging and Quartz lakes, which are in the backcountry and accessible only by hiking trails.

WHERE TO EAT

ABOUT THE RESTAURANTS

Steak houses featuring certified Angus beef are typical of the region; in recent years, resort communities have diversified their menus to include bison meat, fresh fish, and savory vegetarian options. Small cafés offer hearty, inexpensive meals, and you can pick up on local history through conversation with the local denizens. Trout, venison, elk, moose, and bison appear on the menus inside the park. Attire everywhere is decidedly casual.

Jamming in the Park

Harkening back to the early days of automobile touring in the parks, each summer a fleet of red jammers weaves through Glacier and Waterton Lake national parks. Drivers began jamming gears on the vintage coaches in 1936, but today only guides licensed with Glacier Park, Inc. (☎406/892–2525 ⊕www.glacierparkinc.com) operate them. Park visitors ride them for special tours, as well as to traverse the park and go up the incredible Going-to-the-Sun Road.

One of the most popular drivers is Joe Kendall, known as "Jammer Joe"

to passengers. His lively narration and colorful descriptions of Glacier have endeared him to many park visitors. In fact, he has so won the hearts of fans over his 10 years of service that the park has named a pizza parlor (near Lake McDonald Lodge) after him.

Kendall's wife of 54 years, Geri, also works for Glacier Park, Inc., as tour director for the dozen or so six-day Great Lodges of Glacier Tours each summer.

During the off-season, the Kendalls live in Illinois.

–Debbie Harmsen

WHAT IT COSTS					
	¢	$	$$	$$$	$$$$
RESTAURANTS	under $8	$8–$12	$13–$20	$21–$30	over $30

Restaurant prices are for a main course at dinner.

$$–$$$$ ✕**Great Northern Dining Room.** Here you'll enjoy fine dining in a natural mega-log structure with all the amenities of a first-class dining room that was originally a steak place. Though the restaurant now serves pasta, seafood and chicken, prime rib and steaks are still the house specialties. ⊠*Rte. 49, next to railroad station, East Glacier* ☎*406/226–5600* ♺*Reservations not accepted* ▤*D, MC, V* ۩*Closed Oct.–May.*

$$–$$$ ✕**Ptarmigan Dining Room.** Sophisticated cuisine is served in the dining room of early-20th-century chaletlike Many Glacier Hotel. As the sun sets over Swiftcurrent Lake just outside the massive windows, Italian-inflected food is served amid Swiss-style decor. Each night there's a chef's special such as pork prime rib with a huckleberry demi-glace. For a true Montana creation, have a huckleberry daiquiri. ⊠*Many Glacier Rd.* ☎*406/732–4411 or 406/892–2525* ▤*AE, D, MC, V* ۩*Closed late Sept.–early June.*

$–$$ ✕**Curly Bear Café & Pizza Co.** Buffalo burgers, rotisserie chicken, and pizza fill the menu. An ice-cream parlor is next door. ⊠*St. Mary Lodge, U.S. 89 and Going-to-the-Sun Rd., St. Mary* ☎*406/732–4431* ♺*Reservations not accepted* ▤*AE, D, MC, V* ۩*Closed early Oct.–mid-May.*

$–$$ ✕**Lake McDonald Lodge Restaurants.** In Russell's Fireside Dining Room, take in a great view while choosing between standards such as pasta, steak, and salmon. Don't miss the apple bread pudding with caramel-cinnamon sauce for dessert. Across the parking lot is a cheaper alternative, **Jammer Joe's Grill & Pizzeria,** which serves burgers and pasta for lunch and dinner. ⊠ *10 mi north of Apgar on Going-to-the-Sun Rd.* ☎ *406/888–5431 or 406/892–2525* ⊟ *AE, D, MC, V* ✆ *Closed early Oct.–early June.*

$–$$ ✕ **The Park Café and Grocery.** Not far outside the St. Mary entrance, pies call to hungry travelers. With more than 17 different kinds baked fresh every day, it's no wonder their slogan is "Pie for Strength." Breakfast, lunch, and dinner are traditional American fare—great burgers, sandwiches, barbecue chicken, bison steak, and much more. You'll probably have company waiting on the front porch for a table, but it's well worth it. ⊠ *U.S. Hwy. 89, St. Mary 59417* ☎ *406/732–4482* ⚘ *Reservations not accepted* ⊟ *MC, V* ✆ *Closed late Sept.–Memorial Day.*

PICNIC AREAS There are picnic spots at most campgrounds and visitor centers. Each has tables, grills, and drinking water in summer.

★ **Sun Point.** On the north side of St. Mary Lake, this is one of the most beautiful places in the park for a picnic. ⊠ *Sun Point trailhead.*

WHERE TO STAY

ABOUT THE HOTELS

Lodgings in the park tend to be fairly rustic and simple, though there are a few grand lodges and some modern accommodations. A few modern hotels offer facilities such as swimming pools, hot tubs, boat rentals, guided excursions, or fine dining. Although there is a limited supply of rooms, the prices are relatively reasonable. It's best to reserve well in advance, especially for July and August.

ABOUT THE CAMPGROUNDS

There are 10 major campgrounds in Glacier National Park and excellent backcountry sites for backpackers. Reservations for Fish Creek and St. Mary campgrounds are available through the National Park Reservation Service (☎ 877/444–6777 ⊕ *http://reservations.nps.gov/*). Reservations may be made up to five months in advance.

Outside the park, campgrounds vary from no-services, remote state or federal campsites to upscale commercial operations. During July and August it's best to reserve a camp spot. Ask locally about bears and whether food must be stored inside a hard-side vehicle (not a tent).

WHAT IT COSTS				
¢	$	$$	$$$	$$$$
HOTELS under $50	$50–$100	$100–$150	$150–$200	over $200

Hotel prices are for two people in a standard double room in high season, excluding service charges and a 7% bed tax.

$$$$ ⊡ **Sperry Chalet.** This elegant backcountry lodge, built in 1913 by the Great Northern Railway, is accessible only by a steep, 6½-mi trail with a 3,300-foot vertical rise. Either hike in or arrive on horseback. Guest rooms have no electricity, heat, or running water, but who cares when the view includes Glacier's Gunsight Peak, Mt. Edwards, Lake McDonald, and mountain goats in wildflowers. Look for the "horse and rider" in the mountains on the way up to the chalet. Informal meals, such as turkey with the trimmings, are simple yet filling. Note that the reservations office is closed September and October. Pros: Great meals are a welcome reward after a long hike; there are a lot of day hikes from the chalet; the nicest quarter-million-dollar composting toilet you'll ever see. Cons: Be prepared for a tough climb on the hike up to Sperry; it's best to use a horse, but you have to be dropped off. ⌂ *Box 188, Going-to-the-Sun Rd., West Glacier 59936* ☎ *406/387–5654 or 888/345–2649* ⊕ *www.sperrychalet.com* ⤳ *17 rooms* ⌖ *In-room: no a/c, no phone, no TV. In-hotel: restaurant, no-smoking rooms* ⊟ *AE, MC, V* ⊗ *Closed mid-Sept.–early July* ⊚ *FAP.*

$$–$$$$ 🏨 **Glacier Park Lodge.** On the east side of the park, across from the
★   Amtrak station, you'll find this beautiful hotel built in 1913. The full-service lodge is supported by 500- to 800-year-old fir and 3-foot-thick cedar logs. Rooms are sparsely decorated, but have had recent renovations, including new paint and new linens. There are historic posters on the walls in the halls. Cottages and a house are also available on the grounds next to the golf course. If you golf on the spectacular course, watch out for moose. Entertainers delight guests with storytelling and singing in the great hall. Pros: The gardens up front are a gorgeous place for a morning or evening stroll. Cons: You have to take the long way around, via Highway 2, to reach the Glacier Park Lodge instead of taking Going-to-the-Sun Road. ⊠ *Off U.S. 2, East Glacier* ⌂ *Box 2025, Columbia Falls 59912* ☎ *406/892–2525 or 406/226–5600* 🖷 *406/226–9152* ⊕ *www.glacierparkinc.com* ⤳ *154 rooms* ⌖ *In-room: no a/c, no TV. In-hotel: restaurant, bar, golf course, spa, pool, no-smoking rooms* ⊟ *AE, MC, V* ⊗ *Closed late Sept.–Memorial Day* ⊚ *EP.*

$$–$$$$ 🏨 **Many Glacier Hotel.** The most isolated of the grand hotels—it's on Swiftcurrent Lake on the northeast side of the park—this is also one of the most scenic, especially if you nab one of the balcony rooms. There's a large fireplace in the lobby where guests gather on chilly mornings. Rooms are small and sparsely decorated. Every afternoon in the Interlaken Lounge there's a fondue paired with the appropriate wine or microbrew. Pros: You can often spot grizzlies working the slopes from the parking area. This is truly a place to get away from the cell phone or computer. Cons: Fans can be scarce in summer, and the rooms tend to heat up in late afternoon. ⊠ *Many Glacier Rd., 12 mi west of Babb* ⌂ *Box 2025, Columbia Falls 59912* ☎ *406/892–2525 or 406/732–4411* 🖷 *406/732–5522* ⊕ *www.glacierparkinc.com* ⤳ *211 rooms* ⌖ *In-room: no a/c, no TV, no phone. In-hotel: restaurant, bar, no-smoking rooms, no elevator* ⊟ *AE, MC, V* ⊚ *EP.*

$$–$$$ 🏨 **Village Inn.** On Lake McDonald this motel could use some updating, but it is very popular and offers a great view. All of the plain but serviceable rooms, some with kitchenettes, face the lake. A restaurant, bar, and coffee shop are nearby. Pros: Being on the lake is the best place to be in summer. Cons: There are a lot of people in the area between hotel

lodging and the campground, so it's a far cry from wilderness seclusion. ⊠*Apgar Village* ☎*Box 2025, Columbia Falls 59912* ☎☎*406/888–5632 or 406/892–2525* 🖷*406/888–5636* ⊕*www.glacierparkinc.com* ⟿*36 rooms* ⟳*In-room: no a/c, no elevator* ☰*AE, MC, V* ⊙*Closed late Sept.–June* ⟟⟂*EP.*

$$ ⚏**Lake McDonald Complex.** One of the great historic lodges of the West
★ anchors this complex on the shore of lovely Lake McDonald. Take a room in the lodge itself, where public spaces are filled with massive timbers, stone fireplaces, and animal trophies. Cabins sleep up to four and don't have kitchens; there are also motel-style rooms separate from the lodge. Pros: The deck and walkway overlooking Lake McDonald is absolutely lovely in the evening. Cons: This is the closest historic lodge to "civilization," so it's always busy in and around the place. ⊠*Going-to-the-Sun Rd.* ☎*Box 2025, Columbia Falls 59912* ☎*406/892–2525 or 406/888–5431* 🖷*406/888–5681* ⊕*www.glacier parkinc.com* ⟿*30 rooms, 13 cabins* ⟳*In-room: no a/c, no TV. In-hotel: restaurant, bar, no-smoking rooms, no elevator* ☰*AE, MC, V* ⊙*Closed late Sept.–June.*

$–$$ ⚏**Granite Park Chalet.** Early tourists used to ride horses through the park 7 to 9 mi each day and stay at a different chalet each night. The Granite Park is one of two chalets still standing (the other one is the Sperry Chalet). You can reach it only by hiking trails. You must bring sleeping bags and your own food, and you need a reservation. You can park at Logan Pass Visitor Center and hike 7½ mi or at the Loop trailhead and hike uphill 4 mi. Pros: There's something special about hiking in from Logan Pass and seeing the chalet off in the distance. The structures are gorgeous, and you feel very secure. Cons: Having to either pack a sleeping bag or pay for linens is a downside. For those afraid of bears, this isn't the place to stay. ⊠*7½ mi south of Logan Pass* ☎*Box 189, West Glacier 59936* ☎*406/387–5654 or 888/345–2649* ⊕*www. graniteparkchalet.com* ⟿*12 rooms* ☰*AE, D, MC, V* ⊙*Closed mid-Sept.–early July.*

$–$$ ⚏**Swiftcurrent Motor Inn.** For no-frills overnight accommodations, the rooms and cottages here will keep you warm and dry, and offer a solid wall between you and the bears. The complex includes two large traditional motel buildings, plus a fringe of single and duplex cabins with and without private bathrooms. The ones without their own bathroom have a cold-water sink in the cabin, and there are public showers nearby. In summer a naturalist sets up a spotting scope so that guests can look for bears and bighorns on the surrounding slopes. Pros: You'll have a good chance of seeing a grizzly through the summertime wildlife-viewing scope. Camp store and a great restaurant are nearby. Cons: Cabins are very rustic; some are just a small step up from a tent. The token-operated public showers only give you a few minutes to wash up. ⊠*At end of Many Glacier Rd.* ☎*Box 147, East Glacier 59434* ☎*406/732–5531* 🖷*406/732–5595* ⊕*www.glacierparkinc.com* ⟿*88 rooms* ⟳*Restaurant, laundry facilities* ☰*AE, D, MC, V* ⊙*Closed mid-Sept.–early June.*

5

CAMPING   ⚠ **Apgar Campground.** This large, popular campground on the southern shore of Lake McDonald has many activities and services. From here you can hike, boat, fish, or swim and sign up for trail rides. About 25 sites are suitable for RVs. ✉ *Apgar Rd.* ☎ *406/888–7800* ⛺ *194 sites* ♿ *Flush toilets, pit toilets, dump station, drinking water, bear boxes, fire grates, food service, picnic tables, public telephone, general store, ranger station, swimming (lake)* ▤ *AE, D, MC, V* ⊙ *Closed mid-Oct.– early May.*

⚠ **Avalanche Creek Campground.** This peaceful campground is shaded by huge red cedars and bordered by Avalanche Creek. Trail of the Cedars begins here, and it's along Going-to-the-Sun Road. Some campsites and the comfort stations are wheelchair accessible. There are 50 sites for RVs up to 26 feet. There are evening naturalist programs at the Avalanche Ampitheater. ✉ *Going-to-the-Sun Rd.* ☎ *406/888–7800* ⛺ *87 sites* ♿ *Flush toilets, drinking water, fire grates, picnic tables, public telephone* ▤ *AE, D, MC, V* ⊙ *Closed early Sept.–early June.*

⚠ **Bowman Lake Campground.** In the remote northwestern corner of Glacier, this quiet camping spot is a fishermen's favorite for lake and stream fishing. Mosquitoes can be bothersome here, as can the potholes and ruts in the one-lane drive in from Polebridge. Moose sightings are frequent in this area, particularly in fall. ✉ *Bowman Lake Rd.* ☎ *406/888–7800* ⛺ *48 sites* ♿ *Pit toilets, drinking water, bear boxes, fire grates, picnic tables, ranger station, swimming (lake)* ▤ *AE, D, MC, V* ⊙ *Closed Dec.–mid-May.*

⚠ **Fish Creek Campground.** The quietest sites on Lake McDonald are surrounded by thick evergreen forest; 18 sites are suitable for RVs up to 35 feet. Evening programs by a park ranger are held at the Fish Creek Amphitheater. ✉ *2 mi north of Apgar Visitor Center on Camas Rd.* ☎ *406/888–7800* ⛺ *180 sites* ♿ *Flush toilets, dump station, drinking water* ▤ *AE, D, MC, V* ⊙ *Closed Sept.–June.*

⚠ **Kintla Lake Campground.** Beautiful and remote, this is a trout fishermen's favorite. Trails lead into the backcountry. The dirt access road is rough, so RVs are not recommended. ✉ *14 mi north of Polebridge Ranger Station on Inside North Fork Rd.* ⛺ *13 sites* ♿ *Pit toilets, dump station, bear boxes, fire grates, picnic tables* ▲ *Reservations not accepted* ▤ *AE, D, MC, V* ⊙ *Closed Dec.–May.*

★   ⚠ **Many Glacier Campground.** One of the most beautiful spots in the park is also a favorite for bears. Several hiking trails take off from here, and often ranger-led hikes climb to Grinnell Glacier. Always check posted notices for areas closed because of bears. There are 13 sites that can accommodate RVs up to 35 feet. Showers, including an ADA-compliant unisex shower, are at the nearby Swiftcurrent Motor Inn. ✉ *Many Glacier Rd.* ☎ *406/888–7800* ⛺ *110 sites* ♿ *Flush toilets, pit toilets, drinking water, showers, bear boxes, fire grates, food service, picnic tables, public telephone, ranger station, swimming (lake)* ▤ *AE, D, MC, V* ⊙ *Primitive camping Oct.–late May.*

⚠ **Rising Sun Campground.** As the name says, you can watch the sun rise from your camp, across the peaks and grassy knolls here. The campground is near St. Mary Lake and many hiking trails. Ten sites can accommodate vehicles up to 25 feet long. ✉ *Going-to-the-Sun Rd.*

☎406/888–7800 or 800/365–2267 ➧83 sites ♿Flush toilets, drinking water, showers, bear boxes, fire grates, food service, picnic tables, public telephone, swimming (lake) ▭AE, D, MC, V ☯Closed mid-Sept–late May.

♿**St. Mary Campground.** This large, grassy spot alongside the lake and stream has mountain views and cool breezes. It always seems to be the campground that fills first. There are 25 sites for RVs up to 35 feet. ✉Going-to-the-Sun Rd. ☎406/888–7800 ➧148 sites ♿Flush toilets, pit toilets, drinking water, dump station, bear boxes, fire grates, food service, picnic tables, public telephone, swimming (lake) ▭AE, D, MC, V ☯Closed late Sept.–late May.

♿**Sprague Creek Campground.** This sometimes noisy roadside camp spot for tents, RVs, and campers only (no towed units) offers spectacular views of the lake and sunsets, fishing from shore, and great rock skipping on the beach. There's no designated swimming area, though; most campers just wander over to Lake McDonald. Restaurants, gift shops, and a grocery store are 1 mi north on Going-to-the-Sun Road. ✉Going-to-the-Sun Rd., 1 mi south of Lake McDonald Lodge ☎406/888–7800 ➧25 sites ♿Flush toilets, drinking water, bear boxes, fire grates, picnic tables ♺Reservations not accepted ▭AE, D, MC, V ☯Closed mid-Sept.–mid-May.

♿**Two Medicine Campground.** This is often the last campground to fill during the height of summer since it's out of the way. A general store, snack bar, and boat rentals are available. Thirteen sites will accommodate RVs up to 32 feet. ✉Two Medicine Rd. ☎406/888–7800 ➧99 sites ♿Flush toilets, pit toilets, drinking water, bear boxes, fire grates, food service, picnic tables, public telephone, general store, swimming (lake) ▭AE, D, MC, V ☯Closed late Sept.–late May.

GLACIER ESSENTIALS

ACCESSIBILITY

All visitor centers are wheelchair-accessible, and most of the campgrounds and picnic areas are paved, with extended-length picnic tables and accessible restrooms. Three of Glacier's nature trails are wheelchair-accessible: the Trail of Cedars, Running Eagle Falls, and the Oberlin Bend Boardwalk, just west of Logan Pass.

ADMISSION FEES

Entrance fees for Glacier are $25 per vehicle, or $12 for one person on foot or bike, good for seven days; a one-year pass is $35. A day pass to Waterton Lakes costs C$7 (C$3.45 per child), and an annual pass costs C$35. *Passes to Glacier and Waterton must be paid for separately.*

ADMISSION HOURS

The parks are open year-round; however, most roads and facilities close October through May because of snow and road construction.

ATMS/BANKS

You'll find cash machines at Lake McDonald, Many Glacier, St. Mary Lodge, and Glacier Park lodges. First Citizens and Glacier Bank are in Columbia Falls.

AUTOMOBILE SERVICE STATIONS

Contacts **Glacier Highland Store** (⊠ *12555 U.S. 2 E, West Glacier* ☎ *406/888–5427 ⊙ Closed mid-Oct.–Apr.*). **Lodge at St. Mary Exxon** (⊠ *Going-to-the-Sun Rd. at U.S. 2* ☎ *406/732–4431 ⊙ Closed mid-Oct.–Apr.*).

EMERGENCIES

In case of a fire or medical emergency, call 911. In summer the West Glacier Urgent Care Clinic (☎ 406/888–9005), behind the firehouse, is open.

LOST & FOUND

Park headquarters in West Glacier (☎ 406/888–7800).

PERMITS

At Glacier backcountry permits are mandatory. There's a limited number of permits and they're doled out on a first-come, first-serve basis, so the best way to ensure you get a pass is to make an advance reservation. You can print out an application online (⊕ *www.nps.gov/glac/planyourvisit/backcountry.htm*); the reservation costs $30. Mail a request and a check after mid-April to Backcountry Reservations, Glacier National Park Headquarters, Box 395, West Glacier, MT 59936 or fax it in with a credit card number (☎ 406/888–5819). Once you get to the park you'll then need to stop by the Apgar Backcountry Permit Center to pick up your permit, paying an additional $5 per day. If you don't make an advance reservation, you can stop by the Apgar center after mid-April to request a $5 permit for the following day. This is a long shot, though, as permits often run out.

POST OFFICES

Contacts **West Glacier Post Office** (⊠ *110 Going-to-the-Sun Rd.* ☎ *406/888–5591*). **East Glacier Post Office** (⊠ *U.S. 2, north of town* ☎ *406/226–5534*).

PUBLIC TELEPHONES

Find them at Avalanche Campground, Glacier Highland Motel and Store, Apgar, St. Mary Visitor Center, Two Medicine Campstore, and all lodges except Granite Park Chalet and Sperry Chalet. Cell phones do not generally work.

RESTROOMS

Portable toilets are along several roadside pullouts on Going-to-the-Sun Road. Restrooms may be found at the visitor centers and most campgrounds.

SHOPS & GROCERS

Contacts **EddieGrocery and Café** ✉ *157 Apgar Rd., Apgar* ☎ *406/888–5361*. **Lake McDonald Camp Store** (✉ *Adjacent to Lake McDonald Lodge* ☎ *406/888–9953*). **Rising Sun Camp Store** (✉ *6½ mi from St. Mary* ☎ *406/732–5523*) **Swift-current Camp Store** (✉ *Near Many Glacier* ☎ *406/732–5531*). **Two Medicine Camp Store** (✉ *Beside Two Medicine Campground* ☎ *406/226–5582*).

VISITOR INFORMATION

Contacts **Glacier National Park** (🖃 *Box 128, West Glacier, MT 59936* ☎ *406/888–7800* ⊕ *www.nps.gov/glac*).

5

Northwest Montana

WORD OF MOUTH

"I would go for two nights in Missoula and one night in Whitefish, myself. Lots to do in Missoula, great restaurants, very interesting architecture. Ditto Whitefish: a Frank Lloyd Wright building and an incredible railroad station. Try to be there when the Empire Builder arrives in the morning. I would urge you to have room reservations well in advance for Labor Day. Even in July, many hotels and motels were fully booked in both places."

—Ackislander

Updated by
Amy Grisak

WITH MORE THAN 6 MILLION acres of public land, northwest Montana might be America's largest outdoor destination. More than 1,000 secluded mountain lakes with crystal-clear waters and hungry fish provide peaceful isolation for professional and amateur anglers alike. On Flathead Lake you can sail, water-ski, and, if you're lucky, spot the mythical Flathead Lake Monster. Thousands of miles of hiking and biking trails lace the Missoula and Bitterroot valleys and climb and switchback up Big Mountain and the Mission Mountains region. In summer the lush valleys provide

> ## TOP REASONS TO GO
>
> ■ The Daly Mansion for a glimpse of Montana's affluent past.
>
> ■ Gatiss Gardens is a botanical wonderland from spring until late fall.
>
> ■ The Carousel for Missoula is an old-fashioned thrill ride.
>
> ■ Big Mountain's slopes are awash in wildflowers in summer.
>
> ■ The Bison Range comes alive in the spring with all the new babies.

a glorious carpet of native meadow grasses with sky-blue lupine and yellow arnica, beneath white-capped mountains. In winter the land settles under a blanket of snow, and the water under sheets of ice, creating a winter-sports paradise, particularly for skiers.

6

Much of the area's population is concentrated in the Bitterroot, Missoula, Mission, and Flathead valleys. Missoula, with a population of approximately 82,000, is the largest. Home of the University of Montana, it's a business and shopping center and offers many arts and cultural attractions. In friendly towns such as Hamilton, Stevensville, Kalispell, Polson, and Whitefish you'll find well-preserved historical sites and small yet resourceful museums. However, civilization here perches on the edge of seemingly endless wilderness: visit this part of the world for its wildlife, its water, and its pristine lands.

EXPLORING NORTHWEST MONTANA

Rivers, streams, lakes, and mountains dominate landscapes here and attract boaters, fly-fishers, and outdoor adventurers. Once here, they discover playhouses, art galleries, and summer festivals and rodeos. In winter visitors seek out northwest Montana's seven ski areas and scores of cross-country ski trails. But some of the best times to visit are the shoulder seasons, particularly in September, when there are fewer crowds and gorgeous days.

ABOUT THE RESTAURANTS

Although Montana generally isn't known for elegant dining, several sophisticated restaurants are tucked away among the tamaracks and cedars, where professionally trained chefs bring herbed nuances and wide-ranging cultural influences to their menus. More typical of the region are steak houses featuring certified Angus beef; in recent years, particularly in resort communities, these institutions have diversified their menus to include bison meat, fresh fish, and savory vegetarian options. Small cafés offer hearty, inexpensive meals, and you can pick up on local history through photographs and artwork on walls and

PLANNING YOUR TIME

Among the best in the state, northwest Montana's seven alpine ski areas are led by The Whitefish Mountain Resort at Big Mountain in the Flathead Valley. If you come in summer, be sure to take a chairlift ride to the top: from there you can see the Canadian Rockies, the peaks of Glacier, and the valley. Nearby, railroad fans and history buffs will appreciate Whitefish's Stumptown Historical Museum and Kalispell's Central School Museum, both crammed full of local history, plus a few humorous exhibits. Water lovers find ample room for all kinds of sports on Flathead Lake, the West's largest natural freshwater lake. Artsy types should stop in Bigfork, on the lake's northeast shore, where galleries dominate the main street and eateries are often galleries, too.

If your travels include Missoula, you can figure out the lay of the land via a short hike to the M on the mountainside above the University of Montana's Washington-Grizzly Football Stadium. From here you'll see the Clark Fork River, downtown's Missoula Art Museum, and, way off to the west, the Rocky Mountain Elk Foundation Wildlife Visitor Center.

In the forested Bitterroot Valley, where many travelers follow Lewis and Clark's trail, stop at Traveler's Rest State Park for perspective on the expedition. Plan on floating and fishing the Bitterroot and other local rivers, and in early July watch the Senior Pro Rodeo if you're in Hamilton. At one of the valley's guest ranches, be sure to sign up for a trail ride into the Bitterroot or Selway wilderness areas and along surrounding U.S. Forest Service trails. Wherever you go, don't forget your cowboy hat and your "howdy."

conversation with the local denizens. Attire everywhere is decidedly casual: blue jeans, a clean shirt, and cowboy boots or flip-flops are dress-up for most Montana restaurants.

ABOUT THE HOTELS

From massive log lodges to historic bed-and-breakfasts to chain hotels, you'll find the range of lodging options here that you'd expect from a region that makes a business of catering to tourists. Many historic lodges and cabins do not offer air-conditioning, but in general you won't miss it, since summers here are never humid and temperatures rarely reach 90°. During ski season and the summer vacation months, reservations are necessary. Some hotels are open only in summer and early fall.

WHAT IT COSTS					
	¢	$	$$	$$$	$$$$
RESTAURANTS	under $7	$7–$11	$12–$16	$17–$22	over $22
HOTELS	under $70	$70–$110	$110–$160	$160–$220	over $220

Restaurant prices are for a main course at dinner, excluding sales tax of 2%–4% in some resort communities. Hotel prices are for two people in a standard double room in high season, excluding service charges and 7% bed tax.

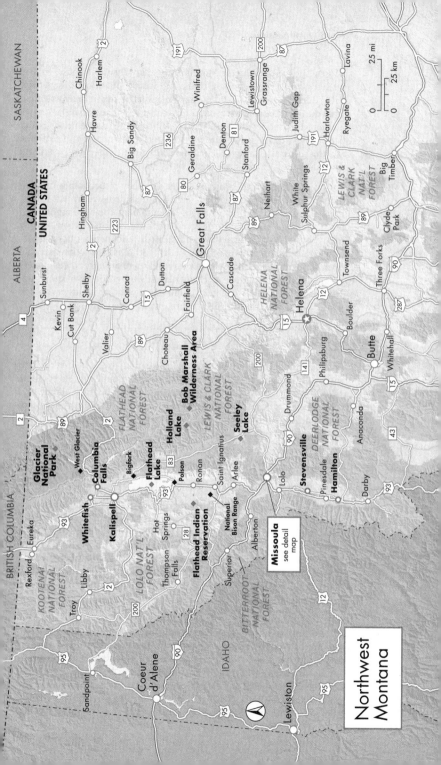

SASKATCHEWAN

ALBERTA

BRITISH COLUMBIA

CANADA
UNITED STATES

Sunburst

Kevin
Cut Bank
Shelby
Conrad
Valier

Chinook
Harlem
Havre
Big Sandy
Hingham

Winifred
Geraldine
Denton
Stanford

Lewistown
Grassrange
Lavina

Judith Gap
Harlowton
Ryegate

White
Sulphur Springs

Big
Timber

Clyde
Park

Three Forks

LEWIS &
CLARK
NAT'L
FOREST

25 mi
25 km

Dutton
Fairfield

Great Falls
Cascade

Neihart

Choteau

Bob Marshall
Wilderness Area

Holland
Lake

Seeley
Lake

LEWIS & CLARK
NATIONAL
FOREST

HELENA
NATIONAL
FOREST

Helena

Townsend

Boulder

Butte
Whitehall

Philipsburg

Drummond

DEERLODGE
NATIONAL
FOREST

Anaconda

Glacier
National
Park

West Glacier

FLATHEAD
NATIONAL
FOREST

Columbia
Falls

Bigfork

Flathead
Lake

Polson
Ronan

Saint Ignatius

Arlee

Whitefish

Kalispell

Hot
Springs

Flathead Indian
Reservation

National
Bison Range

Stevensville

Pinesdale
Hamilton

Darby

Eureka

Rexford

Troy
Libby

KOOTENAI
NATIONAL
FOREST

Thompson
Falls

LOLO NAT'L
FOREST

Lolo

Superior

Alberton

Missoula
see detail map

BITTERROOT
NATIONAL
FOREST

IDAHO

Sandpoint

Coeur
d'Alene

Lewiston

Northwest
Montana

TIMING

Most visitors to northwest Montana come in July and August, enticed by lakes, rivers, golf courses, trails, and fresh mountain air. Arts festivals, rodeos, powwows, and farmers' markets fill the summer calendar. Even during this busiest season, though, you're unlikely to feel cramped among Montana's wide-open spaces. Winter is the second peak season; deep snows attract snowboarders and skiers to the region's seven alpine ski areas. It's also an excellent time to explore cross-country ski and snowshoe trails through the light, fluffy snow.

Spring and fall are the quiet seasons, but they're becoming increasingly popular. In spring wildlife sightings include newborn elk calves, fawns, and an occasional bear cub. Mountain air cools the nights, and the occasional late-spring storm can cloak the region in snow, if only for a day. Fall's dry, warm days and blessedly cool nights offer the best of weather; there are few other tourists, and most attractions are still open. Lodgings offer off-season rates and there are no crowds, unless it's at a local high-school event, where nearly the entire town shows up. No matter the time of year, keep in mind that weather in this part of the world can change rapidly. Be prepared with extra clothing.

FLATHEAD & MISSION VALLEYS

Between the Canadian border and Missoula, tree-lined lakes and snowy peaks punctuate glaciated valleys scoured out by ice sheets some 12,000 years ago. A growing destination for golf, boating, skiing, and other outdoor recreation, the fertile Flathead and Mission valleys support ranching and farming, and are becoming known for some of the state's best restaurants.

FLATHEAD INDIAN RESERVATION

20 mi north of Missoula via U.S. 93.

Home to the Salish and Kootenai tribes, this 1.2-million-acre reservation is a fascinating historical site. Archaeological evidence indicates that Native Americans were here some 14,000 years ago, but it wasn't until the 1700s that the Kootenai, Salish, and Pend d'Oreille shared common hunting grounds in this area. The people hunted bison, descendants of which you can see at the National Bison Range. When Catholic "Black Robes" arrived to convert the Indians, they built the St. Ignatius Mission.

WHAT TO SEE

For nature lovers, the main attractions of the **Flathead Indian Reservation** are fishing and water recreation on numerous lakes and streams and bird-watching in Ninepipe National Wildlife Refuge. A tribal fishing license is required, and available at most licensing agents. Of the approximately 6,950 enrolled tribal members of the **Confederated Salish and Kootenai Tribes** (*Box 278, Pablo 59855* *406/675–2700, 406/657–0160, or 888/835–8766* *www.cskt.org*), about 4,500 live on the reservation, which is interspersed with non–Native American ranches and other property. Both tribes celebrate their heritage during the annual July Powwow. ☎406/675–0160 ⊕*www.indiannations. visitmt.com/flathead.shtm* ☞*Free* ⊙*Weekdays 9–5.*

★ The **Sqelix'u/Aqfsmakni-k Cultural Center (The People's Center)** exhibits artifacts, photographs, and recordings concerning the Salish, Kootenai, and Pend d'Oreille people. The People's Center oversees educational programs, guided interpretive tours, outdoor traditional lodges, and annual festivals. A gift shop sells both traditional and nontraditional work by local artists and craftspeople. ⊠*53253 U.S. 93 W, 6 mi south of Polson, Pablo* ☎406/883–5344 *or* 800/883–5344 ⊕*www.peoples center.org* ☞*$3* ⊙*Apr.–Sept., weekdays 9–6, Sat. 10–6; Oct.–Mar., weekdays 9–5.*

Fodor's Choice The Red Sleep Mountain Drive, a 19-mi loop road at the **National Bison**
★ **Range,** allows close-up views of bison, elk, pronghorn, deer, and mountain sheep. The gravel road rises 2,000 feet and takes about two hours to complete; you're required to begin the drive no later than 6 PM and to finish before the gate closes at dark. The 19,000-acre refuge at the foot of the Mission Mountains was established in 1908 by Theodore Roosevelt. Today the U.S. Fish and Wildlife Service ranches a herd of 400 bison. A visitor center explains the history, habits, and habitat of the bison. To reach the bison range, follow the signs west, then north from the junction of U.S. 93 and Route 200 in Ravalli. ⊠*58355 Bison Range Rd., Moiese* ☎406/644–2211 ⊕*www.fws.gov/bisonrange/* ☞*$5 per vehicle* ⊙*Range 7* AM*–dark throughout year; visitor center mid-May–Sept., daily 7* AM*–9* PM; *Oct.–mid-May, weekdays 8–4:30.*

Established in 1846 as a Hudson's Bay Company trading post, **Fort Connah** was used by fur traders until 1871. Of the original three buildings, one remains today; it's believed to be the oldest building still standing in Montana. You can't go inside, but a historical marker details events and inhabitants. ⊠*U.S. 93 at Post Creek, between St. Ignatius and Charlo* ☎406/676–0256 *or* 406/549–4431 ⊕*www.visitmt.com* ☞*Donations accepted* ⊙*By appointment.*

The **St. Ignatius Mission**—a church, cabin, and collection of other buildings—was built in the 1890s with bricks made of local clay by missionaries and Native Americans. The 61 murals on the walls and ceilings of the church were used to teach Bible stories to the natives. In the St. Ignatius Mission Museum (an old log cabin) there's an exhibit of early artifacts and arts and crafts. The mission is still a functioning church; mass is held several mornings a week in the rectory. To reach the mission from St. Ignatius, take Main Street south to Mission Drive. ⊠*300 Bear Track Ave.* ☎406/745–2768 ☞*Donations accepted* ⊙*Memorial Day–Labor Day, daily 9–7; Labor Day to Memorial Day, daily 9–5.*

Sprawling **Ninepipe National Wildlife Refuge** is *the* place for bird-watchers. This 2,000-acre wetland complex in the shadow of the Mission Mountains is home to everything from marsh hawks to kestrels to red-winged blackbirds. Flanking both sides of U.S. 93 are rookeries for double-crested cormorants and great blue herons; bald eagles fish here in the winter. Roads (includ-ing U.S. 93, where stopping is prohibited within the boundaries) through the center of the refuge are closed March through mid-July during nesting season, but you can drive along the periph-ery throughout the year. Maps are available from the nearby National Bison Range, which manages Ninepipe. ✉*58355 Bison Range Rd.* ☎*406/644–2211* ⊕*www.fws.gov/bisonrange/ninepipe/.*

Symes Hot Springs Hotel and Mineral Baths. Truly a unique find on the western edge of the Flathead Indian Reservation, this rustic 1928 hotel has hot mineral pools from contin-uously flowing springs, spa treat-ments, massage, and live music on weekends. In the restaurant

MACK ATTACK

In an effort to reduce the highly predaceous lake trout numbers, Montana Fish, Wildlife & Parks and the Confederated Salish-Kootenai Tribe co-sponsor the monthlong **Mack Days** events in March and September. As they say, "It only takes one fish to win," and every-one is welcome to participate. ☎ *406/982–3142 or 406/270–3386* ⊕ *www.mackdays.com.* From a flasher and squid com-bination to flutterspoons, you'll find the perfect lures and lots of information at **Zimmer Tackle** ✉ *20024 Hwy. 93, Pablo 59855* ☎*406/675–0068* ⊙ *Daily 8–7.*

($–$$$) steak, seafood, and pasta satisfy hungry soakers. The hotel itself isn't a standout, though the rates (¢–$$) are reasonable. Several historic hot springs in the area attracted Native Americans for centu-ries. **Pros:** A great place to get away from crowds. **Cons:** Quite a ways from larger towns. ✉*209 Wall St., Hot Springs* ☎*406/741–2361 or 888/305–3106* ⊕*www.symeshotsprings.com* 🛁*Pools and baths $7* ⊙*Daily 8* AM–*11* PM.

WHERE TO STAY & EAT

$$$ 🏠**Cheff's Guest Ranch and Outfitters.** This 10,000-acre working cattle ranch at the base of the Mission Mountains lets you take part in ranch-ing life in summer and conducts pack trips from September through November. Hearty breakfasts start off days of trail rides, fishing for trout, bass, bullhead, and perch, and exploration on the nearby Ninepipe National Wildlife Refuge and Kicking Horse Reservoir in the valley below. You can join in on fencing projects, moving stock, and bucking bales of hay. A full range of options is available, from rooms with no services to cabins with all-inclusive packages. **Pros:** The Cheffs have been taking care of folks for a long time and are excellent hosts. Their horses and mules are some of the best in the outfitting world, and they do a good job matching a rider's skill with the right horse. **Cons:** It's a significant drive coming from either Kalispell or Missoula. ✉*30888 Eagle Pass Trail, Charlo 59824* ☎*406/644–2557* 📠*406/644–2611* ⊕*www.cheffguestranch.com* 🛏*7 rooms, 3 with bath; 2 cabins* ♿*In-room: no a/c, no phone, kitchen in cabins. In-hotel: bicycles, laundry facilities, airport shuttle, no-smoking rooms* ▤*AE, MC, V* ⊙*Closed Dec.–May* ⊙*FAP.*

$$$ ✕**Ninepipes Lodge.** On the edge of the Ninepipe National Wildlife Ref-uge, the lodge has views of the snow-tipped Mission Mountains and

the native-grass-edged wetlands full of birds. The restaurant is open seven days a week, and dinners include tasty all-natural Angus beef steaks, seafood, and specials like beer-battered catfish or mushroom quesadillas. You can find reasonable lodging here, too ($), as well as an art gallery, a museum, and a trading post next door. ⊠*69286 U.S. Hwy. 93, Charlo 59824* ☎*406/644–2588* ⚖*Reservations essential* ⊟*AE, MC, V.*

¢–$$ 🖳**Twin Creeks B&B.**The setting is first-rate at this contemporary B&B: ℃ two creeks meander through the property, under the spectacular Mission Mountains, with views of Mission Valley farmland. Two tepees—you may stay in them for the ultimate Western night—and the resident St. Bernard dogs, Hansel and Gretel, are popular with kids. Breakfast consists of homemade biscuits and huckleberry jam, ham, eggs any way you like them, or steel-cut oats. **Pros:** Fresh cookies are always at hand; a beautiful property with stunning views. **Cons:** The owners are sometimes difficult to reach for questions. ⊠*33292 Twin Creek Rd., Ronan 59864* ☎*406/676–8800 or 877/524–8946* 🖷*406/676–2662* ⊕*www.twincreeksbb.com* 🛏*7 rooms, 2 teepees* ⚲*In-room: no a/c, DVD, Ethernet. In-hotel: room service laundry facilities, parking (no fee), no-smoking rooms, some pets allowed, no elevator* ⊟*MC, V* ⦿*BP.*

6

CAMPING   ⚠**Mission Meadows RV.** This grassy meadow near the highway is conveniently located near the bison range and fishing. ⚲*Flush toilets, full hookups, dump station, drinking water, guest laundry, showers, fire pits, picnic tables, food service, electricity, public telephone, general store* 🛏*20 full hookups, 70 partial hookups, 30 tent sites* ⊠*44457 Mission Meadow Dr., 2 mi north of Ronan* ☎*406/676–5182* 🖷*406/676–0854* ⊟*D, MC, V.*

THE ARTS

℃ For more than a century, the four-day powwow during the **Arlee 4th of July Celebration** (⊠*Pow-Wow Rd., ½ mi east of U.S. 93, Arlee* ☎*406/675–2700 Ext. 1222* ⊕*www.arleepowwow.com*) has drawn Native Americans from all over the West. Highlights are drumming, dancing, and singing contests; the parade; the traditional encampment; and arts, crafts, and food vendors. Gambling includes traditional stick games and live cards.

SHOPPING

The **Flathead Indian Museum and Trading Post** (⊠*1 Museum La., on U.S. 93, St. Ignatius* ☎*406/745–2951*) has an extensive collection of authentic artifacts from local Native American tribes. On sale are arts, crafts, books, maps, and gifts.

FLATHEAD LAKE

12 mi north of Ronan via U.S. 93.

The 370-foot-deep Flathead Lake, with 180 mi of shoreline, is the largest natural freshwater lake in the western United States. It's a wonderful—and popular—place for sailing, fishing, and swimming. Wildhorse Island State Park, in the lake, is home to bighorn sheep and other wildlife; the 2,165-acre island can be reached only by private boat. Cherry groves line the lake's shores, and toward the end of July farmers harvest them and sell cherries at roadside stands along the two highways that encircle the lake.

Polson, a quiet community of 4,000 on the southern edge of Flathead Lake, sits under the morning shadow of the jagged Mission Mountains. It's the largest town on the Flathead Indian Reservation. Picnic spots, lake access, and playgrounds are found at Boettcher, Sacajawea, and Riverside parks. Some other parks are for tribal members only; signs identify picnic areas that are closed to the public.

The Swan River empties into Flathead Lake at the small, idyllic resort community of **Bigfork.** The small town is filled with shops, galleries, restaurants, and a cultural center. Many summer events are so popular that you should make dinner and playhouse reservations a month in advance. This is a great spot to browse after you're finished with your outdoor activities.

The rotating exhibits at **Bigfork Art and Cultural Center** (⊠ *525 Electric Ave.* ☎ *406/837–6927)* display bronzes, paintings, and works in other media by Montana artists.

SPORTS & THE OUTDOORS

BOATING **Absolute Water Sport Rentals** (⊠ *303 U.S. 93, Polson* ☎ *406/883–3900 or 800/358–8046)* has everything from canoes and sea kayaks to Jet Skis. At **Dayton Yacht Harbor** (⊠ *399 C St., Dayton* ☎ *406/849–5423 or 800/775–2990)* you can rent a sailboat, take sailing lessons, or moor your own sailboat near Wild Horse and Cromwell islands.

★ One of the most pleasant ways to see the lake is to take a **two-hour sail** (⊠ *150 Flathead Lake Lodge Rd., Bigfork* ☎ *406/837–4391)* on the historic *Questa* or the *Nor'Easter,* both 51-foot Q-class racing sloops built in the 1920s. They depart from Flathead Lake Lodge.

FISHING Take a charter trip on Flathead Lake with **A-Able Fishing Charters & Tours** (⊠ *63 Twin Acres Dr., Kalispell* ☎ *406/257–5214 or 800/231–5214)* to fish for enormous lake trout, as well as pike, perch, and whitefish, or just enjoy the spectacular scenery. They take individuals and groups of up to 18 people. Fly-fish with **Two River Gear and Outfitter** (⊠ *603 Electric Ave., Bigfork* ☎ *406/837–3474)* on local streams, rivers, and lakes.

GOLF Wonderful views of mountains and Flathead Lake from **Eagle Bend Golf Club** (⊠ *279 Eagle Bend Dr., Bigfork* ☎ *406/837–7310 or 800/255– 5641)* are matched by the golfing on the 27-hole course. Each of the 27 holes of the **Polson Bay Golf Club** (⊠ *111 Bayview Dr.* ☎ *406/883–8230)* has a view of the Mission and Swan mountain ranges and Flathead Lake.

HIKING **Jewel Basin Hiking Area** (⊠ *10 mi east of Bigfork via Hwy. 83 and Echo Lake Rd. to Jewel Basin Rd., No. 5392)* provides 35 mi of well-maintained trails among 27 trout-filled alpine lakes. You'll find the nearest phone and hearty to-go trail lunches at the Echo Lake Cafe at the

Fodor'sChoice
★

junction of Highway 83 and Echo Lake Road. The **Swan Lake Ranger District Office** (⊠*200 Ranger Station Rd.* ☎*406/837–7500*) in Bigfork sells hiking maps.

KAYAKING   World-class kayaking on the Swan River's Wild Mile draws boaters and spectators to the white water during spring and summer runoff. The annual **Bigfork Whitewater Festival** (⊠*8155 Hwy. 35, Old Town Center, Bigfork* ☎*406/837–5888* ⊕*www.bigfork.org*) celebrates the torrent every Memorial Day weekend with a water rodeo, races, and entertainment at local pubs and eateries.

RAFTING   Eight white-water miles of the lower Flathead River are covered by **Flathead Raft Co.** (⊠*1503 U.S. 93 S, across from Super 1 Foods in Polson* ☎*406/883–5838 or 800/654–4359* ⊕*www.flatheadraftco.com*). From June through September it provides wild rafting adventures, kayaking, and Native American interpretive trips between Kerr Dam and Buffalo Bridge, overnight trips, charter fishing, and tours of Wild Horse Island. The outfitter will design family floats suitable for any age.

SKIING   As you schuss runs of **Blacktail Mountain Ski Area** (⊠*Blacktail Mountain Rd., Lakeside* ☎*406/844–0999* ⊕*www.blacktailmountain.com*), you'll glimpse Flathead Lake and surrounding peaks. This family-friendly mountain is known for inexpensive lift tickets; uncrowded, mostly intermediate slopes; a lovely log-accented lodge; and friendly staff.

6

WHERE TO EAT

$$$–$$$$ ✕**La Provence.** The garden dining here offers a flower-studded view
★   down Bigfork's main street. Local artists' work decorates the white-washed walls. The owner-chef specializes in French onion soup with Gruyère cheese served inside a large onion, and specials like venison tenderloin with figs and Bordeaux sauce. An international wine list and a traditional chocolate soufflé round out the Mediterranean meals. ⊠*408 Bridge St., Bigfork* ☎*406/837–2923* ▭*AE, MC, V* ☉*Closed Sun.*

$$–$$$$ ✕**Bigfork Inn.** The Swiss-chalet style of the Bigfork Inn is reminiscent of the lodges in Glacier National Park. Inside you'll find a lively atmosphere, with seating for more than 200 patrons between the main dining room, library, deck (summer), balcony, and two private rooms. They have live music Friday and Saturday evenings, and all are welcome on the dance floor. Splurge with Crispy Farmhouse Duck (served with a pecan, cherry, and red currant sauce) or the Australian lobster tail. Only slightly less decadent but delicious nonetheless is the Bigfork Inn Fettuccini made with chicken, red peppers, onions, and basil and topped with an Asiago sauce. ⊠*604 Electric Ave., Bigfork* ☎*406/837–6680* ▭*AE, D, MC, V.*

$$–$$$$ ✕**Showthyme!** In Bigfork's former bank building, built in 1908, diners
★   opt for street- or bay-side seating, or a table in the snug bank vault. The menu changes seasonally, but signature dishes include fresh ahi tuna with sweet soy ginger and wasabi over jasmine rice, and roasted elk tenderloin with porcini mushrooms. Save room for Benedictine chocolate truffle pie. ⊠*548 Electric Ave., Bigfork* ☎*406/837–0707* ▭*AE, D, MC, V* ☉*Closed Mon. No lunch*

Big Country, Brief History

Scraped by receding glaciers and chiseled by weather, the landscape of northwest Montana has a long history, but the region's human history is relatively recent. The earliest Native Americans probably settled here between 10,000 and 12,000 years ago, or traveled through in search of bison herds east of the Rockies. Today, the Confederated Salish and Kootenai tribes live on the Flathead Indian Reservation spread out across the Mission and Flathead valleys; their People's Center is one of the state's best displays of native culture and history.

Explorers such as Lewis and Clark looked at but mostly didn't touch the riches—timber, wild game, and emerald lakes—of northwest Montana, and more permanent white settlers didn't arrive until they had depleted goldfields in other areas of the West. Many of the frontier communities are only now celebrating centennial anniversaries. Even so, the area claims some

of Montana's oldest structures, such as St. Mary's Mission, the first Catholic mission in the Northwest, and Fort Connah, a Hudson's Bay Company fur-trading post. During the race across the continent, three railroads laid track through Glacier Country, leaving in their wake elegant train stations and a heritage of rail travel.

Historic sites throughout northwest Montana offer a glimpse back at the rough-and-tumble old days, but the wild lands and wildlife are what you'll write home about. On the National Bison Range, you'll see descendants of the last few free-roaming American bison. Watch for birds of prey wherever you go. From the Lee Metcalf National Wildlife Refuge to the Bob Marshall Wilderness to Glacier National Park, elk, bighorn sheep, mountain goats, and bears thrive. All of these critters are living reminders of centuries of Montana history.

WHERE TO STAY

$$$$ 🏨 **Averill's Flathead Lake Lodge.** Since 1945 Averill's has been providing
🕐 families a wholesome and active Western getaway. The beautiful green grounds are on the shore of the lake, where beach fires, canoeing, and sailing take place. The lodge, accommodations, and other buildings are all log-and-stone structures. Horseback rides set out both in the morning and evening, and you can learn to rope in the rodeo arena. Many activities such as rafting and guided fishing trips are available for an extra cost. It's BYOB at the bar. October through May, the lodge is open for corporate retreats only. **Pros:** Watching the large herd of horses being turned out to pasture at the end of the day is breathtaking. Well-kept facility with many family activities. **Cons:** The sign on the east side of Highway 35 can easily be missed. The price takes this facility out of reach of most travelers. ✉ *150 Flathead Lake Lodge Rd., Bigfork 59911* ☎ *406/837–4391* 🖶 *406/837–6977* ⊕ *www.averills. com* 🛏 *20 rooms, 20 cottages* 🛆 *In-room: no a/c, no TV, no phone. In-hotel: tennis courts, pool, beachfront, children's programs (ages 3 and up), Wi-Fi in the lodge, airport shuttle, no-smoking rooms* ▭ *AE, MC, V* ❙◯❙ *FAP.*

$$$–$$$$ 🏨 **Mountain Lake Lodge.** This resort perched above crystalline Flathead
★ Lake offers 30 well-appointed suites surrounding an outdoor pool on

meticulously groomed grounds. From your room, enjoy sweeping views of the lake (best from the lakeside lodges) and surrounding mountains. The hotel is well situated for hiking, golfing, rafting, and lake cruising. The log-accented dining room is designed to let you watch the sunset while enjoying smoked pheasant and other delicacies. The dining room is open seasonally; the bar serves light dinners year-round. **Pros:** Beautiful facility with stunning views, great central location. **Cons:** It's a short drive to Bigfork, but Highway 35 is narrow and winding. Be very aware of logging trucks during certain times of the year. ⊠ *1950 Sylvan Dr., at Hwy. 35 mile marker 26.5, Bigfork 59911* ☎ *406/837–3800 or 877/823–4923* 🖷 *406/837–3861* ⊕ *www.mountainlakelodge.com* ⤢ *30 suites* △ *In-hotel: restaurant, bar, pool, exercise room, Wi-Fi on site, no-smoking rooms* ⊟ *AE, DC, MC, V* ⦿ *EP.*

$$–$$$$ 🏨 **Swan River Inn.** Situated in downtown Bigfork with views overlooking Bigfork Bay, the Swan River Inn has eight opulent suites decked out with themes such as Victorian, country French, safari (decorated with antiques gathered from world travels), or Montana-made furnishings. They also have three houses in Bigfork, such as the Carriage House or Trapper Cabin, with the same luxurious amenities. The restaurant ($$–$$$) at the Swan River Inn exudes European elegance, serving filet mignon wrapped in bacon, rack of lamb with a huckleberry demi glace, and Margrit's Famous Spaghetti. There is a brunch on Sunday, and look for celebrations, such as Oktoberfest, at different times of the year. **Pros:** All except one room have great views of the bay. Terrific location for all the restaurants, shops, and entertainment in Bigfork. **Cons:** Downtown Bigfork is a busy place in summer, particularly during festivities such as Whitewater Days. ⊠ *360 Grand Ave., Bigfork 59911* ☎ *406/837–2328* 🖷 *406/837–2327* ⊕ *www.swanriverinn.com* ⤢ *8 suites, 3 cottages* △ *In room: Ethernet, refrigerator* ⊟ *AE, D, MC, V* ⦿ *EP.*

CAMPING   ⛺ **Flathead Lake state parks.** Five lakeside parks are scattered around Flathead, offering quiet camping, boat launches, and good views. Bigfork's Wayfarers, Lakeside's West Shore, and Polson's Big Arm, Finley Point, and Yellow Bay parks are all owned by the State of Montana and run by Montana Fish, Wildlife & Parks. △ *Pit toilets, drinking water, fire grates, picnic tables, swimming (lake)* ⤢ *273 tent sites* ⊠ *490 N. Meridian Rd., Kalispell* ☎ *406/752–5501* 🖷 *406/257–0349* ⊕ *www. fwp.mt.gov* ⊟ *No credit cards* ⦿ *May–Sept.*

☼   ⛺ **Polson/Flathead KOA.** Perched above Flathead Lake with incredible views of the Mission and Swan mountains, this grassy spot is convenient to the lake and town, and hosts can direct you to fossil and arrowhead hunting. △ *Flush toilets, full hookups, dump station, drinking water, guest laundry, showers, fire pits, picnic tables, electricity, public telephone, general store, play area, swimming (pool), Wi-Fi* ⤢ *31 full hookups, 23 partial hookups, 1 cottage with kitchenette, fireplace, and private hot tub* ⊠ *200 Irving Flat Rd., Polson* ☎ *406/883–2130 or 800/562–2130* 🖷 *406/883–0151* ⊕ *www.flatheadlakekoa.com* ⊟ *AE, D, MC, V* ⦿ *Mid-Apr.–mid-Oct.*

6

SHOPPING

Bigfork's Electric Avenue is lined with galleries and eclectic gift shops and is recognized for unparalleled dining and sweets. Try the soft cookies and hot-out-of-the-oven cinnamon rolls baked daily and shipped nationwide from **Brookies Cookies** (✉ *191 Mill St.* ☎ *406/837–2447*). **Electric Avenue Gifts** (✉ *490 Electric Ave.* ☎ *406/837–4994*) carries unique Flathead cherry designs in everything from dishes to napkins, custom wood signs, and a multitude of unique gifts.See award-winning sculptor Eric Thorsen at work daily on clay sculptures and wood carvings in his studio. **Eric Thorsen Fine Art Gallery** (✉ *547 Electric Ave.* ☎ *406/837–4366*).You can pick up a tiny jar of huckleberry jam or flavored honey at **Eva Gates Homemade Preserves** (✉ *456 Electric Ave.* ☎ *406/837–4356 800/682–4283*), or have one of the family-size jars of various treats shipped back home.

EN ROUTE

When the last glacier receded from the area 10,000 years ago, it left a 100-foot depth of fertile soil called glacier loam, perfect for agriculture. Two scenic routes—Highway 35 to Creston and Highway 82 to Kalispell—traverse this land, heading north from Bigfork, over the Flathead River (look for osprey nests atop poles), through fields of mint, seed potatoes, and hay, and past tree nurseries. **Gatiss Gardens** (✉ *4790 Hwy. 35, at Broeder Loop Rd., 8 mi north of Bigfork, Creston* ☎ *406/755–2418*) has a gentle 1¼-mi trail past hundreds of perennials, bulbs, and shrubs that is open to the public from Memorial Day to Labor Day.

KALISPELL

20 mi northwest of Bigfork via Hwy. 35.

WHAT TO SEE

You can ring the old school bell at the **Central School Museum**, an 1894 Romanesque building. In the museum are galleries, activities, and displays concerning regional heritage and history, including local Native American culture. You'll also find a café, museum store, conference rooms, and reference library. ✉ *124 2nd Ave. E* ☎ *406/756–8381* ⊕ *www.yourmuseum.org* 🖃 *$5* ⊙ *June–Sept., Mon.–Sat. 10–5; Oct.–May, weekdays 10–5.*

☾ A town highlight is the **Conrad Mansion National Historic Site Museum**, a 26-room Norman-style mansion that was the home of C. E. Conrad, the manager of a freighter on the Missouri River and the founder of Kalispell. Docents offer specialized tours for kids that focus on the clothing, activities, and food of the turn-of-the-20th-century era. The "Christmas at the Mansion" kicks off the holiday season in October, and the mansion is decorated for the season. There is a special "Tea and Tour" offered every Saturday from late November to the end of December. ✉ *4th St. between 6th and Woodland* ☎ *406/755–2166* ⊕ *www.conradmansion.com* 🖃 *$8* ⊙ *Guided tours mid-May–mid-Oct., Tues.–Sun. 10–4 on the hr; Christmas tours Thanksgiving–late Dec., Fri.–Sun. 11, 1, and 3.*

The **Hockaday Museum of Art,** housed in the renovated Carnegie library, presents contemporary art exhibits focusing on Montana artists. ⊠*302 2nd Ave. E, at 3rd St.* ☎*406/755–5268* ⊕*www.hockadayartmuseum. org* ⊠*$5* ☉*June–Aug., Tues.–Fri. 10–6, Sat. 10–5, Sun. noon–4; Sept.–May, Tues.–Sat. 10–5.*

One of 20 city green spaces, **Woodland Park** has a playground, ball fields, rose gardens, and a picnic area. Geese, ducks, peacocks, and black swans flutter to the pond, which in winter opens for ice skating; there's a warming hut nearby. Open June–August, Woodland Water Park is a popular attraction with a pool, waterslides, and the "Lazy River" float. ⊠*Conrad Dr. and Woodland Dr.* ☎*406/758–7812 or 406/758–7778* ⊕*www. kalispell.com/parks* ⊠*Woodland Park free; water park $5* ☉*Daily dawn–dusk.*

Inside the historic **Great Northern Depot** is visitor information from the Kalispell Chamber of Commerce and the Flathead Convention and Visitors Bureau. Outside is the lovely Depot Park, where live music, arts shows, a gazebo, picnicking, and a playground attract both locals and travelers. ⊠*15 Depot Park* ☎*406/758–2800 or 888/888–2308* ⊕*www.kalispellchamber.com* ⊠*Free* ☉*Weekdays 8–5.*

OFF THE BEATEN PATH

Lone Pine State Park. At an elevation of 2,959 feet, you can view Kalispell, Flathead Lake, and the Whitefish Mountain Range from this 186-acre park. Features include a self-guided nature trail, a visitor center, nature interpretive programs, picnic areas and shelters, horse trails, and a horseshoe pit. ⊠*4 mi southwest of Kalispell on Foyes Lake Rd., then 1 mi east on Lone Pine Rd.* ☎*406/755–2706* ⊕*www.fwp.mt.gov* ⊠*$5 per vehicle* ☉*Mid-Apr.–Oct., daily dawn–dusk.*

SPORTS & THE OUTDOORS

GOLF At **Big Mountain Golf Club** (⊠*3230 U.S. 93 N* ☎*406/751–1950 or 800/255–5641*) the challenging 18-hole links-style course has rolling fairways lined with native grasses and giant pine trees along the Stillwater River. At one time, a private herd of bison grazed on what's now **Buffalo Hill Golf Club** (⊠*1176 N. Main* ☎*406/756–4530 or 888/342–1619* ⊕*www.golfbuffalohill.com*) in the heart of Kalispell. This municipal 27-hole course, built in 1936, has tree-lined fairways along the Stillwater River.

HIKING Every year from May through October, the **Montana Wilderness Association** (⊠*307 1st Ave. E, Suite 1* ☎*406/755–6304* ⊕*www.wildmontana. org*) offers free Wilderness Walks booklets describing dozens of trails in state. Join one of their free guided backcountry hikes, which vary from short wildflower walks to strenuous climbs.

TRAIL RIDING Ride for a couple of hours or an entire day on the beautiful rolling hills and open meadows of this 800-acre ranch with **High Country Trails.** Kids 12 years and older are welcome. (⊠*2800 Foy's Lake Rd.* ☎*406/755–1283 or 406/755–4711*).

WHERE TO STAY & EAT

$$–$$$$ ✕**Capers.** For more than a decade Capers was known as Café Max,
★ and it was the place for upscale dining in Kalispell. The owners decided it was time to provide more moderately priced meals with the same delicious flair. The revamped menu still offers upscale fare, such as the grilled Montana buffalo tenderloin or melt-in-your-mouth seared ahi, but also includes a less pricey, but equally impressive cheeseburger (made with local beef) or vegetarian lasagna. Capers serves outstanding wine and a surprisingly varied selection of local and imported beer. ⊠*121 Main St.* ☎*406/755–7687* ▭*AE, MC, V* ☽*Closed Mon.*

$$–$$$ ✕**The Knead Cafe.** Come here for the best bread and soup in the valley. The café's baked goods, including croissants, fresh baguettes, and chocolate cakes, will entice you in, but it's worth your while to stay for breakfast or lunch—their Reuben sandwiches are sublime, and any one of their salads make a great lunch. The funky, mismatched dining tables and chairs are surrounded by local artwork. ⊠*25 2nd Ave. W* ☎*406/755–7510* ▭*AE, MC, V* ☽*Closed Sun.*

$$$$ ▦**The Master Suite.** If you've ever dreamed of living in a castle overlooking spectacular countryside, this is the place to stay. As the name implies, there is one grand, private suite—actually the entire ground floor of the home—for people seeking privacy as well as plenty of room to stretch out. The 1,500-square-foot accommodation includes two bathrooms, living area, partial kitchen, bedroom, and enclosed patio. Guests are welcome on the main level of the house, as well as on the outdoor decks and gorgeous grounds. Hors d'oeuvres and cocktails are served in the afternoon. Gourmet breakfasts are often made with organic ingredients and can be modified to meet dietary needs. **Pros:** You're the guest of honor here, ideal for a romantic getaway. A facility is nearby where you can board your horses. **Cons:** Having only one room takes away the camaraderie of a typical bed-and-breakfast. ⌖*1031 S. Main St., 59901* ☎*406/752–8512* ⊕*www.mastersuitebedandbreakfast.com* ⤻*1 room* ⌂*In room: DVD, Ethernet.* ▭*MC, V* ⍓*BP.*

$$$–$$$$ ▦**Hampton Inn Kalispell.** This hotel 1 mi west of downtown features an indoor 24-hour guest pool and free extended buffet breakfast. The spacious rooms, Western decor, and river-rock fireplace in the lobby give the place a homey feel. They also have suites with private hot tubs and fireplaces. **Pros:** Very spacious, great room rates often available from the end of September through April. **Cons:** Pool is directly off the lobby, hotel is on the west side of town, which can be bogged down during high traffic times coming from either Whitefish or through Kalispell. No restaurant. ⊠*1140 U.S. 2 W, 59901* ☎*406/755–7900 or 800/426–7866* 🖷*406/755–5056* ⊕*www.hamptoninnkalispell.com* ⤻*120 rooms* ⌂*In-room: Wi-Fi, Ethernet, DVD, refrigerator. In-hotel: fitness center, pool, no-smoking rooms* ▭*AE, D, DC, MC, V* ⍓*CP.*

$–$$$ ▦**The Kalispell Grand Hotel.** The smell of freshly baked cookies greets
★ travelers in the afternoon as soon as they walk into the Kalispell Grand.

The hotel has been a local landmark for nearly a century, welcoming guests since 1912, shortly after Glacier became a national park. The Grand's lobby has wildlife mounts, rich wood, and comfortable furniture, and they rotate interesting exhibits in their art gallery. The rooms are clean and comfortable with nice-size work desks for business travelers. But for those who would rather relax, they have a certified massage therapist available to work out any sore muscles. **Pros:** Feels like a step back in time, very friendly staff, delicious cookies every afternoon, and they also make their own pound cake for the continental breakfast. **Cons:** Immediate vicinity is a little limited except for a few restaurants and some shops. Main Street is very busy in the morning and late in the afternoon with traffic. ⊠*100 Main St., 59901* ☎*406/755–8100 or 800/858–7422* 🖶*406/752–8012* ⊕*www.kalispellgrand.com* 🛏*40 rooms, 2 suites* ⚴*In room: Ethernet. In hotel: spa.* ☐*AE, D, DC, MC, V* ⏺*CP.*

CAMPING ⚠ **Glacier Pines RV Park.** A bit of forest in the city, this spacious campground set among pines has paved roads and no maximum size limit or time limit. There are no tent sites, and it's open year-round. ⚴*Flush toilets, full hookups, dump station, drinking water, guest laundry, showers, fire pits, picnic tables, electricity, Wi-Fi, general store, play area, swimming (pool)* 🛏*75 full hookups* ⊠*1850 Hwy. 35 E, 1 mi east of Kalispell* ☎*406/752–2760 or 800/533–4029* ⊕*www.glacierpines. com* ☐*MC, V.*

NIGHTLIFE

Cowboy boots and sneakers kick up the sawdust and peanut shells on the floor at **Moose's Saloon** (⊠*173 N. Main St.* ☎*406/755–2337*), where tunes from the jukebox get the raucous crowd moving. You can order pizza or a hearty sandwich to go with your beer.

SHOPPING

Noice Studio and Gallery (⊠*127 Main St.* ☎*406/755–5321*) features ongoing exhibits of paintings, pastels, sculptures, fiber arts, and photography by Montana artists such as Rudy Autio, Russell Chatham, and Marshall Noice, in a lovingly restored turn-of-the-20th-century building.

Sportsman Ski Haus (⊠*145 Hutton Ranch Rd.* ☎*406/755–6484 or 406/862–3111*) has a brand new facility in Kalispell to satisfy any outdoor-equipment need. There's also a store in the Whitefish Mountain Mall off Highway 93.

WHITEFISH

15 mi north of Kalispell via U.S. 93.

A hub for golfing, lake recreation, hiking, mountain biking, and skiing, Whitefish sits at the base of Big Mountain Ski and Summer Resort. Skiers descend Big Mountain late fall through early spring, and summer attracts hikers to the Danny On Trail. The trail leads to the mountain summit, which can also be accessed via the Glacier Chaser chairlift. Numerous other activities, such as a kids' bike academy, art treks, art and music festivals, and nighttime stargazing events, keep the mountain busy throughout the warmer months. You can tackle mountain-bike trails, rent mountain scooters, try a 9-hole folf (Frisbee golf) course, and walk in the trees along an 800-foot path in the treetops, 60 feet above the forest floor. A nature center and a few gift shops and restaurants remain open mid-June–mid-September, daily 9–4:30.

If you want to check out a cross section of American life, drop by the Whitefish train station at 6 AM as a sleepy collection of farmers, cowboys, and skiers awaits the arrival of Amtrak's *Empire Builder*, en route from Seattle to Chicago. Inside the half-timber depot is the **Stumptown Historical Society's Museum.** The focus here is the Great Northern Railway, the nation's first unsubsidized transcontinental railway that passed through Whitefish. On display are lanterns, old posters, and crockery, as well as reminders of local history, such as the books of author Dorothy M. Johnson and photos of the Whitefish football team from 1922 through 1954, plus some real fun (look for the fur-covered trout). You can pick up a walking-tour map of Whitefish's historic district here. ⊠ *500 Depot St.* ☎ *406/862–0067* ☞ *Donations accepted* ☉ *June–Sept., weekdays 10–4, Sat. noon–3; Oct.–May, weekdays 11–3, Sat. noon–3.*

SPORTS & THE OUTDOORS

BICYCLING Of the 2,000 mi of county roads in the area, only 400 mi are paved, leaving dirt and gravel roads and innumerable trails open for discovery. You can rent bikes suitable to the terrain at **Glacier Cyclery** (⊠ *326 E. 2nd St.* ☎ *406/862–6446* ⊕ *www.glaciercyclery.com*). Monday-night group rides begin at the shop courtyard and lead to a variety of trails of varying degrees of difficulty. Bike maps, gear, and free air are available at this full-service shop.

DOGSLEDDING The dogs are raring to run at **Dog Sled Adventures** (⊠ *U.S. 93, 20 mi north of Whitefish, 2 mi north of Olney* ☎ *406/881–2275* ⊕ *www. dogsledadventuresmt.com*). Your friendly musher will take care to gear the ride to the passengers, from kids to senior citizens; bundled up in a sled, you'll be whisked through Stillwater State Forest on a 1½-hour ride over a 12-mi trail. The dogs mush trails such as the Eskimo Rollercoaster late November–mid-April. Reservations are necessary.

FISHING Toss a fly on one of the region's trout streams or lakes and you might snag a west slope cutthroat, rainbow trout, or grayling. By winter you can dangle a line through a sawed hole in the ice of Whitefish Lake. The best place for fishing gear in Whitefish is **Lakestream Fly Fishing Shop** (⊠ *334 Central Ave.* ☎ *406/862–1298* ⊕ *www.lakestream.com*). Guided trips to secluded private lakes, equipment, and fly-fishing gear are sold at the shop. Advice is free. The **Tally Lake Ranger District** (⊠ *1335 Hwy. 93 W* ☎ *406/863–5400*) can recommend good fishing spots and provide maps to the Flathead National Forest.

GOLF The 36-hole **Whitefish Lake Golf Club** (⊠ *1200 U.S. 93 W* ☎ *406/862–4000*) had its modest beginning as an airstrip. You'll need reservations to play on the championship course.

SKIING & SNOWBOARDING

☾ ★ The **Whitefish Mountain Resort on Big Mountain** has been one of Montana's top ski areas since the 1930s.

The mountain's most distinctive features are its widely spaced trees, which—when encased in snow—are known as snow ghosts. With 3,000 skiable acres, plus out-of-bounds areas for Sno-Cat skiing, the Big Mountain offers a lot of terrain to explore and many different lines to discover among those widely spaced trees. The pleasure of exploration and discovery—such as finding a fresh cache of powder many days after a snowstorm—is perhaps the main reason to ski the Big Mountain. Easy discovery comes with the help of free mountain tours by mountain ambassadors. They meet intermediate skiers near the bottom of the main quad chair, Glacier Chaser, at 10:30 AM and 1:30 PM daily.

In general the pitch is in the intermediate to advanced-intermediate range; there's not a whole lot of super-steep or super-easy skiing. A sameness in pitch, however, doesn't mean a sameness in skiing. With trails falling away on all sides of the mountain, there is a tremendous variation in exposure and hence in snow texture; also take into consideration the number of trees to deal with and the views (the best being northeast toward Glacier National Park). Kids love the Super Pipe on the front side's Chair 3; they can spend the whole day on the north side, especially in the natural half pipe of George's Gorge, under Chair 7 (the Big Creek Express).

One of the Big Mountain's best features is its long high-speed quad, the Glacier Chaser, meaning that runs using most of the mountain's 2,300-foot vertical are interrupted by less than 10 minutes of lift-riding time. A negative is weather. Foggy days are not uncommon; at those times you're thankful that those snow ghosts are around as points of reference. 🖂 *Box 1400, 59937* ☎ *406/862–2900 or 877/754–3474* 📠 *406/862–2922* ⊕ *www.skiwhitefish.com* ☉ *Early Dec.–early Apr. and mid-June–mid-Sept., daily 9–4; Fri. and Sat. night skiing late Dec.– early Mar. until 8:30.*

Backcountry Skiing & Snowboarding Because of an unusually liberal policy regarding skiing out-of-bounds, backcountry powder skiing and boarding are possible from the top of the Big Mountain. For the most part, the Big Mountain ski patrol does not prevent riders from crossing ski-area boundary ropes, although if you do so and get into trouble, you're responsible for paying rescue costs. Those who choose to travel out-of-bounds run a high risk of getting lost: it's easy to ski too far down the wrong drainage, creating the prospect of a tiring and excruciating bushwhack back to the base. For an introduction to the nearby backcountry, you might want to sign up with Big Mountain Ski and Snowboard School's **Sno-Cat-skiing** (☎ *406/862–2909*) operation, which takes skiers on a four-hour off-piste adventure for the price of a lift ticket plus $120.Although the backcountry avalanche danger varies with the winter snowpack, it's best to check the local avalanche forecast with **Glacier Country Avalanche Center** (☎ *406/257–8402*) and to carry tranceivers, probe poles, shovels, and, most important, a knowledge of backcountry safety and first aid.

Facilities 2,300-foot vertical drop; 3,000 skiable acres; 20% beginner, 50% intermediate, 30% advanced; 3 high-speed quad chairs, 1 quad chair, 5 triple chairs, 3 surface lifts. Snow report ☎406/862–7669 or 877/754–3474.

🕐 **Lessons & Programs** Group instruction in downhill is offered for $56 for a half day (plus a lift ticket); cross-country, telemark skiing, and snowboarding lessons are also available. Specialty clinics such as racing, mogul, and telemark techniques are provided, as well as children's programs. For information call the **Ski and Snowboard School** (☎406/862–2909).

Lift Tickets A full-day ticket is $56; for night skiing the charge is $15.

Nordic Skiing There are two machine-groomed track systems in the Whitefish area: both systems serve their purpose well enough, but don't expect inspiring views or a sense of wilderness seclusion. The **Big Mountain Nordic Center** (☎406/862–1900) has its own 10 mi of groomed trails; the daily fee is $12. One advantage that the **Glacier Nordic Touring Center** (✉1200 U.S. 93 W ☎406/862–4000 for snow report) on Whitefish Lake Golf Course has is that 1.6 mi of its 7 mi of groomed trail is for night skiing. A $5 per person donation is suggested. Rentals and trail maps are available at **the Outpost Lodge on Big Mountain** (☎406/862–2946). Arrangements for cross-country lessons can be made through the **Ski and Snowboard School** (☎406/862–2909).

Rentals Full snowboard or ski rental packages including skis/snowboard, boots, and poles start at $25 per day (☎406/862–1995).

WHERE TO EAT

$$–$$$$ ✕**Pollo Grill.** This Whitefish hot spot on the way to Big Mountain has succulent spit-roasted chicken as well as duck in a huckleberry merlot sauce and pork prime rib. They use Montana-grown products from local farmers and ranchers in much of their menu, and wild game is featured as specials. The side dishes, such as scalloped potatoes with Gorgonzola and rosemary, are as delicious as the main meals. ✉1705 Wisconsin Ave. ☎406/863–9400 ⚘Reservations recommended ▤AE, D, MC, V.

$$–$$$$ ✕**Tupelo Grille.** In homage to the South, native Louisiana chef-owner Pat Carloss cooks up excellent dishes such as Low Country shrimp and grits, herb-crusted rack of lamb, Cajun creole gumbo, and Thai beef tenderloin tips served in a curry-lime coconut cream sauce that is worth cleaning your plate for. Carloss rotates his well-chosen art collection in the dining room and further enlivens the atmosphere with piped-in New Orleans jazz, Dixieland, or zydeco music. ✉17 Central Ave. ☎406/862–6136 ⚘Reservations essential ▤AE, MC, V ⊘No lunch.

$$–$$$$ ✕**Wasabi Sushi Bar and Ginger Grill.** Not your typical Western ski-town eatery, Wasabi is the place for your sushi fix and Japanese cuisine. The restaurant has an urban sophistication with lavender-and-red walls

accented in black with a huge fish mural along one wall. For cooked dishes the Ginger Grill serves family-style meals. As eclectic and innovative as the sushi bar, the grill has small and large plates, including Moroccan lamb, duck, chicken, and seafood fare. ⊠ *419 E. 2nd St.* ☎ *406/863–9283* ⊟ *MC, V* ⊗ *Closed Mon. No lunch.*

$$–$$$$ ✗**Whitefish Lake Restaurant.** In the historic clubhouse on the municipal golf course, dine on locals' favorites such as hand-cut steaks and prime rib, or fresh fish dishes such as halibut steak wrapped in herbs and phyllo dough, baked and served with garlic mashed potatoes. The Napoléon, made with eggplant, caramelized onions, roasted red peppers, and provolone, and topped with a spicy tomato sauce, makes a delicious vegetarian entrée. You can also get a burger at the bar, but always save room for dessert: coffee–ice cream mud pie with Oreo cookie–crumb crust and fudge. ⊠ *1200 U.S. 93 N* ☎ *406/862–5285* ⚐ *Reservations essential* ⊟ *AE, D, MC, V* ⊗ *No lunch mid-Oct.–mid-Apr.*

$–$$$ ✗**Pescado Blanco.** Mountain-Mexican fusion—fine Mexican cuisine with a Rocky Mountain flair—includes handmade tacos, burritos, enchiladas, fresh seafood, wild game, and a fresh salsa bar. Enjoy a cold beer or glass of wine in the summer on the patio with mountain views. ⊠ *235 1st St.* ☎ *406/862–3290* ⊟ *MC, V.*

¢–$ ✗**Buffalo Cafe.** For the classic small-town café experience, this is the

Fodor's Choice place. Locals and visitors happily blend in a casual, friendly atmo-
★ sphere as they dig into well-prepared breakfasts and lunches. You can start your day with pancakes ("bigger than bowling balls," the menu brags, but considerably lighter), biscuits and gravy, or any of a dozen egg dishes. At lunchtime it's burgers, salads, grilled sandwiches, and Tex-Mex-style burritos and tacos; homemade milk shakes are worth the calories. Dinner provides a home-cooked-meal-away-from-home experience such as stroganoff made with sirloin steak and ground beef, steak sandwiches, and pasta entrées. ⊠ *514 3rd St.* ☎ *406/862–2833* ⚐ *Reservations not accepted* ⊟ *AE, MC, V* ⊗ *Closed Mon.*

¢–$ ✗**Montana Coffee Traders.** Coffees, fresh roasted locally, pastries, and homemade gelato are favorites with downtown shoppers. Unique hand-painted furniture, gifts, and bulk coffees and teas line the hangout's brick walls. Browse through the Saddest Pleasure Bookstore in the back of the café for local works, used books, and cards. Or visit the shop where their roasting is done at 5810 Highway 93 South. ⊠ *110 Central Ave.* ☎ *406/862–7667* ⚐ *Reservations not accepted* ⊟ *AE, MC, V.*

¢–$ ✗**Mrs. Spoonover's.** For a lighthearted place to eat with real food—no
☺ deli meats or greasy fried fare here—head for Mrs. Spoonover's. Hearty sandwiches such as the Wild Whitefish Turkey made with bacon and huckleberry spread or the Hungry Horse Rollup are created with fresh and local ingredients. Even the eggs in their tuna-and-egg-salad sandwich are from the area. They also have fresh soups and a kid-friendly menu. Picking a favorite of the 18 flavors of ice cream might be difficult, but not nearly as challenging as drinking their super-thick milk shakes through a straw. Espresso, cappuccino, and smoothies are available, or join them for one of their special tea parties for "children,

6

ladies and gentlemen of refinement." ⊠*131 Central Ave.* ☎*406/862–9381* ▭*No credit cards.*

¢–$ ✕**Quickees Cantina.** You can count on great sandwiches and authentic Mexican dishes here. Try the fish tacos—a Quickees' specialty. ⊠*28 Lupfer* ☎*406/862–9866* ▭*MC, V* ☉*Closed Sun.*

WHERE TO STAY

For lodging at the base of the Big Mountain Ski and Summer Resort, contact **central reservations** (☎*800/858–4152*), which handles everything from upscale Kandahar Lodge to dormitorylike Hibernation House, and various new-and-chic to older-yet-updated condominiums.

$$$$ ▦**The Bar W.** Just a short drive north of Whitefish, the Bar W is a playground for horse people and outdoor-recreation enthusiasts. You can ride the nearby trails or in the indoor arena, watch trainers work with horses, or take lessons yourself. The nonequine minded, can enjoy unlimited hiking opportunities, fishing in the private pond, badminton, archery, and more. The rooms are simple and comfortable with a distinct Western flair. The cabin overlooks pasture and the nearby woods, and it's not uncommon to sit on the deck and watch deer and other wildlife. **Pros:** They provide horse boarding, so you can bring your own to ride the 3,000-plus acres on Forest Service land or train them at one of their clinics. This is a great facility for business or family gatherings with lots of activities and plenty of room. **Cons:** Returning to the ranch from town requires caution—the deer along Highway 93 have a death wish. ⊠*2875 Hwy. 93 W, 59937* ☎*406/863–9099 or 888/828–2900* ▤*406/863–9500* ⊕*www.thebarw.com* ⇆*6 rooms, 1 cabin* ⚿*In-room: refrigerator. In-hotel: Wi-Fi, no elevator* ▭*AE, D, MC, V* ⦿*BP.*

$$$–$$$$ ▦**Grouse Mountain Lodge.** Always a Whitefish favorite, Grouse Mountain is consistently booked solid in July and August. Public tennis courts and cross-country trails border the lodge, and there's a 36-hole golf course next door. Off-season you can book some bargain activity packages. Thoroughly modern, it has a sunny lounge area with a lacquered slate floor, elk-horn chandeliers, soft-cushioned furniture, and a tall fireplace. The Grill at Grouse ($$–$$$$) focuses on steaks, ribs, and Pacific Northwest salmon baked on a cedar plank. Food is also served outside from mid-April to mid-October on the Deck and Patio ($–$$$), where there's shade and a large stone fire pit. The Wine Room can be reserved for a five-course dinner expertly paired with wines from their impressive collection. Recently renovated guest rooms are less refined but have standard modern furnishings and features, including 24-inch flat-screen TVs and high-speed Wi-Fi. Also updated, with a refrigerator, wet bar, and microwave, the loft units are a good choice for families. During the holidays the lodge is decorated with twinkly flair. **Pros:** Grouse Mountain provides free shuttle from the aiport or Amtrak station, daily trips into town, and four trips each day up Big Mountain. They can also provide a rental car at the lodge for those who wish to travel to Glacier or the surrounding area. **Cons:** They are very busy in summer, oftentimes making it difficult to book a room. The hotel is a little too far from town to walk in for shopping or res-

taurants. ⊠*2 Fairway Dr., 59937* ☎*406/862–3000, 877/862–1505* 🖷*406/863–2901* ⊕*www.grousemountainlodge.com* ⚑*133 rooms, 12 suites* ⚒*In-hotel: 3 restaurants, bar, pool, bicycles, airport shuttle* ⊟*AE, D, DC, MC, V.*

$$$–$$$$ 🖫**Kandahar–The Lodge at Big Mountain.** Cafe Kandahar (no lunch, reservations recommended), the small, rustic dining room in this lovely mountain lodge, serves the finest meals on the mountain. In addition to dressed-up standards such as tournedos of beef and New York strip steak, you can choose from game dishes such as roast quail, elk rib chops, and duck with a spice-and-orange-vanilla-bean jus, all prepared with a French provincial touch. In the rest of the lodge, the massive lobby fireplace and the Snug Bar are attractive public spaces, and the wood-accented guest rooms feature tile-and-granite finishes, leather furniture, and down comforters on the beds. Remedies Day Spa provides massage services daily and is on-site. You can catch a free two-minute shuttle to the slopes, then ski back to the lodge. **Pros:** The very accommodating staff knows some of the best ski areas. Having Remdies there is wonderful, especially after that first day on the slope. **Cons:** Even though it isn't ski season, they're closed to the public during some of the nicest times to be on the mountain. ⊠*3824 Big Mountain Rd.* ⚐*Box 278, 59937* ☎*406/862–6247 café, 800/862–6094, 406/862–6098* 🖷*406/862–6095* ⊕*www.kandaharlodge.com* ⚑*50 rooms* ⚒*In-room: refrigerator (some), kitchen (some), Ethernet. In-hotel: restaurant, bar, fitness center, Ethernet, laundry facilities, airport shuttle, parking (no fee), no-smoking rooms* ⊟*AE, D, MC, V* ⊘*Closed early Apr.–June and Oct.–late Nov.* ⦿*BP.*

$$–$$$$ 🖫**Garden Wall Inn B&B.** Most of what you see in this 1923 home is ★ antique, from first-edition books about Glacier National Park and local history to bed linens with lace borders. All rooms are individually decorated and have down duvets. Special extras include a wake-up coffee and tea tray delivered to your room and afternoon beverages and hors d'oeuvres in front of the fireplace. The three-course breakfast in the dining room is served on china from a Glacier National Park lodge. The innkeeper lives on the premises and shares cooking duties with the vivacious owner. The snow bus to the ski resort stops one block away. **Pros:** The industrious chef uses fresh, local produce in many of the dishes. Fresh flowers from the garden brighten up the rooms. The deep, claw-foot tubs can't be beat for a soak after a hard day of hiking or skiing. **Cons:** Spokane Ave. is a very busy street in Whitefish, and it might be tricky making a turn during the morning and afternoon traffic. ⊠*504 Spokane Ave., 59937* ☎*406/862–3440 or 888/530–1700* ⊕*www.gardenwallinn.com* ⚑*3 rooms, 1 suite* ⚒*In-room: no a/c, Wi-Fi, no phone, no TV. In-hotel: restaurant, parking (no fee), no-smoking rooms, no elevator* ⊟*AE, MC, V* ⦿*BP.*

$$–$$$$ 🖫**Kristianna Mountain Resort.** With a selection of condos, town houses, and luxury private homes, Kristianna can accommodate everyone from couples seeking an intimate getaway to large gatherings of family or friends. You can ski to the door in many places, or walk a short distance to the lifts. The places are adorned in Montana-style decor, with comfort, including down comforters and fireplaces, as a priority. The owners/managers take superb care of their guests, including stocking your kitchen ahead of time, if requested, and picking you up at the airport or train station. **Pros:** All of the properties are very well kept, and most guests want for nothing. **Cons:** This isn't the typical hotel or rental complex since the room or homes are in different locations on the mountain, but some of the private homes are large enough to house a large group. ⊠*3842 Winter Lake, 59937* ☎*406/862–2860* 🖷*406/862–0782* ⊕*www.kristianna.com* ⇆*15 condos, 10 town houses, 5 private homes* ⌂*In room: full kitchens, sauna, hot tub, . In hotel: no elevator* ▤*MC, V* ⏹*EP.*

$$–$$$ 🖳**Hidden Moose Lodge B&B.** At the foot of the road that climbs to Big Mountain, this two-story log lodge has a lively ski motif—a child's sled for a coffee table, an antique ski for a handrail. Some of the rooms have their own Jacuzzis, and there's one outdoors as well. Rooms are individually decorated with rough-hewn pine furniture and ironwork, and each has its own entrance off a small deck. The living room's vaulted ceiling creates space for plenty of light and a 20-foot-high fireplace; the scene can be quite social, especially in summer. Breakfasts are a standout, and come evening, a glass of wine or bottle of locally brewed beer is on the house. The skier-owners may even share their favorite powder run on Big Mountain. **Pros:** The lodge is easy to find and away from the hectic downtown traffic. The atmosphere is very welcoming, and you may not want to leave. **Cons:** The stairs could be difficult for some people with physical challenges, or who are stoved up after hitting the slopes for the first time. Not close enough to town to walk for shopping or restaurants. ⊠*1735 E. Lakeshore Dr., 1.9 mi from downtown, 59937* ☎*406/862–6516 or 877/733–6667* 🖷*406/862–6514* ⊕*www. hiddenmooselodge.com* ⇆*13 rooms* ⌂*In-room: refrigerator, DVD. In-hotel: Wi-Fi, bicycles, no-smoking rooms, no elevator* ▤*AE, D, MC, V* ⏹*BP.*

CAMPING   🏕**Whitefish Lake State Park.** On Whitefish Lake in a shady grove of tall pines, this clean campground is very popular and fills early. It has a shallow bay for swimming, a boat launch, and views of the Whitefish Range. One downside is that trains rumble through at all hours. ⌂*Flush toilets, pit toilets, drinking water, fire grates, picnic tables, swimming (lake)* ⇆*25 sites* ⊠*State Park Rd., ½ mi from downtown on U.S. 93 N, then 1 mi north on State Park Rd.* ☎*406/752–5501* 🖷*406/257–0349* ⊕*www.fwp.mt.gov* ▤*No credit cards* ⏲*May–early Oct.; primitive camping Oct.–Apr.*

NIGHTLIFE & THE ARTS

THE ARTS   The **O'Shaughnessy Cultural Arts Center** (⊠*1 Central Ave.* ☎*406/862– 5371*) hosts a variety of year-round live performances and music concerts, as well as classic and independent films, in an intimate theater setting.

The wild and the woolly show up in February for the annual **Whitefish Winter Carnival** (🖃*Box 1120, 59937* ☎*406/862–3501* ⊕*www. whitefishwintercarnival.com*), where you may be chased by a yeti or kissed by a mountain man at the parade. There are activities on the Big Mountain, including a torchlight parade and the Spirit of Winter show by the Ski School. In town, events include snow-sculpting contests and skijoring races (skiers pulled by horse and riders).

NIGHTLIFE A locals' hangout, particularly for the singles crowd, **the Great Northern Bar and Grill** (⊠27 Central Ave. ☎406/862–2816) rocks with local bands, open mike nights, and the occasional sort-of-big-name gig. The stage is surrounded by signs from Whitefish enterprises that are now defunct. Hang out inside or head out to the patio to enjoy a brew and a pile of nachos in the cool summer evenings. The microbrewery **Great Northern Brewing** (⊠2 Central Ave. ☎406/863–1000) is open for free tastings of seven different beers, including the Wild Huckleberry or Wheatfish. They're open daily noon–8.

SHOPPING

From local history to best sellers, you'll find it at **Bookworks** (⊠244 Spokane Ave. ☎406/862–4980), which has a fine selection of kids' books and handmade pottery.

☼ The largest toy shop in northwest Montana, **Imagination Station** (⊠221 Central Ave. ☎406/862–5668) has fun, educational, and creative toys and gifts in all price ranges. It also has a downtown Kalispell location.

Sage and Cedar (⊠214 Central Ave. ☎406/862–9411) sells lotions, soaps, massage products, perfumes, and accessories.

COLUMBIA FALLS

8 mi east of Whitefish via U.S. 93 and Hwy. 40.

☼ Many roadside attractions open during summer between the hard-working lumber town of Columbia Falls and Glacier National Park. Hands down, the most popular place on hot summer days is the **Big Sky Waterpark,** the largest waterpark in Montana. Besides the 10 waterslides there is a huge whirlpool, a kids' pool, a beach volleyball court, a golf course, arcade games, bumper cars, a carousel, barbecue grills, a picnic area, a souvenir shop, and food service. ⊠7211 U.S. 2 E, junction of U.S. 2 and Hwy. 206 ☎406/892–5025 or 406/892–2139 ⊕www.bigskywp.com ☜$22 ☼Memorial Day–Labor Day, daily 11–6.

☼ Get lost in the maze at the **Amazing Ventures Fun Center,** a circuitous outdoor route made of plywood walls and ladders, with viewing areas where parents can watch their kids (and give directions when necessary). Other attractions include Bankshot Basketball, go-karts, 18 holes of miniature golf, thriller bumper boats in a pond, and a picnic area. ⊠10265 U.S. 2 E, Coram ☎406/387–5902 ☜$6 per activity or $17.25 fun pass ☼Memorial Day–mid-Sept., daily 9:30–an hr before dark.

> ### WORD OF MOUTH
>
> If you . . . enjoy kitsch, stop at the House of Mystery. You can't miss it, there's a giant chair in front. Went with a friend and had a really fun time, great for pictures.
>
> –coolbluewater

☼ You've found the power center of Montana at the **House of Mystery–**

Montana Vortex, a wacky roadside attraction where the laws of physics don't apply and other mystifying phenomena prevail. ⊠ *7800 U.S. 2 E,* ☎ *406/892–1210* 🖂 *$7* ⊗ *Apr.–Oct., daily 10–5.*

WHERE TO STAY & EAT

¢–$$ ✕ **The Back Room of the Nite Owl.** Locals wait in line for the fall-off-the-bone barbecue ribs, broasted chicken, and fry bread served with honey butter. The atmosphere is very casual with a large main room, several smaller eating areas (great for families), and seating in the bar. A typical combination platter includes your choice of ribs (country-style or spare) and either broasted or rotisserie chicken served with sides of fry bread, baked beans, coleslaw, and red potatoes—or opt for a side salad. They also serve pasta and have excellent pizza with homemade sauce. ⊠ *Hwy. 2 E* ☎ *406/892–3131* 🖂 *AE, D, MC, V* ⊗ *No lunch.*

$$$–$$$$ 🏨 **Meadow Lake Golf Resort.** As the name indicates, the links are front and center here. The inn is just a few steps from the pro shop, and the veranda has views of the course as well as the surrounding mountains and a pond. Condos and vacation homes, with private decks, barbecue grills, fireplaces, and simple, comfortable furnishings, line the fairways. Puttski's ($$–$$$$) specializes in fresh salads, burgers, and the chef's favorite, Buffalo Tip Stroganoff. You can dine outside in summer. Troop Meadow Lake has many activities for the kids, including swimming-pool games, arts and crafts, outdoor adventures, and movie night. Hucklebear's Zone is a fun part of the pool where kids can spray each other with the water canons or climb the tower and dump buckets of water on unsuspecting friends. **Pros:** Offers free shuttle service to Whitefish Mountain Resort. Very accommodating for families. **Cons:** Outside of Puttski's, fine dining is limited in the Columbia Falls area. Although centrally located to the Big Mountain, Flathead Lake, or Glacier National Park, it's a fair distance to any of the places. ⊠ *100 St. Andrew's Dr., 59912* ☎ *406/892–8700 or 800/321–4653* 🖶 *406/892–0330* ⊕ *www.meadowlake.com* 🛏 *24 rooms, 100 condos, 20 vacation homes* & *In-room: kitchen (some), refrigerator (some), Wi-Fi. In-hotel: restaurant, bar, golf course, pools, Ethernet, fitness room, concierge, laundry facilities, airport and Amtrak shuttle, no-smoking rooms, no elevator* 🖂 *AE, D, DC, MC, V* ⧦ *EP.*

CAMPING 🏕 **Columbia Falls RV Park.** The in-town location, with tall trees to shelter against the breeze, is convenient to the Big Sky Waterpark, shopping, the city pool, and the Flathead River. Pull-through spaces are adequate for large RVs, and the tent area is grassy, with electricity for some sites. & *Flush toilets, full hookups, picnic tables, electricity, public telephone, general store* 🛏 *40 full hookups, 10 tent sites* ⊠ *1000 3rd Ave. E, on U.S. 2* ☎ *406/892–1122 or 888/401–7268* ⊕ *www.columbiafalls rvpark.com* 🖂 *D, MC, V* ⊗ *May–Oct.*

NIGHTLIFE & THE ARTS

THE ARTS   Enjoy plenty of holiday cheer and local color at the early December nighttime parade, **Night of Lights** (⊠ *Nucleus Ave.* ☎ *406/892–2072* ⊕ *www.columbiafallschamber.com*).

The outdoors echoes with the **Summer Concert Series** (⊠ *Marantette Park on U.S. 2 E* ☎ *406/892–2072*) in the Don Lawrence Amphitheater Thursday at 8 PM from mid-June through late August. Types of music vary but are aimed toward a broad audience; the Don Lawrence Big Band has a performance every year.

NIGHTLIFE   Whether the owner's band is playing on the stage or cowboys are serenading a sparse crowd of locals during karaoke, the **Blue Moon Nite Club, Casino and Grill** (⊠ *Hwy. 40 and U.S. 2* ☎ *406/892–9925*) is a hoot. The wooden dance floor gets a good scuffing on Western dance and country-swing nights. Two stuffed grizzly bears rear up near the entrance, and other species decorate the large saloon as well.

SHOPPING

Huckleberry Patch Restaurant & Gift Shop (⊠ *8868 U.S. 2 E, Hungry Horse* ☎ *406/387–5670 or 800/527–7340* ⊕ *www.huckleberrypatch. com*) has been the huckleberry headquarters of the state for more than 50 years, selling the purple wild berry native to the region. Newly remodeled, it has an excellent selection of jams, candies, coffee, fudge, barbecue sauce, and huckleberry-scented lotions (best not wear while hiking in bear country!). Don't miss their outstanding huckleberry pie or milk shakes.

6

SEELEY–SWAN VALLEY

Squeezed between two magnificent mountain ranges—the Missions on the west and the Swan Range on the east—the glacially formed Swan Valley is littered with lakes, sprinkled with homesteads, and frosted with snow for five months of the year. One road, Highway 83, winds along an 80-mi course that follows the Clearwater and Swan rivers, popular for boating and fishing—both winter ice fishing and summer trout fishing. Several trailheads lead into the Bob Marshall Wilderness from the Swan Valley. Modern amenities are as sparse as the population. Only about a thousand people reside here year-round, so you are much more likely to encounter a dozen deer than a dozen humans. With that in mind, it's imperative that you look out for deer and elk on the road, day and night. Summer visitors fill campgrounds and the few guest lodges. Besides snowmobiling and cross-country skiing, winters bring snow, drippy weather, and low clouds. Do as the locals do: put up your hood, grab the gloves and boots, and head outdoors.

SEELEY LAKE

120 mi south of Glacier National Park via U.S. 2, Hwy. 206, and Hwy 83.

Bordered by campgrounds, hiking trails, and wildlife-viewing opportunities, this community of 2,400 centers on lovely Seeley Lake. Nearby is the Big Blackfoot River, a setting in *A River Runs Through It,* Norman McLean's reflection on family and fishing. Host to races and leisure outings, the Seeley Creek Nordic Ski Trails roll across hills and meadows. In winter 350 mi of snowmobile trails rip through the woods. The major industry, logging, which began in 1892, is evident on some hillsides.

Paddling on the 3½-mi **Clearwater Canoe Trail,** along an isolated portion of the Clearwater River, you may see moose and will likely see songbirds, great blue herons, and belted kingfishers. The Seeley Lake Ranger Station has free maps and directions to the put-in for the two-hour paddle. ⊠*3 mi north of Seeley on Hwy. 83* ☎*406/677–2233* ⊕*www.fs.fed.us/r1* ✆*Free* ☉*May–Oct.*

Ten days of events celebrate winter during the January **Seeley Lake Area Winterfest,** including a snow-sculpture contest, Christmas tree bonfire, parade, biathlon, kids' games, cross-country ski events, snowmobile poker runs, and more. ⊠*Hwy. 83 S* ☎*406/677–2880* ⊕*www.seeley lakechamber.com* ☉*Mid–late Jan., daily.*

Logging's colorful past is displayed in the big log barn at **Seeley Lake Museum and Visitors Center,** along with tools of the trade and visitor information. ⊠*2920 Hwy. 83 S at mile marker 13.5* ☎*406/677–2880* ⊕*www.seeleylakechamber.com* ✆*Free* ☉*Memorial Day–Labor Day, daily 9–5; Labor Day–Memorial Day, Mon., Thurs., and Fri. 11–4.*

OFF THE BEATEN PATH

Morrell Falls National Recreation Trail #30. A 2½-mi hike (one way) leads to the lovely cascades of Morrell Falls. It is actually a series of falls, with the longest about a 100-foot drop. This is a moderately difficult family hike, perfect for a picnic (although it's wise to remember this is bear country), and often used by bicyclists and horsemen. Maps and travel information are available at the Seeley Lake Ranger District office. ⊠*From Hwy. 83, turn east on Morrell Creek Rd. and follow signs* ☎*406/677–2233* ⊕*www.fs.fed.us/r1* ✆*Free* ☉*Daily.*

SPORTS & THE OUTDOORS

★ You can romp in deep snows on the **Seeley Creek Nordic Ski Trails** at the edge of town. Trails are groomed for skate and classic skiing. Nearby are dogsled trails. The trail systems share a parking lot and covered picnic area where you can join a campfire to warm your toes. ⊠*Forest Rd. 477; from Hwy. 83, turn east on Morrell Creek Rd., aka Cottonwood Lakes Rd., and drive 1 mi to trailhead* ☎*406/677–2233* ⊕*www.seeleylake chamber.com* ✆*$4 donation requested* ☉*Dec.–Mar., daily.*

CROSS-COUNTRY SKIING

You can ski a few kilometers on the **Double Arrow Resort** (⊠*Hwy. 83 at milepost 12, 2 mi south of Seeley Lake* ☎*406/677–2777 or 800/468–0777*), where you may see moose in the willows.

Ski-touring equipment and maps from **Seeley Lake Recreational Rentals** (⊠*Hwy. 83 N* ☎*406/677–7368* ⊕*www.seeleyfunrentals.com*) will take you to the winter trails. You can also rent snowmobiles, snowshoes, and summer toys like boats and bikes—reserve online.

SNOW-MOBILING Rent snowmobiles, snowshoes, cross-country skis, and all of the accessories from **Seeley Sport Rentals** (⊠*3112 Hwy. 83 S* ☎*406/677–3680* ⊕*www.seeleysportrentals.com*), which also offers a guide service. When the weather warms up, they have pontoon boats, ski boats, wave runners, canoes, and mountain bikes for summer adventures.

WHERE TO EAT

$$–$$$$ ✕**Lindey's Steak House.** Locals will send you here to watch the sun set over the lake while dining on the only thing on the menu: steak. Select cuts, all 16-ounce portions, are served with potatoes, garlic bread, and pickled watermelon rind served family-style. During the summer, grab a burger or chicken breast sandwich at Lindsey's Bay Burgers ($–$$) and enjoy the outside dining. October through March, Bay Burgers moves inside the steak house from 11 to 3. ⊠*Hwy. 83, downtown Seeley Lake* ☎*406/677–9229* ⊟*MC, V.*

$$$ ✕**Kozy Korner Steak House.** From the outside it doesn't look like much, but this out-of-the-way charmer, a 1930s building with a log-cabin dining area, features some of the finest steaks around. Locals crowd into the remote restaurant south of town and east of Salmon Lake for the chicken-fried steak, potato bar, salad bar, and tempura prawns. You can snowmobile directly to the restaurant in the winter. ⊠*6070 Woodworth Rd. (Hwy. 67), 4 mi east of Hwy. 83* ☎*406/677–5699* ⊟*AE, D, MC, V.*

¢–$$ ✕**The Filling Station.** Friendly folks fill up on the simple food at this diner, which doubles as a bar and casino. Old standards are burgers with fries, porterhouse steaks, and huckleberry barbecue ribs served with baked beans and coleslaw. ⊠*Hwy. 83, downtown Seeley Lake* ☎*406/677–2080* ⚑*Reservations not accepted* ⊟*AE, D, MC, V.*

WHERE TO STAY

$$–$$$$ ▦**Double Arrow Resort.** The handsome, 60-year-old log main lodge combines European grace and Western trimmings on a 200-acre spread. The great room's stone fireplace is a guest gathering spot; nearby in Seasons restaurant ($$$–$$$$) the sophisticated and changing menu features blackened buffalo sirloin, grilled shrimp skewers, and crab-stuffed halibut. Guest rooms and log cabins are simply furnished with a few antiques and fluffy comforters on brass beds. Early-20th-century log homes with antiques, knotty-pine interiors, and modern kitchens are popular with families. **Pros:** Excellent location for a family reunion with all the amenities to keep people of all ages entertained. **Cons:** The closest airport is in Missoula, which is 55 mi from Double Arrow. It's 100 mi to Whitefish for those traveling by Amtrak. ⊠*Hwy. 83, milepost 12, 2 mi south of Seeley Lake,* ✉*Box 747, Seeley Lake 59868* ☎*406/677–2777 or 800/468–0777* 📠*406/677–2922* ⊕*www.double arrowresort.com* ➫*3 rooms, 12 cabins, 6 homes* ⚑*In-room: no a/c, kitchen (some), dial-up. In-hotel: restaurant, bar, golf course, tennis*

courts, pool, concierge, laundry facilities, no-smoking rooms, no elevator ⊟ *D, MC, V* ⦿*CP.*

CAMPING 🏕 **Big Larch.** Giant larch trees shade the large site, where fishing and boating are popular. There's a good beach for swimming, a horseshoes pit, handicapped-accessible picnicking, and marked nature trails. Shopping, laundry, and services are nearby. ♿*Flush toilets, dump station, drinking water, fire grates, picnic tables, ranger station, swimming (lake)* 🔺*50 sites* ⊠*Forest Rd. 2199; 1 mi north of Seeley Lake on Hwy. 83, and ½ mi west on Forest Rd. 2199* ☎*406/677-2233* 🖷*406/677-3902* ⊕*www.fs.fed.us/r1* ⊟*No credit cards* ⊙*Mid-May–Sept.; primitive camping (no services or fees) mid-Sept.–May.*

🏕 **Seeley Lake Forest Service Campground.** This busy campground among tall pines is on the lake, so mosquitoes can be pesky. Groceries, sports rentals, and restaurants are about 4 mi away. Reservations are recommended. ♿*Flush toilets, dump station, drinking water, fire grates, picnic tables, ranger station, swimming (lake)* 🔺*29 sites* ⊠*Boy Scout Rd.* ☎*406/677-2233* 🖷*406/677-3902* ⊕*www.fs.fed.us/r1* ⊟*No credit cards* ⊙*Late May–Labor Day.*

HOLLAND LAKE

19 mi north of Seeley Lake via Hwy. 83.

Outdoorsy types come to this 400-acre lake for fishing, boating, swimming, hiking, trail riding, and camping in summer and ice fishing, cross-country skiing, snowshoeing, and snowmobiling in winter. To pursue any of the activities available in this remote setting, you must come equipped with your own canoe, motor launch, or snowmobile: your company will be kokanee salmon, rainbow trout, and bull trout, plus the handful of people who run Holland Lake Lodge. Maps for the numerous trails that depart from the lake area are available at the lodge or through the Forest Service office. Some routes climb the Swan Range into the Bob Marshall Wilderness.

The hike to **Holland Falls** is about 1½ mi from the lodge. The last bit is a steep climb, but it's well worth it for the view. ⊠*Holland Lake Rd.; from Hwy. 83, turn east on Forest Rd. 44 for 3 mi to Holland Lake Rd.* ☎*406/837-7500* ⊕*www.fs.fed.us/r1* ⊡*Free* ⊙*Daily.*

WHERE TO STAY

$–$$ 🏠**Holland Lake Lodge.** When the snow flies, this lodge is nearly buried, which makes for cozy fireside dining and relaxing. The log lodge sits on the lakeshore, where you can cross-country ski or snowshoe from the door. In summer step off the cabin porch for a hike or a swim. Cabins are updated yet rustic. You can dine on trout in the restaurant ($$–$$$) while watching the trout rise. **Pros:** Incredible place nestled at the foot of the mountains. You can't ask for a better place to relax, particularly during the shoulder seasons. **Cons:** The 4 mi of unpaved road can be a bit rough and very congested during the summer. This is a heavily used area in July and August for packers and hikers heading into the backcountry. ⊠*1947 Holland Lake Rd., Swan Valley 59826*

☎406/754–2282 or 877/925–6343 🖷406/754–2208 ⊕www.holland lakelodge.com ⇆9 rooms, 6 cabins ☖In-room: no a/c, no phone, no TV. In-hotel: restaurant, room service, bar, no-smoking rooms, no elevator ☰AE, D, MC, V ⧖FAP.

CAMPING △**Holland Lake Campground.** Large trees provide lots of shade for campers near the lake. The spot is popular with outfitters who pack horses into the nearby Bob Marshall Wilderness. Food service is available nearby at Holland Lake Lodge. ☖Pit toilets, dump station, drinking water, bear boxes, fire grates, picnic tables, swimming (lake) ⇆40 sites ⊠Holland Lake Rd. ☎406/837–7500 🖷406/837–7503 ⊕www. fs.fed.us/r1 ☰No credit cards ⊙Mid-May–Sept.

BOB MARSHALL WILDERNESS AREA

5 mi east of Hwy. 83 via Pyramid Pass Trail, Lion Creek Pass Trail, or Smith Creek Pass Trail.

The Bob Marshall, Scapegoat, and Great Bear wilderness areas take up 1.5 million rugged, roadless, remote acres within the Flathead National Forest. Preservation pioneer, forester, and cofounder of the Wilderness Society, Bob Marshall pushed Congress in 1964 to create the wilderness area that bears his name. Since then, little has altered the landscape, which runs 60 mi along the Continental Divide. More than 1,000 mi of trails enter the wilderness from near Seeley Lake at Pyramid Pass Trail and Holland Lake at Pyramid Pass, Condon's Lion Creek Pass, and Smith Creek Pass, where hikers are sure to meet outfitters and packhorses. An old airstrip at Shafer Meadows is used for float parties on the wild white-water Middle Fork of the Flathead.

Information on the Bob Marshall Wilderness is available through the **Flathead National Forest,** which has maps, listings of outfitters and access points, and safety information regarding travel in bear country. ⊠1935 3rd Ave. E, Kalispell 59901 ☎406/758–5200 ⊕www.fs.fed. us/r1 ⧖Free ⊙Weekdays 8–4.

A complete list of trails, elevations, and backcountry campsites can be found in the book *Hiking Montana's Bob Marshall Wilderness* by Erik Molvar, available at **Books West** (⊠101 Main, Kalispell 59901 ☎406/752–6900 or 800/471–2270).

OFF THE
BEATEN
PATH **Spotted Bear.** At the end of a long and often washboarded gravel road, Spotted Bear is a remote entrance into the Bob Marshall Wilderness. You'll find there a ranger station, outfitter's ranch, campground, swimming, and rafting a short distance down the South Fork of the Flathead River to the Hungry Horse Reservoir. ⊠Forest Service Rd. 38; 55 mi from Hungry Horse on either E. or W. Hungry Horse Reservoir Rd. ☎406/387–3800 ⊕www.fs.fed.us/r1 ⧖Free ⊙Apr.–Oct.

SPORTS & THE OUTDOORS

FISHING Five-day pack and float trips with **Bob Marshall Wilderness Horse Pack and Float Expeditions** (⊠55 mi from Hungry Horse on either E. or W. Hungry Horse Reservoir Rd. toward Spotted Bear Ranger Station

CLOSE UP

Of Dudes & Ranches

By the late 1800s, stories of the jagged peaks and roaring rivers in the Rocky Mountains had caught the nation's imagination. Travelers headed west on the recently completed transcontinental railroads to see these wonders firsthand. They stayed where they could, whichoften meant rustic ranches. It worked out well—ranchers, starved for fresh faces and news from back home, were pleased to have the company. Soon ranches began hosting paying guests. These "dudes" stayed for weeks or months and participated in day-to-day operations. By 1940, there were more than 300 dude ranches in the United States and Canada. Today, you'd be hard pressed to find one of these places calling itself a dude ranch—"guest ranch" sounds better—and the typical stay is about a week. Activities include trail rides, barbecues, hoedowns, and sometimes opportunities to work the livestock. The week often culminates in an O-Mok-See, a series of competitive horseback events.

☎ 800/223–4333 ⊕ www.spottedbear.com) go deep into the backcountry for fly-fishing in the wilderness. This Orvis-endorsed expedition is limited to 12 people per trip. **Wilderness Lodge** (⊠ *West Side Hungry Horse Reservoir Rd., 55 mi east of Hungry Horse* ☎ 406/387–4051) conducts five-day or longer float and fishing trips in the wilderness area from the end of June to mid-September.

TRAIL RIDES   Take a day ride or an overnight pack trip into the wilderness with **Diamond R Guest Ranch** (⊠ *East Side Hungry Horse Reservoir Rd., 55 mi from Hungry Horse* ☎ 406/756–1573 or 800/597–9465). **A-Rawhide Trading Post** (⊠ *12000 Hwy. 2. E, West Glacier* ☎ 406/387–5999 or 800/388–5727) takes riders on excursions from 1 hour to 11 days in the Flathead National Forest, or try a "Saddle and Paddle" adventure, where you ride a horse upstream alongside the Middle Fork of the Flathead River and raft down.

WHERE TO STAY

$$$$ 🏨 **Rich Ranch.** At this small, personal, and beautiful guest ranch bordering the Bob Marshall Wilderness, all-inclusive packages are the rule. You get traditional Western meals and a horse to ride for the duration of your stay; some packages emphasize riding, others fishing, or they have snowmobile tours in the winter. **Pros:** There is plenty to do even if you never leave the ranch. The owners are very accommodating and helpful. **Cons:** It's several hours to visit Glacier National Park, and at least an hour to hit the shopping in Missoula. ⊠ *939 Cottonwood Lakes Rd., Seeley Lake 59868* ☎ 406/677–2317 or 800/532–4350 🖷 406/677–3530 ⊕ www.richranch.com ➷ 4 rooms, 8 cabins ♿ In-room: no a/c, no phone, DVD (some). In-hotel: Wi-Fi in the lodge, bicycles, airport shuttle, no-smoking rooms ▤ MC, V ⟨◎⟩ FAP.

$$$$ 🏨 **Spotted Bear Ranch.** Book well in advance if you wish to stay at this
★   remote yet upscale lodge. The two-bedroom log cabins here among the evergreens are cozy, yet have generator power, flush toilets, showers, fireplaces, and views. The ranch, reachable by a rough road, spe-

6

cializes in fly-fishing expeditions. Dinners are for guests only, and are served family-style in the historic main lodge. **Pros:** The Bob Marshall wilderness is at your fingertips, and the fly-fishing opportunities are phenomenal. **Cons:** Plan on a two- three-hour drive on a winding and teeth-rattling road to reach the lodge. It is very remote and out of range for those dependent on cell phones. ✉ *55 mi from Hungry Horse on either E. or W. Hungry Horse Reservoir Rd. toward Spotted Bear Ranger Station, Whitefish 59937* ✆ *Winter address, Box 4940* ☎ *800/223–4333* ⊕ *www.spottedbear.com* ⏎ *6 cabins* ⌂ *In-room: no a/c, no phone, no TV. In-hotel: no-smoking rooms, no elevator* ▭ *AE, D, MC, V* ⊗ *Closed mid-Sept.–mid-June* ⏐◯⏐ *FAP.*

$$$
Fodor's Choice
★

Seven Lazy P Guest Ranch. A snug haven in a rugged landscape, this 1,200-acre ranch is surrounded by pines and aspens deep in Teton Canyon, an eastern gateway to the Bob Marshall Wilderness. The duplex cabins feel like a second home, with comfortable furniture, wood-paneled ceilings, rough-hewn wainscoting, and picture windows; enveloping sofas and chairs, a large stone fireplace, and more golden wood fill the main lodge. Their 3,600-square-foot three-bedroom home is ideal for larger groups. Three meals daily (included in the room rate) are served family-style, and the food is memorable: a sausage-egg-and-cheese bake with homemade muffins for breakfast, grilled lemon-glazed salmon for dinner, and pies just out of the oven. They'll fortify you for a day of hiking, wildlife viewing, or guided horseback riding (also included in the room rate). In summer multiday pack trips into the Bob Marshall give riders a glimpse of the Rockies as Lewis and Clark saw them. ✆ *Box 178, Choteau 59422* ☎ *406/466–2044* ⊕ *www. sevenlazyp.com* ⏎ *2 duplex cabins, 1 single cabin, 4 family-type cabins, 1 3-bedroom house* ⌂ *In-room: no a/c, no phone, refrigerator, no TV. In-hotel: airport shuttle, no elevator* ▭ *MC, V* ⊗ *Closed end of Nov.–Apr.* ⏐◯⏐ *FAP.*

¢

Wolf Willow Ranch. There are two cabins—one fully equipped, the other rustic—on a family ranch outside of Bynum, 25 mi northwest of Choteau. Both sit just east of the foot of the mountains, with an inspirational view. The hiking and bird- and wildlife-watching for which the Rocky Mountain Front is known are right outside the door. One cabin is just like home, with a full kitchen and bath, living room with TV and VCR, and sleeping space (queen and twin beds) for four to six people, depending on how friendly they are. The other cabin has a loft and four bunk beds, a sofa, a propane stove and refrigerator, and an outhouse (in other words, no running water). ✉ *Bynum, 59419* ☎ *406/469–2231* ⏎ *2 cabins* ▭ *No credit cards.*

CAMPING

⚠ Spotted Bear Campground. Alongside the South Fork of the Flathead River, this remote campground offers flat sites shaded by tall pines. Grizzly bears frequent the area, so a clean camp is imperative. Trailheads lead into wilderness areas. ⌂ *Vault toilets, dump station, drinking water, bear boxes, fire grates, picnic tables, ranger station, swimming (river)* ⏎ *13 sites* ✉ *Forest Service Rd. 38, 55 mi southeast of U.S. 2 at Hungry Horse* ☎ *406/758–5376* 🖷 *406/758–5390* ⊕ *www.fs.fed.us/r1* ▭ *No credit cards* ⊗ *Memorial Day–Labor Day.*

MISSOULA

A fertile valley hemmed in by mountains cradles Missoula, the cultural center of northwest Montana. The largest metropolis around (population 57,000) is the home of the University of Montana. In the aptly nicknamed Garden City, maple trees line the residential streets and the Clark Fork River slices through the center of town; a 6-mi riverside trail passes the university en route to Hellgate Canyon. Missoula makes a good base for regional exploration by way of Interstate 90 east–west, U.S. 93 north–south, and numerous back roads.

In 1860 French trappers dubbed this trading settlement the Hell Gate when they discovered bones and bodies in the canyon after a bloody battle between Blackfeet and other Indians. Settlers did not arrive until more than 50 years after the Lewis and Clark expedition traveled through the area. Gold speculators, homesteaders, and the coming of the Northern Pacific Railroad in 1883 all helped establish the town.

EXPLORING MISSOULA

Numbers in the margin correspond to numbers on the Missoula map.

Missoula is home to the Adventure Cycling Association (formerly Bike Centennial), so it's no surprise that the city has more bicycles than people. Exploring by bicycle is popular and easy: downtown and the university district are relatively flat and have bike paths and bike traffic lanes; many storefronts are adorned with bike racks. Within the center of the city, walking is a good option, too, particularly given that parking is at a premium and that the university itself is a car-free zone. Dozens of walking and biking paths wend through town. The Missoula Valley and sights on the outskirts of town are best explored by car.

WHAT TO SEE

❺ Caras Park. Downtown's favorite green space, the park has a walking path along the Clark Fork River. A summer pavilion hosts live musical performances such as those at Downtown ToNight, a Thursday evening event that also features food and what the chamber of commerce likes to call a "beverage garden." ⊠ *Front and Ryman Sts.* ☎ *406/543–4238* ⊕ *www.missouladowntown.com* ⊠ *Free* ☉ *Daily 6 AM–11 PM.*

❹ A Carousel for Missoula. In downtown Caras Park, kids hop in the saddles of hand-carved steeds. The carousel's horses and chariots gallop on a lovingly restored 1918 frame, accompanied by tunes from the largest band organ in continuous use in the United States. The Dragon Hollow play area next to the carousel features a dragon, a castle, and many play structures. ⊠ *101 Carousel Dr.* ☎ *406/549–8382* ⊕ *www.carrousel.com* ⊠ *Adults $1.50, under 16 and over 55 50¢ per ride; play area free* ☉ *Memorial Day–Labor Day, daily 11–7; Labor Day–Memorial Day, daily 11–5:30.*

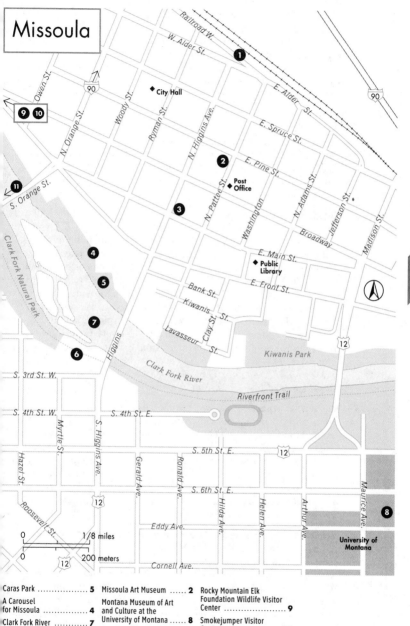

Missoula

City Hall

E. Alder St.

W. Alder St.

Railroad W.

Owen St.

N. Orange St.

Woody St.

Ryman St.

N. Higgins Ave.

E. Spruce St.

E. Pine St.

Post Office

N. Pattee St.

Washington

E. Main St.

Public Library

E. Front St.

Broadway

N. Adams St.

Jefferson St.

Madison St.

S. Orange St.

Clark Fork Natural Park

Bank St.

Kiwanis St.

Lavasseur St.

Clay St.

Higgins

Kiwanis Park

Clark Fork River

Riverfront Trail

S. 3rd St. W.

S. 4th St. W.

S. 4th St. E.

Myrtle St.

S. Higgins Ave.

S. 5th St. E.

Gerald Ave.

Ronald Ave.

Hilda Ave.

Helen Ave.

Arthur Ave.

Maurice Ave.

Hazel St.

Roosevelt St.

Eddy Ave.

S. 6th St. E.

University of Montana

Cornell Ave.

0   1/8 miles

0   200 meters

6

Caras Park **5**

A Carousel
for Missoula **4**

Clark Fork River **7**

Higgins Block **3**

Historical Museum at
Fort Missoula **11**

Missoula Art Museum **2**

Montana Museum of Art
and Culture at the
University of Montana **8**

Northern Pacific
Railroad Depot **1**

Old Milwaukee
Railroad Depot **6**

Rocky Mountain Elk
Foundation Wildlife Visitor
Center **9**

Smokejumper Visitor
Center **10**

7 Clark Fork River. The heart of Missoula is defined by the Clark Fork River, which cuts through Hellgate Canyon between Mt. Sentinel and Mt. Jumbo, passes by the university, and slices through downtown. A 6-mi-long riverside trail and the connecting 2½-mi Kim Williams trail make for easy, pleasant walks, with picnic spots and benches along the way where you can watch the river. Take note: the powerful currents of the Clark Fork are dangerous—they've taken many lives over the years.

3 Higgins Block. This Queen Anne–style commercial structure, a granite, copper-domed corner building with red polychromed brick, occupies a block in the heart of downtown. On the National Register of Historic Places, it's now home to a deli, a bank, and several shops. ⊠*202 N. Higgins Ave.* ⊕*www.missouladowntown.com* ⊠*Free* ⊗*Tues. noon–8, Wed.–Sat. noon–6.*

11 Historical Museum at Fort Missoula. Fort Missoula, at the western edge of town, was established in 1877 at the height of the U.S. Army's conflict with the Nez Perce, led by Chief Joseph. The museum's indoor and outdoor exhibits, including 13 historic structures relocated from nearby sites, depict and explain the early development of Missoula County. The black 25th Infantry of bicycle soldiers arrived in 1888 to test bicycles for military use; near-life-size photos depict the soldiers during an expedition to Yellowstone National Park's Mammoth Terraces. Uniforms and artifacts are also on display. They ultimately rode one-speed bicycles from Missoula to St. Louis. Guided tours are available by appointment. ⊠*Fort Missoula, Bldg. 322, accessed via South Ave.* ☎*406/728–3476* ⊕*www.fortmissoulamuseum.org* ⊠*$3* ⊗*Memorial Day–Labor Day, Mon.–Sat. 10–5, Sun. noon–5; Labor Day–Memorial Day, Tues.–Sun. noon–5.*

2 Missoula Art Museum. Each year, two dozen changing contemporary art
★ exhibits join a permanent collection featuring works by E. S. Paxson, Walter Hook, Rudy and Lela Autio, and modern-day Native American artists. The 1903 Carnegie Library building, reopened in summer 2006 after extensive remodeling adding handicapped accessibility, has much more gallery space and classrooms. ⊠*335 N. Pattee St., 1 block from intersection with W. Broadway* ☎*406/728–0447* ⊕*www.missoulaart museum.org* ⊠*Donations accepted* ⊗*Tues.–Fri. 11–6, Sat. 10–3; call for occasional extended hrs.*

8 Montana Museum of Art and Culture at the University of Montana. The university's art museum, divided into the Meloy and Paxson galleries, hosts traveling exhibitions and has a permanent collection of more than 10,000 works, with an emphasis on historic and contemporary art from the West. ⊠*Performing Arts and Radio/Television Center, University of Montana* ☎*406/243–2019* ⊕*www.umt.edu/montanamuseum* ⊠*Free* ⊗*June–Aug., Wed.–Sat. 11–3; Sept.–May, Tues.–Thurs. 11–3, Fri. and Sat. 4–8:30.*

1 Northern Pacific Railroad Depot. The construction of the Northern Pacific Railroad was instrumental in opening up the West to settlers, and the arrival of the line in Missoula is a key point in the city's history. The depot, opened in 1901, is an example of the Renaissance Revival architecture that dominates the north end of downtown. Today the depot houses private offices, but you can still look around inside, enjoy a picnic outside, and examine the Crossings, a sculpture of giant red enamel Xs representing railroad trestles over mountain ravines. ⊠*N. Higgins Ave.* ☏*406/543–4238* ⊕*www.missouladowntown.com* ✉*Free* ⊙*Weekdays 9–5.*

⑥ Old Milwaukee Railroad Depot. A Missoula landmark along the river's south shore, this 1910 passenger depot, with Romanesque windows, a Spanish-style roof, two towers, and Mission-style parapet walls, is on the National Register of Historic Places. It's now the site of the Boone and Crockett Club national headquarters, an organization founded in 1887 by Theodore Roosevelt to establish conservation of wild habitats. Open to the public is a display of a world-record-size taxidermied elk, bighorn sheep, and other wildlife. ⊠*250 Station Dr., near Higgins Ave. Bridge* ☏*406/542–1888, 888/840–4868 for orders* ⊕*www.boone-crockett.org* ✉*Free* ⊙*Weekdays 8–5.*

⑨ Rocky Mountain Elk Foundation Wildlife Visitor Center. The new visitor center ♻ features natural-history displays (including hands-on displays for kids), films, art, taxidermied animals, a world-record-size pair of elk antlers, and an outdoor nature trail. The foundation works to preserve wild lands for elk and other wildlife; since 1984, the nonprofit organization has saved almost 5 million acres from development. ⊠*5705 Grant Creek Rd.; look for big bronze elk* ☏*406/523–4500 or 800/225–5355* ✉*Donations accepted* ⊙*Jan. 1–Memorial Day, weekdays 8–5, Sat. 10–5; Memorial Day–Dec. 30, weekdays 8–6, weekends 9–6.*

⑩ Smokejumper Visitor Center. A replica 1930s lookout tower, fire photos, ★ videos, and murals explain wildland fire ecology and behavior, firefighting technique, and the nation's history of smoke jumping, which began here in 1942. Today, it's the largest smoke-jumper base in the nation. From Memorial Day through Labor Day, the center offers five tours daily given by firefighter guides who provide firsthand accounts of jumping into blazing forests. ⊠*5765 W. Broadway, 6 mi west of town, next to airport* ☏*406/329–4934* ⊕*www.smokejumpers.com* ✉*Donations accepted* ⊙*Memorial Day–Labor Day, weekdays 8:30–5; Labor Day–Memorial Day by appointment; summer tours on the hr 10–11 and 2–4.*

SPORTS & THE OUTDOORS

BICYCLING

Nearly 30 trails thread through Missoula and can be found on the Missoulian's Hike, Bike, Run map, free online or by calling the **Bicycle and Pedestrian Office** (☏*406/721–7275* ⊕*www.missoulian. com/specials/hikebike/*).

★ The folks at **Adventure Cycling** (⊠*150 E. Pine St.* ☏*406/721–1776 or 800/755–2453* ⊕*www.adv-cycling.org*) in downtown Missoula have good suggestions for nearby bike routes and an extensive selection of regional and national bike maps for sale. You can find bikes to rent or buy, cycling accessories, and cross-country ski gear at **Open Road Bicycles & Nordic Equipment** (⊠ *517 S. Orange St.* ☎ *406/549–2453*).

FISHING

Grizzly Hackle (⊠ *215 W. Front St.* ☎ *406/721–8996*) offers guided fly-fishing and outfitting for half-day float trips on the Bitterroot, Blackfoot, and Clark Fork rivers. Pick up supplies in the retail shop or sign up for a lesson.

GOLF

Highlands Golf Club (⊠ *102 Ben Hogan Dr.* ☎ *406/721–4653*) has 9 holes and provides the best view of Missoula from the restaurant-bar **Shadows Keep**. **Larchmont Golf Course** (⊠ *3200 Old Fort Rd.* ☎ *406/721–4416*), a relatively flat 18-hole municipal course, provides in-town golfing at reasonable rates ($24 for a round in midweek).

RAFTING

Raft and kayak adventures with **Montana River Guides** (⊠ *Sawmill Gulch Rd., 35 minutes west of Missoula on I–90, Exit 70 at Cyr, cross Cyr Bridge, turn left on Sawmill Gulch, and look for yellow rafts* ☎ *406/273–4718 or 800/381–7238*) splash down the Blackfoot and Bitterroot rivers and the rowdy Alberton Gorge of the Clark Fork River.

SKIING

Montana Snowbowl (⊠ *Grant Creek Rd.* ☎ *800/728–2695 or 406/549–9777* ⊕ *www.montanasnowbowl.com*) has slopes for advanced skiers who are hooked on steep, challenging runs, and powdery views of nearby Rattlesnake Wilderness. Telemarkers and geländesprung alpine ski jumpers add a colorful element to the scene. New skiers aren't neglected: groomed beginner and intermediate runs make up more than half the trails on the 950 acres here, 12 mi northwest of Missoula. Services include a restaurant, bar, and Geländesprung Lodge in the base area.

WHERE TO EAT

$$–$$$$ ✕**Blue Canyon Kitchen and Tavern.** Blue Canyon brings a new game to
★ Missoula by pairing the casual Montana atmosphere with excellent food and a unique dining experience. The open kitchen creates hearty dishes for their seasonally inspired, innovative menu. Try the pretzel-crusted trout served in a whole-grain-mustard–caper-butter sauce, or go all out with the beef rib-eye steak with a smoked blue cheese–maple butter. Better yet, plan ahead and reserve the private table to create your own five-course culinary nirvana with their inventive head chef. ⊠ *3720 N. Reserve St.* ☎ *406/451–2583* ▭ *AE, D, DC, MC, V.*

$$$ ✕**Lolo Creek Steakhouse.** For a real taste of Montana, head for this
★ steak house in a rustic log structure 8 mi south of Missoula, in Lolo. The dining room has a hunting-lodge atmosphere, replete with taxidermied wildlife on the walls. Although most diners opt for one of their signature sirloins—cooked over a crackling open-pit barbecue and

available in three sizes—there are other well-prepared meat, chicken, and seafood dishes from which to choose. ✉*6600 U.S. 12 W, Lolo* ☎*406/273–2622* ▤*AE, D, MC, V* ⊘*Closed Mon. No lunch.*

$$ ✕**The Higgins Alley.** Some of the best pizza ever tossed under the Big Sky is baked here with the freshest homemade sauces and mozzarella cheese. An upscale version of the former Zimorino's, the Higgins Alley also makes their own pasta and serves up dishes such as herb-encrusted halibut or a rack of lamb marinated in rosemary and red pepper. Wash it all down with a selection from their extensive wine list or one of the fine Montana microbrews. ✉*424 N. Higgins Ave.* ☎*406/721–7757* ▤*AE, D, MC, V.*

$–$$ ✕**The Shack Cafe.** A longtime Missoula favorite for any meal, this ele-
★ gant restaurant isn't in a shack but rather in a tastefully remodeled auto dealership. Swinging doors take you into the saloon, where there's an oak bar that arrived in Montana via steamship up the Missouri River a century ago. For dinner try the porkloin cutlets or one of the specials. Breakfasts of hearty omelets and huge pancakes are popular with the locals. ✉*222 W. Main* ☎*406/549–9903* ▤*AE, MC, V.*

¢–$$ ✕**Tipus.** One of the few East Indian restaurants in the northern Rockies, vegetarian-only Tipus serves such delectables as traditional samosas, dals, chapatis, and fresh chutneys. The mango chutney is delicious with the traditional flatbread. You can sit at the stainless-steel counter or a cozy table, or order takeout. ✉*115½ S. 4th W* ☎*406/542–0622 or 877/705–9843* ▤*AE, D, MC, V.*

¢–$$ ✕**Worden's Market & Deli.** Floorboards creak beneath you as you explore this old-fashioned market, which spills over with deli delicacies. There's an impressive selection of groceries, along with imported beer, micro-brews, and wine, plus a knowledgeable staff to help you make the best selections. With 150 cheeses to choose from, the sandwich possibili-ties are endless; have them pile on Black Forest ham and horseradish for a creation that will get you down the trail. There's limited seating both inside and outside, where Worden's espresso and fruit-smoothie bar has a walk-up window. ✉*451 N. Higgins Ave.* ☎*406/549–1293* ⌲*Reservations not accepted* ▤*AE, MC, V.*

¢–$ ✕**The Staggering Ox Downtown.** Reading the menu here is as much fun as eating the deli sandwiches, which are served on specialty breads shaped like a tin can. Evocative sandwich names include the Head-banger's Hoagie (with ham, salami, pepperoni, cream cheese, cheddar, Swiss, mozzarella, lettuce, and Italian dressing) and Chernobyl Melt Down (with turkey, salami, Swiss, sharp cheddar, cream cheese, veg-gies, and salsa). The Camel Spit (a yogurt and dill sauce) is a must for the Slammed Saddam sandwich. There are sister restaurants in Helena and Spokane. ✉*123 E. Main* ☎*406/327–9400* ⌲*Reservations not accepted* ▤*AE, D, MC, V.*

¢ ✕**Bernice's Bakery.** Missoula's best bakery sells buttery croissants, muf-fins, scones, quiches, and other treats plus a tempting array of des-serts, breads, and coffee from 6 AM to 8 PM. There's seating inside and outside, or you can eat alongside the nearby river. ✉*190 S. 3rd W* ☎*406/728–1358* ⌲*Reservations not accepted* ▤*D, MC, V.*

6

"Howdy" & Other Highway Encounters

CLOSE UP

Driving through Montana's western valleys, you'll notice that folks wave. Don't be alarmed. It's just a "howdy" and a courtesy along remote roads where neighbors and visitors are few and far between. Wave back and you'll have a new friend.

Under the Big Sky, goodwill is as essential as independence to hardtack survival. Emblems of life's harshness here, white crosses along the highways mark the places where travelers have died on the road. The somber memorials remind you to slow down and enjoy the glorious West described by Norman McLean in "*A River Runs Through It*." Take your time exploring this land, and you're bound to agree with another writer, Bill Kitteredge, who called Montana "The Last Best Place."

¢ ✕**Taco Del Sol.** Locals, professors, and students hang out, study, and chow down on Mission-style burritos and fish tacos. Design your own and try a *horchata* (a sweet Mexican rice drink) or a Mexican soda. Beer and wine are also served. ⊠*422 N. Higgins Ave.* ☎*406/327–8929* ⊟*V, MC.*

WHERE TO STAY

$$$$ **The Resort at Paws Up.** With linens and a "camping butler," even stay-
☾ ing in one of the tents at Paws Up is a long way from roughing it. And
★ for those who desire more refinement, try the Bunkhouse (a great environment for a group of friends to share) or one of their luxury homes. For the wilderness traveler, ride 12 mi back to the Encampment at Bull Creek, where gourmet food and featherbeds await. During your stay, fly-fish in the Blackfoot River, go horseback riding on Paws Up's nearly 40,000-acre "backyard," or pamper yourself at their spa. Never worry about the kids becoming bored with the Kids Corps of Discovery offering daily activities lasting a full or half day. **Pros:** It's difficult to think of any amenity lacking at Paws Up, they've thought of everything. **Cons:** You need a map to find your way around the place. ⊠*40060 Paws Up Rd., Greenough 59823* ☎*406/244–5200 or 866/894–7969* ⊟*406/244–5242* ⊕*www.pawsup.com* ✑*18 homes, 1 bunkhouse, 10 tents (including the Encampment at Bull Run)* ⌂*In room: Ethernet, kitchens (some). In hotel: laundry facilities (some), spa, no elevator* ⊟*AE, D, MC, V* ❘⊙❘*FAP.*

$$$ **Wingate by Wyndham.** Oversize guest rooms and a 24-hour self-
☾ service business center here are designed with the business traveler in mind, but two waterslides at the pool please kids as well. Rooms have cordless phones, lounge chairs, and large TVs; a few have Jacuzzis. The inn has a pleasant lobby that includes a breakfast area, and it's convenient to restaurants, historic sites, and the airport. **Pros:** Great waterslides for the kids, friendly staff, close to the airport. Cons: Check-in is late in the afternoon. ⊠*5252 Airway Blvd., 59808* ☎*406/541–8000 or 866/832–8000* ⊟*406/541–8008* ⊕*www.wingateinnmissoula.com*

⊅100 rooms ௯In-room: refrigerator, Wi-Fi. In-hotel: pool, gym, laundry facilities, airport shuttle, no-smoking rooms ▭AE, D, DC, MC, V ▯○▯CP.

$$–$$$ ▯▯Hilton Garden Inn Missoula. This upscale facility is a business traveler's dream. A fully equipped business center near the lobby, and large desks with ergonomic chairs are functional work areas, and the spacious rooms donned in Montana-lifestyle decor are set up with flat-screen TVs, adjustable beds, DVD players, and video games, making relaxing easy. The Blue Canyon Kitchen and Silver Creek Tavern next door serve lunch and dinner, and the Great American Grill next to the lobby serves breakfast. The Pavilion Pantry convenience mart has the sundries that you forgot, and the helpful staff is able to direct you to the sights and recreational opportunities in the area. **Pros:** Business amenities make working on the road fun. The smoke-free tavern with live games is an enjoyable place to unwind. **Cons:** The view from the Grill overlooks the parking area. Because restaurants are not directly affiliated with the Hilton chain, you have to walk outside to enter the restaurant and tavern. ⊠3720 N. Reserve St., 59808 ☎406/532–5300 or 877/782–9444 ⊟406/532–5305 ⊕www.missoula.stayhgi.com ⊅146 rooms ௯In-room: refrigerator, Ethernet, Wi-Fi. In-hotel: 2 restaurants, bar, pool, gym, laundry facilities, airport shuttle, no-smoking rooms ▭AE, DC, MC, V ▯○▯EP.

$$–$$$ ▯▯Holiday Inn Missoula–Parkside. The Missoula member of the Holiday Inn chain is a large, comfortable hotel with a lush atrium in the center and modern rooms. The property's greatest asset is its location in Missoula's riverfront Bess Reed park, a stone's throw from the Clark Fork River and across the river from the university, a ¾-mi walk. Pets are welcome. This is a great area for walks along the river trail and is an easy walk into town for eating and shopping. ⊠200 S. Pattee St., 59802 ☎406/721–8550 or 800/399–0408 ⊟406/728–3472 ⊕www.himissoula.com ⊅200 rooms ௯In-room: Ethernet, Wi-Fi. In-hotel: restaurant, bar, pool, gym, no-smoking rooms ▭AE, D, DC, MC, V ▯○▯EP.

$$ ▯▯C'mon Inn. This hotel at the bottom of Grant Creek, near the Snowbowl ski area, has easy access to recreation and business in Missoula. The best family lodging in town, it features a spacious, tree-filled indoor courtyard with a pool, baby pool, five hot tubs, and a waterfall. The large guest rooms equipped with flat-screen TVs open onto the pool on the first floor and have balconies on the second. Some rooms have kitchens. **Pros:** Easily accessible off the interstate. This is an ideal location for those skiing at Snowbowl. The friendly staff is quick to help point guests in the right direction for activities in or out of town. **Cons:** It's away from the downtown scene for restaurants and entertainment. ⊠2775 Expo Pkwy., off I–90, 59808 ☎406/543–4600 or 888/989–5569 ⊟406/543–4664 ⊕www.cmoninn.com ⊅119 rooms ௯In-hotel: pool, gym, no-smoking rooms ▭AE, DC, MC, V ▯○▯CP.

$–$$ ▯▯Goldsmith's Bed and Breakfast. Built in 1911 for the first president of ★ the University of Montana, this lodging is on the bank of the Clark Fork River, at the end of a footbridge that leads to the campus. Within the prairie-style building, with big white eaves and a huge porch, are period furnishings, wool carpets, and fresh flowers. Each private room is unique; the honeymoon suite has a Japanese soaking tub, and two suites have gas fireplaces. Public rooms include a library and TV sitting area. Breakfast offerings include frittatas with a basil/cream sauce and apple-walnut pancakes, served in the dining room or on the deck overlooking the Clark Fork River. **Pros:** It's very convenient to walk to many of the outstanding shops and restaurants from here. They have excellent views of the river and are close to the walking path. The chef obviously loves what he does, judging by the quality of the breakfasts. **Cons:** A busy restaurant and ice-cream shop is next door. It is somewhat difficult to find in Missoula's confusing street setup. The main entrance is next to the honeymoon suite's private deck. ⊠ *809 E. Front St., 59801* ☎ *406/728–1585 or 866/666–9945* 🖷 *406/543–0045* ⊕ *www.goldsmithsinn.com* ⤳ *3 rooms, 4 suites* ⟁ *In-hotel: Wi-Fi, no-smoking rooms, no elevator* ▭ *D, MC, V* ⦿*BP.*

CAMPING

↻   ⛰ **Jellystone RV Park.** On the outskirts of town, this lively park is popular with families for the playground, miniature golf, swimming pools, and, a kid favorite, pictures with Yogi Bear. Camping cabins, which sleep four comfortably, have air-conditioning, refrigerators, and microwaves. ⟁ *Flush toilets, full hookups, partial hookups, dump station, drinking water, guest laundry, showers, picnic tables, food service, electricity, public telephone, general store, swimming (pool)* ⤳ *110 full hookups, 10 tent sites; 6 cabins* ⊠ *I-90, Exit 96, ½ mi north* ☎ *406/543–9400 or 800/318–9644* 🖷 *406/543–9405* ⊕ *www.campjellystonemt.com* ▭ *MC, V* ☾ *May–Oct. 1.*

↻   ⛰ **Missoula KOA.** This lovely campsite in the Montana-born KOA chain is easy to reach from the interstate. It has two hot tubs, a game center, miniature golf, bike rentals, a playground, and a bonfire pit area. Nightly ice-cream socials and weekend activities during the summer make this more of a community than a campground. ⟁ *Flush toilets, full hookups, dump station, drinking water, guest laundry, showers, picnic tables, food service, electricity, public telephone, general store, swimming (pool)* ⤳ *146 full hookups, 31 tent sites; 19 cabins* ⊠ *3450 Tina Ave., I-90, Exit 101, 1½ mi south, right on England Blvd.* ☎ *406/549–0881 or 800/562–5366* 🖷 *406/541–0884* ⊕ *www.missoulakoa.com* ⟁ *Reservations essential* ▭ *AE, D, MC, V.*

NIGHTLIFE & THE ARTS

↻   The wildest film stars in the world are up on the big screen at the weeklong **International Wildlife Film Festival** (⊠ *718 S. Higgins Ave.* ☎ *406/728–9380* ⊕ *www.wildlifefilms.org*), which shows natural history documentaries in early May at the Wilma and Roxy theaters in downtown Missoula. The festival includes seminars, panel discussions, a parade, and art displays. The organization also offers a fall festival, "MontanaCINE: Cultures and Issues on Nature and Environment," at the Roxy.

☾ At the **Missoula Children's Theatre** (✉*200 N. Adams* ☎*406/728–1911 or 406/728–7529* ⊕*www.mctinc.org*), year-round productions vary from Broadway musicals to community theater for and by children from 5 to 18 years old. From October to June, you can see local talent and guest artists (usually professionals) perform family favorites like *Seussical*. In summer, there's a theater camp where kids are the stars of the productions.

The University of Montana's Department of Drama and Dance manages the **Montana Repertory Theatre** (☎*406/243–6809* ⊕*www.montanarep. org*). This professional company provides the region with a steady diet of popular Broadway shows on campus as well as in national tours.

SHOPPING

Take a break while touring downtown Missoula and have a cappuccino or a glass of fresh-squeezed orange juice at **Butterfly Herbs** (✉*232 N. Higgins Ave.* ☎*406/728–8780*), or try the Butterfly Ice Cream Coffee Soda—a cold drink with multiple layers of sweetness. The shop also sells baked goods, candies, soaps, candles, china, and other odds and ends.

Works by Montana authors, a fine selection of regional books, and gift items are found at **Fact and Fiction** (✉*220 N. Higgins Ave.* ☎*406/721–2881*). Readings, signings, and other literary events are scheduled year-round at this comfortable shop, where you're likely to rub elbows with an author browsing through the shelves.

At the outdoor **Missoula Farmers' Market** (✉*N. Higgins Ave. on Circle Sq. between Railroad and Alder Sts.* ☎*406/543–4238* ⊕*www.missouladowntown.com*) you can buy flowers, fresh fruits and vegetables, and unique handmade goods. It's held on Market Plaza, a two-block area downtown, every Saturday morning from mid-May to mid-October and Tuesday evenings from July through mid-September.

Whimsical artistry by Missoula natives is available at the **Monte Dolack Gallery** (✉*139 W. Front* ☎*406/549–3248* ⊕*www.montedolack.com*), open Monday–Saturday for your laughing pleasure.

For locally made crafts, come to the **Saturday Arts and Craft Market** (✉*Pine St. between Higgins Ave. and Pattee St.* ☎*406/543–4238* ⊕*www.missouladowntown.com*), open Saturday mornings from mid-May to mid-October.

BITTERROOT VALLEY

This history-filled valley south of Missoula was once home to Nez Perce who helped Lewis and Clark find their way through the mountains. The expedition's campsites, plus historic mansions and missions, are scattered in and around Stevensville, Hamilton, and Darby, towns founded by early settlers attracted by temperate weather and fertile soil. Flanked by the Bitterroot and Sapphire mountains, the valley is named for the state flower, the delicate pink rosette-shape bitterroot, which blooms in late spring; its roots were a staple of the Salish Indian diet. U.S. 93 threads through the heart of the verdant valley and along the Bitterroot River, an excellent fly-fishing spot. Back roads lead to wildlife refuges and numerous remote trailheads for biking and hiking. Beware of hazardous driving: now that the Bitterroot has been discovered, the two-lane roads fill with impatient drivers trying to pass slow-moving farm vehicles and RVs.

STEVENSVILLE

25 mi south of Missoula via U.S. 93.

Stevensville, population 1,550, sits on the site of the state's first non–Native American settlement, St. Mary's Mission, a restored treasure that dates back to 1841. Nearby Fort Owen is a partially restored 1850s trading post. The town itself is named for General Isaac Stevens, who was in charge of the Northwest Territory's military posts and Native American affairs. Today it's a mix of beautiful old homes and haphazard modern construction in a lush valley.

WHAT TO SEE

⟳ The **Lee Metcalf National Wildlife Refuge,** on the edge of town, is nearly as pristine as it was before development encroached upon the wilds in this part of the state. Within its 2,800 acres reside 235 species of birds, 41 species of mammals, and 17 species of reptiles and amphibians. Bald eagles, osprey, deer, and muskrats are frequently seen along the preserve's 2 mi of nature trails and in the wildlife-viewing area. There are children's fishing and waterfowl clinics in the summer and fall. Fishing is permitted on the river, but not on the refuge ponds. Archery season for deer and waterfowl hunting occur during their specific seasons in autumn. ⊠*4567 Wildfowl Lane., 2 mi north of Stevensville* ☎*406/777-5552* ⊕*www.fws.gov/leemetcalf/* ⊠*Free* ⊙*Daily dawn–dusk.*

★ **St. Mary's Mission,** established by Father Pierre DeSmet in 1841, was the first Catholic mission in the Northwest and the site of the first permanent non–Native American settlement in Montana. The site is run by a nonsectarian, nonprofit organization that encourages tour groups, school groups, and individuals to explore the home of Father Anthony Ravalli, an Italian priest recruited to the mission by Father DeSmet in 1845. Ravalli was also Montana's first physician and pharmacist. On the site are a photogenic chapel, a priest's quarters, a pharmacy, Father Ravalli's log house, and the cabin of Chief Victor, a Salish Indian who refused to sign the Hell Gate Treaty and move his people onto the Flathead Reservation. A burial plot has headstones bearing the names of both Native Americans and white settlers. ⊠*4th St.; from Main St., turn west at 4th and drive 3 blocks* ☎*406/777-5734* ⊕*www.saintmarysmission.org* ⊠*$6* ⊙*Mid-Apr.–mid-Oct., daily 10–5.*

Major John Owen established **Fort Owen** as a trading post in 1850. The property also served as the headquarters of the Flathead Agency until

1860. It's worth a half hour to visit the museum to see the restored barracks, artifacts, and some of the fort's original furnishings. ✉ *Hwy. 269, ½ mi east of U.S. 93 at Stevensville* ☎ *406/542–5500* ⊕ *www. fwp.mt.gov* ✏ *$4* ⊙ *Daily dawn–dusk.*

Historical items in the **Stevensville Museum** include the belongings of early settlers, particularly the missionaries who came to convert the Native Americans of the West. Other exhibits provide an overview of the area's original cultures (Salish, Nez Perce, and Lemhi Shoshone), background on Lewis and Clark's two visits, and a look at later residents, from orchard farmers to today's cybercommuters. ✉ *517 Main St.* ☎ *406/777–1007* ✏ *Donations accepted* ⊙ *Memorial Day–Labor Day, Thurs.–Sat. 11–4, Sun. 1–4.*

SPORTS & THE OUTDOORS

FISHING **Anglers Afloat, Inc.** (✉ *2742 Alpenglow Rd.* ☎ *406/777–3421*) leads serious fly-fishermen after the really big trout on floats on the Bitterroot and Blackfoot rivers. During the mayfly, caddis, and salmon fly hatches, fish with **Backdoor Outfitters** (✉ *227 Bell Crossing E* ☎ *406/777–3861*), along spring creeks, in private ponds, or on river float trips on the Bitterroot, Clark Fork, Blackfoot, and Big Hole rivers.

WHERE TO STAY & EAT

$$–$$$$ ✕**Marie's Italian Restaurant.** This family-run sit-down restaurant is known for its gourmet Italian cuisine and fresh seafood. A good way to decide what you like best is to try the sampler, which includes hand-made pasta stuffed with different fillings, spinach gnocchi, fettuccine Alfredo, shrimp, vegetables, and another side. All meals include soup or salad. ✉ *4040 Hwy. 93 N* ☎ *406/777–3681* ⊟ *No credit cards* ⊙ *Closed Dec.–Feb. and Mon.–Thurs. No lunch.*

$–$$ ✕**Frontier Cafe.** For a bit of town gossip and great burgers, stop in this classic small-town café, a dressed-down spot where the locals love to hang out. ✉ *3954 U.S. 93 N* ☎ *406/777–4228* ⊿ *Reservations not accepted* ⊟ *AE, D, MC, V.*

¢–$ ✕**Olde Coffee Mill Bakery and Eatery.** For those looking for delicious baked goods, an espresso/cappuccino fix, or hearty sandwiches, including the popular veggie sandwich, as well as homemade soups and quiches, this place fits the bill at lunch. Or join the hungry crowd for dinner on the first Friday of every month. ✉ *225 Main St.* ☎ *406/777– 2939* ⊿ *Reservations not accepted* ⊟ *No credit cards* ⊙ *Closed Sun. Dinner 1st Fri. of month only.*

$–$$ ⌂**Bitterroot River Bed and Breakfast.** Views of the Bitterroot River give this inn a peaceful, country feel even though it's walking distance to many of the shops and restaurants in downtown Stevensville. The rooms are made with comfort in mind, including down comforters and featherbeds in some rooms, and a cozy fireplace in another. Breakfasts are casual, but with egg casseroles, banana bread French toast, and locally roasted coffee, they'll be sure to fuel you for the day. Children over 12 are welcome. **Pros:** The owners are longtime Montana residents who know the area and are happy to offer advice on activities. **Cons:** There are no phones in the rooms for private conversation, but cell phones should work. ✉ *501 South Ave., 59870* ☎ *406/777–5205*

⊕*www.bitterrootriverbb.com* ⟿*4 rooms* ⌂*In -room: no TV (some).
In-hotel: bicycles, no elevator* ⊟*MC, V* ⚌*BP.*

CAMPING △ **Charles Waters Campground.** Located in the historical area of Stevensville, this is an access point to the Selway-Bitterroot Wilderness. Trails, fishing, picnic spots, and a bicycle campsite are sheltered among trees, affording glimpses of the surrounding mountains. A fire-ecology interpretive trail explores regrowth after recent forest fires. ⌂*Pit toilets, drinking water, fire grates, picnic tables* ⟿*22 sites* ⊠*2 mi west of U.S. 93 on County Rd. 22 (Bass Creek Rd.), then 1 mi northwest on Forest Rd. 1316* ☎*406/777–5461* 🖷*406/777–7423* ⊕*www.fs.fed.us/r1/bitterroot/* ⊟*No credit cards* ☉*Late May–early Sept.*

EN ROUTE

A refreshing stop for wildlife viewing is the **Teller Wildlife Refuge** (⊠*1288 Eastside Hwy., Corvallis* ☎*406/961–3507*), a 1,200-acre private preserve dedicated to conservation, education, and research. Situated along 3 mi of the Bitterroot River, about 8 mi north of Hamilton, the refuge is home to otters, beavers, spotted frogs, and salamanders, as well as pileated woodpeckers, birds of prey, waterfowl, deer, and many native plants. An education center conducts numerous courses, including teachers' workshops, fly-fishing classes, and lectures. Conference groups of up to 26 may arrange to stay in the four homes on the refuge. It's best to call ahead to tour the refuge. To get here, take Route 269 (Eastside Highway) to Quast Lane and follow the signs.

HAMILTON

36 mi south of Stevensville via U.S. 93.

Home to retirees, gentleman ranchers, and the Ravalli County Museum, Hamilton (pop. 5,000) is a gateway to the Selway-Bitterroot Wilderness. It was established by 19th-century industrialist Marcus Daly to house employees at his 22,000-acre Bitterroot Stock Farm. There he raised thoroughbred racehorses, funding the venture with part of the fortune he made mining copper in Montana. His own home, the Daly Mansion, is open for tours.

WHAT TO SEE

Ⓒ ★ Copper king Marcus Daly's 24,000-square-foot, 56-room **Daly Mansion,** with 25 bedrooms, 15 baths, and five Italian marble fireplaces, is the showplace of Hamilton and is undergoing a $1.7 million renovation to preserve its history and elegance. The Georgian Revival–style house is open to the public, and tours run on the hour. There's also a printed walking guide available to the extensive grounds. The "Kids in the Garden" event is held in August. ⊠*251 Eastside Hwy.* ☎*406/363–6004* ⊕*www.dalymansion.org* ▦*$7* ☉*Mid-Apr.–mid-Oct., daily 10–4; and for special events.*

Frequent festivities at the **Daly Mansion** include crafts shows, Missoula Symphony performances, and even a Kentucky Derby Gala that celebrates Daly's dedication to racehorses. Call the **Chamber of Commerce** (☎*406/363–2400* ⊕*www.bitterrootvalleychamber.com*) or the mansion to learn about events.

The **Ravalli County Museum,** in the former courthouse, contains exhibits on natural history, fly-fishing, Native Americans, Lewis and Clark, and other subjects related to the region. During the Sunday Series (most Sundays 2 PM, $5), speakers share local history and lore. ⊠*205 Bedford* ☎*406/363–3338* ⌐*Couple $5, single $3, student $1* ☉*Mon., Thurs., and Fri. 10–4, Sat. (May–Oct.) 9–1 and (Nov.–May) 10–2, Sun. 1–4.*

Hamilton is in the midst of the 1.6-million-acre **Selway-Bitterroot National Forest.** It includes the Bitterroot and Sapphire mountains and parts of the Selway-Bitterroot, Anaconda-Pintler, and Frank Church–River of No Return wildernesses, and is traversed by the Salmon and Selway rivers. More than 1,600 mi of trails wend through the forest, where visitors may encounter bears, elk, moose, deer, and bighorn sheep. There are also songbirds and birds of prey such as eagles and owls. The forest has three historically significant trails: the Continental Divide Scenic Trail, the Lewis and Clark Trail, and the Nez Perce Trail; some parts of the trails are open to hikers, other parts to bikes and vehicles. Wildfires of 2,000 scorched parts of the forest; hikers should be alert to the danger of falling trees in the burned-out areas. ⊠*1801 North Ave.* ☎*406/777–5461* ⊕*www.fs.fed.us/r1* ⌐*Free* ☉*Daily.*

OFF THE BEATEN PATH

Skalkaho Highway. Three miles south of Hamilton, turn east onto Route 38, also known as the Skalkaho Highway, and you'll find yourself on a beautiful, seldom-traveled route leading into the Sapphire Mountains and on to the Georgetown Lake area near Anaconda. This fair-weather road is best traveled in summer, since 20 mi of it are gravel. Mountain bikers tour here, and there are plenty of hiking trails through the 23,000-acre Skalkaho Wildlife Preserve. Note that Forest Road 1352 into the preserve is closed October 15 to December 1, making that a fine time for nonmotorized travel. Only 10 mi of the Skalkaho Highway are plowed in winter, which means the area is excellent for cross-country skiing and snowshoeing.

SPORTS & THE OUTDOORS

FISHING

There are two good options for fishing excursions in the area. You can float and fish with **Fly Fishing Adventures** (⊠*112 Freeze La.* ☎*406/363–2398*) on the Bitterroot River. Fishing trips with **Fly Fishing Always** (⊠*714 S. 4th St.* ☎*406/360–4346*) amble down the Bitterroot River looking for brown trout and west slope cutthroat. Scenic float trips on the Missouri and Clark Fork rivers are also available.

RODEO

See more than 300 of the country's top senior rodeo cowboys and cowgirls—even some 80-year-old team ropers—among the over-50-year-olds who rope and ride at the annual **Senior Pro Rodeo** (⊠*Ravalli County Fairgrounds* ☎*406/363–3411*) in early July. A parade, food, cowboy poetry readings, arts-and-crafts booths, and live music round out the offerings.

TRAIL RIDES

Ride into the Selway-Bitterroot Wilderness on horseback with **Lightning Creek Outfitters** (⊠*1424 Skalkaho Hwy.* ☎*406/363–0320*) Spend a few hours, a full day, or a summer week in the saddle with **Two Bear Outfitters** (⊠*505 Camas Creek Loop* ☎*406/375–0070*).

WHERE TO EAT

¢–$$ ✕ **Spice of Life.** Wednesday night, when live music fills the air, is the time to visit this romantic spot in a historic building. Eclectic fare includes pasta, seafood, steak, Mexican, Thai, and Japanese specials. ⌧ *163 2nd St. S* ☎*406/363–4433* ▤*AE, MC, V* ⊗*No dinner Sun.–Tues.*

¢–$ ✕ **Bitter Root Brewing.** Meet the brewmaster, sample a Sawtooth Ale or "the Brewer's Whim," and enjoy the live music (Thursday and Saturday). This smoke-free brewpub offers free tastings daily and an eclectic menu from the grill, and their specialty, hand-dipped fresh halibut-and-chips. ⌧ *101 Marcus St., 1 block east of town center* ☎*406/363–7468* ⊕*www.bitterrootbrewing.com* ▤*AE, MC, V.*

¢–$ ✕ **A Place to Ponder Bakery and Cafe.** Excellent baked goods available in the small, smoke-free café include croissants, cookies, and cookie bars that go great with a cup of chai. Order a slice of pizza or a bowl of homemade soup, or get a packed lunch for the trail—particularly good is the chicken salad on outfitters bread, similar to croissant dough with cheese baked inside. Their new location has plenty of seating. ⌧ *215 Marcus St.* ☎*406/363–0080* ▤*MC, V* .

WHERE TO STAY

$–$$ ▦ **Deer Crossing B&B.** The two deluxe rooms, two luxury suites, and two cabins are set on 25 acres of property surrounded by pastureland, pines, the Sapphire Mountains, and Como Peak. On this homestead, accommodations are outfitted with fireplaces, hot tubs, and Western furnishings. The hearty ranch breakfast consists of French bread custard, smoked ham, and a fruit platter, served on the deck in summers. Horses and pets are welcome. **Pros:** They have room and facilities for you to bring your own horses. This is a family-friendly accommodation that can host large parties for reunions or weddings. **Cons:** No Wi-Fi for those who can't leave the office behind. It's best to have a map printed out and on hand to find the place. ⌧ *396 Hayes Creek Rd., 59840* ☎*406/363–2232 or 800/763–2232* ▤*406/375–0771* ⊕*www. deercrossingmontana.com* ⬎*2 rooms, 2 suites, 2 cabins* ⌂*In-room: no a/c, no phone. In-hotel: parking (no fee), no-smoking rooms, some pets allowed, no elevator* ▤*AE, D, MC, V* ⎚*BP.*

$ ▦ **Best Western Hamilton Inn.** This clean and convenient hotel is typical of the chain's smaller properties. It's within walking distance of many of the town's sites and restaurants. A continental breakfast and a newspaper are available in the lobby each morning. **Pros:** Easy to find and centrally located in the Bitterroot Valley, this is an ideal base camp for those who are focused on recreation and not lounging indoors. Pets welcome for those traveling with the furry members of the family. **Cons:** The rooms are pretty basic, and this is one of the older facilities in the area. ⌧ *409 S. 1st St., 59840* ☎*406/363–2142 or 800/426–4586* ▤*406/363–2142* ⊕*www.bestwestern.com* ⬎*36 rooms, including 3 larger family-size rooms* ⌂*In-room: refrigerator, Wi-Fi. In-hotel: some pets allowed, no-smoking rooms, no elevator* ▤*AE, D, DC, MC, V* ⎚*CP.*

CAMPING   ⛺ **Blodgett Canyon Campground.** From this undeveloped campsite along a canyon creek you have easy access to hiking and biking trails, fishing, and rock climbing. There's no garbage haul, so cleanliness depends on good camping etiquette. ♿ *Pit toilets, drinking water, fire grates, picnic tables* ⊴*6 sites* ⊠*Blodgett Canyon, 5 mi northwest of Hamilton* ☎*406/777–5461* ⊕*www.fs.fed.us/r1* ♺*Reservations not accepted* ⊟*No credit cards.*

NORTHWEST MONTANA ESSENTIALS

AIR TRAVEL

Northwest Montana has two principal airports: Missoula International, on U.S. 93 just west of Missoula, and Glacier Park International, 8 mi northeast of Kalispell and 11 mi southeast of Whitefish on U.S. 2. Both are serviced by major airlines; if you're coming from outside the Rockies area, the odds are that you'll have a connecting flight through a larger hub such as Denver, Salt Lake City, Minneapolis/St. Paul, Phoenix, or Calgary, Alberta.

Airlines & Contacts **Alaska/Horizon** (☎*800/547–9308* ⊕*www.horizonair. com*). **America West** (☎*800/428–4322* ⊕*www.usairways.com/awa*). **Big Sky** (☎*800/237–7788 or 406/247–3910*). **Delta** (☎*800/221–1212* ⊕*www.delta-air. com*). **Northwest** (☎*800/225–2525* ⊕*www.nwa.com*). **Skywest** (☎*800/453– 9417* ⊕*www.skywest.com*). **United/United Express** (☎*800/864–8331* ⊕*www. united.com*).

Airport Information **Glacier Park International Airport** (⊠*4170 U.S. 2 E, Kalispell* ☎*406/257–5994* ⊕*www.iflyglacier.com*). **Missoula International Airport** (⊠*5225 U.S. 10 W, Missoula* ☎*406/728–4381* ⊕*www.msoairport.org*).

BUS TRAVEL

Commercial buses that travel along U.S. 93 between Missoula and Whitefish depart daily and stop at several small towns en route.

Bus Information **Greyhound** (☎*800/231–2222* ⊕*www.greyhound.com*).

CAR RENTAL

Car rentals are available in East and West Glacier, Hamilton, Kalispell, Missoula, and Whitefish.

Contacts **Alamo/National Car Rental** (☎*406/257–7144, 406/257–7148, or 800/227–7368* ⊕*www.nationalcar.com*). **Avis** (☎*406/257–2727 or 800/331– 1212* ⊕*www.avis.com*). **Budget** (☎*406/755–7500 or 800/527–0700* ⊕*www. budget.com*). **Dollar** (☎*800/457–5335* ⊕*www.montanadollar.com*). **Enterprise** (☎*406/755–4848* ⊕*www.enterprise.com*). **Hertz** (☎*406/758–2220 or 800/654–3131* ⊕*www.hertz.com*). **Thrifty** (☎*406/549–2277 or 800/344–1705* ⊕*www.thrifty.com*).

CAR TRAVEL

Of Montana's 69,000 mi of public roads, there are certainly more gravel and dirt roads than paved. Many of the unpaved routes are in good shape, yet you'll need to slow down and, as on any Montana road, be on the lookout for wildlife, open-range livestock, farm equipment, unexpected hazards such as cattle crossing guards, and changing weather and road conditions. Snow can fall any month of the year. In more remote areas, carry an emergency kit with water, snacks, extra clothing, and flashlights. Gasoline is available along most paved roads. However, if you are traveling in more remote areas, be sure to gas up before leaving town. Note that cell phone coverage has increased in the state recently, yet in mountainous terrain, it's unlikely that you will have cell reception.

Information **Statewide Road Report** (☎ *511 or 800/226-7623* ⊕ *www.mdt. mt.gov/travinfo/*). **Montana Highway Patrol** (☎ *911, 406/329-1500, 406/755-6688, or 800/525-5555* ⊕ *www.doj.mt.gov/enforcement/highwaypatrol*).

EMERGENCIES

Ambulance or Police **Emergencies** (☎ *911*).

24-Hour Medical Care **Kalispell Regional Medical Center** (✉ *310 Sunnyview La., Kalispell* ☎ *406/752-5111* ⊕ *www.krmc.org*). **Marcus Daly Memorial Hospital** (✉ *1200 Westwood Dr., Hamilton* ☎ *406/363-2211* ⊕ *www.mdmh.org*). **North Valley Hospital** (✉ *1600 Hospital Way, Whitefish* ☎ *406/863-3500* ⊕ *www. nvhosp.org*). **St. Joseph Hospital** (✉ *6 13th Ave. E, Polson* ☎ *406/883-5377 or 866/344-2273* ⊕ *www.saintjoes.org*). **St. Patrick Hospital** (✉ *500 W. Broadway, Missoula* ☎ *406/543-7271* ⊕ *www.saintpatrick.org*).

LODGING

Contacts **Montana Bed & Breakfast Association** (☎ *406/582-8440* ⊕ *www. mtbba.com*). **Montana Dude Ranchers' Association** (✐ *Box 589* ✉ *Manhattan, MT 59741* ☎ *888/284-4133* ⊕ *www.montanadra.com*). **Montana Innkeepers Association** (☎ *406/449-8408* ⊕ *www.montanainnkeepers.com*).

CAMPING   Campgrounds across the region vary from no-services, remote state or federal campsites, to upscale commercial operations. During July and August it's best to reserve a camp spot. Ask locally about bears and whether or not food must be stored inside a hard-side vehicle (not a tent). Avoid leaving pets alone at campgrounds because of wildlife confrontations, and because it's against the rules at most campgrounds.

Information **KOA, Kampgrounds of America** (☎ *406/248-7444* ⊕ *www.koa. com*). **Montana Fish, Wildlife & Parks** (☎ *406/444-2535* ⊕ *www.fwp.mt.gov*). **U.S. Forest Service** (☎ *406/329-3511* ⊕ *www.fs.fed.us/r1*).

SPORTS & THE OUTDOORS

If you really want to get away from it all, plan a trip to the roadless 1.5 million acres of the Bob Marshall, Great Bear, and Scapegoat wilderness areas. Access is limited, although once you penetrate this huge wilderness tract, there are trails such as the 120-mi-long Chinese Wall, a reeflike stretch of cliffs in the Bob Marshall Wilderness. Remember that in bear country it's best to pursue outdoor activities in groups of four or more, make plenty of noise, and carry pepper spray.

BICYCLING   Hill climbing, single track, dirt road, or easy cruising bike paths—northwest Montana is flush with cycling opportunities. Bicycle trail maps are available at local sports shops and U.S. Forest Service offices. Note that bicycles are not allowed in designated wilderness areas or on backcountry trails of national parks.

Contacts **Adventure Cycling Association** (☎ *406/721-1776 or 800/755-2453*).

Glacier Cycling (☎ *406/862–6446*).

GUIDES & OUTFITTERS When heading into the backcountry, it's a good idea to hire a guide or outfitter who knows the local trails, weather patterns, and unique features. Outfitters offer rafting, hiking, horse-pack, and other trips into the remote mountains.

Contacts **Fishing Outfitters Association of Montana** (☐ *Box 67, Gallatin Gateway 59730* ☎ *406/763–5436* ⊕ *www.foam-montana.org*). **Montana Outfitters and Guides Association** (☐ *2033 11th Ave. #8, Helena 59601* ☎ *406/449–3578* ⊕ *www.moga-montana.org*).

HIKING Before lacing up your hiking boots, determine where you want to go, what you need to bring, and what you're likely to encounter on the trail. The book *Hiking Montana* by Bill Schneider has useful, basic hiking safety information and offers route details from several trail-heads. U.S. Forest Service offices have local maps, trail guides, and safety information.

Contacts **Montana Fish, Wildlife & Parks** (☎ *406/444–2535* ⊕ *www.fwp.mt.gov*). **U.S. Forest Service regional office** (☎ *406/329–3511* ⊕ *www.fs.fed.us/r1/*).

SKIING Although there is a statewide ski areas' association, the best information for both downhill and cross-country skiing is available through the state tourism bureau. For descriptions of many cross-country ski trails throughout the state, pick up a copy of the book *Winter Trails Montana,* by Jean Arthur, which details 40 trail systems in Montana's snowy regions. Novices to the slopes will be in good hands at the area's well-established ski schools.

Contacts **Travel Montana** (e ✉ *301 S. Park, Helena 59620* ☎ *406/841–2870 or 800/847–4868* ⊕ *www.visitmt.com*).

TRAIN TRAVEL

Amtrak chugs across the Highline and the northwest part of the state, stopping in East Glacier, West Glacier, and Whitefish daily. Flathead Travel partners with Amtrak to offer package excursions to Glacier National Park and other northwest Montana destinations.

Train Information **Amtrak** (☎ *800/872–7245* ⊕ *www.amtrak.com*). **Flathead Travel** (✉ *500 S. Main St., Kalispell 59901* ☎ *800/223–9380 or 406/752–8700* ☎ *406/752–8786* ⊕ *www.flatheadtravel.com*).

VISITOR INFORMATION

Information **Glacier Country** (☐ *Box 1035, Bigfork 59911-1035* ☎ *800/338–5072* ⊕ *www.glaciermt.com*). **Travel Montana** (✉ *301 S. Park, Helena 59620* ☎ *406/841–2870 or 800/847–4868* ⊕ *www.visitmt.com*). **Bigfork Chamber of Commerce** (☐ *Box 237, Bigfork 59911* ☎ *406/837–5888* ⊕ *www.bigfork.org*). **Bitterroot Valley Chamber of Commerce** (✉ *105 E. Main St., Hamilton 59840* ☎ *406/363–2400* ⊕ *www.bitterrootvalleychamber.com*). **Missoula Chamber of Commerce** (☐ *Box 7577, Missoula 59807* ☎ *406/543–6623 or 800/526–3465* ⊕ *www.missoulachamber.com*). **Whitefish Chamber of Commerce** (✉ *520 E. 2nd St., Whitefish 59937* ☎ *406/862–3501 or 877/862–3548* ⊕ *www.whitefishchamber.org*).

The Montana Plains

WORD OF MOUTH

"Traveling through Judith Gap and the wind farm there is sort of surreal. Do check out the windmills; they're huge and there must be over a 100."
                                                        —kureiff

"Slow down and enjoy your trip between Great Falls and Billings. All of the 'Big Sky State' is scenic."
                                                        —RedRock

Updated by Andrew Mckean

SPACE, LOTS OF SPACE IS the hallmark of eastern Montana's gently rolling plains. To escape stifling crowds and urban sprawl, you would do well in the wide-open plains of Big Sky Country. The state as a whole averages six people per square mi, but some of its prairies measure in reverse: one person per six square mi. Although largely devoid of the epic snow-covered peaks of the towering Rockies, the eastern two-thirds of Montana have an expansive beauty that seems to stretch endlessly beyond the horizon, beckoning you to bask in the isolated serenity of one of the least-populated places in the country—in a land of almost too much sky.

That's not to say that eastern Montana is flat and boring. In fact, the grassy plains are often broken up by geographical oddities such as

badlands, glacial lakes, and ice caves. Occasional pine-covered foothills or snowcapped mountains even pop up, looking strangely out of place rising from the surrounding prairie. This topographical diversity makes the region a playground for lovers of the outdoors. Hiking, horseback riding, wrangling, boating, skiing, snowmobiling, caving, and some of the best fishing and hunting in the world are among the greatest attractions here. Beyond the blessings nature has bestowed upon the state are an ample number of historic sites, state parks, museums, and even paleontological digs.

Paradoxically, the first- and third-largest cities in Montana are in the state's highly rural eastern region. The largest city in a 500-mi radius, Billings is a center for culture, shopping, entertainment, and medical care. Great Falls, straddling the Missouri River near a handful of thundering waterfalls, is one of Montana's greatest historical centers, with dozens of museums and interpretive centers that trace the state's varied cultural influences. Scattered in between these two cities are more than 100 small communities, some with no more than two dozen inhabitants living in the shadow of towering clapboard grain elevators. Although diminutive, sleepy, and dependent on the larger cities, each of these towns has its own distinct Western character, adding to the larger flavor of the region.

EXPLORING THE MONTANA PLAINS

Most visitors to Montana neglect the eastern plains in their rush to get to the increasingly crowded forests and peaks farther west, but the grassy prairies that roll ever onward into the Dakotas and Canada should not be overlooked simply because they lack the majesty of a mountain range. Stop on the plains for their isolation, their serenity, and their sky. Unbroken by man-made objects (or even natural ones), the heavens don't just stretch upward—they stretch outward. At night the effect becomes even more intense, as millions of stars, undisguised by the lights of civilization, beam down from every direction onto an otherwise pitch-black landscape.

Major roads are few and far between in this part of the state. I–94 sweeps westward from North Dakota to Billings, where it joins I–90, which comes up from Wyoming's Bighorn Mountains and snakes west through the Rockies into Idaho. The only other interstate is I–15, which threads north out of Idaho and onto the plains outside Helena before looping around Great Falls and heading to Canada. In the vast stretches of prairie out of reach of the interstates, the key thoroughfares are U.S. 2, also known as the Hi-Line, running east–west across the top of the state; U.S. 212, running southeast out of Billings into South Dakota; and U.S. 87, running north out of Billings.

ABOUT THE RESTAURANTS

Showy dress and jewelry matter little to most Montanans. A cowboy in dusty blue jeans, flannel shirt, and worn boots leaning against his rust-eaten Chevy could be a millionaire rancher and stockbroker, and the ponytailed woman behind the counter of the general store might be the town mayor. Because of this, no matter where you go to eat—whether the food is extravagant or simple, the prices expensive or dirt cheap—dress is casual. But despite the universal informality in dining, eastern Montana has a surprising number of upscale restaurants turning out sophisticated dishes. Good ethnic food, with the possible exception of Mexican and Native American cuisine, is scarce, however. Classic steak houses and local ma-and-pa eateries are ubiquitous.

ABOUT THE HOTELS

The strength of eastern Montana's hospitality doesn't lie in luxury resorts, bustling lodges, or crowded dude ranches, which are confined almost entirely to the western third of the state. The crown jewels of lodging on the plains are historic hotels and bed-and-breakfasts. Nearly every town with more than a few hundred residents has at least one of these properties, but no two are alike. From turreted Victorian mansions and rustic log ranch houses to Gothic manors and hulking sandstone inns with intricately carved facades, these lodgings have their own appeal and local flavor that set them apart from chain accommodations and commercial strip motels.

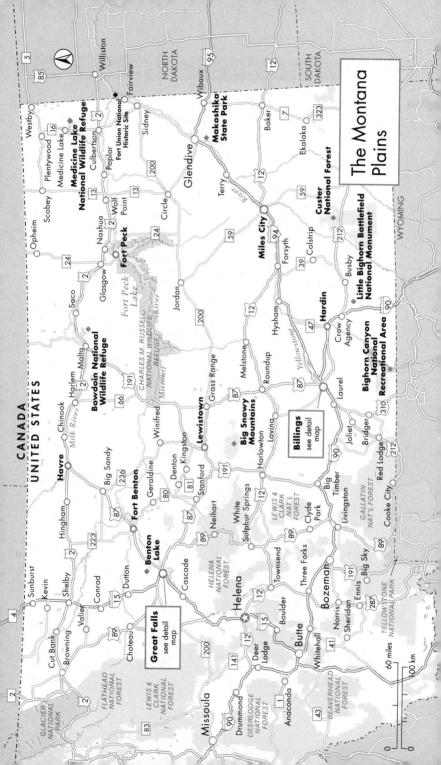

	WHAT IT COSTS				
	¢	$	$$	$$$	$$$$
RESTAURANTS	under $7	$7–$11	$11–$16	$16–$22	over $22
HOTELS	under $70	$70–$110	$110–$160	$160–$220	over $220

Restaurant prices are for a main course at dinner. Hotel prices are for two people in a standard double room in high season, excluding service charges and 4% tax.

TIMING

Each season offers something different in Montana: summer brings warm, dry weather perfect for hiking, biking, and horseback riding; autumn yields throngs of wildlife for animal watchers, and anglers; winter means plenty of snow for skiing, snowmobiling, and ice fishing. Although summer is the busiest season here—with good reason, since freezing temperatures can arrive as early as September and depart as late as May—many travelers are only passing through on their way farther west. The roads may be crowded, but the attractions, hotels, and restaurants are likely not. Winter can sometimes be just as busy as summer, as thousands of avid skiers rush through on their way to the slopes. Road conditions are generally poor in winter, especially when a heavy snowfall closes down entire sections of highway. Spring is a hard season to define, as snowstorms can strike well into May. Autumn weather, although not completely predictable, is usually the most stable. Days are long and sunny, evenings are cool, and there are very few fellow travelers to contend with.

GREAT FALLS

One of Great Falls' greatest assets is its sense of history. Here, along the banks of the Missouri where the plains meet the Rockies, explorers Meriwether Lewis and William Clark encountered one of the more daunting obstacles of their expedition: the thundering waterfalls that gave the city its name. The waterfalls have since been tamed by hydropower dams, but an interpretive center, guided boat trips, and paved trails that recall the passage of the two explorers in 1805 are impressive, and a slew of other museums and attractions celebrate other chapters in the city's history. From prehistoric buffalo jumps and famous Western artists to pioneering cowboys and the Missouri River fur trade, Great Falls has a storied past rich enough to make its people proud. And they are.

With 56,690 residents, Great Falls is no longer Montana's second-largest city, demoted in the 2000 census to third place, below the burgeoning mountain town of Missoula and its 363 extra residents. But Great Falls is still the commercial and social hub for northern Montana and southern Alberta, with a bi-level mall, thriving downtown district, bustling civic center, and near-boundless opportunities for outdoor recreation.

PLANNING YOUR TIME

Space, one of Montana's most abundant natural resources, can make traveling between major communities and attractions tedious. The drive from Great Falls to Billings, for instance, takes four hours. It's tempting to rush the drive to get from point A to point B, but that tactic can make you—and your traveling companions—batty with the vehicular version of cabin fever.

Break up long drives with side trips and random stops. Even if the trip could take only four or five hours, give yourself the entire day. Survey your route on a map before you set out and choose two or three possible stops along the way. Between Great Falls and Billings you might pause in the Big Snowy Mountains for a brisk hike. Break up the drive from Great Falls to Havre with lunch in Fort Benton, at the Union Grille in the Grand Union Hotel. Don't hesitate to stop in the random small town. You may not find much more than a gas station and a diner, but the locals will almost always offer friendly conversation and a few tall tales.

There is plenty to do in the two largest cities on the Montana plains. Lake Elmo State Park, ZooMontana, and Pictograph Cave State Monument are good stops in Billings, and the C. M. Russell Museum, Giant Springs State Park, and the Lewis and Clark National Historic Trail Interpretive Center are must-sees in Great Falls. Both cities make good base camps for further exploration: most of the region's attractions are day trips from these communities.

If you have the time, explore some of the state's smaller towns. These mini-municipalities have few obvious visitor attractions. You just have to do a little creative thinking in these remote villages. It may look a little primitive next to its big-city counterparts, but don't hesitate to pay a visit to the local museum. Remember outdoor recreation opportunities, too: for example, Miles City may look a little dull at first glance, but it's the perfect base from which to float down the Yellowstone River to Pirogue Island State Park or kick around on the rocky shorelines for agates and arrowheads.

Indeed, the great outdoors are probably why you're in Montana to begin with. If you are unaccustomed to so much space, the state's endless plains and wide-open skies may become wearisome after a while, but they can be every bit as beautiful as the mountain peaks that tower in the distance. Appreciate the empty countryside while you can, and stop on the side of the road in this strangely deserted landscape and marvel at the scale of the sky and the horizon. Once you're back home, you'll miss it.

EXPLORING GREAT FALLS

This is a beautiful city for a sightseeing drive. Maple trees line the residential streets, the Missouri River slices through the center of town, and the Rockies sink their teeth into the western horizon. The High-woods and Little Belts mountains frame the views to the north and east of town. Despite the curves of the river, most streets are straight and relatively easy to navigate, thanks largely to the flat terrain. However,

Black Eagle
Falls **4**

C. M. Russell
Museum
Complex **6**

Giant Springs State
Park **2**

Gibson Park **8**

Historic district .. **7**

Lewis and Clark
National Historic
Trail Interpretive
Center **3**

Paris Gibson
Square Museum of
Art **5**

Rainbow Falls ... **1**

with an Air Force base on the east side of town, a commercial airport on the west side, and only four bridges spanning the river in between, traffic can get heavy, especially in late afternoons and on weekends. Pedestrian paths are far less congested. A gorgeous 30-mi-long riverside trail, ideal for walking and cycling, passes the city's largest green space, Gibson Park, and one of the largest cold-water springs in the world.

TIMING   Depending on how much time you want to spend visiting the museums and wandering the historic district, this tour could keep you busy from sunrise to sunset. If you rush things, you might be able to finish in five or six hours. The parks and waterfalls take on their own special beauty when the snow falls, but biting winds might keep you from enjoying them for very long; the warmth of summer and the colors of autumn create perfect conditions for this tour.

THE MAIN ATTRACTIONS

❹ Black Eagle Falls. On the north side of the historic part of town is 40-foot-high, 500-foot-wide Black Eagle Falls, one of the places where the Missouri River takes a sharp dive on its 500-foot descent through town. The adjacent golf courses and baseball diamond give the area plenty of green space and a seminatural feel, although it's hard not to notice the concrete dam looming above. ⊠ *Intersection of U.S. 87 and 25th St. N.*

⑥ C.M. Russell Museum Complex. This 76,000-square-foot complex houses
Fodor's Choice the largest collection of original art and personal objects of legendary
★ cowboy artist Charlie Russell (1864–1926). Russell's more than 4,000
works of art—sculptures, watercolors, oil paintings—primarily portray
the vanishing era of the Old West. His log studio and home, built at the
turn of the 20th century, are adjacent to the main galleries. Also here
are collections of paintings by other 19th-century and modern Western artists, interactive exhibits, and a research library. ⊠*400 13th St.
N* ☎*406/727–8787* ⊕*www.cmrussell.org* ⊠*$9* ⊙*May–Sept., daily
9–6; Oct.–Apr., Tues.–Sat. 10–5, Sun. 1–5.*

② Giant Springs State Park. The freshwater springs here feed a state fish
☾ hatchery that covers 400 acres of parkland. According to residents, the
★ waters that flow from the springs form the shortest river in the world,
the 200-foot-long Roe River (Oregonians hold that their D River is
shorter, but most independent record keepers side with Montana on
the issue). In addition to the hatchery, a visitor center, picnic grounds,
a river drive, hiking and biking trails, and a playground are all on-site
and you can walk up the hill to Fish, Wildlife & Parks' regional headquarters, filled with educational displays featuring life-size mounts of
area wildlife. You can also fish, attend educational programs, and take
tours. Kids will enjoy feeding the hatchery's fish. ⊠*4600 Giant Springs
Rd.* ☎*406/454–5840* ⊕*www.fwp.mt.gov/parks/* ⊠*$5 for nonresi-
dents, free for Montana residents* ⊙*Daily dawn–dusk.*

⑧ Gibson Park. This park, named for the insightful founder of Great Falls,
☾ is the crown jewel of the city's 400-acre park system. The most popular features are the duck pond, the extensive flower gardens, and a
small café. There are also jogging paths, outdoor exercise equipment,
basketball courts, restrooms, a playground, a band shell, and prime
picnicking spots. The restored log cabin of Vinegar Jones, reportedly
Great Falls' first permanent resident, is also on display in the park.
⊠*Park Dr. N and 1st Ave. N* ☎*406/771–1265* ⊕*www.ci.great-falls.
mt.us/people_offices/park_rec/* ⊠*Free* ⊙*Daily dawn–dusk.*

ALSO WORTH SEEING

⑦ Historic district. There are more than 200 historic houses and small businesses here in the historic district, on the east bank of the Missouri
River. The structures reflect various architectural styles, including bun-
galow, prairie, colonial, Queen Anne, Victorian, and Second Empire.
You can obtain a brochure for a one-hour self-guided walking tour of
the area from the **Great Falls Information Center** (⊠*15 Upper River Rd.*
☎*406/771–0885 or 800/735–8535*). The area was laid out in a grid
pattern by city founder Paris Gibson, making it easy to navigate.

③ Lewis and Clark National Historic Trail Interpretive Center. At this hands-on
☾ interpretive center overlooking the Missouri River you can trace the
trail that the Corps of Discovery traveled from 1804 to 1806 while in
search of an overland route to the Pacific Ocean. The center exhibits
materials used by the travelers and the Native Americans they met on
their journey. Films, a self-guided tour, and costumed interpreters who
conduct daily demonstrations further illuminate the history. Don't miss

the pirogue pull, a muscle-straining simulation of the arduous task of pulling the expedition's dugout boats up cactus-studded canyons. The corps spent a month dragging their boats around Great Falls' namesake waterfalls. ⊠ *4201 Giant Springs Rd.* ☎ *406/727–8733* ⊕ *www. fs.fed.us/r1/lewisclark/lcic.htm* ◨ *$5* ⊙ *Memorial Day–Sept., daily 9–6; Oct.–Memorial Day, Tues.–Sat. 9–5, Sun. noon–5.*

❺ Paris Gibson Square Museum of Art. Contemporary artwork of the northwest United States makes up the bulk of the collection here. In addition to several exhibition halls and a photography collection, the museum has a bistro and a gallery. ⊠ *1400 1st Ave. N* ☎ *406/727–8255* ⊕ *www.the-square.org* ◨ *$5* ⊙ *Memorial Day–Labor Day, Tues.–Fri. 10–5, weekends noon–5; Labor Day–Memorial Day, weekdays 10–5, Sat. noon–5.*

❶ Rainbow Falls. One of the waterfalls that gives the city its name, 50-foot-high Rainbow Falls is below Rainbow Dam, about 1½ mi east of Giant Springs State Park. The surrounding land is mostly owned by ranchers, although there are some trails cut into the hills near the falls. ⊠ *Giant Springs Rd.*

OFF THE BEATEN PATH

Smith River. Flowing out of the Helena National Forest in the heart of Montana is the 60-mi Smith River. Like most other waterways in the state, it fluctuates with the seasons, ranging from a trickle in September to a raging torrent in June (thanks to the melting mountain snowpack). Although the river is popular for numerous activities, including camping on its banks, fishing, and swimming, the most prevalent activity on the Smith is floating. Floating is so popular, in fact, that Montana Fish, Wildlife & Parks limits the number of groups boating down the river to 700 per year. Despite the river's popularity, this is still Montana, and the sense of serene isolation that comes from the sight of towering mountains and open prairie will far outweigh any annoyance at seeing a few other boats during your journey. ⊠ *Between I–15 and U.S. 85* ☎ *406/454–5840* ⊕ *www.fwp.mt.gov/parks/smith* ◨ *Charges for use permits vary; call for details. Float applications due mid-Feb.*

First Peoples Buffalo Jump State Park. For centuries Native Americans hunted bison by stampeding them off a cliff at this 2,000-acre park, which is sacred to the state's original residents. This is one of the largest and best-interpreted buffalo jumps in the United States. The mile-long cliff affords a spectacular view of the Rocky Mountains, the Missouri River, and the plains. An interpretive center focuses on the culture of the Plains Indians before white settlement. ⊠ *10 mi south of Great Falls on I–15 to Ulm exit, then 3½ mi northwest* ☎ *406/866–2217* ⊕ *www.fwp.mt.gov* ◨ *$5 for nonresidents, free for Montana residents* ⊙ *Memorial Day–Sept., daily 8–6; Oct.–Memorial Day, Wed.–Sat. 10–4, Sun. noon–4.*

SPORTS & THE OUTDOORS

Unlike some of Montana's more westerly cities, Great Falls does not lie at the base of world-class ski runs or sheer cliffs for rock climbing. It is nevertheless popular with outdoor enthusiasts, largely because of its central location. Ski lodges and climbing trails are a short drive west and stretching out north and south are Montana's famed blue-ribbon fishing streams. Not to be forgotten is the "Mighty Mo"—the Missouri River, a recreational playground that runs straight through the middle of the city.

The 30-mi **River's Edge Trail** (☎ *406/788–3313* ⊕ *www.thetrail.org*) follows the Missouri River through the city on both banks; four bridges connect the trail's two branches. The trail, which attracts bikers, joggers, and strollers, passes Gibson Park, the West Gate Mall, Giant Springs State Park, and several waterfalls and dams. More primitive and challenging trails extend downstream of Rainbow Dam. More than 13 mi of the path, which is still under development, are paved; the remaining 17 mi are gravel. Just blocks from the River's Edge Trail in downtown Great Falls is **Bighorn Wilderness Equipment** (✉ *206 5th St. S* ☎ *406/453–2841*), an outdoors specialty store with everything from camping-stove fuel and freeze-dried food to ice-climbing equipment and kayaks. The store also rents bicycles and equipment. **Craig Madsen's Montana River Outfitters** (✉ *923 10th Ave. N* ☎ *406/761–1677 or 800/800–8218*), facing the river on the north side of town, is known among locals for its guided trips along the river by canoe, raft, or kayak. You can also rent bicycles or get outfitted for a float trip with a wide selection of rental equipment.

WHERE TO EAT

$$–$$$$ ✕**Eddie's Supper Club.** Campfire steak, lobster, prime rib, and shrimp are the entrées of choice at this casual Great Falls mainstay. The large booths and tables may hark back to the 1950s, but Eddie's serves some of the best burgers and steaks in town. There's live piano music on the weekends. ✉ *3725 2nd Ave. N* ☎ *406/453–1616* ⊟ *AE, D, MC, V.*

$$$ ✕**Borrie's.** The dining is family-style at this restaurant in Black Eagle, a small community that borders the northeast edge of Great Falls. Regulars favor the steaks, chicken, lobster, and burgers, although the huge portions of spaghetti, ravioli, and rigatoni are also popular. Historic photos of Great Falls line the walls, but they're hard to appreciate in the dim lighting. ✉ *1800 Smelter Ave., Black Eagle* ☎ *406/761–0300* ⊟ *AE, D, MC, V* ⊘ *No lunch.*

$$$ ✕**The Breaks.** Upstairs in this historic warehouse just south of downtown is a wine bar and restaurant that features cedar-plank salmon, cashew-and-almond-encrusted halibut, and rack of lamb. Downstairs is Machinery Row, a pub where you can shoot pool, throw darts, watch the game, or enjoy live music on weekends. The wine bar features more than two dozen appetizers on the menu and leather couches that invite intimate conversation and casual after-work socializing. ✉ *202 2nd St. S* ☎ *406/453–5980* ⊟ *AE, D, MC, V* ⊘ *Closed Sun.*

$–$$ ✕**Bert & Ernie's.** A casual atmosphere and consistent food has made this downtown eatery a locals' favorite, and live entertainment in its Irish-flavored bar is drawing a younger crowd on weekday evenings. Burgers, pasta, and full-meal salads are featured in the restaurant. The bar features more than a dozen Montana microbrews on tap and a respectable wine list. Live entertainment, including bluegrass pickers, classical guitarists, and Irish pub bands, takes the small stage from 7 to 10 PM. Monday through Saturday. ⊠*300 1st Ave. S* ☎*406/453–0601* ▤*AE, D, MC, V* ☉*Closed Sun.*

WHERE TO STAY

$$–$$$ ⌂ **La Quinta Inn & Suites Great Falls.** Overlooking the Missouri River just southwest of downtown and within easy walking distance of casual restaurants and watering holes, this clean, trendy property is a nice balance between bland franchise hotels and pricey upper-end lodging. Decor is decidedly Western, with a stone fireplace and exposed log beams. **Pros:** Off the main thoroughfares but close to downtown and the 10th Avenue S retail district. Close to restaurants. West-facing rooms have sunset views. **Cons:** The location isn't great for quick in-and-out visits. The area is funky but neglected, giving the neighborhood a slightly disused, even dangerous, feel. ⊠*600 River Dr. S, 59405* ☎*406/761–2600* ⇨*91 rooms, 21 suites* ⌂*In-room: Wi-Fi. In-hotel: laundry facilities, no-smoking rooms, some pets allowed* ▤*AE, D, MC, V* ⏴*CP.*

$ ⌂ **Townhouse Inn.** Frequent travelers to Great Falls return again and again to this modern hotel for its low prices and well-furnished, spacious rooms. Shades of beige, green, red, and blue decorate the motel-style rooms. An indoor courtyard has plants, a swimming pool, and a large hot tub. A small casino also offers distraction for road-weary guests. **Pros:** No-nonsense motor hotel for overnight or longer stays. Clean rooms and attentive service at a fair price. **Cons:** There's nothing charming about frenetic 10th Avenue S. ⊠*1411 10th Ave. S, 59405* ☎*406/761–4600* 🖷*406/761–7603* ⇨*109 rooms* ⌂*In-hotel: pool, no-smoking rooms, no elevator* ▤*AE, D, DC, MC, V.*

¢–$ ⌂ **Great Falls Inn.** The furniture in the common areas of this small but well-appointed downtown hotel is so comfortable you'll want to meet friends in the lobby. Many of the guests of the inn stay here while using the services of the Great Falls Clinic and Benefis Healthcare Center next door. ⊠*1400 28th St. S, 59405* ☎*406/453–6000* 🖷*406/453–6078* ⇨*60 rooms* ⌂*In-room: refrigerator (some). In-hotel: fitness room, no-smoking rooms, some pets allowed* ▤*AE, D, MC, V* ⏴*CP.*

CAMPING

🌣 ⚠ **Fort Ponderosa Campground.** Horseshoes, proximity to outdoor recreation along Belt Creek and in the Little Belt Mountains, and helpful hosts are some of the attractions of this friendly campground tucked in the Belt Creek Canyon, 20 mi south of Great Falls just off U.S. Highway 89. A small store here stocks propane and some basic provisions, and larger stores are in the nearby town of Belt, a short drive—or tube ride down the creek—away. If you don't bring your own shelter, you can stay in the A-frame chalet. There's an extra $3 charge per night if you plan to use your RV's heater or air-conditioner. ⌂*Flush toilets, full hookups, partial hookups (electric and water), drinking water, guest laundry, showers, fire pits, picnic tables, food service, electricity, public telephone, general store, play area, swimming (creek)* ⇨*10 full hook-*

ups, 25 partial hookups, 10 tent sites, 1 chalet ⊠ *568 Armington Rd.* ☏ *406/277–3232* 📠 *406/277–3309* ▤ *MC, V.*

⚠ **Great Falls KOA.** Regular evening entertainment at this campsite on the south edge of town includes bluegrass music, country humor, and a little cowboy poetry. The site is near three golf courses and has a large outdoor pool with a hot tub and sauna, spacious tent sites, and even rental cottages. ⚓ *Flush toilets, full hookups, partial hookups (electric and water), drinking water, showers, picnic tables, food service, electricity, public telephone, Wi-Fi, general store, swimming (pool)* ⚓ *80 full hookups, 60 partial hookups, 30 tent sites, 25 cabins* ⊠ *1500 51st St. S* ☏ *406/727–3191* ⊕ *www.koa.com/where/mt/26153/* ▤ *AE, D, MC, V.*

SHOPPING

★ Thanks to insightful city planners, Great Falls is blessed with a beautiful and extensive **downtown shopping district** full of the kind of old-fashioned stores that in other parts of the country are rapidly giving way to chain stores and shopping malls. Eat ice cream at a soda fountain, play with wooden cars at a toy store, and prepare for a trip down the Missouri at an outfitter's shop. Most of these businesses are in an area bounded by the Missouri River, 8th Street, 4th Avenue North, and 4th Avenue South.

★ A co-op run by a dozen local artists, **Gallery 16** (⊠ *608 Central Ave.* ☏ *406/453–6103*) has creations from more than 100 craftspeople whose works include paintings, jewelry, furniture, pottery, and sculpture.

CENTRAL MONTANA

Although central Montana consists mostly of rolling plains carpeted with golden grasses, the general uniformity of the landscape is broken up by the occasional mountain range or swath of forest. There are other contrasts here as well, in this land where the pinnacles of the Rockies abut the ranches and farms of the prairie, and where old mining camps lie only a few miles from historic cow towns. Among the highlights of the region are its rivers: the Missouri, the Judith, and the Smith. They might not provide the kind of fishing found in Montana's famed Madison and Gallatin rivers, but they also aren't as crowded, and their rich history and stunning landscape make them the most popular Montana destinations you've probably never heard of. If you require regular doses of culture, you'll easily get bored in this land of seeming sameness, where you're considered a newcomer unless your grandparents are buried in the local cemetery.

FORT BENTON

40 mi northeast of Great Falls via U.S. 87.

The gateway to the Upper Missouri River, this town of 1,594 people has a rich and rugged past that's captured in a trio of excellent museums. Lewis and Clark first camped at this site less than an hour downriver from Great Falls in 1805. As a quick and easy way to move people, the Missouri River was the lifeblood of 19th-century Fort Benton. The first steamboat arrived here from St. Louis in 1859, and the city once claimed distinction as the farthest inland port in the world. Throughout the 1860s gold taken from mines across Montana was shipped downriver via Fort Benton; in 1866 alone, the town shipped 2½ tons of gold dust. The river still moves people today, not to seek their fortune in the goldfields but to paddle its placid waters amid the peaceful, serene, and beautiful countryside.

★ The **Missouri Breaks Interpretive Center** puts the fabled Missouri Breaks in perspective, and offers a virtual glimpse of the river to those not floating down the Mighty Mo, and maps for those who do. The front of the building, on Fort Benton's historic levee, looks like the stunning White Cliffs of the Missouri; the rear resembles the deck of a paddlewheel steamer. Inside, photos and films of the river and its wildlife, interactive exhibits, and history lessons await. A complete set of Karl Bodmer lithographs graces one wall of the center. ⊠ *701 7th St.* ☎ *406/622–4000* ⊕ *www.blm.gov/mt/st/en/fo/lewistown_field_office/ UM/interp* 🖃 *$2* ☉ *Memorial Day–Sept. 30, daily 8–5; Oct. 1–Memorial Day, weekdays 8–5.*

Montana's official agriculture museum, the **Museum of the Northern Great Plains** tells the story of three generations of farmers from 1908 until 1980. The 30,000 square feet of exhibition space hold a village of businesses from the homestead era, and a library. On display are the Hornaday-Smithsonian Bison, specimens taken from the Montana plains when it seemed likely that the species faced extinction. In 1886 the six buffalo were stuffed, then exhibited in the Smithsonian for more than 70 years before being returned to their native state. ⊠ *1205 20th St.* ☎ *406/622–5316* ⊕ *www.fortbenton.com/museums/ag_museum.htm* 🖃 *$10* ☉ *May–Sept., daily 10–5; off-season by appointment only.*

Fodor'sChoice
★ Covering the era from 1800 to 1900, the **Museum of the Upper Missouri** highlights the importance of Fort Benton and the role it played as a trading post, military fort, and the head of steamboat navigation. Old Fort Benton is adjacent; considered the birthplace of Montana, with its 1846 blockhouse, this is the oldest standing structure in the state. Highlights of the museum include tours of the restored frontier-era fort. The $10 fee also gives you access to the nearby Museum of the Northern Great Plains and the Missouri Breaks National Monument Interpretive Center. ⊠ *Old Fort Park* ☎ *406/622–5316* 🖃 *$10* ☉ *May–Sept., daily 10–5; off-season by appointment only.*

In 1805–06 Lewis and Clark explored the upper Missouri River and camped on its banks. Today the stretch designated the **Upper Missouri National Wild and Scenic River** runs 149 mi downriver from Fort Benton. Highlights include the scenic White Cliffs area, Citadel Rock, Hole in the Wall, Lewis and Clark Camp at Slaughter River, abandoned homesteads, and abundant wildlife. Commercial boat tours, shuttle service, and boat rentals—including rowboats, power boats, and canoes—are available in Fort Benton and Virgelle. Be aware of seasonal restrictions that prohibit motorized boats and limited campsites on the river. ⊠*Missouri Breaks Interpretive Center, 701 7th St.* ☎*406/622–5185* 🖾*Free.*

SPORTS & THE OUTDOORS

Although sparsely inhabited, this calm stretch of the Mighty Mo is becoming more and more popular with visitors. The benefit is that there's no shortage of outfitters and guides offering their services at competitive prices.

★ The **Lewis and Clark Canoe Expeditions** (⊠*812 14th St.* ☎*406/622–3698 or 888/595–9151* ⊕*www.lewisandclarkguide.com*) guided trips last from one to seven days and can include horseback riding. You can also arrange for canoe rentals and a guide-only service, in which you provide transportation and food for your escort. The **Missouri River Canoe Company** (⊠*7485 Virgelle Ferry Rd. N, Loma* ☎*406/378–3110 or 800/426–2926* ⊕*www.canoemontana.com/index.html*), in the tiny town of Virgelle, provides canoe and kayak rentals by the day, outfitted excursions, and one to four day guided trips. Trips with lodging at Virgelle Merc, a restored homestead-era settlement with accommodations in cabins, B&B rooms, and even a sheepherder's wagon under the stars, are also available.

WHERE TO STAY

$$ 🏨**Grand Union Hotel.** Perhaps the oldest hotel in Montana, the Grand
Fodor'sChoice Union was built on the bank of the Missouri in 1882 to serve steam-
★ boat and stage travelers. Filled with period pieces, the two-story building is as elegant as ever. With its dark-wood accents and Victorian-style lighting, the Union Grille Restaurant ($$$–$$$$) brings to mind the refinement cultivated by the Western frontier's elite. The menu features Montana regional cuisine and fare from afar, including seared sea scallops, charbroiled venison, and grilled buffalo tenderloin, and the wine list is populated by choices from California and Washington vineyards. **Pros:** Full-service hotels are rare in Fort Benton. Many rooms have river views, and beds have best pillows in Montana. **Cons:** Hard to get a reservation in high season. Spacious hallways and public spaces tend to feel lonely during off season. ⊠*1 Grand Union Sq., 59442* ☎*406/622–1882 or 888/838–1882* ⊕*www.grandunionhotel.com* 🛏*26 rooms* ☖*In-hotel: restaurant, bar, no-smoking rooms* ⊟*AE, D, MC, V* ☺*Restaurant closed Mon. in summer, Mon. and Tues. in winter. No lunch* ⦾*CP.*

SHOPPING

There are thousands of bolts of quilting fabric at the **Quilting Hen** (⊠*1156 Buck Bridge Rd., Carter* ☎*406/734–5297*), about halfway between Great Falls and Fort Benton. The store specializes in unusual patterns and kits, including one based on the Lewis and Clark expedition and one that depicts the return of the sacred white buffalo.

LEWISTOWN

90 mi southeast of Fort Benton via Hwys. 80 and 81.

Started as a small trading post in the shadow of the low-lying Moccasin and Judith mountains, Lewistown has evolved into a pleasant town of nearly 7,000 residents. Several locations are listed on the National Register of Historic Places, including the Silk Stocking and Central Business districts, Courthouse Square, Judith Place, and Stone Quarry.

Self-guided-tour brochures are available at the **Lewistown Area Chamber of Commerce** (⊠ *408 N.E. Main St.* ☎ *406/535–5436* ⊕ *www.lewistownchamber.com*).

Nearly half the town—and several hundred visitors from across the country—turn out each year for the **Lewistown Chokecherry Festival.** Held the first Saturday after Labor Day, the annual harvest celebration includes arts and crafts booths, a farmers' market, a cook-off starring the wild-growing sour fruit, and a variety of contests for visitors of all ages, including a chokecherry pit-spitting contest that awards distance and accuracy. ⊠ *Along Main St.* ☎ *406/535–5436* ⊕ *www.lewistownchamber.com.*

Pioneer relics, blacksmith and cowboy tools, guns, and Native American artifacts are displayed at the **Central Montana Museum.** Guided tours are available in the summer; from Labor Day through Memorial Day visitors are on their own to view the array of exhibits, most of which illuminate the human history of the Judith Basin and central Montana. ⊠ *408 N.E. Main St.* ☎ *406/535–3642* ⊑ *Free* ☾ *Memorial Day–Labor Day, daily 9–5.*

☾ Discover the vistas that inspired Western artist Charlie Russell on the
★ **Charlie Russell Chew-Choo,** a vintage 1950s-era train that travels on the old Milwaukee Road tracks through some of the most beautiful and remote landscapes in the state. The tour, which departs from Kingston, about 10 mi northwest of Lewiston, lasts 3½ hours and includes dinner and a cash bar. On weekends before Christmas the Chew-Choo transforms into a prairie Polar Express. ⊠ *U.S. 191 north 2 mi, then Hanover Rd. west for 7½ mi* ☎ *406/538–8721 or 866/912–2980* ⊕ *www.montanacharlierussellchewchoo.com* ⊑ *$90–$125, including dinner* ☾ *June–Oct. and Dec., Sat. Call for departure times.*

☾ At the head of one of the purest cold-water springs in the world is the **Big Springs Trout Hatchery.** The state's largest cold-water production station nurtures several species of trout and kokanee salmon. The show pond, where you can view albino rainbow trout and fish weighing a monstrous 15 pounds, is a popular attraction, but the hatchery grounds are a sight in and of themselves and a wonderful spot to enjoy a picnic under giant willow and cottonwood trees. You can see the place where Big Spring Creek spurts from the earth, and the native wildlife—including white-tailed deer, beavers, wood ducks, and belted kingfishers—make frequent appearances. ⊠ *Hwy. 466, 5 mi south of Lewistown* ☎ *406/538–5588* ⊑ *Free* ☾ *Daily dawn–dusk.*

OFF THE BEATEN PATH

Judith River. The tame, deserted Judith flows more than 60 mi from the Lewis and Clark National Forest through arid plains and sandy mesas before emptying into the Missouri. The scenery is stunning, but the variably low water levels and stifling hot summer sun are not conducive to float trips. This is, however, excellent fossil-hunting ground, and the **Judith River Dinosaur Institute,** based in Malta, sponsors frequent digs here. Most of the land surrounding the river is private, though, so check before you start wandering the banks looking for bones. As always, remember to leave fossils where you find them, and report anything significant to the Dinosaur Institute. ⊠*North of Hwy. 200* ☎*406/696–5842 Dinosaur Institute* ⊕*www.montanadinosaurdigs.com.*

War Horse National Wildlife Refuge. In 1958 this 3,192-acre area was established as a refuge and breeding ground for migratory birds and other wildlife. The refuge comprises three units: War Horse Lake, Wild Horse Lake, and Yellow Water Reservoir. The three units are geographically separate, but all are part of the larger Charles M. Russell National Wildlife Refuge, which encompasses more than 1 million acres along the Missouri River. Note that it's necessary to take gravel roads to reach fishing and wildlife areas. ⊠*48 mi east of Lewistown on U.S. 87* ☎*406/538–8706* ⊕*www.fws.gov/cmr/* ⊠*Free* ☉*Daily; headquarters weekdays 8–4.*

SPORTS & THE OUTDOORS

Lewistown has access to water—and plenty of it. From natural springs to alpine lakes to crystal-clear creeks fed by melting snow, there are all kinds of ways to get wet in town, or within a few short miles. Big Springs Creek flows right through downtown, and even underneath several establishments on Main Street.

Ackley Lake State Park (⊠*U.S. 87 to Hwy. 400, then 7 mi southwest* ☎*406/454–5840* ⊕*www.fwp.mt.gov*) has two boat ramps, great fishing for rainbow trout, and a 23-site campground. It's to the north of the Little Belt Mountains, about 26 mi southwest of Lewistown. In a clearing outside Lewistown you can swim in the **Gigantic Warm Springs** (⊠*North on U.S. 191, then west on Hwy. 81 for 5 mi*), a small spring-fed lake that keeps a constant temperature of 68°F. One of the most popular places in Frank Day City Park is the **Lewistown Municipal Swimming Pool** (⊠*S. 5th Ave.* ☎*406/535–4503*), a 13,000-square-foot water park with two large slides.

WHERE TO STAY & EAT

$–$$$
★
✕**The Mint Bar & Grill.** This quaint bar and grill serves an exceptional array of dishes, but you won't find most of them on the menu. You have a choice of 7 to 10 specials each night, ranging from simple sandwiches to salmon with lemon-tarragon beurre blanc to braised lamb shank over mashed potatoes. The separate bar, housed in the same restored 1914 brick building, has wainscotted walls and a hardwood floor. ⊠*113 4th Ave. S* ☎*406/535–9925* ▭*D, MC, V* ↘*No smoking* ☉*Closed Sun.*

¢–$ **Yogo Inn of Montana.** This sprawling modern hotel on the east side of Lewistown takes its name from the Yogo sapphires mined nearby. Rooms are contemporary, spacious, and well furnished; some have four-poster beds. Many rooms face an indoor courtyard with a swimming pool and hot tub. The hotel and convention center is built around the Centermark Courtyard, which takes its name from surveyor documents buried here in 1912: they proclaimed the spot the geographical center of Montana. You can arrange for Western buggy and sleigh rides and guided tours of nearby ghost towns and Native American petroglyphs. **Pros:** Sprawling hotel has hundreds of rooms in various wings. The restaurant is solid, with lots of hardy food at a fair price, and the bar/casino is a prime meeting place. **Cons:** Pool area is too dim and often too cold for comfortable lounging. The front desk feels crowded and lodgers must walk through the restaurant to access many of the rooms. ⊠*211 E. Main St., 59457* ☎*406/535–8721 or 800/860–9646* ⊕*www.yogoinn.com* ↴*123 rooms* ⌂*In-hotel: restaurant, bar, Wi-Fi, pool, no-smoking rooms, some pets allowed, no elevator* ▤*AE, D, MC, V.*

BIG SNOWY MOUNTAINS

40 mi south of Lewistown via Red Hill Rd.

South of Montana's geographical center, an island of rocky peaks rises more than 3,000 feet from the sea of windswept prairie, beckoning scenery lovers and hard-core adventurers alike. A combination of pine and fir forests and barren tundra, much of the Big Snowy Mountains area is undeveloped. More than 80% of its 106,776 acres are designated federal wilderness study area—there are no homes, no commercial services, no industry, and very few roads. The result is almost total solitude for anyone who treks into the Big Snowies to explore their rocky pinnacles, icy caves, and tranquil forests. The best road accesses are Red Hill Road about 40 mi south of Lewistown or Trail and Neil creeks east of the small town of Judith Gap. Few of the features of the Big Snowies are marked, but you can pick up a map of the area from any of the Lewis and Clark National Forest ranger stations scattered around central Montana, including the **Musselshell Ranger Station** (⊠*809 2nd St. NW, Harlowton* ☎*406/632–4391* ⊕*www.fs.fed. us/r1/lewisclark*), 25 mi southwest of the mountains.

At 8,681 feet, **Greathouse Peak** is the tallest mountain in the Big Snowies. Vehicles are permitted on Forest Service roads that reach partially to the peak, but the simplest way up is to hike the 6 mi of unmarked trails that zigzag up the slope from Halfmoon Canyon. The main trail, which is only mildly strenuous, doesn't quite make it to the top; to reach the summit, you'll need to hike a few yards off the main path. You'll know you've reached the highest point when you see the two stone cairns. The Judith Ranger Station in Stanford is your best source for Snowies information. ⊠*Pack Trail* ☎*406/566–2292* ⊗*Daily; automobile access seasonally restricted by deep snow.*

The second-highest point in the Big Snowies is **Big Snowy,** also called Old Baldy. Just 41 feet shorter than Greathouse Peak, the 8,640-foot-high mountain makes an enjoyable climb. A designated path, Maynard Ridge Trail, follows an old jeep road almost to the summit. The peak is a barren plateau with a small rocky outcropping marking the highest point. ⊠*Red Hill Rd.* ☎*406/566–2292* ☉*Daily; automobile access seasonally restricted by deep snow.*

★ In the higher reaches of the mountains is pristine **Crystal Lake.** There's excellent hiking along interpretive and wildflower trails as well as camping, fossil hunting, and ice-cave exploration. The ice cave is a 6-mi hike from the 28-site campground; June is the best time to see the 30-foot ice pillars formed over the winter. There's a cabin for snowmobilers. No motorized boats are allowed on the lake. ⊠*Crystal Lake Rd.* ☎*406/566–2292* ⊠*Free* ☉*Daily; automobile access generally June–Nov., but can be seasonally restricted by deep snow.*

A pair of 1909 sandstone buildings in the town of Harlowton, 25 mi southwest of the mountains, house the **Upper Musselshell Museum.** The collection primarily contains artifacts of the people who lived in, worked, and developed the land around the Upper Musselshell River. There are also fossils of dinosaurs and bison in the two buildings in Harlow's small but picturesque commercial district. ⊠*11 and 36 S. Central St., Harlowton* ☎*406/632–5519* ⊠*$5* ☉*Memorial Day–Labor Day, Tues.–Sat. 10–5.*

SPORTS & THE OUTDOORS

In the evergreen forests and rocky slopes of the Big Snowies and the Judith and Little Belt mountains, you can pursue numerous outdoor activities, including fishing, hiking, rock climbing, snowmobiling, and cross-country skiing. The utter isolation of the region enhances the experience but get supplied in the larger communities of Lewistown, Great Falls, or Billings before making the trek out to the mountains.

A well-appointed local outfitter, **Don's Store** (⊠*120 2nd Ave. S, Lewistown* ☎*406/538–9408 or 800/879–8194* ⊕*www.dons-store.com*) carries a wide selection of fishing and hunting gear and outdoor wear, plus optics equipment such as binoculars and spotting scopes. **High Plains Bike & Ski** (⊠*924 W. Water St., Lewistown* ☎*406/538–2902*) sells many brands of alpine and bicycling equipment and can rush-order cross-country-skiing equipment.

WHERE TO STAY

¢–$ ⬚**Corral Motel.** Family units, some with two bedrooms, and three full kitchenette units are the specialty of this hotel filled with modern furniture. Most rooms afford unobstructed views of the Musselshell River and the Castle, Crazy, and Big Snowy mountains. **Pros:** Budget lodging with million-dollar views. Kitchenette units and café next door make this a great base. **Cons:** Outdated fixtures, beds could use an upgrade. Proximity to U.S. 191 means you may be jolted out of bed by traffic noise. ⊠*U.S. 12 and U.S. 191, Harlowton 59036* ☎*406/632–4331 or 800/392–4723* ⊜*406/632–4748* ➲*18 rooms, 6 2-bedroom units*

7

♻ *In-room: refrigerator (some). In-hotel: restaurant, bar, no-smoking rooms, no elevator* =AE, D, MC, V.

CAMPING ♨ **Crystal Lake Campground.** Tucked inside the lip of the crater that contains the waters of Crystal Lake, this primitive Forest Service campground may be one of the most dramatic (and cold) places to pitch a tent in the state. There are year-round ice caves nearby, and snow can fly just about any month of the year. There's plenty of space separating the campsites. ♻ *Pit toilets, drinking water, picnic tables, swimming (lake)* ⎆*23 sites* ✉*Crystal Lake Rd., 22 mi west of U.S. 87* ☏*406/566–2292* =*406/566–2408* =*MC, V* ☀*Mid-May–late Sept.; call to verify.*

EN ROUTE Any combination of U.S. 12, U.S. 191, U.S. 87, and I–90 will make a quick route to Billings. However, if you have the time, try getting off the main roads. The square of beautiful country between these four highways is the location of **Halfbreed Lake National Wildlife Refuge** (✉*Molt-Rapelje Rd.* ☏*406/538–8706*), part of the Charles M. Russell National Wildlife Refuge. The several thousand acres of Halfbreed encompass a seasonally wet lake and wetlands, creeks, and grassy plains. Wildlife includes grouse, waterfowl, grasslands birds, deer, and antelope. This is a favorite spot for birders.

BILLINGS

A bastion of civilization on an otherwise empty prairie, Billings is a classic Western city, full of the kind of history that shaped the frontier. The Minnesota and Montana Land and Improvement Company founded the town simply to serve as a shipping point along the Northwestern Railroad. In the spring of 1882 the settlement consisted of three buildings—a home, a hotel, and a general store—but before six months passed, 5,000 city lots had been sold and more than 200 homes and businesses had been erected. The city's immediate and consistent growth earned Billings the nickname "the Magic City."

Billings' population has doubled every 30 years since its founding, and today the metropolitan area has more than 120,000 residents, making it not only the largest city in Montana, but also the largest city for 500 mi in any direction. Since the 1951 discovery of an oil field that stretches across Montana and the Dakotas into Canada, refining and energy production have played a key role in keeping the city vibrant and productive.

EXPLORING BILLINGS

Although city planners in its first century did a fine job of laying out the constantly growing community of Billings, most growth in recent years has been characterized by sprawl, especially to the west along Interstate 90. The primary residential districts are on the northern and western sides, the industrial parks are on the city's southern and eastern perimeters, and a lively downtown commercial district is sandwiched in between. There are plenty of major avenues to ease the flow of traffic between the sectors, and downtown streets are logically numbered, making navigation by car or foot relatively simple. (Note: some of the downtown streets are one-way.) Because of its sprawl expect to do far more driving than walking to reach your destination. Major residential and commercial development continues near Interstate 90 on the town's western edge, producing new freeway interchanges, strip malls, and chain hotels and motels. Keep in mind that I–90, which runs along the southern and eastern edges of Billings, is the primary route many locals use to commute to work, so do your best to avoid it in the early morning and early evening.

TIMING You could easily spend one or even two days on this tour, depending on how much time you want to allocate to the sights and parks. In winter, many of the outdoor sights close or are significantly less enjoyable.

THE MAIN ATTRACTIONS

6 **Alberta Bair Theater.** In the 1930s, 20th Century Fox built this Art Deco movie theater on land homesteaded by a successful sheep-ranching family. Saved from the wrecking ball by community groups in the 1980s, it is now a cultural center for the region. Aside from being home to the Billings Symphony Orchestra, the Alberta Bair hosts dance companies, theater troupes, and national music acts. ⊠*2801 3rd Ave. N* ☎*406/256–6052 or 877/321–2074* ⊕*www.albertabairtheater.org.*

4 **Lake Elmo State Park.** Surrounding a 64-acre reservoir in Billings Heights, this park is a popular spot for hiking, swimming, fishing, and nonmotorized boating. Although it's not far from downtown, the park is still wild enough to seem miles away from civilization. The regional on-site headquarters for Montana Fish, Wildlife & Parks is a source of recreational information and museum-quality wildlife displays. ⊠*U.S. 87* ☎*406/247–2940* ⊕*www.fwp.mt.gov* ✉*$5 for nonresidents, free for Montana residents* ☉*Daily dawn–dusk.*

8 **Moss Mansion.** Dutch architect Henry Hardenbergh, who worked on the original Waldorf-Astoria and Plaza hotels in New York City, designed this house in 1903 for businessman P. B. Moss. The mansion still contains many of the elaborate original furnishings, ranging in style from Moorish to art nouveau. Guided tours are offered on the hour. ⊠*914 Division St.* ☎*406/256–5100* ⊕*www.mossmansion.com* ✉*$7* ☉*Sept.–May, daily 1–4; June–Aug., Mon.–Sat. 9–5, Sun. 1–4.*

10 **Pictograph Cave State Park.** Once home to prehistoric hunters, this spot has yielded more than 30,000 artifacts related to early human history. A paved trail affords good views of the 2,200-year-old cave paintings depicting animal and human figures; if you bring binoculars, you'll be able to appreciate better the subtle detail of the artwork. ⊠*Coburn Rd. (U.S. 87)* ☎*406/247–2940* ⊕*www.pictographcave.org* ✉*$5 per vehicle for nonresidents, free for Montana residents* ☉*May–Sept., daily 11–7.*

Fodor'sChoice
★

1 **Rimrock Trail.** This trail system on the northern edge of Billings is a pleasant mix of paved urban paths and rugged dirt tracks, where elderly

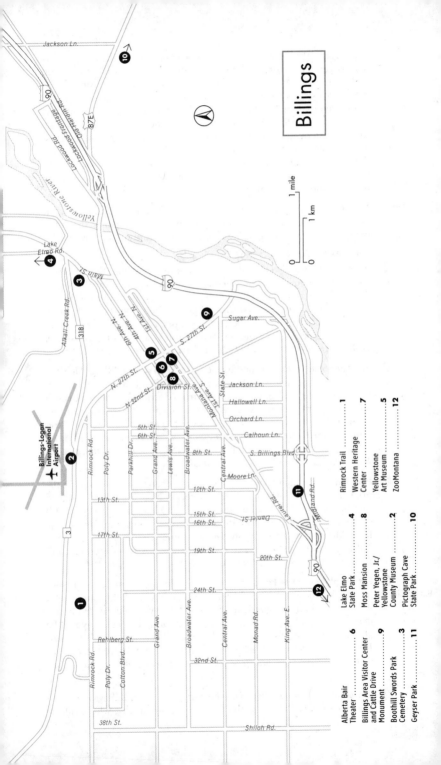

Billings

1 mile
1 km

Jackson Ln.

Billings-Logan International Airport

Yellowstone River

Lake Elmo Rd.

Lockwood Frontage Rd.
Old Hardin Rd.

Sugar Ave.

Jackson Ln.
Hallowell Ln.
Orchard Ln.
Calhoun Ln.
S. Billings Blvd.
Moore Ln.

5th St.
6th St.
8th St.
12th St.
13th St.
15th St.
16th St.
17th St.
19th St.
20th St.
24th St.
32nd St.
38th St.

Division St.

Rehberg St.
Shiloh Rd.

Rimrock Rd.
Poly Dr.
Cotton Blvd.
Grand Ave.
Broadwater Ave.
Central Ave.
King Ave. E.
Monad Rd.
Lewis Ave.
Parkhill Dr.
Daniel St.
Laurel Rd.
Midland Rd.

N. 27th St.
N. 32nd St.
S. 27th St.
Main St.
6th Ave. N.
4th Ave. N.
1st Ave. N.
1st St.
Montana Ave.
State St.

Atkali Creek Rd.

318

Alberta Bair
Theater 6
Billings Area Visitor Center
and Cattle Drive 9
Boothill Swords Park
Cemetery 3
Geyser Park 11

Lake Elmo
State Park 4
Moss Mansion 8
Peter Yegen, Jr./
Yellowstone
County Museum 2
Pictograph Cave
State Park 10

Rimrock Trail 1
Western Heritage
Center 7
Yellowstone
Art Museum 5
ZooMontana 12

A GOOD TOUR

The center of Billings is tucked beneath a distinct rock wall, aptly named the Rimrocks. Running along part of the wall is the **Rimrock Trail** ❶, made up of several smaller trails, which has outstanding views. After your hike, drive east on Highway 3 to **Peter Yegen, Jr./Yellowstone County Museum** ❷ at the entrance to Billings Logan International Airport. Continue east on Route 318, passing **Boothill Swords Park Cemetery** ❸ before heading north on Main Street to **Lake Elmo State Park** ❹, a popular recreational spot on the edge of town near Billings Heights. Head back down Main Street and then drive southwest on 6th Avenue North into the commercial district, where several sights are grouped together. Make a left onto North 27th Street and drive to 4th Avenue North for the **Yellowstone Art Museum** ❺, displaying Western and contempo-

rary art. Continue on foot one block south on North 27th Street to 3rd Avenue North; make a right and walk one block to North 28th Street to reach the **Alberta Bair Theater** ❻. Walk south down North 28th Street to Montana Avenue, where you'll find the **Western Heritage Center** ❼. To reach the turn-of-the-20th-century **Moss Mansion** ❽, head north on North 28th Street for two blocks; make a left onto 2nd Avenue North and follow it west for several blocks to Division Street. Return to your car and drive south on 27th Street until you reach I–90; follow the interstate east for 2 mi to Exit 452. Turn right and follow Highway 87 south a few miles to the border of the Crow Indian Reservation, where you'll find the fascinating **Pictograph Cave State Park** ❿. For a bit of fun, head back into Billings and take I–90 west to **ZooMontana** ⓬.

locals out for a Sunday stroll are just as content as extreme mountain bikers. Several individual trails make up the Rimrock system, which starts at Boothill Cemetery and winds past the airport up into the rocky formations that surround the city and give the trail its name. Expect fantastic views of the open plains and five distinct mountain ranges in some places, and the roar of jet engines and the sight of oil-refinery smokestacks in others. ⌧*Airport Rd.* ☎*406/245–4111.*

❼ **Western Heritage Center.** The permanent exhibits here include oral histories, artifacts, and kid-friendly interactive displays tracing the lives of Native Americans, ranchers, homesteaders, immigrants, and railroad workers who lived in the area between 1880 and 1940. Native American interpretive programs and tours to local cultural sites are available in summer. The impressive castlelike building that houses the center is just as interesting as the exhibits. ⌧*2822 Montana Ave.* ☎*406/256–6809* ⊕*www.ywhc.org* ⌐*$3* ☉*Tues.–Sat. 10–5, closed holidays.*

❺ **Yellowstone Art Museum.** One of the premier art museums in a four-state region, Yellowstone displays Western and contemporary art from nationally and internationally known artists. Among the artists whose works are on permanent display are Charles M. Russell and Will James. ⌧*401 N. 27th St.* ☎*406/256–6804* ⊕*yellowstone.artmuseum.org* ⌐*$7* ☉*Tues., Wed., Fri., and Sat. 10–5, Thurs. 10–8, Sun. noon–5.*

Guest Ranches on the Plains

Most eastern Montana ranchers are busy enough with making a living that their concession to visitors is a two-fingered wave through the windshield. But a few ranches, most in the mountains south of Billings, cater to guests, who take part in calving and branding, trailing cows to summer pasture, fixing fence, and other staples of ranch life.

Dryhead Ranch (⊠ *1062 Road 151 Lovell, WY 82431* ☎ *307/548–6688*) is headquartered in Lovell but sprawls up the arid east slopes of the Pryor Mountains in Montana. A dozen horse-loving guests a week visit from April through November, helping Iris Basset and her family run their thousand head of cattle and 300 horses. "They come for as much horseback riding as we can give them, and we can wear them out in four or five days," says Basset.

Nestled in the Clarks Fork Valley to the west, **Lonesome Spur Ranch** (⊠ *107 Schwend Rd., Bridger, MT*

59014 ☎ *406/662–3460*) also caters to horsey guests, more than half of whom hail from overseas. This is where Nicholas Evans, author of *The Horse Whisperer*, lived as he researched the best-selling novel, and a week at the ranch revolves around saddle horns and bridle bits and includes a trip to see the Pryor Mountains' wild-horse herd.

Just to the west, in the shadow of the Beartooth Mountains, the **Lazy E-L Ranch** (⊠ *East Rosebud Rd., Rosco, MT 59071* ☎ *406/328–6858*) is similarly devoted to horses and includes ranch work.

Don't expect wine tastings or hot-towel spas at these working ranches, but if you want to spend a week in the saddle, experiencing authentic Western landscapes from the back of a horse, these ranches are worth a look. Rates range from $1,500 to $1,800 per week per adult, and some ranches allow groups to book the entire facility.

⑫ **ZooMontana.** Although it specializes in native northern-latitude temperate species, ZooMontana has plenty of exotic plants and animals, making it a favorite destination for locals and visitors alike. A new grizzly bear exhibit is a steady draw, and there's a small children's zoo with kid-friendly exhibits and displays. Because this is one of the only zoos in the region, it can be extremely busy in summer. ⊠ *2100 S. Shiloh Rd.* ☎ *406/652–8100* ⊕ *www.zoomontana.org* 🎟 *$6* ☉ *Daily 10–4.*

ALSO WORTH SEEING

⑨ **Billings Area Visitor Center and Cattle Drive Monument.** A hero-size bronze sculpture of a cattle drover commemorates the Great Montana Centennial Cattle Drive of 1989 (which commemorated the drive of 1889) at this visitor center. You can take guided tours of the center, study the exhibits on the region, and gather all the information you'll need on area attractions. ⊠ *815 S. 27th St.* ☎ *406/252–4016 or 800/735–2635* ⊕ *www.itsinbillings.com* 🎟 *Free* ☉ *Weekdays 8–5.*

❸ **Boothill Swords Park Cemetery.** Many of the city's early residents are buried at this cemetery atop the Rimrocks, north of historic Billings. Among Boothill's residents are H. M. Muggins Taylor, the army scout who carried word of Custer's defeat through 180 mi of hostile territory to Fort Ellis; Western explorer Yellowstone Kelly; and several outlaws executed in the territorial days. ⊠*Airport and Main Sts.* ☎*406/657–8371.*

⓫ Geyser Park. A favorite diversion for area visitors with children, Geyser Park has bumper boats, go-karts, a climbing wall, laser tag, and a miniature-golf course with waterfalls and geyser pools. Concessions are rather pricey, so pack a cooler and eat in the picnic area. ⊠*4910 Southgate Dr.* ☎*406/254–2510* ☜*$4–$6 per game* ⊕*www.geyser park.net* ☉*Apr.–Oct., daily 11–11, weekends year-round.*

❷ Peter Yegen, Jr./Yellowstone County Museum. This log cabin served as a gentlemen's club for many years, frequented by the likes of Teddy Roosevelt and Buffalo Bill Cody, before it was moved in 1949 to its present location at the entrance to Billings Logan International Airport. The structure today serves as a small Montana frontier history museum. Check out the chuck wagon, barbed-wire collection, and creepy-looking tools from the city's first dentist office. A veranda affords unparalleled views of the Bighorn, Pryor, and Beartooth mountains more than 100 mi to the south. ⊠*1950 Terminal Circle* ☎*406/256–6811* ⊕*www.pyjrycm.org* ☜*Free* ☉*Feb.–Dec., weekdays 10:30–5, Sat. 10:30–3.*

SPORTS & THE OUTDOORS

The Rimrocks are easily the dominant feature of Billings. These 400-foot sandstone rock walls provide a scenic backdrop for numerous recreational pursuits. One of the most popular is mountain biking; suitable terrain for beginners, experienced thrill seekers, and everyone in between can be found within a short driving distance. The Yellowstone River flows through town; best access points are East Bridge on the east side of Billings and South Hills access southeast of town off Blue Creek Road.

GOLF

Perhaps surprisingly, Billings has more than half a dozen golf courses. Ranging from quick 9-hole executives in the middle of town to grand 18-hole country-club courses set against the Rimrocks, the golfing venues around the city are diverse in design and often have exceptional views of the surrounding country.

Circle Inn Golf Links (⊠*1029 Main St.* ☎*406/248–4202*), on top of the Rimrocks in Billings Heights, is a 9-hole public course that doesn't discriminate: men and women tee off from the same spot. A creek runs along three of the holes, and there's a bunker on one hole. Just below the Rimrocks near the airport is the 18-hole **Exchange City Golf Course** (⊠*19th St. W* ☎*406/652–2553*), a casual course with a winding creek and plenty of hills on the front nine. A public 18-hole course near Lake Elmo State Park in Billings Heights, the **Lake Hills Golf Club** (⊠*1930 Clubhouse Way* ☎*406/252–9244*) is in a wooded area frequented by grouse, antelope, and pheasant. Its two lakes and 444-yard final hole are its most famous features. The **Yegen Golf Club** (✉ *1390 Zimmer-man Trail* ☎ *406/656–8099*), an 18-hole public course, is set against the walls of the Rimrocks. Although not very wooded, the course has plenty of water hazards and bunkers.

MOUNTAIN BIKING

The **Bike Shop** (✉ *1934 Grand Ave.* ☎ *406/652–1202*), owned by a local family since the 1970s, sells, rents, and services mountain bikes. **DVS Bikes** (✉ *520 Wicks La., Suite 12* ☎ *406/256–3900*) specializes in BMX and freestyle bikes. **Scheels All Sports** (✉ *Rimrock Mall, 1233 W. 24th St.* ☎ *406/656–9220*)sells mountain and street bikes. Head to the **Spoke Shop** (✉ *1910 Broadwater Ave.* ☎ *406/656–8342*) for road bikes, mountain bikes, and equipment.

WHERE TO EAT

$$$–$$$$ ✕ **Juliano's.** Highly regarded Hawaiian-born chef Carl Kurokawa's
Fodor's Choice menu changes monthly; past entrées have included roasted ostrich,
★ grilled elk, spicy watermelon salad, chicken with leeks and roasted tomato, and sea bass. Inspired by Pacific and European flavors, yet distinctly American, Carl's cooking is some of the best in the state. The building, with its tin ceiling, is almost as impressive, having once been a stable for the turn-of-the-20th-century sandstone mansion next door. Lunch is fast and inexpensive. Reservations are a good idea. ✉ *2912 7th Ave. N* ☎ *406/248–6400* ▭ *AE, D, MC, V* ⊗ *Closed Sun. No dinner Mon. or Tues.*

$$–$$$$ ✕ **George Henry's.** With its stained glass and tearoom-style table settings, this restaurant in an 1882 Victorian house is elegant yet surprisingly laid-back. Favorites include steak Oscar (steak with béarnaise sauce, crab, and asparagus), roasted crispy duck, quiche, and seafood pasta. ✉ *404 N. 30th St.* ☎ *406/245–4570* ▭ *AE, D, DC, MC, V* ⊗ *Closed Sun.*

$$–$$$$ ✕ **The Granary.** A restored flour mill houses this restaurant, which ages its own beef and changes its eclectic menu every few months. Seafood, veal, lamb, and organic chicken are mainstays. Like the outdoor seating options at most Billings restaurants, the veranda here is very popular in summer. ✉ *1500 Poly Dr.* ☎ *406/259–3488* ▭ *AE, D, MC, V.*

$$–$$$$ ✕ **The Rex.** Built in 1910 by Buffalo Bill Cody's chef, this restaurant was
★ saved from the wrecking ball and restored in 1975. Today it's one of the best steak houses in the city. The dining room and bar are big and airy, enhanced by wooden beams that impart an almost Southwestern look, but the outdoor patio is perhaps the most popular place to dine on such dishes as roasted buffalo, prime rib, Italian beef sandwiches, jerk steak with mango chutney, and Vietnamese noodle salad. The kitchen stays open until 11 PM, making the restaurant especially popular with the after-theater crowd. ✉ *2401 Montana Ave.* ☎ *406/245–7477* ▭ *AE, D, DC, MC, V.*

$$ ✕ **Enzo Bistro.** People come to this attractive chalet-style building for European, pan-Asian, and American specialties such as fresh fish prepared in flavorful sauces, dry-aged beef dishes, Mediterranean meat loaf with basil, cumin, and kalamata olives, and kids' favorites such as

pizzas and pastas. ✉*1502 Rehberg La., at Grand Ave.* ☎*406/651–0999* ▤*AE, DC, MC, V* ⊘*No lunch.*

$$ ✕**Thai Orchid.** When chef Lex Manraksa moved from Thailand to Billings, he brought with him authentic Thai cooking and spices Montana had never seen before. His downtown eatery is now a community fixture and gets especially popular with the business crowd around lunchtime. Manraksa is happy to talk with Thai-food connoisseurs and then serve them some superspicy traditional dishes; for the uninitiated he has plenty of milder dishes reminiscent of Chinese favorites. Look for entrées highlighting shrimp, oyster, and duck. ✉*2232 St. Andrews Dr.* ☎*406/256–2206* ▤*MC, V* ⊘*Closed Sun.*

$ ✕**Bruno's.** Traditional Italian music and artfully displayed antique pasta machines, old olive-oil cans from Italy, and utensils the owners have picked up over their decades in the restaurant business create a warm dining environment. Locals come for the homemade pasta, the veal, made-from-scratch meatballs, and specialty pizzas. There's a full bar, plus a modest selection of Italian wines and beers. ✉*1911 King Ave.* ☎*406/652–4416* ▤*AE, D, MC, V* ⊘*Closed Sun. No lunch.*

$ ✕**Pug Mahon's.** Good Irish stews, pasties, and traditional fish-and-chips
★ are the highlights of this authentic Irish pub, which serves dozens of imported beers and whiskies. The Sunday brunch is wildly popular. Be sure to try one of the 22 varieties of omelet. ✉*3011 1st Ave. N* ☎*406/259–4190* ▤*D, MC, V* ⊘*No dinner Sun.*

¢ ✕**Poet Street Market.** The distinctive sandwiches include roast beef with blue cheese, turkey with cranberry-apple compote on pumpkin bread, and artichoke hearts with white cheddar cheese on olive bread. The soups, salads, and pizzas are equally creative. It's difficult to leave without ordering dessert: catching sight of fresh concoctions such as chocolate Bavarian torte, bourbon spice cake, or sour cream pear tart is enough to make you hungry again. ✉*905 Poly Dr.* ☎*406/245–9501* ▤*AE, MC, V* ⊘*Closed Sun.*

WHERE TO STAY

$$–$$$$ ▦**Crowne Plaza.** The downtown location of this landmark high-rise is convenient, and the contemporary rooms are spacious and well appointed. Some rooms overlook the mountain ranges outside the city, and the deluxe suites are booked months, even years, in advance. The hotel features a comfortable lobby with large fireplace and in-house Starbucks. **Pros:** Montana's most luxurious hotel. Breathtaking views. **Cons:** The facade and lobby have a gritty urban feel. Restaurant could use some inspiration and more imaginative menu. ✉*27 N. 27th St., 59101* ☎*406/252–7400 or 800/588–7666* ⊕*www.crowneplaza.com* ⌁*289 rooms, 11 suites* ⌂*In-room: refrigerator (some), Wi-Fi. In-hotel: restaurant, bar, gym, no-smoking rooms* ▤*AE, D, DC, MC, V.*

$–$$$ ▦**Josephine Bed and Breakfast.** Within walking distance of downtown is this lovely historic home with five theme rooms—such as the Garden Room, with its floral fabrics. You're welcome to relax in the guest parlor, with a piano, coffee-table books, and newspapers, or in the library. Breakfast is served at your convenience; afterward, you can work off your meal with a free guest pass to the local YMCA. **Pros:** Is like staying in a favorite aunt's house, comfortably appointed and familiar yet not stifling. Thoughtful personal touch, from the food to the check-in and even phone reservations. **Cons:** Kids might feel as though they're being constantly monitored. ⊠ *514 N. 29th St., 59101* ☎ *406/248–5898 or 800/552–5898* ⊕ *www.thejosephine.com* ➦ *5 rooms* ⌂ *In-room: dial-up (some), Wi-Fi. In-hotel: public Internet, no-smoking rooms, no elevator* ☐ *AE, D, MC, V* ⊙ *BP.*

$–$$ 🏨 **C'mon Inn.** Five hot tubs and an indoor pool attract families to this lodging near the major roads and the interstate. Even in winter, there's a garden inside the woodsy, tropical courtyard, and wood-burning fireplaces in the lobby. **Pros:** Bathrooms are spacious and well appointed, attentive service, easy access off the interstate. **Cons:** Details are overlooked: So-so beds and generic rooms. ⊠ *2020 Overland Ave., 59102* ☎ *406/655–1100 or 800/655–1170* ⊕ *www.cmoninn.com* ➦ *72 rooms, 8 suites* ⌂ *In-room: refrigerator, microwave. In-hotel: pool, gym, no-smoking rooms, Wi-Fi* ☐ *AE, D, MC, V* ⊙ *CP.*

$–$$ 🏨 **Quality Inn Homestead.** A delightful outdoor sundeck and an indoor swim center are the main attractions here. The rooms are contemporary in design and average in size; the two-room suites are a favorite among families. The on-site car rentals are a bonus for business travelers. A complimentary full breakfast is made to order. **Pros:** Spacious rooms, made-to-order full breakfast, family-friendly swimming complex. **Cons:** Reservations must be made far in advance. ⊠ *2036 Overland Ave., 59102* ☎ *406/652–1320* ⊕ *www.qualityinn.com* ➦ *119 rooms, 60 suites* ⌂ *In-room: refrigerator (some). In-hotel: pool, laundry facilities, no-smoking rooms, no elevator* ☐ *AE, D, DC, MC, V* ⊙ *BP.*

¢–$ 🏨 **Dude Rancher Lodge.** As you might expect, a Western theme pervades this downtown institution, right down to the lantern-style light fixtures, wood paneling, and custom-made carpet "branded" with the symbols of several area ranches. The hotel has one suite with a full kitchen. Breakfast, which costs extra, is full and hearty. Try to get a room that opens on the courtyard parking lot. **Pros:** Within easy walking distance of attractions and restaurants. In-house restaurant offers affordable comfort food served with nice touches. Bathrooms have jet tubs. **Cons:** Rooms are small and beds need to be upgraded. Bathrooms are crowded. Hallways smell strongly of cigarettes. ⊠ *415 N. 29th St., 59101* ☎ *406/259–5561 or 800/221–3302* ⊕ *www.duderancherlodge. com* ➦ *56 rooms* ⌂ *In-room: refrigerator and microwave (some). In-hotel: restaurant, no-smoking rooms, some pets allowed, Wi-Fi, no elevator* ☐ *AE, D, DC, MC, V.*

¢   🏨 **The Carlin Hotel.** Transport yourself to the heydays of rail travel with a stay here, in rooms that are alternately elegant and classy but with steam-heat authenticity. Opened in 1910 for railroad passengers, the Carlin fell into disrepair, as did much of Billings's downtown district, with the demise of rail travel. But it was luxuriously restored in 2002 and now has suites fully furnished for extended stays (there's a one-week minimum). The suites, decorated almost entirely in black, white, and bright primary colors, are distinctly modern. The bathrooms are tiled, and the kitchens have dishwashers and hardwood floors. There's a restaurant and martini bar on the first floor. **Pros:** Great place for longer stays and location is prime for after-hours socializing or shopping in the funky stores of downtown's west end. **Cons:** Old fixtures work intermittently. Location can be a little sketchy after midnight. Cold in the winter and stifling in the summer. ⊠*2501 Montana Ave., 59101* ☎*406/245-7515* ⊕*www.carlinhotel.com* ⟳*8 suites* ⌂*In-room: refrigerator, Ethernet. In-hotel: restaurant, bar, no-smoking rooms* ⊟*AE, D, MC, V.*

NIGHTLIFE & THE ARTS

NIGHTLIFE

★ The **Carlin Martini Bar and Nightclub** (⊠*Carlin Hotel, 2501 Montana Ave.* ☎*406/245–2503*) offers live entertainment most nights, ranging from rock and blues bands to comedians and DJs. **Casey's Golden Pheasant** (⊠*222 N. Broadway* ☎*406/259-7762*) combines the Old West and the 1950s: the 1870s bar is solid mahogany, but the mural on the ceiling depicts 1950s rock stars, and neon signs hang from the walls. Various bands play almost every night of the week. A young crowd gathers at **Eleven: 11** (⊠*2526 Montana Ave.* ☎*406/238–0011*) to play pinball, air hockey, and pool. The music is almost exclusively punk rock, and modern art by regional artists decorates the walls. No alcohol is served here. After a long and fabled run as the Beanery Bar and Grill, Billings' 19th-century train depot has a new life as **McCleary's Tavern.** Solid food and beverages make this a consistent lunch spot for downtowners, but at night the bar is a favorite hangout for a younger, trendier set. ⊠*2314 Montana Ave.* ☎*406/839–9041.*

THE ARTS

The **Alberta Bair Theater** (⊠*2801 3rd Ave. N* ☎*406/256–6052 or 877/321-2074* ⊕*www.albertabairtheater.org*) presents music, theater, dance, and other cultural events. It's the home theater for the Billings Symphony Orchestra.

From paintings and etchings to sculpture and vintage rifles, the **Meadowlark Gallery** (⊠*118 N. 29th St.* ☎*406/294–8575 or 800/727–3949*) showcases all kinds of Western artwork. The owners are experts on painter-etchers Hans Kleiber and Bill Gollings, and they love to talk with interested customers. The works of modern artists living in the region are shown at the downtown **Toucan Gallery** (⊠*2505 Montana Ave.* ☎*406/252–0122*). The artwork varies from traditional paintings and sculptures to painted quilts, ceramics, jewelry, object collages, and dolls.

SHOPPING

Al's Bootery and Repair Shop (⊠*1820 1st Ave. N* ☎*406/245–4827*) corrals your toes into no-nonsense work boots, moccasins, and fancy cowboy boots ranging from $50 to $1,800. Billing itself as "a deli for the mind," **Barjon's Books** (⊠*221 N. 29th St.* ☎*406/252–4398 or 800/788–4318* ⊕*www.barjonsbooks.com*) sells incense, Celtic statuary, books on Buddhism, and more. The store hosts readings and talks by guests who include New Age authors and Buddhist monks and holds classes on topics as varied as belly dancing and New Age healing. **Rand's Custom Hats** (✉2205 1st Ave. N ☎406/248–7688 or 800/346–9815 ⊕www.randhats.com) creates cowboy hats for working cowboys and movie stars and will custom-fit a felt fur hat. Prices range from $300 to $2,000. Rand's also sells leather carrying cases.

EN
ROUTE ★
Although the route will take you slightly out of the way, take I–94 on your way to Hardin and stop at **Pompey's Pillar National Monument** (✉I–94, 25 mi east of Billings ☎406/875–2400 ⊕www.pompeyspillar.org ✉$7 per vehicle or free when interpretive center is closed ☉April 30–Labor Day, daily 8–8; Labor Day–Oct. 28, 9–4), the only on-site physical evidence of the Lewis and Clark expedition. When William Clark saw this small sandstone mesa rising out of the prairie along the Yellowstone River on July 25, 1806, he climbed to the top to survey the area and then marked it with his signature and the date. His graffiti, along with other engravings by early-19th-century fur traders and homesteaders, is still visible. You can climb to the top of the mesa and view the signature year-round during daylight hours. Festive "Clark Days" are held the last weekend in July, the anniversary of the explorer's visit to the knob. To get to Hardin, continue east on I–94 for a few miles and then head south on Highway 47.

SOUTHEAST MONTANA

Characterized by badlands, shallow canyons, grassy hills, and, above all, treeless plains, the land here survives on annual rainfall that just barely exceeds that of a desert. Aside from the livestock, this land belongs to ranchers and Native Americans—specifically the Crow and Northern Cheyenne, who both have reservations here. Few settlements in the region have more than 1,000 people, but most are friendly and almost always willing to show you around town—which sometimes consists of their home and the general store they run next door.

HARDIN

50 mi east of Billings via I–90.

Although its roots are firmly planted in cattle ranching, Hardin makes a significant portion of its living as a visitor gateway to the Little Bighorn Battlefield National Monument just a few miles to the south. It's also a popular base for exploring the several state parks and national recreation areas nearby. With 3,334 residents, Hardin is among the largest communities in southeast Montana.

The **Arapooish Fishing Access Site,** a mile north of Hardin, is a favorite spot among locals, who pack the family up, set up in a shaded picnic area, cast a line into the Bighorn River, and have a cookout. It's also a prime bird-watching venue. ✉Hwy. 47 ☎406/237–2940 ⊕www.fwp.

mt.gov 🎫*Free for Montana residents, $5 per vehicle for nonresidents* ⏱*Daily dawn–dusk.*

Focusing on Native American and early homestead settlement, the 22-acre **Bighorn County Historical Museum and Visitor Information Center** complex comprises 20 historic buildings that have been relocated to the site. The buildings are open May 1–October 1. ✉*I–90, Exit 497* ☎*406/665–1671* ⊕*www.museumonthebighorn.org* 🎫*Free* ⏱*May–Sept., daily 8–6; Oct.–Apr., daily 9–5.*

★ During the third week in August, a stretch of land along the Bighorn River becomes the "teepee capital of the world" when the **Crow Fair and Rodeo,** official fair of the Crow tribe, begins north of the town of Crow Agency. The festival focuses on traditional dances, activities, and sports tournaments. ✉*Bighorn River north of Crow Agency, 14 mi south of Hardin on I–90* ☎*406/638–3793* 🎫*Free.*

OFF THE BEATEN PATH

The Montana Dinosaur Trail. Eastern Montana 200 million years ago was a swampy, wet place populated by seashore jungles, swamps, and dinosaurs. Today the badlands and breaks of the region are the nation's paleontological hot spots. Many of the best dinosaur fossils have been taken to New York's Museum of Natural History and the Smithsonian, but you can see original inhabitants of the region at dust-country museums and state-of-the-art interpretive centers across Eastern Montana. The Dinosaur Trail includes 13 stops, from Jack Horner's collection at the Museum of the Rockies in Bozeman to a field station at Fort Peck. ☎*800/847–4868* ⊕*www.mtdinotrail.org.*

WHERE TO STAY & EAT

$$ ✕**Purple Cow.** This family eatery with a friendly staff is a favorite among

Fodor's Choice travelers, largely because heading eastward it's one of the last restau-

★ rants for more than 200 mi. The shakes and malts are fantastic, as are the burgers and steaks. Portions are generous, so you might want to consider splitting some items, such as the delectable BLT. ✉*I–90, Exit 495* ☎*406/665–3601* 🟰*MC, V.*

¢–$$ 🏨**American Inn.** The massive waterslide that towers above the outdoor pool is the most noticeable feature of this lodging off I–90. Tans, browns, and dark reds decorate the guest rooms, a bracing change from the sterile beiges and pastels of most chain hotels. **Pros:** Easy access off Interstate 90. Great for families. **Cons:** Rooms are large but bathrooms are tight. ✉*1324 N. Crawford Ave., 59034* ☎*406/665–1870* 🖨*406/665–1492* 🛏*43 rooms* 🛎*In-room: refrigerator. In-hotel: restaurant, bar, pool, Wi-Fi, laundry facilities, no-smoking rooms, some pets allowed, no elevator* 🟰*AE, D, MC, V* 🍴*CP.*

CAMPING 🏕**Grandview Campground.** Cable TV, nightly ice-cream socials, and movie rentals are some of the extras at this full-service campground. On the edge of town, in the narrow corridor between downtown Hardin and I–90, it lies next door to the Hardin Community Activity Center, giving you access to an Olympic-size indoor pool and fitness facilities. The owner is a font of knowledge and takes great pride in the community. The Grandview is open year-round, but only a few electric sites are available in winter. 🛎*Flush toilets, full hookups, dump* *station, drinking water, Wi-Fi, guest laundry, showers, picnic tables, electricity, public telephone, play area, swimming (indoor pool)* ⇌*50 full hookups, 30 tent sites* ⊠*1002 N. Mitchell* ☎*406/665–2489 or 800/622–9890* ⊕*www.grandviewcamp.com* ▭*MC, V.*

LITTLE BIGHORN BATTLEFIELD NATIONAL MONUMENT

17 mi south of Hardin via I–90.

When the smoke cleared on June 25, 1876, neither Lieutenant Colonel George Armstrong Custer (1839–76) nor his 200 or so blue-shirted troopers were alive to tell the story of their battle against several thousand Northern Plains warriors led by Sitting Bull (circa 1831–90) and Crazy Horse (1842–77). It was a Pyrrhic victory for the tribes; the loss pushed the U.S. government to redouble its efforts to clear them off the plains. Now the Little Bighorn Battlefield, on the Crow Indian Reservation, memorializes the warriors who took part in the conflict, with monuments and an interpretive center. The site, a windswept prairie along the Little Bighorn River, remains largely undeveloped. Note that there are rattlesnakes around the area, and also beware of touching the flesh-piercing yucca plants.

The interpretive exhibits at the **Little Bighorn Battlefield Visitor Center** explain the events that led to and resulted from the battle, as well as the deeper issues regarding the historical conflict between white and Native American culture. Talks by park rangers contain surprises for even the most avid history buff. ⊠*Battlefield Rd.* ☎*406/638–3204* ⊙*Memorial Day–July, daily 8–9; Aug.–Labor Day, daily 8–8; Sept. and Oct., daily 8–6; Nov.–Mar., daily 8–4:30; Apr.–late May, daily 8–6.*

The old stone superintendent's house is now the **White Swan Memorial Library,** which has one of the most extensive collections of research material on the Battle of the Little Bighorn. You can view the material by appointment only; contact the visitor center for more information.

Among those interred at **Custer National Cemetery,** near the visitor center, are Custer's second-in-command, Marcus Reno; some of Custer's Native American scouts; and many soldiers from more modern wars, from World Wars I and II to Korea and Vietnam. Note that you can visit the cemetery without paying the park entrance fee.

For more than 120 years the only memorial to those killed in the battle was the towering obelisk of the **7th Cavalry Monument** at the top of Last Stand Hill. Although the hill isn't particularly high, it affords a good overall view of the battlefield site.

★ Until the **Indian Memorial** was unveiled in 2003, the battlefield's only monument paid tribute to the immediate losers. Although they are meant to honor Native Americans who died on both sides (Custer had a few Crow and Arikara scouts), the three bronze riders of this memorial represent the united forces of the Lakota Sioux, Northern Cheyenne, and Arapahoe, who defeated the government troops. The stone opening off to the side forms a "spirit gate" welcoming the dead riders.

Scattered around the battlefield are short white **markers** indicating the places where soldiers died. Although the markers may look like graves, the actual bodies are interred elsewhere, including that of Custer, whose remains at rest at the military academy at West Point. One marker belongs to Custer's younger brother, Thomas, the most decorated soldier of the Civil War. Nineteen red markers represent Native American warriors, in part because no one knows exactly where they fell: the Native American survivors buried their dead immediately after the battle in traditional fashion.

WHERE TO EAT

¢–$ ✕ **Custer Battlefield Trading Post and Cafe.** With its stock of T-shirts, inexpensive jewelry, Indian fry bread mix, and dreamcatchers, the trading post is touristy, but the small attached restaurant is quite good—as evidenced by the locals who regularly congregate here. Steak is the dish of choice, and there are no fewer than three ways to get it on a sandwich. The several variations of Indian taco made by the Crow cooks are especially popular. ⊠*I–90 at U.S. 212* ☎*406/638–2270* ⊕*www.laststand.com* ▭*D, MC, V.*

BIGHORN CANYON NATIONAL RECREATION AREA

7

40 mi southwest of Little Bighorn Battlefield National Monument via I–90 and Hwy. 313.

Centered around a 60-mi-long lake, this park stretches between the Pryor and Bighorn mountains, well into Wyoming. Really just a wide spot on the Bighorn River, the lake fills much of Bighorn Canyon, whose steep walls, carved by geological upheaval and the force of wind and water, are too rugged for casual access. Most people visit the park by boat, which is the only way within the park to get directly from the northern unit, in Montana, to the southern unit, much of which is in Wyoming. Most of the major sights are accessible by boat, but you can also reach them by driving north from Wyoming on Highway 37. If you're visiting from Wyoming, Lovell makes a good base for exploring the area. Check locally about useable boat ramps; fluctuating lake levels can leave the upper 15 mi mostly dry. ☎*307/548–2251 or 406/666–2412* ⊕*www.nps.gov/bica/* ⊠*$5 per vehicle* ☉*Daily 24 hrs.*

The **Yellowtail Dam Visitor Center** in the northern unit features exhibits focusing on the life of Crow Chief Robert Yellowtail, the Crow people, the history of the Bighorn River, the dam's construction, and the wildlife in the area, including the wild mustangs that roam the high grasslands of the Pryor Mountains above the canyon. ⊠*Hwy. 313, Fort Smith* ☎*406/666–3218* ⊕*www.nps.gov/bica/* ⊠*Included in $5 admission to recreation area* ☉*Memorial Day–Labor Day, daily 9–5.*

The old **Hillsboro Dude Ranch** complex is probably the best known and easiest to reach of the four ranch ruins within the recreation area. There are old log cabins, cellars, chicken coops, and other buildings that belonged to Grosvener W. Barry, one of the area's more colorful characters in the early 20th century. He attempted three gold-mining ventures, all of which failed, before opening a dude ranch here. ⊠ *Hwy. 37* ⊕ *www.nps.gov/bica/* ☜ *Included in $5 admission to recreation area.*

Fodor's Choice
★ When Spanish explorers introduced horses to the Americas, some of the animals inevitably escaped and roamed wild across the land. You can see some of the last members of these breeds in the **Pryor Mountain Wild Horse Range,** the first such nationally designated refuge. Some 200 horses, generally broken into small family groupings, roam these arid slopes with bighorn sheep, elk, deer, and mountain lions. Coat variations such as grulla, blue roan, dun, and sabino indicate Spanish lineage, as do markings such as dorsal stripes, zebra stripes on the legs, and a stripe on the withers. The best way to view the herds is simply to drive along Highway 37 and look out your window. ⊠ *Hwy. 37* ☎ *406/896–5013* ⊕ *www.kbrhorse.net/wclo/blmdak01.html* ☜ *Included in $5 admission to recreation area.*

★ **Devil's Canyon Overlook,** a few miles north of the Wyoming border, affords breathtaking views of the point where narrow Devil's Canyon joins sheer-walled Bighorn Canyon. The overlook itself is on a cliff 1,000 feet above the lake. Look for fossils in the colorful rock layers of the canyon walls. ⊠ *Hwy. 37* ⊕ *www.nps.gov/bica/* ☜ *Included in $5 admission to recreation area.*

The **Crooked Creek Ranger Station,** past the south entrance of the park in Wyoming, houses exhibits about the four historic ranches within the recreation area. A small shop sells books related to the local history and geology. ⊠ *Hwy. 37, WY* ☎ *307/548–7326* ⊕ *www.nps. gov/bica/* ☜ *Included in $5 admission to recreation area* ⊙ *Daily; hrs vary by season.*

The main visitor center for the park, the **Bighorn Canyon Visitor Center** has geological and historical exhibits on the area, as well as a film about the canyon. Two shorter movies, one on the Pryor Mountain wild horses and the other about Medicine Wheel National Historic Landmark (east of Lovell), are shown on request. A small store sells books and other regional items. ⊠ *U.S. 310 at U.S. 14A, Lovell WY* ☎ *307/548–2251* ⊕ *www.nps.gov/bica/* ☜ *Free* ⊙ *Memorial Day–Labor Day, daily 8–6; Labor Day–Memorial Day, daily 8–5.*

OFF THE BEATEN PATH

Chief Plenty Coups State Park. Although many Plains Indian tribes opposed the intrusion of whites into their lands, the Crow did not. Hoping that U.S. troops would keep the rival Cheyenne and Lakota off their lands, the Crow allied themselves with the U.S. government. Ultimately, the army protected Crow territory from the other tribes— but only so it could be settled by whites. Despite the betrayal, the last traditional chief of the Crow, Plenty Coups, strongly encouraged his people to adopt modern ways and cooperate with the U.S. government. At his request, his home and general store in the town of Pryor were preserved as a state park after his death. Note the blending of modern and traditional ways, such as the room of honor in the rear of his log home, meant to parallel the place of honor along the back wall

CLOSE UP

Walking Alone

The total isolation possible in this great and empty land is a rare thing. Eastern Montana is one of the few places left in the world where you can feel truly alone.

As any local will tell you, a stroll through a wildlife refuge or a drive along a quiet county road is an excellent way to take some time for yourself. You don't need to pull out your yoga mat to absorb the solitude; just try to make time—even if it's only a few minutes—to take a walk by yourself. No kids, no spouse, not even the family dog—just you, the rocks, the grass, and the incredible sky that stretches endlessly into the distance.

Towering canyon walls make Bighorn Canyon National Recreation Area a good place to withdraw from civilization, so long as you're far enough away from the lake and its motorboats. Another distinctive place to experience Montana's silence is among the eerie rock formations of the badlands in Makoshika State Park.

Near Havre, the Bears Paw Mountains are among the most ancient in the world. The Big Snowy Mountains have miles of peaceful old-growth forest in which to wander, and the Charles M. Russell National Wildlife Refuge is so sprawling that it's easy to lose yourself—no kidding, so be sure to take a map with you wherever you go.

of a teepee. Parks Passports are not valid here. ✉ *1 mi west of Pryor on county road, Pryor* ☎ *406/252–1289* ⊕ *www.mt.gov/parks/* 🖅 *$2* ⊙ *May–Sept., daily 8–8.*

SPORTS & THE OUTDOORS

The Lewis and Clark expedition, and later, fur traders avoided the Bighorn River at all costs, for the narrow channel, high canyon walls, and sharp rocks were treacherous. With the construction of the Yellowtail Dam in the 1960s, however, the water levels in the canyon rose above most rocky obstacles and created new access points along the shore of the now-tamed river. The fishing here—for smallmouth bass, rainbow and brown trout, walleye, yellow perch, and more—is excellent above the dam. Below the dam, the cold, clear water exiting the hydropower facility has created a world-class trout fishery. Many visitors never wet a line, opting instead to simply rest on the water and enjoy the calm winds and pleasant views.

Fluctuating reservoir levels, caused by extended drought and light mountain snowpack, can periodically shut down the lake's marinas and boat launches. Because canyon walls create sharp turns and bottlenecks in the lake, there are some boating speed limits. All the marinas on Bighorn Lake operate during the peak summer season and are closed in the fall, winter and early spring.

Boats can be docked or rented in the northern unit of the park at **Ok-A-Beh Marina** (✉ *Off Hwy. 313, on north end of lake* ☎ *406/665–2216*). The facilities here aren't luxurious, but you'll find a basic eatery, a few groceries, tackle, a swimming area, and reasonable rates. One of the most popular boat launches in the southern unit is **Barry's Landing**

(⊠ *Hwy. 37* ☎ *406/666–2412*). There isn't much here—not even electricity—but the scenic campground, shaded picnic area, and central location are big draws. Many boats in the southern unit are based at **Horseshoe Bend Marina** (⊠ *Hwy. 37, WY*), which has boat rentals, a beach, a small general store, a modest restaurant, and the largest campground in the park. A nearby buildup of silt from the Shoshone and Bighorn rivers has made boat launching here a tricky business.

CAMPING

🏕 **Black Canyon Campground.** This campground, about 5 mi south of the Ok-A-Beh Marina up the tight Black Canyon Creek, is accessible only by boat, and only during high water. It's very primitive, but the isolation is unmatched. ⚭ *Pit toilets, bear boxes, fire pits, picnic tables, swimming (lake)* 🛏 *17 sites* ⊠ *Black Canyon Creek* ☎ *406/666–3218* ⊕ *www.nps.gov/bica/* ⚭ *Reservations not accepted.*

🏕 **Horseshoe Bend Campground.** The proximity to the marina in the southern unit makes this, the largest campground in the park, especially popular, although never very busy. It's open all year, but most services are unavailable in winter. ⚭ *Flush toilets, dump station, drinking water, fire pits, picnic tables, food service, electricity, public telephone, general store, swimming (lake)* 🛏 *54 sites* ⊠ *Hwy. 37, WY* ☎ *307/548–7230* ⊕ *www.nps.gov/bica/* ⚭ *Reservations not accepted.*

🏕 **Medicine Creek Campground.** Just north of Barry's Landing, the isolated site offers a good central location without the summer bustle of some other camping spots. You can boat or hike in. ⚭ *Pit toilets, picnic tables, swimming (lake)* 🛏 *6 sites* ⊠ *Medicine Creek* ☎ *307/548–2251* ⊕ *www.nps.gov/bica/* ⚭ *Reservations not accepted.*

MILES CITY

160 mi northeast of Bighorn Canyon National Recreation Area via Hwy. 313 and I–94.

History buffs enjoy the ranch town of Miles City (population 8,487), at the confluence of the cottonwood-lined Tongue and Yellowstone rivers. The federal Fort Laramie Treaty of 1868 stated that this land would be "Indian country as long as the grass is green and the sky is blue." The government reneged on its promise only six years later, when gold was found in the Black Hills of South Dakota to the southeast. White settlers streamed into the area, setting in motion events that led to the Battle of the Little Bighorn. After the battle the army built a new post less than 2 mi from where Miles City would be founded. In time the ranchers took over, and in 1884, the last of the great herds of bison was slaughtered near here to make room for cattle. Ranching has been a way of life ever since.

★ The third weekend in May, Miles City holds its famed **Bucking Horse Sale,** a three-day event with a rodeo, a concert, and a giant block party. Rodeo-stock contractors come from all over the country to buy the spirited horses sold here. Faded Wranglers and cowboy boots are proudly displayed downtown, along with open containers and a sort of rowdy civic pride. ⊠*Fairground Rd. at Main St.* ☎*406/234–2890 or 877/632–2890* ⊕*www.buckinghorsesale.com* ▣*$8.*

★ Although the holding tanks of an old water-treatment plant don't seem like the best location for fine art, the **Custer County Art Museum**, in the town's 1910 wastewater facility overlooking the Yellowstone River, is actually very attractive. The permanent exhibit reflects the town's Western heritage; the traveling shows are a bit more varied. The museum store features a variety of original artworks, reproductions, ceramics, and a good selection of Western history books. ⊠*Water Plant Rd.* ☎*406/234–0635* ⊕*www.ccac.milescity.org* ▣*Free* ☉*Oct.–May, daily 1–5, June–Sept., daily 9–5.*

★ Wind and water carved holes in the sandstone pillars north of Ekalaka, creating an eerie and barren landscape. Embracing the terrain's mystery, Native Americans used the site for rituals to conjure spirits centuries ago. Teddy Roosevelt was struck by the area's unique beauty when he visited in the late 19th century. In 1957 the area was designated **Medicine Rocks State Park**. The 320-acre park is largely undeveloped; aside from a few picnic tables, a short hiking trail, and a handful of unmarked campsites, the land is exactly how it was when Native Americans first performed their ceremonies here. ⊠*Hwy. 7* ☎*406/234–0900* ⊕*www. fwp.mt.gov/parks/* ▣*Free* ☉*Daily 24 hrs.*

The **Range Riders Museum**, built on the site of the 1877 Fort Keogh, is jammed to the rafters with saddles, chaps, spurs, guns, and other frontier artifacts. Some of the nine museum buildings of this complex were once part of the fort, which was abandoned in the 1920s after being used as a remount station during World War I. The volunteers and staff love to talk about local history and are great sources for information about modern amenities, too. ⊠*435 L.P. Anderson Rd., across Tongue River Bridge on west end of Main St., Exit 135 off I-94* ☎*406/232–4483 or 406/232–6146* ▣*$5* ☉*Apr.–Oct., daily 8–5:30.*

Pirogue Island State Park, a 269-acre chunk of land in the middle of the Yellowstone River, is completely undeveloped; the only way to access the park is by floating down the river or fording in times of low water. The cottonwood trees are an excellent habitat for waterfowl, raptors, and deer, and the geology of the island makes it prime agate-hunting ground. ⊠*1 mi north of Miles City on Hwy. 59, 2 mi east on Kinsey Rd., then 2 mi south on county road* ☎*406/234–0900* ⊕*www.fwp. mt.gov/lands/site_283962.aspx* ▣*Free* ☉*Daily 24 hrs.*

WHERE TO STAY & EAT

¢–$$$ ✕**Mama Stella's Pizza.** You can always opt for traditional pies, but you may want to try one of Mama Stella's imaginative creations, such as pizza topped with white Alfredo sauce. Unusual toppings include sauerkraut and asparagus. There are also several sandwiches with Italian and domestic flairs. Mama delivers and stays open until 10 PM on weeknights and until midnight on weekends—no small accomplishment in a town with fewer than 9,000 residents. ⊠*Trail's Inn Bar and Comedy Club, 607 Main St.* ☎*406/234–2922* ▭*AE, D, MC, V.*

¢–$ 🏨 **Best Western War Bonnet Inn.** The two-room family suites and complimentary hot breakfast make this chain hotel stand out. It's on the edge of town near I–94. **Pros:** Easy access off Interstate 90, and fairly easy walk or short drive to the vehicle-friendly cafés and gas stations off the highway. Serviceable rooms and decent breakfast. **Cons:** Restaurant is dated and even a little dingy. Stay here for a quick overnight, not for the amenities. Truck traffic can be distracting. ✉ *1015 S. Haynes Ave., 59301* ☎ *406/234–4560* ⊕ *www.bestwestern.com* ↗ *53 rooms, 4 suites* ♿ *In-hotel: pool, fitness center, Wi-Fi, no-smoking rooms* ▤ *AE, D, DC, MC, V* ⦿ *CP, BP.*

CAMPING   △ **Medicine Rocks Campground.** Although these campsites are primitive—they aren't even marked—the weathered rocks here make an incredible backdrop for a night sleeping under the stars. ♿ *Pit toilets, drinking water, picnic tables* ↗ *12 tent sites; 12 RV sites* ✉ *Off Hwy. 7* ☎ *406/234–0900* ⊕ *www.fwp.mt.gov/parks/* ⟐ *Reservations not accepted.*

NIGHTLIFE

The downtown **Trail's Inn Bar and Comedy Club** (✉ *607 Main St.* ☎ *406/234–2922*) draws regional and national comedy acts. Satisfy your munchies at the on-site Mama Stella's Pizza restaurant.

SHOPPING

★   The craftspeople at **Miles City Saddlery** (✉ *808 Main St.* ☎ *406/232–2512*), in business since 1909, custom-design saddles of legendary quality. They also craft saddlebags, holsters, and other leather goods. Even if you're not buying, this is worth a stop.

THE BIG OPEN

Revel in wild grasslands, stark badlands, unhindered skylines, and spectacular sunsets, far from the rumble of jetliners, the roar of traffic, and the ringing of cell phones. A great triangle bounded by the Yellowstone River to the south, the Missouri River to the north, and U.S. 87 to the west, the region comprises nearly 10% of the state of Montana. Its residents, however, represent less than 1% of the state's total population, and the number is shrinking. This is a region with barely 1,000 people between the two largest towns (Jordan, with 364 residents, and Circle, with 644), where the livestock outnumbers the people 100 to 1. One winter the tumbleweeds clogged a highway so badly that the state had to send out snowplows to clear the way.

MAKOSHIKA STATE PARK

84 mi northeast of Miles City via I–94 and N. Merrill Ave.

★   Named after the Lakota word for "bad land," Makoshika State Park encompasses more than 11,000 acres of Montana's badlands, distinct rock formations also found in Wyoming and the Dakotas. The bare rock walls and mesas of the park create an eerie moonscape that is only occasionally broken by a crooked pine or juniper tree warped by the hard rock and lack of water. Practically a desert, the badlands are excellent fossil grounds, and the remains of tyrannosaurs and triceratops have been found here.

At the entrance of the park, the largest in Fish, Wildlife & Parks' state-parks system, is the small **Visitor Information Center,** with information on the park's history and geology. A few fossils are on display, including a triceratops skull. ☎406/377–6256 ⊕*www.fwp.mt.gov/lands/ site_283890.aspx* ⊙*Daily 9–5.*

Interpretive signs explain the geology of the rock layers visible on the ½-mi loop of the **Cap Rock Nature Trail,** which begins on Cains Coulee Road, a few miles from the park entrance. The trail affords excellent views of a natural rock bridge. Beginning at the campground, the 1½-mi **Diane Gabriel Trail** loops through both badlands and prairie terrain. At the halfway point a duck-billed-dinosaur fossil is embedded in a cliff. The ½-mi **Kinney Coulee Trail** starts about 4 mi south of the park entrance and leads 300 feet down a canyon. The terrain here is a bit more forested than elsewhere in the park, but the rock formations are the real stars. ⊠*Makoshika State Park Rd.* ☎406/377–6256 ⊕*www.fwp.mt.gov/parks/* 🖅*$5 per vehicle for nonresidents, free for Montana residents* ⊙*Daily 24 hrs.*

WHERE TO STAY

$ 🏠**Charley Montana Bed & Breakfast.** Built by ranching mogul Charles Krug in 1907, this solid brick home looks like a fortress compared with its stick-built Victorian contemporaries. Indeed, with more than 25 rooms and 8,000 square feet, this place sometimes seems more like a castle than a B&B. The interior is decidedly soft, however, and much of the Krug family's period furniture is still in use. **Pros:** Owners are friendly and helpful. This is a great base to explore the Yellowstone river and nearby badlands. **Cons:** The building and some fixtures feel old. Downtown location is handy, but there are few remarkable places to eat or drink. ⊠*103 N. Douglas, Glendive 59330* ☎888/395–3207 ⊕*charley-montana.com* 🖅*5 rooms* ⚲*In-room: refrigerators (some). In-hotel: no-smoking rooms, no elevator* ⊟*AE, D, MC, V* ⊙*BP.*

CAMPING ⚐**Makoshika State Park Campground.** This small campground doesn't offer much in the way of amenities, but the views of the surrounding sheer cliffs and stone bluffs are incredible. There's a Frisbee-golf course nearby. Some facilities are at the nearby visitor center. ⚲*Flush toilets, drinking water, fire pits, picnic tables, electricity, public telephone, ranger station* 🖅*22 sites* ⊠*Makoshika State Park Rd.* ☎406/377–6256 ⊕*www.fwp.mt.gov/parks/* ⊟*No credit cards.*

EN ROUTE The drive from Makoshika State Park to Fort Peck will take you along the Hi-Line, otherwise known as U.S. 2, through the **Fort Peck Indian Reservation** (⊠*U.S. 2* ☎406/768–5155). Like most of Montana, much of the land here is empty; at nearly 2 million acres, the reservation is home to only 6,800 tribal members. However, the reservation does have a bustling industrial center, a community college, and an interesting tribal cultural center and museum in Poplar.

FORT PECK

147 mi northwest of Makoshika State Park via Hwy. 200S, Hwy. 13, U.S. 2 and Hwy. 117.

Fort Peck itself is nearly a ghost town today, with 240 residents; at night, the lights of ranch houses here are few and far between. It owes its existence to Fort Peck Dam, built on the Missouri River during the Great Depression. One of President Franklin Roosevelt's earliest and largest New Deal projects, the Fort Peck Dam provided a source of water and jobs.

★ The 18,000-square-foot **Fort Peck Interpretive Center** features interpretive displays recounting the history and significance of the dam's construction, wildlife of the lower river and Missouri River Breaks, and one of the most striking life-size dinosaur displays in the West. It's a replica of Peck's Rex, a tyrannosaurus rex found near Fort Peck, and other local dinosaur discoveries are also detailed here. The center also features the largest aquariums in Montana, filled with the native and introduced fish species of Fort Peck Reservoir and the Missouri River. Guided tours of the dam and its power plants are available April through October. ⊠*Lower Yellowstone Rd.* ☎*406/526–3493* ⊕*www.corpslakes. us/fortpeck* ⊠*Free* ☉*Oct. 1–Apr. 30, weekdays 10–4; May 1–Sept. 30, daily 9–5.*

At the peak of dam construction, nearly 11,000 workers lived in Fort Peck; together with their families, they made up a thriving population center of 50,000. To help keep the populace entertained, the Army Corps of Engineers built a movie house in 1934. It was supposed to be a temporary structure, but instead it eventually became the **Fort Peck Summer Theatre.** The chalet-style building is a venue for live entertainment weekend nights in summer. ⊠*110 5th St.* ☎*406/228–9219* ⊕*www. fortpecktheatre.org/* ⊠*$15* ☉*June–Aug., Fri.–Sun. 7–midnight.*

SPORTS & THE OUTDOORS

Stretching 134 mi across the border between the Big Open and the Hi-Line (U.S. 2), Fort Peck Reservoir is a prime outdoor-adventure destination. Fishing is especially popular here, with Walleye being the lake's most well-known fish. Other species include northern pike, lake trout, smallmouth bass, and Chinook salmon. Outfitters are hard to come by, so be sure to get most of your supplies before you arrive. The lake is the venue for the annual **Governor's Cup Walleye Tournament** (☎*406/228–2222* ⊕*www.mtgovcup.com/*) held the second weekend in July.

The **Fort Peck Dredge Cuts** (⊠*Hwy. 117* ☎*406/228–3700*), also known as the Fort Peck Trout Pond, is a state fishing access site just below Fort Peck Dam off the Missouri River. It has a boat launch and family-friendly swimming beaches. The **Rock Creek Marina** (⊠*652 S. Rock Creek Rd.* ☎*406/485–2560*) has marina facilities, a boat launch, and a modern campground on the remote Big Dry Arm of the lake. **Fort Peck Marina** on the west side of Fort Peck Dam is probably the most accessible concession on the big lake. The store has basic and walleye-specific fishing tackle, bait, boat gas, and a boat-repair facility. The associated bar has beverages to go or for on-site consumption, and a simple restaurant. (⊠ *West End Dr.* ☎*406/526–3442*)

WHERE TO STAY

¢–$ 🏨 **Fort Peck Hotel.** Just about every piece of furniture in this lodgelike wooden building dates from the hotel's construction during the Great Depression. Inside, the thick beams, sturdy rafters, and Western style transport you back to the 1930s. Accommodations are small and modest, and most bathrooms have showers, but some have massive clawfoot bathtubs. The adjoining rustic dining room serves three square meals a day for an additional charge. The hotel, listed on the National Historic Registry, is popular with hunters in the fall and with arts patrons in the summer. Packages that include lodging, meals, and theater tickets are available. **Pros:** Authentic 1930s feel. The restaurant is spacious and the front porch is a wonderful place to wind down. **Cons:** Creaking floors, dripping faucets, and creaking beds make this seem more like a summer camp than a hotel. In the summertime the mosquitoes can drive you inside. ⊠*175 S. Missouri St., 59223* ☎*406/526–3266 or 800/560–4931* 🖷*406/526–3472* ⬎*38 rooms* ⏦*In-room: no phone, no TV. In-hotel: no-smoking rooms, public Wi-Fi no elevator* 🚫*D, MC, V.*

CAMPING   ⛺ **Downstream Campground.** Known locally as Kiwanis Park, this large and wooded campground sits just below Fort Peck Dam on the shores of the Missouri River. If Kiwanis is full—and it's popular with Hi-Liners on holiday weekends—then drive past Fort Peck Marina to West End Campground. ⏦*Flush toilets, pit toilets, partial hookups (electric), dump station, drinking water, showers, picnic tables, electricity, public telephone, play area, swimming (lake)* ⬎*71 partial hookups, 3 tent sites* ⊠*Hwy. 24 N* ☎*406/526–3224* 🖷*406/526–3593* 🚫*AE, D, MC, V.*

7

CHARLES M. RUSSELL NATIONAL WILDLIFE REFUGE

1 mi south of Fort Peck via Missouri Ave.

Bordering the shores of Fort Peck Lake—and extending west more than 100 mi to U.S. Highway 191—is the massive Charles M. Russell National Wildlife Refuge, a 1.1-million-acre preserve teeming with more than 200 species of birds, including bald eagles and game birds; 45 different mammals, including elk, antelope, prairie dogs, and deer; and a variety of fish and reptiles. But this is also a refuge for history: each year scientists from around the country march into the preserve, and each year they find something new, whether it's dinosaur bones, buffalo jumps, teepee rings, or an old homesteader's shack. The refuge is open for hiking, horseback riding, fishing, boating, and other activities. Several access roads run through the area; most of these are unpaved, aside from U.S. 191, which runs north–south through the western edge of the refuge. ☎*406/538–8706* ⊕*cmr.fws.gov* 🏷*Free* ⏰*Daily 24 hrs.*

There are three staffed **field stations** (✉ *U.S. 91, Hwy. 200, and Hwy. 24* ☎ *406/538–8706* ⊕ *cmr.fws.gov*) in the refuge: the **Sand Creek Wildlife Station**, the **Jordan Wildlife Station**, and the **Fort Peck Wildlife Station**. Although they have no public facilities, they are conveniently scattered around the park, and are sources for maps, road conditions, and points of interest. If they're in, the rangers will help you with directions or problems.

★ Hundreds of elk congregate in evening in the fall at the **Slippery Ann Wildlife Viewing Area** (✉ *U.S. 191*). During the autumn mating season, the bulls violently lock horns while herds of cows come to watch and be courted. Be sure to bring binoculars and zoom lenses for your camera, because you must keep your distance from these massive animals.

A refuge within a refuge, the **UL Bend National Wildlife Refuge** consists of more than 20,000 acres of wilderness entirely within the boundaries of the Charles M. Russell National Wildlife Refuge. Its primary mission at the moment is to rescue one of the nation's most endangered animals: the black-footed ferret. The ferrets depend on the high concentration of prairie dog towns for food. There are also plenty of grouse and burrowing owls, who use abandoned prairie dog tunnels for homes. ✉ *UL Bend National Wildlife Refuge Rd.* ☎ *406/538–8706* ⊕ *cmr.fws.gov* 💲 *Free* 🕑 *Daily 24 hrs.*

THE HI-LINE

The Hi-Line is named for U.S. 2, which connects Houlton, Maine, with Everett, Washington. The most northerly road traveling east–west across the United States, the highway plows a path almost straight through northern Montana until it reaches the Rockies. Remote prairies, northern wetlands, and scattered forests make this area a haven both for wildlife and for the few people who live here. There may not be a Starbucks on every corner, or even a movie theater within 100 mi, but Hi-Line residents wouldn't have it any other way.

MEDICINE LAKE NATIONAL WILDLIFE REFUGE COMPLEX

230 mi northeast of Charles M. Russell National Wildlife Refuge via Larb Creek Rd. and U.S. 2.

Established in 1935, this refuge sandwiched between U.S. 2 and the Canadian border encompasses more than 30,000 acres of wetlands that provide habitat for dozens of mammal species, including beaver, muskrat, and bobcats, and a variety of shorebirds and upland birds. Medicine Lake hosts one of the largest concentrations of American pelicans in the nation. There are few facilities available, but that's the point.

Winding through the central unit of the refuge is the **Auto Tour Route,** an excellent way to get a peek at the animals that call this pristine park home. Most of the route is open only during daylight hours.

The **Observation Tower,** adjacent to the refuge headquarters, provides a good overview of the lakes in the refuge and the surrounding terrain. From above the trees and tall reeds, you can see the distinct lakes and ponds, as well as the sand hills around the borders. Birders often congregate in the **Grouse Observation Blind,** 2¼ mi east of the refuge headquarters, to take a good look at the resident bird species. The covered area is also good for watching other wildlife. ⊠*223 North Shore Rd.* ☎*406/789–2305* ⊕*medicinelake.fws.gov/* ▭*Free* ⊙*Daily dawn–dusk.*

BOWDOIN NATIONAL WILDLIFE REFUGE

200 mi west of Medicine Lake National Wildlife Refuge via U.S. 2.

An oxbow of the Missouri River before the last ice age, Bowdoin National Wildlife Refuge is a massive series of lakes and wetlands a few miles east of Malta. Before the government started to administer the refuge, water levels would drastically vary by season, making it a poor breeding ground for birds—but an excellent breeding ground for disease. Since the construction of several dikes and water channels in the 1930s, however, the water levels of the lakes have remained fairly constant, and the 15,000-acre preserve now shelters numerous birds and mammals. Aside from typical prairie animals and field songbirds, there are sizeable populations of pelicans, gulls, and herons. Several protected species also live here, including the piping plover, black-footed ferret, bald eagle, and peregrine falcon.

As the main road through the refuge, the **Bowdoin Refuge Auto Tour Route** affords excellent views of the terrain and wildlife. Old U.S. 2 is another main route, but it doesn't compare to the slower and far more scenic experience of the Auto Tour.

The **Bowdoin Wildlife Refuge Headquarters,** at the main entrance to Bowdoin, provides information on refuge conditions, species lists, a variety of mounted birds and mammals, and instructions for a drivable tour route. ⊠*Bowdoin Refuge Auto Tour Rte.* ☎*406/654–2863* ⊕*bowdoin.fws.gov* ▭*Free* ⊙*Weekdays 8–5.*

Birders and wildlife photographers come to the **Pearce Waterfowl Production Area Bird Blind,** on the northeast edge of the refuge, for great views. ☎*406/654–2863* ⊕*bowdoin.fws.gov* ▭*Free* ⊙*Daily during daylight hrs.*

OFF THE BEATEN PATH

Phillips County Historical Museum. This museum, and the Dinosaur Field Station next door, is an official repository for fossils found in the Judith River basin. The highlight of the dinosaur display is a reconstructed albertosaur skeleton, which towers above the rest of the collection. There are also exhibits on outlaws who spent time here: Butch Cassidy, the Sundance Kid, Kid Curry, the Tall Texan, and other members of the Wild Bunch gang. Ask about tours of the Robinson House and gardens next door. The house, ordered from a Sears & Roebuck catalog and erected in 1900, is an example of frontier simplicity. ⊠*431 U.S. 2, Malta* ☎*406/654–1037* ⊕*www.montanadinosaurdigs.com/museum.htm* ▭*$4* ⊙*Mon.–Sat., 10–5, Sun. 12:30–5.*

7

WHERE TO STAY

¢ ⊞**Maltana Hotel.** Easy to find, this downtown hotel is within walking distance of Malta's Amtrak station and a few blocks from the junction of U.S. 2 and 191. The rooms are modest but modern, with Wi-Fi and coffeemakers—unusual finds in a small, isolated town. **Pros:** Well-tended small hotel with great service and comfortable rooms. **Cons:** Hot in the summer and a little breezy in the winter. Beds are lumpy. ⊠*138 1st Ave. E, Malta 59538* ☎*406/654–2610* ⊟*406/654–2905* ⬠*19 rooms* ⚷*In-room: refrigerator. In-hotel: airport shuttle, no-smoking rooms, no elevator* ⊟*AE, D, MC, V.*

> ### RESTORING THE PRAIRIE
>
> The **American Prairie Foundation** wants to heal the prairie by returning bison and associated wildlife species to the landscape, and they're starting south of Malta, where ranch managers are building a small herd of bison, restoring streams and rangeland, and even rehabilitating a country school. You can visit their properties and learn more about their vision of temperate grasslands conservation around the world by arranging tours. ⊠*Dry Fork Rd., Malta 59538* ☎*406/585–4600* ⊕*www.americanprairie.org.*

HAVRE

103 mi west of Bowdoin National Wildlife Refuge via U.S. 2.

Mainly a place to stay when visiting Fort Assinniboine, the town of Havre (population 9,621) is the trading center for a wide area of extreme north-central Montana and southern Alberta and Saskatchewan. It lies in the Milk River valley in the shadow of the Bears Paw Mountains, and in a preserve south of town you can fish, picnic, or just enjoy the view.

Displays at the **H. Earl Clack Memorial Museum** include murals, artifacts, dioramas, and military exhibits that explore the lives of Plains Indians and Havre's early settlers and ranchers. The museum arranges tours of Fort Assinniboine and the Wahkpa Chu'gn Archaeological Site, a major buffalo jump. ⊠*1753 U.S. Hwy. 2 W, #30* ☎*406/265–4000* ⬠*Free* ☉*Labor Day–Memorial Day, Tues.–Sat. 1–5; Memorial Day–Labor Day, daily 11–6.*

★ Once the largest military reservation west of the Mississippi, **Fort Assinniboine** was established in 1879 in the aftermath of the Battle of the Little Bighorn. At its peak, the fort had more than 100 brick and stone buildings and nearly 500 men. The soldiers stationed here brought along their families, who lived on the post. As a result, the Victorian-era fort became a cultural center as well as a military one, hosting plays and dances along with parades and training exercises. The fort is now a museum, and many of the imposing buildings still stand, although they appear eerily deserted. In fact, a few are storage or administrative facilities for the Northern Research Agricultural Center. Others are open to public tours, which begin at the H. Earl Clack Memorial Museum. ⊠*1753 U.S. Hwy. 2 W in Holiday Village Mall* ☎*406/265–4000* ⬠*$6* ☉*May–Sept., tours at 11:30 and 5 daily or by appointment.*

★ The **Havre Beneath the Streets** tour takes you to a bordello, an opium den, a bakery, and other stops in an underground business center dating from the early days of the frontier—the equivalent of a modern underground mall. The subterranean businesses were mainly built and operated by the town's Asian population, drawn to the area by the Great Northern Railroad and its attendant business opportunities. Reservations for tours are recommended. ⊠*120 3rd Ave.* ☎*406/265–8888* ⊠*$10* ☉*Sept.–May, Mon.–Sat. 10–4; June–Aug., daily 9–5.*

Set in the ancient Bears Paw Mountains, about 10 mi south of town, is the 10,000-acre **Beaver Creek Park**, the largest county park in the country. It's a favorite spot for locals, who come here to fish in the two lakes and winding Beaver Creek, camp, picnic, and enjoy the grassy foothills and timbered ridges of this island mountain range surrounded by dryland wheat fields. ⊠*1786 Beaver Creek Rd.* ☎*406/395–4565* ⊠*$7 per vehicle* ☉*Daily 24 hrs.*

WHERE TO STAY & EAT

¢–$$ ✕**Lunch Box.** There are daily soup and sandwich specials at this family-style deli; two soups are made fresh daily. The menu lists a lot of healthful choices, with 70 sandwiches, as well as salads, nachos, baked potatoes, lattes, and espresso. ⊠*213 3rd Ave.* ☎*406/265–6588* ⊟*AE, D, MC, V* ☉*Closed Sun.*

$ 🏨**Best Western Great Northern Inn.** A clock tower, colorful flags, and off-white stones and bricks decorate the proud exterior of this spacious hotel that offers one of the best continental breakfasts on the Hi-Line. Contemporary furnishings fill the rooms. **Pros:** Great hot breakfast in the morning and comfortable rooms. Good beds and spacious bathrooms. **Cons:** Parking can be tight, the rail-yard behind the hotel can get noisy. ⊠*1345 1st St., 59501* ☎*406/265–4200 or 888/530–4100* ⊕*www.bestwestern.com* ⇥*63 rooms, 12 suites* ⌂*In-hotel: bar, pool, laundry facilities, airport shuttle, no-smoking rooms, Wi-Fi* ⊟*AE, D, DC, MC, V* ⋈*CP.*

THE ARTS

Focusing on the pencil drawings of local artist Don Graytak, the **Old Library Gallery** (⊠*439 4th Ave.* ☎*406/265–8165*) also displays paintings and pottery; most have a connection with local history and culture.

THE MONTANA PLAINS ESSENTIALS

AIR TRAVEL

Within eastern Montana, commercial flights—generally via Salt Lake City, Seattle, Denver, or Phoenix—are available only to Billings and Great Falls; small commuter and charter flights serve other towns. Because the region is so isolated, flights here from anywhere in the country can be pricey—often more expensive than coast-to-coast flights.

Airlines & Contacts **Big Sky** (☎*800/237–7788* ⊕*www.bigskyair.com*). **Delta** (☎*800/221–1212* ⊕*www.delta.com*). **Horizon** (☎*800/252–7522* ⊕*horizo-*

nair.alaskaair.com). **Northwest** (☎ *800/225-2525* ⊕ *www.nwa.com*). **United** (☎ *800/864-8331* ⊕ *www.ual.com*).

AIRPORTS

Both Billings Logan and Great Falls are full-service airports, with several flights daily from a variety of carriers. Because Billings and Great Falls have direct service to only a few cities in the western part of the country, some residents of the region drive as far as Bismarck, North Dakota; Rapid City, South Dakota; or Gillette, Wyoming, to catch departing flights.

Airport Information Billings Logan International Airport (☎ *406/238-3420* ⊕ *www.flybillings.com*). **Great Falls International Airport** (☎ *406/727-3404* ⊕ *www.gtfairport.com*).

BUS TRAVEL

A dwindling number of bus companies connect most communities of 1,000 residents or more; smaller towns may not have service. Expect high ticket prices; depending on where you're going, taking the bus can be almost as expensive as flying, and because of the great expanse of Montana, it can take infinitely longer.

Bus Information Greyhound Bus Lines (☎ *406/245-5116 or 800/231-2222* ⊕ *www.greyhound.com*). **Karst Stage** (☎ *406/556-3500* ⊕ *www.karststage. com*). **Powder River Transportation** (☎ *307/674-6188*). **Rimrock Stages** (☎ *406/245-7696 or 800/255-7655* ⊕ *www.rimrocktrailways.com*). **Silver Eagle Shuttle Inc.** (☎ *406/256-9793* ⊕ *www.montanacustomtours.com*).

CAR RENTAL

The airports in Billings and Great Falls are your best bet for rental cars.

Contacts Avis (☎ *800/831-2847* ⊕ *www.avis.com*). **Budget** (☎ *800/527-0700* ⊕ *www.budget.com*). **Hertz** (☎ *800/654-3131* ⊕ *www.hertz.com*). **National** (☎ *800/227-7368* ⊕ *www.nationalcar.com*).

CAR TRAVEL

It is virtually impossible to travel around the Montana plains without a car. One of the best things about driving here is the lack of traffic. Aside from a little bustle in Great Falls or Billings on weekdays in the late afternoon, gridlock and traffic jams are unheard of. The largest driving hazards will be slow-moving farming or ranching equipment, wranglers on horseback, herds of grazing livestock that refuse to move off the highway, and deer bounding over ditches in the evening. Driving gets a little hairy in winter, but not because of the amount of snow that falls, which is generally very little. Whiteouts, when winds tearing across the plains whip up the tiniest bit of snow into ground blizzards, are the most common hazard. Large drifts and slick roads become more problematic at higher elevations.

For information on road conditions, contact the Montana Department of Transportation.

Information Montana Department of Transportation (☎ *800/226–7623 or 511* ⊕ *www.mdt.mt.gov/travinfo*). **Montana Highway Patrol** (☎ *406/444–3780* ⊕ *www.doj.mt.gov/enforcement/highwaypatrol*).

EMERGENCIES
Ambulance or Police Emergencies (☎ *911 or 800/525–5555*).

24-Hour Medical Care Benefis Healthcare (✉ *1101 26th St. S, Great Falls* ☎ *406/455–5000* ⊕ *www.benefis.org*). **Deaconess Billings Clinic** (✉ *2800 10th Ave. N, Billings* ☎ *406/657–4000* ⊕ *www.billingsclinic.com*). **St. Vincent Healthcare** (✉ *1233 N. 30th St., Billings* ☎ *406/657–7000* ⊕ *www.stvincent healthcare.org*).

LODGING
The Montana Innkeepers Association's simple Web site accesses a large database of lodgings throughout most of the state. Many of the smaller inns and motels in eastern Montana are not listed.

Contacts Montana Innkeepers Association (☎ *406/449–8408* ⊕ *www.mon tanainnkeepers.com*).

CAMPING Many federal and state-owned lands allow camping for little or no charge, and you can often set up shop wherever you like, so long as you don't light a fire. In the more developed towns and cities there is almost always a campground or two with more modern conveniences, such as hot showers and flush toilets. It's a testament to this treeless terrain that most commercial campgrounds advertise their shade before their other amenities.

Contact Montana Fish, Wildlife & Parks for information on camping in state parks and the U.S. Forest Service for information on camping at national parks in the area.

Information Montana Fish, Wildlife & Parks (☎ *406/444–2535* ⊕ *www.mt.gov/ parks*). **U.S. Forest Service** (☎ *406/329–3511* ⊕ *www.fs.fed.us/r1*).

SPORTS & THE OUTDOORS
BOATING Motorized boating, including jet skiing, is usually not restricted, even in the massive Charles M. Russell National Wildlife Refuge. Marinas rent out boats on Fort Peck Lake, Bighorn Lake, and a few of the other reservoirs scattered around the plains. Extended droughts can sometimes put the marinas out of business—at least temporarily—or force them to move to another location. If you're interested in boat rentals on a specific lake or river, call Travel Montana.

Contacts Travel Montana (☎ *406/841–2870 or 800/847–4868* ⊕ *www.visitmt. com*).

FISHING Although the eastern two-thirds of Montana are decidedly drier than the western regions, small mountain-fed creeks and reservoirs on a few major rivers are plentiful. Unlike the blue-ribbon streams of the higher elevations, the muddy, slow-moving streams of the lowlands seldom attract crowds, though the fishing for channel catfish, walleye, and northern pike can be quite good.

Contacts **Montana Fish, Wildlife & Parks** (☎ *406/444–2535* ⊕ *www.mt.gov/ parks*).

TRAIN TRAVEL

Amtrak serves the isolated communities of the Hi-Line with its Empire Builder line, running one train each way daily from Chicago to Seattle. The tracks run nearly parallel to U.S. 2 the entire length of the state. Trains stop in the towns of Glasgow, Malta, Havre, Wolf Point, and Cut Bank, among others.

Train Information **Amtrak** (☎ *800/872–7245* ⊕ *www.amtrak.com*).

VISITOR INFORMATION

Tourist Information **Billings Convention and Visitors Bureau** (☎ *406/252–4016 or 800/735–2635* ⊕ *www.billingscvb.visitmt.com*). **Great Falls Convention and Visitors Bureau** (☎ *406/761–4434* ⊕ *greatfallscvb.visitmt.com*). **Travel Montana** (☎ *406/841–2870 or 800/847–4868* ⊕ *www.visitmt.com*).

Cody, Sheridan & Northern Wyoming

WORD OF MOUTH

"Devils Tower . . . is a spectacular natural creation (former core of a volcano), and conjures up memories of "Close Encounters", of course. The scenery as you drive around out there is hard to describe. Parts of Wyoming were like being on the moon, isolated and just plain desolate—but then you would come to sheer beauty, too."

—RetiredVermonter

Updated by
Gil Brady
& Shauna
Stephenson

PINE-CARPETED HILLSIDES AND SNOWY MOUNTAIN summits give way to windswept prairies and clean-flowing rivers where the Great Plains meet the mighty Rocky Mountains. Northern Wyoming's epic landscape is replete with symbols of the American frontier: the ranch, the rodeo, and the cowboy.

It may be that no state in the union exalts cowboy life as Wyoming does. The concept of the dude-ranch vacation—where urban folk learn to rope, ride, and rodeo with weathered ranchers and professional cattle drivers—started in northern Wyoming, at Eaton's Guest Ranch 18 mi outside Sheridan in the town of Wolf. Numerous other guest ranches are strewn across the grassy plains here, from the dusty prairies east of Cody to the alpine meadows of the Big Horn Mountains. Most Big Horn–area dude ranches run pack trips into these high, rugged peaks, sometimes for days at a time. Even if you prefer a warm bed to sleeping under the stars, don't be deterred, and certainly don't leave the state without getting on a horse at least once: try a shorter trail ride or a pack trip that ends at a furnished cabin.

The outdoors is northern Wyoming's primary draw. Take the time to appreciate the wide-open spaces before you: take a hike, go fishing, ride a bike, or get out into the snow. Much of this territory is just as empty as it was when the first white people arrived here two centuries ago. Even though Europeans settled in Wyoming as early as 1812, the state's population is the smallest in the nation, at only 515,004 permanent residents. But the few who have dwelt in this place have been history makers. This part of Wyoming has a rich and storied past that encompasses icons such as gunslingers, gamblers, miners, mule skinners, and warriors. Some of the most famous (and infamous) figures of the Old West passed through here, including Buffalo Bill Cody, Wild Bill Hickok, Calamity Jane, Chief Washakie, Butch Cassidy, and the Sundance Kid, the latter of whom took his name from one of the region's towns.

EXPLORING NORTHERN WYOMING

Northern Wyoming is a point of convergence. Here mountains meet prairies, forests meet ranches, and country towns meet Western cities. Most settlements have no more than a few hundred people; only three surpass 10,000 residents. Casper, on the banks of the North Platte River in the center of Wyoming, is on or near five of the major pioneer trails of the mid-19th century, including the Oregon and Mormon trails. Gillette, in the Powder River basin near Devils Tower National Monument, and Sheridan, on the edge of the Big Horn Mountains 104 mi to the northwest, are both in Wyoming's energy country, although ranching (both dude and cattle) are mainstays of the communities. Cody, with about 9,100 residents, is the largest community between the Big Horn Mountains and Yellowstone National Park, a convenient stop for visitors on their way to the natural treasures farther west.

ABOUT THE RESTAURANTS

Although not every community here has the eclectic mix of dining options common in more urban areas, there are plenty of small restaurants and local cafés with inimitable appeal. The larger communities often have several ethnic eateries from which to choose, serving everything from traditional Mexican and Native American specialties to old-world Italian and modern Korean dishes. The real strength of the region's dining, however, lies with the basics. In almost any small-town watering hole, you can order up some of the freshest and best-tasting beef and buffalo in the world. Whether it's prime rib and mashed potatoes with sunflower bread, or charred rib eye with corn on the cob, the area's best meals are simple yet filled with a flavor found only in the West.

ABOUT THE HOTELS

Just as diverse as the area's landscape, which fades from small Western cities into vast lengths of open prairie and forested mountains, are its accommodations. In the population centers, lodgings range from new chain hotels with wireless Internet access to elegant and historic stone inns decorated with buffalo skins and Victorian furniture. Move beyond these cities, however, and everything changes. Campgrounds abound in the open countryside. On the prairie, expect sprawling guest ranches alongside cold mountain-fed creeks. In the higher elevations, look for charming bed-and-breakfasts on mountain slopes with broad alpine vistas. But whatever the type of accommodation, all kinds of amenities are available, from the ordinary to the unconventional, including saunas, hot tubs, horseback riding, fly-fishing lessons, and square dancing. Perhaps the greatest benefit of all, however, is the isolation. In what some might call a welcome change in this era of information overload, many rural lodgings don't have in-room televisions or telephones, and vast stretches don't have cell phone service.

WHAT IT COSTS					
	¢	$	$$	$$$	$$$$
RESTAURANTS	under $7	$7–$11	$12–$16	$17–$22	over $22
HOTELS	under $70	$70–$110	$111–$160	$161–$220	over $220

Restaurant prices are for a main course at dinner, excluding sales tax of 4%–7%. Hotel prices are for two people in a standard double room in high season, excluding service charges and 5%–10% tax.

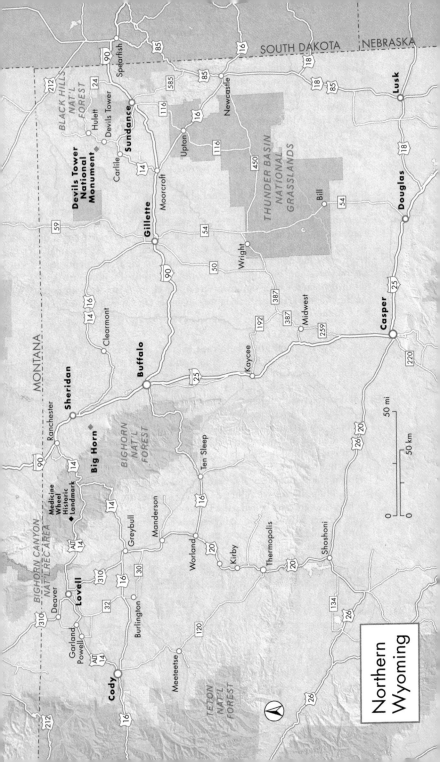

SOUTH DAKOTA   NEBRASKA

85
90
Spearfish
212
BLACK HILLS NAT'L FOREST
24
Hulett
Devils Tower
116
585
85
16
18
Newcastle
18
85
Lusk
16
Upton
116
Devils Tower National Monument
Carlile
14
Moorcroft
116
Sundance
450
18
Douglas
THUNDER BASIN NATIONAL GRASSLANDS
Bill
54
59
Gillette
54
Wright
50
90
25
MONTANA
14 16
Clearmont
387
Midwest
387
259
Casper
220
Sheridan
Ranchester
Buffalo
25
Kaycee
192
50 mi
90
14
Big Horn
BIGHORN NAT'L FOREST
Ten Sleep
26 20
50 km
Medicine Wheel Historic Landmark
14
16
Manderson
BIGHORN CANYON NAT'L REC AREA
14
ALT 14
Greybull
20
Kirby
Thermopolis
20
Shoshoni
Deaver
310
16
30
Worland
Lovell
32
Burlington
134
26
Garland
Powell
ALT 14
310
120
Meeteetse
Cody
16
TETON NAT'L FOREST
26
212

Northern Wyoming

TIMING

People come to experience northern Wyoming in all four seasons—sometimes all in the same week. The weather here is notoriously difficult to predict, as warm Chinook winds can shoot January temperatures into the 70s and freak storms can drop snow in July. On the whole, however, Mother Nature behaves herself and gives the area pleasantly warm summers and refreshingly snowy winters. Most travelers flock to the region between June and August, availing themselves of the higher temperatures optimal for outdoor activities. Many more come to ski or snowmobile the pristine powder of the Big Horn Mountains in winter.

Temperatures in both seasons can be extreme, however. Thermometers often register a week of triple digits in August in the lower elevations. Snow begins to blanket the mountain slopes in late September and begins to recede only in late May. Spring, especially in the mountains, is sometimes nothing more than a week or two of rain between the last winter snowfall and the warm sunshine of summer. Autumn, on the other hand, is full of pleasantly warm days, cooler nights, and vivid colors. Additionally, the only crowds to fight are small pockets of hunters, anglers, and local leaf peepers.

THE BIG HORN BASIN

Rich in Native American history, Old West flavor, and natural wonders, this broad basin is flanked by the Absaroka and Owl mountains to the west and the Big Horns to the east. The Bighorn River flows north along the eastern edge of the basin and up into Montana. Here, straddling the two states, is Bighorn Canyon National Recreation Area; most of the recreation area lies in Montana, but the southern portion is easily accessible in Wyoming via Highway 37.

8

LOVELL

49 mi northeast of Cody via Alternate U.S. 14.

This small community makes a convenient, if bare-bones, base for exploring the Bighorn Canyon National Recreation Area, which overlaps the Wyoming–Montana border. On the Wyoming side, Bighorn Lake is popular with boaters and anglers; most of the main attractions, including the majority of the Pryor Mountain Wild Horse Range, lie on the Montana side. (⇨ *Chapter 7.*)

The main visitor center for the Bighorn Canyon National Recreation Area, the **Bighorn Canyon Visitor Center** has geological and historical exhibits, as well as a film about the canyon. ✉ *U.S. 310 at Alternate U.S. 14* ☎ *307/548–2251* ⊕ *www.nps.gov/bica/* ✉ *$5, 1-yr pass $30* ☉ *Memorial Day–Labor Day, daily 8–6; Labor Day–Memorial Day, daily 8:30–4:30.*

More than 155 species of birds, including white pelicans, pheasant, bald eagles, and great blue herons, inhabit the 19,424-acre **Yellowtail**

Wildlife Habitat Management Area, as do numerous other animal species, including red fox, mule deer, and cottontail rabbits. ⊠*Hwy. 37, 33 mi east of Lovell* ☎307/527–7125 ☑*Free* ⊙*Daily.*

OFF THE BEATEN PATH

Fodor'sChoice

★

Medicine Wheel National Historic Landmark. A ring of rocks 75 feet in diameter, this ancient site is the best preserved of nearly 150 Native American stone wheels found in Wyoming, South Dakota, Montana, Alberta, and Saskatchewan. Evidence such as the 28 spokes (one for each day of the lunar cycle) leading from the edge of the wheel to a central cairn has persuaded some that the wheel was an ancient spiritual observatory much like England's Stonehenge may have been. To protect the area, access to the wheel is restricted to foot travel; it's a 1½-mi hike to the site from the parking lot (people with disabilities may drive to the site). Up in the Big Horn Mountains, at an elevation of 9,642 feet, the site affords views of the entire Big Horn Basin. At this elevation, you'll want to bring a coat or sweatshirt. ⊠*30 mi east of Lovell on Alternate U.S. 14* ☎307/548–6541 ⊕*wyoshpo.state.wy.us/medwheel. htm* ☑*Free* ⊙*Daily 24 hrs.*

★ **Hyart Theatre.** Near the town's sugar beet factory, this arty-looking, 975-seat movie palace, built in 1950 by film-lover Hyrum Bischoff, is the heart and soul of this 2,300 person outpost, known as the "Rose City," at the foot of the Big Horn Mountains. Due to the popularity of home video rentals, the Hyart shut down in 1992 until being revived by a citizen's committee of volunteers who raised funds to restore the theatre, its spacious lobby, sunken lounge, sloping balcony, "cry room" for babies and neon painter's palette high above the marquee to its former Truman-era glory, reopening it in 2004. ⊠*251 E. Main St.* ☎307/548–7021 ⊕*www.hyarttheater.com* ☑*Tickets generally $5 and under* ⊙*Fri. and Sat.*

WHERE TO STAY & EAT

¢–$ ✕**Lange's Kitchen.** This homey diner-style grill is a local institution, partly because it used to be the only restaurant in town. Workers at the nearby sugar refinery and bentonite plants come here for the kind of down-home cooking that sticks to your insides: biscuits and gravy, homemade oatmeal, hamburgers, shrimp baskets, tacos, halibut strips, and liver and onions. If you're not in the mood for a full meal, you can enjoy brewed coffee and tea in the coffee shop out front. Lange's is open from 6 AM to 2 PM, so you won't be able to get late lunch or dinner here. ⊠*483 Shoshone Ave.* ☎307/548–9370 ▤*MC, V* ⊙*No dinner.*

¢ ✕**The Switchback Grill.** Catering to late-lunch and early-bird dinner crowds, this place serves Philly cheesesteak sandwiches, fried chicken, hoagies, hamburgers, and steaks with grilled onions and fries. ⊠*384 W. Main St.* ☎307/548–4595 ▤*MC, V.*

¢–$ ▥**Horseshoe Band Motel.** This low-slung, one-story throwback from 1969 is straight out of a Sam Shepard play and has free parking, clean rooms, some with kitchenettes, a swimming pool and gas grill for guests, and picnic tables, and dutifully supports hunters, allowing their dogs to stay, too. According to locals, the nearby Yellowtail Game Management Area is a favorite of sportsmen. **Pros:** Clean rooms, some with kitchenettes, attentive staff, hunter friendly. **Cons:** Fills up quick, no-smoking rooms. ⊠*375 E. Main St., 82431* 🕾*307/548–2221* 🖅*22 rooms* ⌂*In-hotel: Wi-Fi, some pets allowed, no-smoking rooms, no elevator* 🖃*AE, MC, V.*

CODY

84 mi northwest of Thermopolis via Hwy. 120; 52 mi east of Yellowstone via U.S. 14/16/20.

Cody, founded in 1896 and named for Pony Express rider, army scout, Freemason, and entertainer William F. "Buffalo Bill" Cody, is the eastern gateway community for Yellowstone National Park. The North Fork Highway—as the route leading east to Yellowstone is locally known—follows the North Fork of the Shoshone River past barren rock formations strewn with tumbleweeds, then enters lush forests and green meadows as the elevation increases roughly 3,000 feet in 70 mi. Cody is within easy reach of Shoshone National Forest, the Absaroka Range, the Washakie Wilderness, and the Buffalo Bill Reservoir.

But Cody is much more than a base for exploring the surrounding area. Several excellent museums make up the outstanding Buffalo Bill Historical Center, and the Western lifestyle is alive and well on dude ranches and in both trendy and classic shops. Part of the fun in Cody is sauntering down Main Street, stopping by the Irma Hotel (built by Buffalo Bill and named for his daughter) for some refreshment, and attending the nightly rodeo.

Pick up a brochure ($1 donation) with a self-guided walking tour of the town's historic sites at the Chamber of Commerce on Sheridan Avenue.

The **Wyoming Vietnam Veterans Memorial** is a small-scale version of the Vietnam Veterans Memorial wall in Washington, DC. The Cody memorial recognizes the Wyoming residents who died during the conflict. ⊠*U.S. 14/16/20, east of Cody.*

The **Cody Mural,** at the Church of Jesus Christ of Latter-day Saints, is an artistic interpretation of Mormon settlement in the West. Edward Grigware painted the scene on the domed ceiling in the 1950s. ⊠*1010 Angler Ave.* 🕾*307/587–3290 or 307/587–9258* 🖾*Free* 🕙*June–mid-Sept., Mon.–Sat. 8–8, Sun. 3–8.*

Fodor's Choice
★ On the west side of Cody are some of the finest museums anywhere and true jewels of the West: the **Buffalo Bill Historical Center,** which houses five museums in one. The **Buffalo Bill Cody Museum** is dedicated to the incredible life of William F. "Buffalo Bill" Cody. Shortly after Cody's death, some of his friends took mementos of the famous scout and Wild West showman and opened the Buffalo Bill Museum in a small log building. The museum has since been moved to the historical center and includes films, huge posters from the original Wild West shows, and illustrated books as well as personal effects such as clothing, guns, saddles, and furniture. The **Cody Firearms Museum** traces the history

of firearms through thousands of models on display, from European blunderbusses to Gatling guns and modern firearms. Included are examples of Winchester and Browning arms, as well as a model of an arms-manufacturing plant. There are also the 1881 Navy revolvers belonging to Cody friend James "Wild Bill" Hickok. Legend has it that Hickok's revolvers had to be sold after his death, following a lethal card game in Deadwood, to bury him. At the time of his death, Hickok was holding a pair of black aces and a pair of eights—since known as a "Dead Man's Hand." Through exhibits, outdoor activities, tours, and seminars, the **Draper Museum of Natural History** explores the Yellowstone ecosystem. There are children's discovery areas in addition to life-size animal mounts. Recordings play the sounds of wolves, grizzly bears, birds, and other animals that make their home in the Yellowstone area. At the **Plains Indian Museum,** interactive exhibits and life-size dioramas explore the history and culture of the Lakota, Blackfeet, Cheyenne, Shoshone, and Nez Perce tribes. Among the exhibits are rare medicine pipes, clothing, and an earth-house interpretive area. The **Whitney Gallery of Western Art** is devoted to the West's greatest artists. On display are works by such masters as Frederic Remington, Charles M. Russell, Albert Bierstadt, George Catlin, and Thomas Moran, plus contemporary artists such as Harry Jackson, James Bama, and Peter Fillerup. ⊠ *720 Sheridan Ave.* ☎ *307/587–4771* ⊕ *www.bbhc.org* ⊠ *$15 (2 days)* ⊘ *Apr., Tues.–Sun. 10–5; May, Tues.–Sun. 8–8; June–mid-Sept., Tues.–Sun. 8–8; mid-Sept.–Oct., Tues.–Sun. 8–5; Nov. and Dec., Tues.–Sun. 10–3, Jan.–Mar., Tues.–Sun. 10–3.*

☉ **Cody Nite Rodeo,** more dusty and intimate than big rodeos such as Cheyenne Frontier Days, offers children's events, such as goat roping, in addition to the regular adult events. Contact the Cody Chamber of Commerce for more information. ⊠ *West Cody Strip* ☎ *800/207–0744* ⊕ *www.codyniterodeo.com* ⊠ *$8–$20; seat prices vary with location* ⊘ *June–Aug., daily at 8:30 PM.*

☉ Summer evenings, the **Cody Gunslingers Shootout** takes place on the porch at the Irma Hotel. ⊠ *1192 Sheridan Ave.* ☎ *307/587–4221* ⊠ *Free* ⊘ *June–late Sept., daily at 6 PM.*

If you give the folks at **Cody Trolley Tours** an hour of your time, they'll take you on a journey through 100 years of Cody history. The tour takes in historic sites, scenery, geology, and wildlife attractions. A combination ticket also grants you admission to the Buffalo Bill Historical Center. ⊠ *Ticket booth in front of Irma Hotel, 1192 Sheridan Ave.* ☎ *307/527–7043* ⊕ *www.CodyTrolleyTours.com* ⊠ *Tour ticket $20, combination ticket with Buffalo Bill Historical Center $30* ⊘ *Early June–Sept., Mon.–Sat. at 9, 11, 1, 3, and 6:30; Sun. at 9, 11, 1, and 3.*

☉ On Cody's western outskirts, off the West Yellowstone Highway, is **Old Trail Town,** a collection of historic buildings from Wyoming's frontier days. Also here are a cemetery for famous local mountain men, and Native American and pioneer artifacts. The buildings aren't fancy and the displays are rustic, so you really get a feel for an Old West town.

Sometimes in summer Bobby Bridger, great-grandnephew of mountain man Jim Bridger, performs his "Ballad of the West" ($12) in the barn here. The three-night program describes the settlement of the West and includes stories of mountain men, Buffalo Bill Cody, and the Lakota. ⊠*1831 Demaris Dr.* ☎*307/587–5302* ⌨*$6* ⊗*Mid-May–mid-Sept., daily 8–8.*

Fishing and boating on the Buffalo Bill Reservoir are popular activities at **Buffalo Bill State Park,** west of Cody. A visitor center here focuses on the history of the reservoir, which was completed in 1910. ⊠*47 Lakeside Rd., west of Cody on U.S. 24/26/20; then State Rte. 291* ☎*307/587–9227* ⊕*wyoparks.state.wy.us/Parks/BuffaloBill/index.asp* ⌨*Park $4, camping $12* ⊗*Park daily 24 hrs, visitor center May–Sept., daily 8–8.*

The **Shoshone National Forest** was the country's first national forest, established in 1891. You can hike, fish, mountain bike, and ride horses in warmer weather, and snowmobile and cross-country ski in winter. There are picnic areas and campgrounds. ⊠*U.S. 14/16/20, west of Cody* ☎*307/527–6241* ⊕*www.fs.fed.us/r2/shoshone/* ⌨*Free* ⊗*Daily 24 hrs.*

OFF THE BEATEN PATH

Chief Joseph Scenic Byway. In 1877, a few members of the Nez Perce tribe killed some white settlers in Idaho as retribution for earlier killings by whites. Fearing that the U.S. Army would punish the guilty and innocent alike, hundreds of Nez Perce fled on a five-month journey toward Canada that came to be known as the Nez Perce Trail. Along the way they passed through what is now Yellowstone National Park, across the Sunlight Basin area north of Cody, and along the Clarks Fork of the Shoshone River before turning north into Montana. To see the rugged mountain area they traveled through, follow Highway 120 north 17 mi to Highway 296, the Chief Joseph Scenic Byway. The byway eventually leads to Cooke City and Red Lodge, Montana. Along the way you'll see open meadows, pine forests, and a sweeping vista of the region from the top of Dead Indian Pass.

8

SPORTS & THE OUTDOORS

CANOEING, KAYAKING & RAFTING

To get out on the Shoshone River, charter a guided trip. In Cody it's not possible to rent equipment for unguided trips.

Family river trips on the Shoshone River are offered by **River Runners** (⊠*1491 Sheridan Ave.* ☎*307/527–7238*). **Wyoming River Trips** (⊠*Buffalo Bill Village, 1701 Sheridan Ave.* ☎*307/587–6661 or 800/586–6661*) arranges Shoshone River trips.

FISHING

The fish are big at the private **Monster Lake** (☎*800/840–5137*), filled with rainbow, brook, and brown trout weighing up to 10 pounds. For a fee you can fish all or part of the day at this lake on the east side of town; accommodations are available as well.

You can buy fishing tackle, get information on fishing in the area, or take a guided half- or full-day trip with **Tim Wade's North Fork Anglers** (⊠*1107 Sheridan Ave.* ☎*307/527–7274* ⊕*northforkanglers.com*).

GOLF

Olive Glenn Golf and Country Club (⊠*802 Meadow La.* ☎*307/587–5551 or 307/587–5308*) is a highly rated 18-hole course open to the public; a Jacuzzi, pool, and two tennis courts are also here.

HORSEBACK RIDING

Ride for one to four hours or all day with **Cedar Mountain Trail Rides** (⊠*U.S. 14/16/20, 1 mi west of rodeo grounds* ☎*307/527–4966*). You can ride horses into Shoshone National Forest with **Goff Creek Lodge** (⊠*995 E. Yellowstone Hwy.* ☎*307/587–3753 or 800/859–3985* ⊕*goffcreek.com*); lunch rides are also available.

SKIING

In the Wood River valley near Meeteetse, 32 mi south of Cody, **Wood River Ski Touring Park** (⊠*1010 Park Ave.* ☎*307/868–2603*) has 32 km (20 mi) of cross-country trails.

WHERE TO EAT

$–$$$ ✕**Proud Cut Saloon.** At this popular downtown eatery and watering hole, owner Del Nose serves what locals call "kick-ass cowboy cuisine": butterfly steaks, prime rib, shrimp, fish, and chicken. Western paintings, vintage photographs of Cody country, and large-game mounts decorate the place. ⊠*1227 Sheridan Ave.* ☎*307/527–6905* ▭*D, MC, V.*

$$ ✕**Maxwell's.** A turn-of-the-20th-century Victorian structure with huge windows and a porch houses this upscale contemporary restaurant that serves free-range beef entrées, homemade soups, pastas, and sandwiches. The baby back pork ribs are always a good bet, and the Mediterranean pizza with Greek olives, feta cheese, and fresh tomatoes is also a good, very filling choice. In summer there's outdoor dining on the deck. ⊠*937 Sheridan Ave.* ☎*307/527–7749* ▭*AE, D, MC, V.*

$–$$ ✕**Granny's.** This family-style diner has a kids' and senior menu and is
☺ popular with locals and old-timers, serving good coffee, omelets, biscuits with gravy, patty melts, hot sandwiches, fried chicken, soups, and salads. ⊠*1550 Sheridan Ave.* ☎*307/587–4829* ▭*MC, V.*

¢–$$ ✕**La Comida.** Making no claim to authentic Mexican cooking, this restaurant nevertheless receives praise for its "Cody-Mex" cuisine. You may order enchiladas, burritos, tacos, and chiles rellenos, but they won't be as spicy as similar foods would be in the Southwest. Mexican wall hangings contribute to the festive atmosphere. ⊠*1385 Sheridan Ave.* ☎*307/587–9556* ▭*AE, D, DC, MC, V.*

WHERE TO STAY

$$$$ ▦**Rimrock Dude Ranch.** Dating to 1956, this is one of the oldest guest ranches on the North Fork of the Shoshone River. Rimrock offers both summer and winter accommodations and activities, from horseback riding in the surrounding mountain country to snowmobile trips in Yel-

lowstone National Park. Lodging is in one- and two-bedroom cabins. There's a one-week minimum stay. **Pros:** Excellent long-standing reputation, near Yellowstone, open winters. **Cons:** Minimum stays, might be too expensive for families on tight budgets. ⊠*2728 North Fork Rte., 82414* ☎*307/587–3970 or 800/208–7468* 🖷*307/527–5014* ⊕*www.rimrockranch.com* 🛏*9 cabins* ♨*In-room: no a/c, refrigerator, no TV. In-hotel: pool, airport shuttle, no-smoking rooms, no elevator.* ▤*MC, V* ⦿*FAP.*

$$$–$$$$ 🖫**UXU Ranch.** One of the cabins at the UXU guest ranch is a historic ☾ late-19th-century stage stop moved to the site and decorated with Molesworth-style furnishings made by New West of Cody; other cabins here date to the 1960s or 1920s. The ranch, along the North Fork of the Shoshone River, offers outstanding horseback riding, pack trips into the nearby mountains, and the opportunity to really get away from it all. There's a minimum one-week stay. It's open year-round; inquire about winter rates. **Pros:** Gorgeous setting, 17 mi from Yellowstone, expert management, new and ongoing renovations, excellent food and accommodations. **Cons:** Currently, undergoing renovations, no pets. ⊠*1710 North Fork Hwy., Wapiti 82450* ☎*800/373–9027* 🖷*307/587–8307* ⊕*www.uxuranch.com* 🛏*11 cabins* ♨*In-room: no a/c, no phone. In-hotel: bar, children's programs (ages 6 and up), no-smoking rooms, no elevator* ▤*MC, V* ⦿*FAP.*

$–$$$$ 🖫**Cody Guest Houses.** You have several house-rental options here, from ★ a Victorian guesthouse with lace curtains and antique furnishings to a four-bedroom lodge with a fireplace. The 10 different guesthouses have one to four bedrooms, and all of them have been lovingly restored and elegantly decorated. These houses are meant to make you feel truly at home, so you'll find refrigerators, full kitchens, outdoor barbecue grills, and children's play areas at most of them. **Pros:** Near Yellowstone, ideal for families and reunions. Guest homes offer additional privacy. **Cons:** Additional toiletries and supplies required on extended stays, payment in full upon arrival. ⊠*1525 Beck Ave., 82414* ☎*307/587–6000 or 800/587–6560* 🖷*307/587–8048* ⊕*www.codyguesthouses.com* 🛏*10 houses* ♨*In-room: no a/c (some), kitchen, no TV (some). In-hotel: laundry facilities, no-smoking rooms, no elevator* ▤*AE, D, MC, V.*

$–$$ 🖫**Buffalo Bill Village.** This downtown development comprises three lodgings, which share many facilities. The Buffalo Bill Village Resort consists of log cabins with modern interiors, and the Holiday Inn Convention Center and the Comfort Inn are typical chain hotels. The downtown shopping district begins one block to the west, and there's also a grocery store a block away. **Pros:** Clean, comfortable, good location, restaurant on premises. **Cons:** Relatively pricey in off-season, no complimentary breakfast, one guest washing machine. ⊠*1701 Sheridan Ave., 82414* ☎*307/587–5544 or 800/527–5544* ⊕*www.blairhotels. com* 🛏*Buffalo Bill Village Resort 83 cabins; Comfort Inn 74 rooms; Holiday Inn 188 rooms* ♨*In-hotel: restaurant, bar, pool, gym, airport shuttle, no-smoking rooms* ▤*AE, D, DC, MC, V.*

$–$$ 🖫**Lockhart Inn.** The former home of Cody author Caroline Lockhart, this inn has rooms named after her characters and books. Western antiques decorate the rooms, many of which have claw-foot tubs.

It's on the main western strip of Cody, which is convenient to area attractions. **Pros:** Beautiful and imaginatively decorated and appointed rooms, good location, hearty country breakfast included. **Cons:** Limited amenities, privacy. For sale. ⊠*109 W. Yellowstone Ave., 82414* ☎*307/587–6074 or 877/377–7255* ⊕*stayincody.com/lockhartinn1. htm* ⇆*7 rooms* ⌂*In-hotel: no-smoking rooms, no elevator* ▤*D, MC, V* ⊙*|BP.*

$–$$ ⊡ **Yellowstone Valley Inn.** Located 16 mi west of Cody and 30 mi east of Yellowstone National Park's east entrance, this sprawling and peaceful property offers basic accommodations in a mountain setting. Rooms are in the motel or duplex cabins, and campsites are available. **Pros:** Nice, clean rooms, recently remodeled, rustic but with amenities, beautiful location. **Cons:** Travelers have had mixed impressions: noisy bar crowd at times, unhelpful service. ⊠*3324 Northfolk Hwy., 82414* ☎*307/587–3961 or 877/587–3961* ⊟*307/587–4656* ⊕*www.yellow-stonevalleyinn.com* ⇆*15 motel rooms, 20 cabin rooms* ⌂*In-room: no phone. In-hotel: restaurant, bar, pool, laundry facilities, no-smoking rooms, some pets allowed, no elevator* ▤*AE, D, MC, V.*

¢–$$ ⊡ **Irma Hotel.** This 106-year-old Victorian hotel named for Buffalo Bill's
★ daughter retains some frontier charm and rough edges, with period furniture, pull-chain commodes in many rooms, a large restaurant ($–$$$) and an elaborate cherrywood bar. For those looking for modern amenities and trappings, this probably isn't it. But if you want true history, be sure to stay in one of the 15 rooms of the original 1902 hotel named after local legends and not in the annex, which has standard hotel-style contemporary rooms. In summer, locals stage a gunfight on the porch Tuesday–Saturday at 6 PM. **Pros:** Tons of character, history and charm. Located in town. Nice rooms. **Cons:** Late night front desk help sometimes lacking in grace, those looking for finer amenities may be disappointed. ⊠*1192 Sheridan Ave., 82414* ☎*307/587–4221 or 800/745–4762* ⊟*307/587–1775* ⊕*www.irmahotel.com* ⇆*40 rooms* ⌂*In-hotel: restaurant, bar, no-smoking rooms, no elevator* ▤*AE, D, DC, MC, V.*

CAMPING

There are 31 campgrounds within **Shoshone National Forest** (☎*307/527–6241* ⊕*www.fs.fed.us/r2/shoshone*); some have only limited services, and others have hookups and campground hosts.

⚠ **Cody KOA.** This campground on the southeast side of town serves free pancake breakfasts. There's also a free shuttle to the Cody Nite Rodeo, and you can arrange to take a horseback ride. ⌂*Flush toilets, full hookups, partial hookups (electric and water), drinking water, guest laundry, showers, picnic tables, general store, swimming (pool)* ⇆*78 tent sites, 68 full hookups, 54 partial hookups, 21 cabins, 1 cottage* ⊠*5561 U.S. 20 (Greybull Hwy.)* ☎*800/562–8507* ⊟*307/587–2369* ⊕*www.codykoa.com* ▤*AE, D, DC, MC, V* ☉*May–Oct.*

⚠ **Dead Indian Campground.** You can fish in the stream at this tent campground adjacent to the Chief Joseph Scenic Byway (Highway 296). There are hiking and horseback-riding trails, plus nearby corrals for horses. ⌂*Pit toilets, drinking water, bear boxes, fire grates, picnic* *tables, swimming (creek)* 🛏*12 sites* ✉*17 mi north of Cody on Hwy. 120, 17 mi to WY 296, then 25 mi northwest on Hwy. 296* ☎*307/527–6241* ⊕*www.fs.fed.us/r2/shoshone* ▬*No credit cards* ⊙*May–Oct.*

🏕 **Deer Creek Campground.** At the head of the South Fork of the Shoshone River, this small, tree-shaded campground for tents provides hiking access to the Absaroka Range and the Washakie Wilderness. ♿*Pit toilets, drinking water, fire pits, picnic tables* 🛏*7 sites* ✉*47 mi west of Cody on South Fork Hwy. (Hwy. 291)* ☎*307/527–6241* ⊕*www. fs.fed.us/r2/shoshone* ⊙*May–Oct.*

🏕 **Ponderosa Campground.** Within walking distance (three blocks) of the Buffalo Bill Historical Center, this is a large facility with separate areas for tents and RVs. You can even stay in a teepee or pitch your own tent or tepee in a primitive camping area (without any nearby facilities) known as the OK Corral in the canyon above the Shoshone River. ♿*Flush toilets, full hookups, dump station, drinking water, guest laundry, showers, picnic tables, public telephone, Wi-Fi, general store, play area* 🛏*137 full hookups, 50 tent sites; 8 teepees* ✉*1815 8th St.* ☎*307/587–9203* ▬*No credit cards* ⊙*Mid-Apr.–mid-Oct.*

NIGHTLIFE & THE ARTS

NIGHTLIFE

A trip to Cody isn't complete without a chance to scoot your boots to live music, usually provided by the local band West, at **Cassie's Supper Club and Dance Hall** (✉*214 Yellowstone Ave.* ☎*307/527–5500*). The tunes are a mix of classic country, the band's Western originals, and today's hits.

THE ARTS

Impromptu jam sessions, nightly concerts, and a symposium of educational and entertaining events related to cowboy music are all part of the **Cowboy Songs and Range Ballads** (☎*307/587–4771* ⊕*www.bbhc. org*). In addition to classic range ballads there's original music by performers from across the West. Events are held over the course of a few days in early April at the Buffalo Bill Historical Center and other venues.

☼ The two-day **Plains Indian Powwow** (✉*720 Sheridan Ave.* ☎*307/587–4771* ⊕*www.bbhc.org*), in late June, brings together hoop dancers, traditional dancers, and jingle dancers from various tribes. The performances take place at the Buffalo Bill Historical Center.

Sculptures and paintings by such artists as James Bama, Chris Navarro, Frank McCarthy, and Howard Post are displayed at **Big Horn Galleries** (✉*1167 Sheridan Ave.* ☎*307/527–7587*). **Simpson Gallagher Gallery** (✉*1161 Sheridan Ave.* ☎*307/587–4022*) showcases and sells contemporary representational art by Harry Jackson, Margery Torrey, and Julie Oriet.

SHOPPING

★ Sheridan Avenue, Cody's main drag, is a great place to browse and shop among its many Native American and Western-theme shops. Most carry high-quality goods, but for those desiring the real McCoy, beware of those items claiming to be true in Native American handcraft or from local tribes. While judging an item's authenticity, be sure to determine whether it's made from natural or artificial materials. Head to the **Custom Cowboy Shop** (⊠ *1286 Sheridan Ave.* ☎ *800/487–2692*) to stock up on top-quality cowboy gear and clothing, ranging from hats and vests for men to women's shirts and jackets; there's even gear for your horse here. Also available are CDs by top Western recording artists such as Ian Tyson, Don Edwards, and Michael Martin Murphey.

★ **Indian Territory** (⊠ *1212 Sheridan Ave.* ☎ *307/527–5522*) lacks the variety of its imitators, but this small shop sells a high percentage of handmade Arapaho, Shoshone, Aztec jewelry, wall art, shadowboxes, clothing, hair shirts, dream catchers, walking sticks, and headdresses. **Flight West** (⊠ *1155 Sheridan Ave.* ☎ *307/527–7800*) sells designer Western women's wear, leather goods for men and women, books, gifts, and jewelry. Women shop at the **Plush Pony** (⊠ *1350 Sheridan Ave.* ☎ *307/587–4677*) for "uptown Western clothes" ranging from leather belts to stylish skirts, jackets, and dresses. The **Wyoming Buffalo Company** (⊠ *1270 Sheridan Ave.* ☎ *307/587–8708 or 800/453–0636*) sells buffalo-meat products, such as sausage and jerky, in addition to specialty foods such as huckleberry honey.

POWDER RIVER BASIN & THE BLACK HILLS

The rolling grassland of the Powder River Basin, in the far northeastern corner of Wyoming, is the ancestral homeland of the Lakota Sioux. On its western edge, the Big Horn Mountains are both a popular winter recreational area and a beautiful backdrop for the communities of Sheridan, Big Horn, and Buffalo. As you drive east, the mountains give way to coal mines (particularly around Gillette), oil fields, and family ranches, many of which were established in the 19th century by Basque sheepherders. Now one of the least-populated parts of America, the basin encompasses the vast Thunder Basin National Grasslands.

The Black Hills border the Powder River Basin to the east, where a couple of hundred thousand acres of Black Hills National Forest spill out of South Dakota into Wyoming. Thickly wooded with pine, spruce, and fir trees, the rocky slopes stand in stark contrast to the prairie below. Some of the most famous characters of the American West roamed across this soil, including Wild Bill Hickok, Calamity Jane, and the Sundance Kid, who took his name from a local town.

Dropping a Line

CLOSE UP

Casting into a clear stream or placid blue lake is a popular pastime all over Wyoming, with good reason: the waters of the entire state teem with trout, pike, whitefish, catfish, and bass of all kinds. Most fishing enthusiasts stick to the land near Yellowstone, leaving the blue-ribbon streams of northern Wyoming relatively underutilized. The Bighorn River, Powder River, Crazy Woman Creek, Keyhole Reservoir, and Buffalo Bill Reservoir are all excellent angling venues.

Fly-fishing is especially big here, and there's no shortage of outfitters to equip you, both in the towns and in the wilderness. Anyone with a pole—be it an experienced fly-fisher or novice worm dangler—is respected out here. All the same, if you're a beginner, you'd do well to hire a guide. Tackle-shop staff can direct you to some good fishing spots, but you're more likely to find the choicest locations if you have an experienced local at your side.

SHERIDAN

147 mi north of Casper via I–25 and I–90.

Proximity to the Big Horn Mountains and Bighorn National Forest makes Sheridan a good base for hiking, mountain biking, skiing, snowmobiling, and fly-fishing, and the small city's European-flavored cowboy heritage makes it an interesting stop for history buffs. Soon after trappers built a simple cabin along Little Goose Creek in 1873, the spot became a regional railroad center. Cattle barons, many of them English and Scottish noblemen, established ranches that remain the mainstay of the economy. Sheridan still has ties to Britain's aristocracy; in fact, Queen Elizabeth II herself has paid the town a visit. Recently, coal mines and oil wells to the east have brought much-needed jobs and tax income to this community of 16,429 residents.

Built in 1923 as a vaudeville theater called the Lotus, the **Wyo Theater** was closed and nearly demolished in the early 1980s. A strong show of support from the community saved the building, and now the refurbished art deco structure hosts everything from orchestras and ballets to lectures and Broadway revivals, especially in the summer. ⊠*42 N. Main St.* ☎*307/672–9084* ⊕*www.wyotheater.com.*

Local cowboy legend Don King owns **King's Saddlery and Ropes.** A saddle maker since the 1940s, King now lets his sons run the business. Besides selling high-quality equipment to area ranchers and professional rodeo performers, King's has crafted gear for many celebrities, including Queen Elizabeth II. Behind the store is a museum full of King's own collection, including saddles from the pre–Civil War era and medieval Japan. ⊠*184 N. Main St.* ☎*307/672–2702* ⊠*Free, donations accepted* ☉*Mon.–Sat. 8–5.*

★ A Flemish Revival mansion built in 1913 for John B. Kendrick, cattleman and one of Wyoming's first governors and senators, is now the **Trail End State Historic Site.** The furnishings and exhibits in the home are designed to depict early-20th-century ranching on the Plains. Highlights include elegant hand-carved woodwork and a third-floor ballroom. ⊠*400 Clarendon Ave.* ☎*307/674–4589* ⊕*www.trailend.org* ☜*$2* ⊙*Mar.–May and Sept.–mid-Dec., daily 1–4; June–Aug., daily 9–6.*

Fodor'sChoice
★
Evidence of the area's old-world ties can be found at the **Sheridan Inn,** just a few miles from downtown near the old railroad depot. Modeled after a hunting lodge in Scotland, the 1893 building sports 69 gables in a show of architectural splendor not often seen around these parts. On the National Register of Historic Places, the inn once lured the likes of Herbert Hoover, Will Rogers, and Ernest Hemingway, and Buffalo Bill auditioned performers here for his Wild West Show. The original Buffalo Bill Bar, an oak-and-mahogany monstrosity on the main floor, is said to have been a gift sent from England by Queen Victoria. Lunch and dinner are served all year, although patrons are no longer permitted to bring their horses inside. ⊠*856 Broadway, Box 6393, 82801* ☎*307/674–5440* ⊕*www.sheridaninn.com* ☜*Free, self-guided tour $2, guided tour $5* ⊙*Hrs vary by season; call for current schedule.*

SPORTS & THE OUTDOORS

FLY-FISHING
More of a custom adventure company than an outfitter, **Angling Destinations** (⊠*151 Powder Horn Rd.* ☎*800/211–8530*) arranges multi-day fishing trips to some of the most remote locations of Wyoming, Montana, and Idaho, as well as international destinations. For the less experienced angler, **Big Horn Mountain Sports** (⊠*334 N. Main St.* ☎*307/672–6866*) provides fly-fishing lessons and guided trips and rents and sells complete fly-fishing gear (including flies, rods, reels, waders, and hats). The full-service **Fly Shop of the Big Horns** (⊠*227 N. Main St.* ☎*800/253–5866*) offers sales, rentals, guided trips, and a fly-fishing school, a 2½-day class covering everything from casting to landing and releasing.

WHERE TO EAT

$$–$$$$
Fodor'sChoice
★
✕**Oliver's Bar and Grill.** Yellows, greens, and soft light accent this industrial-feeling restaurant with big-city ambience. Oliver's has an open kitchen, paintings from local artists on the walls, and perennially high marks from its loyal clientele. The ever-changing and eclectic menu carries Western favorites like burgers, salads, and chicken dishes as well as osso buco, pan-roasted Alaskan halibut, gnocchi, shrimp, and pasta. Seasonal items include Copper River salmon from Alaska, available here in early summer for only three weeks. From the kitchen bar you can watch chefs prepare your meal, and there's a diverse and inviting wine list, too. Afterward, such fine desserts as crème brûlée and cheesecake with port or cognac offer decadent possibilities. ⊠*55 N. Main St.* ☎*307/672–2838* ▤*AE, D, MC, V.*

$$
☾
✕**Sanford's Grub and Pub.** This replica of a hole-in-the-wall founded by a bunch of college buddies inhabits a massive old building but evokes the TV-land junk alley that inspired its name. With its mishmash of vintage signs, crusty car tags, sports team ephemera, and scrap heaps of memorabilia, it's no surprise that Sanford's menu of miscellany would be unlike most found in Wyoming. Here, Cajun and Southwestern-style dishes,

seafood pasta, and big juicy steaks compete with whimsically named half-pound burgers, salads, sandwiches, and Dixie-land favorites, including a huge selection of beers and a couple of in-house brews that might offend some finer folks. Oh yeah, try the Rocky Mountain Oysters if you dare! ⊠*1 E. Alger St.* ☎*307/674–1722* ▭*D, DC, MC, V.*

WHERE TO STAY

$$$$ 🏚**The Ranch at Ucross.** If you're looking to get in touch with yourself—or your traveling companion—the banks of Piney Creek may well be the place. In the foothills of the Big Horns, this tranquil Old West–style ranch is as relaxed as it gets. The four bedrooms in the restored 1912 house, as well as modern rooms and cabins around the property, are given a warm Western feel by gnarled wood lamps, quilt-covered beds, and comfy throws for cool nights. Most accommodations open onto spacious decks where you can read, watch the sun set, or just gaze at the Canada geese, grazing horses, and towering cottonwoods. Do some mountain-stream fishing or take a pack trip to mountain lakes. Good for family reunions and retreats. ⊠*2673 U.S. Hwy. 14, Clearmont 82835* ☎*307/737–2281 or 800/447–0194* ⊕*www.blairhotels. com* 🛏*31 rooms, 5 cabins* ♿*In-room: no TV, dial-up. In-hotel: bar, tennis courts, pool, no-smoking rooms, some pets allowed, no elevator* ▭*AE, D, MC, V* ⦿*FAP.*

$$–$$$$ 🏚**Sheridan Holiday Inn.** The soaring atrium of this five-story lodging, which is five minutes from downtown by car, has a waterfall and is filled with overstuffed chairs and couches. The rooms are typical of chain hotels, but most have some Western-style touches, and some look out on the Big Horn Mountains. Two restaurants ($–$$$$), the Brew Garden and Sugarland Mining Company, serve burgers, steak, chicken, and pasta. You can also grab a bite at Scooter's Bar. The Sunday brunch buffet starts at $10.95. ⊠*1809 Sugarland Dr., 82801* ☎*307/672–8931 or 877/672–4011* 🖷*307/672–6388* ⊕*www.holidayinnrockies. com* 🛏*212 rooms, 7 suites* ♿*In-hotel: 2 restaurants, bar, pool, gym, Wi-Fi, airport shuttle, no-smoking rooms, pets allowed free if paying by credit card* ▭*AE, D, DC, MC, V.*

$$$ 🏚**Eaton's Guest Ranch.** This spread is credited with inventing the dude ranch, back in the late 19th century, and it's still going strong as a working cattle ranch. Its location, west of Sheridan on the edge of the Bighorn National Forest, makes it ideal for horseback riding, fishing, cookouts, and pack trips. The ranch can accommodate 125 guests, and reservations for the summer should be made by March. The facilities are a collection of one-, two-, and three-bedroom cabins and the main lodge. There's a one-week minimum stay mid-June through August and a three-day minimum stay the rest of the season. ⊠*270 Eaton's Ranch Rd., Wolf 82844* ☎*307/655–9285 or 800/210–1049* 🖷*307/655–9269* ⊕*www.eatonsranch.com* 🛏*51 cabins* ♿*In-room: no a/c, no TV. In-hotel: pool, laundry facilities, airport shuttle, no-smoking rooms, no elevator* ▭*MC, V* ⊙*May 31–Sept. 30* ⦿*FAP.*

$ 🏚**The Mill Inn.** A former flour mill near a bridge has been converted into this motel with generic rooms on the east side of town, some facing a busy street. The building has six stories, but the top four floors are business offices. Furniture from a dude ranch fills much of the motel,

8

giving it a definite Western style. **Pros:** Near downtown, complimentary breakfast, hospitable staff, historic accents. **Cons:** Some think the inn is overpriced with some rooms too close to outside traffic and the bathrooms unaccommodating to those with handicaps. ⊠*2161 Coffeen Ave., 82801* ☎*307/672–6401 or 888/357–6455* 🖷*307/672–6401* ⊕*www.sheridanmillinn.com* 📼*45 rooms* 👤*In-hotel: gym, no-smoking rooms, restaurant, some pets allowed* ▤*AE, D, MC, V* ⭘|*CP.*

CAMPING   🏕 **Big Horn Mountain KOA Campground.** On the banks of Big Goose Creek minutes away from downtown Sheridan is this KOA, a well-developed campground with a basketball court, horseshoe pits, and a miniature-golf course. 👤*Flush toilets, full hookups, drinking water, showers, picnic tables, food service, electricity, Wi-Fi, public telephone, play area, swimming (pool)* 📼*40 full hookups, 12 tent sites; 6 cabins* ⊠*63 Decker Rd.* ☎*307/674–8766* ⊕*www.koakampgrounds.com* ⚓*Reservations essential* ▤*AE, D, MC, V.*

🏕 **Foothills Motel and Campground.** In the tiny town of Dayton, 20 mi west of Sheridan, this campground nestles in a cottonwood grove on the Tongue River, at the base of the Big Horns. In addition to tent and RV sites, there are cabins here. They are clean and well equipped with cable TV and showers, except for one: an aged and rustic log cabin heated by a woodstove. 👤*Flush toilets, full hookups, partial hookups (electric and water), drinking water, guest laundry, showers, picnic tables, electricity, public telephone, play area, swimming (river)* 📼*12 full hookups, 10 partial hookups, 30 tent sites; 10 cabins* ⊠*101 N. Main St., Dayton* ☎*307/655–2547* ⊕*www.foothillscampground.com* ▤*No credit cards.*

SHOPPING

The suburban malls that have drained so many downtowns are absent in Sheridan; instead, Main Street is lined with mostly homegrown—and sometimes quirky—shops.

In a break from typical gift stores stocked with rubber tomahawks, the **Best Out West Mall** (⊠*109 N. Main St.* ☎*307/674–5003*) is a two-story bazaar of Western paraphernalia, with booths hawking everything from spurs to rare books. Some items are new, but most are antiques. For an excellent selection of both local and general-interest books, try **The Book Shop** (⊠*117 N. Main St.* ☎*307/672–6505*). On occasion, local authors will spend several hours here signing their books. The **Crazy Woman Trading Company** (⊠*120 N. Main St.* ☎*307/672–3939* ⊕*crazywomantradingco.com*) sells unique gifts and antiques, including deluxe coffees and T-shirts sporting a black bear doing yoga. Murphy McDougal, the store's CEO (and the owners' golden retriever), is usually sleeping near the front door.

BIG HORN

9 mi south of Sheridan via Hwy. 335.

Now a gateway to Bighorn National Forest, this tree-lined town with mountain views was originally a rest stop for emigrants heading west.

An outpost on the Bozeman Trail, which crossed Bozeman Pass, Big Horn City in the mid-19th century was a lawless frontier town of saloons and roadhouses. After pioneers brought their families to the area in the late 1870s, the rowdy community quieted down. It never officially incorporated, so although it has a post office, fire department, and school, there is no bona-fide city government.

🕙 A hand-hewn-log blacksmith shop, built in 1879 to serve pioneers on their way to the goldfields of Montana, houses the **Bozeman Trail Museum,** the town's historical repository and interpretive center. The jewel of its collection is the Cloud Peak Boulder, a stone with names and dates apparently carved by military scouts just two days before the Battle of the Little Bighorn, which was fought less than 100 mi to the north in 1876. The staff is very friendly to children, and there are some old pipe organs that kids are encouraged to play. ✉335 Johnson St. ☎307/674–1600 ☞Free ☉Memorial Day–Labor Day, weekends 11–6.

If you're not staying at a ranch and you want to get a look at one of the West's finest, visit the **Bradford Brinton Memorial,** south of Big Horn on the old Quarter Circle A Ranch. The Brinton family didn't exactly rough it in this 20-room clapboard home, complete with libraries, fine furniture, and silver and china services. A reception gallery displays changing exhibits from the Brinton art collection, which includes such Western artists as Charles M. Russell and Frederic Remington. ✉239 Brinton Rd. ☎307/672–3173 ⊕www.bradfordbrintonmemorial.com/ ☞$4 ☉Memorial Day–Labor Day, daily 9:30–5.

Big Horn is an access point to the 1.1-million-acre **Bighorn National Forest,** which has lush grasslands, alpine meadows, rugged mountaintops, canyons, and deserts. There are numerous hiking trails and camping spots for use in the summer, and it's a popular snowmobiling area in the winter. ✉Ranger station, 2013 Eastside 2nd St., Sheridan ☎307/674–2600 ⊕www.fs.fed.us/r2/bighorn.

WHERE TO STAY & EAT

$–$$$ ✗**Bozeman Trail Inn.** A wood-slat building with a false front and tin roof, this is the oldest operating bar in Wyoming, established in 1882. The inn's only sign is painted on a mock covered wagon that's perched above the door. The kitchen serves standard burgers and sandwiches for lunch, steak and seafood for dinner, and prime rib on the weekends. ✉158 Johnson St. ☎307/672–9288 ☰MC, V ☉Closed Sun. and Mon.

$–$$$$ 🏠**Wagon Box Resort.** On the edge of the tiny town of Story, about 16 mi south of Big Horn, the Wagon Box, named after a conflict between Sioux warriors and loggers, lies at the base of the Big Horn Mountains. The rooms and cabins are furnished modestly in Western style; the cabins have fireplaces and porches with swings. This is a great spot for outdoor recreation—from hiking and fishing to horseback riding and barbecuing—and your hosts are happy to help you plan whatever activity suits your fancy. There are even horse corrals at the campground next door, so planning a quick ride or a major expedition into

8

neighboring Bighorn National Forest is a breeze. **Pros:** Rustic location, historic ambience. **Cons:** No pets, few modern amenities. ⊠*108 N. Piney Rd., Story 82842* ☎*307/683–2444* 🖷*307/683–2443* ⊕*www. wagonbox.com* 🛏*15 rooms, 5 cabins* ⚏*In-room: no a/c, no phone, kitchen (some), no TV. In-hotel: restaurant, bar, no-smoking rooms, some pets allowed, no elevator* ▤*AE, D, MC, V.*

$$–$$$ ▦ **Spahn's Big Horn Mountain Bed and Breakfast.** Ron and Bobbie Spahn have guest rooms and cabins at their soaring log home in the Big Horn Mountains. The rooms have tongue-and-groove woodwork, peeled-log beams, ruffled curtains, and peeled-log beds, and overlook Native American lands, mountain peaks, and Montana in the distance. It's more than a traditional B&B: you can participate in horseback riding, cookouts, and guided tours that include a wildlife-viewing trip. Family-style dinners, including fresh grilled steaks, are served by arrangement. **Pros:** Secluded, short drive to Big Horn (7.5 mi), (16.5 mi to Sheridan). **Cons:** Solar-powered electricity and limited hot water showers might exasperate those unaccustomed to more luxuries. ⊠*Hwy. 335, 7 mi south of Big Horn, Box 579, 82833* ☎*307/674–8150* 🖷*307/674–8150* ⊕*www.bighorn-wyoming.com* 🛏*5 rooms, 2 cabins* ⚏*In-room: no a/c, no phone, kitchen (some), no TV. In-hotel: no-smoking rooms, no elevator* ▤*No credit cards* ⑩*BP.*

BUFFALO

34 mi south of Big Horn via I–90, U.S. 87, and Hwy. 335.

Buffalo is a trove of history and a hospitable little town in the foothills below Big Horn Pass. Here cattle barons who wanted free grazing and homesteaders who wanted to build fences fought it out in the Johnson County War of 1892. Nearby are the sites of several skirmishes between the U.S. military and Native Americans along the Bozeman Trail. Buffalo is 182 mi due west on I-90 of Sturgis, South Dakota (⇨ Chapter 10). The first week of every August, Sturgis hosts a very popular and legendary biker's conclave. So, if you're passing through at this time of year, don't be surprised to hear the occasional roar of hogs.

Fodor's Choice The **Jim Gatchell Memorial Museum** is the kind of small-town museum
★ that's worth stopping for if you're interested in the frontier history of the region, including the Johnson County War. It contains Native American, military, outlaw, and ranching artifacts collected by a local druggist who was a close friend of area Native Americans. In 2007 this nationally accredited museum celebrated its 50th anniversary after undergoing a $300,000 upgrade. ⊠*100 Fort St.* ☎*307/684–9331* ⊕*www.jimgatchell.com* 🛏*$5* ⊙*Mid-Apr.–late Oct., weekdays 9–8.*

★ Signs bearing a buffalo symbol mark the **Clear Creek Trail** (☎*307/684–5544 or 800/227–5122*), which consists of about 11 mi of trails following Clear Creek through Buffalo and past historic areas. The trail has both paved and unpaved sections that you can traverse on foot or by bicycle. Along it you see the Occidental Hotel (made famous by Owen Wister's novel *The Virginian*), a brewery and mill site, and the site of

Fort McKinney, now the Veterans' Home of Wyoming. You can also use the trail for wildlife viewing, photography, and access to fishing.

★ The frontier army occupied the military installation at **Fort Phil Kearny State Historic Site** for only a couple of years in the mid-1860s. Considered a hardship post by officers and enlisted men alike, the fort protected travelers headed to Montana's goldfields and later distracted Native Americans from the construction of the transcontinental railroad to the south. Eventually the constant attacks by the Plains Indians paid off, and the fort was abandoned in 1868 as part of the Fort Laramie Treaty. No original buildings remain at the site—they were likely burned by the Cheyenne as soon as the soldiers left—but fort buildings are marked and the visitor center has good details. The stockade around the fort was re-created after archaeological digs in 1999. ⊠ *15 mi north of Buffalo on I–90* ☎ *307/684–7629* ⊕ *www.philkearny.vcn.com* ✉ *$2* ⊙ *Interpretive center: mid-May–Sept., daily 8–6.*

SPORTS & THE OUTDOORS

The forested canyons and pristine alpine meadows of the Big Horn Mountains teem with animal and plant life, making this an excellent area for hiking and pack trips by horseback. The quality and concentration of locals willing to outfit adventurers are high in Buffalo, making it a suitable base camp from which to launch an expedition.

The folks at **South Fork Mountain Outfitters** (⊠ *16 mi west of Buffalo on U.S. 16* ☎ *307/267–2609* ⊕ *southfork-lodge.com*) can customize about any sort of adventure you'd like to undertake in the Big Horns, whether it's hiking, fishing, horseback riding, snowmobiling, or cross-country skiing. The company can arrange for all of your food and supplies and provide a guide, or render drop-camp services for more experienced thrill seekers.

FLY-FISHING The **Sports Lure** (⊠ *66 S. Main St.* ☎ *800/684–7682*) stocks rods, reels, flies, books, and outdoor wear. You can also arrange for lessons and guided fishing trips.

HORSEBACK RIDING & PACK TRIPS Located on a 24,000-acre working ranch, the **Powder River Experience** (⊠ *U.S. 14, Clearmont* ☎ *307/758–4381 or 888/736–2402*) gives you the chance to ride on the open range or to pack into the backcountry for an overnight stay at a log cabin. You're also encouraged to watch or personally experience as many ranch activities as you wish, whether it's branding, cattle driving, or calving.

Trails West Outfitters (⊠ *259 Sunset Ave.* ☎ *307/684–5233 or 888/283–9793* ⊕ *www.trailswestoutfitters.com*) arranges multiday pack trips in the Bighorn and Shoshone national forests. The company also operates shorter wilderness excursions and drop camps for more independent adventurers.

WHERE TO EAT

$$–$$$$ ✕ **The Virginian Restaurant.** Named for the 1902 Owen Wister novel that Fodor'sChoice made Buffalo famous, this is the dining salon of the beautifully restored ★ Occidental Hotel. Dishes made from organic beef range from buffalo rib eye to chateaubriand and filet mignon with béarnaise sauce. Further

delights include shrimp scampi, swordfish, and chicken marsala, all served amid the splendor of antique mirrors, Western art, and Victorian lamps; many fixtures are from the original building. Period lamps light the 19th-century brass-color tin ceiling, and wainscoting accents the maroon-colored walls. There's also a kids' menu, and starry-eyed couples can dine in candlelit seclusion within the old Stockmen's bank vault. ✉ *10 N. Main St.* ☎ *307/684–0451* ▭ *AE, D, MC, V.*

$$–$$$$ ★ ✕ **Winchester Steak House.** You can tie up your car in front of the hitch racks before this Western-style eatery in a false-front building. The Winchester has prime rib, steak, and more steak, plus appetizers, a good wine list, and a large rock fireplace and small bar. Locals rave about the place. ✉ *117 Hwy. 16 E* ☎ *307/684–8636* ▭ *MC, V* ⊙ *Closed Sun. and Mon. No lunch.*

$$$ ✕ **Colonel Bozeman's Restaurant and Tavern.** This eatery, which is literally on the Bozeman Trail, serves decent food, from chicken, taco, and Cobb salads to local favorites such as prime-rib melts and club sandwiches or bison steak, burgers, and king-cut prime-rib plates amid Western memorabilia. You can also dine outdoors on the deck and sip from the large selection of microbrews. ✉ *675 E. Hart St.* ☎ *307/684–5555* 🌐 *bozemancrossing.com/restaurant.htm* ▭ *D, MC, V.*

¢–$$ ★ ✕ **Deerfield Boutique and Espresso Bar.** For a change from steak and potatoes, try this café in a renovated historic theater with high ceilings and old wallpaper. The place serves a wide selection of simple soups, salads, tortilla wraps, and specialty sandwiches such as lemon-ginger chicken pita, and turkey and Swiss on focaccia. In summer there are chilled soups like tomato wine, cream of cantaloupe, and spinach cucumber. The Polynesian and mandarin orange salads are equally refreshing. Deerfield is next to Clear Creek in downtown Buffalo. ✉ *7 N. Main St.* ☎ *307/684–7776* ▭ *MC, V.*

WHERE TO STAY

$$$–$$$$ Fodor's Choice ★ **Paradise Guest Ranch.** Not only does this dude ranch 13 mi west of Buffalo have a stunning location at the base of some of the tallest mountains in the range, but it's also one of the oldest (circa 1905) and most progressive, as evidenced by its adults-only month (September) and two ladies' weeks. The rest of the summer has extensive children's programs, with everything from overnight pack trips to a kids' rodeo, crafts, and pony rides as well as nature hikes. Adult programs involve sing-alongs, fancy barbecues with wine, gourmet meals, and square dances. The wranglers are very careful about matching riders to appropriate horses; multiday trips for veterans venture into the Bighorn National Forest and Cloud Peak Wilderness Area. Cabins are simple. Some have fireplaces; all have full baths and kitchenettes. There's a one-week minimum stay. **Pros:** Clean cabins with rustic, beautiful views, hospitable staff, good children's programs, ask about 30% June discounts. **Cons:** Minumum stays, 11.5 mi to Buffalo, cold mornings until late spring. ✉ *282 Hunter Creek Rd., off U.S. 16, Box 790, 82834* ☎ *307/684–7876* 📠 *307/684–7380* 🌐 *www.paradiseranch.com* *18 cabins* *In-room: no a/c, no phone, kitchen, no TV. In-hotel: bar, pool, children's programs (ages 6–18), laundry facilities, airport shuttle, no elevator.* ▭ *No credit cards* ⊙ *Closed Oct.–Apr.* *FAP.*

$–$$$ ⌂**Occidental Hotel.** Voted a True West magazine's "Best" two years
Fodor'sChoice   running, this enchanting, fully restored grand hotel, founded in 1880,
★   served emigrants on the Bozeman Trail, two U.S. presidents, and some
of Wyoming's most colorful characters. Owen Wister immortalized
the Occidental in his 1902 novel, *The Virginian*, about the Johnson
County Cattle War. After winning a high-stakes poker game in 1918,
one family held on to the hotel for 58 years, keeping intact all of its
original furnishings and architectural accents. A lavish $1 million-plus
restoration under current owners John and Dawn Wexo spruced up
the Victorian-style rooms and tin-ceiling lobby, saloon, and restaurant,
sparing this living treasure from the wrecking ball. Most spectacular
among the many nostalgic suites are the Clear Creek, with its six-post
cherrywood bed, adjoining sitting room, and spacious bathroom, and
the elegant Teddy Roosevelt Suite, furnished with a high-back walnut
bed, an antique hardwood desk, and a claw-foot tub. Making the time
machine complete are the ubiquitous old-timey tube radios playing
such yesteryear classics as "Calling All Cars," "The Lone Ranger," and
early cowboy crooner Gene Autry. Down in the saloon, the 25-foot
bar, stained-glass shade, and tin ceiling look brand new—except for
23 bullet holes, revealing its origins in the cutthroat, quick-draw era.
On Thursday nights nowadays, there's usually a bluegrass hootenanny
jam-packed with friendlies. **Pros:** Well-stocked library, gracious ser-
vice, owners on premises, well-appointed rooms, gourmet restaurant.
Cons: No pool, Wi-fi signal can be weak in certain areas, old plumbing.
⊠*10 N. Main St., 82834* ☎*307/684–0451* ⊕*occidentalwyoming.com*
⤶*14 rooms, 9 suites* ⚷*In-hotel: 2 restaurants, Wi-Fi, no-smoking
rooms, some pets allowed, no elevator* ⊟*AE, D, MC, V.*

$ ⌂**Blue Gables Motel.** Old West collectibles and quilts add warmth to
this highway-side motel's homey log cabins clustered in a U-shape.
A few tent sites and a two-bedroom house are also available nearby.
Pros: Owners on premises, tent sites, heated pool, laundry facilities,
café. Close to town. **Cons:** Not geared to executive business travelers
or upscale vacationers. ⊠*662 N. Main St., 82834* ☎*307/684–2574 or
800/684–2574* ⊕*www.bluegables.com* ⤶*17 cabins* ⚷*In-hotel: pool,
no-smoking rooms, no elevator.* ⊟*D, MC, V.*

CAMPING   ⛰**Deer Park Campground.** Although one section of this campground is
quiet and relaxed, reserved for campers over 55, the main campsites
are busy. In addition to a heated pool and a hot tub, Deer Park offers
guided fishing excursions during the day (for a fee) and free ice-cream
socials at night. Rates vary dramatically, depending on the number of
site occupants. ⚷*Flush toilets, full hookups, partial hookups (electric
and water), drinking water, showers, picnic tables, electricity, public
telephone, swimming (pool)* ⤶*33 full hookups, 33 partial hookups,
34 tent sites, 3 cabins* ⊠*146 U.S. 16* ☎*307/684–5722 or 800/222–
9960* ⊕*www.deerparkrv.com* ⚐*Reservations essential* ⊟*MC, V*
☾*May–Sept.*

8

NIGHTLIFE

Regulation pool tables and live country music and dancing every Friday and Saturday night (no cover charge) make the **White Buffalo Saloon** (⌧*106 U.S. 16* ☎*307/684–0101*) a local favorite. The gift shop sells T-shirts, shot glasses, and other kitsch emblazoned with the White Buffalo logo.

SHOPPING

★ Cast-iron chandeliers with a Western flair are the signature products of **Frontier Iron Works** (⌧*659 Trabing Rd.* ☎*307/684–5154 or 800/687–6952*). They also craft distinctive furniture ranging from bar stools and patio sets to wall sconces and fireplace screens.

GILLETTE

70 mi east of Buffalo on I–90.

With 19,646 residents, Gillete is the metropolis of the Powder River Basin. Thanks to the region's huge coal mines, it's one of Wyoming's wealthiest cities, and as a result it has an excellent community infrastructure that includes the Cam-Plex, a multiuse events center that hosts everything from crafts bazaars and indoor rodeos to concerts and fine-arts exhibits. Gillette is also a gateway town for Devils Tower National Monument, the volcanic plug that is one of the nation's most distinctive geological features and a hot spot for rock climbers.

Gillette has worked hard to make itself presentable, but you don't have to look very hard to find a shovel bigger than a house at one of its giant strip mines. Once a major livestock center, from which ranchers shipped cattle and sheep to eastern markets, the city now mines millions of tons of coal each year and ships it out to coal-fired power plants. In fact, if Gillette (and surrounding Campbell County) were its own nation, it would be the world's sixth-greatest producer of coal. Currently the county turns out nearly a third of all American-mined coal. Gillette, however, is a big fish in a small pond, one of only two incorporated towns in the county (the other is Wright, population 1,347).

WHAT TO SEE

Anything from a rodeo or crafts show to a concert or melodrama could be going on at the **Cam-Plex,** Gillette's multiuse facility. There's something scheduled almost every day; call or check the Web site for details. ⌧*1635 Reata Dr.* ☎*307/682–0552, 307/682–8802 for tickets* ⊕*www.cam-plex.com* ☽*Check Web site for schedule.*

You can fish, boat, swim, and camp at **Keyhole State Park.** Bird-watching is a favorite activity here, as up to 225 species can be seen on the grounds. ⌧*353 McKean Rd.* ☎*307/756–3596, 307/756–9529 marina information* ⊕*wyoparks.state.wy.us/index.asp* ⌑*$2 resident vehicle, $4 nonresident vehicle; camping $6 resident vehicle, $12 nonresident vehicle.*

Local artifacts, including bits, brands, and rifles, make up the collection at the Campbell County–run **Rockpile Museum.** The museum's name comes from its location next to a natural rock-pile formation that served as a landmark for pioneers. ✉*900 W. 2nd St.* ☎*307/682–5723* ⊕*www.rockpilemuseum.com* 🖃*Free* ☉*June–Aug., Mon.–Sat. 9–7, Sun. 1–5; Sept.–May, Mon.–Sat. 9–5.*

At the **Eagle Butte Coal Mine,** 17 mi south of Gillette, shovels and haul trucks dwarf anything you're likely to see in a science-fiction movie. There's a surprising amount of wildlife, from falcons to deer to bobcats, dwelling in and around the huge pits. You can register for the summer tours of the mine at the Gillette Visitors Center. ✉*Gillette Visitors Center, Flying J Travel Plaza, 1810 S. Douglas Hwy. #A* ☎*307/686–0040 or 800/544–6136* 🖃*Free* ☉*Tours June–Aug., daily 9* AM *and 11* AM.

OFF THE BEATEN PATH

Thunder Basin National Grasslands. An 890-square-mi wilderness preserve that stretches from the edge of the Black Hills almost to the center of Wyoming, Thunder Basin truly is the outback of America. Except for a handful of tiny towns, deserted highways, and coal mines, it is entirely undeveloped. Farmers from the east settled this area at the end of the 19th century, hoping to raise crops in the semiarid soil. Experienced only with the more humid conditions east of the Rockies, the farmers failed, and the region deteriorated into a dust bowl. Most of the land has reverted to its natural state, creating millions of acres of grasslands filled with wildlife. Among the many species is one of the largest herds of pronghorn in the world (numbering approximately 26,000), prairie dogs, and burrowing owls that live in abandoned prairie dog holes. U.S. 116 and U.S. 450 provide the best access; a few interior dirt roads are navigable only in dry weather. The grasslands, though, are most impressive away from the highways. Take a hike to get a real sense of the vast emptiness of this land. ✉*U.S. 450* ☎*307/745–2300* ⊕*www. fs.fed.us/r2/mbr/* 🖃*Free* ☉*Daily 24 hrs.*

WHERE TO EAT

★ $$–$$$$ ✕**The Chophouse.** In the middle of a ranching town in the middle of ranching country, it's no surprise that more than half of this restaurant's menu is devoted to beef. Chef Ray Marini, who helped open the first American restaurant in the Soviet Union, uses only certified Angus, and only cuts that have been aged to his standards. The remainder of the menu is split between pasta and dishes made with fresh fish flown in at Marini's request. Of course, the beef dishes—including the massive 22-ounce bone-in rib eye—remain house favorites. The two dining rooms are on the ground floor of a renovated century-old hotel: one is cheerfully decorated in a Western motif, and the other is accented with dark-wood trim and artwork by Frank Sinatra, one of the owner's favorite celebrities. ✉*113 S. Gillette Ave.* ☎*307/682–6805* ▭*AE, MC, V.*

¢–$$ ✕**Hong Kong.** Lunches here are served fast and cheap (between $5 and $6) and include more than 30 different dishes, such as Mongolian beef and cashew chicken. They're popular with the business crowd, so you might want to avoid the noon lunch rush. ✉*1612 W. 2nd St.* ☎*307/682–5829* ▭*AE, D, MC, V.*

8

WHERE TO STAY

$$–$$$ 🛅**Clarion Western Plaza.** Travelers with a yen for exercise appreciate the gym and a pool of lap-swimming proportions at this motel with everything under one roof. Rooms are decorated in burnt red and cream colors. **Pros:** Visitors can grab a cup of coffee at the Mountain Mudd Espresso shop, on-site, or take a dip in the mineral pool. **Cons:** The location provides little variety for nearby restaurants except fast food. ✉2009 S. Douglas Hwy., 82718 ☎307/686–3000 or 800/686–3068 🖷307/686–4018 ⊕www.westernplaza.com ⏎146 rooms, 13 suites △In-room: refrigerator (some). In-hotel: restaurant, pool, gym, Wi-Fi, no-smoking rooms ⊟AE, D, DC, MC, V.

$–$$ 🛅**Best Western Tower West Lodge.** Shades of beige and teal decorate the large, comfortable rooms of this hotel on the west side of town. Among the public spaces are an outdoor courtyard and a lobby with leather couches and chairs grouped around the fireplace. **Pros:** Close to a variety of restaurants and easy interstate access. **Cons:** Located a fair distance from the downtown area. ✉109 N. U.S. 14/16, 82716 ☎307/686–2210 🖷307/682–5105 ⊕www.bestwestern.com ⏎189 rooms △In-hotel: restaurant, bar, pool, gym, no-smoking rooms, no elevator, Wi-Fi ⊟AE, D, DC, MC, V.

SHOPPING

The people of Campbell County take their gardening seriously, as any observer can tell by walking into the **Sunrise Greenhouse** (✉7568 Hwy. 59, 38 mi south of Gillette, Wright ☎307/464–0889 or 888/820–0889 ⊕www.sunrisegreenhousewy.com) in the springtime. A community institution, this greenhouse not only keeps local and exotic plants in stock but also carries an extensive selection of flowers for special occasions.

DEVILS TOWER NATIONAL MONUMENT

★ *65 mi northeast of Gillette via I–90 and U.S. 14.*

As you drive east from Gillette, the highways begin to rise into the forested slopes of the Black Hills. A detour north will take you to Devils Tower, a rocky, grooved butte that juts upward 1,280 feet above the plain of the Belle Fourche River. Native American legend has it that the tower was corrugated by the claws of a bear trying to reach some children on top, and some tribes still revere the site, which they call Bear Lodge. Geologists attribute the butte's strange existence to ancient volcanic activity. Rock climbers say it's one of the best crack-climbing areas on the continent. The tower was a tourist magnet long before a spaceship landed here in the movie *Close Encounters of the Third Kind.* Teddy Roosevelt made it the nation's first national monument in 1906, and it has attracted a steadily increasing throng of visitors ever since—up to nearly half a million people a year.

When you visit Devils Tower, take some time to stop at the **visitor center,** a few miles beyond the park entrance. Exhibits here explain the geology, history, and cultural significance of the monument, and a bookstore carries a wide selection of materials relating to the park.

Park rangers can provide updated information on hiking and climbing conditions. ⊠*Hwy. 110* ☎*307/467–5283* ⊕*www.nps.gov/deto/* 🚗*Cars and motorcycles $10; bicycles and pedestrians $5* ☉*Butte daily 24 hrs; visitor center daily 9–5* PM, *May–Nov.*

SPORTS & THE OUTDOORS

HIKING Aside from affording excellent views of Devils Tower and the surrounding countryside, the hiking trails here are a good way to view some of the geology and wildlife of the Black Hills region. The terrain that surrounds the butte is relatively flat, so the popular **Tower Trail**, a paved 1 - mi path that circles the monument, is far from strenuous. It's the most popular trail in the park, though, so if you're looking for more isolation, try the 1½-mi **Joyner Ridge Trail** or the 3-mi **Red Beds Trail.** They're a bit more demanding, but the views from the top of Joyner Ridge and the banks of the Belle Fourche River are more than adequate rewards. Both the Tower and Red Beds trails start at the visitor center; Joyner Ridge Trail begins about a mile's drive north from there.

ROCK CLIMBING Climbing is the premier sporting activity at Devils Tower. Acclaimed as one of the best crack-climbing areas in North America, the monument has attracted both beginners and experts for more than a century. There are few restrictions when it comes to ascending the granite cone. Although climbing is technically allowed all year, there is generally a voluntary moratorium in June to allow for peaceful religious rites performed by local Native American tribes. Additionally, the west face of the formation is closed intermittently in the summer to protect the prairie falcons that nest there.

Before ascending Devils Tower you should sign in at the **visitor center** (⊠*Hwy. 110* ☎*307/467–5283*) and discuss conditions with park officials. You can obtain a list of park-licensed guides here; courses are offered at all skill levels and sometimes include excursions into the Rockies or South Dakota. Some tour operators continue to guide climbs during the voluntary ban in June.

CAMPING

⚠ **Belle Fourche Campground.** Tucked away in a bend of the Belle Fourche River, this campground is small and spartan, but it is the only place in the park where camping is allowed. ♿*Flush toilets, drinking water, picnic tables* 🏕*30 sites* ⊠*Hwy. 110* ☎*307/467–5283* 🖨*307/467–5350* ⊕*www.nps.gov/deto/* ⚠*Reservations not accepted* ▤*No credit cards* ☉*Apr.–Nov.*

⚠ **Devils Tower KOA.** Less than a mile from Devils Tower, this campground literally lies in the shadow of the famous stone monolith. The view of the sheer granite walls above red river bluffs is one of the property's greatest assets. Another is the bordering Belle Fourche River, which nurtures several stalwart cottonwood and ash trees that provide at least some areas with shade. Weather permitting, the campground stages a nightly outdoor showing of *Close Encounters of the Third Kind.* ♿*Flush toilets, full hookups, partial hookups (electric and water), drinking water, guest laundry, showers, picnic tables, public telephone, general store, play area, swimming (pool)* 🏕*56 full*

8

hookups, 30 tent sites; 11 cabins ✉*Hwy. 110* ☎*307/467–5395 or 800/562–5785* ⊕*www.devilstowerkoa.com* ⊟*AE, D, DC, MC, V* ⊙*May–Sept.*

SHOPPING

At **Devils Tower Trading Post** (✉*57 Hwy. 110* ☎*307/467–5295*), at the entrance to Devils Tower National Monument, you can purchase informative books, Western art, buffalo hides, clothing, knickknacks, and souvenirs. A giant Harley-Davidson flag (supposedly the world's largest) flies over the store, so it's no wonder that bikers overrun the place during the massive Sturgis Motorcycle Rally the first week of August. The old-fashioned ice-cream parlor, which also serves a mean sarsaparilla, is a real treat in the heat of summer.

SUNDANCE

31 mi southeast of Devils Tower National Monument via U.S. 14.

A combination of traditional reverence and an infamous outlaw's date with destiny put Sundance on Wyoming's map, and continues to draw visitors today. Native American tribes such as the Crow, Cheyenne, and Lakota consider Sundance Mountain and the Bear Lodge Mountains to be sacred. Before whites arrived in the 1870s the Native Americans congregated nearby each June for their Sun Dance, an important ceremonial gathering. The event gave its name to this small town, which in turn gave its name to the outlaw Harry Longabaugh, the Sundance Kid, who spent time in the local jail for stealing a horse. Ranch country and the western Black Hills surround the town.

★   Thousands of buffalo bones are piled atop each other at the **Vore Buffalo Jump,** where Native Americans forced buffalos to plunge to their deaths in the era when hunting was done with spears rather than fast horses and guns. ✉*Frontage Rd.* ☎*307/283–1000* ⊕*www.sundance wyoming.com/vore.htm* ▣*Free* ⊙*Daily.*

Projects by local young people are displayed at the **Crook County Fair and Rodeo** during the first week in August, from cooking and clothing to livestock projects. There also are live music shows, basketball tournaments, a Dutch oven cook-off, pig wrestling, and a rodeo with sheepdog trials and team roping events. ✉*Fairgrounds Loop Rd.* ☎*307/283–2644* ⊕*www.wyomingfairs.org* ▣*Free.*

WHERE TO EAT

$–$$$ ✗**Aro Restaurant and Lounge.** This large family diner in downtown Sundance has a cowboys-and-Indians theme and an extensive, well-priced menu. Standards include burgers, prime rib, Southwestern smothered burritos, Reuben sandwiches, and a huge Devils Tower brownie sundae dessert. ✉*203 Cleveland St.* ☎*307/283–2000* ⊟*D, MC, V.*

¢–$$ ✗**Country Cottage.** This one-stop shop in the center of town sells flowers, gifts, and simple meals, including submarine sandwiches. There's a modest seating area with some booths and small tables. ✉*423 Cleveland St.* ☎*307/283–2450* ⊟*MC, V.*

¢–$$ ✕**Log Cabin Café.** Locals crowd this small log-cabin restaurant full of country crafts for burgers, steaks, and seafood. Because the place is always packed, service can be slow, but the staff is always friendly. ⊠*1620 E. Cleveland St.* ☎*307/283–3393* ☐*MC, V.*

WHERE TO STAY

¢–$$$ 🛏**Best Western Inn at Sundance.** Brown carpeting and red drapes decorate the spacious rooms of this hotel. With its inlaid cedar accents and comfortable deck chairs, the room housing the indoor pool is surprisingly stylish for a chain hotel. **Pros:** Contemporary furnishings. **Cons:** At the edge of town. ⊠*2719 Cleveland St., 82729* ☎*307/283–2800 or 800/238–0965* 🖨*307/283–2727* ⊕*www.blackhillslodging.com* ⤶*44 rooms* 🜲*In-hotel: pool, laundry facilities, no-smoking rooms, some pets allowed, Wi-Fi, no elevator* ☐*AE, D, DC, MC, V* �🍴*CP.*

¢–$$$ 🛏**Rodeway Inn.** Clean but basic rooms, friendly service, and a comfortable poolside area make this one-story ranch-style motor inn a nice place to stay. It's convenient to I–90 and across the street from area restaurants. **Pros:** New furniture and carpeting in rooms. **Cons:** Rooms all open to the outside. ⊠*26 Hwy. 585, 82729* ☎*307/283–3737* 🖨*307/283–3738* ⊕*www.choicehotels.com* ⤶*42 rooms* 🜲*In-room: refrigerators (some). In-hotel: pool, laundry facilities, no-smoking rooms, some pets allowed, no elevator* ☐*AE, D, DC, MC, V* �🍴*CP.*

¢–$$ 🛏**Bear Lodge Motel.** A cozy lobby, a stone fireplace, and wildlife mounts on the walls distinguish this downtown motel. Hardwood furniture and patterned bedspreads add a slightly Western touch to the spacious, simple bedrooms. DVDs and players are available for use at no charge. **Pros:** Accepts pets, downtown location. **Cons:** Slightly outdated appearance. ⊠*218 Cleveland St., 82729* ☎*307/283–1611* 🖨*307/283–2537* ⊕*www.bearlodgemotel.com* ⤶*33 rooms* 🜲*In-room: refrigerator (some). In-hotel: no-smoking rooms, no elevator, Wi-Fi* ☐*AE, D, DC, MC, V.*

THE NORTH PLATTE RIVER VALLEY

Sweeping down from the Colorado Rockies into the very center of Wyoming, the North Platte River was a key waterway for emigrants because its valley was one of the few places where wagons could safely cross the mountains. A deep pioneer legacy survives here, where several trails converged along the Platte and Sweetwater rivers and snaked through South Pass. Some of the travelers put down roots, and the North Platte River valley remains one of Wyoming's important agricultural areas.

Much of this area is cattle country, for one simple reason: it's flat and dry. On some of the westernmost ranges of short grassland before the Rockies thrust up from the plains, the land is relatively treeless. The human presence consists largely of fences, livestock, a few small cow towns, and the bustling Western city of Casper. Today a hefty share of central Wyoming's wealth derives from its deposits of oil, uranium, and bentonite.

LUSK

140 mi northeast of Cheyenne via I–25 and U.S. 18.

Proudly rural, the 1,500 townspeople of Lusk often poke gentle fun at themselves, emblazoning T-shirts with phrases such as "End of the world, 12 miles. Lusk, 15 miles." You'll see what they mean if you visit this seat of Niobrara County, whose population density averages 524 acres of prairie per person. If you find yourself traveling the main route between the Black Hills and the Colorado Rockies, a stop in this tiny burg is worth the time for a quick lesson in frontier—particularly stagecoach—history. You can also find gasoline and food, rare commodities on the open plain.

Artifacts from early settlement days and the period when the Cheyenne–Deadwood Stage Line was in full swing are some of the displays at the **Stagecoach Museum.** You also can get information about the Texas Cattle Trail. ⊠*322 S. Main St.* ☎*307/334–3444 or 800/223–5875* ⊡*$2* ⊙*May–Aug., weekdays 10–6; Sept. and Oct., weekdays 10–4.*

You can still see the remains of one of the Cheyenne–Deadwood Stage Line stops at the **Historic Hat Creek Stage Station.** Also here are an old schoolhouse and post office out in the tallgrass plains. You can wander among the buildings whenever you like, but to see the insides you must call for a tour. ⊠*15 mi north of Lusk on U.S. 85, then 2 mi east on gravel road* ☎*307/334–2950, 307/334–2134 for private tour* ⊡*Free* ⊙*Daily.*

WHERE TO STAY & EAT

¢–$ ✕**Pizza Place.** A casual atmosphere and good food come together at this downtown eatery. Pizza, calzones, and sub sandwiches made with homemade bread are on the menu, and there's also a salad bar. ⊠*218 S. Main St.* ☎*307/334–3000* ⊟*No credit cards.*

$ 🏨**Covered Wagon.** With a covered wagon on the front portico, an indoor pool, and an outdoor playground, this U-shape hotel is an inviting place for families with kids. **Pros:** Newly installed playground for the kids. **Cons:** Books up quickly in the summer, so plan ahead. ⊠*730 S. Main St., 82225* ☎*307/334–2836 or 800/341–8000* ⊟*307/334–2977* ⇆*51 rooms* ⚫*In-hotel: pool, laundry facilities, no-smoking rooms, no elevator* ⊟*AE, DC, MC, V* ⓘ○*CP.*

¢–$$ 🏨**Best Western Pioneer Court.** Although the exterior of this motel near downtown and the Stagecoach Museum is unremarkable, the lobby is attractive, with a ceramic-tile floor, hardwood trim, and wrought-iron tables and lamps. There are some extra-large rooms that can accommodate up to eight people. **Pros:** Nice furnishings. **Cons:** Outdoor pool open only part of the year. ⊠*731 Main St., 82225* ☎*307/334–2640* ⊟*307/334–2660* ⊕*www.bestwestern.com* ⇆*30 rooms* ⚫*In-room: refrigerator. In-hotel: restaurant, bar, pool, no-smoking rooms, no elevator, Wi-Fi* ⊟*AE, D, DC, MC, V.*

¢ 🏨**Rawhide Motel.** The standard-size rooms are rustic but warm, and service is friendly at this affordable, locally owned motel in downtown Lusk. It's within walking distance of area restaurants. **Pros:** Good location **Cons:** No pool. ⊠*805 S. Main St., 82225* ☎*307/334–2440 or*

888/679–2558 🖷307/334–2440 ↩19 rooms ⟁In-room: refrigerator. In-hotel: no-smoking rooms, some pets allowed, Wi-Fi ▭AE, D, MC, V.

EN ROUTE A few miles east of **Glendo State Park** lies a vast stone quarry initially mistaken for the work of early Spanish explorers. Archaeologists later determined the site, known as the **Spanish Diggings**, to be the work of various indigenous tribes on and off for the past several thousand years. Tools and arrowheads carved from the stone quarried here, including quartzite, jasper, and agate, have been found as far away as the Ohio River valley. To see the diggings you'll have to drive through Glendo State Park. ✉State Rd. 319 ☎307/735–4433 ⊕wyoparks.state.wy.us/ Parks/Glendo/index.asp ⛟$4 per vehicle ☉Daily.

DOUGLAS

55 mi west of Lusk via U.S. 18 and I–25.

Douglas is best known for two things: the Wyoming State Fair, which has been held here annually since 1905, and the jackalope. A local taxidermist assembled the first example of the mythical cross between a jackrabbit and an antelope for display in a local hotel. There's an 8-foot-tall concrete jackalope statue in Jackalope Square in downtown Douglas, and many businesses sell jackalope figures and merchandise.

The weeklong **Wyoming State Fair and Rodeo,** held in early August each year at the Wyoming State Fairgrounds, includes a carnival, livestock judging, commercial exhibits, and a Professional Rodeo Cowboys Association rodeo. ✉400 W. Center St. ☎307/358–2398 ⊕www. wystatefair.com ⛟$4 ☉Early Aug.; call for exact dates.

At the **Wyoming Pioneer Memorial Museum,** the emphasis is on the Wyoming pioneer settlers and overland immigrants, but this small state-operated museum on the state fairgrounds also has displays on Native Americans and the frontier military. ✉400 W. Center St. ☎307/358–9288 ⊕www.wypioneermuseum.com ⛟Free ☉June–Aug., weekdays 8–5, Sat. 1–5; Sept.–May, by appointment.

Overland immigrants sometimes visited **Ayres Natural Bridge** (✉Off I–25 ☎307/358–3532), a rock outcrop that spans LaPrele Creek. It's now a small but popular picnic area and campsite where you can wade in the creek or simply enjoy the quiet. No pets are allowed at the campsite.

Built in 1867 to protect travelers headed west, the army post here is preserved today as the **Fort Fetterman State Historic Site.** Two buildings, the ordnance warehouse and officers' quarters, survived decades of abandonment and today house interpretive exhibits and artifacts related to the area's history and the fort's role in settling the West. The remains of other fort buildings can still be seen, as can the ruins of Fetterman City, which died out when Douglas was founded several miles to the south. ✉752 Hwy. 93 ☎307/684–7629, 307/358–2864 for res-

8

ervations ⊕*wyoparks.state.wy.us/sites/fortfetterman/index.asp* 🖅*$1 residents, $2 nonresidents* ⊙*Memorial Day–Labor Day, daily 9–5.*

The **Medicine Bow National Forest, Douglas District** (⊠*Douglas Ranger District, 2250 E. Richards St.* ☎*307/358–4690* ⊕*www.fs.fed.us/r2/ mbr/),* southwest of Douglas in the Laramie Peak area, includes four campgrounds ($5 for camping; campground closed in winter) and areas where you can fish and hike.

WHERE TO STAY & EAT

$–$$$ ✕ **Plains Trading Post.** Antique furnishings and portions of old bank buildings set the scene at this restaurant, where the menu is diverse but basic—chicken, burgers, steaks—and the portions are large. It's open 24 hours a day, a rarity even in the larger cities. ⊠*628 Richards St.* ☎*307/358–4489* ▭*MC, V.*

$–$$ 🏨 **Morton Mansion.** The huge, covered wraparound porch of this inn on a quiet, residential street is perfect for relaxing. The mansion was built in 1903 in the Queen Anne style. Antiques and floral patterns decorate the guest rooms, and the attic suite has two bedrooms, a private living room, and a full kitchen. **Pros:** Beautiful, historic lodging with a full breakfast. **Cons:** Slightly off the beaten path in Douglas. ⊠*425 E. Center St., 82633* ☎*307/358–2129* ⊕*www.mortonmansion.com* ↜*3 rooms, 2 suites* ⚹*In-hotel: Wi-Fi, no-smoking rooms, no elevator* ▭*AE, D, MC, V* ⦿*CP.*

$ 🏨 **Best Western Douglas Inn.** With its cathedral ceiling and fireplace, the atrium lobby is an impressive entranceway into this chain hotel. The location is convenient, next to I–25 on the north side of town and close to the Wyoming State Fairgrounds. The restaurant's menu ($$–$$$) of mostly American dishes includes exotic choices such as ostrich and buffalo steak. **Pros:** Cozy atmosphere and good location. **Cons:** Books up quickly. ⊠*1450 Riverbend Dr., 82633* ☎*307/358–9790* 🖷*307/358– 6251* ⊕*www.bestwestern.com* ↜*118 rooms* ⚹*In-room: refrigerator (some). In-hotel: restaurant, pool, gym, laundry facilities, no-smoking rooms, some pets allowed, no elevator, Wi-Fi* ▭*AE, D, DC, MC, V.*

CAMPING ⛺ **Esterbrook Campground.** Nestled among pine trees near Laramie Peak, 30 mi south of Douglas, Esterbrook is only a few miles from Black Mountain Lookout, one of the few staffed fire lookouts remaining in the country. During fire season (generally mid-June through September) be sure to ask the ranger-in-residence before exploring his or her home. ⚹*Pit toilets, drinking water, fire grates, picnic tables, ranger station* ↜*12 sites* ⊠*Forest Rd. 633* ☎*307/358–4690 or 307/358–1604* ⊕*www.fs.fed.us/r2/mbr/recreation/camping/douglas/esterbrook.shtml* ▭*No credit cards* ⊙*Mid-May–mid-Oct.*

CASPER

50 mi west of Douglas via I–25.

Several excellent museums in Casper illuminate central Wyoming's pioneer and natural history. The state's second-largest city, it's also one of the oldest. Some of the first white people to venture across Wyoming spent the winter here in 1811, on their way east from Fort Astoria in Oregon. Although they didn't stay, they helped to forge several pioneer trails that crossed the North Platte River near present-day Casper. A permanent settlement eventually arose, and was named for Lieutenant Caspar Collins; the spelling error occurred early on, and it stuck. The town has grown largely as a result of oil and gas exploration, and sheep and cattle ranchers run their stock on lands all around the city.

WHAT TO SEE

Fodor'sChoice
★

Five major immigrant trails passed near or through Casper between 1843 and 1870. The best known are the Oregon Trail and the Mormon Trail, both of which crossed the North Platte River in the vicinity of today's Casper. The **National Historic Trails Interpretive Center** examines the early history of the trails and the military's role in central Wyoming. Projected onto a series of screens 11 feet high and 55 feet wide, a film shows Wyoming trail sites and scenes of wagon travelers. You can climb into a wagon to see what it was like to cross the river, or learn about Mormon pioneers who traveled west with handcarts in 1856. ⊠*1501 N. Poplar* ☎*307/265-8030* ☞*$6* ☉*Apr.–Oct., daily 8–7; Nov.–Mar., Tues.–Sat. 9–4:30.*

The **Fort Caspar Historic Site** re-creates the post at Platte Bridge, which became Fort Caspar after the July 1865 battle that claimed the lives of several soldiers, including Lieutenant Caspar Collins. A post depicts life at a frontier station in the 1860s, and sometimes soldier reenactors go about their tasks. Museum exhibits show the migration trails. ⊠*4001 Fort Caspar Rd.* ☎*307/235-8462* ⊕*www.fortcasparwyoming.com* ☞*May–Sept. $2, Oct.–Apr. $1* ☉*Museum May and Sept., daily 8–5, June–Aug., daily 8–7; Oct.–Apr., Tues.–Sat. 8–5. Fort buildings May and Sept., daily 8:30–4:30; June–Aug., daily 8:30–6:30.*

The **Casper Planetarium** has multimedia programs on astronomy. There are also interactive exhibits in the lobby and a gift shop. Public programs, which last an hour, are scheduled regularly in the summer. ⊠*904 N. Poplar St.* ☎*307/577-0310* ⊕*www.natronaschools.org/ planetarium* ☞*$2.50* ☉*Lobby exhibits weekdays 8:30–5. Public programs June–Aug., Tues.–Sat. 7 PM–8 PM; Sept.–June, Sat. 7 PM–8 PM; call for group rates.*

The **Werner Wildlife Museum,** near the Casper College campus, has displays of birds and animals from Wyoming and around the world. ⊠*405 E. 15th St.* ☎*307/268-2676, 307/235-2108 for tours* ⊕*www. caspercollege.edu/community/campus/Werner/index.html* ☞*Free* ☉*Weekdays 10–4.*

Casper College's **Tate Earth Science Center and Geological Museum** displays fossils, rocks, jade, and the fossilized remains of a brontosaurus, plus other dinosaur bones. ⊠*125 College Dr.* ☎*307/268-3068* ⊕*nw4.caspercollege.edu/community/campus/tate/index.html* ☞*Free* ☉*Weekdays 9–5, Sat. 10–4.*

A showcase for regional artists and mostly modern artwork, the **Nico-**
★ **laysen Art Museum and Discovery Center** also exhibits works by national

artists. The building's early-20th-century redbrick exterior and contemporary interior are an odd combination, but this makes the museum all the more interesting. There are hands-on activities, classes, children's programs, a research library, and a Discovery Center. ⊠*400 E. Collins Dr.* ☎*307/235–5247* ⊕*www.thenic.org* ⊠*Donations accepted* ☼*Tues.–Sat. 10–5, Sun. noon–4.*

SPORTS & THE OUTDOORS

With thousands of acres of empty grassland and towering mountains only miles away, the landscape around Casper is full of possibilities for enjoying the outdoors. Casper Mountain rises up 8,000 feet no more than 20 minutes from downtown, providing prime skiing and hiking trails.

Edness Kimball Wilkins State Park (⊠*I–25, 6 mi east of Casper* ☎*307/577–5150*) is a day-use area with picnicking, swimming, fishing, and a 3-mi walking path.

HIKING   Much of Casper Mountain is taken up by private land, but there are some public trails, including mountain-bike routes and the Braille Trail, a simple hike with plaques (in Braille) that describe the views and ecology of the mountain. The trails can get a little crowded in the summer. Contact the **Casper Convention and Visitors Bureau** (⊠*992 N. Poplar St.* ☎*307/234–5362 or 800/852–1889* ⊕*www.casperwyoming.info*) for more information.

The **Platte River Parkway** hiking trail runs adjacent to the North Platte River in downtown Casper. Access points are at Amoco Park at 1st and Poplar streets, or at Crosswinds Park, on North Poplar Street near the Casper Events Center.

SKIING   Perched on Casper Mountain a few miles outside of town is **Hogadon Ski Area** (⊠*Casper Mountain Rd.* ☎*307/235–8499*), with a vertical drop of 600 feet. Less than a quarter of the runs are rated for beginners; the rest are evenly divided between intermediate and expert trails. Also here are a separate snowboard terrain park and a modest lodge. **Mountain Sports** (⊠*543 S. Center* ☎*307/266–1136*) provides more than just ski and snowboard sales. It also runs Wyomaps, which sells personal Global Positioning System products and provides custom mapping services.

WHERE TO EAT

$$–$$$$ ✕**Poor Boys Steakhouse.** Reminiscent of a frontier mining camp or Western town, this steak house has blue-and-white-check tablecloths and chair backs, quick service, and large portions of steak, seafood, and chicken. Salad comes in a bucket and is served with fresh, hot bread. Try the Moonshine Mama—grilled chicken breast smothered in mushrooms and Monterey Jack and cheddar cheeses—or enjoy a tantalizingly tender filet mignon with shrimp. For dessert try the Dutch apple pie or Ashley's Avalanche—a huge plate of ice cream, a white-chocolate brownie, cherry-pie filling, chocolate sauce, and whipped cream. ⊠*739 N. Center St.* ☎*307/237–8325* ▭*AE, D, DC, MC, V.*

$–$$$ ✕ **El Jarro.** Usually crowded and always noisy, this place serves hearty portions of Mexican cuisine. The beef fajitas are a favorite, second only to the fine margaritas, which come in glasses the size of bowls. The place is decorated with bright colors, which only seem to encourage the generally rowdy bunch at the bar. ⊠ *500 W. F St.* ☎ *307/577–0538* ▤ *AE, MC, V.*

$–$$$ ✕ **Sanfords Grub and Pub.** This lively spot decorated with 20th-century memorabilia may be a brewery, but children are welcome here in the heart of downtown. The extensive menu includes pastas, pizzas, and calzones. If you're a vegetarian, this is your best bet in Casper for its variety of meatless dishes. ⊠ *241 S. Center St.* ☎ *307/234–4555* ▤ *AE, D, DC, MC, V.*

WHERE TO STAY

$ ⊞ **Hampton Inn.** The rooms in this clean and very quiet lodging have coffeemakers, large cable TVs, white fluffy comforters, and easy chairs with ottomans. You can also make use of the business center, fitness center, and continental breakfast. **Pros:** Recently remodeled, and Cloud Nine beds give rooms a cozy feel. **Cons:** No longer allows pets. ⊠ *400 W. F St., 82601* ☎ *307/235–6668* 📠 *307/235–2027* ⊕ *www.hamptoninn.com* ⌦ *120 rooms* ♿ *In-room: refrigerator (some). In-hotel: restaurant, pool, no-smoking rooms, Wi-Fi, no elevator* ▤ *AE, D, DC, MC, V* ⏏ *CP.*

$ ⊞ **Parkway Plaza.** With a large convention center, the Parkway is one of Casper's busiest motels. The rooms are quiet and large, with double vanities, one inside the bathroom and one outside. Furnishings are contemporary in the rooms but Western in the public areas. The pool has wading and diving sections. Attached to the hotel is Old Town, a small amusement park with an arcade, a miniature-golf course, and a NASCAR-sanctioned go-kart track. **Pros:** With the attached amusement park there is plenty for the kids. **Cons:** This is a winding maze of a hotel. ⊠ *123 W. E St., 82601* ☎ *307/235–1777 or 800/270–7829* 📠 *307/235–8068* ⊕ *www.parkwayplaza.net* ⌦ *285 rooms* ♿ *In-hotel: restaurant, bar, pool, gym, laundry facilities, no-smoking rooms, elevator, Wi-Fi* ▤ *AE, D, MC, V.*

¢ ⊞ **Best Western Ramkota Hotel.** This full-service location, off I–25, has everything under one roof, from dining options to business services. Muted blues, greens, and mauves decorate the large, contemporary rooms, some of which have whirlpool tubs. ⊠ *800 N. Poplar St., 82601* ☎ *307/266–6000* 📠 *307/473–1010* ⊕ *www.bestwestern.com* ⌦ *229 rooms* ♿ *In-room: dial-up. In-hotel: restaurant, bar, pool, no-smoking rooms* ▤ *AE, D, DC, MC, V.*

THE ARTS

Both the Casper Symphony Orchestra and the Casper College Theater Department perform at the 465-seat **Gertrude Krampert Theater** (⊠ *Casper College, 125 College Dr.* ☎ *307/268–2500*). **Stage III Community Theater** (⊠ *904 N. Center St.* ☎ *307/234–0946*) presents plays and other dramatic performances at various times.

8

SHOPPING

The largest shopping center in a 175-mi radius, the **Eastridge Mall** (✉ *601 S.E. Wyoming Blvd.* ☎ *307/265–9392*), anchored by such standbys as Sears, JCPenney, Target, and Macy's, is popular and important to locals. There are also a few local stores here, including JAAG Racing, the largest NASCAR store in the state, and Corral West Ranchwear, which occasionally hosts roping competitions in the central court.

CODY, SHERIDAN & NORTHERN WYOMING ESSENTIALS

AIR TRAVEL

For the most part, airlines connect the region only to Denver, Minneapolis, or Salt Lake City, although some carriers occasionally have seasonal routes to smaller cities such as Billings.

Delta Air Lines serves Casper and Cody from Salt Lake City. Northwest Airlines connects Casper and Minneapolis. United Airlines flies from Denver into Casper, Gillette, Sheridan, and Cody.

Airlines & Contacts **Delta Air Lines** (☎ *800/221–1212* ⊕ *www.delta.com*). **Northwest Airlines** (☎ *800/225–2525* ⊕ *www.nwa.com*). **United Airlines** (☎ *800/241–6522* ⊕ *www.ual.com*).

AIRPORTS

The region's major airports are Casper's Natrona County International Airport, Gillette's Campbell County Airport, and Cody's Yellowstone Regional Airport. Sheridan County Airport has one or two flights daily to and from Denver, plus charter service.

The Campbell County Airport is 6 mi north of Gillette and 106 mi east of Sheridan. Natrona County International Airport is 12 mi west of Casper. Yellowstone Regional Airport is on the edge of Cody, about a mile from downtown.

Airport Information **Campbell County Airport** (✉ *2000 Airport Rd., Gillette* ☎ *307/686–1042* ⊕ *www.ccgov.net/departments/airport/index.html*). **Natrona County International Airport** (✉ *8500 Airport Pkwy., Casper* ☎ *307/472–6688* ⊕ *www.iflycasper.com*). **Sheridan County Airport** (✉ *908 W. Brundage La.* ☎ *307/674–4222* ⊕ *www.sheridancountyairport.com*). **Yellowstone Regional Airport** (✉ *3001 Duggleby Dr., Cody* ☎ *307/587–5096* ⊕ *www.flyyra.com*).

BUS TRAVEL

National bus service from Greyhound Lines is available only through Powder River Transportation, a regional carrier that connects the area to the larger hub cities of Cheyenne and Rapid City, South Dakota. Casper, Gillette, Sheridan, Cody, and nearly every smaller town in northern and central Wyoming are well served by Powder River Transportation.

Information **Greyhound Lines** (☎ *307/587–6993 or 800/231–2222* ⊕ *www. greyhound.com*). **Powder River Transportation** (☎ *307/682–0960*).

CAR RENTAL

The three major airports in the region are the best places to find car rentals. Make rental reservations early; between business travelers and tourists, which both peak in summer, rental agencies are often booked.

Contacts **Avis** (☎ 800/831–2847 ⊕ www.avis.com). **Budget** (☎ 800/527–0700 ⊕ www.budget.com). **Dollar** (☎ 800/800–4000 ⊕ www.dollar.com). **Hertz** (☎ 800/654–3131 ⊕ www.hertz.com). **National** (☎ 800/227–7368 ⊕ www.nationalcar.com).

CAR TRAVEL

Unless you're traveling with a package tour, a car is essential here. I–90 cuts directly through northeastern Wyoming, hitting the towns of Sheridan, Buffalo, Gillette, and Sundance. I–25 runs south from Buffalo through the Big Horns to Casper, Douglas, Cheyenne, and eventually Denver. There are no interstate highways west of the Big Horns, so U.S. 14—one of two routes that cross the mountain range—is the main road in this part of the state, connecting Cody with I–90.

Because the territory in this part of the world is so sparsely populated, it's almost impossible to find gas and repair shops at your convenience. There are few towns along the major routes here, including the interstates, so it's wise to plan your trip in advance. Although most of the country has gone to 24-hour credit-card gas pumps, these pieces of technology haven't hit the smaller towns in Wyoming, and it's rare to find a gas station open past the early evening unless you're in Gillette, Sheridan, Casper, or Cody. If you're driving in a particularly remote region, it's wise to take along extra water. Although the communities here employ great fleets of snowplows in the winter, it can sometimes take them time to clear the upper elevations. Some passes in the Big Horns close entirely. Keep in mind, too, that residents are used to driving in a little snow and ice, so the plows will come out only if accumulations are substantial.

Contact the Wyoming State Highway Patrol for information on road conditions.

Information **Wyoming State Highway Patrol** (☎ 888/996–7623 or 800/442–9090 ⊕ dot.state.wy.us).

EMERGENCIES

Ambulance or Police **Emergencies** (☎ 911).

24-Hour Medical Care **Campbell County Memorial Hospital** (⌧ 501 S. Burma St., Gillette ☎ 307/682–1000 ⊕ www.ccmh.net). **Sheridan County Memorial Hospital** (⌧ 1401 W. 5th St., Sheridan ☎ 307/672–1000 ⊕ www.sheridanhospital.org). **West Park Hospital** (⌧ 707 Sheridan Ave., Cody ☎ 800/654–9447 ⊕ www.westparkhospital.org). **Wyoming Medical Center** (⌧ 1233 E. 2nd St., Casper ☎ 307/577–7201 ⊕ www.wmcnet.org).

LODGING

CAMPING The opportunities to camp in this region are almost limitless. There are countless campgrounds in the Big Horns, and a few on the prairies below. Most of the public land within the national forests and parks is open for camping, provided that you don't light any fires. Keep in mind when selecting your campsite that the majestic peaks of the Big Horns are home to black bears and mountain lions.

SPORTS & THE OUTDOORS

FISHING Besides the local chambers of commerce, the Wyoming Game and Fish department is your best bet for updated information on the numerous fishing opportunities in this region. The countless local outfitters, guides, and community organizations can also provide information.

Contact **Wyoming Game and Fish** (⊠ *5400 Bishop Blvd., Cheyenne 82006* ☎ *307/777–4600* ⊕ *gf.state.wy.us/*).

SKIING The Big Horns receive a substantial amount of snow each year, turning the mountains into a winter playground. Even the flatter land that lies below is conducive to scenic sledding and cross-country skiing, and there are miles of groomed trails for that purpose. Because there is no one agency that keeps track of conditions in the area, your best sources of information on winter sports are individual outfitters and businesses, or the local chambers of commerce.

VISITOR INFORMATION

There are plenty of publications, ranging from small booklets to thick magazines, geared to visitors to the area, especially for those headed to the Black Hills. Many of these publications can be found at hotels and restaurants, usually for free (although you should expect 50%–75% of these magazines to be dedicated to advertisements).

Wyoming Tourist Information **Buffalo Chamber of Commerce** (⊠ *55 N. Main St., Buffalo 82834* ☎ *307/684–5544 or 800/227–5122* ⊕ *www.buffalowyo. com*). **Campbell County Chamber of Commerce** (⊠ *314 S. Gillette Ave., Gillette 82716* ☎ *307/682–3673 or 307/686–0040* ⊕ *www.gillettechamber.com*). **Casper Chamber of Commerce** (⊠ *500 N. Center St., Casper 82601* ☎ *307/234–5311 or 866/234–5311* ⊕ *www.casperwyoming.org*). **Casper Convention and Visitors Bureau** (⊠ *992 N. Poplar St., Casper 82602* ☎ *307/234–5362 or 800/852–1889* ⊕ *www.casperwyoming.info*). **Cody Country Chamber of Commerce** (⊠ *836 Sheridan Ave., Cody 82414* ☎ *307/587–2777* ⊕ *www.codychamber.org*). **Gillette Convention and Visitor's Bureau** (⊠ *1810 S. Douglas Hwy., Gillette 82718* ☎ *307/686–0040 or 800/544–6136*). **Park County Travel Council** (⊠ *Box 2454, Cody 82414* ☎ *307/587–2297 or 800/393–2639* ⊕ *www.yellowstonecountry.org*). **Sheridan Chamber of Commerce** (⊠ *Box 707, Sheridan 82801* ☎ *307/672–2485 or 800/453–3650* ⊕ *www.sheridanwyomingchamber.org*).

Cheyenne, Laramie & Southern Wyoming

WORD OF MOUTH

"If you do stop off in Laramie you might consider taking a side trip up into the Medicine Bow National Forest for a view of Lake Marie, the peak, etc. It is a pleasant drive and the forest entrance is just above Centenniel a brief 33 miles away. Also on your way from Laramie to Cheyenne you might find the rock formations at Vedauwoo worth checking out."

—Dukey

Updated
by Shauna
Stephenson

A JOURNEY ACROSS SOUTHERN WYOMING takes you through a wonderfully diverse landscape, from the wheat fields of the southeast to the mountains of the Snowy Range to the stark and sometimes hauntingly beautiful Red Desert, where wild horses still roam freely. Cheyenne, the largest city in Wyoming and the state capital, is the cornerstone community at the eastern edge of the state.

Several smaller communities with unique museums, access to diverse recreational opportunities, and one-of-a-kind personality lure travelers away from I–80, the main route through the region. Medicine Bow has a rich cowboy heritage portrayed in Owen Wister's 1902 Western novel *The Virginian*. Saratoga has a resort flavor and some of the best dining and lodging of any small town in the state. Encampment and Baggs are little, slow-paced, historically rich towns. In these and other towns across the region you can travel back in time by attending re-creations of mountain-man rendezvous, cowboy gatherings, and other historical events.

Once covered by an ocean and now rich in fossils, southwest Wyoming's Red Desert, or Little Colorado Desert, draws people in search of solitude (there's plenty of it), pioneer trails (more miles of 19th-century overland emigrant trails than anywhere else in the country), and recreation ranging from wildlife watching to fishing and boating on Flaming Gorge Reservoir, south of the town of Green River. The region is rich in history as well: here, John Wesley Powell began his 1869 and 1871 expeditions down the Green River, and Jim Bridger and Louis Vasquez constructed the trading post of Fort Bridger, now a state historic site. And all across the region, evidence remains of the Union Pacific Railroad, which spawned growth here in the 1860s as workers laid the iron rails spanning the continent.

EXPLORING SOUTHERN WYOMING

Once you explore this region, it becomes apparent why Wyoming has earned the nickname the "Cowboy State." The plains remain a prime grazing spot for wild horses, cattle, and sheep. As you drive west, the plains give way to the snowcapped mountains of the appropriately named Snowy Range. After a few more hours driving west you'll reach the Red Desert, with unique rock formations and herds of wild horses and pronghorn.

I–80 is the major artery through this region, running from Cheyenne at the southeast corner of the state west to Evanston in the southwest corner of the state.

ABOUT THE RESTAURANTS

Almost anywhere you dine in southern Wyoming, beef plays a prominent role on the menu; prime rib and steak are often specialties. Standard fare at many small-town restaurants includes burgers and sandwiches, and several eateries serve outstanding Mexican dishes. The pickings can be a bit slim for vegetarians, although most menus have at least one vegetable pasta dish or meatless entrée. Jeans and a T-shirt are acceptable attire for most places (even if the folks at the next table happen to be dressed up). Cowboy hats are always welcome.

ABOUT THE HOTELS

Because I–80 traverses this region, there are countless chain motels, but many other interesting accommodations are available. Southern Wyoming has a large number of independent lodging properties ranging from bed-and-breakfasts to lodges to historic hotels. Dude ranches are a unique lodging experience that let you sample a taste of wrangling life, and you can even stay in a remote mountain cabin in the heart of the national forest.

WHAT IT COSTS					
	¢	$	$$	$$$	$$$$
RESTAURANTS	under $7	$7–$11	$12–$16	$17–$22	over $22
HOTELS	under $70	$70–$110	$111–$160	$161–$220	over $220

Restaurant prices are for a main course at dinner, excluding sales tax of 4%–7%. Hotel prices are for two people in a standard double room in high season, excluding service charges and 5%–10% tax.

TIMING

The best time to visit southern Wyoming is in summer or fall, when most lodging properties and attractions are open (some smaller museums, sights, and inns close between Labor Day and Memorial Day). Summer is the season for most local community celebrations, including the region's longest-running and biggest event, Cheyenne Frontier Days (⇨ box below), held the last full week in July

Some areas, particularly around Laramie, Centennial, Saratoga, and Encampment, are great for winter sports, including cross-country skiing, snowmobiling, and ice fishing. Bear in mind that in parts of southern Wyoming it can—and often does—snow every month of the year, so even if you're visiting in July, bring some warm clothes, such as a heavy jacket and sweater.

Southern Wyoming

SD
NE
COLORADO
IDAHO
UTAH

Cheyenne see detail map

Laramie see detail map

TETON NAT'L FOREST

GRAND TETON NATIONAL PARK

SHOSHONE NATIONAL FOREST

BRIDGER NAT'L FOREST

THUNDER BASIN NATIONAL GRASSLAND

MEDICINE BOW NATIONAL FOREST

MEDICINE BOW NATIONAL FOREST

Fort Laramie National Historic Site

Medicine Bow

Centennial

Saratoga

Encampment

Baggs

Rawlins

Rock Springs

Green River

Kemmerer

Fossil Butte National Monument

Seedskadee Nat'l Wildlife Refuge

Flaming Gorge National Recreation Area

Fort Bridger State Historic Site

Casper

Douglas

Glendo

Wheatland

Guernsey

Torrington

Yoder

Chugwater

Rock River

Hanna

Elk Mountain

Wamsutter

Bairoil

Sweetwater Station

South Pass City

Atlantic City

Lander

Ethete

Riverton

Shoshoni

Thermopolis

Kirby

Worland

Ten Sleep

Kaycee

Midwest

Lusk

Van Tassell

Pine Bluffs

Granger

Lyman

Evanston

Cokeville

Big Piney

La Barge

Pinedale

Farson

Dubois

Moran Junction

Hoback Junction

Jackson

Alpine

Thayne

Afton

Driggs

18
85
18
270
26
34
211
210
25
85
313
25
80
287
130
230
30
487
80
130
70
789
530
191
430
80
287
220
487
25
59
450
50
387
192
25
16
20
134
132
135
789
28
189
191
189
30
30
189
89
26
191
89
120
26 20

35 miles
45 km
0

PLANNING YOUR TIME

All across southern Wyoming you can immerse yourself in cowboy and Old West heritage. Some of your driving can take you along pioneer emigrant trails; you can hike or ride horses on other segments. A good place to start your explorations is at one of the two major frontier-era forts, Fort Laramie (northeast of Cheyenne) and Fort Bridger (in the southwest), that served emigrants heading to Oregon, California, and Utah. From Fort Laramie, drive to Cheyenne, where you can see one of America's most complete horse-drawn wagon collections. Continue west to learn about territorial and frontier justice at the historic prisons in Laramie and Rawlins. For a rare treat, spend some time visiting the region's small museums, which preserve evocative relics of the past. Start with the Grand Encampment Museum, Medicine Bow Museum, Little Snake River Valley Museum (in Baggs), and Carbon County Museum (in Rawlins), then head west to tour the Sweetwater County Historical Center in Green River and Ulrich's Fossil Museum west of Kemmerer.

If you like to spend time in the outdoors, by all means take the scenic routes. From Cheyenne, follow Highway 210, which provides access to Curt Gowdy State Park. Traveling west of Laramie, head into the Snowy Range and Sierra Madre Mountains by taking Highway 130, which links to Saratoga by way of Centennial, or take Highway 230 to Encampment and then travel over Battle Highway (Highway 70) to Baggs. The mountain country of the Snowy Range and Sierra Madres provides plenty of opportunity for hiking, horseback riding, mountain biking, fishing, and camping. There are hundreds of thousands of acres to explore on trails ranging from wheelchair-accessible paths to incredibly difficult tracks for experienced backcountry travelers only. The action continues in winter, when snowmobilers ride free-style across open country (rather than on trails), cross-country skiers glide through white landscapes, and snowshoers explore hushed forests. The lakes that attract anglers during summer are equally busy in winter, when ice fishing rules.

For a firsthand Western experience, stay at one of the guest ranches near Cheyenne, Laramie, or Saratoga, where you can take part in cowboy activities and ride horses. Wild horses range freely in southwest Wyoming's Red Desert, even though the area is being heavily developed for energy production. You can spot the magnificent creatures west of Baggs and north and south of Rock Springs.

CHEYENNE

Cheyenne is Wyoming's largest city, but at just over 50,000 people it is not a place where you'll have to fight traffic or wait in lines—except, perhaps, during the last nine days in July, when the annual Cheyenne Frontier Days makes the city positively boom. Throughout the year it offers a decent variety of shopping, plus attractions ranging from art galleries to museums to parks.

A GOOD TOUR

Park your car at the **Old West Museum ❶**, within Frontier Park; this museum houses displays on the history of the region, plus the largest collection of horse-drawn vehicles anywhere in Wyoming. After you tour the museum, cross the street for a stroll through the **Cheyenne Botanic Gardens ❷**.

Head south on Carey Avenue; make a left on 24th Street to reach the **Wyoming State Capitol ❸**. Park along the street or turn right onto

Central Avenue to look for parking. Take a self-guided tour of the capitol building, and note the statue out front of Esther Hobart Morris, who helped make Wyoming the first state to grant women the right to vote. Cross Central Avenue to the **Wyoming State Museum ❹**, housing artifacts from across the state.

TIMING

You could visit all of the sights within the city in a day. Several sights close on Sunday.

Cheyenne became the state capital in 1890, at a time when the rule of the cattle barons was beginning to weaken after harsh winter storms in the late 1880s and financial downturns in the national economy. But Cheyenne's link to ranching didn't fade, and the community launched its first Cheyenne Frontier Days in 1897, an event that continues to this day. During the late July celebration—the world's largest outdoor rodeo extravaganza—the town is up to its neck in bucking broncs and bulls and joyful bluster. The parades, pageantry, and parties require the endurance of a cattle hand on a weeklong drive.

EXPLORING CHEYENNE

Numbers correspond to points of interest on the Cheyenne map.

I–25 runs north–south through the city; I–80 runs east–west. Central Avenue and Warren Avenue are quick north–south routes; the former goes north one way and the latter runs south one way. Several major roads can get you across town fairly easily, including 16th Street (U.S. 30), which gives you easy access to downtown. Most places of interest are in the downtown area. Most shopping is also downtown or along Dell Range Boulevard on the north side of town. Note that there are a few one-way streets in the downtown area.

THE MAIN ATTRACTIONS

❷ **Cheyenne Botanic Gardens.** A vegetable garden, roses and other flowers, cacti, and both perennial and annual plants bloom within the greenhouse conservatory and on the grounds here. ⊠ *710 S. Lions Park Dr.* ☎ *307/637–6458* ⊕ *www.botanic.org/* ☜ *Donations accepted* ⊙ *Conservatory weekdays 8–4:30, weekends 11–3:30; grounds stay open into evening.*

❻ **Curt Gowdy State Park.** You can fish, boat, hike, and picnic at this park named for Wyoming's most famous sportscaster, who got his start at local radio stations in the 1940s. The park, which is 20 mi west of the

Cheyenne Botanic
Gardens **2**

Curt Gowdy
State Park **6**

Historic
Governor's
Mansion **5**

Old West
Museum **1**

Wyoming State
Capitol **3**

Wyoming State
Museum **4**

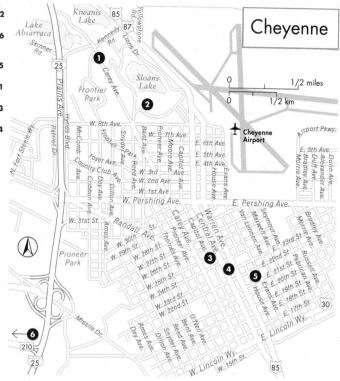

city, is particularly pleasant in summer and spring, when the wildflowers are in bloom. ✉ *1351 Hyndslodge Rd., off Hwy. 210 (Happy Jack
Rd.)* ☎ *307/632–7946* ⊕ *http://wyoparks.state.wy.us/index.asp* ✉ *$2
resident vehicles, $4 nonresident vehicles* ⊙ *Daily 24 hrs; entrance fee
station, 7 AM–11 PM.*

❶ Old West Museum. This museum within Frontier Park houses some
30,000 artifacts—including more than 150 carriages, the largest collection of horse-drawn vehicles in the state—relating to rodeos, ranching, and Cheyenne Frontier Days. Guided tours are geared to children.
During Frontier Days the museum hosts the Governor's Invitational
Western Art Show and Sale, which exhibits works by top Western wildlife and landscape artists from across the country. The museum also
features an interactive learning center for children. ✉ *4610 N. Carey
Ave.* ☎ *307/778–7290 or 800/266–2696* ⊕ *www.oldwestmuseum.org*
✉ *$6* ⊙ *Weekdays 9–5, weekends 10–5, with extended hrs during
Frontier Days, in late July.*

❸ Wyoming State Capitol. Construction on this Corinthian-style building,
now on the National Register of Historic Places, was authorized by
the Ninth Territorial Legislative Assembly in 1886. The dome, covered
in 24-karat gold leaf and visible from all roads leading into the city, is
50 feet in diameter at the base and 146 feet high. Standing in front is a

**Fodor's Choice
★**

9

statue of Esther Hobart Morris, a proponent of women's suffrage. One of Wyoming's nicknames is the "Equality State" because of its early advocacy of women's rights. Thanks to Wyoming's informal ways, it's not unusual to find the governor wandering the halls of the capitol. You can take a self-guided tour of state offices and the Senate and House chambers. ⊠ *Capitol Ave.* ☎ *307/777–7220* ⊕ *http://ai.state. wy.us/capitoltour/index.htm* 🖃 *Free* ☉ *Weekdays 8–5.*

4 **Wyoming State Museum.** Several permanent exhibits are dedicated to exploring the heritage, culture, and landscape of Wyoming, covering everything from natural resources to wildlife to historical events. There's a hands-on exhibit geared to children, and the museum hosts several additional temporary exhibits each year. ⊠ *Barrett Building, 2301 Central Ave.* ☎ *307/777–7022* ⊕ *wyomuseum.state.wy.us* 🖃 *Free* ☉ *May–Oct., Tues.–Sat. 9–4:30; Nov.–Apr., Tues.–Fri. 9–4:30, Sat. 10–2.*

ALSO WORTH SEEING

5 **Historic Governor's Mansion.** Between 1905 and 1976 (when the state built a new residence for the governor), 19 Wyoming first families made their home in this Colonial Revival building. Period furnishings and ornate chandeliers remain in nearly every room. ⊠ *300 E. 21st St.* ☎ *307/777–7878* ⊕ *wyoparks.state.wy.us/HGMslide.htm* 🖃 *Free* ☉ *Tues.–Sat. 9–5.*

WHERE TO EAT

$$–$$$$ ✕**Little Bear Steakhouse.** Locals rave about this classic American steak
★   house decorated with a Western theme. The seafood selections are diverse and well prepared. Try the New York strip steak or the rib eye; salmon is fixed in several ways. ⊠ *1700 Little Bear Rd.* ☎ *307/634– 3684* 🖃 *AE, D, DC, MC, V.*

$–$$$ ✕**The Albany.** Historic photographs of early Cheyenne set the tone for this downtown icon, a place that seems as old as the city itself (the structure was built circa 1900). It's a bit dark, and the booths are a bit shabby, but the American food is solid. Now if only you could get the walls to tell their stories. No doubt they've heard it all, as many of the movers and shakers in Cheyenne's past (and a few in its present) have eaten here. The menu lists hot and cold sandwiches, salads, and burgers, plus prime rib, steak, pork, lamb, and seafood. ⊠ *1506 Capitol Ave.* ☎ *307/638–3507* 🖃 *AE, D, DC, MC, V.*

$–$$$ ✕**Texas Roadhouse.** Close to the Dell Range Boulevard shopping district, this steak house also serves chicken, pork, and pasta. Favorite menu items include the portobello-mushroom chicken sandwich and barbecue ribs. The Western atmosphere includes buckets of peanuts; when you eat the peanuts, throw the shells on the hardwood floor just like cowboys did in the 1800s. You can wet your whistle at the bar. ⊠ *1931 Bluegrass Circle* ☎ *307/638–1234* 🖃 *AE, D, MC, V.*

$–$$ ✕**Los Amigos.** Mexican sombreros, serapes, and artwork on the walls complement the south-of-the-border food at this local favorite south of downtown. Deep-fried tacos and green chili are popular items, and

CLOSE UP

Cheyenne Frontier Days

One of the premier events in the Cowboy State is Cheyenne Frontier Days, held the last full week of July every year since 1897. The event started as a rodeo for ranch-riding cowboys who liked to show off their skills; now it consumes all of Cheyenne for nine days, when 250,000 to 300,000 people come into town.

Parades, carnivals, concerts, and more fill the streets and exhibition grounds, but rodeo remains the heart of Frontier Days, drawing the best cowboys and cowgirls each year. There is no rodeo quite like this one, known by the trade-marked nickname "Daddy of 'Em All."

BY THE NUMBERS
Cheyenne Frontier Days includes nine afternoon rodeos; nine nighttime concerts; eight days of Native American dancing (Saturday–Saturday); four parades (Saturday, Tuesday, Thursday, and Saturday); three pancake breakfasts (Monday, Wednesday, and Friday); one U.S. Air Force air show (Wednesday); and one art show (all month).

THE RODEOS
Dozens of the top Professional Rodeo Cowboys Association contenders come to Cheyenne to face off in bull riding, calf roping, saddle bronc or bareback bronc riding, and steer wrestling. Women compete in barrel racing; trick riders and wisecracking rodeo clowns break up the action. In one of the most exciting events, three-man teams catch a wild horse and saddle it, then one team member rides the horse around a track in a bronc-busting rendition of the Kentucky Derby. Frontier Days wraps up with the final rodeo, in which the top contestants from a week's worth of rodeos compete head-to-head.

EXTRACURRICULARS
Each night, concerts showcase top country entertainers such as Kenny Chesney, Toby Keith, and Tim McGraw (be sure to buy tickets in advance). Members of the Northern Arapaho and Eastern Shoshone tribes from the Wind River Reservation perform dances at a temporary Native American village where they also drum, sing, and share their culture. The parades show off a huge collection of horse-drawn vehicles, and the free pancake breakfasts feed as many as 12,000 people in two hours. Crowds descend on the midway for carnival rides and games.

BOOTS & BOOKS
Of course, there's plenty of shopping: at the Western wear and gear trade show you can buy everything from boots and belts to home furnishings and Western art. And you can pick up regional titles at book signings by members of the Western Writers of America.

PLAN AHEAD
Cheyenne Frontier Days entertains both kids and adults, in large numbers. It not only takes over Cheyenne but fills lodgings in nearby Laramie, Wheatland, Torrington, and even cities in northern Colorado. If you plan to attend, make your reservations early—some hotels book a year out.

For further information and to book rodeo and concert tickets, contact **Cheyenne Frontier Days** (✉ *Box 2477, Cheyenne 82003* ☎ *307/778-7222 locally, 800/543–2339 in WY, 800/227–6336 elsewhere* ⊕ *www.cfdrodeo.com*). The Web site is a useful resource: you can buy tickets online, see a schedule of activities, and order a brochure, all well in advance of the event itself.

9

the portions are big. ⊠ *620 Central Ave.* ☎*307/638–8591* ▤*MC, V, AE, D* ☺*Closed Sun. and Mon.*

$–$$ ✕**Shadows.** This downtown spot in the historic Union Pacific Railroad Depot has its own brewery. The bar looks out on the trains that still pass through Cheyenne. Eat sandwiches, stone-oven pizzas, pasta, fresh fish, or steak in the bar or the adjacent restaurant. ⊠*115 W. 15th St., Suite 1* ☎*307/634–7625* ▤*AE, D, MC, V.*

WHERE TO STAY

$$ ▦**Best Western Hitching Post Inn.** State legislators frequent this hotel, known to locals as "The Hitch." With its dark-wood walls, the hotel has an elegance not found elsewhere in Cheyenne. It books country-and-western performers in the lounge. The Cheyenne Cattle Company restaurant ($$–$$$$) serves steak and other dishes in a quiet, relaxed dining room. Next door at the Taco Johns Center are miniature golf, laser tag, and ice-skating. Pros: There's lots to keep the kids entertained. Cons: While the Hitching Post Inn itself is well kept, the neighborhood is not. ⊠*1700 W. Lincolnway, 82001* ☎*307/638–3301* 🖷*307/778–7194* ⊕*www.hitchingpostinn.com* ↩*166 rooms* ⚐*In-room: refrigerator, dial-up. In-hotel: restaurant, room service, bar, pool, gym, laundry service, airport shuttle, no-smoking rooms* ▤*AE, D, DC, MC, V.*

$$ ▦**Nagle Warren Mansion.** This delightful Victorian mansion B&B, built
Fodor'sChoice in 1888, has gorgeous woodwork, ornate staircases, and period fur-
★ niture and wallpaper. Antiques furnish the lavish rooms, which are named for figures associated with the mansion's history; some rooms have gas fireplaces. Close to downtown, the B&B is near restaurants and within walking distance of shops. Pros: Elegant, historical surroundings with many services such as English high tea and concierge. Cons: High demand for lodging here requires that you plan ahead for accommodations. ⊠*222 E. 17th St., 82001* ☎*307/637–3333 or 800/811–2610* 🖷*307/638–6879* ⊕*www.naglewarrenmansion.com* ↩*12 rooms* ⚐*In-room: no a/c, dial-up. In-hotel: gym, no-smoking rooms, no elevator* ▤*AE, MC, V* ▯*BP.*

$–$$ ▦**Little America Hotel and Resort.** An executive golf course and driving
Fodor'sChoice range are the highlights of this resort at the intersection of I–80 and
★ I–25. Most guest rooms are spread among several buildings clustered around the swimming pool, and some are attached to the common public areas via a glassed-in breezeway. Carol's Cafe (¢–$) serves sandwiches, chicken, steak, and seafood (try the hot turkey sandwich); or sit at linen-covered tables in Hathaway's or in large booths in the dining room ($–$$$$), which has piano music. On the menu there you will find seafood, steak, and prime rib. Pros: Newly remodeled rooms and 37-inch high-definition televisions. Cons: The golf course is only 9 holes. ⊠*2800 W. Lincolnway, 82001* ☎*307/775–8400 or 800/445–6945* 🖷*307/775–8425* ⊕*www.littleamerica.com* ↩*188 rooms* ⚐*In-room: refrigerator (some), Wi-Fi. In-hotel: restaurant, room service, bar, golf course, pool, gym, laundry service, airport shuttle, no-smoking rooms* ▤*AE, D, DC, MC, V.*

CAMPING

Curt Gowdy State Park. In rolling country with pine forest and a profusion of wildflowers during spring and summer, Curt Gowdy is a good camping spot about 20 mi west of the city. The park has picnic sites and areas for swimming, boating, and fishing. The campsites can be used for tents or trailers. *Flush toilets, pit toilets, dump station, drinking water, fire pits, picnic tables, public telephone, play area, swimming (lake) 150 sites 1319 Hyndslodge Rd., off Hwy. 210 307/632–7946 or 877/996–7275 http://wyoparks.state.wy.us/index.asp No credit cards.*

Terry Bison Ranch. In addition to being a full-service campground and RV park with a restaurant and occasional entertainment, this is a working bison ranch, with nearly 2,500 head on the property. *Flush toilets, full hookups, drinking water, guest laundry 88 full hookups, 100 tent sites; 7 cabins, 17 bunkhouse rooms I–25 Service Rd. near the Colorado state line 307/634–4171 307/634–9746 www. terrybisonranch.com D, DC, MC, V.*

Wyoming Campground and Mobile Home Park. Two of the attractions at this campground are a swimming pool and Internet service. It's on the south side of Cheyenne. *Flush toilets, full hookups, partial hookups (electric), dump station, drinking water, guest laundry, showers, picnic tables, electricity, public telephone, play area, swimming (pool) 50 full hookups, 20 partial hookups, 50 tent sites I–80, Exit 377 307/547–2244 AE, D, DC, MC, V May–Oct.*

NIGHTLIFE & THE ARTS

For an evening of live rock and roll (country and western during Cheyenne Frontier Days) that you can enjoy on a large dance floor, try the **Cheyenne Club** (1617 Capitol Ave. 307/635–7777). The dance floor and rock and roll beckon at **The Crown Bar** (222 W. 16th St. 307/778-9202). You'll find live country and western plus rock and roll Tuesday through Saturday, dancing, and drinks at **The Outlaw** (312 S. Greeley Hwy. 307/635–7552).

A wide variety of cultural events, including concerts, theater productions, dance recitals, and performances by the Cheyenne Symphony Orchestra take place at **Cheyenne Civic Center** (510 W. 20th St. 877/691–2787 www.cheyenneciviccenter.org). Original oil paintings, sculpture, and other art is sold at **Manitou Gallery** (1715 Carey Ave. 307/635–0019).

SHOPPING

For the best women's Western-style clothing in the city, ranging from belts, pants, shirts, and skirts to leather jackets, visit **Just Dandy** (212 W. 17th St. 307/635–2565). **Wrangler** (16th and Capitol Sts. 307/634–3048) stocks a full line of traditional Western clothing, ranging from Wrangler and Rocky Mountain jeans to Panhandle Slim shirts, Resistol hats, and Laredo boots. There are sizes and styles for the entire family. Handcrafted furniture, artwork, and Western home items are available at **Wyoming Home** (509 W. Lincolnway 307/638–2222).

SIDE TRIP TO FORT LARAMIE NATIONAL HISTORIC SITE

🕐 *105 mi north of Cheyenne via Hwys. 25 and 26.*

Fodor's Choice
★

Fort Laramie is one of the most important historic sites in Wyoming, in part because its original buildings are extremely well preserved, but also because it played a role in several significant periods in Western history. Near the confluence of the Laramie and North Platte rivers, the fort began as a trading post in 1834, and it was an important provisioning point for travelers on the Oregon Trail in 1843, the Mormon Trail in 1847, and the California Trail in 1849, when it also became a military site. In 1851 the first treaty between the U.S. government and the Northern Plains Indians was negotiated near the fort, and in 1868 a second Fort Laramie Treaty led to the end of the First Sioux War, also known as Red Cloud's War. Costumed interpreters reenact scenes of military life and talk about the fur trade, overland migration, and relations between settlers and Native Americans. ⊠ *Goshen County Rd. 270, 3 mi west of town of Fort Laramie* ☎ *307/837–2221* ⊕ *www.nps. gov/fola* ☒ *$3* ⊙ *Site daily 8–dusk; visitor center daily 9–5:30.*

EN ROUTE

Although I–80 connects Cheyenne and Laramie more quickly, the drive between the two cities on **Happy Jack Road** (Highway 210) is very scenic, particularly in spring and early summer, when wildflowers are in full bloom. The road winds over the high plains, past Curt Gowdy State Park, and provides access to the Vedauwoo Recreation Area before linking back to I–80, 7 mi east of Laramie at the **Lincoln Monument.** At this state rest area you can obtain information about the region and view a larger-than-life sculpture of the 16th president.

The **Vedauwoo Recreation Area,** in the Medicine Bow–Routt National Forest, is a particularly unusual area and a great place for a picnic. Springing out of high plains and open meadows are glacial remnants in the form of huge granite boulders piled skyward with reckless abandon. These one-of-a-kind rock formations, dreamscapes of gray stone, are great for hiking, climbing, and photography. There's also camping here. ⊠ *31 mi west of Cheyenne off I–80 or Hwy. 210* ☎ *307/745–2300* ⊕ *www.fs.fed.us/r2/mbr* ☒ *Free, camping $10* ⊙ *Daily 24 hrs.*

LARAMIE

The historic downtown of Laramie, nestled in a valley between the Medicine Bow Mountains and the Laramie Range, has several quaint buildings, some of which date back to 1868, the year after the railroad arrived and the city was established. For a time it was a tough "end-of-the-rail" town. Vigilantes took care of lawbreakers, hanging them from convenient telegraph poles. Then, in 1872, the city constructed the Wyoming Territorial Prison on the bank of the Little Laramie River. One of its most famous inmates was Butch Cassidy. The prison has since closed, and things have calmed down in this city of approximately 30,000. It's now the center of open-plains ranching country and the site of the University of Wyoming, Wyoming's only state university.

American Heritage
Center **6**

Laramie Plains
Museum **2**

University of
Wyoming **4**

University of
Wyoming
Geological
Museum **5**

Wyoming
Children's Museum
and Nature
Center **3**

Wyoming
Territorial Prison
State Historic
Site **1**

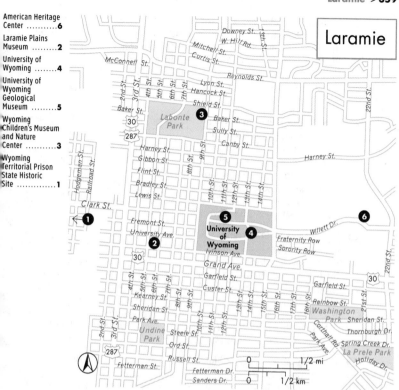

You can get brochures from the Laramie Chamber of Commerce, on South 3rd Street, for a self-guided tour of the late-19th-century Victorian architecture. Also available are the "Architectural Walking Tour" brochure, which focuses on the historic residences in the downtown area, and the "Laramie Antique Trail" guide, with locations of antiques shops in and around downtown.

EXPLORING LARAMIE

I–80 skirts the south and then west sides of town; U.S. 287 (3rd Street within the city) bisects Laramie from north to south. Grand Avenue, which borders the University of Wyoming, is the primary east–west route through Laramie.

THE MAIN ATTRACTIONS

6 **American Heritage Center.** The center houses more than 10,000 photographs, rare books, collections of papers, and memorabilia related to such subjects as American and Western history, the petroleum industry, conservation movements, transportation, and the performing arts. Permanent and temporary art displays also fill the museum space. ✉2111 Willet Dr. ☎307/766–4114 ⊕www.uwyo.edu/ahc ✉Free ☉Sept.–May, weekdays 8–5; June–Aug., weekdays 7:30–4:30.

❷ **Laramie Plains Museum.** Edward Ivinson, a businessman and philanthropist and one of Laramie's first settlers, built the mansion that houses this museum in 1892; it's now on the National Register of Historic Places. Inside is a growing collection of historical artifacts from the Laramie plains area. ⊠ *603 Ivinson Ave.* ☎ *307/742–4448* ⊕ *www. laramiemuseum.org* ⊠ *$7* ⊗ *Mid-June–mid-Aug., Tues.–Sat. 9–5, Sun. 1–4; mid-Aug.–mid-June, Tues.–Sat. 1–4.*

❺ **University of Wyoming Geological Museum.** This is one of the University of Wyoming's most notable museums, in a building with a dinosaur statue out front. Inside, a skeleton of an apatosaurus is 15 feet high and 75 feet long; it's believed the animal would have weighed 30 tons. Other exhibits explore the dinosaur family tree, meteorites, fossils, and earthquakes. ⊠ *Northwest corner of University of Wyoming campus* ☎ *307/766–2646 or 307/766–4218* ⊕ *www.uwyo.edu/geomuseum* ⊠ *Free* ⊗ *Weekdays 8–5, weekends 10–3.*

❸ **Wyoming Children's Museum and Nature Center.** Here children are encouraged to explore, make noise, experiment, play, imagine, discover, and invent. The hands-on exhibits emphasize wildlife, nature, and some local history. Live animals include Hissy, a great horned owl. The museum is on the edge of Labonte Park, which has playground equipment and plenty of grassy space in which children can burn off some energy. ⊠ *968 N. 9th St.* ☎ *307/745–6332* ⊕ *www.wyshs.org/mus-wychildrens.htm* ⊠ *$3* ⊗ *Memorial Day–Labor Day, Tues.–Thurs. 9–4, Fri. 1–5, Sat. 10–3; Labor Day–Memorial Day, Tues.–Thurs. 9–4, Sat. 10–3.*

❶ **Wyoming Territorial Prison State Historic Site.** Perhaps because of the bedlam of the early days, Laramie became the site of the Wyoming Territorial Prison in 1872. Until 1903 it was the region's federal and state penal facility, locking down Butch Cassidy and other infamous frontier outlaws. Today the restored prison is a state historic site that brings to life the legends of frontier law and justice. The warden's house and a broom factory are being restored and may open in 2008. ⊠ *975 Snowy Range Rd.* ☎ *307/745–6161* ⊕ *www.wyoprisonpark.org* ⊠ *$5* ⊗ *Park, May 1–Oct. 31, daily 9–6; frontier town, June–Aug., weekends 9–6.*

ALSO WORTH SEEING

❹ **University of Wyoming.** In addition to having several museums and attractions, the university hosts year-round events—from concerts to football games. You can join a tour or just pick up information on the university at the **UW Visitor Center** (⊠ *14th and Ivinson Sts.* ☎ *307/766–4075*). The **Anthropology Museum** (☎ *307/766–5136*) houses numerous Native American exhibits. Among the artworks displayed in the **Art Museum** (☎ *307/766–6622*) are paintings, sculpture, photography, and folk art from America, Europe, Africa, and Asia. Kids especially enjoy looking at the butterflies, mosquitoes, and other crawling and flying critters at the **Insect Museum** (☎ *307/766–2298*). You can learn about the stars and watch laser shows at the university's **planetarium** (☎ *307/766–6514*). The **Rocky Mountain Herbarium** (☎ *307/766–2236*) focuses on Rocky Mountain plants but also includes other examples of flora from the Northern Hemisphere. Call individual museums for opening times and fees (most of them are free). ⊠ *13th St. and Ivinson Ave.* ⊕ *www.uwyo.edu.*

SPORTS & THE OUTDOORS

BICYCLING

Mountain-biking trails are scattered throughout the Medicine Bow–Routt National Forest and the Happy Jack recreation area, east of Laramie. For information, trail maps, and rentals, see Carl Gose at the **Pedal House** (⊠207 S. 1st St. ⊕www.pedalhouse.com ☎307/742–5533).

CROSS-COUNTRY SKIING

The Medicine Bow–Routt National Forest and the Happy Jack recreation area have numerous cross-country trails. For information and rentals, contact **Cross Country Connection** (⊠117 Grand Ave. ☎307/721–2851).

WHERE TO STAY & EAT

$$$–$$$$ ✕**Cavalryman Supper Club.** It's the food, not the look of the place, that attracts people to this restaurant on the plains, 1 mi south of Laramie on U.S. 287. Menu highlights include prime rib, steak, fresh fish, and lobster. Every dinner includes deep-fried mushrooms, soup and salad, and dessert. Brunch is served on Sunday. The lounge features mounts from local game animals. ⊠4425 S. 3rd St. ☎307/745–5551 ⊟AE, DC, MC, V ⊘No lunch.

$–$$$ ✕**The Overland Fine Eatery.** Patio dining and a superb wine list enhance
Fodor'sChoice the food—pasta, chicken, quiche, beef, and seafood—at this restaurant
★ in the historic district, right on the railroad tracks. Sunday brunch might include such unique entrées as yellowfin tuna and eggs, a buffalo-chili omelet, or avocados Benedict. Hours change in winter. ⊠100 Ivinson Ave. ☎307/721–2800 ⊟AE, D, MC, V.

$$–$$$ 🏨**Laramie Comfort Inn.** On busy Grand Avenue, this Comfort Inn is close to restaurants and fast-food chains, as well as War Memorial Stadium at the University of Wyoming. Pros: Many rooms have been recently remodeled, and it is close to the stadium and conference center. Cons: Rooms fill up fast on game weekends. ⊠3420 Grand Ave., 82070 ☎307/721–8856 🖷307/721–5166 ⊕www.comfortinn.com ☞55 rooms, 3 suites, 1 efficiency apartment ♿In-hotel: pool, gym, Wi-Fi, no-smoking rooms ⊟AE, D, DC, MC, V ⊠CP.

¢–$ 🏨**Howard Johnson Inn.** At this white-brick motel, the lobby and halls are rustic Western knotty pine, and the rooms are basic, with contemporary furnishings. The property includes a convenience store, a restaurant, and a liquor store. It's on the western edge of town, at the Snowy Range Road exit off I–80. Pros: Close to the interstate. Cons: No pets. ⊠1555 Snowy Range Rd., Exit 311 off I–80, Box 580, 82070 ☎307/742–8371 🖷307/742–0884 ☞112 rooms ♿In-hotel: restaurant, bar, pool, Internet, no-smoking rooms, no elevator ⊟AE, D, DC, MC, V.

CAMPING

🏕️**Laramie KOA.** This campground on the west side of town has lots of grassy space and some trees. For an extra fee you can have satellite TV and telephone service for your RV. Modem service is also available at no extra charge. There are one- and two-bedroom cabins. ♿Flush toilets, full hookups, drinking water, picnic tables, general store, play *area* ⇄*116 full hookups, 30 tent sites; 8 cabins* ✉*1271 W. Baker St., I–80 at Curtis St. exit* ☎*307/742–6553* 🖷*307/742–5039* ⊕*www.koa. com* ▤*D, DC, MC, V.*

⚠ **Sugarloaf Campground.** At 10,700 feet, this is the highest campground in Wyoming. Don't be surprised if you get snowed on in July. With stunning views of the mountains, getting a site here can be difficult, so plan accordingly. ⬧ *Picnic tables, fire rings, trash pick up, vault toilet* ⇄*16 sites* ✉*40 mi west of Laramie on Hwy. 130 and then 1 mi north on Forest Service Rd. 346* ☎*307/745–2300 or 877/444–6777* ⊕*www. reserveusa.com* ▤*No credit cards* ⊘*July–Sept.*

⚠ **Libby Creek Pine.** Wake up to the sound of Libby Creek as it rushes past your campsite. This campground is small and shady and tucked away from the main road. All sites are first-come, first-served. ⬧ *Picnic tables, fire rings, trash pick up, vault toilet* ⇄*6 sites* ✉*32 mi west of Laramie on Hwy. 130 to Libby Recreation Area, then ½ mi on Forest Rd. 351* ☎*307/745–2300 or 877/444–6777* ⊕*www.reserveuse.com* ▤*No credit cards* ⊘*May–Oct.*

NIGHTLIFE

On weekends you can kick up your heels to live country-and-western music at the **Buckhorn** (✉*114 Ivinson Ave.* ☎*307/742–3554*), or listen to a DJ upstairs at the Parlour Bar Wednesday–Saturday. Take a spin around the dance floor at the **Cowboy Saloon** (✉*108 S. 2nd St.* ☎*307/721–3165*) on weekends. On Thursday September through May the place hops with college kids who aren't old enough to be in the bar at other times; no alcohol is served then, but there is usually live music, dance contests, and other events. A young set often congregates at the **Drawbridge Tavern** (✉*1622 Grand Ave.* ☎*307/745–3490*), which hosts rock bands. College students gather and shoot pool at **Mingles** (✉*3206 Grand Ave.* ☎*307/721–2005*).

SHOPPING

Laramie's most interesting shopping is found in a shopping district called **Landmark Square** along Ivinson and Grand avenues. Stores here sell artwork, clothing, and handcrafted items.

IN & AROUND THE SNOWY RANGE

Mountain lakes and streams, aspens and pines, camping areas, and trails for hiking, cross-country skiing, and snowmobiling draw outdoor enthusiasts to the Snowy Range, which encompasses portions of both the Laramie and Brush Creek districts of Medicine Bow–Routt National Forest. The Snowy Range Pass, a stretch of Highway 130 running west from Centennial toward Saratoga, climbs as high as 10,847 feet; driving through the pass, which is open only in summer, takes you past stunning views of the surrounding peaks, including 12,013-foot Medicine Bow Peak. The high elevation means snow caps the mountain peaks in the range year-round.

MEDICINE BOW

60 mi northwest of Laramie via U.S. 30.

When novelist Owen Wister (1860–1938) first visited Medicine Bow—the town he would immortalize in his 1902 classic Western tale *The Virginian*—he noted that the community looked "as if strewn there by the wind." Today the town still looks somewhat windblown, although the small business district is anchored by the Virginian Hotel, built in the early 1900s and named in honor of the book. This is a community of 320 struggling for survival, with an economy based on the vagaries of agriculture and mining. Although the town sits at the intersection of U.S. 30 (Lincoln Highway) and Wyoming Route 487, you'll seldom encounter much traffic here, except during the fall hunting season (the area is particularly noted for its antelope hunting) and when there are football or basketball games at the University of Wyoming. On those days, expect a crowd on the road and fans talking of sports at the Virginian Hotel.

You can learn about the history of this small town at the **Medicine Bow Museum,** housed in an old railroad depot built in 1913. Owen Wister's summer cabin was relocated to the premises and stands next door. ⊠*405 Lincoln Pl.* ☎*307/379–2383* ⊕*www.medicinebow.org/museum.htm* 🖃*Free* ⊙*Memorial Day–Sept., weekdays 10–5 and by appointment.*

WHERE TO STAY

¢ **Virginian Hotel.** Inspired by the Owen Wister novel *The Virginian,* this sandstone hotel was built in 1909 and has been operating nearly continuously ever since. Claw-foot tubs, tulip-shape lights, and brass beds with comforters fill the Victorian-style rooms. The rooms in the main hotel don't have TVs, phones, or radios (most don't even have electrical outlets), but the atmosphere more than makes up for the lack of amenities. In the main hotel, only the suites have private bathrooms; rooms in the Bunkhouse Motel annex have TVs and bathrooms. The dining room ($$–$$$), with antique oak furniture and 19th-century photographs, serves American fare such as steak and chicken. ⊠*404 Lincoln Hwy., Box 127, 82329* ☎*307/379–2377* 🛏*32 rooms, 4 suites in hotel; 12 rooms in Bunkhouse Motel* ⌕*In-room: no a/c, no phone (some), no TV (some). In-hotel: restaurant, bar, no-smoking rooms, no elevator* ⊟*MC, V.*

9

CENTENNIAL

30 mi west of Laramie via Hwy. 130; 90 mi south of Medicine Bow via U.S. 30 and Hwy. 130.

Snuggled up against the mountains of the Snowy Range, Centennial lies at the head of the glacial Centennial Valley. As the community closest to the Snowy Range, the town makes a good base from which to take part in numerous recreational activities, including hiking, cross-country skiing, snowmobiling, and downhill skiing. This small town has a few hardy year-round residents, and many more people who summer in the area.

The former Centennial Railroad Depot now houses the **Nici Self Museum,** at the eastern edge of town. The museum displays ranching, farming, and mining equipment, plus artifacts typical of what you'd find in a pioneer home; there's also an outdoor-equipment exhibit. ✉2740 Hwy. 130 ☎307/742–7158 or 307/634–4955 ⊕http://wyshs.org/mus-nici. htm 🖎Donations accepted ☉Mid-June–Labor Day, Fri.–Mon. 1–4.

You can hike, picnic, fish, ski, snowmobile, or take photographs in the 400,000 acres of **Medicine Bow–Routt National Forest, Laramie District** (✉Laramie office: 2468 Jackson St., Laramie 82070 ☎307/745–2300, 877/444–6777 for camping ⊕www.fs.fed.us/r2/mbr/), and that is the short list. The Laramie District has 19 developed campgrounds; dispersed camping is also allowed. Lodgings such as cabins, forest guard stations, and even a fire lookout tower high in the Snowy Range are available for rent in summer.

SPORTS & THE OUTDOORS

CROSS-COUNTRY SKIING
The same trails that serve hikers in summer cater to cross-country skiers in winter in the Lower Snowy Range trail system. You can access several trails on Highway 130 west of Centennial in the Medicine Bow–Routt National Forest, including the Corner Mountain Trail (3 mi west of Centennial), Little Laramie Trail (5 mi west of Centennial), and the Green Rock Trail (9 mi west of Centennial). There is also a cross-country-skiing trail system at Snowy Range Ski and Recreation Area. Many of the trails are interconnected, so you can combine short trails for a longer ski trip.

HIKING
Dozens of miles of hiking trails slice through the Medicine Bow–Routt National Forest west of town. Major trailheads are on Highway 130, including trailheads for the 7-mi Corner Mountain Trail (3 mi west of Centennial), 7-mi Little Laramie Trail (5 mi west of Centennial), and 9-mi Medicine Bow Peak Trail (9 mi west of Centennial). The easy 1-mi Centennial Trail takes off from the Centennial Visitor Center at the forest boundary. More difficult is the 4½-mi Barber Lake Trail, which starts at Barber Lake and incorporates ski trails and old forest roads. Most hikers follow this trail downhill one way and instead of doubling back use two vehicles to shuttle between Barber Lake and the Corner Mountain trailhead (the Barber Lake Trail hooks up with part of the Corner Mountain trail).

Trail maps and information are available at the **Centennial Visitor's Center** (✉Hwy. 130, 1 mi west of Centennial ☎307/742–6023).

SKIING & SNOWBOARDING
Downhill skiing and snowboarding are available 7 mi west of Centennial at the **Snowy Range Ski and Recreation Area** (✉6416 Mountain Mist Ct. ☎307/745–5750 or 800/462–7669 ⊕www.snowyrange. com). There are slopes for beginners and experienced skiers, plus some cross-country-skiing trails.

WHERE TO STAY

$$–$$$ 🛏 **Vee Bar Guest Ranch.** Along the Centennial Valley's Little Laramie River, 21 mi west of Laramie and 9 mi east of Centennial, this family-operated guest ranch builds its summer activity program around

horseback riding. Other activities include fishing, hiking, river tubing, and trap shooting. Lodging is in nine individual cabins and four lodge suites. You can buy an all-inclusive week or stay as a nightly B&B guest; October through May, only the B&B plan is offered. B&B guests, and those not staying at the ranch, may eat in the dining room ($$$–$$$$) by reservation only. Pros: Beautiful scenery and plenty to keep you busy. Cons: Located a short jaunt from the downtown. ⊠ *2091 Hwy. 130, Laramie 82070* ☎ *307/745–7036 or 800/483–3227* 🖷 *307/745–7433* ⊕ *www.veebar.com* ❑ *9 cabins, 4 lodge rooms* ⟁ *In-room: no a/c, no TV, refrigerator, Wi-Fi. In-hotel: laundry facilities, no-smoking rooms* ☰ *AE, D, MC, V* Ⓨ *FAP.*

$–$$$ ⬚ **Winter Creek Condos and Cabins.** Just outside town in a forest of pine and aspen, these cabins afford views of the Centennial Valley. The cabins sleep 3 to 10 people and have full kitchens and outdoor gas grills; there's a two-night minimum stay. A common area has a basketball court and a horseshoe-pitching area. Condos have satellite television. ⊠ *75 Rainbow Valley Rd., Box 135, 82055* ☎ *307/721-9859* ⊕ *www. wintercreekcondos.com* ❑ *9 units* ⟁ *In-room: no a/c, no phone, kitchen, no TV. In-hotel: no-smoking rooms, no elevator* ☰ *MC, V.*

¢–$ ⬚ **Old Corral Hotel & Steak House.** A crowd of Western carved-wood characters greets you on the front lawn of this log restaurant and hotel. Walking into the steak house ($$–$$$$), with its woodstove and ranch decorations, is like stepping into the Old West. Hand-hewn pine beds and dressers decorate the hotel rooms, and you have access to a deck with picnic tables and a hot tub, a pool room, and a TV room with videos. The lower level of the on-site gift shop sells T-shirts and Christmas decorations; upstairs there are antique replicas, including Native American pipes and outlaw paraphernalia. In winter you can rent snowmobiles. Pros: Just down the road from the Snowy Mountains. Cons: Hotel closings vary by season. ⊠ *2750 Hwy. 130, 82055* ☎ *307/745–5918* 🖷 *307/742–6846* ⊕ *www.oldcorral.com* ❑ *35 rooms* ⟁ *In-room: no a/c, VCR (some), dial-up. In-hotel: restaurant, laundry service, no-smoking rooms, some pets allowed, no elevator* ☰ *D, MC, V* ⊙ *Closed mid-Oct.–mid-Dec. and mid-Apr.–mid-May.*

CAMPING In addition to the campgrounds listed here, there are several others in both the Laramie and Brush Creek districts of the **Medicine Bow–Routt National Forest** (☎ *877/444–6777, 307/745–2300 Laramie District, 307/326–5258 Brush Creek District* ⊕ *www.fs.fed.us/r2/mbr/*).

⛺ **Brooklyn Lake.** On the east side of Snowy Range Pass, at an elevation of 10,200 feet, this small campground sits beside Brooklyn Lake and is surrounded by pine forest. You can fish in the lake and use non-motorized boats. All campsites have views of the lake. ⟁ *Pit toilets, fire pits, picnic tables* ❑ *19 sites* ⊠ *Hwy. 130, 7 mi west of Centennial on Hwy. 130, then 2 mi east on Brooklyn Lake Rd./Forest Rd. 317* ☎ *307/745–2300* ⊕ *www.fs.fed.us/r2/mbr/* ⟁ *Reservations not accepted* ☰ *No credit cards* ⊙ *July–Sept.*

⛺ **Nash Fork.** Pine trees surround this simple campground at an elevation of 10,200 feet. Each site can accommodate an RV or a tent, but there are no hookups. ⟁ *Pit toilets, drinking water, fire grates,*

9

fire pits, picnic tables ⊐*27 sites* ⊠*Hwy. 130, 8 mi west of Centennial* ☎*307/745–2300* ⊕*www.fs.fed.us/r2/mbr/* ⚓*Reservations not accepted* ⊟*No credit cards* ☾*July–Oct.*

⚠**Ryan Park.** During World War II this was the site of a camp for German prisoners, and you can still see some of the building foundations. The campground on the east side of Snowy Range Pass lies at an elevation of 8,000 feet. It has access to stream fishing as well as to hiking on forest trails and two-track roads. Just west of the small community of Ryan Park, it is 20 mi southeast of Saratoga. ⚓*Pit toilets, drinking water, fire pits, picnic tables* ⊐*19 sites* ⊠*Hwy. 130, 20 mi southeast of Saratoga* ☎*877/444–6777* ⊕*www.reserveusa.com* ⊟*No credit cards* ☾*June–Oct.*

SHOPPING

★ Leather purses, children's and regional-history books, clothing, ice cream, and baked goods are sold at the **Country Junction** (⊠*2742 Hwy. 130* ☎*307/745–3318*), on the eastern edge of Centennial and within walking distance of the Nici Self Museum. Antiques, wood furniture, and a 5¢ cup of coffee are available at **J&N Mercantile** (⊠*2772 Hwy. 130* ☎*307/745–0001*), along with Wyoming products such as goat's-milk lotion, "cowboy bubble bath" (a bag of beans), and jewelry.

EN ROUTE Highway 130 between Centennial and Saratoga is known as the **Snowy Range Scenic Byway.** This paved road, which is in excellent condition, crosses through the Medicine Bow–Routt National Forest, providing views of 12,013-foot Medicine Bow Peak and access to hiking trails, 10 campgrounds (6 right near the road), picnic areas, and 100 alpine lakes and streams. Gravel roads lead off the route into the national forest. Maps are available from the **Centennial Visitor's Center** (⊠*Hwy. 130, 1 mi west of Centennial* ☎*307/742–6023*).

At the top of the 10,847-foot Snowy Range Pass, about 10 mi west of Centennial, take a short walk to the Libby Flats Observation Site for views of the Snowy Range and, on clear days, Rocky Mountain National Park to the southwest in Colorado. Lake Marie, a jewel of a mountain lake at an elevation of approximately 10,000 feet, is also here. On the Saratoga side of the mountain, the road passes through pine forest and descends to the North Platte River valley, with cattle ranches on both sides of the highway. Note that there is ongoing construction near the junction of Highways 130 and 230, 8 mi south of Saratoga. Also, the byway is impassable in winter and therefore is closed between approximately mid-October and Memorial Day.

SARATOGA

49 mi west of Centennial via Hwy. 130, Memorial Day–early Oct.; rest of year, 140 mi west of Centennial via Hwy. 130 east to Laramie, Hwy. 230 west to Encampment, and Hwy. 130 north or east to Laramie, I–80 west to Hwy. 130 and then south.

Tucked away in a valley formed by the Snowy Range and Sierra Madre mountains, Saratoga is a rarely visited treasure. Fine shopping and dining happily combine with elegant lodging facilities and a landscape that's ideal for outdoor activities. This is a good spot for river floating and blue-ribbon fishing: the North Platte River bisects the region, and there are several lakes and streams nearby in the Medicine Bow–Routt National Forest. You can also cross-country ski and snowmobile in the area. The town first went by the name Warm Springs, but in an attempt to add an air of sophistication to the place, townsfolk changed the name to Saratoga in 1884 (after Saratoga Springs, New York).

★ Hot mineral waters flow freely through the **Hobo Pool Hot Springs,** and the adjacent swimming pool is heated by the springs. People have been coming here to soak for generations, including Native Americans, who considered the area neutral territory. Hardy folk can do as the Native Americans did and first soak in the hot water, then jump into the adjacent icy waters of the North Platte River. ⊠*201 S. River St.* ☎*307/326–5417* ⊠*Free* ☉*Hot springs daily 24 hrs; pool Memorial Day–Labor Day, daily 9–8 (sometimes closed for lessons).*

The former Union Pacific Railroad depot houses the **Saratoga Historical and Cultural Association Museum,** with displays of local artifacts related to the history and geology of the area. Outdoor exhibits include a sheep wagon and a smithy. A nearby gazebo is used for occasional musical and historical programs in summer. ⊠*104 Constitution Ave.* ☎*307/326–5511* ⊕*www.saratoga-museum.com* ⊠*Donations accepted* ☉*Memorial Day–Labor Day, Tues.–Sat. 1–4.*

SPORTS & THE OUTDOORS

CANOEING & RAFTING
★ **Stoney Creek Outfitters** (⊠*216 E. Walnut St.* ☎*307/326–8750* ⊕*www.grmo.com*) offers guided canoe and raft expeditions on the North Platte River, plus canoe and drift-boat rentals.

CROSS-COUNTRY SKIING
Extensive trail networks in the Medicine Bow–Routt National Forest are good for novice and experienced cross-country skiers and snowmobilers. For trail conditions, contact the **Hayden/Brush Creek Ranger District** (☎*307/326–5258 or 307/327–5481* ⊕*www.fs.fed.us/r2/mbr*) of the Medicine Bow–Routt National Forest.

FISHING
Brook trout are prevalent in the lakes and streams of Medicine Bow–Routt National Forest, and you can also find rainbow, golden, cutthroat, and brown trout, as well as splake. You can also drop a fly in the North Platte River. **Stoney Creek Outfitters** (⊠*216 E. Walnut St.* ☎*307/326–8750* ⊕*www.grmo.com*) rents tackle and runs fishing trips on the Upper North Platte.

WHERE TO STAY & EAT

$–$$$ ✕**Lazy River Cantina.** Mexican music and sombreros greet you at this downtown restaurant, which also includes a bar and lounge where locals and visitors take their shot at darts. The entrées include tacos, enchiladas, burritos, and chimichangas, served in one of two small rooms. You can sit in a booth and watch folks and traffic on busy Bridge Avenue. ⊠*110 E. Bridge Ave.* ☎*307/326–8472* ▤*MC, V* ☉*Closed Tues.*

9

$-$$ 🏨 **Saratoga Inn Resort.** With leather couches in the common areas, pole-
Fodor'sChoice   frame beds, and Western art, this inn is as nice as any place in Wyo-
★   ming. Some rooms are in the main lodge, which has a double fireplace
lounge that opens both to the central sitting room and the back porch;
other rooms are in separate buildings surrounding a large expanse of
lawn and a hot-mineral-water swimming pool. There are five outdoor
hot tubs filled with mineral water, three of them covered with tepees,
a 9-hole public golf course, and tennis courts. The Silver Saddle Res-
taurant ($$–$$$$) serves steak, pasta, and seafood in a quiet, cozy set-
ting with a fireplace to warm you in fall or winter. ⊠*601 E. Pic-Pike
Rd., Box 869, 82331* ☎*307/326–5261* 🖷*307/326–5234* ⊕*www.
saratogainn.com* ➪*50 rooms* ⚲*In-hotel: restaurant, room service,
bar, golf course, tennis courts, pool, no-smoking rooms, no elevator*
▭*AE, DC, MC, V.*

¢–$ 🏨 **Riviera Lodge.** Locally owned and simplistic in nature, the Riviera is
located right on the slow-moving Encampment River, a haven for trout
and waterfowl. Rooms are decorated in a western theme. An empty
lobby and one of the owner's pets usually greet you as you enter. Out
back you will find a large grassy area making the property one of the
few pet-friendly places in Saratoga. Anglers will appreciate the loca-
tion as it is within walking distance from local fly shops. Pros: Only
two blocks from downtown. Cons: Relatively few amenities. ⊠*104
E. Saratoga St., 82331* ☎*307/326–5651 or 866/326/5651* ⊕*www.
therivieralodge.com* ➪*40* ⚲*In-room: no a/c, refrigerators, Wi-Fi*
▭*AE, D, MC, V.*

¢–$ 🏨 **Wolf Hotel.** This downtown 1893 hotel on the National Register of
Fodor'sChoice   Historic Places is well maintained by its proud owners. Although some
★   of the guest rooms are small, all of them have simple Victorian charm
(note that the rooms are on the second and third floors, and there
is no elevator; there also is no way to control the heat in individual
rooms). The fine restaurant ($–$$$$), bar, and lounge also have Vic-
torian furnishings, including dark-green wallpaper, antique oak tables,
crystal chandeliers, and lacy drapes. Prime rib and steaks are the spe-
cialties, and seafood and lamb are also on the menu. Dinner reserva-
tions are strongly recommended. Pros: Beautiful and historic at a great
price. Cons: No pets. ⊠*101 E. Bridge Ave., 82331* ☎*307/326–5525*
⊕*www.wolfhotel.com* ➪*5 rooms, 5 suites* ⚲*In-room: no a/c, no
TV (some). In-hotel: restaurant, bar, no-smoking rooms, no elevator*
▭*AE, MC, V.*

ENCAMPMENT

18 mi south of Saratoga via Hwys. 130 and 230.

This is the gateway community to the Continental Divide National
Scenic Trail, accessed at Battle Pass, 15 mi west on Highway 70. When
completed, this trail will run from Canada all the way south to Mex-
ico along the Continental Divide. Encampment is also a good place
to launch trips into four nearby wilderness areas in the Hayden Dis-
trict of Medicine Bow–Routt National Forest—Platte River, Savage
Run, Encampment River, and Huston Park—where you can go hik-

ing, fishing, mountain biking, snowmobiling, and cross-country skiing. Although, recreation is a quickly emerging industry, there's still a lot of quiet mountain country to explore, and it's not yet crowded in this town of 400 residents.

FodorśChoice
★
The modern interpretive center at the **Grand Encampment Museum** holds exhibits on the history of the Grand Encampment copper district and logging and mining. A pioneer town of original buildings includes the Lake Creek stage station, the Big Creek tie hack cabin, the Peryam homestead, the Slash Ridge fire tower, a blacksmith shop, a transportation barn, and a two-story outhouse. Among the other relics are three original towers from a 16-mi-long aerial tramway built in 1903 to transport copper ore from mines in the Sierra Madres. You can take guided tours, and there's also a research area. A living-history day, with music, costumes, and events, takes place the third weekend in July. ⊠*807 Barnett Ave.* ☎*307/327–5308* ⊕*www.grandencampmentmuseum.org* ✉*Donations accepted* ☉*Memorial Day weekend 10–5; June–Labor Day, Mon.–Sat. 10–5, Sun. 1–5; Sept., weekends 1–5.*

The ranching and cowboy lifestyle is the focus of the three-day **Grand Encampment Cowboy Gathering** (⊠*807 Barnett Ave.* ☎*307/326–8855*), held in mid-July. Cowboy musicians and poets perform during afternoon and evening concerts, and there's a stick-horse rodeo for children. Events take place at the Grand Encampment Museum and other venues around town.

The **Medicine Bow–Routt National Forest, Hayden District** covers 586,000 acres, including the Continental Divide National Scenic Trail and the Encampment River, Huston Park, Savage Run, and Platte River wilderness areas. The local **Forest Service office** (⊠*204 W. 9th St.* ☎*307/326–5258* ⊕*www.fs.fed.us/r2/mbr*) can provide information on hiking, fishing, camping, cross-country skiing, and snowmobiling trails.

9

SPORTS & THE OUTDOORS

CROSS-
COUNTRY
SKIING
A network of cross-country trails in Medicine Bow–Routt National Forest, the **Bottle Creek Ski Trails** (⊠*Hwy. 70, 6 mi southwest of Encampment* ☎*307/327–5720*) include several backcountry trails suitable only for expert skiers. There are also easier routes for skiers of all levels. Some trails double as snowmobile trails. All of them are free. For more information in town, go to the Trading Post.

For ski rentals and sales as well as trail information contact Mark Rauterkus at the **Trading Post** (⊠*Junction of Hwys. 70 and 230* ☎*307 /327–5720*).

HIKING
There are extensive trails in the Sierra Madre range west of Encampment, ranging from developed paths around Bottle Creek to wilderness trails through Huston Park and along the Encampment River. For hiking information, contact the Forest Service office of the **Medicine Bow–Routt National Forest, Hayden District** (⊠*204 W. 9th St.* ☎*307/326–5258*).

HORSEBACK
RIDING
Rick Stevens of **Horseback Adventures** (☎*307/326–5569*) can lead a trail ride geared to your riding level. You can choose among rides in the Snowy Range, Sierra Madres, or desert country throughout Carbon County. Rides rage in length from half-day to overnight pack trips.

WHERE TO STAY & EAT

$–$$$ ✕ **Bear Trap Cafe.** People come for the large portions of hearty but basic food at this log building with the look and feel of a Western hunting lodge. The menu is strong on burgers, steaks, fish, and chicken. ✉ *120 E. Riverside Ave., 2 mi northeast of Encampment, Riverside* ☎ *307/327–5277* ▭ *MC, V.*

$–$$ ✕ **Pine Lodge Restaurant.** Regular offerings here include homemade pizza, burgers, and sandwiches; on some evenings there is Mexican food or prime rib. The bar is in a separate room. ✉ *518 McCaffrey St.* ☎ *307/327–5203* ▭ *MC, V.*

$–$$ 🏠 **Cottonwood Cabins.** In the quiet little town of Riverside, just across the street from the town park, these cabins have wood furniture, country quilts, outdoor grills, picnic tables, and full kitchens. Pros: Close to outdoor recreation. Cons: Open only through the summer. ✉ *411 1st St., Riverside 82325* ☎ *307/327–5151* 🖨 *307/327–5151* 🛏 *3 cabins* 🔥 *In-room: no a/c, no phone, kitchen. In-hotel: no-smoking rooms, no elevator* ▭ *D, MC, V.*

$ 🏠 **Spirit West River Lodge.** Beside the Encampment River, this massive log structure has walls of lichen-covered rocks and large windows overlooking the water and surrounding scenery. Stained glass and Western artwork—most of it by owner R.G. Finney, who is known for his wildlife bronzes and paintings—fill the lodge. His wife, Lynn, who serves the full breakfast, is a Senior Olympic gold medalist in cycling and a native of the area. She can direct you to the best cycling routes and cross-country-skiing trails. The lodge has a mile of private-access fishing on the Encampment River, and each room has a private entrance off a deck overlooking the river. The three-bedroom guesthouse ($–$$$$) has a full kitchen and private access, as well as river frontage. Some units have television and full kitchens. Pros: Quiet, secluded location. Cons: A short jaunt from downtown. ✉ *¼ mi east of Riverside on Hwy. 230, Box 605, 82325* ☎ *307/326–5753* 🖨 *307/327–5753* 🛏 *6 rooms* 🔥 *In-room: no a/c, no TV (some), kitchen (some). In-hotel: no-smoking rooms, no elevator* ▭ *MC, V* ⦿ *BP.*

Fodor's Choice
★

CAMPING   ⛺ **Hog Park.** In the Sierra Madres west of Encampment, this large campground sits beside a high mountain lake at 8,400 feet; some of the campsites have views of the water. You can use motorized boats and other watercraft on the lake. Hiking, horseback riding, and mountain-biking roads and trails abound, and there is a boat dock here as well. 🔥 *Pit toilets, drinking water, fire pits, picnic tables* 🛏 *50 sites* ✉ *20 mi southwest of Encampment; 5 mi west on Hwy. 70, then 15 mi southwest on Forest Rd. 550* ☎ *307/326–5258* ⊕ *www.fs.fed.us/r2/mbr/* 🔥 *Reservations not accepted* ▭ *No credit cards* ⊙ *Mid-June–Sept.*
★

⛺ **Lazy Acres Campground.** The Encampment River runs past this small campground with plenty of big cottonwood trees for shade. There are pull-through RV sites, tent sites, one small cabin (you provide bedding, stove, and cooking utensils), and four no-frills motel rooms, which have cable television and Wi-Fi. 🔥 *Flush toilets, full hookups, dumpsite, guest laundry, showers,* 🛏 *17 full hookups, 14 partial hookups, 2 tent sites; 1 camping cabin, 4 motel rooms.* ✉ *Hwy. 230, River-*

side ☎307/327–5968 ⊕*www.lazyacreswyo.com* ▤*MC, V* ☽*May 15–Oct. 31.*

⛺**Six Mile Gap.** There are only nine sites at this campground on a hillside above the North Platte River. Some are pull-through camper sites and others are walk-in tent sites. Trails follow the river, which you can cross during low water to reach the Platte River Wilderness Area. ♿*Pit toilets, drinking water, fire pits, picnic tables* ⛺*19 sites* ⊠*Hwy. 230, 26 mi east of Encampment, then 2 mi east on Forest Rd. 492* ☎*307/326–5258* ⊕*www.fs.fed.us/r2/mbr/* ☝*Reservations not accepted* ▤*No credit cards* ☽*May–Oct.*

EN ROUTE

As you make your way west to Baggs over the **Battle Highway** (Highway 70), you'll cross the Continental Divide and the Rocky Mountains. This route takes you through the mining country that was developed during the 1897–1908 copper-mining boom in the Sierra Madres; interpretive signs along the way point out historic sites. In 1879, Thomas Edison was fishing near Battle Pass with a bamboo rod when he began to ponder the idea of a filament, which led to his invention of the incandescent lightbulb. Note that this section of the highway closes to car travel in winter, though it stays open for snowmobiles.

BAGGS

60 mi west of Encampment via Hwy. 70.

Settled by cattle and sheep ranchers, the Little Snake River valley—and its largest community, Baggs—is still ranch country. Two emigrant trails passed nearby: the south branch of the Cherokee Trail (circa 1849–50) crosses near the community, and the Overland Trail (1862–65) lies farther to the north. Notorious outlaw Butch Cassidy frequented the area, often hiding out here after pulling off a train or bank robbery. To the west of Baggs, large herds of wild horses range freely on public lands. The town is on the southern edge of what is now a major oil, gas, and coalbed methane field, so large numbers of equipment trucks, big water trucks, and field workers ply the roads. Motels and restaurants stay busy.

Ranch paraphernalia, handmade quilts, a doll collection, and the original 1870s-era cabin of mountain man James Baker are exhibited at the **Little Snake River Valley Museum** ⊠*No. 2 N. Savery Rd.* ☎*307/383–7262* ⊕*www.littlesnakerivermuseum.com* 🏷*Donations accepted* ☽*Memorial Day–late Oct., daily 11–5.*

WHERE TO STAY & EAT

¢–$$$ ✕**El Rio.** Mexican food is the specialty in this small restaurant. Burritos, fajitas, and red and green chili are local favorites. The menu also includes hamburgers, chicken strips, and a steak-and-shrimp meal. ⊠*20 N. Penland St.* ☎*307/383–7515* ▤*MC, DC, V.*

$ 🏨**Drifter's Inn.** Drifter's has no-frills motel rooms adjacent to a restaurant ($–$$$) and lounge. Menu items range from burgers and steaks to chicken and fish. Friday nights there's prime rib, and Saturday nights are reserved for steak and shrimp. Pros: The attached restaurant is reg-

9

ularly open, unlike many other eateries in Baggs. Cons: This is pretty much the only game in town. ✉ *210 Penland St., 82321* ☎ *307/383–2015* 🖷 *307/383–6282* 🛏 *52 rooms* ⚐ *In-hotel: restaurant, bar, no-smoking rooms, some pets allowed, no elevator* ☰ *AE, D, MC, V.*

RAWLINS

70 mi northeast of Baggs via Hwy. 789 and I–80.

The northern gateway to the Medicine Bow–Routt National Forest, Rawlins stands at the junction of U.S. 287 and I–80. Started as one of the Union Pacific's hell-on-wheels towns, this was an important transportation center as early as 1868, when miners heading for the goldfields at South Pass to the north rode the rails to Rawlins or points nearby, then went overland to the gold diggings. The town became a large sheep-raising center at the turn of the 20th century. Kingpins in the sheep industry, such as George Ferris and Robert Deal, also backed the development of the Grand Encampment Copper Mining District in the Sierra Madres after miner Ed Haggarty discovered copper there in 1897.

Declines in sheep raising, long Rawlins's mainstay industry, have hurt the community economically, as have downturns in regional mineral production. But the city of 10,000 is still home to many railroad workers and employees of the Wyoming State Penitentiary outside of town. In summer there are weekly free concerts in the park.

About 70 mi north of Rawlins via U.S. 287 and Highway 220 are several sights of interest that are grouped together: Independence Rock State Historic Site, Devil's Gate, and Handcart Ranch (⇨ *Chapter 8*).

You can fish, boat, and water-ski on the Seminoe Reservoir, the primary attraction within **Seminoe State Park.** This is also a popular spot for camping and picnicking. It's on a Bureau of Land Management backcountry byway, Carbon County Road 351, which links Sinclair with Alcova. ☎ *307/320–3013* ⊕ *http://wyoparks.state.wy.us* ✉ *$2 resident vehicle, $4 nonresident vehicle; $6 camping* ◷ *Daily 24 hrs.*

Cold steel and concrete, the Death House, and the Yard are all part of the tour of the **Wyoming Frontier Prison,** which served as the state's penitentiary from 1901 until 1981. There are occasional midnight tours, and there's a Halloween tour. ✉ *500 W. Walnut St.* ☎ *307/324–4422* ✉ *$6* ◷ *Memorial Day–Labor Day, daily 8–5:30; Apr.–Memorial Day and Labor Day–Oct., call for limited hrs; rest of yr by appointment.*

WHERE TO EAT

$–$$$ ✕ **Cappy's.** The chicken-fried steak, T-bone steak, and enchiladas are all equally good at this family-owned restaurant on the west side of the city. The dining room has a homey feel and sunlight streams in the big banks of windows giving the space a bright, clean feel. ✉ *2351 W. Spruce St.* ☎ *307/324–4847* ☰ *AE, D, MC, V.*

$–$$$ ✕ **Sanfords Grub & Pub.** This downtown restaurant looks like an antiques store packed with road signs, memorabilia from the 1960s and later, and other vintage decorations. The huge menu includes beef, chicken,

CLOSE UP

Wyoming's Cowboy Symbol

Ask any old-timer in Cheyenne, Laramie, Lander, or Pinedale who the cowboy is on the Wyoming license plate's bucking-horse symbol, and you'll probably get four different answers. Artist Allen True, who designed the symbol, once said he had no particular rider in mind, but that hasn't stopped Wyoming residents from attributing the rider to regional favorites. Several well-known cowboys are often mentioned, including Stub Farlow of Lander and Guy Holt of Cheyenne (who later ranched near Pinedale).

True was not the first person to create this bucking-horse design, however. The symbol evolved over a number of years, beginning with a 1903 photograph by Professor B. C. Buffum of cowboy Guy Holt riding Steamboat, one of five horses recognized as the most difficult bucking horses of all time. In 1921, the University of Wyoming used that photograph as a model for the bucking-horse-and-cowboy logo on its sports uniforms.

But by that time there was already another Wyoming bucking-horse symbol. During World War I, George Ostrom, a member of the Wyoming National Guard serving in Germany, had a bucking-horse-and-rider design painted on a brass drum. His 148th Field Artillery unit soon adopted the logo for its vehicles as well, and it became known as the Bucking Bronco Regiment from Wyoming. And which horse was the symbol modeled after? In the case of the Wyoming National Guard logo, the horse was Ostrom's own mount, Red Wing.

Using Allen True's design, the state of Wyoming first put the bucking bronco on its license plate in 1936, and the well-known, trademarked symbol has been there ever since.

pasta, sandwiches, and salads, but specializes in sandwiches, many of which include a small slab of cream cheese The restaurant is also known for it's wide selection of beers, including both domestic and imported. Keep an eye out for semi-local brews from Jackson or Fort Collins, Colorado, as they can be difficult to find outside the Rocky Mountain West. ✉ *401 Cedar St.* ☎ *307/324–2921* ▭ *AE, D, DC, MC, V.*

¢–$$ ✕ **Su Casa.** One of Wyoming's best Mexican menus is here, 6 mi east of Rawlins in Sinclair. The menu includes shrimp, beef, and chicken fajitas, green chili, enchiladas, and Navajo tacos. Try the chiles rellenos (fried cheese-stuffed peppers) or shredded beef enchiladas. Takeout is available. ✉ *705 E. Lincoln Ave., Sinclair* ☎ *307/328–1745* ▭ *MC, V.*

WHERE TO STAY

$–$$$ ⌂ **Quality Inn.** Formerly the Lodge at Rawlins, this motel on the east side of town near the 287 bypass has just about everything you could ask for under one roof, from a game room to business services to a barbershop. It's convenient to shops and a grocery store; a free pass gives you full gym access at the Rawlins Recreation Center. Fat Boys Bar & Grill ($–$$$) serves sandwiches, steak, meat loaf, pot roast, and shepherd's pie. Pros: Easy interstate access, provides most amenities you could need. Cons: Outdoor pool is closed once cold weather sets in. ✉ *1801 E. Cedar St., 82301* ☎ *307/324–2783* 🖷 *307/328–1011*

9

⊕*www.choicehotels.com* ⟿*131 rooms* ⟵*In-room: refrigerator, dial-up, Wi-Fi. In-hotel: restaurant, bar, pool, laundry service, parking (no fee), no-smoking rooms, some pets allowed* ⊟*AE, D, DC, MC, V.*

$–$$ ⊞**Best Western Cottontree Inn.** This is Rawlins's finest motel, with spacious guest rooms decorated in greens and mauves. The inviting public areas with easy chairs are great for relaxing. There are regular water aerobics classes at the indoor pool. The Hungry Miner ($–$$$) restaurant serves melt-in-your-mouth corn bread and homemade soups. Pros: Welcoming atmosphere, the pool is open until 11 PM. Cons: Location leaves a bit to be desired. ⊠*23rd and W. Spruce Sts., Box 387, 82301* ☎*307/324–2737* 🖶*307/324–5011* ⊕*www.cottontree.net* ⟿*122 rooms* ⟵*In-room: Wi-Fi, refrigerator. In-hotel: restaurant, bar, pool, laundry service, parking (no fee), no-smoking rooms, some pets allowed* ⊟*AE, D, DC, MC, V.*

CAMPING   △**RV World Campground.** There are pull-through RV sites and tent sites at this campground on the west side of Rawlins. ⟵*Flush toilets, full hookups, dump station, drinking water, guest laundry, showers, picnic tables, swimming (pool)* ⟿*90 full hookups, 11 tent sites* ⊠*3101 Wagon Circle Rd.* ☎🖶*307/328–1091* ⊟*MC, V* ⊙*Mid-Apr.–Sept.*

△**Western Hills Campground.** There are pull-through RV sites, grassy tent sites, and an 18-hole miniature golf course at this year-round campground on the west side of Rawlins. Barbecue, play horseshoes, or browse the gift shop. You have access to immediate phone hookup, a TV area, and a public computer. ⟵*Flush toilets, full hookups, drinking water, guest laundry, showers, fire pits, picnic tables, play area* ⟿*115 full hookups, 80 tent sites* ⊠*2500 Wagon Circle Rd.* ☎🖶*307/324–2592* ⊟*MC, V.*

▎EN
ROUTE   If you're heading west from Rawlins to Rock Springs on I–80, you'll be following the path of the Cherokee Trail, the Overland Trail, and the Union Pacific Railroad into the **Great Divide Basin and Red Desert**, a landscape of flat sands and sandstone outcrops and bluffs. The best time to appreciate the beauty of this desert country, which spreads for thousands of acres west of Rawlins, is early morning (traveling west) and late afternoon (traveling east), when the sun creates wonderful shadows and makes the land glow. If you're headed east in the morning or west in the afternoon, you'll be driving with the sun in your eyes, so this may be a good time to take a break from driving.

SOUTHWEST WYOMING

Known as the Red Desert or the Little Colorado Desert, this is a unique area of Wyoming, with a combination of badlands, desert, and mountains. Although it may appear to be desolate, there's a wealth of wildlife in this region, including the largest free-ranging herd of pronghorn in the world (numbering around 50,000) and one of the largest herds of wild horses (numbering in the hundreds) in the United States. Southwest Wyoming is known for its mineral resources and for the dinosaur fossils that have been found here.

GREEN RIVER

12 mi west of Rock Springs via I–80.

A town of more than 13,000, Green River attracts those who want to explore the waterways of the Green River drainage in the nearby Flaming Gorge National Recreation Area. Of all the towns along the Union Pacific Railroad, this is the only one that predated the arrival of the rails in the late 1860s. It began as a Pony Express and stage station on the Overland Trail. In 1869 and again in 1871, explorer John Wesley Powell (1834–1902) launched expeditions down the Green and Colorado rivers from nearby sites.

A golf tournament, parade, arts festival in the park, and concerts are all part of **Flaming Gorge Days** (☎*307/875–5711* ⊕*www.flaminggorgedays. com*), a two-day celebration held each June in Green River. Tickets can be purchased for individual events, and concert tickets start at $25.

OFF THE BEATEN PATH

Seedskadee National Wildlife Refuge. Prairie and peregrine falcons, Canada geese, and various species of hawks and owls inhabit this 25,000-acre refuge. Trumpeter swans also occasionally use the area. Within or near the refuge there are homestead and ranch sites, Oregon Trail crossings, and ferries that cross the Green River, as well as the spot where Jim Bridger and Henry Fraeb built a trading post in 1839. Visitor information and restrooms are available during daylight hours. ✉*37 mi north of Green River on Hwy. 372* ☎*307/875–2187* ⊕*www.fws. gov/seedskadee* ✉*Free.*

SPORTS & THE OUTDOORS

A stroll on the paved path by the Green River takes you along the route that John Wesley Powell followed on his expedition down the waterway in 1869. Along the way you can visit Expedition Island, the Green Belt Nature Area, and the Scotts Bottom Nature Area. Access **Expedition Island** off 2nd Street, southwest of the railroad yard in Green River; wild birds, squirrels, and rabbits inhabit the grassy, tree-shaded island. Downstream from Expedition Island on the south bank of the river is the **Green Belt Nature Area,** with interpretive signs, nature paths, and numerous birds, including waterfowl. Farther south is **Scotts Bottom Nature Area,** where you'll find more interpretive signs related to the wildlife that lives in this riparian habitat.

WHERE TO EAT

$–$$$ ✕**Krazy Moose.** Moose-theme decor abounds in this American steak house. Locals favor the chicken-fried steaks, which are handmade and enormous in size. The menu also includes items such as sandwiches, burgers, and steaks. ✉*211 E. Flaming Gorge Way* ☎*307/875–5124* ▭*DC, MC, V.*

¢–$$$ ✕**Don Pedro's Family Restaurant.** Heaping plates of sizzling fajitas, enchiladas, burritos, and other traditional Mexican fare are served in a two-room restaurant where serapes, Mexican sombreros, and cactus provide decoration. ✉*520 Wilkes, Suite 10* ☎*307/875–7324* ▭*AE, D, MC, V.*

★

9

¢–$$ ✗ **Penny's Diner.** The name pretty much says it all—a 1950s-style 24-hour diner with a bright shiny look, reminiscent of a railcar, and flashing neon lights. Try a burger, fries, and a milk shake. The diner is part of the Oak Tree Inn. ⊠ *1172 W. Flaming Gorge Way* ☎ *307/875– 3500* ⊟ *AE, D, DC, MC, V.*

WHERE TO STAY

$–$$ ⬚ **Little America.** This one-stop facility stands alone in the Red Desert, and it can be a real haven if the weather becomes inclement. The hotel, founded in 1934, is the original of the small chain. The rooms are large and comfortable, with mauve-and-green comforters and lots of floral pillows; a small number of them have only showers, and no bathtubs, in the bathrooms. A full-service fuel station and a convenience store are also on the premises. Pros: Newly remodeled, all rooms have 37-inch flat-screen TVs. Cons: The closest town is 20 mi away. ⊠ *I–80, 20 mi west of Green River, Box 1, Little America 82929* ☎ *307/875–2400 or 800/634–2401* ☐ *307/872–2666* ⊕ *www.littleamerica.com* ⤺ *140 rooms* ☐ *In-room: refrigerator (some), Ethernet. In-hotel: restaurant, bar, pool, gym, laundry facilities, no-smoking rooms, no elevator* ⊟ *AE, D, DC, MC, V.*

$ ⬚ **Oak Tree Inn.** This two-story inn in four buildings on the west side of town is 20 mi from Flaming Gorge and has views of unique rock outcroppings above the city. Contemporary furnishings fill the rooms, which are decorated in shades of mauve and green. ⊠ *1170 W. Flaming Gorge Way, 82935* ☎ *307/875–3500* ☐ *307/875–4889* ⤺ *192 rooms* ☐ *In-room: refrigerator (some). In-hotel: restaurant, laundry facilities, no-smoking rooms, Wi-Fi, some pets allowed* ⊟ *AE, D, DC, MC, V.*

FLAMING GORGE NATIONAL RECREATION AREA

20 mi south of Green River via Hwy. 530 or Hwy. 191.

The Flaming Gorge Reservoir of the Flaming Gorge National Recreation Area is formed by Green River water held back by Flaming Gorge Dam. Here you can boat and fish, as well as watch for wildlife. The area is as rich in history as it is spectacularly beautiful. Mountain men such as Jim Bridger and outlaws such as Butch Cassidy found haven here, and in 1869, on his first exploration down the Green River, John Wesley Powell named many local landmarks: Flaming Gorge, Horseshoe Canyon, Red Canyon, and the Gates of Lodore. The recreation area straddles the border between Wyoming and Utah; most of the park's visitor services are in Utah. There are marinas, lodging, food, campgrounds, places to rent horses and snowmobiles, and trails for mountain bikes. The Ashley National Forest administers the area. ☎ *435/784–3445, 800/752–8525 for information on reservoir elevations and river flows, 877/444–6677 TDD, 877/444–6777 for campground reservations* ⊕ *www.fs.fed.us* ☒ *Free, but $2 daily recreation pass to use the boat ramp* ☉ *Daily 24 hrs.*

SPORTS & THE OUTDOORS

BOATING **Buckboard Marina** (✉ *Hwy. 530, 25 mi south of Green River* ☎ *307/875–6927*) provides full marina services, including boat rentals, a marina store, and an RV park.

CAMPING

🏕 **Buckboard Crossing.** The campsites at this campground on the west side of Flaming Gorge can be used for tents or RVs, though only a few sites have electrical hookups for RVs. There's a boat dock here. ⚐ *Flush toilets, dump station, drinking water, showers, fire pits, picnic tables, general store* ⥲*68 sites* ✉*23 mi southwest of Green River on Hwy. 530, then 2 mi east on Forest Rd. 009* ☎*435/784-3445 for information, 307/875–6927, 877/444–6777 for reservations* ⊕*www. reserveusa.com* ▭*AE, D, MC, V* ◷*Mid-May–mid-Sept.*

🏕 **Firehole Canyon.** Located in the Flaming Gorge National Recreation Area, this campground has great canyon views. You can pitch a tent or park an RV on the campsites here, but there are no hookups for RVs. There's a beach area nearby, plus a boat ramp. ⚐ *Flush toilets, drinking water, showers, fire pits, picnic tables* ⥲*38 sites* ✉*13 mi south of Green River on Hwy. 191, then 10 mi west on Forest Rd. 106* ☎*435/784–3445 for information, 877/444–6777 for reservations* ⊕*www.reserveusa.com* ▭*AE, D, MC, V* ◷*Mid-May–mid Sept.*

FORT BRIDGER STATE HISTORIC SITE

◷ *51 mi west of Green River via I–80.*

★ Started in 1843 as a trading post by mountain man Jim Bridger and his partner Louis Vasquez, Fort Bridger was under the control of Mormons by 1853 after they either purchased the fort or forced the original owners to leave—historians aren't sure which. As the U.S. Army approached during a conflict known as the Mormon War of 1857, the Mormons deserted the area and burned the original Bridger post. Fort Bridger then served as a frontier military post until it was abandoned in 1890. Many of the military-era buildings remain, and the Bridger post has been rebuilt and is staffed by a mountain man and woman. You can attend interpretive programs and living-history demonstrations during the summer, and the museum has exhibits about the fort's history. The largest mountain-man rendezvous in the intermountain West occurs annually at Fort Bridger over Labor Day weekend, attracting hundreds of buckskinners and Native Americans plus thousands of visitors. ✉*Exit 34 off I–80* ☎*307/782–3842* ⊕*http://wyoparks.state. wy.us/sites/fortbridger/index.asp* ▱*$2–$4* ◷*Grounds daily 8–dusk. Museum May–Oct., 9–4:30, weekends or by appointment when staff is available.*

CAMPING

🏕 **Fort Bridger RV Camp.** There's plenty of grass for tents, and room for RVs as well at this campground near Fort Bridger. ⚐ *Flush toilets, full hookups, drinking water, guest laundry, showers, picnic tables* ⥲*39 full hookups, 20 tent sites* ✉*64 Groshon Rd.* ☎*307/782–3150* ▭*No credit cards* ◷*Apr.–mid-Oct.*

9

SHOPPING

★   The fort's re-created **Bridger/Vazquez Trading Post** sells goods typical of the 1840s, when the post was first established, including trade beads, clothing, and leather items. It's open May–September, daily 9–4:30.

KEMMERER

34 mi north of Fort Bridger via Hwy. 412, 35 mi north of Evanston via Hwy. 189.

This small city serves as a gateway to Fossil Butte National Monument. Probably the most important person in Kemmerer's history was James Cash Penney, who in 1902 started the Golden Rule chain of stores here. He later used the name J. C. Penney Company, which by 1929 had 1,395 outlets. Penney revolutionized merchandising in western Wyoming. Before the opening of Penney's stores, the coal-mining industry dominated the region, and miners were used to working for the company and purchasing their supplies at the company store—which often charged whatever it wanted, managing to keep employees in debt. But when Penney opened his Golden Rule, he set one price for each item and stuck to it. Later he developed a catalog, selling to people unable to get to town easily.

A unique concentration of creatures is embedded in the natural limestone outcrop at **Fossil Butte National Monument,** indicating clearly that this area was an inland sea more than 50 million years ago. Many of the fossils—which include fish, insects, and plants—are remarkably clear and detailed. Pronghorn, coyotes, prairie dogs, and other mammals find shelter within the 8,198-acre park, along with numerous birds, such as eagles and falcons. You can hike the fossil trails and unwind at the picnic area. A visitor center here houses an information desk and exhibits of fossils found in the area, including a 13-foot crocodile. ⊠ *15 mi west of Kemmerer via U.S. 30* ☎ *307/877–4455* ⊕ *www.nps.gov/fobu* ✉ *Free* ☉ *Park daily 24 hrs. Visitor center June–Aug., daily 8–7; Sept.–May, daily 8–4:30.*

The **Fossil Country Frontier Museum,** housed in a former church, has fossils and displays related to early settlement in the area. ⊠ *400 Pine Ave.* ☎ *307/877–6551* ✉ *Free* ☉ *June–Aug., Mon.–Sat. 9–5; Sept.–May, Mon.–Sat. 10–4.*

At **Ulrich's Fossil Gallery** you can view fossils from around the world and even buy some specimens, particularly fish fossils. Ulrich's also runs fossil-digging excursions at private quarries; call for more information. ⊠ *U.S. 30* ☎ *307/877–6466* ✉ *Gallery free, fossil-digging excursions $85. Reservations required* ⊕ *www.ulrichsfossilgallery.com* ☉ *Daily 8–6; fossil digs June–Sept., daily at 9.*

WHERE TO STAY & EAT

$ ✕ **Busy Bee.** This local favorite on the main street of town serves hearty homemade fare such as chicken-fried steak, chicken dinners, hamburgers, and omelets. The theme is cows: cow pictures and ceramic heifers dot the walls and counters. ⊠*919 Pine St.* ☏*307/877–6820* ▭*No credit cards.*

¢ ⌖**Energy Inn.** Southwestern colors decorate the basic rooms, and you have access to a fax machine and a microwave in the lobby. A few miles south of Kemmerer in Diamondville, the motel caters to energy-industry workers; 10 ground-floor kitchenette units are for extended stays. Pros: Wallet-friendly price. Cons: Accommodations are a bit shabby, and it can be difficult to get a room with the influx of energy workers. ⊠*3 Hwy. 30, Diamondville 83116* ☏☏*307/877–6901* ⊕*www.energyinn.net* ⤴*31 rooms, 10 kitchenette units* ⌂*In-room: kitchen (some), refrigerator, Wi-Fi. In-hotel: no-smoking rooms, no elevator* ▭*AE, D, DC, MC, V.*

SHOPPING

To understand Kemmerer's roots, stop at the **JC Penney store** (⊠*722 JC Penney Dr.* ☏*307/877–3164*), which is where James Cash Penney began his merchandising career. This small retail establishment, known as the "mother store," sells clothing.

SOUTHERN WYOMING ESSENTIALS

To research prices, get advice from other travelers, and book travel arrangements, visit www.fodors.com.

AIR TRAVEL

CARRIERS Great Lakes Airlines/United Express connects Cheyenne, Laramie, and Rock Springs to Denver, Colorado.

Airlines & Contacts Great Lakes Aviation/United Express (☏*307/432–7000 in Cheyenne, 307/742–5296 in Laramie, 800/554–5111* ⊕*www.greatlakesav. com/).*

AIRPORTS

Cheyenne, Laramie, and Rock Springs' Sweetwater County Airport are the major airports in the area, with service to and from Denver only; there is no commercial service to other communities in the region. Many visitors to southeastern Wyoming prefer to fly into Denver International Airport and drive the 90 mi north to Cheyenne.

If you only need to get to and from the airport or bus station and the capitol area from Cheyenne Airport, you can make do with cabs. Try Checker Cab or Yellow Cab.

Airport Information Cheyenne Airport (⊠*200 E. 8th Ave., Cheyenne* ☏*307/634–7071* ⊕*www.cheyenneairport.com).* **Laramie Airport** (⊠*3 mi west of Laramie off Hwy. 130* ☏*307/742–4165* ⊕*www.laramieairport.com).* **Sweetwater County Airport** (⊠*382 Hwy. 370, Rock Springs* ☏*307/352–6880* ⊕*www.rockspringsairport.com).*

Taxis Checker Cab (☏*307/635–5555).* **Yellow Cab** (☏*307/638–3333).*

BUS TRAVEL

Greyhound Lines connects Cheyenne, Evanston, Laramie, Rawlins, and Rock Springs to such hubs as Denver and Salt Lake City.

Bus Information **Greyhound Lines** (☎ 800/231–2222 ⊕ www.greyhound.com ✉ 120 N. Greeley Hwy., Cheyenne ☎ 307/635–1327 ✉ 289 Bear River, Evanston ☎ 307/783–5930 ✉ 375 W. Lyon St., Laramie ☎ 307/742–1136 ✉ 102 W. Cedar St., Rawlins ☎ 307/324–4196 ✉ 1695 Sunset Dr., Suite 118, Rock Springs ☎ 307/362–2931).

CAR RENTAL

Rental agencies can be found at airports and at other locations in the larger cities.

Local Agencies **Avis** (✉ Cheyenne Airport ☎ 307/632–9371 ✉ Sweetwater County Airport, Rock Springs ☎ 307/362–5599). **Enterprise** (✉ 2200 Missile Dr., Cheyenne ☎ 307/632–1907 ✉ Sweetwater County Airport ☎ 307/362–0416). **Hertz** (✉ Cheyenne Airport ☎ 307/634–2131 ✉ Laramie Airport ☎ 307/745–0500 ✉ Sweetwater County Airport, Rock Springs ☎ 307/382–3262).

CAR TRAVEL

A car is essential to explore southern Wyoming. I–80 is the major route through the region, bisecting it from east to west. In places it runs parallel to U.S. 30. Other major access roads include U.S. 287, connecting Laramie and Medicine Bow; Highway 130, serving Centennial and Saratoga; Highway 230, running through Encampment; and Highway 70, connecting Encampment and Baggs.

Although distances between towns can be extensive, gasoline and other automobile services are available in each community and at various points roughly 20 to 40 mi apart along I–80. When traveling here in winter, be prepared for whiteouts and road closings (sometimes for hours, occasionally for more than a day). Always carry a blanket and warm clothing when driving in winter, along with a safety kit that includes snack food and water. Cell-phone service is getting better but is still sporadic in areas where mountains might interfere with cell towers.

Note that the Snowy Range Pass section of Highway 130, between Centennial and Saratoga, and the Battle Highway section of Highway 70, west of Encampment, close during cold weather, generally from mid-October until Memorial Day.

Contact the Wyoming Department of Transportation for information on road conditions.

Information **Wyoming Department of Transportation** (☎ 307/777–4484, 307/772–0824 from outside Wyoming for road conditions, 888/996–7623 from within Wyoming for road conditions ⊕ www.wyoroad.info/). **Wyoming Highway Patrol** (☎ 307/777–4301, 800/442–9090 for emergencies, #4357 (#HELP) from a cell phone for emergencies ⊕ http://whp.state.wy.us/index.htm).

EMERGENCIES

Ambulance or Police **Emergencies** (☎ 911).

24-Hour Medical Care **Evanston Regional Hospital** (✉ 190 Arrowhead Dr., Evanston ☎ 307/789–3636 or 800/244–3537 ⊕ www.evanstonregionalhospital. com). **Ivinson Memorial Hospital** (✉ 255 N. 30th St., Laramie ☎ 307/742–2141 ⊕ www.ivinsonhospital.org). **Memorial Hospital of Carbon County** (✉ 2221 Elm

St., Rawlins ☎ *307/324–2221* ⊕ *www.imhcc.com*). **Memorial Hospital of Sweet-water County** (✉ *1200 College Dr., Rock Springs* ☎ *307/362–3711*). **Cheyenne Regional Medical Center East** (✉ *2600 E. 18th St., Cheyenne* ☎ *307/634–2273* ⊕ *www.crmcwy.org*). **Cheyenne Regional Medical Center West** (✉ *214 E. 23rd St., Cheyenne* ☎ *307/634–2273* ⊕ *www.crmcwy.org*).

LODGING

CAMPING   Just about every community in the region has private campgrounds and RV parks. The Wyoming Campground Association can provide information on these campgrounds.

You can also camp on public lands managed by the U.S. Forest Service and local Bureaus of Land Management; these camping opportunities range from dispersed camping with no facilities to campgrounds with water, fire pits, and picnic tables. Some of the best camping spots are in the Medicine Bow–Routt National Forest near the communities of Centennial, Saratoga, Encampment, and Baggs. Camping near lakes and reservoirs is possible west of Cheyenne at Curt Gowdy State Park and south of Green River at Flaming Gorge National Recreation Area.

Information Curt Gowdy State Park (☎ *307/632–7946* ⊕ *http://wyoparks.state. wy.us/parks/curtgowdy/index.asp*). **Flaming Gorge National Recreation Area** (☎ *801/784–3445, 877/833–6777 for campground reservations* ⊕ *www.fs.fed. us/r4/ashley/recreation/flaming_gorge*). **Kemmerer District Bureau of Land Management** (☎ *307/828–4500* ⊕ *www.wy.blm.gov/kfo/info.htm*). **Medicine Bow–Routt National Forest** (☎ *307/745–2300* ⊕ *www.fs.fed.us/r2/mbr*). **Rawlins District Bureau of Land Management** (☎ *307/328–4200* ⊕ *www.blm.gov/wy/st/ en/field_offices/Rawlins.htm/*). **Rock Springs District Bureau of Land Management** (☎ *307/352–0256* ⊕ *www.blm.gov/wy/st/en/field_offices/Rock_Springs. html*). **U.S. Forest Service** (☎ *303/275–5350* ⊕ *www.fs.fed.us/r2*). **Wyoming Campground Association** (☎ *307/684–5722* ⊕ *www.campwyoming.org/*).

DUDE   If you want to experience a bit of the wrangling life, consider a stay at
RANCHES   a dude ranch. Professional cattle drivers and ranchers will teach you to rope, ride, and rodeo. The Wyoming Dude Ranchers Association can help you find a ranch to suit your interests and needs.

Contacts Wyoming Dude Ranchers Association (☎ *307/684–7157* ⊕ *www. wyomingdra.com*).

SPORTS & THE OUTDOORS

SKIING &   Numerous trail systems in the Medicine Bow–Routt National Forest,
SNOWMOBILING   Snowy Range, and Sierra Madres are popular with cross-country skiers and snowmobilers. Centennial, Encampment, Laramie, and Saratoga make particularly good bases for cross-country skiing, and you can access some downhill-skiing terrain from Centennial as well.

TOURS

The Cheyenne Trolley takes a $10, 1½-hour tour of the historic down-town area and Frances E. Warren Air Force Base, including 20–25 minutes at the Old West Museum. The trolley runs from mid-May to mid-September, Monday–Saturday at 10 and 1:30, Sunday at 11:30. Tickets are sold at the Cheyenne Area Convention and Visitors Bureau on weekdays and at the Wrangler shop on weekends. For a self-guided walking tour of the downtown and capitol area in Cheyenne, contact the Cheyenne Area Convention and Visitors Bureau.

Large herds of wild horses range freely on public lands west of Baggs, and you can see the animals by taking a four-wheel-drive tour with Wild Horse Country Tours. Tours start at $200 for two people. Having grown up here, guides John and Esther Clark are very knowledgeable about the area.

Rick Stevens of Horseback Adventures in Saratoga will take you out for a day, or on an overnight pack trip into the mountain and desert country of south-central Wyoming.

Tour Operators **Cheyenne Trolley Ticket Sales** (✉ *Cheyenne Area Convention and Visitors Bureau, One Depot Sq., 121 W. 15th St., Suite 202* ☎ *307/778–3133 or 800/426–5009* ⊕ *www.cheyenne.org* ✉ *Wrangler shop, 16th and Capitol Sts.* ☎ *307/634–3048*). **Horseback Adventures** (✉ *Box 1681, Saratoga 82331* ☎ *307/326–5569*). **Wild Horse Country Tours** (✉ *Box 11, Baggs 82391* ☎ *307/383–6865*)

VISITOR INFORMATION

Tourist Information **Albany County Tourism Board (Laramie)** (✉ *210 E. Custer St., Laramie 82070* ☎ *307/745–4195 or 800/445–5303* ⊕ *www.laramie-tourism. org*). **Carbon County Visitor's Council** (✉ *Box 1017, Rawlins 82301* ☎ *800/228–3547* ⊕ *www.wyomingcarboncounty.com*). **Cheyenne Area Convention and Visitors Bureau** (✉ *One Depot Square, 121 W 15th St., Suite 212, Cheyenne 82001* ☎ *307/778–3133 or 800/426–5009* ⊕ *www.cheyenne.org*). **Evanston Chamber of Commerce** (✉ *36 10th St., Evanston 82931* ☎ *307/783–0370* ⊕ *www.etown chamber.com*). **Green River Chamber of Commerce** (✉ *132 E. Flaming Gorge Way, Green River 82935* ☎ *307/875–5711 or 800/354–6743* ⊕ *www.grchamber. com*). **Kemmerer Chamber of Commerce** (✉ *800 Pine Ave., Kemmerer 83101* ☎ *307/877–9761* ⊕ *www.kemmererchamber.com/*). **Laramie Chamber of Commerce** (✉ *800 S. 3rd St., Laramie 82070* ☎ *307/745–7339 or 866/876–1012* ⊕ *www.laramie.org*). **Medicine Bow–Routt National Forest** (✉ *2468 Jackson St., Laramie 82070* ☎ *307/745–2300* ⊕ *www.fs.fed.us/r2/mbr*). **Rawlins–Carbon County Chamber of Commerce** (✉ *519 W. Cedar St., Rawlins 82301* ☎ *307/324–4111 or 800/228–3547* ⊕ *www.rawlinscarboncountychamber.com*). **Rock Springs Chamber of Commerce** (✉ *1897 Dewar Dr., Rock Springs 82902* ☎ *307/362–3771 or 800/463–8637* ⊕ *www.tourwyoming.com*). **Saratoga–Platte Valley Chamber of Commerce** (✉ *106 N. 1st St.* ✉ *Box 1095, Saratoga 82331* ☎ *307/326–8855* ⊕ *www.saratogachamber.info*). **Sweetwater County Joint Travel & Tourism Board** (✉ *79 Winston Dr., Rock Springs 82902* ☎ *307/382–2538* ⊕ *www.tourwyoming.com*). **Visitors Information Center/Depot Square** (✉ *920 Front St., Evanston 82930* ☎ *307/789–1472*).

The South Dakota Black Hills

WITH BADLANDS & WIND CAVE NATIONAL PARKS

WORD OF MOUTH

"Mount Rushmore must be seen at day and at night, as the nighttime view has massive spotlights on the faces and patriotic music, as I recall. The Crazy Horse Monument is also an interesting stop. It is a work in progress for over 50 years now."

—jeff

10

By T.D. Griffith
& Dustin D.
Floyd

"AN EMERALD ISLE IN A sea of prairie," as they are sometimes called, the Black Hills rise up from the western South Dakota plains just over the Wyoming state line and about 150 mi east of the Big Horn range of the Rocky Mountains. They aren't as high—Harney Peak, their tallest summit, measures 7,242 feet—and they cover a territory only 50 mi wide and 120 mi long, but these ponderosa-covered mountains have a majesty all their own. Alpine meadows, thick forests, and creek-carved canyons: the landscape of the Black Hills and Badlands region more closely resembles Big Horn and Yellowstone country than it does South Dakota's typical flat farmland.

The Black Hills are anchored by Rapid City; with 62,715 residents, it's the largest city for 350 mi in any direction. Perhaps better known, however, are the region's 19th-century frontier towns, including Spearfish, Lead, and Deadwood. The Black Hills also can claim one of the highest concentrations of public parks, monuments, and memorials in the world. Among the more famous are Badlands National Park, Jewel Cave National Monument, and Mount Rushmore National Memorial, whose giant stone carvings of four U.S. presidents have retained their stern grandeur for more than 60 years.

As in neighboring Wyoming and Montana, outdoor recreation reigns supreme in the Black Hills. Whatever your pleasure—hiking, mountain biking, rock climbing, horseback riding, fishing, boating, skiing, snowmobiling, cross-country skiing—you can do it here, before a backdrop of stunning countryside.

EXPLORING THE SOUTH DAKOTA BLACK HILLS

The 2 million acres of the Black Hills are about evenly split between private property and the Black Hills National Forest. Fortunately for visitors, the national forest is one of the most developed in the United States. Roads are numerous and generally well maintained, and navigation is easy. Towns with services are plentiful (compared with the Wyoming plains to the west), so you needn't worry about how much gas you've got in your tank or where you'll find a place to stay at night. Rapid City, the largest community in the region, is the most popular base for exploring the Black Hills. The northern towns of Deadwood and Spearfish have almost as many services, with less traffic and fewer tourists.

ABOUT THE RESTAURANTS

Like neighboring Wyoming, the Black Hills are not known for culinary diversity, and no matter where you go in this part of the world, beef is king. Nevertheless, thanks to a growing population and increasing numbers of visitors, the area is beginning to see more dining options. Rapid City and Spearfish have an abundance of national chain restaurants, and both communities have local eateries that specialize in Continental, contemporary, Native American, and traditional American cooking. Although dining in Deadwood's casinos usually involves an all-you-can-eat buffet, the tiny town also claims some of the best-ranked restaurants in South Dakota. Don't be afraid to try wild game

PLANNING YOUR TIME

Every small town in the Black Hills has something to offer—a fact that you may find surprising. This region has the highest concentration of parks, monuments, and memorials in the United States, qualifying the Black Hills and badlands as more than just a stopover on the way to and from the huge national parks of western Montana and Wyoming. If you have the time, your must-see list should include Rapid City, Mount Rushmore, the Crazy Horse Memorial, Deadwood, and Custer State Park. Sure, you can see the highlights of southwestern South Dakota in 24 or 48 hours—but if you spend five days or more here you will be amply rewarded.

You might consider a top-down approach, first exploring the Northern Hills around Deadwood. The historic sites, scenery, and casinos will keep you busy, but don't be afraid to explore the hidden treasures of the outlying towns: The new Tri-State Museum in Belle Fourche, the High Plains Western Heritage Center in Spearfish, and the Homestake Visitor Center in Lead are all worth seeing. Afterward, you can move into the

central Black Hills, spending some time in Rapid City to shop, check out the Journey Museum, and sample the local cuisine. Rapid City is also a good base for a day trip to nearby Mount Rushmore and Hill City, a tiny town with a vibrant art-gallery district and its own winery and vintage steam train. When you've covered the central region, shift down to the southern hills and visit Wind Cave National Park, Crazy Horse Memorial, Jewel Cave National Monument, the Mammoth Site, and the historic towns of Custer and Hot Springs—where naturally warm water still bubbles up from the earth. You can approach Badlands National Park to the east as a separate region if you have the time, or you might simply make it a day trip.

Spending a day in each subregion will allow you to explore most of the key attractions in the Black Hills. If you have time to spare, you will probably want to add the central and northern Black Hills, which are relatively unpopulated and offer exceptional natural wonders such as Spearfish Canyon.

10

dishes: buffalo, pheasant, and elk are relatively common ingredients in the Black Hills.

ABOUT THE HOTELS

New chain hotels with modern amenities are plentiful in the Black Hills, but when booking accommodations consider a stay at one of the area's historic properties. From grand brick downtown hotels to intimate Queen Anne homes converted to bed-and-breakfasts, historic lodgings are easy to locate. Many have been carefully restored to their late-19th-century grandeur, down to antique Victorian furnishings and authentic Western art. Other distinctive lodging choices include the region's mountain lodges and forest retreats. Usually built along creeks or near major trails, these isolated accommodations often attract outdoor enthusiasts.

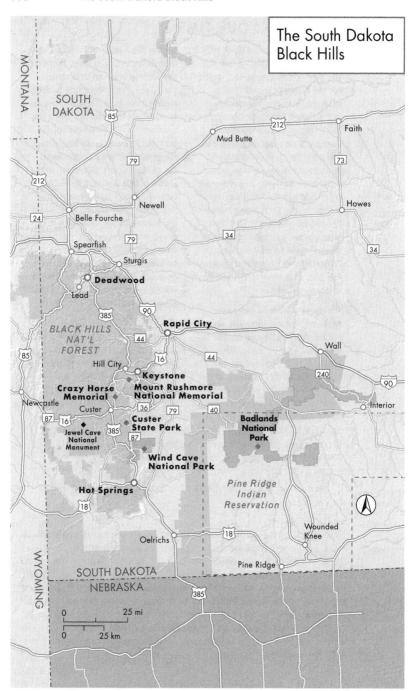

The South Dakota
Black Hills

MONTANA

SOUTH
DAKOTA

85

Mud Butte

212

Faith

73

212

79

24

Newell

Howes

Belle Fourche

79

34

Spearfish

34

Sturgis

Deadwood

Lead

385

90

Rapid City

BLACK HILLS
NAT'L
FOREST

44

Wall

85

16

44

240

90

Hill City

Keystone

**Crazy Horse
Memorial**

**Mount Rushmore
National Memorial**

Interior

Newcastle

Custer

36

79

40

**Badlands
National
Park**

87

16

**Custer
State Park**

Jewel Cave
National
Monument

385

87

**Wind Cave
National Park**

Pine Ridge
Indian
Reservation

Hot Springs

18

Wounded
Knee

Oelrichs

18

WYOMING

SOUTH DAKOTA

Pine Ridge

NEBRASKA

385

0   25 mi

0   25 km

WHAT IT COSTS					
	¢	$	$$	$$$	$$$$
RESTAURANTS	under $8	$8–$12	$13–$20	$21–$30	over $30
HOTELS	under $70	$70–$110	$110–$160	$160–$220	over $220
CAMPING	under $10	$10–$17	$18–$35	$36–$49	over $50

Restaurant prices are for a main course at dinner, excluding sales tax of 4%–7%. Hotel prices are for two people in a standard double room in high season, excluding service charges and 5%–10% tax. Camping prices are for standard (no hookups, pit toilets, fire grates, picnic tables) campsite per night.

TIMING

Weather forecasters hate the Black Hills. Snow can fall in the upper elevations every month of the year, and temperatures in January occasionally register above 60°F. However, anomalies like these rarely last more than a day or two. For the most part, expect the thermometer to range between 80°F and 100°F in summer, and know that winter temperatures can plunge below 10°F. Most visitors come in the warmer months, June to September, which is an optimal time for outdoor activities. Thanks to an average annual snowfall of 150 inches, more wintersports enthusiasts are beginning to discover the area's many skiing and snowmobiling opportunities. Nevertheless, the colder months are the least crowded in the Black Hills.

The shoulder seasons are increasingly popular times to visit, a trend that should continue as the baby boomers begin to retire. Spring in the Black Hills is generally snowy and rainy, but autumn is the perfect time to visit. The days are pleasantly warm, the nights are cool, and if you arrive before mid-October, you'll be treated to an incredible display of fall colors. Your only competition for space will be small groups of sportsmen and the occasional photographer out capturing images of colorful leaves.

DEADWOOD

10

Fodor'sChoice ★ *42 mi northwest of Rapid City via I–90 and U.S. 14A.*

Its brick-paved streets plied by old-time trolleys, illuminated by period lighting, and lined with original Victorian architecture, Deadwood today owes much of its historical character to casinos. In 1989 South Dakota voters approved limited-stakes gaming for the town, on the condition that a portion of revenues be devoted to historic preservation. Since then more than $200 million has been dedicated to restoring and preserving this once infamous gold-mining boomtown, which has earned recognition as a National Historic Landmark. Small gaming halls, good restaurants, and hotels occupy virtually every storefront on Main Street, just as they did back in Deadwood's late-19th-century heyday. You can walk in the footsteps of legendary lawman Wild Bill Hickok, cigar-smoking Poker Alice Tubbs, and the fabled Calamity Jane, who swore she could outdrink, outspit, and outswear any man—and usually did.

Several of the storefronts on **Main Street** belong to souvenir shops that typically peddle rubber tomahawks and plastic pistols to tourists. Some of the more upscale stores carry high-quality Western wear, Black Hills–gold jewelry, and fine art. Ice-cream parlors are never hard to find during summer.

EXPLORING DEADWOOD

Because most of Deadwood was laid out before the advent of automobiles, the city today is entirely walkable. Strung in a roughly straight line along the bottom of a gulch, the main points of interest are difficult to miss. The best strategy is to park in one of the lots on Main or Sherman street and begin your pedestrian adventure from there.

THE MAIN ATTRACTIONS

A tour of the restored **Adams House** includes an explanation of the tragedies and triumphs of two of the community's founding families (the Franklins and the Adamses) who lived here. The 1892 Queen Anne–style mansion was closed in the mid-1930s and sat empty for more than 50 years, preserving the original furniture and decor that you see today. ⊠ *22 Van Buren Ave.* ☎ *605/578–3724* ⊕ *www.adamsmuseum andhouse.org* ⊒ *$5* ☉ *May 1–Sept. 30, daily 9–5; Oct. 1–Apr. 30, Tues.–Sat. 10–4.*

☉ The **Adams Museum,** between the massive stone-block post office and the old railroad depot, houses three floors of displays, including the first locomotive used in the area, photographs of the town's early days, and a reproduction of the largest gold nugget (7¾ troy ounces) ever discovered in the Black Hills. ⊠ *54 Sherman St.* ☎ *605/578–1714* ⊕ *www.adamsmuseumandhouse.org* ⊒ *Donations accepted* ☉ *May 1–Sept. 30, daily 9–5; Oct. 1–Apr. 30, Tues.–Sat. 10–4.*

☉ **Broken Boot Gold Mine.** You can pan for gold, and even if you don't find any, you'll leave with a souvenir stock certificate. ⊠ *U.S. 14A* ☎ *605/578–1876* ⊕ *www.brokenbootgoldmine.com* ⊒ *Tour $5, gold panning $5* ☉ *Mid-May–mid-Sept., daily 8:30–5:30.*

The annual Days of '76 Rodeo—five days of parades, gallantry, horsemanship, and the best of the Old West, held at the end of July—pays homage to Deadwood's storied past. The **Days of '76 Museum** began almost by accident as the horse-drawn carriages and stagecoaches used in the event's parade became an attraction in their own right. Over the years cowboy memorabilia, photographs, and historical clothing have been added to the collection, and the museum is currently trying to raise $6 million to build a world-class facility to better present the artifacts. ⊠ *17 Crescent St.* ☎ *605/578–2872* ⊕ *www.daysof76.com/ museum* ⊒ *Donations accepted* ☉ *Mid-Apr.–mid-Oct., daily 9–5.*

Mount Moriah Cemetery, also known as Boot Hill, is the final resting place of Wild Bill Hickok, Calamity Jane, and other notable Deadwood residents. The aging landmark was revitalized by extensive restoration work in 2003, including the addition of a visitor center that houses a leather Bible, a stained-glass window, and pulpit chairs from the first and second

Methodist churches of Deadwood, which were destroyed in 1885 and 2003, respectively. From the top of the cemetery you'll have the best panoramic view of the town. ✉ *Top of Lincoln St.* ☎ *605/722–0837* 💵 *$1* 🕙 *Memorial Day–Labor Day, daily 7* AM*–8* PM*; Labor Day–end of Sept., daily 9–5.*

A heroic-scale bronze sculpture of three Native Americans on horseback driving 14 bison off a cliff is the centerpiece of **Tatanka: Story of the Bison,** on a ridge above Deadwood. The attraction, owned by *Dances with Wolves* star Kevin Costner, also includes an interpretive center; Lakota guides explain Plains Indian life circa 1840. ✉ *U.S. 85* ☎ *605/584–5678* 🌐 *www.storyofthebison.com* 💵 *$7.50* 🕙 *Mid-May–Sept., daily 9–5.*

OFF THE BEATEN PATH

🐄 **High Plains Western Heritage Center.** Founded to honor the pioneers and Native Americans of a region now covered by five states—the Dakotas, Wyoming, Montana, and Nebraska—the center features artifacts such as an original Deadwood-Spearfish stagecoach and life-size dioramas of an American cattle drive. Outdoor exhibits include a log cabin, a one-room schoolhouse, herds of bison and longhorn steers, antique farm equipment, and, in summer, an entire antique farm. Often on the calendar are cowboy poetry, live music, festivals, reenactments, talks on area ghost towns, and the Campfire Series of historical talks. ✉ *825 Heritage Dr., Spearfish* ☎ *605/642–9378* 🌐 *www.westernheritagecenter.com* 💵 *$7* 🕙 *Daily 9–5.*

SPORTS & THE OUTDOORS

Deadwood makes a good base for a winter sports vacation in the Black Hills, particularly if you like snowmobiling and cross-country skiing. The surrounding Northern Hills are especially popular, both for their stunning scenery and heavy snows. The rocky peaks and deep canyons are most dramatic here, and the snowfall is the heaviest. In some years the area around Deadwood sees as much as 180 inches of the white stuff, although the yearly average hovers around 150 inches. The climate here is more variable than in the Rockies, so snow doesn't blanket the region all winter. Warm spells of 50°F, 60°F, or even 70°F weather often hit the region for a week or so after big snowfalls, quickly melting the fresh powder. Before you make firm plans, be sure to check weather reports.

The community of **Sturgis** becomes South Dakota's largest city during the first week of August each year, when more than half a million motorcyclists invade for the **Sturgis Motorcycle Rally** (✉ *13 mi east of Deadwood on U.S. 14* ☎ *605/720–0800* 🌐 *www.sturgismotorcycle rally.com*). Begun in 1940 by a handful of bike owners, the event has grown into one of the largest gatherings of Harley-Davidson owners in

10

the world. Motorcycle shows, concerts, motorcycle tours, and national racing events are just some of the activities that fill this 10-day festival. Most hotels within a 100-mi radius of the town are totally booked for the festival up to a year in advance.

HIKING & BICYCLING

Beginning in Deadwood and running the length of the Black Hills from north to south, the **Mickelson Trail** (⊕ *www.ridethetrail.com*) incorporates more than 100 converted railroad bridges and four tunnels in its 109-mi-long course. Although the grade seldom exceeds 4%, parts of the trail are strenuous. A $2 day pass lets you hike or bike on the trail ($10 for an annual pass); passes are available at self-service stations along the trail, some state park offices, and through the South Dakota Game, Fish and Parks Web site (www.sdgfp.info/Index.htm). A portion of the trail is open for snowmobiling in winter.

Deadwood Bicycles (⊠ *180 Sherman St.* ☎ *605/578–1345*), in a restored engine house at the beginning of the Mickelson Trail, provides bike sales, service, and rentals, including bikes for men, women, and children, plus tandems. There's also a modest selection of rock-climbing equipment.

SKIING

Heavy snowfalls and lovely views make the Black Hills prime cross-country skiing territory. Many trails are open to snowmobilers as well as skiers, but most skiers stick to the quieter trails that are closed to motorized traffic. Many of these trails run along the rim or at the bottom of narrow canyons and gulches, affording outstanding views of some spectacular country. Depending on the freeze-thaw cycle, you may catch a glimpse of frozen waterfalls, particularly in Spearfish Canyon.

Although the Black Hills don't have the massive peaks that give Colorado, Wyoming, and Montana some of the best downhill skiing in the world, a couple of rocky slopes in the Northern Hills are both steep enough and snowy enough to support modest ski resorts, with respectable intermediate-level runs.

The groomed **Big Hill Trails** (⊠ *7 mi south of Spearfish on Tinton Rd., 15 mi west of Deadwood* ☎ *605/673–9200*) travel all around Spearfish Canyon. The trees here are gorgeous, ranging from the ubiquitous ponderosa and Black Hills spruce to quaking aspen and paperbark birch. The towering canyon walls, abundant wildlife, and stark contrast between the evergreens and the bare trees make this a particularly outstanding trail.

The runs at **Deer Mountain Ski Area** (⊠ *3 mi south of Lead on U.S. 85* ☎ *605/717–0422* ⊕ *www.skideermountain.com*) aren't as challenging as those on nearby Terry Peak, but this slope has a massive beginner's area and the only night skiing in the Black Hills. There are also about 10 mi of groomed cross-country trails. Rentals, regular classes, and inexpensive personal lessons are available, and there's a modest lodge. Perched on the sides of a 7,076-foot mountain, **Terry Peak Ski Area**

(⊠ *2 mi south of Lead on U.S. 85* ☎ *605/584–2165 or 800/456–0524* ⊕ *www.terrypeak.com*) claims the second-highest mountain summit in the Black Hills. The runs here are challenging for novice and intermediate skiers (and should at least keep experts entertained). The view from the top is spectacular; on a clear day you can see into Wyoming, Montana, Nebraska, and North Dakota.

SNOWMOBILING

Trade and travel magazines consistently rank the Black Hills among the top snowmobiling destinations in the country for two simple reasons: dramatic scenery and an abundance of snow. You'll find both throughout the area, but especially in the Northern Hills.

Trailshead Lodge (⊠ *21 mi southwest of Deadwood on U.S. 85* ☎ *605/584–3464* ⊕ *www.trailsheadlodge.com*), near the Wyoming border, has a small restaurant, a bar, gas, a repair shop, and dozens of brand-new snowmobiles for rent by the day. In summer (or during warm spells in winter when the snow melts) the lodge caters to bicyclists, horseback riders, hunters, and hikers.

WHERE TO EAT

$$–$$$ ✕ **Deadwood Thymes Bistro.** Across from the historic courthouse, away
★ from the Main Street casinos, this bistro has a quieter, more intimate feel than other town restaurants—and the food is among the best. The menu changes frequently, but expect dishes like brioche French toast, salmon quiche, Parisian grilled ham and Swiss, Thai burrito with peanut sauce, and lamb chops marinated in white wine and mustard and served with parsley-gin sauce. The wine list features imports, and desserts are incredible. You might find raspberry cheesecake or chocolate angel food cake with a whiskey-bourbon sauce. ⊠ *87 Sherman St.* ☎ *605/578–7566* ⊟ *MC, V.*

$$–$$$ ✕ **Jakes.** This restaurant, owned by actor Kevin Costner, is among
★ South Dakota's classiest dining experiences. Cherrywood pillars inlaid with etched-glass lights, white-brick fireplaces, and a pianist add to the elegance of the atrium dining room. Among the menu's eclectic offerings are buffalo roulade, Cajun seafood tortellini, filet mignon, and fresh fish. ⊠ *677 Main St.* ☎ *605/578–1555* 🍴 *Reservations essential* ⊟ *AE, D, DC, MC, V.*

10

$–$$$ ✕ **Deadwood Social Club.** On the second floor of historic Saloon No. 10,
Fodor'sChoice this warm restaurant surrounds you with wood and old-time photo-
★ graphs of Deadwood's past. Light jazz and blues play over the sound system. The decor is Western, but the food is northern Italian, a juxtaposition that keeps patrons coming back. The menu stretches from wild-mushroom pasta-and-seafood nest with basil cream to chicken *piccata* (sautéed and served with a lemon and parsley sauce) and melt-in-your-mouth Black Angus rib eyes. The wine list had nearly 200 selections at last count. Reservations are a good idea. ⊠ *657 Main St.* ☎ *605/578–1533* ⊟ *AE, MC, V.*

¢ ✕ **Moonshine Gulch Saloon.** Although it's 25 mi south of Deadwood in the middle of a very empty section of the forest, the ghost town of

Rochford is worth visiting. Once the site of a prosperous gold camp, the town now has about 15 residents and even fewer buildings. The saloon (between the Rochford Mall, the self-proclaimed "Small of America," and one-room Rochford University) stays quite busy in the summer despite its remote location. After you order your sarsaparilla soda and hamburger, look up to admire the collection of baseball caps and currency on the ceiling. ⊠ *Rochford Rd., Rochford* 🕾 *605/584–2743* 🖃 *MC, V.*

WHERE TO STAY

$$$ 🛏 **Mineral Palace.** As at the other hotels built in town since gaming was reintroduced in 1989, the architecture of Mineral Palace blends in with the historic buildings of Deadwood. The rooms have modern furnishings, but floral bedspreads, burgundy carpeting, and hardwood trim give them a slightly Victorian look. A recent multimillion-dollar expansion added amenities like Jacuzzis and flat-panel TVs to VIP and Royal suites. **Pros:** Recent expansion offers some of the best accommodations in Deadwood, on-site steak house is one of the tastiest in town. **Cons:** No-smoking rooms still have a hint of smoke smell, only a small on-site parking area. ⊠ *601 Main St., 57732* 🕾 *605/578–2036 or 800/847–2522* 🖷 *605/578–2037* ⊕ *www.mineralpalace.com* ❧ *59 rooms, 12 suites* ⚒ *In-room: dial-up. In-hotel: restaurant, room service, bar, laundry facilities, no-smoking rooms* 🖃 *AE, D, MC, V.*

$$$ 🛏 **Spearfish Canyon Lodge.** About midway between Spearfish and Dead-
★ wood, near the bottom of Spearfish Canyon, this lodge-style hotel commands some of the best views in the Black Hills. Limestone cliffs rise nearly 1,000 feet in all directions. The rush of Spearfish Falls is only a ¼-mi hike away, and the gentle flow of Roughlock Falls is a mile-long hike through pine, oak, and aspen from the lodge's front door. **Pros:** Scenery unmatched by any hotel in the area, a mile from one of the most breathtaking waterfalls in the region, on snowmobile trail that offers riders more than 300 mi of groomed trails. **Cons:** Secluded—nearly 15 mi from the closest amenities, winding approach road can be dangerous during the winter months. ⊠ *10619 Roughlock Falls Rd., Lead 57754* 🕾 *877/975–6343 or 605/584–3435* 🖷 *605/584–3990* ⊕ *www.spfcanyon.com* ❧ *54 rooms* ⚒ *In-room: Ethernet. In-hotel: no elevator, restaurant, room service, bar, laundry facilities, no-smoking rooms* 🖃 *AE, D, MC, V.*

$–$$$ 🛏 **Bullock Hotel.** A casino occupies the main floor of this meticulously restored, pink granite hotel, which was built by Deadwood's first sheriff, Seth Bullock, in 1895. Rooms are furnished in Victorian style with reproductions of the original furniture. **Pros:** Centrally located with on-site parking, staff is friendly and attentive, and on-site ghost tour is fun and unique. **Cons:** Front desk not in the most accessible of locations because of the era in which the hotel was built, slot machines commanding the front lobby can be disconcerting in such a finely restored hotel. ⊠ *633 Main St., 57732* 🕾 *605/578–1745 or 800/336–1876* 🖷 *605/578–1382* ⊕ *www.historicbullock.com* ❧ *29 rooms, 7 suites*

In-hotel: restaurant, room service, bar, no-smoking rooms ⊟AE, D, MC, V.

$–$$$ **Franklin Hotel.** Built in 1903, this imposing hotel has housed many
Fodor's Choice famous guests, including John Wayne, Teddy Roosevelt, and Babe
★ Ruth. It still has its original banisters, ceilings, and fireplace. The guest
rooms are Victorian-style, with reproduction furniture, lace on hard-
wood tables, and flowery bedspreads. A bar on the second floor spills
out onto the veranda above the white-columned hotel entrance, afford-
ing a great view down Main Street. The hotel had a major face-lift in
2006, which included an expanded casino and conference room. **Pros:**
Recent renovations offer guests one of the nicest casinos in town, great
views of the historic town. **Cons:** Parking is often a hike from the hotel
with no valet service, and more room renovations are pending. ⊠*700
Main St., 57732* ☎*605/578–2241 or 800/688–1876* ⊟*605/578–3452*
⊕*www.silveradofranklin.com* ⊲*81 rooms* In-hotel: room service,
bar, no-smoking rooms ⊟AE, D, DC, MC, V.

NIGHTLIFE

There are more than 80 gaming establishments in Deadwood, most
of them small and personal. They generally serve other functions as
well—as restaurants, saloons, and gift shops—and usually have only a
few blackjack and poker tables and slot machines.

Expect a family crowd in the day and a rowdier bunch at night at
the **Bodega and Big Al's Buffalo Steakhouse Stockade** (⊠*658 Main St.*
☎*605/578–1300*). Most evenings you can listen to live country or
rock music; the entertainment moves outdoors in summer, when bands
play in the stockade section. The Bodega has a rough past; from the
1890s until 1980, the upper floors were used as a brothel. The rooms
now sit empty, although the secret buzzers and discreet back doors
were removed only in the 1990s. It doesn't offer live music, but the
casino **Midnight Star** (⊠*677 Main St.* ☎*605/578–1555*) is owned by
actor Kevin Costner and decorated throughout with props and cos-
tumes from his movies. The bar on the first floor is named for and
modeled after the bar in the film *Silverado,* in which Costner starred.
Wood accents, stained glass, and plush carpeting give the structure an
elegant Victorian look.

★ Billing itself as "the only museum in the world with a bar," the **Old Style
Saloon No. 10** (⊠*657 Main St.* ☎*605/578–3346*) is littered with thou-
sands of artifacts, from vintage photos and antique lighting to a stuffed
two-headed calf and the chair in which Wild Bill Hickok was suppos-
edly shot. A reenactment of his murder takes place four times daily in
the summer. At night come for some of the region's best bands, lively
blackjack tables, and quiet bartenders who cater to noisy customers.
The **Silverado** (⊠*709 Main St.* ☎*605/578–1366 or 800/584–7005*),
sprawling over half a city block at the top of Main Street, is among
Deadwood's largest gaming establishments. Although the wood panel-
ing and brass accents around the bars recall Deadwood's Wild West
past, the red carpets, velvet ropes, and bow tie–clad staff give the place

10

modern polish. The prime rib–and-crab buffet on Friday and Saturday nights attracts regulars from more than 100 mi away.

RAPID CITY

42 mi southeast of Deadwood via U.S. 14A and I–90.

The central Black Hills, one of the most developed and best-traveled parts of the region, is anchored by Rapid City (population 62,715). The largest population center in a 350-mi radius, it's the cultural, educational, medical, and economic hub of a vast region. Most of the numerous shops, hotels, and restaurants in the city cater specifically to tourists, including a steady flow of international visitors; some signage displays information in multiple languages and includes metric measurements. Locals refer to Rapid City as "West River," meaning west of the Missouri. Cowboy boots are common here, and business leaders often travel by pickup truck or four-wheel-drive vehicle. At the same time, the city supports a convention center and a modern, acoustically advanced performance hall. A four-lane highway, U.S. 16, links the city to Mount Rushmore National Memorial.

EXPLORING RAPID CITY

★ **Journey Museum.** The interactive exhibits here explore the history of the Black Hills from the age of the dinosaurs to the days of the pioneers. The complex combines the collections of the **Sioux Indian Museum,** the **Minnilusa Pioneer Museum,** the **Museum of Geology,** the **State Archaeological Research Center,** and a private collection of Native American artifacts into a sweeping pageant of the history and evolution of the Black Hills. A favorite among visitors is the tepee in the Sioux Indian Museum; you have to crouch down and peer inside to watch a holographic Lakota woman talk about the history and legends of her people. ⊠*222 New York St.* ☎*605/394–6923* ⊕*www.journeymuseum.org* ▤*$7* ☾*Memorial Day–Labor Day, daily 9–5; Labor Day–Memorial Day, Mon.–Sat. 10–5, Sun. 1–5.*

The **South Dakota Air & Space Museum** has a model of a Stealth bomber that's 60% actual size. Also here are General Dwight D. Eisenhower's Mitchell B-25 bomber and more than two dozen other planes, as well as a once-operational missile silo. The museum is open year-round, but tours are not available in winter. ⊠*2890 Davis Dr.* ☎*605/385–5188* ▤*Free, tour $5* ☾*Mid-May–mid-Sept., daily 8:30–6; mid-Sept.–mid-May, daily 8:30–4:30.*

Although they were released in the early 1990s, the films *Dances with Wolves* and *Thunderheart* continue to generate interest and business in the Black Hills. The **Ft. Hays** *Dances with Wolves* **Movie Set** displays photos and shows a video taken during the making of the film. A chuckwagon dinner show ($15) is offered Memorial Day through Labor Day. ⊠*Ft. Hays Dr. and U.S. 16* ☎*888/394–9653* ⊕*www.rushmoretours. com/forthays.html* ▤*Free* ☾*Mid-May–mid-Sept., daily 7:30* AM*–8* PM.

☺ On the west side of Rapid City is **Storybook Island,** a park on the banks of Rapid Creek that lets children romp through scenes from fairy tales and nursery rhymes. A children's theater troupe, sponsored by the Black Hills Community Theater, performs regular shows on a modest outdoor stage here and hosts workshops and acting programs. ✉*1301 Sheridan Lake Rd.* ☎*605/342–6357* ⊕*www.storybookisland.org* 💰*Donations accepted* ⊙*May–Sept., daily 9–7.*

☺ **Reptile Gardens.** On the bottom of a valley between Rapid City and
★ Mount Rushmore is western South Dakota's answer to a zoo. In addition to the world's largest private reptile collection, the site also has a raptor rehabilitation center. No visit is complete without watching some alligator wrestling or letting the kids check out the giant tortoises. ✉*8955 S. U.S. 16* ☎*605/342–5873* ⊕*www.reptilegardens. com* 💰*$12* ⊙*Memorial Day–Labor Day, daily 8–7.*

☺ **Bear Country U.S.A.** Encounter black bears and wolves at this drive-through wildlife park. There's also a walk-through wildlife center. ✉*13820 S. U.S. 16* ☎*605/343–2290* ⊕*www.bearcountryusa.com* 💰*$13* ⊙*May–Nov., daily 8–7.*

Black Hills Caverns. Frost crystal, amethyst, logomites, calcite crystals, and other specimens fill this cave, first discovered by pioneers in the late 1800s. Half-hour and hour tours are available. ✉*2600 Cavern Rd.* ☎*605/343–0542* ⊕*www.blackhillscaverns.com* 💰*$9 per hr, $7 per ½ hr* ⊙*May–mid-June and mid-Aug.–Sept., daily 8:30–5:30; mid-June–mid-Aug., daily 8–7.*

Museum of Geology. This South Dakota School of Mines and Technology museum hosts a fine collection of fossilized bones from giant dinosaurs. It also contains extensive collections of agates, fossilized cycads, rocks, gems, and minerals. ✉*501 E. St. Joseph St., O'Harra Memorial Building* ☎*605/394–2467 or 800/544–8162* 💰*Free* ⊙*Memorial Day–Labor Day, Mon.–Sat. 8–6, Sun. noon–6; Labor Day–Memorial Day, weekdays 8–5, Sat. 9–4, Sun. 1–4.*

10

SPORTS & THE OUTDOORS

The Black Hills are filled with tiny mountain creeks—especially on the wetter western and northern slopes—that are ideal for fly-fishing. Rapid Creek, which flows down from the Central Hills into Pactola Reservoir and finally into Rapid City, is a favorite fishing venue for the city's anglers, both because of its regularly stocked population of trout and for its easy accessibility (don't be surprised to see someone standing in the creek casting a line as you drive through the center of town on Highway 44). Also popular are nearby Spearfish, Whitewood, Spring, and French creeks, all within an hour's drive of Rapid City.

Although they'll take you on a guided fly-fishing trip any time of the year, the folks at **Dakota Angler and Outfitter** (✉*513 7th St.* ☎*605/341–2450*) recommend fishing between April and October. The guides lead individuals and groups on half- and full-day excursions, and they cater to all skill levels.

WHERE TO EAT

$–$$$$ ✕**Firehouse Brewing Company.** Brass fixtures and firefighting equipment ornament the state's first brewpub, located in a 1915 firehouse. The five house-brewed beers are the highlight here, and the menu includes such hearty pub dishes as pastas, salads, and gumbo. Thursday nights buffalo prime rib is the specialty. Kids' menus are available. ⊠*610 Main St.* ☎*605/348–1915* ⊕*www.firehousebrewing.com* ⌲*Reservations not accepted* ▤*AE, D, DC, MC, V* ⊘*No lunch Sun.*

$$ ✕**Flying T Chuckwagon.** Ranch-style meals of barbecued beef, grilled chicken, potatoes, and baked beans are served on tin plates in this converted barn. Dinner, served between 5 and 6:30, is followed by a Western show with music and cowboy comedy. The prix-fixe price includes dinner and the show. In summer it's a good idea to buy tickets in advance. ⊠*U.S. 16, 6 mi south of town* ☎*605/342–1905 or 888/256–1905* ⊕*www.flyingt.com* ▤*MC, V* ⊘*Closed mid-Sept.– mid-May. No lunch.*

$–$$ ✕**Botticelli Ristorante Italiano.** With a wide selection of delectable veal and
★   chicken dishes as well as creamy pastas, this Italian eatery provides a welcome respite from Midwestern meat and potatoes. The artwork and traditional Italian music in the background give the place a European atmosphere. ⊠*523 Main St.* ☎*605/348–0089* ▤*AE, MC, V.*

WHERE TO STAY

$$–$$$$ 🏨**Radisson Hotel Rapid City/Mount Rushmore.** Murals of the surrounding landscape and a large Mount Rushmore mosaic in the marble floor distinguish the lobby of this nine-floor hotel in the heart of downtown Rapid City. Decorated in gold and beige, the rooms here are unremarkable, with one exception: most feature Sleep Number beds, whose comfort level can be adjusted by users. The popular accommodation stands between Interstate 90 and U.S. 16, the highway that leads into the southern Black Hills and Mount Rushmore. **Pros:** Centrally located downtown, Sleep Number beds in all rooms, boasts one of the premiere fine dining restaurants in the area, immaculate rooms. **Cons:** Rooms on the "bar side" can be noisy during busy nights, and on-site parking can be crowded because of the popularity of the restaurant. ⊠*445 Mt. Rushmore Rd., 57701* ☎*605/348–8300* 📠*605/348–3833* ⊕*www.radisson.com/rapidcitysd* 🛏*176 rooms, 5 suites* ♿*In-hotel: pool, gym, public Wi-Fi, no-smoking rooms* ▤*AE, D, DC, MC, V.*

$$–$$$ 🏨**Audrie's Bed & Breakfast.** This secluded, romantic B&B, set in a thick
★   woods 7 mi west of Rapid City, is filled with Victorian antiques. Suites, cottages, and creek-side cabins sleeping two come with old-world furnishings, fireplaces, private baths, hot tubs, and big-screen TVs. Bicycles and fishing poles can be obtained free from the office. **Pros:** Large, clean, well-furnished suites; great privacy, perfect for couples. **Cons:** Not allowing the use of credit cards can be an unexpected problem for some travelers. ⊠*23029 Thunderhead Falls Rd., 57702* ☎*605/342– 7788* ⊕*www.audriesbb.com* 🛏*2 suites, 7 cottages and cabins* ♿*In-hotel: no elevator, bicycles, no-smoking rooms, no kids under 21* ▤*No credit cards* ⏸⃝*BP.*

CAMPING

⏱ 🏕 **Whispering Pines Campground and Lodging.** Block party–style cookouts are followed by movies every night here as long as the weather is good. Located 16 mi west of Rapid City in Black Hills National Forest, the campground lies exactly midway between Deadwood (22 mi to the north) and Mount Rushmore (22 mi to the south). In addition to RV and tent sites, cabins are available at a reasonable price. ⚐ *Flush toilets, full hookups, partial hookups (electric and water), dump station, drinking water, guest laundry, showers, fire pits, picnic tables, food service, electricity, public telephone, general store, play area, swimming (lake)* ⏚*26 full hookups, 2 partial hookups, 45 tent sites; 5 cabins* ⊠*22700 Silver City Rd.* ☎*605/341–3667* 🖷*605/341–3667* ⊕*www.blackhillscampresort.com* ⚑*Reservations essential* ▭*D, MC, V* ☉*May–Sept.*

MOUNT RUSHMORE NATIONAL MEMORIAL

Fodor'sChoice *24 mi southwest of Rapid City via U.S. 16 and U.S. 16A.*
★

At Mount Rushmore, one of the nation's most famous sights, 60-foot-high likenesses of Presidents George Washington, Thomas Jefferson, Abraham Lincoln, and Theodore Roosevelt grace a massive granite cliff, which, at an elevation of 5,725 feet, towers over the surrounding countryside and faces the sun most of the day. The memorial is equally spectacular at night in June through mid-September, when a special lighting ceremony dramatically illuminates the carving.

EN ROUTE The fastest way to get from Mount Rushmore to Crazy Horse Memorial and the southern Black Hills is along Highway 244 west and U.S. 16/U.S. 385 south. This route, like all of the drives in the Black Hills, is full of beautiful mountain views, but the **Peter Norbeck National Scenic Byway** is an even more stunning, though much longer, route. Take U.S. 16A south into Custer State Park, where buffalo, bighorn sheep, elk, antelope, and burros roam free, then drive north on Highway 87 through the Needles, towering granite spires that rise above the forest. A short drive off the highway reaches 7,242-foot Harney Peak, the highest point in North America east of the Rockies. Highway 87 finally brings you to U.S. 16/U.S. 385, where you head south to the Crazy Horse Memorial. Because the scenic byway is a challenging drive (with one-lane tunnels and switchbacks) and because you'll likely want to stop a few times to admire the scenery, plan on spending two to three hours on this drive. Note that stretches of U.S. 16A and Highway 87 may close in winter.

10

WHERE TO EAT

¢–$ ✕**Buffalo Dining Room.** The only restaurant within the bounds of the memorial affords commanding views of Mount Rushmore and the surrounding ponderosa pine forest, and exceptional food at a reasonable price. The menu includes New England pot roast, buffalo stew, and homemade rhubarb pie. It's open for breakfast, lunch, and dinner. ⊠*Beginning of Ave. of Flags* ☎*605/574–2515* ▭*AE, D, MC, V* ☉*No dinner mid-Oct.–early Mar.*

America's Shrine of Democracy

Like most impressive undertakings, Mount Rushmore's path to realization was one of personalities and perseverance.

When Gutzon Borglum, a talented and patriotic sculptor, was invited to create a giant monument to Confederate soldiers in Georgia in 1915, he jumped at the chance. The son of Danish immigrants, Borglum was raised in California and trained in art in Paris, even studying under Auguste Rodin, who influenced his style. Georgia's Stone Mountain project was to be massive in scope—encompassing the rock face of an entire peak—and would give Borglum the opportunity to exercise his artistic vision on a grand scale.

But the relationship with the project backers and Borglum went sour, causing the sculptor to destroy his models and flee the state as a fugitive. Fortunately, state officials in South Dakota had a vision for another mountain memorial, and Borglum was eager to jump on board. His passion and flamboyant personality were well matched to the project, which involved carving legends of the Wild West on a gigantic scale. In time, Borglum persuaded local officials to think larger, and the idea of carving a monument to U.S. presidents on a mountainside was born.

Borglum began carving Mount Rushmore in 1927 with the help of some 400 assistants. In consultation with U.S. Senator Peter Norbeck and State

Historian Doane Robinson, Borglum chose the four presidents to signify the birth, growth, preservation, and development of the nation. In 6½ years of carving over a 14-year period, the sculptor and his crew drilled and dynamited a masterpiece, the largest work of art on Earth. Borglum died in March 1941, leaving his son, Lincoln, to complete the work only a few months later—in the wake of the gathering storm of World War II.

Follow the Presidential Trail through the forest to gain excellent views of the colossal sculpture, or stroll the Avenue of Flags for a different perspective. Also on-site are an impressive museum, an indoor theater where films are shown, an outdoor amphitheater for live performances, and concession facilities. The nightly ranger program and lighting of the memorial is reportedly the most popular interpretive program in all of the national parks system.

The **Mount Rushmore Information Center,** between the park entrance and the Avenue of Flags, has a small exhibit with photographs of the presidents' faces as they were being carved. There's also an information desk here, staffed by rangers who can answer questions about the memorial or the surrounding Black Hills. A nearly identical building across from the information center houses restrooms, telephones, and soda machines. ⊠ *Beginning of Ave. of Flags* ☎ *605/574–3198* ⊕ *www. nps.gov/moru* ☑ *Free; parking $10* ☉ *May–Sept., daily 8* AM*–10* PM*; Oct.– Apr., daily 8–5.*

MOUNT RUSHMORE ATTRACTIONS

Avenue of Flags. Running from the entrance of the memorial to the museum and amphitheater at the base of the mountain, the avenue represents each state, commonwealth, district, and territory of the United States.

Lincoln Borglum Museum. This giant granite-and-glass structure underneath the viewing platform has permanent exhibits on the carving of the mountain, its history, and its significance. There also are temporary exhibits, a bookstore, and an orientation film. Admission is free, and it is open year-round.

Presidential Trail. This easy hike along a boardwalk and down some stairs leads to the very base of the mountain. Although the trail is thickly forested, you'll have more than ample opportunity to look straight up the noses of the four giant heads. The trail is open year-round, so long as snow and/or ice don't present a safety hazard.

Sculptor's Studio. Built in 1939 as Gutzon Borglum's on-site workshop, it displays tools used by the mountain carvers, a 1:12-scale model of the memorial, and a model depicting the unfinished Hall of Records. Admission is free. Open May–September only.

10

SHOPPING

The **Mount Rushmore Bookstore** (⊠ *Lincoln Borglum Museum, end of Ave. of Flags* ☎ *800/699–3142*) carries a selection of books, CDs, and videos on the memorial, its history, and the entire Black Hills region. There are also some titles on geology and Native American history. The **Mount Rushmore Gift Shop** (⊠ *Beginning of Ave. of Flags* ☎ *605/574– 2515*), across from the Buffalo Dining Room, sells any number of souvenirs, from shot glasses and magnets to T-shirts and baseball caps. You can also buy Black Hills–gold jewelry and Native American art.

KEYSTONE

2 mi northwest of Mount Rushmore National Memorial via Hwy. 244 and U.S. 16.

Founded in the 1880s by prospectors searching the central Black Hills for gold deposits, this small town now serves the millions of visitors who pass through each year on their way to Mount Rushmore, 2 mi away. The touristy town has some 700 hotel rooms—more than twice the number of permanent residents. Its 19th-century buildings house dozens of gift shops, restaurants, and attractions that range from wax museums and miniature-golf courses to alpine slides and helicopter rides.

WHAT TO SEE

Beautiful Rushmore Cave. Stalagmites, stalactites, flowstone, ribbons, columns, helicites, and the "Big Room" are all part of the worthwhile tour into this cave. In 1876 miners found the opening to the cave while digging a flume into the mountainside to carry water to the gold mines below. The cave was opened to the public in 1927, just before the carving of Mount Rushmore began. ⊠ *Rte. 40, Keystone* ☎ *605/255– 4384 or 605/255–4634* ⊕ *www.beautifulrushmorecave.com* 🎫 *$8.50* ☉ *June–Aug., daily 8–8; Sept. and Oct., daily 9–5.*

☯ **Big Thunder Gold Mine.** Take a guided tour through an underground gold mine, get some free gold ore samples, and do a little gold panning yourself at this Keystone attraction. ⊠ *Rte. 40, Keystone* ☎ *605/666–4847 or 800/314–3917* ⊕ *www.bigthundermine.com* 🎫 *$8* ☉ *May–mid-Oct., daily 8–8.*

WHERE TO STAY & EAT

$$–$$$ ✕ **Creekside Dining.** Dine on very good American cuisine at this casual Keystone restaurant with a patio view of Mount Rushmore. Chef Bear's finest dishes are the hearty platters of prime rib, buffalo, lamb, chicken, and fish. Desserts, which include bread pudding, crème brûlée, and peach cobbler, are also excellent. A kids' menu is available. ⊠ *610 U.S. 16A, Keystone* ☎ *605/666–4904* ▤ *MC, V* ☉ *Closed Nov.–May.*

$-$$$ 🛏**Roosevelt Inn.** This mid-size inn less than 1 mi from the east entrance of Mount Rushmore is one of the closest hotels to the "faces" (although you cannot see them from the inn itself). Standard motel-style furnishings fill the rooms, some of which have balconies. Mountain-view rooms are especially inviting in autumn. **Pros:** Great location near Mount Rushmore, great value for money spent, very warm and friendly staff. **Cons:** Go to dinner early, because the restaurant closes by 8 PM. ⊠*206 Old Cemetery Rd., Keystone 57751* ☎*605/666–4599 or 800/257–8923* 🖷*605/666–4535* ⊕*www.rosyinn.com* 🛏*21 rooms* ♿*In-hotel: restaurant, pool, no-smoking rooms* ▤*AE, MC, V* ⫴❘*CP.*

$-$$ 🛏**Best Western Four Presidents.** In the shadow of Mount Rushmore in downtown Keystone, the hotel lies within walking distance of the town's major attractions, including several restaurants. Short pack tours into the hills by horseback can be arranged next door. **Pros:** Great location near Mount Rushmore, great food, hotel overall is spotless. **Cons:** On the edge of town, away from most activities. ⊠*24075 U.S. 16A, 57751* ☎*605/666–4472* 🖷*605/666–4574* ⊕*www.bestwestern. com* 🛏*45 rooms, 5 suites* ♿*In-hotel: room service, pool, gym, laundry facilities, no-smoking rooms* ▤*AE, D, DC, MC, V* ☯*All but 3 rooms closed Nov.–Apr.* ⫴❘*CP.*

$-$$ 🛏**K Bar S Lodge.** Set on 31 acres of lush green forest on the Norbeck Wildlife preserve, the K Bar S Lodge is the perfect location for a weekend getaway or a destination business conference (groups up to 200 can easily be accommodated). Be sure to request one of the rooms with a private deck, which offer picture-perfect views of Mount Rushmore. **Pros:** Premier lodging in the Black Hills, can see Mount Rushmore off room balconies, staff is extremely personable. **Cons:** Can be crowded if special events are going on, be sure to ask during booking. ⊠*434 Old Hill City Rd.* ✉*Box 208, Keystone 57751* ☎*605/666–4545, 866/522–7724* 🖷*605/666–4202* ⊕*www.kbarslodge.com* 🛏*64 rooms* ♿*In-hotel: laundry facilities, Ethernet* ▤*AE, D, MC, V.*

CRAZY HORSE MEMORIAL

Fodor's Choice   *15 mi southwest of Mount Rushmore National Memorial via Hwy.*
★   *244 and U.S. 16.*

Designed to be the world's largest sculpture (641 feet long by 563 feet high), this tribute to Crazy Horse, the legendary Lakota leader who defeated General Custer at Little Bighorn, is a work in progress. So far the warrior's head has been carved out of the mountain, and the head of his horse is starting to emerge; when work is under way, you can expect to witness frequent blasting. Self-taught sculptor Korczak Ziolkowski conceived this memorial to Native American heritage in 1948, and after his death in 1982 his family took on the project. The completion date is unknown, since activity is limited by weather and funding. Near the work site stands a vast new orientation center, the Indian Museum of North America, Ziolkowski's studio/home and workshop, indoor and outdoor sculpture galleries, and a restaurant.

10

✉ *Ave. of the Chiefs* ☎ *605/673–4681* 💳 *Free* 🕐 *May–Sept., daily 8* AM*–9* PM; *Oct.–Apr., daily 8–4:30.*

Indian Museum of North America. When Ziolkowski agreed to carve Crazy Horse at the invitation of a Lakota elder, he determined that he wouldn't stop with the mountain. He wanted an educational institution to sit at the base of the mountain, complete with a center showcasing examples of Native American culture and heritage. The construction in 1972 of the Indian Museum of North America, built from wood and stone blasted from the mountain, was the initial step in that direction. The permanent collection of paintings, clothing, photographs, and artifacts represents many of the continent's tribes. There is also a space for temporary exhibits that often showcases works by modern Native American artists. ☎ *605/673–4681* ⊕ *www.crazyhorse.org* 💳 *$10 per adult or $24 per carload for more than 2 adults* 🕐 *May–Sept., daily 8* AM*–9* PM; *Oct.–Apr., daily 8–4:30.*

WHERE TO STAY & EAT

$–$$ ✕ **Laughing Water Restaurant.** This airy pine restaurant with windows facing the mountain sculpture is noted for its fry bread and buffalo burgers. There's also a soup-and-salad bar, but you'd do well to stick to the Native American offerings; try the Indian taco or "buffaloski" (a Polish-style sausage made with Dakota buffalo). A kids' menu is available. ✉ *Ave. of the Chiefs* ☎ *605/673–4681* ▤ *AE, D, MC, V* 🕐 *Closed Nov.–Apr.*

$–$$ ▦ **Strutton Inn B&B.** Set on 4 acres, this three-story Victorian home is a
★   few miles from Crazy Horse. The 140-foot veranda with a gazebo on each corner looks out over a lovely garden and the Black Hills beyond. Most of the guest rooms of the well-furnished retreat are decorated with pastels, frills, and floral patterns. Rooms have king-size beds, but no TVs; there is, however, a 46-inch TV in the common room. **Pros:** Quiet setting, friendly service, unique decor is very inviting. **Cons:** Rooms can be on the small side, lack of modern amenities can be difficult for some. ✉ *U.S. 16* 🏠 *R.R. 1, Box 55 S, Custer 57730* ☎ *605/673–2395 or 800/226–2611* 🖷 *605/673–2395* ⊕ *www.struttoninn.com* 🛏 *9 rooms* 🛠 *In-room: no phone, no TV. In-hotel: no elevator, no-smoking rooms* ▤ *MC, V* ⑩*BP.*

CUSTER STATE PARK

13 mi southeast of Mount Rushmore National Memorial via Hwy. 244 and U.S. 16.

Down the road less traveled, in 71,000-acre Custer State Park, scenic backcountry is watered by crisp, clear trout streams. Elk, antelope, deer, mountain goat, bighorn sheep, mountain lion, wild turkey, prairie dog, and the second-largest publicly owned herd of bison in the world (after the one in Yellowstone National Park) walk the pristine land. Some of the most scenic drives in the country roll past fingerlike granite spires and panoramic views. Each year at the Buffalo Roundup and Arts Festival, thousands of spectators watch the park's 1,500 bison thunder through the hills at the start of a Western-theme art and food expo. ⊠*U.S. 16A, 4 mi east of Custer* ☎*605/255–4515* ⊕*www.sdgfp.info/parks/Regions/ Custer* ⊠*$2.50–$23. There are several options, including day passes for individuals and cars, as well as season passes for both* ☉ *Year-round.*

BUFFALO ROUNDUP

In October, don't miss the nation's largest buffalo roundup. It's one of South Dakota's most exciting events. Cowboys and park crews saddle up and corral the Custer State Park's 1,500 head of bison so that they may later be vaccinated ☎605/255–4515.

OFF THE BEATEN PATH

★

Jewel Cave National Monument. Even though its 125 mi of surveyed passages make this cave the world's second largest (to Kentucky's Mammoth Cave), it isn't the size of Jewel Cave that draws visitors, it's the rare crystalline formations that abound in the cave's vast passages. Wander the dark passageways, and you'll be rewarded with the sight of tiny crystal Christmas trees, hydromagnesite balloons that would pop if you touched them, and delicate calcite deposits dubbed "cave popcorn." Year-round, you can take ranger-led tours, from a simple half-hour walk to a lantern-light or wild caving tour. Costs vary by tour and group size. ⊠*U.S. 16, 15 mi west of Custer* ☎*605/673–2288* ⊕*www. nps.gov/jeca* ⊠*$4–$27* ☉*Sept.–Apr., daily 8–4:30; May–Aug., daily 8–7.*

WHERE TO STAY & EAT

$$ ✕**Blue Bell Lodge and Resort.** Feast on fresh trout or buffalo, which you can have as a steak or a stew, in this rustic log building within the boundaries of Custer State Park. There's also a kids' menu. On the property, hayrides and cookouts are part of the entertainment, and you can sign up for trail rides and overnight pack trips on old Native American trails with the nearby stable. ⊠*About 6 mi south of U.S. 16A junction on Hwy. 87, in Custer State Park, Custer* ☎*605/255– 4531 or 800/658–3530* ⊕*www.custerresorts.com* ☰*AE, D, MC, V* ☉*Closed mid-Oct.–mid-May.*

$–$$$ ✕▦**Sylvan Lake Resort.** This spacious stone-and-wood lodge in Custer
☉ State Park affords fantastic views of pristine Sylvan Lake and Harney
★ Peak beyond. The rooms in the lodge are large and modern, and there are rustic cabins, some with fireplaces, scattered along the cliff and in the forest. The Lakota Dining Room ($–$$) has an exceptional view of the lake; its lovely veranda constructed of native stone is the perfect place to sip tea and watch the sunrise. On the menu are buffalo selections and rainbow trout. You can canoe, fish, and swim in the lake, and numerous hiking trails make this a great choice for active families. **Pros:** Remodeled section offers spacious rooms with balconies, unbelievable scenery, good food for all meals. **Cons:** The walk back from the lake can be strenuous, as it's all uphill. ⊠*16 mi east of Custer on U.S. 16A, Hill City* ✆*HC 83, Box 74, Custer 57730* ☎*605/574–2561*

10

or 800/658–3530 ☐605/574–4943 ⊕www.custerresorts.com ↘35 rooms, 31 cabins ☖In-hotel: restaurant, no-smoking rooms ▭AE, D, MC, V ☉Closed Oct.–Mother's Day.

HOT SPRINGS

8 mi south of Wind Cave National Park via U.S. 385.

A small and historic community of about 4,000 residents, Hot Springs is the gateway to Wind Cave National Park. It's also the entry point to scores of other natural and historical sites, including Evans Plunge, a large naturally heated indoor-outdoor pool; the Mammoth Site, where more than 50 woolly and Columbian mammoths have been unearthed; and the Black Hills Wild Horse Sanctuary.

WHAT TO SEE

Black Hills Wild Horse Sanctuary. Hundreds of wild mustangs inhabit this 11,000-acre preserve of rugged canyons, forests, and grasslands along the Cheyenne River. Take a guided tour or hike, and sign up for a chuck-wagon dinner. Drive 14 mi south of Hot Springs until you see signs off Route 71. ⊠*Rte. 71* ☎605/745–5955 or 800/252–6652 ⊕www.wildmustangs.com ☞$15 ☉Memorial Day–Labor Day, Mon.–Sat. 9:30–5; tours at 10, 1, and 3.

Mammoth Site. During the construction of a housing development in the 1970s, earthmoving equipment uncovered this sinkhole where giant mammoths supposedly came to drink, got trapped, and died. More than 50 of the fossilized woolly beasts have been unearthed since digging began, and many can still be seen in situ. You can watch the excavation in progress and take guided tours. ⊠*U.S. 18, 15 mi south of Wind Cave National Park* ☎605/745–6017 or 800/325–6991 ⊕www.mammothsite.com ☞$7 ☉Daily; hrs vary, call ahead.

Wind Cave
National Park

If you don't get out of your car at Wind Cave, you haven't scratched the surface—literally. The park has more than 121 mi of underground passageways. Curious cave formations include 95% of the world's mineral box-work, gypsum beard so sensitive it reacts to the heat of a lamp, and delicate helictite balloons that would burst at the touch of a finger. Some are partly hollow; some are partly filled with minerals. No one seems to have a clear understanding of how exactly these intriguing formations are created. Wind Cave is the sixth-longest cave in the world, and experts believe 95% of it is yet to be mapped.

WELCOME TO WIND CAVE

TOP REASONS TO GO

★ **Underground exploring:** Wind Cave offers visitors the chance to get their hands and feet dirty on a four-hour guided tour through one of American's longest and most complex caves.

★ **The call of the wild:** Wind Cave National Park boasts a wide variety of animals: bison, coyote, deer, antelope, elk, prairie dogs, and 37 species of birds, to name just a few.

★ **Education by candlelight:** Wind Cave offers numerous educational and interpretive programs, including the Candlelight Cave Tour, which allows guests to explore the cave only by candlelight.

★ **Noteworthy neighbors:** On the north border of Wind Cave sits Custer State Park, one of South Dakota's can't-miss areas. With its close proximity to numerous other national parks, state parks, and other monuments and memorials, Wind Cave is situated perfectly to explore some of American's greatest national treasures.

1 The Surface. Wind Cave lies at the confluence of Western mountains and central plains, which blesses the park with a unique landscape. A series of established trails weaves in and out of forested hillsides and grassy meadows, providing treks of varying difficulty.

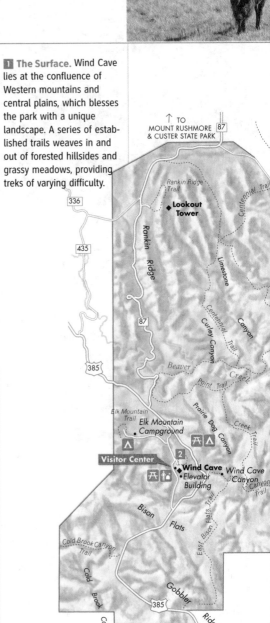

↑ TO
MOUNT RUSHMORE 87
& CUSTER STATE PARK

Rankin Ridge Trail

Centennial Trail

336

◆ Lookout Tower

435

Rankin Ridge

Limestone

Centennial Trail

Curley Canyon

Canyon

87

Beaver

Point Trail

Creek

385

Prairie Dog Canyon

Creek Trail

Elk Mountain Trail

Elk Mountain Campground

Visitor Center

2

◆ Wind Cave   Wind Cave Canyon

Elevator Building

Canyon Canyon Trail

Bison

East Bison Flats Trail

Flats

Cold Brook Canyon Trail

Cold Brook Canyon

Gobbler Ridge

385

2 **The Cave.** With an explored maze of caverns totaling 121 mi, Wind Cave is considered one of the largest caves in the world. Notably, scientists estimate that only 5% of the cave has been explored to date. It is also estimated that 95% of the world's boxwork formations are found in Wind Cave, which means that visitors here are treated to some of the rarest geological features on the planet.

SOUTH DAKOTA

GETTING ORIENTED

Bounded by Black Hills National Forest to the west and windswept prairie to the east, Wind Cave National Park, in southwestern South Dakota, encompasses the transition between two distinct ecosystems: mountain forest and mixed-grass prairie. Abundant wildlife, including bison and elk, roam the 28,295 acres of the park's diverse terrain. Underground, a year-round 53°F temperature gives summer visitors a cool oasis—and winter visitors a warm escape.

WIND CAVE NATIONAL PARK

10

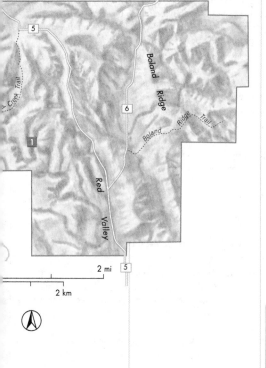

5

Boland Ridge

6

Boland Ridge Trail

1

Creek Trail

Red Valley

2 mi 5

2 km

KEY	
	Ranger Station
	Campground
	Picnic Area
	Restaurant
	Lodge
	Trailhead
	Restrooms
	Scenic Viewpoint
	Walking/Hiking Trails
	Bicycle Path

WIND CAVE PLANNER

When to Go

The heaviest crowds come to Wind Cave from June to September, but the park and surrounding Black Hills are large enough to diffuse the masses.

Neither the cave nor grounds above are ever too packed, except during the first full week in August, when the Black Hills play host to one of the world's largest biker gatherings. ⇨ *Sturgis Motorcycle Rally, above.*

The colder months are the least crowded, though you can still explore underground, thanks to the cave's constant 53°F temperature. The shoulder seasons are also unpopular, though autumn is a perfect time to visit.

Flora & Fauna

About three-quarters of the park is grasslands. The rest is forested, mostly by the ponderosa pine. Poison ivy and poison oak are common in wetter, shadier areas, so wear long pants and boots when hiking.

The convergence of forest and prairies makes an attractive home for bison, elk, coyotes, pronghorn antelope, and mule deer. Wild turkey, prairie dogs, marmots, and squirrels are less obvious but commonly seen by the observant hiker.

Mountain lions also live in the park; although usually shy, they will attack if surprised or threatened. Make noise while hiking to prevent chance encounters.

Bison appear docile but can be dangerous. The largest land mammal in North America, they weigh up to a ton and run at speeds in excess of 35 mph. When park rangers tell you not to approach them, it's wise to heed their warning.

Getting There & Around

Wind Cave is 56 mi from Rapid City, via U.S. 16 and Highway 87, which runs through the park, and 73 mi southwest of Badlands National Park. The nearest commercial airport is in Rapid City. Bus lines service Rapid City and Wall.

Gray Line of the Black Hills (☎ *605/342–4461* ⊕ *www.blackhillsgrayline.com*) offers regional tours.

U.S. 385 and Highway 87 travel the length of the park on the west side. Additionally, two unpaved roads, Forest Service roads 5 and 6, traverse the northeastern part of Wind Cave. Forest Service Road 5 joins Highway 87 at the park's north border. There's ample free parking at the visitor center, although it can get full in midsummer.

WIND CAVE IN ONE DAY

Pack a picnic lunch, then head to the visitor center to purchase tickets for a morning tour of Wind Cave. Visit the exhibit rooms in the center after the tour. By the time you complete your tour, you will probably be ready for lunch. Drive or walk the quarter mile to the picnic area north of the visitor center. The refreshing air and deep emerald color of the pine woodlands will flavor your meal.

In the afternoon take a leisurely drive through the parklands south of the visitor center, passing through Gobbler Pass and Bison Flats, for an archetypal view of the park and to look for wildlife. On the way back north, follow U.S. 385 east toward Wind Cave Canyon. If you enjoy bird-watching, park your car at a turnout and hike the 1.8-mi trail into the canyon, where you can spot swallows and great horned owls in the cliffs and woodpeckers in the dead trees at the bottom. Next, get back on the highway going north, take a right on Highway 87, and continue a half mile to the turnout for Centennial Trail. Hike the trail about 2 mi to the junction with Lookout Point Trail, turn right, and return to Highway 87. The whole loop is about 4¾ mi. As you continue driving north to the top of Rankin Ridge, a pullout to the right serves as the starting point for 1¼-mi Rankin Ridge Trail. It loops around the ridge, past Lookout Tower—the park's highest point and a great place to view the whole park—and ends up back at the pullout. This trail is an excellent opportunity to enjoy the fresh air, open spaces, and diversity of wildlife in the park. Conclude your day by exiting the park on Highway 87 and driving through Custer State Park.

SCENIC DRIVES

★ **Rankin Ridge Drive (North Entrance).** Entering the park across the north border via Highway 87 is perhaps the most beautiful drive into the park. As you leave behind the grasslands and granite spires of Custer State Park and enter Wind Cave, you see the prairie, forest, and wetland habitats of the backcountry and some of the oldest rock in the Black Hills. The silvery twinkle of mica, quartz, and feldspar crystals dot Rankin Ridge east of Highway 87, and gradually give way to limestone and sandstone formations.

WHAT TO SEE

Rankin Ridge Lookout Tower. Some of the best panoramic views of the park and surrounding hills can be seen from this 5,013-foot tower. Hike the 1-mi Rankin Ridge loop to get there. ✉ *6 mi north of visitor center on Hwy. 87.*

★ **Wind Cave.** Discovered by the Bingham brothers in 1881, Wind Cave was named for the strong currents of air that blow in or out of the entrance. This is related to the difference in atmospheric pressure between the cave and the surface. When the atmospheric pressure is higher outside than inside the cave, the air blows in, and vice versa.

WIND CAVE NATIONAL PARK

10

With more than 100 mi of known passageway divided into three different levels, Wind Cave ranks as the sixth longest worldwide. It's host to an incredibly diverse collection of geologic formations, including more boxwork than any other known cave, plus a series of underground lakes. The cave tours sponsored by the National Park Service allow you to see examples of unusual and beautiful formations with names such as button popcorn, starburst, Christmas trees, frostwork, nail quartz, helictite bushes, and gypsum flowers. ⊠ *U.S. 385 to Wind Cave Visitor Center.*

DID YOU KNOW?

Theodore Roosevelt made Wind Cave the country's seventh national park, and the first dedicated to preserving a cave, on January 3, 1903. It is one of the largest caves in the world, with 125.9 mi of mapped passages.

VISITOR CENTER

Wind Cave Visitor Center. The park's sole visitor center is the primary place to get general information. Located on top of the cave, it has three exhibit rooms, with displays on cave exploration, the Civilian Conservation Corps, park wildlife, and resource management. ⊠ *Off U.S. 385, 3 mi north of park's southern border* ☎ *605/745–4600* ⊕ *www.nps.gov/wica* ➤ *Free* ⊙ *Mid-Apr.–mid-Oct., daily 8–5; mid-Oct.–early Apr., daily 8–4:30.*

SPORTS & THE OUTDOORS

BIRD-WATCHING

★ **Wind Cave Canyon.** Here's one of the best birding areas in the park. The limestone walls of the canyon are ideal nesting grounds for cliff swallows and great horned owls, and the standing dead trees on the canyon floor attract red-headed and Lewis woodpeckers. As you hike down the trail, the steep-sided canyon widens to a panoramic view east across the prairies. ⊠ *About ½ mi east of visitor center.*

Rankin Ridge. See large birds of prey here, including turkey vultures, hawks, and golden eagles. ⊠ *6 mi north of visitor center on Hwy. 87.*

HIKING

There are more than 30 mi of hiking trails within the boundaries of Wind Cave National Park, covering ponderosa forest and mixed-grass prairie. The landscape has changed little over the past century, so a hike through the park is as much a historical snapshot of pioneer life in the 1890s as it is exercise. Be sure to hit the Wind Cave Canyon Trail, where limestone cliffs attract birds like cliff swallows and great horned owls, and the Cold Brook Canyon Trail, a short but fun trip past a prairie-dog town to the park's edge. Besides birds and small animals like squirrels and marmots, you're apt to see deer and pronghorn while hiking, and probably some bison.

Hiking into the wild, untouched backcountry is perfectly safe, provided you have a map (available from the visitor center) and a good sense of direction. Don't expect any developments, however; bathrooms are available only at the visitor center, and the trails are dirt or gravel. Since

CAVEMAN-SPEAK

You'll sound like a serious spelunker with this cavemen cheat sheet. These *Speleothems* (cave formations) are ones you may see in Wind Cave.

Cave balloons: Thin-walled formations resembling partially deflated balloons, usually composed of hydromagnesite.

Boxwork: Composed of interconnecting thin blades that were left in relief on cave walls when the bedrock was dissolved away.

Flowstone: Consists of thin layers of a mineral deposited on a sloping surface by flowing or seeping water.

Frostwork: Sprays of needles that radiate from a central point that are usually made of aragonite.

Gypsum beard: Composed of bundles of gypsum fibers that resemble a human beard.

Logomites: Consist of a hollowed-out stalagmite that superficially resemble popcorn.

Pool Fingers: Deposited underneath water around organic filaments.

Ribbons: Thin, layered formations found on sloping ceilings or walls that resemble curtains or scarves.

Stalagmites: Mineral deposits that build up on a cave floor from dripping water.

Stalactites: Carrot-shape formations that hang down from a cave ceiling and are formed by dripping water.

there are no easily accessible sources along the trails, and water from backcountry sources must be treated, pack your own.

EASY **Wind Cave Canyon Trail.** This easy 1.8-mi trail follows Wind Cave Canyon to the park boundary fence. The canyon, with its steep limestone walls and dead trees, provides the best opportunity in the park for bird-watching. Be especially vigilant for cliff swallows, great horned owls, and red-headed and Lewis woodpeckers. Deer, marmots, least chipmunks, and other small animals also are attracted to the sheltered environment of the canyon. Even though you could probably do a round-trip tour of this trail in less than an hour and a half, be sure to spend more time here to observe the wildlife. This trail represents one of your best chances for seeing the park's animal inhabitants, and a little patience will almost certainly be rewarded. ⊠ *Begins on east side of Hwy. 385, 1 mi north of the southern access road to visitor center.*

MODERATE **Centennial Trail.** Constructed to celebrate South Dakota's 100th birthday, this trail bisects the Black Hills, covering 111 mi from north to south. Designed for bikers, hikers, and horses, the trail is rugged but accommodating (note, however, that bicycling on the trail is not allowed within park boundaries). It will take you at least a half day to cover the 6 mi of this trail that traverse the park. ⊠ *Begins off Hwy. 87, 2 mi north of visitor center.*

Cold Brook Canyon Trail. Starting on the west side of U.S. 385, 2 mi south of the visitor center, this 1½-mi, mildly strenuous hike runs past a former prairie-dog town, the edge of an area burned by a controlled fire in 1986, and through Cold Brook Canyon to the park boundary fence.

GEAR UP!

Edge Sports—Lead. On the way to the ski slopes in the northern Black Hills, this outfitter maintains a good stock of winter sports equipment. ✉ *32 Baltimore St., Lead* ☎ *605/722-7547.*

Edge Sports—Rapid City. Rock climbers and hikers will find a good selection of equipment. Cavers will find a solid inventory of clothing and gear. ✉ *922 Main St., Rapid City* ☎ *605/716-9912.*

Granite Sports. Several miles north of the park, this outfitter sells hiking boots, Gore-Tex jackets, packs, water bottles, and more. ✉ *201 Main St., Hill City* ☎ *605/574-2121.*

Scheels All Sport. In Rushmore Mall, Scheels carries a wide selection of all-weather hiking clothes and binoculars suitable for bird-watchers. ✉ *2200 N. Maple Ave., Rapid City* ☎ *605/342-9033.*

Experienced hikers will conquer this trail and return to the trailhead in an hour or less; allow more time if you plan to walk at a more leisurely pace. ✉ *Begins on west side of U.S. 385, 2 mi south of visitor center.*

DIFFICULT **Boland Ridge Trail.** Get away from the crowds for half a day via this strenuous, 2½-mi round-trip hike. The panorama from the top is well worth it, especially at night. ✉ *The trailhead is off Forest Service Rd. 6, 1 mi north of junction with Forest Service Rd. 5.*

Highland Creek Trail. This difficult, roughly 8½-mi trail is the longest and most diverse trail within the park, traversing mixed-grass prairies, ponderosa pine forests, and the riparian habitats of Highland Creek, Beaver Creek, and Wind Cave Canyon. Even those in good shape will need a full day to cover this trail round-trip. ✉ *The southern trailhead stems from Wind Cave Canyon trail 1 mi east of U.S. 385. Northern trailhead is on Forest Service Rd. 5.*

SPELUNKING

★ You may not explore the depths of Wind Cave on your own, but you can choose from five ranger-led cave tours, available from June through August; the rest of the year, only one or two tours are available. On each tour you pass incredibly beautiful cave formations, including extremely well-developed boxwork. The least crowded times to visit in summer are mornings and weekends. The cave is 53°F year-round, so bring a sweater. Note that the uneven passages are often wet and slippery. Rangers discourage those with heart conditions and physical limitations from taking the organized tours. However, with some advance warning (and for a nominal fee) park rangers can arrange private, limited tours for those with physical disabilities. The park provides hard hats, knee pads, and gloves, and all cavers are required to have long pants, a long-sleeve shirt, and hiking books or shoes with nonslip soles. If you prefer lighted passages and stairways to dark crawl spaces, a tour other than the Wild Caving Tour might appeal to you.

Tours depart from the visitor center. A schedule can be found online at ⊕*www.nps.gov/wica*. To make a reservation, call 605/745–4600.

EASY **Garden of Eden Cave Tour.** You don't need to go far to see boxwork, popcorn, and flowstone formations. Just take the relatively easy, one-hour tour, which covers about ¼ mi and 150 stairs. It's available seven times daily, early June through Labor Day, and three times daily, October through early June. (It is unavailable most of September.) The cost is $7.

Natural Entrance Cave Tour. This 1¼-hour tour takes you ½ mi into the cave, over 300 stairs (most heading down), and out an elevator exit. Along the way are some significant boxwork deposits on the middle level. The tour costs $9 and leaves nine times daily from early June through Labor Day, and seven times daily for the rest of September.

MODERATE **Candlelight Cave Tour.** Available twice daily, early June through Labor ★ Day, this tour goes into a section of the cave with no paved walks or lighting. Everyone on the tour carries a lantern similar to those used in expeditions in the 1890s. The $9 tour lasts two hours and covers 1 mi; reservations are essential. Children under eight are not admitted.

Fairgrounds Cave Tour. View examples of nearly every type of calcite formation found in the cave on this 1½-hour tour, available five times daily, early June through Labor Day. There are some 450 steps, leading up and down; the cost is $9.

DIFFICULT **Wild Caving Tour.** For a serious caving experience, sign up for this chal-
Fodor'sChoice lenging, extraordinary, four-hour tour. After some basic training in spe-
★ lunking, you crawl and climb through fissures and corridors, most lined with gypsum needles, frostwork, and boxwork. Expect to get dirty. Wear shoes with good traction, long pants, and a long-sleeve shirt. The park provides knee pads, gloves, and hard hats with headlamps. You must be at least 16 to take this tour, and 16- and 17-year-olds must show signed consent from a parent or guardian. Tours cost $23 and are available at 1 PM daily, early June through mid-August, and at 1 PM weekends mid-August through Labor Day. Reservations are essential.

WIND CAVE NATIONAL PARK

10

WHERE TO STAY & EAT

ABOUT THE RESTAURANTS

If you're determined to dine in Wind Cave National Park, be sure to pack your own meal, because the only dining venues inside park boundaries are the two picnic areas near the visitor center and Elk Mountain Campground. The towns beyond the park offer additional options. Nearby **Hot Springs** and **Custer** offer a variety of dining choices; **Rapid City** (⇨*above*) and **Deadwood** (⇨*above*) claim some of the best-ranked restaurants in South Dakota.

ABOUT THE HOTELS

Wind Cave claims a singular campground, so you'll have to look outside park boundaries if you want to bed down in something more substantial than a tent. New chain hotels with modern amenities are

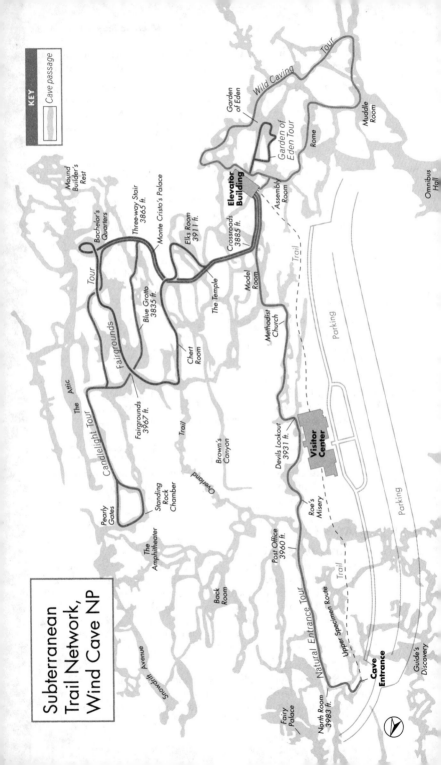

Subterranean Trail Network, Wind Cave NP

KEY
Cave passage

Mound Builder's Rest

Bachelor's Quarters

Three-way Stair 3865 ft.

Monte Cristo's Palace

Blue Grotto 3835 ft.

Fairgrounds Tour

The Attic

Fairgrounds 3967 ft.

Candlelight Tour

Standing Rock Chamber

Chert Room

Pearly Gates

The Amphitheater

Snowdrift Avenue

Trail

Overland

Brown's Canyon

Back Room

Fairy Palace

North Room 3983 ft.

Cave Entrance

Upper Specimen Route

Natural Entrance Tour

Post Office 3960 ft.

Roe's Misery

Devils Lookout 3931 ft.

Visitor Center

Methodist Church

Model Room

The Temple

Elks Room 3911 ft.

Crossroads 3885 ft.

Elevator Building

Assembly Room

Garden of Eden Tour

Garden of Eden

Rome

Wild Caving Tour

Muddle Room

Omnibus Hall

Guide's Discovery

Trail

Parking

Parking

Trail

plentiful in the Black Hills, but when booking accommodations consider a stay at one of the area's historic properties.

ABOUT THE CAMPGROUNDS

Although there is only one primitive campground (Elk Mountain Campground) within the park, there are countless campgrounds in the Black Hills. The public campgrounds in the national forest are accessible by road but otherwise secluded and undeveloped; private campgrounds typically have more amenities. If you're looking for a more adventurous experience, most of the public land within the Black Hills is open for backcountry camping, provided you don't light any fires and obtain a permit (usually free) from the appropriate park or forest headquarters.

> HATS OFF TO THE CAVE
>
> Homesteaders Jesse and Tom Bingham first discovered Wind Cave when they heard air whistling through the rocky opening. Legend goes that the airflow was so strong that day that it knocked Tom's hat clean off his head. Jesse came back a few days later to show the trick to some friends, but it didn't happen quite as he'd planned. The wind, now flowing in the opposite direction, stole Jesse's hat and vacuumed it into the murky depths of the cave.

For additional campgrounds, see Rapid City, above.

CAMP-GROUNDS & RV PARKS

$$ ⚠**Happy Holiday RV Resort.** Outside of Rapid City on U.S. 16, this year-round campground has the advantage of easy access to Mount Rushmore and beautiful forest surroundings. There are also on-site cabins and motel rooms. You get 10% off on gas when you stay here. **Pros:** One of only a few campgrounds in the Black Hills open year-round, great location between Rapid City and Mount Rushmore, a plethora of on-site activities for kids. **Cons:** Located off high-traffic highway. ✉*8990 U.S. 16 S, Rapid City 57701* ☎*605/342–7365* 🖷*605/342–1122* ⊕*www.happyholidayrvresort.com* ⇗*258 sites (170 with full hookups, 88 with partial hookups)* ⛲*Flush toilets, full hookups, partial hookups (electric and water), dump station, drinking water, guest laundry, showers, fire grates, picnic tables, electricity, public telephone, general store, play area, service station, swimming (pool).*

$$ ⚠**Mount Rushmore KOA–Palmer Gulch Lodge.** This huge commercial
☿ campground on Route 244 west of Mount Rushmore offers shuttles
★ to the mountain, bus tours, horse rides, and car rentals. There are also large furnished cabins and primitive camping cabins, as well as a new lodge shadowed by the massive granite ramparts of Harney Peak. With its pools, waterslide, outdoor activities, and kids' programs, this is a great place for families, and parents will appreciate the three hot tubs. A free shuttle takes you to Mount Rushmore and Crazy Horse. ✉*12620 Rte. 244, Hill City 57745* ☎*605/574–2525* 🖷*605/574–2574* ⊕*www.palmergulch.com* ⇗*500 sites (130 with full hookups, 192 with partial hookups), 85 cabins* ⛲*Kitchen (some), Wi-Fi, restaurant, pool, some pets allowed, flush toilets, full hookups, partial hookups (electric and water), dump station, drinking water, guest laundry, showers, fire grates, picnic tables, electricity, play area, service station, no a/c (some), no phone (some)* ☾*May–Sept.*

10

$$ ⚠ **Whistler Gulch Campground.** In a canyon overlooking the town of Deadwood, this well-developed campground—and its modern log lounge—has a spectacular view. ✉ *235 Cliff St., U.S. 85 S, Deadwood* ☎ *605/578–2092 or 800/704–7139* 🖶 *605/578–2094* ⊕ *www.whistlergulch.com* ⟿ *126 sites (110 with full hookups), 2 cabins* ⚘ *Flush toilets, full hookups, guest laundry, showers, fire grates, picnic tables, electricity, public telephone, general store, swimming pool* ⊙ *May–Sept.*

¢–$ ⚠ **Elk Mountain Campground.** If you prefer a relatively developed camp-
★ site and relative proximity to civilization, Elk Mountain is an excellent choice. You can experience the peaceful pine forests and wild creatures of the park without straying too far from the safety of the beaten path. Most of the campers who stay here pitch tents, but there are 25 pull-through sites for RVs, and Sites 24 and 69 are reserved for campers with disabilities. Note that water is shut off during winter. ✉ *½ mi north of visitor center* ☎ *605/745–4600* ⟿ *75 sites* ⚘ *Flush toilets, running water (nonpotable), fire grates, public telephone* ▤ *No credit cards* ⊙ *Apr.–late Oct.*

WIND CAVE ESSENTIALS

ACCESSIBILITY

The visitor center is entirely wheelchair accessible, but only a few areas of the cave itself are navigable by those with limited mobility. Arrangements can be made in advance for a special ranger-assisted tour for a small fee.

ADMISSION FEES

There's no fee to enter the park; cave tours cost $7–$23.

ADMISSION HOURS

The park is open year-round. It is in the Mountain time zone.

EMERGENCIES

Dial 911 for emergencies, then call the visitor center at 605/745–4600. Rangers can provide basic first aid. Further medical attention is available at Custer Community Hospital in Custer, Southern Hills Hospital in Hot Springs, or Rapid City Regional Hospital. Report a fire at the visitor center.

PERMITS

The requisite backcountry camping and horseback riding permits are both free from the visitor center.

VISITOR INFORMATION

Contacts Wind Cave National Park ✉ *U.S. 385 (Box 190), Hot Springs 57747* ☎ *605/745–4600* 🖶 *605/745–4207* ⊕ *www.nps.gov/wica.*

Badlands National Park

So stark and forbidding are the chiseled spires, ragged ridgelines, and deep ravines of South Dakota's Badlands that Lieutenant Colonel George Custer once described them as "hell with the fires burned out."

Although a bit more accessible than the depths of the underworld, the landscape is easily the strangest in the Great Plains. Ruthlessly ravaged over the ages by wind and rain, the 380 square mi of wild terrain continue to erode and evolve, sometimes visibly changing shape in a few days. Prairie creatures thrive on the untamed territory, and animal fossils are in abundance.

WELCOME TO BADLANDS

TOP REASONS TO GO

★ **Here a fossil, there a fossil:** From the mid-1800s, the fossil-rich Badlands area has welcomed paleontologists, research institutions, and fossil hunters who have discovered the fossil remnants of numerous species from ancient days.

★ **A world of wildlife:** Badlands National Park is home to a wide array of wildlife: antelope, deer, black-footed ferret, prairie dogs, rabbits, coyotes, foxes, badgers.

★ **Ready at a moment's notice:** The Minuteman Missile Silo, at the entrance to the park, represents the only remaining intact components of a nuclear-missile field that consisted of 150 Minuteman II missiles and 15 launch control-centers, and covered more than 13,500 square mi of southwestern South Dakota.

★ **Stars Aplenty:** Because of its remote location and vastly open country, Badlands National Park contains some of the clearest and cleanest air in the country, which makes it perfect for viewing the night sky.

1 North Unit. This is the most easily accessible of the three units and attracts the most visitors. It includes the Badlands Wilderness Area.

2 Palmer Creek Unit. This is the most isolated section of the park—no recognized roads pass through its borders. You must obtain permission from private landowners to pass through their property (contact the White River Visitor Center on how to do so). If you plan on exploring here, count on spending two days—one day to hike in and one day out.

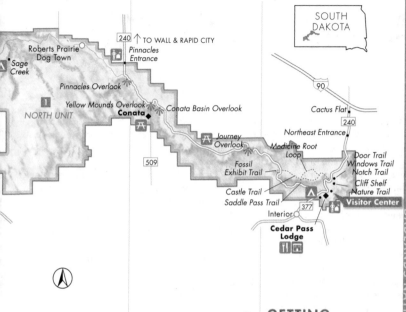

SOUTH DAKOTA

240 ↑ TO WALL & RAPID CITY
Pinnacles Entrance
Roberts Prairie Dog Town
Sage Creek
Pinnacles Overlook
Yellow Mounds Overlook
Conata
NORTH UNIT
1
Conata Basin Overlook
Cactus Flat
90
240
Northeast Entrance
Journey Overlook
Medicine Root Loop
Fossil Exhibit Trail
509
Door Trail
Windows Trail
Notch Trail
Cliff Shelf Nature Trail
Castle Trail
Saddle Pass Trail
377
Visitor Center
Interior
Cedar Pass Lodge

0   4 mi
0   4 km

PALMER CREEK UNIT
2
WOUNDED KNEE

KEY
- Ranger Station
- Campground
- Picnic Area
- Restaurant
- Lodge
- Trailhead
- Restrooms
- Scenic Viewpoint
- ---- Walking/Hiking Trails
- ····· Bicycle Path

3 Stronghold Unit. This was used as a gunnery range for the United States Air Force and the South Dakota National Guard from 1942 until the late 1960s. Discarded remnants and unexploded ordnance make this area potentially dangerous, so mind your step here. If you do find fragments of this era, do not handle them. Report the location to a ranger.

GETTING ORIENTED

The park is divided into three units: the North Unit, and the southern Stronghold and Palmer units. The two southern units are within Pine Ridge Indian Reservation and are jointly managed by the National Park Service and the Oglala Sioux Tribe. Much of the southern units is accessible only on foot or horseback, or by a high-clearance four-wheel drive or ATV.

BADLANDS NATIONAL PARK PLANNER

When to Go

Most visitors frequent the park between Memorial Day and Labor Day. Fortunately, **the park's vast size and isolation prevents it from ever being too packed, except possibly the first week of August,** when hundreds of thousands of motorcycle enthusiasts flock to the Black Hills for the annual Sturgis Motorcycle Rally. On the flip side, it's possible to drive Badlands Loop Road in winter without seeing more than one or two other vehicles. In summer, temperatures typically hover around 90°F—though it can get as hot as 116°F—and sudden midafternoon thunderstorms are not unusual. It rarely rains for more than 10 or 15 minutes (the average annual rainfall is 15 inches). Autumn weather is generally sunny and warm. Snow usually appears by late October. Winter temperatures can drop to as low as -40°F. Early spring is often wet, cold, and unpredictable, and freak snowstorms appear as late as April. By May the weather usually stabilizes, once again bringing pleasant 70°F days.

Flora & Fauna

Little grows among the sharp rock formations and sandy buttes of the Badlands. Most of the park, however, is made up of mixed-grass prairies, where more than 460 species of hardy grasses and wildflowers flourish in the warmer months. Prairie coneflower, yellow plains prickly pear, pale-green yucca, buffalo grass, and side oats grama are just a few of the plants that carpet the Badlands plateau.

For wildlife viewing, keep a sharp lookout around sunrise and sunset. It's not unusual to see herds of pronghorn antelope and mule deer dart across the flat plateaus, American bison grazing along the buttes, prairie dogs barking warnings, and sharptail grouse running through the tall grass, as golden eagles, turkey vultures, and hawks soar on the updrafts.

Getting There & Around

In southwestern South Dakota, Badlands National Park is 70 mi east of Rapid City and 73 mi northeast of Wind Cave National Park. It is accessed via Exit 110 or 131 off Interstate 90, or Route 44 east to Route 377.

Badlands is one of the least developed places on Earth, and few roads, paved or otherwise, pass within park boundaries. Badlands Loop Road (Route 240) is the most traveled and the only one that intersects Interstate 90. It's well maintained and rarely crowded. Portions of Route 44 and Route 27 run at the fringes of the Badlands, connecting the visitor centers and Rapid City. Some roads through the park are unpaved, and should be traveled with care when wet. Sheep Mountain Table Road, a 7-mi road carved out by homesteaders in the early 20th century, is the only public road into the Stronghold Unit of the park. It's impassable when wet, with deep ruts—sometimes only high-clearance vehicles can get through. Off-road driving is prohibited. There's plenty of free parking at the visitor centers, scenic overlooks, and trailheads.

SCENIC DRIVES

★ **Badlands Loop Road.** The simplest drive is on two-lane Badlands Loop Road (Route 240). The drive circles from Exit 110 off Interstate 90 through the park and back to the interstate at Exit 131. Start from either end and make your way around to the various overlooks along the way. Pinnacles and Yellow Mounds overlooks are outstanding places to examine the sandy pink- and brown-toned ridges and spires distinctive to the Badlands. At a certain point the landscape flattens out slightly to the north, revealing spectacular views of mixed-grass prairies. In the rugged Cedar Pass area, the drive takes you past some of the park's best trails.

WHAT TO SEE

HISTORIC SITES

The Big Pig Dig. Daily, from June through August, paleontologists dig for fossils and field questions from curious visitors at this site named for a large fossil originally thought to be of a prehistoric pig (it actually turned out to be a small, hornless rhinoceros). ⊠ *Conata Picnic Area, 17 mi northwest of Ben Reifel Visitor Center.*

Stronghold Unit. With few paved roads and no campgrounds, the park's southwest section is difficult to access without a four-wheel-drive or high-clearance vehicle. However, if you're willing to trek, the unit's isolation provides a rare opportunity to explore Badlands rock formations and prairies completely undisturbed. From 1942 to 1968 the U.S. Air Force and South Dakota National Guard used much of the Stronghold Unit as a gunnery range. Hundreds of fossils were destroyed by bomber pilots, who frequently targeted the large fossil remains of an elephant-size titanothere (an extinct relative of the rhinoceros), which gleamed bright white from the air. Beware of such remnants as old automobiles-turned-targets, unexploded bombs, shells, rockets, and other hazardous materials. If you see unexploded ordnance (UXO) while hiking in the Stronghold Unit, steer clear of it and find another route—however, note the location so you can report it to a ranger later. All visitors who previously haven't visited the area are requested by park officials to first go to the White River Visitor Center. ⊠ *North and west of White River Visitor Center; entrance off Hwy. 27.*

Stronghold Table. This 3-mi-long plateau can be reached only by crossing a narrow land bridge just wide enough to let a wagon pass. It was here, just before the Massacre at Wounded Knee in 1890, that some 600 Sioux gathered to perform one of the last known Ghost Dances, a ritual in which the Sioux wore white shirts that they believed would protect them from bullets. Permission from private landowners is required to gain access to the table; contact the White River Visitor Center for details. ⊠ *Within Stronghold Unit.*

BADLANDS NATIONAL PARK

10

BADLANDS IN ONE DAY

With a packed lunch and plenty of water, arrive at the park via the northeast entrance (off I–90 at Exit 131), and follow Route 240 (Badlands Loop Road) southwest toward the **Ben Reifel Visitor Center.** You can pick up park maps and information here, and also pay the park entrance fee (if the booth at the entrance is closed).

Next, stop at the **Big Badlands Overlook,** just south of the northeast entrance, to get a good feel for the landscape. As you head toward the visitor center, hike any one of several trails you'll pass, or if you prefer guided walks, arrive at the visitor center in time to look at the exhibits and talk with rangers before heading down to the Fossil Exhibit Trail, where you can join the Fossil Talk at 10:30 AM (with repeats at 1:30 and 3:30 PM), usually available from early June to mid-August. Even if you miss the talk, hike this ¼-mi trail before your morning is over. The Badlands are one of the richest fossil fields in the world, and along the trail are examples of six extinct creatures, now protected under clear plastic domes. After your walk, drive a couple of miles to the **Journey Overlook,** up on the right. Here you can enjoy a packed lunch amid grassy prairies, with the sharp, rocky badland formations all around you.

After lunch, continue driving along Badlands Loop Road, stopping at the various overlooks for views and a hike or two. Near the Conata Picnic Area, you'll find the **Big Pig Dig,** a fossil site still being excavated by paleontologists. When you reach the junction with **Sage Creek Rim Road,** turn left and follow it along the northern border of the 100-square-mi **Badlands Wilderness Area,** which is home to hundreds of bison. Provided the road is dry, take a side trip 5 mi down Sage Creek Rim Road to **Roberts Prairie Dog Town,** inhabited by a huge colony of the chattering critters. Children will love to watch these small rodents, which bark warning calls and dive underground if you get too close to their colony. The animals built burrow networks that once covered the Great Plains, but since European settlers established ranches in the region during the late 19th century, prairie dogs have become a far rarer sight. The park is less developed the farther you travel on Sage Creek Rim Road, allowing you to admire the sheer isolation and untouched beauty of Badlands country. Hold out for a glorious sunset over the shadows of the nearby Black Hills, and keep your eyes open for animals stirring about.

SCENIC STOPS

Ancient Hunters Overlook. Perched above a dense fossil bed, this overhang, adjacent to the Pinnacles overlook, is where prehistoric bison hunters drove herds of buffalo over the edge. ⊠ *22 mi northwest of Ben Reifel Visitor Center.*

★ **Badlands Wilderness Area.** Covering about 25% of the park, this 100-square-mi area is part of the United States' largest prairie wilderness. About two-thirds of the Sage Creek region is mixed-grass prairie, making it the ideal grazing grounds for bison, pronghorn, and many of the park's other native animals. The Grassy Tables Overlook 2 mi northwest on Sage Creek Rim Road and the Pinnacles Overlook 1 mi south of the Pinnacles entrance are the best places to get an overview of the wilderness area. Feel free to park beside the road and hike your own route into the untamed, unmarked prairie—just remember that all water in this region is unfit for drinking. ⌂ *25 mi northwest of Ben Reifel Visitor Center.*

Big Badlands Overlook. From this spot just south of the park's northeast entrance, 90% of the park's 1 million annual visitors get their first views of the White River Badlands. ⌂ *5 mi northeast of Ben Reifel Visitor Center.*

Journey Overlook. See where Sioux chief Big Foot and his band traveled through the Badlands on their way to the battle at Wounded Knee, December 29, 1890. ⌂ *7 mi northwest of Ben Reifel Visitor Center.*

Roberts Prairie Dog Town. Once a homestead, the site today contains one of the largest colonies (if not *the* largest colony) of black-tailed prairie dogs in the country. ⌂ *5 mi west of Badlands Loop Rd. on Sage Creek Rim Rd.*

Yellow Mounds Overlook. Contrasting sharply with the whites, grays, and browns of the Badlands pinnacles, the mounds viewed from here greet you with soft yet vivid yellows, reds, and purples. ⌂ *16 mi northwest of Ben Reifel Visitor Center.*

VISITOR CENTERS

Ben Reifel Visitor Center. This is the park's main information hub and is open year-round. Definitely stop here first to pick up brochures and maps. June through August, a 22-minute video about Badlands geology and wildlife runs continually. The facility is named for a Sioux activist and the first Lakota to serve in Congress. Born on the nearby Rosebud Indian Reservation, Ben Reifel went on to Harvard University for his Ph.D and served in the U.S. Army during World War II. ⌂ *On Badlands Loop Rd., near Hwy. 377 junction, just over 8 mi from northeast entrance* ☎605/433–5361 ⊙*June 3–Oct. 13, daily 8 AM–6 PM; Oct. 14–Apr. 15, daily 9–4; Apr. 16–June 2, daily 8–5.*

White River Visitor Center. Open only three months out of the year, this small center serves almost exclusively serious hikers and campers venturing into the Stronghold or Palmer units. If you're heading into one of the southern units, stop here for maps and details about road and trail conditions. The center is on the Pine Ridge Indian Reservation, which co-manages Badlands National Park, and is staffed by the Oglala Sioux Parks and Recreation Authority. While here, you can see fossils and Lakota artifacts, and learn about Sioux culture. ⌂ *25 mi south of Hwy. 44 via Hwy. 27* ☎605/455–2878 ⊙*June–Aug., daily 9–5.*

10

BADLANDS NATIONAL PARK

TOURS

Affordable Adventures Badlands Tour. Take a seven-hour narrated tour through the park and surrounding Badlands for $100 per person. Tours can easily be customized. ⌂ *Box 546, Rapid City 57709* ☎ *605/342–7691* ⊕ *www.affordableadventuresbh.com* 🔖 *$100* ⊙ *Daily year-round.*

Golden Circle Tours. This company gives a seven-hour, narrated van tour out of Custer to several venues, including Mount Rushmore, Crazy Horse Monument, and Custer State Park. Other Black Hills tours are available. ✉ *40 5th St. N, Custer* ☎ *605/673–4349* ⊕ *www.goldencircletours.com* 🔖 *$59 for main tour* ⊙ *Apr. 15–Oct. 15, weather permitting.*

Gray Line of the Black Hills. This outfit offers bus tours from Rapid City to Mount Rushmore, Black Hills National Forest, Custer State Park, and Crazy Horse Monument. ✉ *1600 E. St. Patrick St., Rapid City* ☎ *800/456–4461* ⊕ *www.blackhillsgrayline.com* 🔖 *$35–$52* ⊙ *Apr. 15–Oct. 5.*

Mount Rushmore Tours. Beginning at Fort Hayes on the *Dances with Wolves* film set and then moving to Mount Rushmore, Custer State Park, and Crazy Horse Monument, this nine-hour trip around the Black Hills includes a cowboy show plus breakfast and dinner (guests are responsible for their own lunch at the State Game Lodge). ✉ *2255 Fort Hayes Dr., Rapid City* ☎ *888/343–3113* ⊕ *www.rushmoretours.com* 🔖 *$64* ⊙ *Mid-May–Oct.*

SPORTS & THE OUTDOORS

Pure, unspoiled, empty space is the greatest asset of Badlands National Park, and it can be experienced to its highest degree only if you're on foot. Spring and autumn are the best times of the year to do wilderness exploring, since the brutal extremes of summer and winter can—and do—kill. In fact, the two biggest enemies to hikers and bicyclists in the Badlands are heat and lightning. Before you venture out, make sure you have at least 1 gallon of water per person per day, and be prepared to take shelter from freak thunderstorms, which often strike in the late afternoon with little warning.

AIR TOURS

Most people prefer to see the Badlands from an earthbound perspective, but one ballooning outfitter provides visitors with an airborne perspective of the park.

OUTFITTER & EXPEDITIONS **Black Hills Balloons.** Owned and operated for 22 years by Steve Bauer, this company provides amazing bird's-eye views of some of the Black Hills' most picturesque locations. Reservations are essential. ⌂ *Box 210, Custer 57730* ☎ *605/673–2520* 🔖 *$225–$500* ⊕ *www.blackhillsballoons.com.*

BICYCLING

Bicycles are permitted only on designated roads, which may be paved or unpaved. They are prohibited from closed roads, trails, and the backcountry. Flat-resistant tires are recommended.

Sheep Mountain Table Road. This 7-mi dirt road in the Stronghold Unit is ideal for mountain biking, but should be biked only when dry. The terrain is level for the first 3 mi; then it climbs the table and levels out again. At the top you can take in great views of the area. ⊠ *About 14 mi north of White River Visitor Center.*

OUTFITTER **Two Wheeler Dealer Cycle and Fitness.** This family-owned and family-operated outfitter, founded in 1972, stocks more than 1,000 new bikes for sale or rent. Service is exceptional here, and you can get trail and route information for Badlands National Park and the Black Hills at the counter. ⊠ *100 East Blvd. N, Rapid City* ☎ *605/343–0524* ⊕ *www.twowheelerdealer.com.*

BIRD-WATCHING

Especially around sunset, get set to watch the Badlands come to life. More than 215 bird species have been recorded in the area, including herons, pelicans, cormorants, egrets, swans, geese, hawks, golden and bald eagles, falcons, vultures, cranes, doves, and cuckoos. Established roads and trails are the best places from which to watch for nesting species. The Cliff Shelf Nature Trail and the Castle Trail, both of which traverse areas with surprisingly thick vegetation, are especially good locations. You may even catch sight of a rare burrowing owl at the Roberts Prairie Dog Town. Be sure to bring along a pair of binoculars.

HIKING

Fossil Exhibit Trail and Cliff Shelf Nature Trail are must-dos, but even these popular trails are primitive, so don't expect to see bathrooms or any hiking surfaces other than packed dirt and gravel. Because the weather here can be so variable, rangers suggest that you be prepared for anything. Wear sunglasses, a hat, and long pants, and have rain gear available. It's illegal to interfere with park resources, which includes everything from rocks and fossils to plants and artifacts. Stay at least 100 yards away from wildlife. Because of the dry climate, open fires are never allowed. Tell friends, relatives, and the park rangers if you're going to embark on a multiday expedition. If you have a cell phone with you, assume that it won't get a signal in the park. But most important of all, be sure to bring your own water. Sources of water in the park are few and far between, and none of them are drinkable. All water in the park is contaminated by minerals and sediment, and park authorities warn that it's untreatable. If you're backpacking into the wilderness, bring at least a gallon of water per person per day. For day hikes, rangers suggest you drink at least a quart per person per hour.

EASY **Fossil Exhibit Trail.** The trail, in place since 1964, has fossils of early
☺ mammals displayed under glass along its ¼-mi length, which is now
Fodor's Choice completely wheelchair-accessible. Since October 2006, the trail has
★ new fossil casts that are touchable. Give yourself at least an hour to

fully enjoy this popular hike. ⊠*5 mi northwest of Ben Reifel Visitor Center on Hwy. 240.*

Window Trail. This 200-yard round-trip trail ends at a natural hole, or window, in a rock wall. Looking through, you'll see more of the distinctive Badlands pinnacles and spires. ⊠*2 mi north of Ben Reifel Visitor Center.*

MODERATE **Castle Trail.** This easy hike stretches for 5½ mi one-way from the Fossil Exhibit trailhead on Badlands Loop Road to the parking area for the Door and Windows trails. If you choose to follow the Medicine Root Loop, which detours off the Castle Trail, you'll add ½ mi to the trek. If you plan to walk the entire trail, give yourself three hours—slightly more if you want to take extended breaks. Experienced hikers will do this one more quickly. ⊠*5 mi north of Ben Reifel Visitor Center.*

★ **Cliff Shelf Nature Trail.** This ½-mi loop winds through a wooded prairie oasis in the middle of dry, rocky ridges and climbs 200 feet to a peak above White River Valley for an incomparable view. Look for chipmunks, squirrels, and red-wing blackbirds in the wet wood, and eagles, hawks, and vultures at hilltop. Even casual hikers can complete this trail in far less than an hour, but if you want to observe the true diversity of wildlife present here, stay longer. ⊠*1 mi east of Ben Reifel Visitor Center.*

Door Trail. The ¾-mi round-trip trail leads through a natural opening, or door, in a Badlands rock wall. The eerie sandstone formations and passageways beckon, but it's recommended that you stay on the trail. The first 100 yards of the trail are on a boardwalk. Even a patient and observant hiker will take only an hour here. ⊠*2 mi east of Ben Reifel Visitor Center.*

Notch Trail. One of the park's more interesting hikes, this 1½-mi round-trip trail takes you over moderately difficult terrain and up a ladder. Winds at the notch can be fierce, but it's worth lingering for the view of the White River Valley and the Pine Ridge Indian Reservation. If you take a couple of breaks and enjoy the views, you'll probably want to plan on spending a little more than an hour on this hike. ⊠*2 mi north of Ben Reifel Visitor Center.*

DIFFICULT **Badlands Wilderness Area.** If you want a challenge, you might consider trekking this 100-square-mi parcel of grassy steppes and rocky canyons east of the highway and south of Sage Creek Rim Road, near the Pinnacles entrance. There are no services here and very few visitors, even in summer. Before venturing out, check in with park staff at one of the visitor centers. ⊠*25 mi northwest of Ben Reifel Visitor Center on Hwy. 240.*

Saddle Pass Trail. This route, which connects with Castle Trail and Medicine Root Loop, is a steep, ¼-mi climb up and down the side of "The Wall," an impressive rock formation. Plan on spending about an hour on this climb. ⊠*2 mi west of Ben Reifel Visitor Center.*

HORSEBACK RIDING

★ The park has one of the largest and most beautiful territories in the state in which to ride a horse. Riding is allowed in most of the park except for some marked trails, roads, and developed areas. The mixed-grass prairie of the Badlands Wilderness Area is especially popular with riders. However, note that the weather in the Badlands Wilderness Area can be very unpredictable. Only experienced riders or people accompanied by experienced riders should venture far from more developed areas.

There are several restrictions and regulations that you must be aware of if you plan to ride your own horse. Potable water for visitors and animals is a rarity. Riders must bring enough water for themselves and their stock. Only certified weed-free hay is approved in the park. Horses are not allowed to run free within the borders of the park. It's essential that all visitors with horses contact park officials for other restrictions that may apply.

> **GEAR UP!**
>
> Located in the Rushmore Mall, **Scheels All Sports** is an everyday, all-purpose outfitter. Whatever outdoor activity you have in mind, Scheels provides equipment and advice for locals and visitors alike. Whether it's for golf, paintball, biking, or hiking, Scheels offers top-of-the-line equipment at only slightly inflated prices. At this writing, Scheels was planning to open a larger store a few miles east, just off Exit 60 along I-90, of its current Rapid City location in Spring 2009. ⊠ *480 Rushmore Mall, 2200 N. Maple Ave., Rapid City* ☎ *605/342–9033* ⊕ *www.scheelssports.com.*

OUTFITTER **Gunsel Horse Adventures.** A local outfitter since 1968, Gunsel arranges
★ pack trips into the Badlands, Black Hills National Forest, and Buffalo Gap National Grassland. The four-day trips are based in one central campsite and are all-inclusive; you bring your own sleeping bag and personal effects (7- and 10-day trips are also available). Reservations are essential. ✉ *Box 1575, Rapid City 57709* ☎ *605/343–7608* ⊕ *www.gunselhorseadventures.com* ✉ *$325 per day.*

NEARBY TOWNS

Built against a steep ridge of badland rock, **Wall** was founded in 1907 as a railroad station, and is today the town nearest to Badlands National Park, 8 mi from the Pinnacles entrance to the North Unit. **Pine Ridge,** about 35 mi south of the Stronghold Unit, is on the cusp of Pine Ridge Indian Reservation. The town was established in 1877 as an Indian agency for Chief Red Cloud and his band of followers. With 2,800 square mi, the reservation, home, and headquarters of the Oglala Sioux is second in size only to Arizona's Navajo Reservation. **Rapid City** (⇨ *above*) is a good base from which to explore the treasures of the state's southwestern corner.

WHERE TO EAT

Inside the park, there's only one restaurant. The food is quite good, but don't hesitate to explore other options farther afield. You'll find the most choices in Wall. For restaurant recommendations in Rapid City, *see Where to Eat, above.*

$-$$ ✕ **Cedar Pass Lodge Restaurant.** Cool off within dark, knotty-pine walls under an exposed-beam ceiling, and enjoy a hearty meal of steak, trout, or Indian tacos and fry bread. ⊠ *1 Cedar St. (Rte. 240), Interior* ☎ *605/433–5460* ▭ *AE, D, MC, V* ⊙ *Closed Nov.–Mar.*

¢–$$ ✕ **Cactus Family Restaurant and Lounge.** Delicious hotcakes and pies await you at this full-menu restaurant in downtown Wall. In summer you'll find a roast-beef buffet large enough for any appetite. ⊠ *519 Main St., Wall* ☎ *605/279–2561* ▭ *D, MC, V.*

¢–$$ ✕ **Elkton House Restaurant.** For a terrific hot roast-beef sandwich served on white bread with gravy and mashed potatoes, make your way to this comfortable, family-friendly restaurant. The dining room is sunlit and the service is fast. ⊠ *203 South Blvd., Wall* ☎ *605/279–2152* ⊕ *www. blackhillsbadlands.com/elkton* ▭ *D, MC, V.*

¢–$$ ✕ **Western Art Gallery Restaurant.** This large restaurant in the Wall Drug Store displays more than 200 original oil paintings, all with a Western theme. Try a hot beef sandwich or a buffalo burger; the doughnuts here are the best in South Dakota. An old-fashioned soda fountain serves milk shakes and homemade ice cream. ⊠ *510 Main St., Wall* ☎ *605/279–2175* ⊕ *www.walldrug.com* ▭ *AE, D, MC, V.*

PICNIC AREAS **Bigfoot Pass/Journey Overlook.** There are only a handful of tables here and there's no water, but the incredible view makes it a lovely spot to have lunch. Restrooms are available. ⊠ *7 mi northwest of Ben Reifel Visitor Center on Badlands Loop Rd.*

Conata Picnic Area. A dozen or so covered picnic tables are scattered over this area, which rests against a Badlands wall ½ mi south of Badlands Loop Road. There's no potable water, but there are bathroom facilities; you can enjoy your lunch in peaceful isolation at the threshold of the Badlands Wilderness Area. The Conata Basin area is to the east, and Sage Creek area is to the west. ⊠ *15 mi northwest of Ben Reifel Visitor Center on Conata Rd.*

White River Visitor Center Directly behind this visitor center are four covered tables, where you can picnic simply and stay protected from the wind. ⊠ *25 mi south of Rte. 44 on Rte. 27.*

WHERE TO STAY

IN THE PARK

Badlands National Park is oft visited by families on a vacation to see the American West, but very few opt to stay overnight here, especially when there's a profusion of accommodations in the Black Hills, situated a mere 50 mi west. As a result there are very few lodging options in and around the park. If you're determined to bed down within park boundaries, you have only one choice: Cedar Pass Lodge. Though rustic, it's comfortable and inexpensive.

$ 🏨 **Cedar Pass Lodge.** Each small, stucco, white cabin has two twin beds
★ and views of the Badlands peaks. A gallery at the lodge displays the
work of local artists, and the gift shop is well stocked with local crafts,
including turquoise and beadwork. There are also hiking trails on the
premises. **Pros:** One of only a few accommodations available in the
Badlands, scenery is truly a sight to behold, nature watching is a must.
Cons: Isolation means long stays can seem repetitive. ⊠*1 Cedar St.,
Hwy. 240, Interior 57750* ☎*605/433–5460* 🖷*605/433–5560* ⊕*www.
cedarpasslodge.com* ⏎*24 cabins* 🖏*In-room: no phone, no TV. In-
hotel: no elevator, restaurant, no-smoking rooms, some pets allowed*
🖃*AE, D, MC, V* ⊙*Closed Oct.–Apr.*

CAMPGROUNDS   Pitching a tent and sleeping under the stars is one of the greatest ways
to fully experience the sheer isolation and unadulterated empty spaces
of Badlands National Park. You'll find two relatively easy-access campgrounds within park boundaries, but only one has any sort of amenities. The second is little more than a flat patch of ground with some
signs. Unless you desperately need a flush toilet to have an enjoyable
camping experience, you're just as well off hiking into the wilderness
and choosing your own campsite. The additional isolation will be well
worth the extra effort. You can set up camp anywhere that's at least
½ mi from a road or trail.

$ 🏕 **Cedar Pass Campground.** Although it has only tent sites, this is the
★ most developed campground in the park, and it's near the Ben Reifel Visitor Center, Cedar Pass Lodge, and a half dozen hiking trails.
It's undergoing a face-lift; new features will include paved interior
roads, a new dump station, and improved facilities. You can buy $1
or $2 bags of ice at the lodge. ⊠*Hwy. 377, ¼ mi south of Badlands
Loop Rd.* ☎*605/433–5361* ⊕*www.cedarpasslodge.com* ⏎*96 sites*
🖏*Flush toilets, pit toilets, dump station, drinking water, public telephone, ranger station* 🖎*Reservations not accepted* 🖃*No credit cards*
⊙*Mid-Apr.–mid-Oct.*

¢   🏕 **Sage Creek Primitive Campground.** The word to remember here is
primitive. If you want to get away from it all, this lovely, isolated spot
surrounded by nothing but fields and crickets is the right campground
for you. There are no designated campsites, and the only facilities are
pit toilets and horse hitches. ⊠*25 mi west of Badlands Loop Rd. on
Sage Creek Rim Rd.* ☎*No phone* 🖏*Pit toilets.*

OUTSIDE THE PARK
*For lodging recommendations in Rapid City and the Black Hills, see
above.*

$–$$ 🏨 **Coyote Blues Village B&B.** This European-style lodge on 30 Black Hills
acres (12 mi north of Hill City) displays an unusual mix of antique
furnishings and contemporary art. Hearty Swiss-American breakfasts
include homemade bread. Some rooms have a private deck with a hot
tub. A creek runs through the property. There is no smoking inside
the inn. **Pros:** Unique and beautiful decor sets this B&B apart from
others, owners treat guests like kings and queens, never a bad stay.
Cons: Driveway can be difficult in shoulder seasons. ⊠*Off U.S. 385,*

Hill City 57745 ☎605/574–4477 *or* 888/253–4477 🖷605/574–2101 ⊕*www.coyotebluesvillage.com* 🛏*9 rooms* ⬧*In-room: refrigerator. In-hotel: no elevator, gym, no-smoking rooms* ▭*D, MC, V.*

¢–$$ 🏨**Badlands Ranch and Resort.** This 2,000-acre ranch is just outside the national park, and both the ranch house and cabins have spectacular views of the Badlands. The grounds—complete with gazebo, duck ponds, picnic areas, and a bonfire site—are ideal for summer family vacations and reunions. The ranch house has a Jacuzzi tub set in a wooden deck. Hunting guides are provided in season. Also on the grounds is an RV park with 35 hookup sites. **Pros:** Views from the cabins allow for wonderful photo opportunities, unique mix of modern amenities and rustic feel. **Cons:** Some visitors have said upkeep lacks at times. ✉*Hwy. 44, HCR 53, Box 3, Interior 57750* ☎605/433–5599 *or 877/433–5599* 🖷605/433–5598 ⊕*www.badlandsranchandresort. com* 🛏*4 rooms, 8 cabins* ⬧*In-room: kitchen. In-hotel: no elevator, pool, no-smoking rooms, play area* ▭*AE, D, MC, V.*

$ 🏨**Ann's Motel.** This motel, one block from Wall Drug, has small but clean rooms, each equipped with a coffeemaker and full-size bathtub. **Pros:** Great value, great location to downtown stores and restaurants. **Cons:** Limited services for business travelers. ✉*114 4th Ave., Wall 57790* ☎605/279–2501 🛏*12 rooms, 6 cabins* ⬧*In-room: refrigerator. In-hotel: no elevator* ▭*AE, D, MC, V.*

$ 🏨**Badlands Inn.** At this inn where every room faces Badlands National Park, awaken to a panoramic view of sunrise over Vampire Peak and the other rugged peaks of the Badlands. **Pros:** Rustic feel attracts many visitors, great views and great location. **Cons:** Walls are on the thin side. ✉*Rte. 377, Interior 57750* ☎605/433–5401 ⊕*www.badlandsinn.com* 🛏*18 rooms* ⬧*In-hotel: no elevator, no-smoking rooms, some pets allowed* ▭*AE, D, MC, V* ⊗*Closed Nov.–Mar.*

CAMPGROUNDS ⛺**Badlands/White River KOA.** Southeast of Interior, this campground's
$$ green, shady sites spread over 31 acres are pleasant and cool after a
⊗ day among the dry rocks of the national park. White River and a small creek border the property on two sides. Cabins and cottages are also available. **Pros:** Shady sites are great for hot summer months, plenty of room at most sites. **Cons:** No direct views of the Badlands formations. ✉*4 mi south of Interior on Hwy. 44, Interior 57750* ☎605/433–5337 ⊕*www.koa.com* ⬧*Flush toilets, full hookups, partial hookups (electric and water), dump station, drinking water, showers, fire grates, picnic tables, public telephone, general store, play area, swimming (pool)* 🛏*144 sites (44 with full hookups, 38 with partial hookups), 62 tent sites* ▭*MC, V* ⊗*Mid-Apr.–early Oct.*

$–$$ ⛺**Arrow Campground.** Since this campground is managed together with a small motel, good facilities are easily accessible. From Interstate 90, take Exit 109 or 110 into Wall. The grounds are two blocks from downtown Wall. **Pros:** Great value and location near downtown shops and restaurants. **Cons:** Some sites can be difficult for large rigs to get into. ✉*515 Crown St., Wall 57790* ☎605/279–2112 *or 800/888–1361* ⊕*www.blackhillsbadlands.com/arrow* 🛏*100 sites (36 with full hookups, 36 with partial hookups)* ⬧*Flush toilets, full hookups, partial hookups (electric and water), dump station, drinking water,* *showers, fire grates, electricity, public telephone, play area, swimming (pool) ⊙ May–Oct. 15.*

See also Badlands Ranch and Resort above, where there is an RV park on-site.

BADLANDS ESSENTIALS

ACCESSIBILITY

The visitor centers and Cedar Pass Lodge are all fully wheelchair-accessible. Two trails—the Fossil Exhibit Trail and the Window Trail—have reserved parking and are accessible by ramp, although they are quite steep in places. The Door, Cliff Shelf, and Prairie Wind trails are accessible by boardwalk. Cedar Pass Campground has two fully accessible sites, plus many other sites that are sculpted and easily negotiated by wheelchair users. The campground's office and amphitheater also are accessible. The Bigfoot picnic area has reserved parking, ramps, and an accessible pit toilet. Other areas of the park are very rugged and can be difficult or impossible to navigate by those with limited mobility.

ADMISSION FEES

The entrance pass is $7 per person or $15 per vehicle, and is good for seven days. A $30 annual pass allows admission to the park for an entire year.

ADMISSION HOURS

The park is open 24 hours, daily, year-round. Badlands National Park is in the Mountain time zone.

EMERGENCIES

In case of a fire or medical emergency, call 911. Rangers can provide basic first aid. For assistance, call 605/433–5361, or go to either visitor center or the Pinnacles entrance ranger station. The nearest large hospital is 50 mi away in Rapid City; it has an air ambulance service.

PERMITS

A backcountry permit isn't required for hiking or camping in Badlands National Park, but it's a good idea to check in at park headquarters before setting out on a backcountry journey. Backpackers may set up camps anywhere except within a half mile of roads or trails. Open fires are prohibited.

VISITOR INFORMATION

Contacts **Badlands National Park** ⌂ Box 6, Interior, 57750 ☎ 605/433–5361 ⊕ www.nps.gov/badl.

SOUTH DAKOTA BLACK HILLS ESSENTIALS

AIR TRAVEL

CARRIERS Delta Air provides a connection to the Black Hills from Salt Lake City, Northwest Airlines offers service from Minneapolis, United Airlines flies direct from Denver and Chicago, and Allegiant Air has weekly service from Las Vegas and Phoenix. Frontier Airline's new service from Denver connects Rapid City to the low-cost carrier's hub.

Airlines & Contacts Allegiant Air (☎ *800/432–3810* ⊕ *www.allegiantair.com*). **Delta Air** (☎ *800/221–1212* ⊕ *www.delta.com*). **Frontier Airlines** (☎ *800/432–1359* ⊕ *www.frontierairlines.com*). **Northwest Airlines** (☎ *800/225–2525* ⊕ *www.nwa.com*). **United Airlines** (☎ *800/241–6522* ⊕ *www.ual.com*).

AIRPORTS

Although there are several landing strips and municipal airports in the Black Hills, the only airport with commercial service is in Rapid City. Rapid City Regional Airport, one of the fastest-growing airports in the United States, is 11 mi east of town on Highway 44.

Airport Information Rapid City Regional Airport (✉ *4550 Terminal Rd., Rapid City* ☎ *605/393-9924* ⊕ *www.rapairport.org*).

BUS TRAVEL

Greyhound Lines provides national service out of Rapid City. Jefferson Lines serves Wall and Rapid City, with connections to most Midwestern and Southern cities. Powder River Transportation connects Rapid City with the smaller towns in eastern and northern Wyoming. Gray Line of the Black Hills provides charter service and tours within the Black Hills region.

Information Gray Line of the Black Hills (☎ *605/342-4461* ⊕ *www.blackhills-grayline.com*). **Greyhound Lines** (☎ *307/634-7744 or 800/231-2222* ⊕ *www.greyhound.com*). **Jefferson Lines** (☎ *888/864-2832* ⊕ *www.jeffersonlines.com*). **Powder River Transportation** (☎ *307/682-0960*).

CAR RENTAL

Rapid City Regional Airport is the best place to find car rentals. Make rental reservations early; Rapid City is visited by many business travelers, and rental agencies are often booked.

Contacts Avis (☎ *800/831-2847* ⊕ *www.avis.com*). **Budget** (☎ *800/527-0700* ⊕ *www.budget.com*). **Casey's Auto Rental Service** (✉ *1318 5th St., Rapid City* ☎ *605/343-2277* ⊕ *www.caseyscorner.com*). **Dollar** (☎ *800/527-0700* ⊕ *www.dollar.com*). **Hertz** (☎ *800/654-3131* ⊕ *www.hertz.com*). **National** (☎ *800/227-7368* ⊕ *www.nationalcar.com*).

CAR TRAVEL

Unless you come to the Black Hills on an escorted package tour, a car is essential. I–90 cuts directly through South Dakota from west to east, connecting the northern towns of Spearfish, Sturgis, and Deadwood (which lies about 14 mi off the interstate) with Rapid City. From there the interstate turns straight east, passing Wall and Badlands National Park on its way to Sioux Falls.

Minor highways of importance include U.S. 385, which connects the interior of the Black Hills from south to north, and U.S. 16, which winds south of Rapid City toward the Mount Rushmore and Crazy Horse memorials. Highway 44 is an alternate route between the Black Hills and the Badlands. Within the Black Hills, seven highway tunnels have limited clearance; they are marked on state maps and in the state's tourism booklet.

Snowplows work hard to keep the roads clear in winter, but you may have trouble getting around immediately after a major snowstorm, especially in upper elevations. Unlike the Rockies, where even higher elevations make some major roads impassable in winter, the only Black Hills roads that close permanently in the snowy months are minor dirt- or gravel Forest Service roads.

Contact the South Dakota State Highway Patrol for information on road conditions.

Information **South Dakota State Highway Patrol** (☎ *511* ⊕ *http://hp.state. sd.us*).

EMERGENCIES
Ambulance or Police **Emergencies** (☎ *911*).

24-Hour Medical Care **Rapid City Regional Hospital** (✉ *353 Fairmont Blvd., Rapid City* ☎ *605/719–1000* ⊕ *www.rcrh.org*). **Spearfish Regional Hospital** (✉ *1440 N. Main St., Spearfish* ☎ *605/644–4000* ⊕ *www.rcrh.org*).

LODGING
CAMPING Camping is one of this region's strengths. There are countless campgrounds in the Black Hills and the Badlands. Most of the public land within the national forests and parks is open for camping, provided that you don't light any fires. Keep in mind when selecting your campsite that although the Black Hills don't have any native bears, there is a significant population of mountain lions.

LODGING RESERVATIONS Black Hills Central Reservations, also known as CenRes, offers vacation packages and handles reservations for air travel, car rental, hotels, campgrounds, lodges, ranches, and B&Bs in the Black Hills.

Information **Black Hills Central Reservations** (☎ *866/329–7566* ⊕ *www. blackhillsvacations.com*).

SPORTS & THE OUTDOORS
FISHING Besides the local chambers of commerce, the South Dakota Game, Fish and Parks Department is your best bet for updated information on regional fishing locations and their conditions. Local outfitters, guides, and community organizations can also provide information.

Contacts **South Dakota Game, Fish and Parks** (✉ *523 E. Capitol Ave., Pierre 57501* ☎ *605/773–3485* ⊕ *www.sdgfp.info/Index.htm*).

TOURS
Gray Line of the Black Hills offers bus tours of the region, including trips to Mount Rushmore and Black Hills National Forest.

Information **Gray Line of the Black Hills** (☎ *605/342–4461* ⊕ *www.blackhillsgrayline.com*).

VISITOR INFORMATION

South Dakota Visitor Information **Black Hills, Badlands and Lakes Association** (⊠ *1851 Discovery Circle, Rapid City 57701* ☏ *605/355–3600* ⊕ *www.blackhillsbadlands.com*). **Deadwood Area Chamber of Commerce & Visitor Bureau** (⊠ *735 Main St., Deadwood 57732* ☏ *605/578–1876 or 800/999–1876* ⊕ *www.deadwood.com*). **Rapid City Chamber of Commerce and Convention & Visitors Bureau** (⊠ *Civic Center, 444 N. Mt. Rushmore Rd. Box 747, Rapid City 57709* ☏ *605/343–1744 or 800/487–3223* ⊕ *www.visitrapidcity.com*). **USDA Forest Service Buffalo Gap National Grasslands Visitor Center** (⊠ *708 Main St. ☐ Box 425, Wall 57790* ☏ *605/279–2125*).

Montana & Wyoming Essentials

PLANNING TOOLS, EXPERT INSIGHT, GREAT CONTACTS

There are planners and there are those who, excuse the pun, fly by the seat of their pants. We happily place ourselves among the planners. Our writers and editors try to anticipate all the issues you may face before and during any journey, and then they do their research. This section is the product of their efforts. Use it to get excited about your trip to Montana & Wyoming, to inform your travel planning, or to guide you on the road should the seat of your pants start to feel threadbare.

GETTING STARTED

We're really proud of our Web site: Fodors.com is a great place to begin any journey. Scan "Travel Wire" for suggested itineraries, travel deals, restaurant and hotel openings, and other up-to-the-minute info. Check out "Booking" to research prices and book plane tickets, hotel rooms, rental cars, and vacation packages. Head to "Talk" for on-the-ground pointers from travelers who frequent our message boards. You can also link to loads of other travel-related resources.

■ RESOURCES

ONLINE TRAVEL TOOLS

All About Montana **Montana Fish, Wildlife & Parks** (⊕ fwp.mt.gov/default.html) links to pages for outdoor-enthusiast information, including fishing and hunting licenses and permits, state parks and angler and hunter information, and a Montana Field Guide. **The National Park Service** (⊕ www.nps.gov/state/mt) Web site has links to information about Big Hole, Big Horn Canyon, Glacier National Park, Grant-Korhs Ranch, Little Bighorn Battlefield, the Lewis and Clark National Historic Trail, and Yellowstone National Park. **Montana Kids.com** (Montana Travel ⊕ montanakids.com) gives information about places that will make your family vacation kid approved. **Montana Travel's Montana Big Sky Country's** link (⊕ wintermt.com) has information on all of the places for skiing, snowboarding, and snowmobiling, including a free winter vacation planning guide. **Pacific Northwest Ski Areas Association** (PNSAA ⊕ pnsaa.org) provides weather conditions, information on upcoming events, snow reports, summer activities, and trip planning for Whitefish Mountain Resort and Big Mountain.

All About Wyoming **Wyoming Department of Tourism's** Web site (⊕ www.wyomingtourism.org) has informative links to Wyoming's regions, visitor services, trip planning, state parks, and more. This extensive site has a great link for planning your trip to Yellowstone, links to statewide ski and snowmobiling resorts, and tips and links to sites for outdoor enthusiasts.

Safety **Transportation Security Administration** (TSA ⊕ www.tsa.gov).

Time Zones **Timeanddate.com** (⊕ www.timeanddate.com/worldclock) can help you figure out the correct time anywhere.

Weather **Accuweather.com** (⊕ www.accuweather.com) is an independent weather-forecasting service with good coverage of hurricanes. **Weather.com** (⊕ www.weather.com) is the Web site for the Weather Channel.

VISITOR INFORMATION

At each visitor center and highway welcome center, you can obtain maps and information; most facilities have staff on hand to answer questions. You'll also find conveniences such as phones and restrooms.

Contacts **Travel Montana** (✉ Department of Commerce, 301 S. Park Ave., Helena, MT 59601 ☎ 406/841–2700 or 800/847–4868 🖷 406/841–2701 ⊕ www.visitmt.com). **Wyoming Department of Tourism** (✉ 1520 Etchepare Circle, Cheyenne, WY 82007 ☎ 307/777–7777 or 800/225–5996 🖷 307/777–2877 ⊕ www.wyomingtourism.org).

Trip Insurance Resources

INSURANCE COMPARISON SITES		
Insure My Trip.com	800/487–4722	www.insuremytrip.com
Square Mouth.com	800/240–0369	www.quotetravelinsurance.com
COMPREHENSIVE TRAVEL INSURERS		
Access America	866/807–3982	www.accessamerica.com
CSA Travel Protection	800/873–9855	www.csatravelprotection.com
HTH Worldwide	610/254–8700 or 888/243–2358	www.hthworldwide.com
Travelex Insurance	888/457–4602	www.travelex-insurance.com
Travel Guard International	715/345–0505 or 800/826–4919	www.travelguard.com
Travel Insured International	800/243–3174	www.travelinsured.com
MEDICAL-ONLY INSURERS		
International Medical Group	800/628–4664	www.imglobal.com
International SOS	215/942–8000 or 713/521–7611	www.internationalsos.com
Wallach & Company	800/237–6615 or 504/687–3166	www.wallach.com

■ THINGS TO CONSIDER

PASSPORTS

Montana borders Canada, and if you plan to enter that country, have the proper papers with you. Citizens and legal residents of the United States do not need a passport or a visa to enter Canada, but proof of citizenship (a birth certificate or valid passport) and some form of photo identification will be requested. Naturalized U.S. residents should carry their naturalization certificate. Permanent residents who are not citizens should carry their "green card." Citizens of the United Kingdom need only a valid passport to enter Canada for stays of up to six months.

U.S. Passport Information **U.S. Department of State** (☎877/487–2778 ⊕http://travel.state.gov/passport).

TRIP INSURANCE

What kind of coverage do you honestly need? Do you even need trip insurance at all? Take a deep breath and read on.

We believe that comprehensive trip insurance is especially valuable if you're booking a very expensive or complicated trip (particularly to an isolated region) or if you're booking far in advance. Who knows what could happen six months down the road? But whether or not you get insurance has more to do with how comfortable you are assuming all that risk yourself.

Comprehensive travel policies typically cover trip cancellation and interruption, letting you cancel or cut your trip short because of a personal emergency, illness, or, in some cases, acts of terrorism in your destination. Such policies also cover evacuation and medical care. Some also cover you for trip delays because of bad weather or mechanical problems as well as for lost or delayed baggage. Another type of coverage to look for is financial default—that is, when your trip is disrupted because a tour operator, airline, or cruise line goes out of business. Generally you must buy this when you book your trip or shortly thereafter, and it's available to you only if your operator isn't on a list of excluded companies.

If you're going abroad, consider buying medical-only coverage at the very least. Neither Medicare nor some private insurers cover medical expenses anywhere outside of the United States (including time aboard a cruise ship, even if it leaves from a U.S. port). Medical-only policies typically reimburse you for medical care (excluding that related to preexisting conditions) and hospitalization abroad, and provide for evacuation. You still have to pay the bills and await reimbursement from the insurer, though.

Expect comprehensive travel-insurance policies to cost about 4% to 7% or 8% of the total price of your trip (it's more like 8% to 12% if you're over age 70). A medical-only policy may or may not be cheaper than a comprehensive policy. Always read the fine print of your policy to make sure that you are covered for the risks that are of most concern to you. Compare several policies to make sure you're getting the best price and range of coverage available.

BOOKING YOUR TRIP

Unless your cousin is a travel agent, you're probably among the millions of people who make most of their travel arrangements online.

But have you ever wondered just what the differences are between an online travel agent (a Web site through which you make reservations instead of going directly to the airline, hotel, or car-rental company), a discounter (a firm that does a high volume of business with a hotel chain or airline and accordingly gets good prices), a wholesaler (one that makes cheap reservations in bulk and then re-sells them to people like you), and an aggregator (one that compares all the offerings so you don't have to)?

Is it truly better to book directly on an airline or hotel Web site? And when does a real live travel agent come in handy?

■ ONLINE

You really have to shop around. A travel wholesaler such as Hotels.com or Hotel-Club.net can be a source of good rates, as can discounters such as Hotwire or Priceline, particularly if you can bid for your hotel room or airfare. Indeed, such sites sometimes have deals that are unavailable elsewhere. They do, however, tend to work only with hotel chains (which makes them just plain useless for getting hotel reservations outside of major cities) or big airlines (so that often leaves out upstarts like jetBlue and some foreign carriers like Air India).

Also, with discounters and wholesalers you must generally prepay, and everything is nonrefundable. And before you fork over the dough, be sure to check the terms and conditions, so you know what a given company will do for you if there's a problem and what you'll have to deal with on your own.

■ TIP→ To be absolutely sure everything was processed correctly, confirm reservations made through online travel agents, discounters, and wholesalers directly with your hotel before leaving home.

Booking engines like Expedia, Travelocity, and Orbitz are actually travel agents, albeit high-volume, online ones. And airline travel packagers like American Airlines Vacations and Virgin Vacations—well, they're travel agents, too. But they may still not work with all the world's hotels.

An aggregator site will search many sites and pull the best prices for airfares, hotels, and rental cars from them. Most aggregators compare the major travel-booking sites such as Expedia, Travelocity, and Orbitz; some also look at airline Web sites, though rarely the sites of smaller budget airlines. Some aggregators also compare other travel products, including complex packages—a good thing, as you can sometimes get the best overall deal by booking an air-and-hotel package.

■ WITH A TRAVEL AGENT

If you use an agent—brick-and-mortar or virtual—you'll pay a fee for the service. Travel agents that specialize in a destination may have exclusive access to certain deals and insider information on things such as charter flights. Agents who specialize in types of travelers (senior citizens, gays and lesbians, naturists) or types of trips (cruises, luxury travel, safaris) can also be invaluable.

■ TIP→ Remember that Expedia, Travelocity, and Orbitz are travel agents, not just booking engines. To resolve any problems with a reservation made through these companies, contact them first.

Agent Resources American Society of Travel Agents (☎703/739–2782 ⊕www. travelsense.org).

Montana Travel Agents **Montana Travel**
(✉1102 W. Babcock, Box 100, Bozman, MT
59771 ☎406/587–1188 ⊕www.mttravel.
com).

■ ACCOMMODATIONS

Accommodations in the Rockies and
plains vary from the posh resorts in ski
areas such as Jackson Hole to basic chain
hotels and independent motels. Dude and
guest ranches often require a one-week
stay, and the cost is all-inclusive. Bed-
and-breakfasts can be found throughout
the Rockies and plains.

The lodgings we list are the cream of
the crop in each price category. We list
available facilities, but we don't specify
whether they cost extra. When pricing accommodations, always ask what's
included and what costs extra. In almost
all cases, parking is free, and only in a
resort area like Jackson Hole's Teton Village will you have to pay a charge.

Most hotels and other lodgings require
you to give your credit-card details before
they will confirm your reservation. If you
don't feel comfortable e-mailing this
information, ask if you can fax it (some
places even prefer faxes). However you
book, get confirmation in writing and
have a copy of it handy when you check
in.

Be sure you understand the hotel's cancellation policy. Some places allow you
to cancel without any kind of penalty—
even if you prepaid to secure a discounted
rate—if you cancel at least 24 hours in
advance. Others require you to cancel a
week in advance or penalize you the cost
of one night. Small inns and B&Bs are
most likely to require you to cancel far
in advance. Most hotels allow children
under a certain age to stay in their parents' room at no extra charge, but others
charge for them as extra adults; find out
the cutoff age for discounts.

■TIP→ Assume that hotels operate on the
European Plan (**EP**, no meals) unless we

specify that they use the Breakfast Plan (**BP**,
with full breakfast), Continental Plan (**CP**,
continental breakfast), Full American Plan
(**FAP**, all meals), Modified American Plan
(**MAP**, breakfast and dinner) or are all-inclusive (**AI**, all meals and most activities).

General Information **Travel Montana**
(✉Department of Commerce, 301 S. Park
Ave., Helena, MT 59620 ☎406/841–2700,
800/548–3390 in Montana, 800/847–4868
nationwide 🖷407/841–2701 ⊕www.visitmt.
com). **Wyoming Department of Tourism**
(✉1520 Etchepare Circle, Cheyenne, WY
82007 ☎307/777–7777 or 800/225–5996
⊕www.wyomingtourism.org).

BED & BREAKFASTS

Charm is the long suit of these establishments, which generally occupy a restored
older building with some historical or
architectural significance. They tend to be
small, with fewer than 20 rooms. Breakfast is usually included in the rates.

Reservation Services **Bed & Breakfast.com**
(☎512/322–2710 or 800/462–2632 ⊕www.
bedandbreakfast.com) also sends out an online
newsletter. **Bed & Breakfast Inns Online**
(☎310/280–4363 or 800/215–7365 ⊕www.
bbonline.com). **BnB Finder.com** (☎212/432–
7693 or 888/547–8226 ⊕www.bnbfinder.
com). **Cody Lodging Co.** (✉1302 Beck Ave.,
Suite B, Cody, WY 82414 ☎307/587–6000
or 800/587–6560 🖷307/587–1150 ⊕www.
codyguesthouses.com). **Jackson Hole Central
Reservations** (✉140 E. Broadway, Suite 24,
Jackson, WY 83001 ☎888/838–6606 ⊕www.
jacksonholewy.com).

CONDO & CABIN RENTALS

There are rental opportunities throughout Montana and Wyoming, with the
best selection in resort areas such as Big
Sky and Whitefish (Big Mountain), Montana; and Jackson and Cody, Wyoming.
You'll find a variety of properties ranging from one-bedroom condos to mul-
tibedroom vacation homes. The widest
selection is offered by developer-owner
consortiums.

Local Montana Agents Glacier Village Property (✉3840 Big Mountain Rd., Whitefish, MT 59937 ☎406/862–3687 or 800/858–5439 🖷406/862–0658 ⊕www.stayatbigmountain. com). **Mountain Home–Montana Vacation Rentals** (✉Box 1204, Bozeman, MT 59771 ☎406/586–4589 or 800/550–4589 ⊕www. mountain-home.com). **Resort Property Management** (✉3080 Pine Dr. , Big Sky, MT 59716 ☎406/995–4800 or 866/995–4455 🖷406/993–9561 ⊕www.rpmbigsky.com).

Local Wyoming Agents Cody Area Central Reservations/Absaroka Travel (✉1236 Sheridan Ave., Box 984, Powell, WY 82435 ☎307/754–7287, 800/777–4307 or 888/468–6996 🖷307/754–3493 ⊕www. buffalo-wy.worldweb.com). **Cody Lodging Co.** (✉1302 Beck Ave., Suite B, Cody, WY 82414 ☎307/587–6000 or 800/587–6560 ⊕www. codyguesthouses.com). **Jackson Hole Central Reservations** (✉140 E. Broadway, Suite 24, Jackson, WY 83001 ☎307/733–4005 or 800/443–6931 ⊕www.jacksonholewy.com). **Jackson Hole Resort Lodging** (✉3200 McCollister Dr., Teton Village, WY 83025 ☎307/733–3990 or 800/443–8613 ⊕www. jhresortlodging.com).

GUEST RANCHES

If the thought of sitting around a campfire after a hard day on the range makes your heart beat faster, consider playing dude on a guest ranch. These range from wilderness-rimmed working ranches that accept guests and encourage them to pitch in with chores and other ranch activities to luxurious resorts on the fringes of small cities, with an upscale clientele, swimming pools, tennis courts, and a lively roster of horse-related activities such as breakfast rides, moonlight rides, and all-day trail rides. Rafting, fishing, tubing, and other activities are usually available; at working ranches you may even be able to participate in a cattle roundup. In winter, cross-country skiing and snowshoeing keep you busy. Lodgings can run the gamut from charmingly rustic cabins to the kind of deluxe quarters you expect at a first-class hotel. Meals may be gourmet or plain but hearty. Many ranches offer packages as

well as children's and off-season rates. The various state tourism offices also have information on dude ranches.

Information Montana Dude Ranchers' Association (✉Box 599, Manhattan, MT 59714 ☎888/284–4133 ⊕www.montanadra. com). **Wyoming Dude Ranchers' Association** (✉Box 93, Buffalo, WY 82834 ☎307/684–7157 ⊕www.wyomingdra.com).

HOSTELS

Hostels offer bare-bones lodging at low, low prices—often in shared dorm rooms with shared baths—to people of all ages, though the primary market is young travelers, especially students. Most hostels serve breakfast; dinner and/or shared cooking facilities may also be available. In some hostels you aren't allowed to be in your room during the day, and there may be a curfew at night. Nevertheless, hostels provide a sense of community, with public rooms where travelers often gather to share stories. Many hostels are affiliated with Hostelling International (HI), an umbrella group of hostel associations with some 4,000 member properties in more than 60 countries. Other hostels are completely independent and may be nothing more than a really cheap hotel.

Membership in any HI association, open to travelers of all ages, allows you to stay in HI–affiliated hostels at member rates. One-year membership is about $28 for adults. Rates in dorm-style rooms run about $15 to $25 per bed per night; private rooms are more, but are still generally well under $100 a night. Members have priority if the hostel is full; they're also eligible for discounts around the world, even on rail and bus travel in some countries.

Montana has hostels in Bozeman, East Glacier, Polebridge, and Whitefish that cater mainly to backpackers. Wyoming has a hostel in Teton Village.

Hostelling International is also an especially helpful organization for road cyclists.

Information **Hostelling International—USA** (☎301/495–1240 ⊕www.hiusa.org).

HOTELS

In Montana and Wyoming most city hotels cater to business travelers, with such facilities as restaurants, cocktail lounges, swimming pools, exercise equipment, and meeting rooms. Room rates usually reflect the range of amenities offered. Most cities also have less expensive hotels that are clean and comfortable but have fewer facilities. In resort towns, hotels are decidedly more deluxe, with every imaginable amenity in every imaginable price range; rural areas generally offer simple, and sometimes rustic, accommodations.

Many properties offer special weekend rates, sometimes up to 50% off regular prices. However, these deals are usually not extended during peak summer months, when hotels are normally full. The same discounts generally apply for resort-town hotels in the off-seasons.

All hotels listed have private bath unless otherwise noted.

RESORTS

Ski towns throughout the Rockies—including Big Sky and Whitefish in Montana and Jackson Hole in Wyoming—are home to dozens of resorts in all price ranges; the activities lacking in any individual property can usually be found in the town itself, in summer as well as winter. In the national parks there are both wonderfully rustic and luxurious resorts, such as Jackson Lake Lodge and Jenny Lake Lodge in Grand Teton National Park, Lake Yellowstone Hotel and the Old Faithful Snow Lodge in Yellowstone, and Many Glacier Lodge in Glacier National Park.

▌ AIRLINE TICKETS

Most domestic airline tickets are electronic; international tickets may be either electronic or paper. With an e-ticket the only thing you receive is an e-mailed receipt citing your itinerary and reservation and ticket numbers.

The greatest advantage of an e-ticket is that if you lose your receipt, you can simply print out another copy or ask the airline to do it for you at check-in. You usually pay a surcharge (up to $50) to get a paper ticket, if you can get one at all.

The sole advantage of a paper ticket is that it may be easier to endorse over to another airline if your flight is canceled and the airline with which you booked can't accommodate you on another flight.

▌TIP➔ Discount air passes that let you travel economically in a country or region must often be purchased before you leave home. In some cases you can only get them through a travel agent.

The least expensive airfares to the Rockies and plains are often priced for round-trip travel and must usually be purchased in advance. Airlines generally allow you to change your return date for a fee; most low-fare tickets, however, are nonrefundable.

▌ RENTAL CARS

Rates in most Montana and Wyoming cities run about $50 a day and $275 to $325 a week for an economy car with air-conditioning, automatic transmission, and unlimited mileage. In resort areas such as Jackson or Kalispell, you'll usually find a variety of 4X4s and SUVs for rent, many of them with ski racks. Unless you plan to do a lot of mountain exploring, a four-wheel drive is usually needed only in winter, but if you do plan to venture onto any back roads, an SUV (about $85 a day) is the best bet because it will have higher clearance. Rates do not include tax on car rentals, which is 6% in Wyoming. There is no tax in Montana, but if you rent from an airport location, there is an airport-concession fee.

Car Rental Resources

AUTOMOBILE ASSOCIATIONS		
U.S.: American Automobile Association AAA	315/797–5000	www.aaa.com
	most contact with the organization is through state and regional members.	
National Automobile Club	650/294–7000	www.thenac.com
	membership is open to California residents only.	
MAJOR AGENCIES		
Alamo	800/462–5266	www.alamo.com
Avis	800/230–4898	www.avis.com
Budget	800/527–0700	www.budget.com
Hertz	800/654–3131	www.hertz.com
National Car Rental	800/227–7368	www.nationalcar.com

Rental rates are similar whether at the airport or at an in-town agency. Many people fly into Salt Lake City or Denver and drive a rental car from there to cut travel costs. This makes sense if you're traveling to southern Wyoming, but if your goal is Jackson or Cody, that's a 10- to 11-hour drive from Denver. From Salt Lake City, it's about a six-hour drive to Jackson and a nine-hour trip to Cody.

In the Rockies and plains you must be 21 to rent a car with a valid driver's license; some companies charge an additional fee for drivers ages 21 to 24, and others will not rent to anyone under age 25; most companies also require a major credit card.

Surcharges may apply if you're under 25 or if you take the car outside the area approved by the rental agency. You'll pay extra for child seats, which are compulsory for children under five (under eight in Wyoming) and cost $5 to $10 a day, and usually for additional drivers (up to $25 a day, depending on location).

CAR-RENTAL INSURANCE

Everyone who rents a car wonders whether the insurance that the rental companies offer is worth the expense. No one—including us—has a simple answer. It all depends on how much regular insur-ance you have, how comfortable you are with risk, and whether or not money is an issue.

If you own a car and carry comprehensive car insurance for both collision and lia-bility, your personal auto insurance will probably cover a rental, but read your policy's fine print to be sure. If you don't have auto insurance, then you should probably buy the collision- or loss-dam-age waiver (CDW or LDW) from the rental company. This eliminates your lia-bility for damage to the car.

Some credit cards offer CDW coverage, but it's usually supplemental to your own insurance and rarely covers SUVs, minivans, luxury models, and the like. If your coverage is secondary, you may still be liable for loss-of-use costs from the car-rental company (again, read the fine print). But no credit-card insurance is valid unless you use that card for *all* transactions, from reserving to paying the final bill.

■TIP➡ Diners Club offers primary CDW coverage on all rentals reserved and paid for with the card. This means that Diners Club's company—not your own car insur-ance—pays in case of an accident. It *doesn't* mean that your car-insurance company won't raise your rates once it discovers you had an accident.

You may also be offered supplemental liability coverage; the car-rental company is required to carry a minimal level of liability coverage insuring all renters, but it's rarely enough to cover claims in a really serious accident if you're at fault. Your own auto-insurance policy will protect you if you own a car; if you don't, you have to decide whether you are willing to take the risk.

U.S. rental companies sell CDWs and LDWs for about $15 to $25 a day; supplemental liability is usually more than $10 a day. The car-rental company may offer you all sorts of other policies, but they're rarely worth the cost. Personal accident insurance, which is basic hospitalization coverage, is an especially egregious rip-off if you already have health insurance.

■ TIP→ You can decline the insurance from the rental company and purchase it through a third-party provider such as Travel Guard (www.travelguard.com)—$9 per day for $35,000 of coverage. That's sometimes just under half the price of the CDW offered by some car-rental companies.

In most states (including Montana and Wyoming), you don't need a CDW if you have personal auto insurance or other liability insurance.

TRANSPORTATION

I BY AIR

Absolutely the best connections to Montana and often the shortest flights to Wyoming are through the Rockies hub cities, Salt Lake City and Denver. Montana also receives transfer flights from Minneapolis, Seattle, and Phoenix.

Once you have made your way to Denver or Salt Lake City, which are two of the major hubs providing air service to Montana and Wyoming, you will still have one or two hours of flying time to reach your final airport destination. Many of the airports in these states are served by commuter flights that have frequent stops, though generally with very short layovers. There are no direct flights from New York to the area, and most itineraries from New York take between seven and nine hours. Likewise, you cannot fly direct from Los Angeles to Montana or Wyoming; it will take you four or five hours to get here from the West Coast. To reach Wyoming and most Montana cities, you will have to take a connecting flight.

At smaller airports, you may need to be on hand only an hour before the flight.

If you're traveling during snow season, allow extra time for the drive to the airport, as weather conditions can slow you down. If you'll be checking skis, arrive even earlier.

■TIP➜ If you travel frequently, look into the TSA's Registered Traveler program. The program, which is still being tested in several U.S. airports, is designed to cut down on gridlock at security checkpoints by allowing prescreened travelers to pass quickly through kiosks that scan an iris and/or a fingerprint. How sci-fi is that?

Airlines & Airports Airline and Airport Links.com (⊕ www.airlineandairportlinks.com)

has links to many of the world's airlines and airports.

Airline-Security Issues Transportation Security Administration (⊕ www.tsa.gov) has answers for almost every question that might come up.

AIRPORTS

The major gateways include, in Montana, Missoula International Airport (MSO) and Glacier Park International Airport (GPI; in Kalispell); and in Wyoming, Jackson Hole Airport (JAC), Cheyenne Regional Airport (CYS), Natrona County International Airport (CPR; in Casper), and Yellowstone Regional Airport (COD; in Cody).

■TIP➜ Long layovers don't have to be only about sitting around or shopping. These days they can be about burning off vacation calories. Check out www.airportgyms.com for lists of health clubs that are in or near many U.S. and Canadian airports.

Colorado Airport Information Denver International Airport (☎303/342-2000, 800/247-2336, 800/688-1333 TTY ⊕www.flydenver.com).

Montana Airport Information Glacier Park International Airport (☎406/257-5994 ⊕www.glacierairport.com). Missoula International Airport (☎406/728-4381 ⊕www.msoairport.org).

Utah Airport Information Salt Lake City International Airport (☎801/575-2400 ⊕www.slcairport.com).

Wyoming Airport Information Cheyenne Regional Airport (☎307/634-7071 ⊕www.cheyenneairport.com). Jackson Hole Airport (☎307/733-7682 ⊕www.jacksonholeairport.com). Natrona County International Airport (☎307/472-6688 ⊕iflycasper.com). Yellowstone Regional Airport (☎307/587-5096 ⊕www.flyyra.com).

FLIGHTS

United and Delta have the most flights to the region. The regional carrier Big Sky connects Montana cities; America West and Northwest (among others) provide connections to Big Sky from outside the state.

Airline Contacts Air Canada (☎888/247–2262 ⊕www.aircanada.com). **Alaska Airlines** (☎800/252–7522 ⊕www.alaskaair.com). **America West** (☎800/428–4322 ⊕www.americawest.com). **American Airlines** (☎800/433–7300 ⊕www.aa.com). **ATA** (☎800/435–9282 or 317/282–8308 ⊕www.ata.com). **Big Sky** (☎800/237–7788). **British Airways** (☎800/247–9297 ⊕www.ba.com). **Continental Airlines** (☎800/523–3273 for U.S. and Mexico reservations, 800/231–0856 for international reservations ⊕www.continental.com). **Delta Airlines** (☎800/221–1212 for U.S. reservations, 800/241–4141 for international reservations ⊕www.delta.com). **Frontier** (☎800/432–1359 ⊕www.frontierairlines.com). **Horizon Air** (☎800/547–9308 ⊕www.alaskaair.com). **jetBlue** (☎800/538–2583 ⊕www.jetblue.com). **Mesa Airlines** (☎800/637–2247 ⊕www.mesa-air.com). **Midwest Airlines** (☎800/452–2022 ⊕www.midwestairlines.com). **Northwest Airlines** (☎800/225–2525 ⊕www.nwa.com). **Southwest Airlines** (☎800/435–9792 ⊕www.southwest.com). **United Airlines** (☎800/864–8331 for U.S. reservations, 800/538–2929 for international reservations ⊕www.united.com). **USAirways** (☎800/428–4322 for U.S. and Canada reservations, 800/622–1015 for international reservations ⊕www.usairways.com).

▌ BY BUS

Greyhound Lines has regular intercity routes throughout Montana and Wyoming, with connections from Cheyenne, Rawlins, and Rock Springs to Salt Lake City, which also connects with Bozeman and Missoula. Smaller bus companies provide service within state and local areas.

Bus Information Coach America/Powder River Transportation (☎800/442–3682 or 888/864–2832). **Greyhound Lines** (☎800/231–2222 ⊕www.greyhound.com). **Rimrock/Trailways** (☎800/255–7655).

▌ BY CAR

You'll seldom be bored driving through the Rockies and plains, which offer some of the most spectacular vistas and challenging driving in the world. Montana's interstate system is driver-friendly, connecting soaring summits, rivers, glacial valleys, forests, lakes, and vast stretches of prairie, all capped by that endless "Big Sky." Wyoming's interstates link classic, open-range cowboy country and mountain-range vistas with state highways headed to the geothermal wonderland of Yellowstone National Park. In Wyoming everything is separated by vast distances, so be sure to leave each major city with a full tank of gas and be prepared to see lots of wildlife and few other people.

Before setting out on any driving trip, it's important to make sure your vehicle is in top condition. It's best to have a complete tune-up. At the least, you should check the following: lights, including brake lights, backup lights, and emergency lights; tires, including the spare; oil; engine coolant; windshield-washer fluid; windshield-wiper blades; and brakes. For emergencies, take along flares or reflector triangles, jumper cables, an empty gas can, a fire extinguisher, a flashlight, a plastic tarp, blankets, water, and coins or a calling card for phone calls (cell phones don't always work in high mountain areas).

In the Rockies and plains, as across the nation, gasoline costs fluctuate often.

BORDER CROSSING

Driving a car across the U.S.–Canadian border is simple. Personal vehicles are allowed entry into the neighboring country, provided they are not to be left behind. Drivers must have owner registration and proof of insurance coverage handy. If the car isn't registered in your name, carry a letter from the owner that authorizes your use of the vehicle. Drivers in rental cars that are permitted to cross the border should bring along a copy of the rental contract, which should bear an endorsement stating that the vehicle is permitted to cross the border.

ROAD CONDITIONS

Roads range from multilane blacktop to barely graveled backcountry trails. Many twisting switchbacks are considerately marked with guardrails, but some primitive roads have a lane so narrow that you must back up to the edge of a steep cliff to make a turn. Scenic routes and lookout points are clearly marked, enabling you to slow down and pull over to take in the views.

FROM	TO	DISTANCE
Billings	Bozeman	140 mi
Billings	Helena	239 mi
Billings	Missoula	340 mi
Billings	Great Falls	222 mi
Billings	Butte	221 mi
Jackson	Cheyenne	436 mi
Jackson	Cody	178 mi
Cheyenne	Rock Springs	258 mi
Cheyenne	Sheridan	329 mi

Road-Condition Information Montana (☎511 toll-free from any phone, or 800/226–7623 ⊕www.mdt.mt.gov/travinfo/511). **Wyoming** (☎511 toll-free from any phone, or 888/996–7623 ⊕www.wyoroad.info).

You'll find highways and the national parks crowded in summer, and almost deserted (and occasionally impassable) in winter. You may turn right at a red light after stopping if there is no sign stating otherwise and no oncoming traffic. When in doubt, wait for the green. Follow the posted speed limit, drive defensively, and make sure your gas tank is full. In Montana and Wyoming the law requires that the driver and all passengers wear seat belts.

SNOWY DRIVING

Highway driving through mountains and plains is safe and generally trouble free even in cold weather. Although winter driving can present challenges, road maintenance is good and plowing is prompt. In mountain areas, tire chains, studs, or snow tires are essential. If you're driving into high elevations, check the weather forecast and call for road conditions beforehand. Even main highways can close. Winter weather isn't confined to winter months in the high country, so be prepared: carry an emergency kit containing warm clothes, a flashlight, food and water, and blankets. It's also good to carry a cell phone, but be aware that the mountains, and distance from cell towers, can disrupt service. If you get stalled by deep snow, do not leave your car. Wait for help, running the engine only if needed (keep the exhaust clear, and occasionally open a window for fresh air). Assistance is never far away.

▌BY TRAIN

Amtrak connects the Rockies and plains to both coasts and all major American cities. Trains run through northern Montana, with stops in Essex and Whitefish, near Glacier National Park. Connecting bus services to Yellowstone National Park are provided in the summer from Amtrak's stop in Pocatello, Idaho.

Canada's passenger service, VIA Rail Canada, stops at Jasper, near the Canadian entrance to Waterton/Glacier International Peace Park.

Information **Amtrak** (☎800/872-7245 ⊕www.amtrak.com). **VIA Rail Canada** (☎888/842-7245 ⊕www.viarail.ca).

ON THE GROUND

▍EATING OUT

Dining in Montana and Wyoming is generally casual. Menus are becoming more varied with such regional specialties as trout, elk, or buffalo, but you can nearly always order a hamburger or a steak. Authentic ethnic food—other than Mexican—is hard to find outside of cities. Dinner hours are from 6 PM to 9 PM. Outside the large cities and resort towns in the high seasons, many restaurants close by 9 or 10 PM. The restaurants we list are the cream of the crop in each price category.

MEALS & MEALTIMES

You can find all types of cuisine in the major cities and resort towns, but don't forget to try native dishes such as trout, elk, and buffalo (the latter two have less fat than beef and are just as tasty); organic fruits and vegetables are also readily available. When in doubt, go for a steak, forever a Rocky Mountain and northern plains mainstay.

Rocky Mountain oysters, simply put, are bull testicles. They're generally served fried, although you can get them lots of different ways. You can find them all over the West, usually at down-home eateries, steak houses, and the like.

Unless otherwise noted, the restaurants listed in this guide are open daily for lunch and dinner.

Contacts **OpenTable** (⊕www.opentable. com). **DinnerBroker** (⊕www.dinnerbroker. com).

WINES, BEER & SPIRITS

Microbreweries throughout the region produce a diverse selection of beers. Snake River Brewing Company in Jackson Hole, Wyoming, has won awards for its lager, pale ale, Zonker Stout, and numerous other releases. Missoula, Montana–based Big Sky Brewing Company's best seller is Moose Drool (a brown ale);

the company also markets an award-winning pale ale and several other brews.

Most retail stores are open from 9 or 9:30 until 6 or 7 daily in downtown locations and until 9 or 10 in suburban shopping malls and in resort towns during high seasons. Downtown stores sometimes stay open later Thursday night. Normal banking hours are weekdays 9 to 5; some branches are also open on Saturday morning.

▍MONEY

First-class hotel rooms in Missoula and Cheyenne cost from $85 to $225 a night, "value" hotel rooms might go for $60 to $75, and, as elsewhere in the United States, rooms in national budget chain motels go for around $60 nightly. Weekend packages, offered by most city hotels, cut prices up to 50% (but may not be available in peak winter or summer seasons). As a rule, costs outside cities are lower, except in the deluxe resorts.

In both cities and rural areas, sit-down restaurants charge between 50¢ and $1 for a cup of coffee (specialty coffeehouses charge $2 to $5) and between $4 and $8 for a hamburger. A beer at a bar generally costs between $1.50 and $5, with microbrews and imports at the higher end of the range. Expect to pay double for food and drink in resort towns.

ITEM	AVERAGE COST
Cup of Coffee	$1.50
Glass of Wine	$6
Glass of Beer	$3
Sandwich	$6

Prices throughout this guide are given for adults. Substantially reduced fees are almost always available for children, students, and senior citizens.

CREDIT CARDS

Throughout this guide, the following abbreviations are used: **AE**, American Express; **D**, Discover; **DC**, Diners Club; **MC**, MasterCard; and **V**, Visa.

Reporting Lost Cards American Express (☎800/528–4800 in U.S., 336/393–1111 collect from abroad ⊕www.americanexpress. com). **Diners Club** (☎800/234–6377 in U.S., 303/799–1504 collect from abroad ⊕www. dinersclub.com). **Discover** (☎800/347–2683 in U.S., 801/902–3100 collect from abroad ⊕www.discovercard.com). **MasterCard** (☎800/627–8372 in U.S., 636/722–7111 collect from abroad ⊕www.mastercard.com). **Visa** (☎800/847–2911 in U.S., 410/581–9994 collect from abroad ⊕www.visa.com).

▌SAFETY

Regardless of which outdoor activities you pursue or your level of skill, safety must come first. Remember: know your limits.

Many trails in the Rockies and northern plains are remote and sparsely traveled. In the high altitudes of the mountains, oxygen is scarce. Hikers, bikers, and riders should carry emergency supplies in their backpacks. Proper equipment includes a flashlight, a compass, waterproof matches, a first-aid kit, a knife, a cell phone with an extra battery (although you may have to climb atop a mountain ridge to find a

signal), and a light plastic tarp for shelter. Backcountry skiers should add a repair kit, a blanket, an avalanche beacon, and a lightweight shovel to their lists. Always bring extra food and a canteen of water, as dehydration is a common occurrence at high altitudes. Never drink from streams or lakes, unless you boil the water first or purify it with tablets. Giardia, an intestinal parasite, may be present.

▌TIP→ **Distribute your cash, credit cards, IDs, and other valuables between a deep front pocket, an inside jacket or vest pocket, and a hidden money pouch. Don't reach for the money pouch once you're in public.**

ALTITUDE

You may feel dizzy and weak and find yourself breathing heavily—signs that the thin mountain air isn't giving you your accustomed dose of oxygen. Take it easy and rest often for a few days until you're acclimatized. Throughout your stay drink plenty of water and watch your alcohol consumption. If you experience severe headaches and nausea, see a doctor. It is easy to go too high too fast. The remedy for altitude-related discomfort is to go down quickly, into heavier air. Other altitude-related problems include dehydration and overexposure to the sun because of the thin air.

EXPOSURE

The high elevation, severe cold temperatures, and sometimes windy weather in Montana and Wyoming can often combine to create intense and dangerous outdoor conditions. In winter, exposure to wind and cold can quickly bring on hypothermia or frostbite. Protect yourself by dressing in layers, so you don't become overheated and then chilled. Any time of year, the region's clear air and high elevation make sunburn a particular risk. Always wear sunscreen, even when skies are overcast.

FLASH FLOODS

Flash floods can strike at any time and any place with little or no warning. Mountainous terrain can become dangerous when distant rains are channeled into gullies and ravines, turning a quiet streamside campsite or wash into a rampaging torrent in seconds. Similarly, desert terrain floods quickly when the land is unable to absorb heavy rain. Check weather reports before heading into the backcountry and be prepared to head for higher ground if the weather turns severe.

WILD ANIMALS

One of the most wonderful parts of the Rockies and plains is the abundant wildlife. And although a herd of grazing elk or a bighorn sheep high on a hillside is most certainly a Kodak moment, an encounter with a bear or mountain lion is not. To avoid such a dangerous situation while hiking, make plenty of noise, keep dogs on a leash, and keep small children between adults. While camping, be sure to store all food, utensils, and clothing with food odors far away from your tent, preferably high in a tree (also far from your tent). If you do come across a bear or big cat, do not run. For bears, back away quietly; for lions, make yourself look as big as possible. In either case, be prepared to fend off the animal with loud noises, rocks, sticks, and so on. And as the saying goes, do not feed the bears—or any wild animals, whether they're dangerous or not.

When in the wilderness, give all animals their space and never attempt to feed any of them. If you want to take a photograph, use a long lens rather than a long sneak to approach closely. This is particularly important for winter visitors. Approaching an animal can cause it stress and affect its ability to survive the sometimes brutal climate. In all cases remember that the animals have the right-of-way; this is their home, and you are the visitor.

▌TAXES

Sales tax is 4% in Wyoming; Montana has no sales tax. Some areas have additional local sales and lodging taxes, which can be quite significant.

If you are crossing the border into Canada, be aware of Canada's goods and services tax (better known as the GST). This is a value-added tax of 7%, applicable on virtually every purchase except basic groceries and a small number of other items. Visitors to Canada, however, may claim a full rebate of the GST on any goods taken out of the country as well as on short-term accommodations. Rebates can be claimed either immediately on departure from Canada at participating duty-free shops or by mail within 60 days of leaving Canada. Rebate forms can be obtained from certain retailers, duty-free shops, and customs officials, or by going to the Canada Revenue Agency Web site and searching for document GST176.

Purchases made during multiple visits to Canada can be grouped together for rebate purposes. Instant cash rebates up to a maximum of $500 are provided by some duty-free shops when leaving Canada, and most provinces do not tax goods that are shipped directly by the vendor to the purchaser's home. Always save your original receipts from stores and hotels (not just credit-card receipts), and be sure the name and address of the establishment are shown on the receipt. Original receipts are not returned. To be eligible for a refund, receipts must total at least $200, and each individual receipt must show a minimum purchase of $50.

Canada Tax Refund **Canada Revenue Agency** (⊕ www.cra-arc.gc.ca).

▌ TIPPING

It is customary to tip 15% at restaurants; 20% in resort towns is increasingly the norm. For coat checks and bellhops, $1 per coat or bag is the minimum. Taxi drivers expect 10% to 15%, depending on where you are. In resort towns, ski technicians, sandwich makers, coffee baristas, and the like also appreciate tips.

TIPPING GUIDELINES FOR MONTANA & WYOMING	
Bartender	$1 to $5 per round of drinks, depending on the number of drinks
Bellhop	$1 to $5 per bag, depending on the level of the hotel
Hotel Concierge	$5 or more, if he or she performs a service for you
Hotel Doorman	$1 to $2 if he helps you get a cab
Hotel Maid	$1 to $3 a day (either daily or at the end of your stay, in cash)
Hotel Room-Service Waiter	$1 to $2 per delivery, even if a service charge has been added
Porter at Airport or Train Station	$1 per bag
Skycap at Airport	$1 to $3 per bag checked
Taxi Driver	15% to 20%, but round up the fare to the next dollar amount
Tour Guide	10% of the cost of the tour
Valet-Parking Attendant	$1 to $2, but only when you get your car
Waiter	15% to 20%, with 20% being the norm at high-end restaurants; nothing additional if a service charge is added to the bill

INDEX

A

Absaroka-Beartooth Wilderness, *139–140*
Absaroka Western Designs & Tannery, *125*
Accommodations, *440–442*
Adams House, *388*
Adams Museum, *388*
Adventure Cycling, *247–248*
Aerial Tramway, *107*
Airline tickets, *442*
Airports, *445*
Alberta Bair Theater, *281*
Albright Visitor Center, *41*
Alder Gulch Shortline Railroad, *178*
Alta, WY, *113–114*
Amazing Ventures Fun Center, *235*
Amangani ☐, *102–103*
American Heritage Center, *359*
Amusement parks
  Billings, *285*
  Northwest Montana, *235–236*
Anaconda, MT, *171–173*
Anaconda-Pintlar Wilderness, *172*
Anaconda Smoke Stack State Park, *171–172*
Anthropology Museum, *360*
Apgar, MT, *194*
Arapooish State Fishing Access Site, *290–291*
Archie Bray Foundation, *168–169*
Art galleries and museums
  Billings, *283, 289*
  Cheyenne, *353*
  Great Falls, *269, 270, 273*
  Laramie, *359, 360*
  Missoula, *246*
  Montana Plains, *269, 270, 273, 283, 297*
  Northern Wyoming, *316, 321, 341–342*
  Northwest Montana, *220, 224, 225, 246*
  Northwest Wyoming, *96, 106*
  Southwest Montana, *138, 148, 156–157, 158, 165, 171, 175*
Artist Point, *36*
Atlantic City, WY, *117–119*
Atlantic City Mercantile ✕, *118*
Atlas Building, *165*
Audrie's Bed & Breakfast ☐, *396*

Avalanche Peak, *48*
Avenue of Flags, *399*
Ayres Natural Bridge, *339*

B

B Bar Ranch ☐, *146*
Back Basin, *36–37*
Badlands Loop Road, *421*
Badlands National Park, *418–431*
  accessibility, *431*
  admission fees, *431*
  camping, *429, 430–431*
  dining, *428*
  emergencies, *416*
  flora and fauna, *420*
  lodging, *428–429, 430*
  permits, *431*
  scenic drives, *421*
  sports and the outdoors, *424–427*
  tours, *424*
  transportation, *420*
  visitor information, *431*
  when to go, *420*
Badlands Wilderness Area, *422–423*
Baggs, WY, *371–372*
Baldwin Locomotive No. 12, *178*
Bannack, MT, *184–185*
Bar J Chuckwagon ✕, *111*
Battle Highway, *371*
Bear Country U.S.A., *395*
Bear essentials, *112*
Beartooth Nature Center, *134–135*
Beartooth Pass, *139*
Beartrap Canyon, *180–181*
Beaver Creek Park, *305*
Beaverhead County Museum, *182*
Bed & breakfasts, *440*
Ben Reifel Visitor Center, *423*
Berkeley Open Pit Mine, *174*
Bicycling, *19*
  Billings, *286*
  Glacier National Park, *197–198*
  Grand Teton National Park, *73, 78*
  Jackson, *98*
  Laramie, *361*
  Missoula, *247–248*
  Northern Wyoming, *317*

Northwest Montana, *19, 213, 228, 247–248, 260–261*
South Dakota Black Hills, *19, 390, 425*
Southern Wyoming, *361*
Southwest Montana, *19, 131, 159, 166, 172, 188*
Yellowstone National Park, *43*
Big EZ, The ☐, *155*
Big Hole National Battlefield, *185–186*
Big Horn, WY, *326–328*
Big Pig Dig, *421*
Big Sky, *15, 150–157*
Big Sky Ski and Summer Resort, *150*
Big Sky Waterpark, *235*
Big Snowy Mountains, *278–280*
Big Springs Trout Hatchery, *263*
Big Timber, MT, *140–143*
Bigfork, MT, *203, 220*
Bighorn Canyon National Recreation Area, *293–296*
Bighorn Canyon Visitor Center, *294*
Bighorn County Historical Museum and Visitor Information Center, *291*
Bighorn National Forest, *327*
Billings, MT, *280–290*
  children, activities for, *281, 283, 284, 285*
  dining, *286–287*
  emergencies, *307*
  exploring, *280–281, 283–285*
  lodging, *287–289*
  nightlife and the arts, *289*
  shopping, *289–298*
  sports and the outdoors, *285–286*
  visitor information, *308*
Billings Area Visitor Center and Cattle Drive Monument, *284*
Bird-watching
  Grand Teton National Park, *66, 73–74*
  Montana Plains, *277, 280, 290–291, 297, 301, 303*
  Northern Wyoming, *313–314*
  Northwest Montana, *217–218, 238*
  South Dakota Black Hills, *410, 425*

Southern Wyoming, *375*
Southwest Montana, *131, 175,
182*
Black Eagle Falls, *268*
Black Hills Caverns, *395*
Black Hills Wild Horse Sanctu-
ary, *404*
Black Sand Basin, *37*
Blue Canyon Kitchen and Tav-
ern ✕, *248*
Boating
Glacier National Park, *198*
Grand Teton National Park,
74–75, 78–79
Montana Plains, *295–296, 307*
Northwest Montana, *220*
Southern Wyoming, *377*
Southwest Montana, *144–145,
149, 166*
Yellowstone National Park,
43–44
Bob Marshall Wilderness Area,
241–243
Booking the trip, *439*
Boot Hill cemetery *(Virginia
City), 178*
Boothill Swords Park Cemetery,
284–285
Botticelli Ristorante Italiano
✕, *396*
Boulder River, *140–143*
Bowdoin National Wildlife
Refuge, *303–304*
Bozeman, MT, *157–162*
Bozeman Hot Springs, *159*
Bozeman Trail Museum, *327*
Bradford Brinton Memorial,
327
Bridger Raptor Fest, *160*
Bridger-Teton National Forest,
114, 115
Bridger/Vazquez Trading Post,
378
Broken Boot Gold Mine, *388*
Brooks Lake Lodge 🗇, *124*
Brooks Lake Recreation Area,
123
Browning, MT, *203*
Bucking Horse Sale, *296–297*
Buffalo, WY, *328–332*
Buffalo Bill Cody Museum, *315*
Buffalo Bill Historical Center,
315–316
Buffalo Bill State Park, *317*
Buffalo Cafe ✕, *231*
Buffalo Dining Room ✕, *397*
Bunnery, The ✕, *101*
Burke's Chop House ✕, *100*
Butte, MT, *173–177*

C
C. M. Russell Museum
Complex, *269*
Camping
Glacier National Park, *205,
208–209*
Grand Teton National Park,
83, 88–89
Montana Plains, *272–273, 280,
291–292, 296, 298, 299,
301, 307*
Northern Wyoming, *317,
320–321, 326, 331, 340*
Northwest Montana, *219, 223,
227, 234, 236, 240, 241,
243, 252, 256, 258–259, 260*
Northwest Wyoming, *105, 121,
127–128*
South Dakota Black Hills, *387,
415–416*
Southern Wyoming, *357,
370–371, 374, 377*
Southwest Montana, *138, 142–
143, 147, 150, 156, 168,
171, 173, 177, 179, 181,
184, 185, 186, 187–188*
Yellowstone National Park,
51–52, 58–60
Cam-Plex, *332*
Candlelight Cave Tour, *413*
Canoeing, kayaking and
rafting
Glacier National Park, *198,
201*
Grand Teton National Park,
74–75
Missoula, *20, 248*
Montana Plains, *275*
Northern Wyoming, *20, 317*
Northwest Montana, *221, 238,
248*
Northwest Wyoming, *20, 99*
Southern Wyoming, *367*
Southwest Montana, *20, 135,
143–144, 152, 166*
Canyon, *22, 35*
Canyon Ferry Mansion 🗇, *168*
Canyon Visitor Center, *41*
Capers ✕, *226*
Caras Park, *244*
Carbon County Arts Guild &
Depot Gallery, *138*
Carbon County Historical Soci-
ety Museum, *135*
Carlin Martini Bar and Night-
club, *289*
Carousel for Missoula, *213,
244*

Carousels, *163, 213, 244*
Casper, WY, *340–344*
Casper Planetarium, *341*
Cateye Café ✕, *160*
Cathedral of St. Helena, *163*
Caves
Billings, *281*
South Dakota Black Hills, *395,
406, 409–410*
Southwest Montana, *149*
Cemeteries
Montana Plains, *284–285, 292*
South Dakota Black Hills,
388–389
Cedar Pass Campground ⚠,
429
Cedar Pass Lodge 🗇, *429*
Centennial, WY, *363–366*
Central Montana Museum, *276*
Central School Museum, *224*
Chambers House B&B 🗇, *116*
Chapel of the Transfigura-
tion, *71*
Charles M. Russell National
Wildlife Refuge, *263,
301–302*
Charles Russell Chew-Choo,
276
Chatham Fine Art *(gallery), 148*
Cheyenne, WY, *11–12,
351–358*
camping, *357*
children, activities for, *352–353,
354*
dining, *354, 356*
exploring, *352–354*
festivals, *355*
lodging, *356*
nightlife and the arts, *357*
shopping, *357*
side trips, *358–362*
visitor information, *382*
Cheyenne Botanic Gardens,
352
Cheyenne Frontier Days, *355*
Chico Hot Springs Resort 🗇,
146–147
Chief Joseph Scenic Byway,
317
Chief Plenty Coups State Park,
294–295
Chophouse, The ✕, *333*
Churches. ⇨Also Missions
Grand Teton National Park, *71*
Helena, *163*
Clark Chateau Museum, *175*
Clark Fork River, *246*
Clark's Lookout State Park, *182*
Clear Creek Trail, *328–329*

Clearwater Canoe Trail, *238*

Cliff Shelf Nature Trail, *426*

Climate, *13*

Cody, WY, *11, 50, 315–322*

camping, *320–321*

children, activities for, *316–317, 321*

dining, *318*

exploring, *315–317*

lodging, *318–320*

nightlife and the arts, *321*

shopping, *322*

sports and the outdoors, *317–318*

visitor information, *346*

Cody Firearms Museum, *315–316*

Cody Guest Houses ⌨, *319*

Cody Gunslingers Shootout, *316*

Cody Mural, *315*

Cody Nite Rodeo, *316*

Cody Trolley Tours, *316*

Coleman Gallery and Studio, *138*

Colter Bay Campground ⚠, *88*

Colter Bay Visitor Center, *73*

Columbia Falls, MT, *203, 235–237*

Condo and cabin rentals, *440–441*

Conrad Mansion National Historic Site Museum, *224*

Cooke City, *51*

Copper King Mansion, *174–175*

Copper Village Museum and Arts Center, *171*

Cowboy Connection *(shop), 148*

Craig Thomas Discovery & Visitor Center, *73*

Crazy Horse Memorial, *401–402*

Crazy Mountain Museum, *141*

Credit cards, *5*

Crook County Fair and Rodeo, *336*

Crooked Creek Ranger Station, *294*

Cross Ranch Cookhouse ✕, *183*

Crow Fair and Rodeo, *291*

Crystal Lake, *279*

Curt Gowdy State Park, *352–353*

Custer County Art Museum, *297*

Custer National Cemetery, *292*

Custer National Forest, *139*

Custer State Park, *402–404*

Custom Cowboy Shop, *322*

D

Daly Mansion, *213, 256*

Days of '76 Museum, *388*

Deadwood, SD, *387–394*

children, activities for, *388, 389*

dining, *391–392*

exploring, *388–389*

lodging, *392–393*

nightlife, *393–394*

sports and the outdoors, *389–391*

visitor information, *434*

Deadwood Social Club ✕, *391*

Deadwood Thymes Bistro ✕, *391*

Deer Lodge, MT, *169–171*

Deerfield Boutique and Espresso Bar ✕, *330*

Devil's Canyon Overlook, *294*

Devils Tower National Monument, *334–336*

Di Tommaso Galleries, *106*

Dillon, MT, *182–184*

Dining, *15, 448.* ⇨*Also specific cities and towns*

symbols related to, *5*

Dinosaur and fossil sites

Montana Plains, *277, 279, 291, 294*

South Dakota Black Hills, *404, 421, 425–426*

Southern Wyoming, *360, 378*

Dogsledding, *99, 228*

Don Pedro's Family Restaurant ✕, *375*

Dornan's Chuck Wagon ✕, *84–85*

Douglas, WY, *339–340*

Draper Museum of Natural History, *316*

Dubois, WY, *50, 82, 122–125*

Dude ranches, *381*

Dumas Brothel Museum, *175*

E

Eagle Butte Coal Mine, *310, 333*

East Glacier, *190, 203*

Elk Mountain Campground ⚠, *416*

Emergencies

Glacier National Park, *210*

Grand Teton National Park, *89–90*

Montana Plains, *307*

Northern Wyoming, *345*

Northwest Montana, *260*

Northwest Wyoming, *127*

South Dakota Black Hills, *433*

Southern Wyoming, *380*

Yellowstone National Park, *61–62*

Emerson Cultural Center, *157–158*

Encampment, WY, *368–371*

Ennis, MT, *180–181*

Essex, MT, *203*

Exploration Works, *163*

F

Festival of Nations, *134*

Firehole Canyon Drive, *35–36*

Firehole Lake Drive, *36*

First Peoples Buffalo Jump State Park, *270*

Fishing, *21*

Glacier National Park, *199*

Grand Teton National Park, *66, 75, 79*

Montana Plains, *277, 279, 291–292, 295, 300–301, 307–308*

Northern Wyoming, *21, 317–318, 323, 324, 329, 346*

Northwest Montana, *21, 216, 220, 228, 241–242, 248, 255, 257*

Northwest Wyoming, *115, 119, 128*

South Dakota Black Hills, *395, 433*

Southern Wyoming, *21, 364, 367*

Southwest Montana, *21, 131, 135, 141, 143, 145, 151, 159, 166, 175, 181, 182, 188*

Yellowstone National Park, *21, 28, 44*

Fishing Bridge Visitor Center, *41–42*

Flaming Gorge Days, *375*

Flaming Gorge National Recreation Area, *376–377*

Flathead Indian Reservation, *216–219*

Flathead Lake, *213, 219–224*

Flathead National Forest, *241*

Fly Fishing Discovery Center, *143*

Fort Assinniboine, *304*

Fort Benton, MT, *273–275*

Fort Bridger State Historic Site, *377–378*

Fort Casper Historic Site, *341*

Fort Connah, *217*
Fort Fetterman State Historic Site, *339–340*
Ft. Hays Dances with Wolves Movie Set, *394*
Fort Laramie National Historic Site, *358*
Fort Owen, *254–255*
Fort Peck, *300–301*
Fort Peck Indian Reservation, *299*
Fort Peck Interpretive Center, *300*
Fort Peck Reservoir, *263*
Fort Peck Summer Theater, *300*
Fort Phil Kearny State Historic Site, *329*
Forts
Montana Plains, *300–301, 304*
Northern Wyoming, *329, 339–340, 341*
Northwest Montana, *217, 254–255*
Southern Wyoming, *358, 377–378*
Fossil Butte National Monument, *378*
Fossil Country Frontier Museum, *378*
Fossil Exhibit Trail, *425–426*
Franklin Hotel 📷, *393*
Frontier House Museum, *178*
Frontier Iron Works, *332*
Frontier Montana Museum, *170*

G
Gallatin National Forest, *139*
Gallatin River, *151*
Gallery 16, *273*
Garden Wall, *195*
Garden Wall Inn B&B 📷, *233*
Gardens, *213, 224, 352*
Gardiner, *50–51*
Gates of the Mountains, *166*
Gatiss Gardens, *213, 224*
Geyser Hill Loop, *37*
Geyser Park, *285*
Giant Springs State Park, *269*
Gibbon Falls, *37*
Gibson Park, *269*
Gillette, WY, *332–334*
Glacier National Park, *10, 190–211*
accessibility, *209*
admission fees, *209*
camping, *205, 208–209*
children, activities for, *194, 196, 201–202, 203, 204*
dining, *203–205*

emergencies, *210*
exploring, *194–197*
flora & fauna, *193*
itineraries, *22*
lodging, *205–207*
permits, *210*
price categories, *204, 205*
safety, *193*
scenic drives, *194*
service stations, *210*
sports and the outdoors, *190, 197–201*
telephones, *210*
tours, *193, 203*
transportation and services, *192*
visitor information, *211*
when to go, *192*
Glacier Park Boat Company, *198*
Glacier Park Lodge 📷, *206*
Glendo State Park, *310, 339*
Goat Lick Overlook, *196*
Going-to-the Sun Road, *194, 195*
Goldsmith's Bed and Breakfast 📷, *251–252*
Golf
Billings, *285–286*
Glacier National Park, *199*
Missoula, *248*
Northern Wyoming, *318*
Northwest Montana, *220, 225, 229, 236, 248*
Southwest Montana, *135, 151, 172–173*
Grand Canyon of the Yellowstone, *37*
Grand Encampment Cowboy Gathering, *369*
Grand Encampment Museum, *369*
Grand Hotel 📷, *142*
Grand Prismatic Spring, *37*
Grand Teton National Park, *6–7, 66–90*
accessibility, *89*
admission fees, *89*
camping, *83, 88–89*
children, activities for, *70, 71, 75–76, 77, 81, 84, 85–86*
dining, *82–83, 84–85*
emergencies, *89–90*
exploring, *71–73*
festivals & seasonal events, *69*
flora & fauna, *68*
lodging, *86–88*
lost and found, *90*
permits, *90*
picnic areas, *85–86*

price categories, *83*
scenic drives, *70*
service stations, *89*
sports and the outdoors, *73–81*
tours, *80–81*
transportation and services, *69*
visitor information, *90*
when to go, *68*
Grand Union Hotel 📷, *275*
Granite Hot Springs, *98*
Grant-Kohrs Ranch National Historic Site, *170*
Grant Village, WY, *28, 42*
Great Divide Basin, *374*
Great Falls, MT, *263*
camping, *272–273*
children, activities for, *269–270*
dining, *271–272*
exploring, *267–270*
lodging, *272*
shopping, *273*
sports and the outdoors, *270–271*
visitor information, *308*
Great Fountain Geyser, *36, 37–38*
Great Northern Carousel, *163*
Great Northern Depot, *225*
Greathouse Peak, *278*
Green River, WY, *375–376*
Greycliff Prairie Dog Town State Park, *141*
Grinnell and Salamander Glaciers, *196*
Grinnell Glacier Trail, *200*
Guest ranches, *441*
Gunsel Horse Adventures, *427*
Guy's Lolo Creek Steakhouse ✕, *248*

H
H. Earl Clack Memorial Museum, *304*
Halfbreed Lake National Wildlife Refuge, *280*
Hamilton, MT, *256–259*
Happy Jack Road, *358*
Hardin, MT, *290–292*
Havre, MT, *304–305*
Havre Beneath the Streets, *305*
Headwaters Heritage Museum, *149*
Helena, MT, *162–169*
Hidden Falls, *85–86*
Hidden Lake Nature Trail, *199*
Hidden Lake Overlook, *195*
Hide Out Leather, *106*
Higgins Block, *246*

High Plains Western Heritage Center, *389*
Highline Trail, *200*
Hiking, *18*
  Glacier National Park, 180, 199–200
  Grand Teton National Park, 75–77, 80
  Montana Plains, 279
  Northern Wyoming, 317, 335, 342
  Northwest Montana, 18, 213, 220–221, 225, 240, 261
  Northwest Wyoming, 99
  South Dakota Black Hills, 390, 410–412, 425–426
  Southern Wyoming, 364, 369
  Yellowstone National Park, 18, 45–49
Hillsboro Dude Ranch, *293–294*
Historic Crail Ranch, *151*
Historic Governor's Mansion, *354*
Historic Hat Creek Stage Station, *338*
Historical Museum at Fort Missoula, *246*
Hobo Pool Hot Springs, *367*
Hockaday Museum of Art, *225*
Hog Park, *370*
Holland Falls, *240*
Holland Lake, *240–241*
Holter Museum of Art, *165*
Horseback riding/trail rides, *16*
  Glacier National Park, 200–201
  Grand Teton National Park, 79, 80
  Montana Plains, 275
  Northern Wyoming, 16, 317, 318, 329
  Northwest Montana, 16, 226, 242, 257
  Northwest Wyoming, 120
  South Dakota Black Hills, 427
  Southern Wyoming, 16, 369
  Southwest Montana, 135, 141–142, 145, 151–152, 175, 181, 182–183
  Yellowstone National Park, 16
Hostels, *441–442*
Hot springs
  Northwest Montana, 218
  Northwest Wyoming, 98
  Southern Wyoming, 367
  Southwest Montana, 133, 146–147, 159, 180
  Yellowstone National Park, 28, 35
Hot Springs, SD, *404*
House of Mystery, *235–236*
Houses of historic interest
  Billings, 281
  Cheyenne, 354
  Great Falls, 269
  Helena, 163, 165, 166
  Laramie, 360
  Northern Wyoming, 327
  Northwest Montana, 256, 316–317
  South Dakota Black Hills, 388
  Southwest Montana, 165, 174–175
Hyart Theatre, *314*

Indian Arts Museum, *71*
Indian Caves Pictographs, *281*
Indian Memorial, *292–293*
Indian Museum of North America, *402*
Indian Territory *(shop), 322*
Insect Museum, *360*
Irma Hotel 🏨, *320*
Itineraries, *22, 24–26*

Jackson, WY, *50, 82, 95–107*
Jackson Glacier Overlook, *195*
Jackson Hole Mountain Resort, *98, 108*
Jackson Hole Museum, *96*
Jackson Lake, *72*
Jackson Lake Lodge Mural Room ✕, *84*
Jakes ✕, *391*
Jenny Lake, *66, 72*
Jenny Lake 🏕, *88*
Jenny Lake Lodge Dining Room ✕, *84*
Jenny Lake Scenic Drive, *70*
Jenny Lake Trail, *77*
Jenny Lake Visitor Center, *73*
Jewel Basin Hiking Area, *220–221*
Jewel Cave National Monument, *403*
Jim Gatchell Memorial Museum, *328*
Journey Museum, *394*
Journey Overlook, *423*
Judith River, *277*
Judith River Dinosaur Institute, *277*
Juliano's ✕, *286*

K
Kalispell, MT, *203, 224–227*
Kalispell Grand Hotel 🏨, *227*
Kayaking. ⇨*Canoeing, kayaking and rafting*
Kemmerer, WY, *378–379*
Keyhole State Park, *332*
Keystone, SD, *400–401*
King's Saddlery and Ropes, *323*

L
La Provence ✕, *221*
Lake Butte, *38*
Lake Elmo State Park, *281*
Lake McDonald, *196, 198*
Lake McDonald Complex 🏨, *207*
Lake Overlook, *38*
Lake Yellowstone Hotel 🏨, *54–55*
Lake Yellowstone Hotel Dining Room ✕, *52*
Lamar Valley, *39–40*
Lander, WY, *119–122*
Laramie, WY, *11–12, 358–362*
Laramie Plains Museum, *360*
Last Chance Gulch, *163*
Last Chance Ranch ✕, *167*
Laurance S. Rockefeller Preserve & Center, *72*
Lee Metcalf National Wildlife Refuge, *254*
LeHardy Rapids, *38*
Lehrkind Mansion 🏨, *161*
Lewis and Clark Canoe Expeditions, *275*
Lewis and Clark Caverns, *149*
Lewis and Clark National Historic Trail Interpretive Center, *269–270*
Lewistown, MT, *276–278*
Lewistown Chokecherry Festival, *276*
Libraries, *292*
Lincoln Borglum Museum, *399*
Little America Hotel and Resort 🏨, *356*
Little Bear Steak House ✕, *354*
Little Bighorn Battlefield National Monument, *292–293*
Little Snake River Valley Museum, *371*
Livingston, MT, *51, 143–148*
Livingston Depot Center, *143*
Livingston Roundup Rodeo, *144*

Lodging. ⇨*Also specific cities and towns*
symbols related to, 5
Logan Pass, *190, 195, 196*
Lola Creek Steakhouse ✕, *248–249*
Lone Mountain Ranch ⌑, *152, 154*
Lone Pine State Park, *225*
Lovell, WY, *313–315*
Lower Geyser Basin, *38–39*
Lusk, WY, *338–339*

M

Madison, WY, *28, 32, 42*
Madison Buffalo Jump, *149*
Mai Wah Museum, *175*
Makoshika State Park, *298–299*
Mammoth Hot Springs, WY, *28, 35*
Mammoth Hot Springs Terraces, *39*
Mammoth Site, *404*
Many Glacier Campground ⌂, *208*
Medicine Bow, WY, *363*
Medicine Bow Museum, *363*
Medicine Bow National Forest, *340*
Medicine Bow-Routt National Forest, *364, 369*
Medicine Lake National Wildlife Refuge Complex, *302–303*
Medicine Rocks State Park, *297*
Medicine Wheel National Historic Landmark, *314*
Menor's Ferry Historic Area, *71–72*
Merry Piglets ✕, *111*
Midway Geyser Basin, *39*
Miles City, MT, *296–298*
Miles City Saddlery, *298*
Mineral Museum, *175*
Mines
Northern Wyoming, 310, 333
South Dakota Black Hills, 388
Southwest Montana, 174
Minnilusa Pioneer Museum, *394*
Mint Bar & Grill, The ✕, *277*
Missions
Northwest Montana, 217, 223, 254
Missoula, MT, *244–253*
camping, 252
children, activities for, 244, 247

dining, 248–249
exploring, 244, 246–247
lodging, 250–252
nightlife and the arts, 252–253
shopping, 253
sports and the outdoors, 247–248
visitor information, 261
Missoula Art Museum, *246*
Missouri Breaks Interpretive Center, *274*
Missouri Headwaters State Park, *149*
Money, *448–449*
Montana. ⇨*Montana Plains; Northwest Montana; Southwest Montana*
Montana Auto Museum, *170*
Montana Club, *166*
Montana Dinosaur Trail, *291*
Montana Governor's Mansion, *163*
Montana Historical Society Museum, *165*
Montana Museum of Art and Culture at the University of Montana, *246*
Montana Plains, *11, 263–308.* ⇨*Also Billings, MT; Great Falls, MT*
Big Open, 298–302
camping, 272–273, 280, 291–292, 296, 298, 299, 301, 307
Central Montana, 273–275
children, activities for, 269–270, 276, 277, 283, 284, 294–295
dining, 264, 271–272, 277, 286–287, 291, 293, 297, 305
emergencies, 307
festivals, 276, 291, 296–297
Great Falls, 266–273
Hi-Line, 302–305
itineraries, 267
lodging, 264, 272, 275, 278, 279–280, 287–289, 291, 298, 299, 301, 304, 305, 307
nightlife and the arts, 289, 298, 305
price categories, 266
shopping, 273, 275, 289–290, 298
Southeast Montana, 290–298
sports and the outdoors, 263, 270–271, 275, 277, 279, 285–286, 295–296, 300–301, 307–308

transportation and services, 305–307, 308
visitor information, 308
when to tour, 13, 266
Montana State Old-Time Fiddlers Contest, *134*
Moonlight and Steam Trains, *178*
Moose Visitor Center, *66*
Morrell Falls National Recreation, *238*
Moss Mansion, *281*
Moulton Ranch Cabins ⌑, *87*
Mount Moriah Cemetery, *388–389*
Mount Rushmore KOA-Palmer Gulch Lodge ⌂, *415*
Mount Rushmore National Memorial, *397–400*
dining, 397
shopping, 400
Mountain Lake Lodge ⌑, *222–223*
Mountaineering. ⇨*Rock climbing and mountaineering*
Mud Volcano, *39*
Museum of Geology, *394, 395*
Museum of the Mountain Man, *114–115*
Museum of the Northern Great Plains, *274*
Museum of the Rockies, *158*
Museum of the Upper Missouri, *274*
Museums. ⇨*Also Art galleries and museums; Houses of historic interest*
agriculture, 182, 274
air and space, 394
anthropology, 360
Asian settlers, 175
automobiles, 170
bighorn sheep, 97, 122
in Billings, 281, 285
brothels, 175, 305
Buffalo Bill, 315–316
in Cheyenne, 353, 354
children's, 360
clock, 304
firearms, 135, 170, 315–316
fishing, 257
fossils, 158, 277, 279, 291, 303, 378
frontier, 170, 178, 274, 285, 295, 297, 303, 304, 328, 338, 339, 341, 353, 378
geology, 122, 341, 360, 367, 395
in Great Falls, 269, 270

history, 96, 98, 114–115, 117,
   122, 135, 141, 143–144,
   149, 158–159, 165, 170,
   171, 175, 178, 182, 224,
   228, 246, 255, 257, 274,
   276, 277, 285, 291, 292,
   297, 303, 304, 315–316,
   327, 332, 332–333, 338,
   339, 341, 353, 360, 363,
   367, 369, 371, 388, 394,
   399, 402
insects, 360
Lewis and Clark, 257
logging, 238, 369
military, 246, 274, 304, 328,
   339, 341
mining, 135, 170, 175, 364
missionaries, 255
   in Missoula, 246
   in Montana Plains, 269–270,
   274, 276, 279, 283, 285,
   291, 292, 297, 303, 304
mountain men, 114–115, 371
Native American life, 135,
   143–144, 158–159, 170, 182,
   224, 255, 257, 269–270,
   283, 292, 304, 316, 328,
   339, 394, 402
natural history, 303, 360
   in Northern Wyoming, 315–
   316, 327, 332–333, 338,
   341
   in Northwest Montana, 217,
   219, 224, 225, 228, 238,
   246, 255, 257
   in Northwest Wyoming, 96, 97,
   98, 114–115
pioneers, 141, 143–144,
   158–159, 165, 255, 274,
   276, 279, 283, 297, 304,
   338, 339, 360, 394
prison, 169–170, 360
railroads, 143, 228, 283
ranching, 96, 182, 304, 328,
   364
rodeo, 135, 141
   in South Dakota Black Hills,
   388, 394, 395, 399, 402
   in Southern Wyoming, 354,
   360, 363, 364, 367, 369,
   371, 378
   in Southwest Montana, 135,
   141, 143–144, 149, 158–159,
   163, 165, 169–170, 171,
   175, 178, 182
stagecoaches, 338
toys and dolls, 170
wildlife, 341
Music in the Mountains, 156

N

Nagle Warren Mansion 🏨,
   356
**National Bighorn Sheep Inter-
   pretive Center,** 122
National Bison Range, 217
National Elk Refuge, 96–97
**National Historic Trails Inter-
   pretive Center,** 341
**National Museum of Wildlife
   Art,** 97
Native American sites
   Billings, 281
   Montana Plains, 269–270, 281,
   290, 291, 294–295, 299
   Northern Wyoming, 314, 317
   Northwest Montana, 203,
   216–217, 219
   South Dakota Black Hills,
   400–401
   Southwest Montana, 143–144,
   149, 158–159, 165, 185
Natural Bridge, 39
**Natural Bridge State Monu-
   ment,** 141
**Nevada City Open Air
   Museum,** 178
**Nez Perce National Historic
   Park,** 185
Nici Self Museum, 364
**Nicolaysen Art Museum and
   Discovery Center,** 341
**Ninepipe National Wildlife
   Refuge,** 217–218
Nora's Fish Creek Inn ✕,
   111
Norris, WY, 28, 32, 35
Norris Geyser Basin, 39
Norris Hot Springs, 180
North Rim Trail, 47
Northeast Entrance Road,
   39–40
Northeastern Grand Loop, 36
**Northern Pacific Railroad
   Depot,** 143, 246–247
Northern Wyoming, 11, 310–
   315. ⇨Also Cody; Sheridan
   Bighorn Basin, 313–315
   camping, 317, 320–321, 326,
   331, 340
   children, activities for, 313,
   316–317, 319, 321, 324–325,
   327, 330, 335–336, 341–342
   dining, 311, 314, 318,
   324–325, 327, 329–330, 333,
   336–337, 338, 340, 342–343
   emergencies, 345
   festivals, 321

lodging, 311, 314–315,
   318–320, 325–326, 327–328,
   330–331, 333, 337, 338–339,
   340, 343, 346
nightlife and the arts, 321,
   332, 343
North Platte River Valley,
   337–344
*Powder River Basin and the
   Black Hills,* 322–337
price categories, 311
shopping, 322, 326, 332, 333,
   336, 343
sports and the outdoors,
   317–318, 324, 329, 335,
   342, 346
transportation and services,
   344–345
visitor information, 346
when to tour, 13, 313
Northwest Montana, 10, 213–
   261. ⇨Also Glacier National
   Park; Missoula, MT
Bitterroot Valley, 253–259
camping, 219, 223, 227, 234,
   236, 240, 241, 243, 252,
   256, 258–259, 260
children, activities for, 219,
   220–221, 222, 223, 234,
   225, 228, 229, 230,
   231–232, 235–236, 242, 244,
   247, 250–251, 252–253,
   254, 256
dining, 213–214, 218–219,
   221, 226, 230–232, 236,
   239, 248–250, 255, 258
emergencies, 260
festivals, 238, 252
Flathead and Mission Valleys,
   216–237
lodging, 214, 218, 219,
   222–223, 226–227, 232–234,
   236, 239, 240–241, 242–243,
   250–252, 255–256, 258
Missoula, 244–253
nightlfe and the arts, 219,
   234–235, 237, 252–253
price categories, 214
Seeley-Swan Valley, 237–243
shopping, 219, 227, 235, 237,
   253
sports and the outdoors, 218,
   220–221, 228–230, 238–239,
   241–242, 247–248, 255, 257,
   260–261
transportation and services,
   259–260, 261
visitor information, 261
when to tour, 13, 216

Northwest Wyoming, 7, 92–129. ⇨Also Grand Teton National Park

camping, 105, 121, 127–128

children, activities for, 96–97, 98, 100, 113, 114–115, 121, 122, 123

dining, 93, 100–102, 110, 111, 115–116, 118, 120, 123–124

emergencies, 127

Jackson, 95–107

Jackson Hole area, 107–111

lodging, 93, 102–105, 110–111, 113, 114, 116–117, 118–119, 120–121, 124–125, 127

nightlife and the arts, 105–106, 113, 121

price categories, 94

safety, 128

shopping, 106–107, 117, 119, 122, 125

sports and the outdoors, 98–100, 108–109, 113, 115, 119–120, 123, 128

tours, 128

transportation, 125–127

visitor information, 129

when to tour, 94–95

Wind River range, 114–125

O

Obsidian Dining Room ✕, 52

Occidental Hotel 🏨, 331

Old Faithful, 28, 32, 40, 42–43

Old Faithful Inn 🏨, 55

Old Faithful Visitor Center, 42

Old Milwaukee Railroad Depot, 247

Old Montana Prison Museum, 169–170

Old Style Saloon No. 10, 393

Old Trail Town, 316–317

Old West Museum, 353

Oliver's Bar and Grill, ✕, 324

Opera House (Virginia City), 180

Our Lady of the Rockies, 174

Overland Fine Eatery, The ✕, 361

Oxbow Bend, 66, 72

P

Paradise Guest Ranch 🏨, 330

Paradise Valley Loop, 144

Paris Gibson Square Museum of Art, 270

Park Ranger tips, 42

Parks. ⇨Also Glacier National Park; Grand Teton National Park; Yellowstone National Park

Billings, 281, 285

Cheyenne, 352–353

Great Falls, 269, 270

Missoula, 244

Montana Plains, 269, 270, 277, 281, 285, 294–295, 297, 298–299, 305

Northern Wyoming, 310, 317, 332, 338, 342

Northwest Montana, 225, 234, 244

South Dakota Black Hills, 402–404, 405–431

Southern Wyoming, 352–353, 370, 372

Southwest Montana, 149, 150, 184

Parkway Inn 🏨, 103

Passports, 436–437

Paya Deli Pizza & Catering ✕, 123

Pebble Creek ⚠, 60

Peter Norbeck National Scenic Byway, 397

Peter Yegen Jr./Yellowstone County Museum, 285

Phillips County Historical Museum, 303

Pictograph Cave State Monument, 281

Pine Ridge, SD, 427

Pinedale, WY, 82, 114–117

Pintlar Scenic Highway, 172

Pioneer Cabin, 165

Pioneer Mountain Scenic Byway, 185

Pioneer Museum, 158–159

Pirogue Island State Park, 297

Plains Indian Museum, 316

Planetariums, 158, 341, 360

Polebridge, MT, 203

Pollard Hotel 🏨, 137

Polson, MT, 220

Pompey's Pillar National Historic Landmark, 290

Powell County Museum, 170

Powwows, 14

Presidential Trail, 399

Price categories

Glacier National Park, 204, 205

Grand Teton National Park, 83

Montana Plains, 266

Northern Wyoming, 311

Northwest Montana, 214

Northwest Wyoming, 94

Southern Wyoming, 349

Southwest Montana, 132

Yellowstone National Park, 52

Prisons

Southern Wyoming, 360, 372

Southwest Montana, 169–170

Pryor Mountain Wild Horse Range, 294

Pug Mahon's ✕, 287

Purple Cow ✕, 291

R

Rainbow Falls, 270

Rainbow Ranch Lodge 🏨, 155–156

Range Riders Museum, 297

Rankin Ridge Drive, 409

Rankin Ridge Lookout Tower, 409

Rapid City, SD, 394–397, 427

Ravalli County Museum, 257

Rawlins, WY, 372–374

Red Lodge, MT, 51, 134–135, 137–139

Red Rock Lakes National Wildlife Refuge, 182

Reeder's Alley, 165

Rendezvous at Red Lodge, 134

Rental cars, 442–444

Reptile Gardens, 395

Resort at Paws Up, The 🏨, 250

Resorts, 442

Rex, The ✕, 286

Rimrock Trail, 281–282

Roberts Prairie Dog Town Overlook, 423

Rock climbing and mountaineering

Grand Teton National Park, 75, 78–79

Montana Plains, 279

Northern Wyoming, 335

Southwest Montana, 131

Rockpile Museum, 332–333

Rocky Mountain Brewing Company ✕, 173

Rocky Mountain Elk Foundation Wildlife Visitor Center, 247

Rocky Mountain Herbarium, 360

Rodeos, 14

Cheyenne, 355

Montana Plains, 291, 296–297

Northern Wyoming, 316, 336, 339

Northwest Montana, 257

Southern Wyoming, 355

Southwest Montana, 144, 180, 182

Running Eagle Falls, *196*
"Running of the Sheep" Sheep
   Drive, *141*
Rustic Pine Steakhouse ✕, *123*

S

Safety, *449–450*
St. Ignatius Mission, *217*
St. Mary Lake, *195*
St. Mary's Mission, *222, 254*
Sanders Bed and Breakfast
   ⬚, *168*
Saratoga, WY, *366–368*
Saratoga Historical and Cul-
   tural Museum, *367*
Saratoga Inn Resort ⬚, *368*
Scenic drives
Glacier National Park, *194*
Grand Teton National Park, *70*
Northern Wyoming, *317*
Northwest Montana, *190, 195,
   196, 257*
South Dakota Black Hills,
   397, 409
Southern Wyoming, *358, 366,
   371, 374*
Southwest Montana, *131, 133,
   139, 144, 172, 185*
Yellowstone National Park,
   35–36
Sculptor's Studio, *399*
Seedskadee National Wildlife
   Refuge, *375*
Seeley Creek Nordic Ski Trails,
   238
Seeley Lake, *238–240*
Seeley Lake Museum and Visi-
   tors Center, *238*
Selway-Bitterroot National For-
   est, *257*
Seminoe State Park, *372*
Seven Lazy P Guest Ranch
   ⬚, *243*
7th Cavalry Monument, *292*
Shack Cafe, The ✕, *249*
Sheepshead Mountain Recre-
   ation Area, *175*
Sheridan, WY, *11, 323–326*
camping, *326*
dining, *324–325*
exploring, *232–324*
lodging, *325–326*
shopping, *326*
sports and the outdoors, *324*
visitor information, *346*
Sheridan Inn ⬚, *324*
Shoshone National Forest, *317*
Showthymel ✕, *221*
Signal Mountain Road, *70*

Sinks Canyon State Park, *119*
Sioux Indian Museum, *394*
Skalkaho Highway, *257*
Skiing *(cross-country)*
Glacier National Park, *201*
Grand Teton National Park, *79*
Montana Plains, *279*
Northern Wyoming, *310, 317,
   318, 342, 346*
Northwest Montana, *221, 229–
   230, 238–239, 248, 261*
Northwest Wyoming, *100,
   108–109*
South Dakota Black Hills,
   390–391
Southern Wyoming, *361, 364,
   367, 369, 381*
Southwest Montana, *131, 135,
   154, 159, 172, 183, 186, 188*
Yellowstone National Park,
   49–50
Skiing *(downhill)*, *17*
Missoula, *248*
Northern Wyoming, *310, 342,
   346*
Northwest Montana, *17, 221,
   229–230, 248, 261*
Northwest Wyoming, *108–109*
Southern Wyoming, *364, 381*
Southwest Montana, *17, 135,
   152–153, 159, 172, 183, 188*
Sleigh rides, *100*
Slippery Ann Wildlife Viewing
   Area, *302*
Slough Creek ⌂, *60*
Slough Creek Trail, *48*
Smith River, *270*
Smokejumper Visitor Center,
   247
Snow King Resort, *82*
Snowboarding, *17*
Northwest Montana, *229–230*
Northwest Wyoming, *108–109*
Snowmobiling
Grand Teton National Park, *80*
Jackson, *100*
Montana Plains, *279*
Northern Wyoming, *317*
Northwest Montana, *239*
South Dakota Black Hills, *391*
Southern Wyoming, *364, 367*
Southwest Montana, *131, 152*
Yellowstone National Park,
   49–50
Snowshoeing
Glacier National Park, *201*
Northwest Montana, *239*
Southwest Montana, *152*

Yellowstone National Park,
   49–50
Snowy Range Scenic Byway,
   366
South Dakota Air & Space
   Museum, *394*
South Dakota Black Hills, *12,
   384–404.* ⇨*Also Dead-
   wood; Mount Rushmore and
   the Black Hills; Badlands
   National Park*
camping, *387, 415–416*
children, activities for, *388,
   389, 395, 397, 400, 403–
   404, 411–412*
Crazy Horse Memorial,
   401–402
Custer State Park, *402–404*
Deadwood, *387–394*
dining, *384–385, 391–392,
   396, 397, 400, 402, 403–
   404, 413*
emergencies, *433*
flora & fauna, *408*
Hot Springs, *404*
lodging, *385, 392–393, 396,
   401, 402, 403–404, 413,
   415, 433*
Mount Rushmore National
   Memorial, *397–400*
nightlife, *393–394*
price categories, *387*
Rapid City, *394–397*
scenic drives, *409*
shopping, *400*
sports and the outdoors,
   389–391, 395, 433
tours, *433*
transportation and services,
   431–433
visitor information, *434*
when to tour, *13, 387*
Wind Cave National Park,
   406–416
South Pass City State Historic
   Site, *117–118*
South Rim Trail, *48*
Southern Wyoming, *11–12,
   348–382.* ⇨*Also Cheyenne,
   WY*
camping, *357, 370–371, 374,
   377*
children, activities for, *352–353,
   354, 358, 360, 369, 377*
dining, *349, 354, 356, 361,
   367, 370, 371, 372–373,
   375–376, 378–379*
emergencies, *380–381*
festivals, *375*

itineraries, 351
Laramie, 358–362
lodging, 349, 356, 361, 363, 364–365, 368, 370, 371–372, 373–374, 376, 379, 381
nightlife and the arts, 357, 362
price categories, 349
shopping, 357, 362, 366, 378, 379
Snowy Range area, 362–374
Southwest Wyoming, 374–379
sports and the outdoors, 361, 364, 367, 369, 375, 377, 381
tours, 381–382
transportation and services, 379–380
visitor information, 382
when to tour, 13, 349
Southwest Montana, 7, 10, 131–188
Bozeman, 157–162
Butte, 173–177
camping, 138, 142–143, 147, 150, 156, 168, 171, 173, 177, 179, 181, 184, 185, 186, 187–188
children, activities for, 134–135, 138, 141, 149, 151–152, 153, 158, 159, 163, 165, 169, 170, 173, 183
dining, 132, 137, 142, 145–146, 149–150, 154–155, 159–160, 166–167, 170, 173, 176, 179, 181, 183
festivals, 134, 141,
Helena, 162–169
lodging, 132, 137–138, 142, 146–147, 150, 155–156, 160–161, 168, 170–171, 173, 176–177, 179, 181, 183–184, 186, 187
nightlife & the arts, 138, 143, 147–148, 161–162, 168, 180, 181
north of Yellowstone, 132, 134–135, 137–157
price categories, 132
shopping, 139, 148, 157, 168–169, 177
southwest corner, 169–186
sports and the outdoors, 135, 140, 141–142, 144–145, 149, 151–154, 159, 166, 172–173, 175, 179, 181, 182–183, 188
transportation and services, 186–187
visitor information, 188
when to tour, 13, 132
Spanish Diggings, 338

Spearfish Canyon Lodge ▥, 392
Spelunking, 412–413
Spirit West River Lodge ▥, 370
Spotted Bear, MT, 241
Spotted Bear Ranch ▥, 242–243
Sqelix'u/Aqfsmakni-k Cultural Center, 217
Stagecoach Museum, 338
State Archaeological Research Center, 394
State Capitol Building (Montana), 165
Stevensville, MT, 254–256
Stevensville Museum, 255
Stewart's Trapline Gallery & Indian Trading Post, 125
Stockmen's Restaurant ✕, 115
Stoney Creek Outfitters, 367
Storm Point Trail, 46
Storybook Island, 395
Strutton Inn B&B ▥, 402
Stumptown Historical Society's Museum, 228
Sulphur Caldron, 40
Summit at Big Sky ▥, 156
Sundance, WY, 336–337
Svilars Bar & Dining Room ✕, 120
Swimming, 277
Sylvan Lake Resort ▥, 403–404
Symbols, 5
Symes Hot Springs Hotel and Mineral Baths, 218

T

Tatanka: Story of the Bison, 389
Tate Earth Science Center and Geological Museum, 341
Taxes, 450
Teller Wildlife Refuge, 256
Teton Thai ✕, 102
Teton Village, WY, 82, 107–111
Theater buildings
Billings, 280
Montana Plains, 280, 300
Northern Wyoming, 314, 323
Southwest Montana, 171
Thompson-Hickman Memorial Museum, 178
Three Forks, MT, 148–150
Thunder Basin National Grasslands, 333
Tipping, 451

Toad Hall Manor Bed and Breakfast ▥, 176
Toi's Thai ✕, 167
Tower Fall, 40
Trail End State Historic Site, 323–324
Trail rides. ⇨Horseback riding
Transportation, 445–447
Trip insurance, 437–438
Trout hatcheries
Montana Plains, 263, 269, 276
Southwest Montana, 140
Two Medicine Valley, 196

U

UL Bend National Wildlife Refuge, 302
Ulrich's Fossil Gallery, 378
University of Wyoming, 360
Upper Geyser Basin, 40
Upper Missouri National Wild and Scenic River, 274–275
Upper Musselshell Museum, 279

V

Vedauwoo Recreation Area, 358
Virginia City, MT, 178–180
Virginian Restaurant, The ✕, 329–330
Visitor information, 436
Grand Teton National Park, 90
Montana Plains, 308
Northern Wyoming, 346
Northwest Montana, 261
Northwest Wyoming, 129
South Dakota Black Hills, 434
Southern Wyoming, 382
Southwest Montana, 188
Yellowstone National Park, 63
Vore Buffalo Jump, 336
Voss Inn ▥, 161

W

Wall, SD, 427
War Horse National Wildlife Refuge, 277
Washoe Theatre, 171
Waterfalls
Glacier National Park, 196, 203
Grand Teton National Park, 85–86
Great Falls, 268, 270
Northwest Montana, 238, 240
Yellowstone National Park, 37, 40
Web sites, 437, 443

Werner Wildlife Museum, *341*
West Glacier, *190, 203*
West Thumb Geyser Basin,
    40–41, 43
West Yellowstone, *50*
Western Heritage Center, *283*
When to go, *13*
White River Visitor Center, *423*
White Swan Memorial Library,
    292
Whitefish, MT, *203, 227–235*
Whitefish Mountain Resort on
    Big Mountain, *229–230*
Whitney Gallery of Western
    Art, *316*
Wild Caving Tour, *413*
Wildlife preserves
Missoula, 247
*Montana Plains, 263, 277, 280,
    301–304*
*Northern Wyoming, 313–314,
    333*
*Northwest Montana, 217–218,
    241–243, 247, 254, 256*
Northwest Wyoming, 96–97
*South Dakota Black Hills, 395,
    422–423*
Southern Wyoming, 375
*Southwest Montana, 172, 175,
    182*
Willow Flats, *72*
Wilsall Rodeo, *144*
Wilson, WY, *111, 113*
Winchester Steak House ✕,
    330
Wind Cave, *409–410*
Wind Cave Canyon, *410*
Wind Cave Canyon Trail, *411*
Wind Cave National Park,
    406–416
accessibility, 416
admission fees, 416
camping, 415–416
dining, 413
emergencies, 416

lodging, 413, 415
permits, 416
scenic drives, 409
*sports and the outdoors,
    410–413*
visitor information, 410, 416
Wind River Historical Center,
    122
Windbag Saloon & Grill ✕,
    167
Winter Carnival (Red Lodge),
    134
Wolf Hotel 🛏, *368*
Woodland Park, *225*
Wort Hotel ✕, *104*
Wyo Theater, *323*
Wyoming. ⇨*Northern
    Wyoming; Northwest
    Wyoming; Southern
    Wyoming; Yellowstone
    National Park*
Wyoming Children's Museum
    and Nature Center, *360*
Wyoming Frontier Prison, *372*
Wyoming Pioneer Memorial
    Museum, *339*
Wyoming State Capitol,
    353–353
Wyoming State Fair and
    Rodeo, *339*
Wyoming State Museum, *354*
Wyoming Territorial Prison,
    360
Wyoming Vietnam Veterans
    Memorial, *315*

Y

Yellowstone Art Museum, *283*
Yellowstone Association Insti-
    tute, *45*
Yellowstone Gateway Museum,
    143–144
Yellowstone Lake, *29, 35, 41*
Yellowstone Lake Scenic
    Cruises, *44*

Yellowstone National Park, *6,
    28–63*
accessibility, 60–61
admission fees, 61
camping, 51–52, 58–60
Canyon area, 28, 35
*children, activities for, 37, 39,
    40–41, 44, 46, 55, 58*
dining, 51, 52–54
emergencies, 61–62
exploring, 32, 35–43
Fishing Bridge, 41–42
flora & fauna, 30
Grant Village, 32, 42
itineraries, 22
lodging, 51, 54–60
Madison, 28, 32
Mammoth Hot Springs, 28, 35
Norris, 28, 32, 35
*Old Faithful area, 28, 32, 40,
    42–43*
permits, 62
price categories, 52
scenic drives, 35–36
service stations, 61
sports and the outdoors, 43–50
Tower-Roosevelt, 28
*transportation and services,
    31, 62*
visitor information, 63
when to go, 30
Yellowstone River, *143–148*
Yellowstone River Trout Hatch-
    ery, *140*
Yellowtail Dam Visitor Center,
    293
Yellowtail Wildlife Habitat
    Management Area, *313–314*
Yesterday's Playthings, *170*

Z

ZooMontana, *284*
Zoos, *284, 395*

PHOTO CREDITS

14, *Eric Horan/age fotostock.* 15, *Michael Javorka/viestiphoto.com.* **Chapter 2: Grand Teton National Park:** 66 (top and bottom), National Park Service. **Chapter 5: Glacier National Park:** 190, *Glacier
National Park/National Park Service.* 193, *David Restivo/Glacier National Park/National Park Service.* 195, *Terry Reimink/iStockphoto.* **Chapter 10: The South Dakota Black Hills:** 398, *nagelestock.com/
Alamy.* 404-08, *South Dakota Tourism.* 417 (top), *John Coletti/age fotostock.* 417 (bottom), *Jim Par-
kin/iStockphoto.* 418-19, *South Dakota Tourism.*

NOTES

ABOUT OUR WRITERS

Before moving to Jackson Hole, **Gil Brady** traveled America for seven years, working as a movie hand, script analyst, filmmaker, columnist, reporter, and journalist. Gil's work has appeared in the *Los Angles Times,* the *Casper Star-Tribune, New West.net,* and *Planet Jackson Hole.* He now lives in Oregon with his wife and dog and writes about the adventures and misadventures of outsiders and insiders coexisting in the inscrutable West.

For more decades than she cares to tally, **Joyce Dalton** has roamed the globe, exploring some 160 countries. Her travel articles and photos have appeared in numerous trade and consumer publications. She has contributed to several Fodor's guides and is traditional-cultures editor at www.travellady.com. She lives in Red Lodge, Montana.

For nearly a decade **Amy Grisak** worked on natural-history films for National Geographic television and gained extensive knowledge of Montana's wildlife. Amy and her family enjoy Montana's great outdoors year-round, and she is an avid gardener. Her writing appears in *Montana Magazine, Natural Home, Mother Earth News, Hobby Farms,* and the *Great Falls Tribune.*

After graduating from the University of Wisconsin, **Tom Griffith** pursued a newspaper career that took him to Arizona, Montana, and South Dakota. He served as director of communications for the Mount Rushmore Preservation Fund and wrote three books about the colossal carving, including *America's Shrine of Democracy,* with a foreword by President Reagan. He has contributed to more than two dozen Fodor's guides, and his articles have appeared in newspapers and magazines around the world. A member of the Society of American Travel Writers and Western Writers of America, Tom enjoys motorcycling and fly-fishing in the Black Hills of South Dakota.

Andrew McKean writes about fishing, hunting, wildlife conservation, and natural history from his home outside Glasgow, Montana. He travels the West's backcountry extensively as a field editor and contributor for several national publications. Andrew is hunting editor for *Outdoor Life* magazine and writes a weekly column on the natural history of the Northern Plains for the *Billings Gazette.* He lives on a small farm in the Milk River Valley with his wife and three children.

Steve Pastorino loved every minute of his three trips to Yellowstone to research this book. After a 16-year career managing professional sports franchises, counting bears instead of ticket stubs was a refreshing change. He is a regular contributor to the *Salt Lake Tribune,* and you can also read him at notjustahatrack. typepad.com. He lives in Salt Lake City with his wife, Teri, and three children.

The experiences **Ray Sikorski** gained working in Yellowstone, Grand Teton, Glacier, and Denali national parks helped shape his novel *Driftwood Dan and Other Adventures.* The Bozeman-based writer's work appears in *Via,* Outside's *Go,* the *Christian Science Monitor,* and several regional publications. When not writing, Sikorski enjoys skiing, hiking, mountain biking, rock climbing, and exploring Montana's less-traveled areas.

Shauna Stephenson is the outdoors editor for the *Wyoming Tribune-Eagle* in Cheyenne. After graduating from Iowa State University, she began a career in newspapers. Covering Wyoming's outdoors has taken her to all corners of the state—making her all but useless for any sort of desk job. Most days she can be found rollicking across the wide open spaces of the high plains.